Readings in Economic Development

WALTER L. JOHNSON
Associate Professor of Economics
University of Missouri
Columbia, Missouri

DAVID R. KAMERSCHEN
Professor of Economics
University of Missouri
Columbia, Missouri

Published by

H07 **SOUTH-WESTERN PUBLISHING CO.**

Cincinnati   Chicago   Dallas   New Rochelle, N.Y.   Burlingame, Calif.   Brighton, England

34889

HD
82
.J593
1972

ISBN: 0-538-08070-1

Library of Congress Catalog Card Number: 76-164955

2 3 4 5 K 6 5 4 3 2

Printed in the United States of America

PREFACE

This selection of readings in economic development was chosen with careful thought as to how a readings book could facilitate the task of a professor trying to design and teach a course in development. The editors felt that a readings book in any field could and should serve the purpose of providing depth to the chosen textual materials, as well as updating the courses in which otherwise adequate texts are not current or available. A readings book should also present sharply defined issues which will form the basis for class discussion and stimulate the interest of the student. These considerations and others have figured in the process of selecting the articles for this volume.

We have also given attention to what we consider the shortcomings of readings books we have used and have tried to eliminate them from this one. Too often the editors of readings books seek to include many levels of sophistication in one volume. They present fine selections which require an understanding of the very basic concepts, along with selections which require a mastery of the field to fully appreciate certain aspects of the article. We have tried to avoid this difficulty and present a collection which can be appreciated by the average college student in a beginning course in economic development. The prerequisite to beginning the course in development was presumed to be a demanding course in principles of economics. The selections do not require much mathematical expertise, although in a couple of articles, due to their nature in dealing with models of growth, a hazy understanding of calculus is helpful. If more advanced students of mathematics find the volume useful the editors will, of course, be delighted. However, this book was not specifically intended to be used by the most serious undergraduate student, or by entering graduate classes.

We have chosen articles from a wide variety of sources. Some are available in almost any college library, but would not be accessible to a large number of students seeking that reserve volume simultaneously. Some are fine articles that appear in rather inaccessible places; thus, the student would not have access to them, on the reserve shelf or on any other shelf. In all cases the articles are presented in their entirety, as they originally appeared with the exception of minor typographical corrections. We are fortunate in having the cooperation of Dr. Theodore W. Schultz of the University of Chicago in presenting an original paper in the collection. Professor Bert F. Hoselitz, also of the University of Chicago, kindly assisted in the preparation of his paper for this volume.

Turning now to the construction of the book, we have introduced each group of articles with a short description of what the articles are all about and how they fit in with the remaining articles in that section of the book. Having read the section leaders, the student should begin the articles with some idea of what to look for as he goes through the argument.

Each section is concluded with a number of questions pertaining to the articles in the section. It is important for the student to note that many of the questions have no "right" or "wrong" answers. The queries bring up important matters for discussion and thought on the part of the student. If, after having read the articles, he can construct a coherent, logical argument answering the question, he has succeeded in his task.

In many respects, Sections I and VI of the volume are the most important, since they are the sections that define the question of what economic development is all about and look at the worth of development as opposed to other alternatives which society might reasonably consider. The other sections of the book look at specific parts of the subject.

There is a rather extensive bibliography included at the end of the book. We have also left all footnotes and bibliographies that appeared in the original articles in their respective positions. This was done in order to give the student as large a selection of references as practical for his use in pursuing further work in development or in writing reports or papers on subjects within economic development.

Our reviewers were very helpful in assisting us in putting together a coherent volume. Joseph J. Spengler of Duke University saw the project at two stages and made useful suggestions each time. Stephen Enke of General Electric TEMPO also had criticisms which helped shape the final product. We are indebted to them. It would be fun to have them join in sharing the blame for any errors of omission or commission, but since they would deny any knowledge of such, we will, as demanded by long tradition, and by the fact that our names appear on the spine of the volume, jointly share responsibility while giving abundant credit to those named above and to many others who have helped in producing this volume.

WALTER L. JOHNSON
DAVID R. KAMERSCHEN

TABLE OF CONTENTS

v

TO OUR WIVES, PATTI AND MARY-ANGELA

Section I

INTRODUCTION AND METHODOLOGY

The student beginning a course in economic development hopes that he will learn from the course the theory of economic development. _The_ theory does not exist. If it did exist there would be no development problem left. The less developed countries would be well on the way to eliminating the gaps which separate them from the more developed (assuming that they actually wanted to eliminate the gaps). In beginning the study of approaches to economic development, then, we must ask ourselves "What can we expect from a theory of economic development?" Harvey Leibenstein asks precisely that question and concludes that theories of economic development in order to be useful need not provide large models showing all relationships that exist in an economy. The mere fact that two variables are positively related may be of assistance in planning and in policy. He is careful to point out the error of assuming that correlation implies causality and to point out that correlations may lead to misinterpretation of the development process since the wrong variables have been correlated. There is, for instance, a positive relationship between literacy and per capita income. A correlation showing this relationship might, in the hands of the unsuspecting policy maker, tempt a country to embark on placing large amounts of resources in the promotion of literacy with little result on the level of per capita income, · since literacy is related to a set of variables, including time available after the production of subsistence, health, and so forth, which are themselves related to per capita income.

Next, should a theory "predict" or "explain?" Leibenstein points out that prediction is all well and good, but the fact that a theory predicts accurately in certain cases is no indication that it will continue to do so. He asserts that, "Prediction without explanation is of no consequence from a scientific standpoint." The identification of loosely defined relations which are understood is, however, progress, since the direction of a result, given some action of policy, may be determinable.

1

Leibenstein, then, is rather pessimistic about the development of full blown models of economic development, particularly those that pretend to show the dynamic emergence of an economy over a large number of rather arbitrarily defined time periods. He brings us down to earth rather quickly in our quest for *the* approach to economic development by questioning the analytical apparatus and finding it of only limited assistance. This is the important message that economists should remember. There is a real question as to whether Leibenstein's important article should appear at the beginning or at the end of a book such as this one. It should probably appear in both places, but publishers of books would look upon that as redundancy and throw up their hands about costs of production. The student would do well, however, to read the article at the beginning of his study of economic development, and to refresh himself as to the message of the article periodically in his career as a developmental economist.

P. T. Bauer's essay on economic development seeks to demonstrate many of the same things that Leibenstein's paper is concerned with. Bauer stresses the importance of institutions, of communication with large markets, of the role of ethnic minorities in development, pointing out that the economist has difficulty in putting these into a clearly defined model of an economy. He reviews the attempts of Harrod and Domar and of Rostow (the stages of growth approach) and finds them both lacking. These approaches will be considered in Section III of this volume. He points out as Leibenstein does, that certain relationships are observable, and that these relationships can be helpful in assisting in development. He appeals for an interdisciplinary approach to development in order to cope with some of the social, historical, institutional and anthropological aspects of the problem which are not amenable to economic analysis.

Both papers in Section One, then, point out that the problem of economic development is not at all simple and that economists do not have all of the answers. On the other hand, Leibenstein, from a rather abstract point of view, and Bauer, from one closer to the practical problems, maintain that economics has quite a good deal to offer in the progress toward economic development.

The balance of this book, with the exception of the last part, is concerned with aspects of the problems mentioned by Leibenstein and Bauer. Population, the size of the capital stock, savings ratios, terms of trade, sectoral interdependence, and the like are all parts of the problem.

Harvey Leibenstein†

1. WHAT CAN WE EXPECT FROM A THEORY OF DEVELOPMENT?*

The Romantic View of Economic Theory and the Predictability Test

Various kinds of knowledge are used in an economy. Most of the knowledge employed does not involve ideas about how the economy as a whole works. But some decisions, especially those taken at the central governmental level, do or should involve conception about the operation of the economy as a whole. This is an age when experts are frequently asked to give advice on governmental policies. Economic development theories may, to some extent, influence the advice given. It is therefore of interest to examine the nature of such knowledge. In this paper I will discuss what we may expect from economic growth theories as they are presently developed; and also what, in principle, we may expect from the kinds of theories that are likely to be created in the near future. For the most part, development theories of an aggregative nature are under consideration.

A prejudice against methodological work is part of the tradition in English speaking countries. As a consequence, many economists do not write on the subject of knowledge or examine their own methodological preconceptions in a rigorous fashion. Nevertheless, there is some discussion of these matters on an informal basis and certain views have been developed that, to the extent one can judge, seem to have a fairly high degree of acceptance. I believe that these views, many of which have developed informally, and some of which have developed as a consequence of Professor Friedman's famous essay,[1] represent what might be called a "romantic" approach to economic theory. To be specific, we might look upon the following assertions as part of the romantic view: (1.) an economic theory should be testable; (2.) it should lead to prediction of at least a conditional character; (3.) it should be conceivably

†Harvey Leibenstein, Andalot Professor of Economics and Population, Harvard University.
*From *Kyklos*, Vol. 19 (1) (1966), pp. 1–21. Reprinted by permission of the publisher and the author.
[1]M. Friedman, "The Methodology of Positive Economics," in *Essays in Positive Economics* (Chicago: University of Chicago Press, 1953), pp. 3–43.

falsifiable by events in the outside world, if it is to be considered as a meaningful theory; (4.) if it is true, then it should not have been falsified by events; and (5.) it should pass the same tests in principle, and possibly in practice, as theories in laboratory sciences.

I think that most of the above statements, or their equivalents, would be agreed upon by a great many economists. Yet I want to argue that all of the above statements are either wrong or inapplicable with respect to a very important class of economic theories, but in particular, with respect to economic development theories. The essence of the romantic view is that prediction is the only criterion of really meaningful "scientific" knowledge.

Why should there be so much concern about prediction? The virtue of prediction as a test of a theory is that it can be a *sharp* test. That is to say, it is a test that is less subject to argument than other tests. This is especially true of laboratory prediction. If *A* claims that his theory produces a certain result and states the nature of his experiment to prove it, then *B* can replicate the experiment and determine whether or not the claim is justified. But as a *sharp* test, prediction functions most effectively as a rejection rule. That is to say, if the prediction does not work out, then the theory should be rejected. It shows that, within its sphere, the theory does not have universal predictive capacity. We cannot have a prediction test that is also an acceptance test since there is always the possibility that the next prediction will fail. Acceptance is always tentative.

It is also important to note that the importance of prediction as a scientific test is open to debate. However, it is not a matter that scholars will necessarily agree about, since it depends neither on logic nor on empirical matters. Although it may be true that the majority view in economics is that the purpose and test of scientific propositions is prediction, this is, nevertheless, simply a matter of faith or of taste. It is just as reasonable, in my view, to argue (indeed I believe it to be more reasonable) that the purpose of scientific theories is to obtain coherent explanations of phenomena and events. And it so happens that increased predictive power is often a by-product of having a *coherent explanation*.[2] It is from this point of view that prediction is sometimes used as a test. However, predictive capacity without explanatory capacity is really worthless. Mere clairvoyance, irrespective of its sharpness, does not itself have scientific standing. It is only predictive capacity, that arises out of having coherent and *communicable* explanations, that does have scientific standing. The power to predict is really subsidiary to the power to explain. In other words, explanation without prediction is sufficient, *but prediction without explanation is of no consequence from a scientific standpoint.*

---

[2]Science creates bridges between facts. We integrate these bridges and facts with other experience. It is this awareness of "bridges" and their integration that enables us to understand relationships. These "bridges" are frequently facts arranged in precisely describable patterns — sometimes expressed in equations. These patterns or sets of patterns sometimes have a time dimension, hence they make prediction possible. But prediction is a frequent, although not a necessary consequence of explanation.

The prediction test is frequently restricted to "conditional prediction." That is, the theory is supposed to work only under some specified set of conditions, and in some sciences these conditions can be established artificially in a laboratory. But where the specified conditions cannot be established artificially, or where the effects of changing conditions cannot be calculated exactly, then the prediction test ceases to be a sharp test. Aggregative economic theories fall into a category where conditional prediction cannot, strictly speaking, be applied.

Ideally, economic development theories are theories about unfolding segments of history in an environment that remains constant. But since we cannot stop one segment of the world while another segment of the same world is allowed to develop, conditional prediction cannot readily be applied as a sharp test that yields true or false answers to the questions of validity. The experience that such theories attempt to analyze is imbedded in an essential way in the matrix of general history. It is usually impossible to separate clearly from the total historical experience only those elements that we arbitrarily choose to study. Hence, if a prediction test is to apply generally,[3] it must predict actual events.

The Prediction Engine and the Separability Hypothesis

Theories are more than simply prediction engines. Indeed even when they fail as prediction engines, they may still have many useful properties. This, in part, accounts for the fact that theories may be retained even after they have clearly failed as predictive devices. What, then, are some of the other properties we may look for in a theory?

From a theory of development we expect at least a fruitful vocabulary — a set of concepts that enables us to reduce the multiplicity of detailed observations into a small enough bundle of general concepts that they may be discussed efficiently. But we also want something more — something that tells us how development works. The term development usually encompasses a number of events that occur and must be understood. Since development is an abstract term, we want to "explain" its components at a somewhat lower level of abstraction; such as is evident in the growth in per capita income, the changing rate of investment, changes in labor productivity, the process of capital accumulation, the nature of population growth, and so on. We assume that many of these factors are related to each other and we want to understand, if possible, how they change, especially in their relations to each other.

I have suggested some minimal expectations from a theory: (1.) a consistent vocabulary, and (2.) some notions about the relations between the various components of "development phenomena" to enable a partial understanding

---

[3]Of course, a conditional prediction test may be possible in some instances or some individual development hypotheses.

of how they operate simultaneously. But still we probably want something more. Let us now pause for a moment and see what we *cannot* expect from such a theory. *We cannot expect a theory that will tell us how history unfolds indefinitely, given certain data to begin with.* Although economic theories are often written so that they appear to do this, they in fact cannot, and we must keep this in mind at the outset in order to avoid misunderstanding. For example, some theories of the business cycle appear to suggest that if only we could determine the parameters underlying the difference or differential equations in which such theories are couched, we would be able to predict how the cycle will unfold, given certain initial data. Of course, we are usually not surprised when it does not quite work out in that way. But I believe that we should not blame our failures on our lack of ingenuity in measuring parameters. Rather, the difficulty lies in some intrinsic qualities of social phenomena that are frequently likely to make it impossible to succeed at such efforts; qualities that are frequently forgotten because we seek theories analogous to theories in physics.

By the very nature of things our theories must be partial — they cannot take into account all human and social phenomena. But the unfolding of economic history is a consequence of the totality of the interactions of all human and social relationships. This, in itself, would not be crucial if the set of phenomena that economists choose to study were *separable* from other phenomena; i.e., if economic events were determined only by the economic relationships considered within our theories and not influenced by anything else. But since they are influenced by other matters, and since these are matters that cannot be accounted for on the basis of existing knowledge, we cannot determine the unfolding of economic history simply on the basis of economic theory.

Another way of looking at the matter is to distinguish between two types of parameters and to recognize that some parameters are likely to change, irrespective of our ingenuity in measurement. We may distinguish between *environmental parameters* and the *internal parameters* of the system. By the internal parameters we have in mind the values of the constants of the equations that describe the relations of the system. By the environmental parameters we have in mind the values of those elements that describe the environment under which the system operates. In fact, when economists elaborate their theories they assume the environment to remain constant but they do not specify the nature of the environment in detail. It is obvious that the environmental parameters change constantly and that the operation of the system is not empirically independent of the values of these parameters. Hence, a correct system in the predictive sense — a system that will, in fact, predict what will actually happen — is, in principle, impossible. Even if we knew all of the necessary initial data, as the system unfolds the environmental parameters would change; they would influence some of the variables within the system and the results would not be in accordance with what we would have predicted at the outset.[4] To see what is involved we note that this is precisely the sort of thing that the laboratory scientist is able to get away from by creating an artificial environment in the laboratory whose state he is able to control. Until the economist is able to obtain laboratory controlled economic conditions, he will not be able to test many of his theories in the same sense that the laboratory scientist is often able to. This is not to suggest that the laboratory scientist never runs into situations similar to those that face the economist, it is to suggest that the economist cannot create the situation for his work that the laboratory scientist is *often* able to create.

But the problem of predicting economic history is really deeper than that. If a partial theory were correct it would still not be possible to predict changes in the environmental parameters, because this involves a knowledge of the total system that, in fact, the economist does not even attempt to know. The problem is really more difficult, since it is impossible to know *in principle*, as well as in fact, whether the partial system is correct or not.

The system that the economist is interested in is really part of a larger system of relations that is unknown in its totality. Thus, he is interested in part of a total system. Can we know the part without knowing the system as a whole. To see what is involved consider the simplified case in which the system as a whole is a three variable system and the part is a two variable system. Let X, Y, and Z be the variables in the larger system. The relations between X, Y, and Z will form a surface in three dimensional space. Now suppose that we could only observe X and Y without taking into account the relations between X and Z, and Y and Z. Suppose our theory assumes that X is a certain function of Y. We may, in fact, observe historical values of X and historical values of Y and attempt to draw a regression line from these two sets of values. However, an infinite number of such lines can occur because the value of X that happens depends not only on the value of Y that occurs, but also on the value of Z that occurs simultaneously. Hence, the regression line so obtained is not really a reflection of the relation between X and Y but may be much more a reflection of the way in which Z happens to change historically. Similarly, any

---

[4]The French mathematician and physicist Henri Poincare developed this idea from a somewhat different viewpoint. "I imagine a world in which the various parts can conduct heat so perfectly that they maintain a constant equilibrium of temperature. . . .

Now let us imagine that this world cools slowly through radiation; the temperature will remain everywhere uniform, but will diminish with time. I imagine also that one of the inhabitants falls into a state of lethargy and awakens after a few centuries. Let us grant, since we have already assumed so many things, that he is able to live in a cooler world and that he can remember previous experiences. He will notice that his descendants still write treatises on physics, that they still make no mention of thermometry, but that the laws which they teach are very different from those which he knew. For example, he has been told that water boils at a pressure of 10 millimeters of mercury, and the new physicists observe that in order for water to boil the pressure must be decreased to 5 millimeters. A body which he had known in the liquid state will now be found only in the solid state, and so forth. The mutual relations among the various parts of the universe all depend on temperature, and as soon as the temperature changes, everything is upset." *Mathematics and Sciences: Last Essays* (1912 ed.; Dover), p. 11.

set of relations of the partial system obtained while ignoring the rest of the system, are really *pseudo-relationships* that depend, to some extent, on historical circumstances.

This problem would not arise if the partial system could, in fact, be entirely *separated* from the total system. Suppose that all but one of the equations of the partial system did not involve any variables of the total system. And suppose further, that the one equation involving such a variable connecting the partial system to the total system, could for some reason be predicted in each instance on other grounds. In that case the degree of separability of the two systems would be virtually complete and it would clearly make sense to consider the partial system as a system in its own right. But, in fact, it is hardly likely that this is the case for that set of phenomena that involves economic development. The consequence of this condition is that if we work with the partial system and try to estimate its parameters on the basis of historical data, the estimates will have no relation to the parameters of the total system even in those equations that are the same in the two systems. These parameters are, in principle, of a type that will appear to change from time to time even if the parameters of the total system are in fact stable and fixed. Of course, we do not know whether the parameters of the total system are in some sense or other given for all time.[5] But even if they were, the sub-system that we work with would still be one that would appear to be changing all the time. On the basis of these considerations we could not expect our economic sub-system to be a theory that predicts the unfolding of economic history if the theory is really a partial system rather than a complete system.

Analytical Frameworks, Theories, and Models

Not all theoretical work ends in the creation of theories in the narrow sense. In what follows I will try to distinguish between various types of theoretical efforts, in order to help determine the sort of "theoretical entities" we might expect in the development field. Unfortunately, there is no standardized vocabulary in this area. But it may be useful to distinguish three types of theoretical work.

(1.) We want especially to distinguish an analytical framework from a theory proper. By a theory we have in mind a set of relations that are sufficiently specified so that some conceivably falsifiable conclusions can be reached. At least some of the conclusions resulting from the theory are, at least in principle, in a form that makes it possible for facts not in conformity with the theory to

---

[5]F.S.C. Northrop emphasizes the importance of the law of conservation in classical physics and the lack of a counterpart postulate in economics. His essential point seems to be that the specific properties of economic relations are not based on parameters that are fixed over time. In fact he argues that relations in economics are specified only in terms of their generic properties whereas, in the physical sciences, both the generic and the specific properties are specified. See his "The Method and Limited Predictive Power of Classical Economic Sciences," in *The Logic of the Sciences and Humanities* (Meridian ed., Cleveland: World Publishing Co., 1962), pp. 235–254.

occur. In other words, such a theory does say something about the world of facts. Usually this requires that the parameters of at least some of the equations describing the relationships be sufficiently specified that the variables of the system can take on only some values and not *all* values. In sum, we might say that theories enable us to make assertions about the world of events. In laboratory situations these would often enable us to make predictions under controlled conditions.

(2.) By an analytical framework I have in mind a set of relationships that do not lead to specific conclusions about the world of events. In other words, in an analytical framework the parameters are not sufficiently specified to lead to conceivable falsifiable conclusions. An example should illustrate the distinction between an analytical framework and a theory. Consider the relations usually employed in price theory, the simple demand and supply functions. If we say simply that price is determined by these two relations: (a.) the quantity demanded as a function of price; and (b.) the quantity supplied as a function of price, then we have an analytical framework. As long as the parameters are not specified, then specific events cannot possibly contradict the confluence of these two relationships. However, once we say that the relationships are of a certain specific type so that we can draw a conclusion as to what would happen in the event that there is, say, an increase in demand, then we have a theory rather than an analytical framework. The analytical framework may be looked upon as the mold out of which the specific types of theories are made. The sort of predictions that the theory has to yield in principle for it to be a theory need not be a specific numerical character. It may be sufficient that it predicts a specific direction of change and no more. If this direction could be falsified by the facts, then we have a theory that explains changes in direction.

It is worth noting that very often it may not be possible to tell when we have a theory and when an analytical framework. The distinction may often be very subtle. For example, price theory may be written in such a way, and so many forms of the basic relations may be considered and discussed, that all events could, with hindsight, be explained on the basis of shifts in some of the basic relationships. Textbooks in economics, from this point of view, usually provide us with analytical frameworks rather than theories. In other words, they may be looked upon as toolboxes from which we can fashion theories to explain events, but they are not themselves such theories.

(3.) Another distinction often made is between a theory and a model. Here, especially, there is no standardized and well recognized usage. Sometimes the words are used interchangeably while at others they are meant to refer to different types of abstract entities. Sometimes models appear to be used in the sense of what we have described as an analytical framework. However, I wish to use the term in a somewhat different way. Roughly speaking, by a model I will have in mind a less rich form of a theory. For instance, let us assume that Keynesian theory should have, say, 14 equations and 14 unknowns. Now a theoretical construct that gives some of the same results as the Keynesian theory with fewer equations and fewer unknowns may be looked upon as a model of the Keynesian theory. Clearly, the model allows for a smaller range of possibilities and considers a narrower range of phenomena than the theory, but it reaches some of the same *qualitative* conclusions. As a consequence, models are especially useful for didactic and illustrative purposes. Another variant of a model would be to have the same set of relationships as the theory but with the parameters restricted to a much greater degree to bring out some of the conclusions more clearly. Thus, a theory may be said to have a large variety of models that are consistent with it. For example, if in the theory of price we assume that the demand relation is negatively inclined, then a model of the theory may assume that the demand relation is not negatively inclined, but that it is also linear. It would be easy to think of many models of this kind. Very often we have exceedingly broad, and to some extent, unstated conceptions of our theories and to elucidate their nature we are forced to use models. It is easier to understand a model than a theory since it is either simpler or, by assuming simple specific relations, it is more sharply drawn.

Notes on What We Can Expect from Development Theory

The main viewpoint I wish to propound is that knowledge is incomplete, and that the known and unknown aspects of social and economic phenomena are usually not completely separable, but are organically intertwined as part of entities larger than the entity being studied. I assume that this is an essential fact connected with the study of many aspects of economic development. My aim is to see how, in view of the nature of the knowledge involved, the "known" elements can be used in a theory of economic development. Clearly, the idea of something being "known" is different in this area than it is in areas where knowledge is *separable*.

In considering the previous argument about the difficulty of prediction in economics, a sharp distinction must be made between predictions that involve the operation of an economy as a whole, and those that involve only propositions about the operation of *some* economic entities under controlled conditions. For example, some economic propositions may turn out to be testable for the behavior of individuals or firms under controlled conditions. There is nothing in principle to eliminate this possibility. From this point of view it is conceivable that an economic theory as a whole may eventually contain parts that are based on "tested propositions," just as in some of the biological sciences. However, at present economics is, at least in this respect, not as well developed as biology in which at least some of the propositions are based on laboratory tests.

If we cannot count on the predictive test, then what conditions should we expect our theories to fulfill? There are some conditions that can be stated but ultimately they depend on a belief in the nature of the empirical world that is warranted by experience. Let me suggest three major conditions that a theory should fullfill: (1.) logical consistency; (2.) sound behavior assumptions; and

(3.) consistency with *some* past experience. The meaning of these three conditions is far from obvious, although the meaning of logical consistency is probably the easiest to agree upon.

Consider the second condition. Theories usually have two types of assumptions: (1.) those that indicate the area under which the theory is supposed to work; and (2.) those that indicate how the various elements or entities in the theory are assumed to behave. For example, in the theory of price an assumption about the nature of the market falls into the former category, while the assumption of profit maximization falls into the latter. Assumptions about the area encompassed by the theory are in a sense arbitrary, but assumptions about behavior are not. The entities either do or do not behave as the theory says, and I suggest that these behavior assumptions should usually be consistent with experience, where comparisons with experience can be made.

The third criterion is the most difficult to interpret. Historical experience is determined by a larger system than the one under study. Hence, what can we mean by consistency with past experience? We mean that there may be events that are so clearly not suppressed or distorted by changes in the environmental parameters that we can suppose them to be determined largely by the economic system. In that case, theory should be consistent with the *possibility* of such events. Of course, whether or not the events are of the kind indicated may be a matter of dispute. Nevertheless, this does form a desirable condition, for the theory should have some contact with the world of experience and there are at least some experiences for which such contact exists.

But if we cannot expect theories to tell us the detailed sequence of events that will occur, then what degree of consistency between theory and fact can we expect? At the very least we should expect theory to throw light on the events that are not submerged by changes in the value of the environmental parameters. But we may inquire, how can the theory tell us anything, if in principle we cannot obtain the correct values for the parameters of a model, because the model is really a part of a larger and unknown model? The situation, however, may at times be one in which the parameters obtained are for periods in which the other variables do not play too great a role in determining events. As a consequence, the sub-system that we used may, for the time being, give some degree of reasonable consistency with the events that occur. That is, the model has temporary predictive value.

But note that prediction in the strict sense is still out of the question. We cannot know whether in the future the environmental parameters will or will not be relatively stable. But we may be able to use the system for an assessment of events in the past. For with respect to past events we may be able to determine whether the general situation was one of tranquility or not, and whether the environmental parameters changed greatly or little. Even though we may not know this with respect to small changes, we may believe that there has been considerable stability so that the environment had little influence in determining large changes, i.e., we may reasonably expect the theory to help explain large changes.

Now, a theory of development and the estimates of its parameters should, in many situations, be able to at least explain some general trends. Hence, one thing we might expect of a theory of development is the explanation of trends that are not submerged by environmental influences. For example, the theory should not lead us to expect a long run decline in per capita income when in fact persistent increases are observed.

A more difficult matter arises with respect to turning points. Since a turning point is likely to be the consequence of opposing influences that to some extent balance each other out, and since close to the turning point such opposing influences are near to being balanced, we would expect the difference between them to be sufficiently small so that they in fact will be submerged by the environmental influences. However, if significant turning points are, in fact, observed then our theory must, at the very least, permit such turning points to occur in principle. In addition, there should be states on either side of the turning point, where the theory would suggest that prior to the turning point the trend direction is one way, and after it, another.

Major Uses of Development Theory — Diagnosis and Policy

Although a sharp test for a development theory may not exist, a theory may nevertheless be judged by its general effectiveness in the work that it is expected to do. Such judgments would not lead to definitive conclusions. But there are many scientific matters that cannot be settled beyond any shadow of doubt. There is really no reason to expect definitive judgments. Therefore, a theory's effectiveness can form the basis for some degree of judgment about its "validity" given the evidence about its effectiveness.

The area in which a theory should prove its effectiveness needs to be clarified. The view taken here is that the two main jobs of a theory are: (1.) as an engine of analysis of an existing situation, or as a means of explaining a historical situation; and (2.) as an instrument for policy determination. These elements are closely related.

My basic underlying assumption is that *diagnosis should precede prescription.* In an economic system policies cannot be determined once and for all in such a way as to set the system right for ever after. As a consequence, there is a need for continuous diagnosis. Diagnostic tools should, if possible, be of an organized rather than of a random nature. Therefore, a theory that *in some way* (and to some degree) provides an organized set of diagnostic tools, is desirable from this viewpoint.

I have spoken previously about analytical frameworks. I have also suggested that the job of the theorist is, in part, to provide the frameworks that function as a mold for different kinds of models. This, it would seem to me, is one of the things we might expect from theoretical efforts in the development field. Now the models that result from such frameworks should be seen to contain *sample* propositions. These propositions are essentially relationships that in themselves are not necessarily true. They are samples in the sense that they suggest the form that the theory should take. After investigation, the actual relationships decided upon may be different from the initial samples. But obviously it is desirable to have samples at the outset.

Now some of the sample relations should involve propositions that in this initial form, or in some modified form, are likely to work *frequently*. It is useful, in this context, to conceive a theory to be constructed from an integrated and organized system of sample relations, at least some of which are presumed to work "frequently."

I have suggested that although sharp prediction employed as a rejection rule is an inappropriate criterion, I have by no means eliminated some degree of prediction as a quality of some aspects of a theory. An example from medicine should help to clarify this idea. We may know, for example, that a given quantity of aspirin will frequently cure a headache. This type of knowledge contains some of the qualities that we might expect in a good economic development theory. (1.) It is certainly a useful bit of information. (2.) It is knowledge that does not pass the prediction test employed as a rejection rule. There are some headaches that aspirin does not cure. Nevertheless, we do not throw out the information because of this discovery. (3.) It is the sort of knowledge that lacks precision but is nonetheless highly useful. The term "headache" is not clearly defined. Nor for that matter is the term "frequently" defined. Yet if this is all we know about the relation between aspirins and headaches, it would certainly be useful. Also, we can look upon it as a sample relation. We may, if we wish, get a more precise relation for some specific individual. Thus, we can take a sample and study its effectiveness with specific individuals and thereby improve upon the precision of the relation in this context. For some individuals we may find that a given dosage cures headaches all the time. For others, it may work but with certain undesirable side effects. And for some individuals it may not work at all. Nevertheless, it is quite obvious that as a sample relation it was certainly a useful one and further that it contained some degree of predictability.

Previously, we spoke about the prediction of trends. Trends may be predicted because a few relatively well understood elements that function in a given direction are seen to operate with sufficient magnitude in that direction that we believe this direction will continue for some indefinite time in the foreseeable future. Again, some degree of predictibility is involved. There is also a relation between the magnitude of the independent variable and our feelings about the degree of predictability. In the previous example we may believe that very small dosages of aspirin are unlikely to cure the headaches. But that if we increase the dosage, the likelihood of cure might increase accordingly, at least up to some point. Similarly, in driving an automobile it is unnecessary to know the exact relation between pressure on the accelerator and the speed that will be achieved. All we need know is that under given road conditions an increase in pressure will yield an increase in speed. Indeed, knowing this about any automobile certainly operates as a useful sample relation despite the fact that the actual relation will differ in degree for different types of automobiles. Similarly, an economic theory may contain relations of a monotonic nature between increase in capital and increases in output. This relation may be a useful sample relation despite the fact that it lacks precision. Indeed, as with the aspirin example it would be useful even if, in fact, it did not work all the time but if it did work frequently.

Frequency is a matter of degree. However, we cannot say on *a priori* grounds what degree of frequency is adequate. Of course, on a *ceteris paribus* assumption, a theory whose relations work more frequently is superior to one that works less frequently. But the *ceteris paribus* assumption may not hold in different instances. In addition, some degrees of frequency may be so low as to make the theory uninteresting from an applied viewpoint. But the concept "interesting" is admittedly a subjective notion. This means, in essence, that judgments on these matters cannot be mechanized.

But we do want theories that enable us to predict broad stable equilibrium paths for some time period with some reasonable degree of frequency, where "reasonable" is a subjective, undefined term. The sample relations of the theory should suggest real relations so that prediction within some bounds may follow. The bounds will deal with time if the prediction is only of a directional character, and with the value of the variables that are predicted if the predictions are numerical. In other words, on the basis of some initial condition, there should be a time period such that within that time period we predict the values to fall within a certain broad path. This is illustrated in Figure 1-1. Time is shown on the x axis and the predicted variable on the y axis. The area I is the area in which the initial conditions fall, and the area P is the area in which the predicted path should fall. At each time point the predicted path has a width W and the time dimension of the path is T.

Now, normally we would expect that the frequency with which the prediction holds would depend on the variable width vector W and the time, T. Thus, we would have a functional relation:

$$F = g\,(W,\,T)$$

To say that a theory works, in the sense that we have used the term, means that F is greater than zero for some values of W and T. Of course, to be interesting, the value of F would have to be greater than some minimum for a value of W less than some maximum, and a value of T greater than some minimum. While this introduces matters of judgment into what we mean by working, our concept is nevertheless meaningful, even if there are some subjective judgment elements involved.

How are these ideas related to the notion of theory as an engine of analysis? The sample relations suggest the areas we should investigate in an actual economy in order to see the extent to which any of them have worked frequently. The analytical framework would suggest additional sample relations and would operate as a means of organizing disparate relationships. To the extent that a number of the relations seem to have worked frequently we may, after

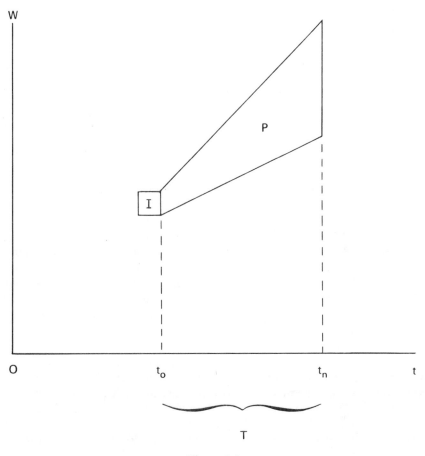

Figure 1-1

study, come to understand some periods in that economy's development. Furthermore, we may come to understand enough of various elements in its development that we can point to the aspects of the economy that presented bottlenecks to further growth as well as those that were conducive to growth. It is clearly such knowledge that should enable us to diagnose current difficulties, and the relation between current difficulties, current events, and the presumed aims that the analyst assumes exist for the economy. This is obviously the stage where some prescriptions could be attempted. I see this as a continuous process in which there is a continuous interaction between theory refinement, the analysis of a particular economy, and prescription.

Return now to the basic notion that although detailed prediction is out of the question in many cases, it may be possible to predict the direction of events. But even that may not be possible in all cases because the environmental parameters or variables may be more important at times than the forces considered in the theory. However, *some policy instruments may be of such a kind that they can be used in various sizes or to various degrees, and for some sizes or degrees their impact will be larger than that of the environmental parameters.* Under such circumstances it may be possible to determine the direction of the change by using the policy instrument to a sufficient degree. Where this is done successfully it would surely prove the usefulness of a theory (even if it would not prove its "correctness").

Consider a Keynesian type theory in a situation of underemployment. The theory may suggest that an increase in the rate of investment is necessary to increase the level of employment. It may not be possible, however, to determine the exact relation between a given increase in investment and a given increase in employment. The environmental parameters make such a determination impossible. But we would expect, if the theory is a good one, that an increase in investment would increase employment. Perhaps a small increase in investment would not do so. In that case we would increase the investment rate still further and see what happens. If the theory about the direction of change is correct, then we would expect that under normal circumstances a sufficiently large increase in investment would overcome any environmental forces operating in the opposite direction. Thus, each increase in investment would result in a change that would tell us whether we have gone in the right direction. If not, then we could correct the situation by increasing the dose. In such a way we should eventually be able to approach a full employment state. A theory that would lend itself to procedures of this sort would clearly be more persuasive than one that would not. It is similar to a capacity to drive a car on unknown and unmarked roads in order to reach a certain destination with the aid of only a compass, and with only a knowledge of the initial point and the end point. We cannot determine the optimum way of getting to the destination. Nor can we always be sure that we will get on to a road that will always go in the right direction. But the compass enables us, every so often, to check our progress with respect to direction, to correct errors, and eventually to reach the destination. Clearly, some predictive power is necessary in such cases. But it need not be a power that is universally correct and the quality of the prediction is of a much lower order than that required by the strict prediction-rejection test.

Now what should we expect from a development theory? Briefly put, we should expect a conceptual framework that would facilitate the creation of theories or models that contain manipulable variables whose dosages can be raised sufficiently to swamp the environmental effects and sufficiently to obtain accurate directional predictions for a limited period of time. This leaves room for many unsettled issues.

In this connection a special problem might arise with respect to manipulable variables whose impact appears at remote periods of time. For example, suppose that investment in education has a ten year lag in perceptible impact on output, while investment in capital has only a one year lag. Here, a heroic decision may have to be made as whether or not to use investment in education on the basis of partial data, but not on the basis of a strict test of the model. A sharp test of the kind used in the exact sciences is out of the question. The decision would have to be made with judgments based on bits of data here and there, as well as with general impressions. This approach clearly differs from that of the exact sciences, but we simply have to face the fact that the nature of the problems we deal with do not lend themselves to the methods of the exact sciences, and there is no point in seeking "pseudo-tests" based on imitation.

Summary and Conclusions

Although many of the points I have made are well known, the general viewpoint I end up with is radically different from that currently accepted. I have dealt with both negative and positive aspects of the problem. On the negative side I have argued against the prediction test as a rejection rule. On the positive side I have put forth a view of theory as a set of sample relations that are helpful in the discovery of specific relations in specific contexts and that we hope will work frequently in a loosely fitting servomechanism type of arrangement.

We cannot really determine whether or not an aggregative development theory is correct in the strict sense. There are no strictly true theories in this area that we would expect to work on the basis of precise prediction. In the same sense, we should not expect any universally true statements about the direction of change or about turning points. The denial of the expectation of finding *universal* truths in this area certainly differs from the contemporary view of the matter.

The views presented also have implications for economic planning. If exact numerical relations are out of the question, then precise planning cannot be based on "true" relations. In addition it would appear that planning schemes that require optimization procedures must be based on illusory relations or what we have called pseudo-relations, given the inseparability of the highly abstracted submodel that we have to handle and the larger model whose real nature is beyond our understanding. If "planning" is to take place without being illusory, it must be of a rather loose fitting type consistent with the nature of our knowledge.

What we can hope to do is to say something about the adequacy of certain theories within given contexts. But such assessments are to a considerable extent separate from the theory itself, or from the accuracy with which it reflects the phenomena it deals with. Rather, it may depend on the factors that happen to be socially manipulable (i.e., on available policy instruments) and on the degree to which the environmental variables happen to be stable during the historical period in question. Thus, theory A may be more adequate than theory B in one period and less adequate in another. In this connection some current arguments about the desirability of having an all-embracing economic growth theory that would apply equally well to both developed and underdeveloped countries strikes me as ill conceived, since the environmental variables are likely to operate differently during different stages. There is no reason why a different theory should not apply to each stage.

Finally, what is the job of the development theorist? It is twofold: (1.) to create analytical frameworks; and (2.) to create *sample* theories consistent with the analytical framework. But in the absence of specific historical studies, or in the absence of specific policy situations, the sample theories are not to be looked upon as working theories but simply as illustrations of the kinds of working theories or working models that could be created. Furthermore, a working model should not be expected to work indefinitely. From time to time we would expect that old working models would have to be retired and replaced by new ones.

This view of the matter also means that our sample hypotheses or relations need to be based on fact. The view that looked upon theories as entities that are to be subjected to a rejection rule did not need to concern itself with the manner in which the hypotheses were arrived at. All that mattered was whether they passed the prediction test time after time. But if we no longer expect our theories to work in a precise predictive sense, but view them only as samples, then it is important that our sample hypotheses have some degree of credibility. And credibility would depend in part on experience. We would expect hypotheses that consistently flout experience to be poorer samples than those that frequently agree with experience in some sense.

In essence, this view is based on what appears to be a realistic judgment of the nature of economic hypotheses. There is a variety of types of scientific information. Some of it fits the categories utilized in such laboratory sciences as chemistry and physics. But not all scientific information is of this type. I have suggested a view of theory that is more complex, apparently more realistic, and one that also seems to fit the contemporary notion of cybernetic devices of a loosely fitting sort that is probably more applicable to social organization, than interpretation based on a stricter, more mechanistic viewpoint.

Questions for discussion and analysis pertaining to this article may be found at the end of Article 2.

Peter Bauer †

2. THE STUDY OF UNDERDEVELOPED ECONOMIES*

I

I want to put before you today a few thoughts on the study and relevance of economics in the context of underdeveloped, i.e. poor, countries. I shall suggest that economic analysis is widely relevant to the explanation of many phenomena in the underdeveloped world, and to the assessment of many measures of policy. On the other hand it cannot explain so readily the various factors behind economic progress, let alone forecast the likelihood of their occurrence, though it may eventually succeed better in the former task at any rate, especially if it were to work with other disciplines. In discussing these matters I shall touch on several topics lightly, rather than try to discuss one subject more thoroughly. This may help to convey some feeling of the vastness and diversity of the underdeveloped world, of the range and variety of the intellectual and practical problems it presents, and perhaps also of the amorphous nature of this branch of economics.

Although dissentient voices are still heard, the relevance of economic analysis to poor countries is now more readily accepted than a decade or two ago. Over a wide range it is not in question, since some of the propositions of economics derive directly from the universal limitation of resources. Their relevance is recognised in the practice of governments in underdeveloped countries of taxing commodities and activities to be discouraged, and subsidising those to be encouraged. This practice makes sense only if the demand for particular commodities is a positive and their supply a negative function of price and reward (that is, if people wish to attain their objectives, whatever these may be, at least cost in terms of scarce resources), which accords with the postulates of elementary economic theory. Indeed, the applicability of economic analysis emerges in unexpected contexts. In the 1940's bride-prices

†Peter T. Bauer, Professor of Economics of Underdeveloped Countries and Economic Development, London School of Economics. The author wishes to thank Sir Sydney Caine and Professor Richard J. Hammond for their suggestions which were of great help.

*From *Economica*, N.S., Vol. 30 (November, 1963), pp. 360–371. Reprinted by permission of the publisher and the author.

in Nigeria rose greatly with the general rise in the prices of assets. Government control over bride-prices was widely canvassed and officially considered, but was rejected when the difficulties of allocation were perceived.

Simple macroeconomics has also been successfully applied in underdeveloped countries. In the Gold Coast in 1947 the late H. S. Booker predicted in an unpublished paper that, unless taxation were raised or import controls relaxed, an acute shortage of consumer goods would develop in the forthcoming cocoa season, so severe that it might lead to civil disturbances. The prediction, based largely on the technique of national income and expenditure analysis, was ignored but was completely fulfilled.

II

The study of underdeveloped economies encounters certain special but familiar difficulties, yet at the same time may offer rather unsuspected opportunities.

An obvious difficulty is the inadequacy or absence of certain types of statistics, especially demographic, national income and occupational statistics. Even when available, these are often subject to conceptual and practical limitations, notably statistics of national income where subsistence output is important, and occupational statistics where specialization is incomplete. On the other hand, as I shall suggest shortly, there are often excellent and illuminating statistics for certain sectors of these economies.

Another difficulty is to find one's way and to observe uniformities in the often unfamiliar social landscape, unfamiliar because the institutions, and especially the values and mores, often differ from our own, which requires an adjustment of our sights. In East Africa cattle are often kept for aesthetic reasons or for prestige. But in the West also, substantial resources are absorbed in the maintenance of animals not designed for work or food. Differences in values and institutions may affect the comparative importance of different economic variables, making it more difficult to discern their operation, without affecting the relevance and validity of economic analysis. Thus, for example, within the opportunities open to them, the responses of people to changes in the relevant variables, for instance prices and wages, are over a wide range of countries and activities much the same as in the West, and, as I have just suggested, this is recognised in Government policy throughout the underdeveloped world. And when new profitable opportunities arise the responses are often massive and rapid, as in the spread of the cultivation of profitable cash crops by Asian and African smallholders, or in the large-scale migration of South Indian labourers to Malaya and Ceylon, which, when it was permitted, responded very closely to the changes in relative economic conditions. These major changes occurred in communities supposedly subject rigorously to the sway of custom and tradition.

The conditions of underdeveloped countries offer some useful and possibly unexpected opportunities for economic inquiry.

Much of the information in underdeveloped economies, or about them, is suitable for the examination of economic hypotheses, and for the establishment and even measurement of the relationships between economic variables. This is so for at least two reasons. First, a large part of output in these countries is in unprocessed primary products, which avoids some of the difficult or intractable problems presented by differences and variations in the quality of commodities and in the composition of output. Second, costs of transport are often heavy, and communication between local markets difficult. This results in situations identical in all, or most, relevant aspects, except one or two variables whose operations and relationship can be investigated.

A single illustration suffices here. In the purchase of Nigerian groundnuts, the combination of a standardised commodity with clearly separate sub-markets, and differences in the number of buyers, has made possible investigations into the effects of the number of buyers on the prices received by the producers. In Nigeria, groundnuts for sale are produced in two widely separated regions. In 1949–1950, when the enquiry was conducted, in one region there were only two merchants buying groundnuts; in the other region there were about twenty merchants buying, although the numbers at work in each market were appreciably fewer. In both regions minimum prices payable by merchants were officially prescribed. In the first region the actual market prices nowhere exceeded the official minima, while in the other region they much exceeded them in many markets. There was a very high positive correlation in the individual markets between the number of merchants and the excess of actual over prescribed prices. This example at any rate bears on the suggestion that an increase in the number of merchants tends only to inflate costs, without improving the terms of trade of their customers.

The interaction of economic variables and the general environment, a notable aspect of development, can also be well observed in underdeveloped countries, that is to say the interaction of incomes, prices, quantities and other familiar economic variables, with other factors or influences, such as attitudes, wants and institutions, variations in which are deliberately ignored for most purposes of economic analysis. For example, in many underdeveloped countries the cultivation of profitable cash crops has provoked the emergence of individual tenure of land. In Malaya and Ghana rubber or cocoa trees are already individually owned, while much of the adjoining land under subsistence crops is still under some sort of communal tenure, though this can be seen to be losing ground. Thus, one can observe, and at times vividly, processes on the contemporary scene similar to those which happened centuries ago in the now developed countries.

Altogether, economics explains satisfactorily much of what goes on in underdeveloped countries. It readily explains the very wide seasonal and year-to-year price fluctuations of the local agricultural produce, a general phenomenon in the underdeveloped world, which reflects a marked degree of inelasticity of short-period supply and demand. This in turn reflects the narrowness of markets in space and time, due largely to the low level of transport and storage facilities. Moreover, economic analysis helps to assess the effects of certain specific measures of policy, often encountered in underdeveloped countries, such as the charging of rents on officially alienated land varying only with the crop cultivated and not with location or fertility, or the prohibition of exports falling below certain physical standards, and many others. It is also obviously relevant for the assessment of the simpler effects of tax changes and, indeed, for the assessment of major implications of more far-reaching policies, such as taxation for development by way of compulsory saving.

III

These matters are often of considerable interest. But they are not the main attraction of the underdeveloped countries to economists and to others. Since the eighteenth century at least, the primary interest in this sphere has been and still is in the determinants of economic progress, or the causes of the wealth of nations for short.

Two widely canvassed approaches to this range of problems have, I think, been unsuccessful.

The first approach regards development as largely or wholly determined by capital accumulation, an approach often expressed in formal growth models. (Such models usually derive from the growth models of Harrod and Domar. But these pioneers and their immediate followers were not primarily concerned with the long-term historical development of societies. Their main concern was with the conditions of steady growth in advanced industrial societies.)[1] In their emphasis on capital these models bear some family resemblance to discussions in classical economics. But this similarity is rather superficial. The classical writers, notably including Adam Smith and Marx, closely related capital accumulation as an engine of development to the activities and conduct of particular groups, organizations and classes, such

---

[1]These models are largely Keynesian in their main aims and assumptions in that they are chiefly concerned with the conditions of long-run full employment, notably the rate of growth of income necessary for this; and they disregard changes (and the effects of different kinds of change) in tastes, knowledge and other resources, attitudes, customs, degree of monetization of the economy, political systems, and often also in population and techniques. This greatly reduces their relevance to the study of economic development.

Keynes' own formulation of his assumptions shows this clearly. "We take as given the existing skill and quantity of available labour, the existing quality and quantity of available equipment, the existing technique, the degree of competition, the tastes and habits of the consumer, the disutility of different intensities of labour and of the activities of supervision and organization, as well as the social structure . . .," *General Theory*, p. 245. This model treats as given the essential variables or determinants of development.

as traders, governments and the bourgeoisie, and to social attitudes, relationships and institutions, and to changes in these. Some of the most influential
growth models abstract these forces, and apparently treat long-term progress
as dependent on capital expenditure alone; and this abstraction differentiates
this approach from that of the classical writers.

More recently the inadequacy of this emphasis on capital has come to be
increasingly realized for various reasons, including the obvious failure of
many large-scale investment programmes, especially in underdeveloped countries; recognition of the very limited explanatory power of the capital-output
ratio; renewed emphasis on the dependence of the productivity of physical
assets on the market for their output and on the presence of complementary
factors, notably skills and appropriate attitudes; and, more generally, recognition that expenditure does not become productive simply because it is termed
investment.

These and other grounds for skepticism have been confirmed by statistical
studies showing that neither in Britain nor America can the growth of physical
capital possibly account for all or even most of the secular growth of income.
And it is not obvious how the special but not unusual case of economic decline
can fit into a theory of development based largely or wholly on the growth
of capital.

The recognition of the inadequacy of physical capital, and *a fortiori* of
investment expenditure, as an instrument of development has come to influence
policy. Foreign aid programmes increasingly acknowledge that money expenditure by itself will not achieve much without changes in institutions and
attitudes. It is more generally recognised that aid to many underdeveloped
countries comes up against difficulties and constraints quite different from
those confronting Marshall Aid to Western Europe after the war. Western
Europe was demonstrably lacking in capital, while at the same time it had the
necessary co-operant resources and market opportunities as well as institutions,
attitudes and motivations favourable to growth, as indeed is obvious from the
past performance of Western Europe for centuries before the Second World
War.

Thus, while the accumulation of physical capital can contribute substantially
to economic progress, it is certainly not a sufficient and often not a major
factor. The opening of new markets, the establishment of external contacts,
changes in attitudes, conduct, customs and wants, the spread of knowledge and
of skills, generally play at least as great a part in development as does the growth
of physical capital, particularly in pre-industrial societies, and especially before
the society has been pervaded by the money economy.

The other widely canvassed, but I think unfruitful, approach to a general
theory of development is the stages-of-growth approach, which seeks to
express history as a predictable sequence of necessarily successful stages.
The approach is not new. I believe I am correct in reporting that economic
historians generally have not found this approach useful in explaining the

progress (or decline) of societies. In some of the most widely canvassed recent formulations it is not clear what the theory has to say about the causes of development, since at times it emphasises certain key variables, while at others it suggests that development depends on an indefinite number of often unspecified factors, saying in effect that growth depends on the presence of factors making for growth. It is precisely because the long-term movement of any society depends in large part on unpredictable forces and events that the stages-of-growth approach may necessarily involve formulations so vague and open-ended as to be unserviceable. This consideration points to the limitations in the study and analysis of economic development of the usefulness of techniques and methods of thought (including economic analysis) which are appropriate to the study of phenomena which in practice or in principle are repeated or repeatable. This is true only to a very limited extent of historical progress of entire societies. This problem is an aspect of the essential difference between the assessment of a situation or the prediction of the probable result of a change in specified variables on one hand, and the forecasting of the unknown future on the other. I need not labour this point, since it would be only an inadequate reflection of Professor Popper's classic treatment of this problem.

IV

Neither formal growth models nor stages-of-growth theories help to explain or predict the long-term development of entire societies. But this does not preclude the possibility of specific generalizations about some of the major aspects or determinants of material progress. Indeed, such specific generalizations about these matters, rather than the framing of complete systems, are in the tradition of the literature, even though they may not be expressed in terms of conventional or formal analysis. Examples include the relationship between the extent of the market, specialization and productivity, and the importance for development of the habits of "order, economy, and attention, to which mercantile business naturally forms a merchant."[2] Generalizations of this type are not so narrow as growth models preoccupied with capital expenditure, nor so ambitious as the well-nigh universal theory of history reflected, for example, in the stages-of-growth approach. But such generalizations, even apparently simple ones, may reveal some factors in the process of development.

To begin with a rather straightforward though negative suggestion. Physical natural resources, notably fertile soil or rich minerals, are once again not the only or even major determinants of material progress (though differences in the bounty of nature may well account for differences in levels and ease of living in different parts of the underdeveloped world). It has always been known that physical resources are useless without capital and skills to develop them, or without access to markets. And the diminishing importance of land

---

[2]Adam Smith, *Wealth of Nations*, Book III, Chapter IV.

and other natural resources in production is also familiar. But the recent rapid development of some underdeveloped countries poorly endowed with natural resources has come as a surprise, though perhaps it should not have done so in view of the Japanese experience. A recent but already classic case is that of Hong Kong, which has practically no raw materials, very little fertile soil, no fuel, no hydro-electric power, and only a very restricted domestic market, but which in spite of these limitations has progressed phenomenally.

The natural rubber industry which has been the mainspring of the rapid development of Malaya, and indeed of the economic transformation of that country and of much of South-East Asia, owes little to scarce natural resources, or to any *local* resources. The rubber tree, which is indigenous in South America, does not require particularly fertile soil, and thrives practically anywhere in the tropical rain forest. The soil of Malaya and Sumatra, the two principal producing countries, is generally poor, nor had their territories appreciable labour forces or supplies of capital when the rubber industry began there only about sixty years ago. The main reasons for its development there were the presence of European merchants and of a stable administration, and access to large reservoirs of labour in South India, China and Java, and to the capital markets of Western Europe.

V

Another range of issues concerns the conspicuous differences between individuals and groups in economic capacities and faculties, such as industry, enterprise, curiosity and ability to perceive and exploit economic opportunity. In a subsistence economy they are largely irrelevant and unobtrusive. But they come into play quite soon in emerging economies, especially with the advance of the money economy. There are obvious examples in the progress of certain distinct ethnic groups, especially, but not only, immigrants, in a number of underdeveloped countries. Throughout the underdeveloped world, originally penniless and often quite uneducated immigrants have within a few years completely out-distanced the local population. Familiar instances include the Chinese in South-East Asia, the Indians in East Africa and the Lebanese in West Africa. The difference in economic performance between some of these groups and the local population, for instance, between the Chinese and the Malays, is often striking. Two examples will suggest that the special circumstances of migration alone do not explain this. In Malaya there is a large Indian as well as large Chinese population. The great bulk of both communities came within recent decades as very poor, illiterate coolies. Within a few years the Chinese drew far ahead of the Indians. The other example is from Israel. The authorities there established a number of separate villages in the same region for recent immigrants from different countries, whom they provided as nearly as possible with the same amount of capital and identical facilities per family.

Differences in economic qualities bear on many aspects and problems of economic development, including, for instance, those of overpopulation. The Chinese can make a living in areas often regarded as hopelessly over-crowded, as for instance Hong Kong and the West Indies. In the latter, which are generally considered as severely overpopulated, prospective Chinese and Lebanese migrants have to be statutorily excluded.

Very little is known about the climatic, biological, cultural and social factors which may lie behind these differences in economic qualities and performance, and their emergence, persistence or disappearance. It is probable that climatic and other geographic factors play an important part. It is noteworthy that, with the exception of a few small areas with which the developed world has established direct and intimate contacts, all tropical countries are underdeveloped. Conversely, almost all countries in the temperate zone are comparatively highly developed. Even allowing for the much lower requirements for shelter and clothing, the concentration of poverty within the tropics is notable. Differences in achievement between the tropical world and the temperate zones go back for many centuries.[3]

Again, much of the now widely canvassed difference in prosperity between North and South Italy goes back at least to the Middle Ages. Since then the North has been well ahead of the South in scientific, intellectual, artistic, commercial and industrial achievement, and it was also the source of the Italian voyages of discovery. It seems unknown how much of the Northern advantage reflects ethnic or climatic factors, or how much was contributed by migrants from the South, or by their recent descendants.

Although some of these differences in economic qualities are longstanding, some, especially the capacity to handle technical objects and processes, can change comparatively quickly. The rapid emergence of Japan as an industrial nation in the nineteenth century is well known. Less familiar and in some ways even more striking was the economic transformation of Sweden in the latter part of the nineteenth century. And again, until very recently, the peoples of sub-Saharan Africa had neither invented the wheel, nor taken to it even when it was brought to their notice. But now they are readily accepting modern equipment and modern technology. Some attitudes and customs which much affect economic development seem very tenacious at home, while they are largely absent abroad. The South Indian communities in Malaya come from parts of rural Madras where caste is strictly observed, as it has been for many centuries; yet they largely abandon it when they leave India.

The study of the often very pronounced ethnic differences in economic performance, and of the climatic, genetical and other factors that may underlie

---

[3]There is a curious contrast which is perhaps worthy of note in this context, as well as in others. There has been much travel and exploration from the West (including at times the Levant) to Asia and Africa since at least the time of Herodotus, and on a large scale since the fourteenth century. There was little reverse movement, even though throughout the ages there have been rich and powerful individuals and groups in many areas of Asia and Africa.

them, might now be more illuminating and rewarding than in the past, because of advances in biology, biometrics, genetics and climatology. These should enable us to observe, assess and perhaps even control some of the effects of climate on economic performance, even long-term performance.

There is no cause for surprise, much less for indignation, at this explicit recognition of the pronounced and often sustained differences in economic qualities between individuals and groups, any more than at noting differences in physical or intellectual attributes and qualities between individuals and groups. Moreover, even if it is found that such differences are deep-seated and persistent, this would not point to any specific prescriptions for policy.

VI

Throughout the underdeveloped world, in the tropics and elsewhere, the most prosperous regions and sectors at present are those with which the developed world has established contacts: the cities and ports of India and their vicinity; the cash crop producing areas and the entrepot ports of South-East Asia, West Africa and Latin America; and the mineral-producing areas of Africa, the Middle East and the Caribbean. Conversely, the poorest and most backward are usually populations with few or no external contacts in Africa, Asia and Latin America, the aborigines being the extreme case. Although there may be odd exceptions, in the nature of curiosa perhaps, the general connection between external contacts, at any rate peaceful contacts, and economic advance is familiar from economic and social history. In the Middle Ages the more advanced regions of backward Eastern and Central Europe and Scandinavia were those in touch with France, the Low Countries and Italy. The difference in the material prosperity of the coastal regions and the centre of Spain has been a notable feature of Spanish history, and one of the determinants of its course.

The connection in underdeveloped countries between comparative material prosperity and external contacts is not surprising. These are the channels through which human and material resources, skills and capital from developed countries reach the underdeveloped world. They open up new markets and sources of supply, and they bring new commodities, wants, crops and methods of cultivation to the notice of the local population. They also engender a new outlook towards material possessions and the means of obtaining them. And perhaps most important, they undermine customs, attitudes and values which obstruct material advance. Again, in poor countries the sectors in contact with richer communities also attract groups and individuals from the local population most responsive to economic opportunities. Such matters obviously greatly affect economic performance in underdeveloped countries, especially in the early stages of development. In the widest sense such contacts promote that dissatisfaction with the existing situation which has been termed the first condition of progress. Their importance can hardly be exaggerated.

Altogether, these contacts draw parts of the underdeveloped world into a wider system of international economic life; and, by enabling their peoples to draw on the resources of the outside world, they help to raise and maintain the economy above subsistence production.[4]

These simple considerations reflect on the curious and influential argument that the presence of developed countries, and the contacts with them, somehow prejudice the advance of poorer countries, a suggestion which is contrary to massive empirical evidence, including the clear connection at present between economic prosperity and progress in the underdeveloped world and contact with richer countries, which I have already mentioned. They also show up certain implications of the severance of contact between the underdeveloped countries and the developed countries by restrictions on migration, trade and capital movements, whether from political motives or pressure of sectional interests.

Indeed, at present these contacts offer exceptional opportunities. Because of the presence of advanced countries and highly developed communications, the underdeveloped world has readier access to the fruits of scientific and technical progress elsewhere than the now developed countries had in the past. Access to this accumulated knowledge could be as helpful as access to unused land was to other countries in times past. The ability of underdeveloped countries to take advantage of this depends greatly on the attitudes and skills of their own peoples, as well as on government policies promoting or restricting international contacts.

External contacts of course are by themselves not sufficient to ensure progress if other factors are missing. The spread of material progress from advanced sectors to others depends on human, institutional, cultural and political factors, besides physical and occupational obstacles to mobility. In Latin America the Peruvian Indians have remained very poor in spite of external contacts, while in Mexico Indians are often prominent and prosperous. Again, in the Middle Ages North Africa had extensive contacts with the prosperous regions of Europe, but this did not prevent its decline. Ibn Khaldun, the Arab philosopher-historian of the fourteenth century, attributed the decay of North Africa, and the failure of the advanced city civilizations to pervade

---

[4]Some of the pervasive changes engendered by external contacts in the contemporary underdeveloped world, notably in South-East Asia and West Africa, are familiar. External contacts have largely transformed these areas. I might perhaps mention a less pervasive and much less well known change, which is nevertheless noteworthy and substantial, to which Professor H. M. Robertson of the University of Cape Town has drawn attention. He has repeatedly stressed the revolutionary effects of the activities of European traders on the life of the Bantu of South Africa. The use of the blanket as a garment is often thought as typical of the tribal Bantu. In fact, until late in the nineteenth century they were unknown to the Bantu who used a skin covering known as the *kaross*. Enterprising traders brought blankets to the notice of the tribal Africans and had blankets specially made for them in Yorkshire. What are regarded as traditional tribal patterns were in fact designed in England at the instigation of merchants wishing to differentiate their products.

the Arab world, to a feckless and careless attitude of the rural population reflected in, and reinforced by, a nomadic life.

VII

Some of the observations in this lecture have taken me far from the usual preoccupations of contemporary economics. The economist may well ask whether they can help him in his academic or professional pursuits. I think they are relevant both to the explanation of much of the scene, and to the assessment of policies for the promotion of economic development of poor countries generally, or of particular areas. But of course they are no more than tentative generalizations, and they share this tentative quality with most other generalizations on the process of economic development. Whatever this validity, consideration of these topics seems necessary for any worthwhile study of development.

And many of these observations and generalizations are largely unrelated to conventional formal economic reasoning (at least to the formal economic analysis of recent decades). Insistence on the wide relevance of economic reasoning in explaining phenomena in underdeveloped countries, and in illuminating situations, or explaining some aspects and conditions of development, is quite consistent with recognition of its limitations in predicting the course of development. This is because long-term development depends, I repeat, so largely on general conditions not susceptible to economic analysis, and what is equally important, on unpredictable changes in these conditions. And further, I do not think that the economist is particularly qualified to assess the wider implications of economic development and of the different methods of attempting to promote it, either in terms of personal happiness or in terms of social and political results.

Von Karman, the distinguished physicist who died recently, used to say that prophecy was not a scientific activity and therefore not the task of science. This applies even more in the social than in the natural sciences. Our task is in some ways very similar to that assigned by Collingwood to historians, that is "to reveal the less obvious features hidden from a careless eye in the present situation." This is very different from speculation about the remote unknown future of a society. The claims of chemistry have always been more modest than those of alchemy. I believe that in economics, especially in the economics of underdeveloped countries, as in other disciplines, it is a sign of maturity and not of obscurantism when the practitioners recognize the limitations of their subject.

VIII

In the study of underdeveloped economies there may be scope for inter-disciplinary co-operation, especially but not only between anthropologists, economists and historians. Various situations and phases of development as yet imperfectly understood might be fruitfully studied through such co-operation. They might include parts of the vast field of the responses of different groups to changes in economic conditions and opportunities. Again, within the extremely important and interesting range of issues in the transmission of knowledge, skills, attitudes and inducements between countries and groups, there are many examples which might perhaps be usefully investigated jointly by anthropologists, economists and historians.

And there are more specific episodes or phenomena the interdisciplinary study of which might prove illuminating. They could include instances of the rapid spread of cash crops produced by the local population, or of the present organization of some of these industries, such as smallholders' rubber in the former Netherlands India (where millions of acres were planted to rubber by smallholders in a few years in the 1920's and 1930's), or kola nuts in Nigeria. These are among the examples of massive development of cash crop production which passed unnoticed for many years, and which in kola nuts, at any rate, has involved a high degree of organization of production, transport and trade, entirely by the local population. Another possible example of such worthwhile study would have been the Gold Coast cocoa hold-up of 1937–38, which was a remarkable farmers' strike by well over 100,000 producers, who for seven months sold practically no cocoa to the merchants. Close interdisciplinary enquiry into this episode might well have yielded worthwhile results on the transmission of information, the organization by a few people of large numbers of producers, and on the ability of farmers and labourers to obtain food and other necessities. Again, the frequently reported wide differences in the prices of local food stuffs in nearby areas could also be examined on an inter-disciplinary basis, to ascertain how far they are illusory or real, and if they are real, how far they are explained in different instances by transport costs, inertia, ignorance, custom, lack of response or quasi-monopoly, which have widely different implications. In suggesting these topics, I may add that serious discussion of underdeveloped countries and their problems is much affected by an acute dearth of scholarly monographs and essays on particular countries or subjects.

In the study of these other aspects of underdeveloped economies and of economic development, inter-disciplinary co-operation may perhaps yield another incidental but possibly important benefit. It may help to convey the value of direct observation and of unprocessed material, and conversely, the pitfalls of reliance on second-hand or third-hand material, including reliance on statistics without examination of their sources or background. Statistics are necessarily a form of abstraction, and they are most effectively used if other aspects of the situation are also known, that is other than those quantified in the statistics.

Some may fear that this approach or method of study will tempt us into excessive detail. However, concern with detail, whether in interdisciplinary

studies or otherwise, can be very fruitful in   ular field of study.
I think the emphasis in recent years has been to   opposite direction.
Perhaps we would do well to remind ourselves of   n maxim (recently
quoted by Professor C. H. Philips) that it "comet   s that mean and
small things discover *great* better than great can   l."

Questions for Discussion and

Article 1

1. *How can economists be sure that they   the proper
   variables in attempting to determine th   causes of   economic
   growth?*
2. *What are the distinctions between a theory   an analytical framework, and a model? Are these distinction   of any importance
   to the developmental economist or to the government of a developing country?*
3. *If a theory is capable of prediction of event   it is usable, and
   if it can not furnish predictive information   it is not usable.
   Comment.*

Article 2

4. *Are ethnic differences important in promoting economic development? How does one explain that certain ethnic groups
   in a society may develop economically and culturally much
   more rapidly than the balance of the society?*
5. *How could it be possible that changes in the market for one
   commodity, cocoa, could make such a difference to the inhabitants of Nigeria or Ghana?*
6. *Bauer cites a case involving two markets for the production of
   Nigerian groundnuts (we call them peanuts) in which different
   prices prevailed. Why were the prices different in the two markets? Is there a policy implication for governments in less developed countries involved in Bauer's discovery of the two
   prices?*
7. *What factors other than the growth of the capital stock have
   been important in increasing the level of per capita income?
   If these factors are important, why do we not see more of their
   use?*

Section II

DIMENSIONS OF UNDERDEVELOPED COUNTRIES

The articles in this section are aimed at trying to give the reader a profile of what a "typical" underdeveloped country might be like. Unfortunately this may not be possible. It is as difficult to find a "representative" underdeveloped country as it is to find a "typical" student in an economic development course. But the first three selections by Leibenstein, Kuznets, and Hoselitz should give the reader some feel for the common elements in these countries. The final three selections by Haberler, Blase, and Kamerschen criticize some of the popular generalizations made about the less developed nations.

Leibenstein merely presents a list of economic, demographic, cultural, political, and technological factors that he feels are characteristic of many economically backward nations. While it is no doubt true that some economists would quibble with some of his characteristics — e.g., I., A., 3, regarding "disguised unemployment" — there are also a large number of economists who would accept many of the items on his list, e.g., I., A., 1, regarding the high proportion of the population in agriculture.

The Kuznets article is, in a sense, a companion to the Leibenstein list in that he elaborates on several of the items in the list as well as developing some new ones. Comparing the conditions in presently underdeveloped countries with those in the developed countries in their preindustrialization phase, Kuznets notes that:

(1.) per capita output is lower;
(2.) per capita supply of agricultural land is lower;
(3.) per capita productivity is lower;
(4.) the size distribution of income is at least as wide;
(5.) social and political factors are less favorable;
(6.) political independence is rather recent;
(7.) the inherited civilizations are quite different;
(8.) the stock of technological knowledge is greater; and
(9.) there are more developed countries in existence.

Thus, the presently developing countries possess both advantages and disadvantages over their counterparts in the past.

The Hoselitz article concentrates on the social factors in economic growth. He considers the changes in culture and social structure which the transition from a social system displaying a "traditional" form of economic organization — featuring underdeveloped, often stagnating economies — to one displaying a "more advanced" economic organization — featuring permanent, indigenous economic growth — calls forth. He argues that this process involves not merely a reshaping of the "economic order," but also a restructuring of social relations in general, or at least of those that are relevant to the performance of the productive and distributive tasks of the society. Hence, he feels that a development plan must embrace not only prescriptions for economic adjustments, but also for the channeling of associated social and cultural changes.

Haberler critically discusses four ideas that have been prominent in economic development literature regarding underdeveloped nations:

(1.) "disguised unemployment";
(2.) "balanced growth" ("big push");
(3.) the demonstration effect; and
(4.) secular deterioration in the terms of trade.

He feels that economists' preoccupation with the importance of a few highly mechanized large plants or industries goes a long way in explaining the first two of these ideas. He is equally unimpressed with the theoretical and empirical support for the last two notions. In short, all these misleading notions are based on the tenuous belief that the consumers and producers in the developing countries are irrational, ignorant, and incompetent, whereas the development economists studying these areas are alert, informed, and brilliant!

In addition to interpreting the human consequences of some recent statistics concerning the world food-population problem, Blase attempts to exploit certain common myths surrounding the food-population dilemma. In particular, he discusses five old myths that characterize the food-population problem in developing countries:

(1.) that people are lazy;
(2.) that industry is the answer to development;
(3.) that technology can be easily imported;
(4.) that importing agricultural products from developed nations is feasible; and
(5.) that there is no food-population problem.

The final article by Kamerschen is also critical of one important notion in economic development. It is believed by some social scientists that underdeveloped countries are typically plagued by the problem of overurbanization. The basic idea of overurbanization is that the developing countries are felt to have too many agricultural workers in the urban areas as a result of having been "pushed" out of rural areas because of great and increasing population pressures. Kamerschen finds both the analytical foundation and the empirical evidence supporting this theory very weak indeed.

Harvey Leibenstein†

3. CHARACTERISTICS OF UNDERDEVELOPED AREAS (COMBINED LIST)*

I. Economic

A. General

1. A very high proportion of the population in agriculture, usually some 70 to 90 percent.
2. "Absolute overpopulation" in agriculture, that is, it would be possible to reduce the number of workers in agriculture and still obtain the same total output.
3. Evidence of considerable "disguised unemployment" and a lack of employment opportunities outside agriculture.
4. Very little capital per head.
5. Low income per head and, as a consequence, existence near the "subsistence" level.
6. Practically zero savings for the large mass of the people.
7. Whatever savings do exist are usually achieved by a landholding class whose values are not conducive to investment in industry or commerce.
8. The primary industries, that is, agriculture, forestry, and mining, are usually the residual employment categories.
9. The output in agriculture is made up mostly of cereals and primary raw materials, with relatively low output of protein foods. The reason for this is the conversion ratio between cereals and meat products; that is, if one acre of cereals produces a certain number of calories, it would take between five and seven acres to produce the same number of calories if meat products were produced.
10. Major proportion of expenditures on food and necessities.
11. Export of foodstuffs and raw materials.

†Harvey Leibenstein, Andalot Professor of Economics and Population, Harvard University.
*From *Economic Backwardness and Economic Growth* (New York: John Wiley & Sons, Inc., 1957), pp. 40–41. Reprinted by permission of the publisher and the author.

12. Low volume of trade per capita.
13. Poor credit facilities and poor marketing facilities.
14. Poor housing.

B. Basic Characteristics in Agriculture

1. Although there is low capitalization of the land, there is simultaneously an uneconomic use of whatever capital exists due to the small size of holdings and the existence of exceedingly small plots.

2. The level of agrarian techniques is exceedingly low, and tools and equipment are limited and primitive in nature.

3. Even where there are big landowners as, for instance, in certain parts of India, the openings for modernized agriculture production for sale are limited by difficulties of transport and the absence of an efficient demand in the local market. It is significant that in many backward countries a modernized type of agriculture is confined to production for sale in foreign markets.

4. There is an inability of the small landholders and peasants to weather even a short-term crisis, and, as a consequence, attempts are made to get the highest possible yields from the soil, which leads to soil depletion.

5. There is a widespread prevalence of high indebtedness relative to assets and income.

6. The methods of production for the domestic market are generally old-fashioned and inefficient, leaving little surplus for marketing. This is usually true irrespective of whether or not the cultivator owns the land, has tenancy rights, or is a sharecropper.

7. A most pervasive aspect is a feeling of land hunger due to the exceedingly small size of holdings and small diversified plots. The reason for this is that holdings are continually subdivided as the population on the land increases.

II. Demographic

1. High fertility rates, usually above 40 per thousand.
2. High mortality rate and low expectation of life at birth.
3. Inadequate nutrition and dietary deficiencies.
4. Rudimentary hygiene, public health, and sanitation.

III. Cultural and Political

1. Rudimentary education and usually a high degree of illiteracy among most of the people.

2. Extensive prevalence of child labor.
3. General weakness or absence of the middle class.
4. Inferiority of women's status and position.
5. Traditionally determined behavior for the bulk of the populace.

IV. Technological and Miscellaneous

1. Low yields per acre.
2. No training facilities or inadequate facilities for the training of technicians, engineers, etc.
3. Inadequate and crude communication and transportation facilities, especially in the rural areas.
4. Crude technology.

Questions for discussion and analysis pertaining to this article may be found at the end of Article 8.

Simon Kuznets †

4. PRESENT UNDERDEVELOPED COUNTRIES AND PAST GROWTH PATTERNS*

Underdeveloped Countries Identified

By underdeveloped countries we mean those with a per capita product so low that material deprivation is widespread and reserves for emergency and growth are small. The number and identity of such countries depends, of course, upon the level at which marginal per capita income is drawn. For present purposes I prefer to set the dividing line low in order to bring the problem into sharp focus. Specifically, using the per capita national product estimates for 1952–54 (and some earlier years) prepared by the United Nations, I have placed the maximum income for underdeveloped countries at roughly $100 (in purchasing power of 1952–54).[1] By this criterion, most of the populous countries of Asia (China, India, Pakistan, Indonesia, Burma, South Korea) and many in Africa would fall within this group. It is significant that not a single reported Latin American country falls below $100 per capita. Close to half of the world population is in this group and would be even if other criteria were used, not only today, but in the 1930's and for some time back in the past.

That we have come to designate these countries as "underdeveloped" implies that their current low rates of economic performance are far short of the potential. This, as distinct from actual rates of per capita production (no matter how crude), is a presumption rather than a statement of fact. However, it seems plausible to us because in many other countries rates of economic production are at much higher per capita levels; because strikingly high rates of

†Simon Kuznets, Professor of Economics, Harvard University.

*From *Economic Growth: Rationale, Problems, Cases,* edited by Easton Nelson (Austin: University of Texas Press, 1960); reprinted in Simon Kuznets, *Economic Growth and Structure* (New York: Norton, 1965), pp. 176–193. Reprinted by permission of the publisher and the author.

[1]See United Nations, *Per Capita National Product of Fifty-five Countries: 1952–54,* Statistical Papers Series E, No. 4 (New York, 1957), and *National and Per Capita Incomes of Seventy Countries: 1949,* Statistical Papers, Series E, No. 1 (New York, October, 1950). The countries listed in the text are from both publications, with some allowance for maximum growth in countries covered for 1949 but not for 1952–54.

growth have been attained over varying long periods within the last two centuries; and because the stock of tested useful knowledge at the disposal of mankind is large and has been increasing apace. But it is, nevertheless, a presumption and we should be wary of applying patterns of economic growth observed in a few countries, accounting for at most a fifth of mankind, to the large population masses included in the underdeveloped countries as defined above. Indeed, our main purpose in stressing certain basic characteristics of these underdeveloped countries is to point up the differences between them and comparable characteristics of the presently developed countries in the decades preceding their industrialization and growth.

In such an attempt, statistical evidence, even if available, has to be treated summarily, and the choice of characteristics necessarily reflects implicit notions of factors important in economic growth, without providing explicit exposition, analysis, and defense. Nevertheless, the attempt seems worth while. Much of the writing and thinking on problems of economic growth in underdeveloped countries is unconsciously steeped in the social and economic background of the developed Western nations, and there is a temptation to extrapolate from the past growth patterns of these nations to the growth problems and potentials of the underdeveloped areas. An emphasis on the differences, viewed as obstacles to such extrapolation, may contribute to a more realistic appraisal of the magnitude and recalcitrance of the problems.

Summary Results of Comparisons

The present levels of per capita product in the underdeveloped countries are much lower than were those in the developed countries in their preindustrialization phase.

This statement can be supported by a variety of evidence and appears to be true, except in reference to Japan, where per capita income before industrialization was as low as in most of Asia today. The preindustrialization phase may be defined either as the decade when the share of the labor force in agriculture was at least six tenths of the total and was just ready to begin its downward movement, or as the decade just before those which Professor W. W. Rostow characterizes as the "take-off into self-sustained growth."[2] In either case, the evidence that we have on the presently developed countries — in Western and Central Europe, in North America, and in Oceania — shows that the per capita incomes in their preindustrial phases were already much higher than those now prevailing in the underdeveloped countries. They ranged well above $200 (in 1952–54 prices) compared with the present well below $100 for the populous underdeveloped countries of Asia and Africa. Even

---

[2]See the *Economic Journal*, LXVI, 261 (March, 1956), pp. 25–83, particularly the table of dates on p. 31.

in Russia, per capita income around 1885 was probably more than $150 (in 1952–54 prices), on the assumption that the present level is about $500.[3]

The supply of agricultural land per capita is much lower in most underdeveloped countries today than in most presently developed countries even today, let alone their preindustrial phase. Comparison of the supply of agricultural land per agricultural worker would yield similar findings.

This statement conforms to our general knowledge of the higher density of population settlement and the greater pressure of population on land in such countries as China, India, Pakistan, and Indonesia than in the older Western European countries now or even more before their industrialization, not to mention the vast empty spaces of Canada, the United States, and other Western European offshoots overseas or for that matter of the USSR. Statistical evidence assembled by Colin Clark relates agricultural land (reduced to standard units) to male workers in agriculture, and yields ratios of 1.2 workers per land unit for the United States, slightly more than 3 in the USSR, about 10 in Germany and France, and as many as 31 in India and Pakistan, 25 in China, and 73 in Egypt (post-World War II).[4] More directly relevant are the data provided by Professor Bert F. Hoselitz on the density of agricultural settlement in countries with more than half of the active labor force in agriculture, which show that in England and Wales in 1688 and in many European countries in the mid-ninteenth century the number of hectares per male worker (or household) ranged mostly between 5 and 10, whereas similar calculations for Asian countries and Egypt today show a range from well below 1 to at most 2.5 hectares.[5]

The lower per capita (and per worker) income in the underdeveloped countries — relative to that in the preindustrialization phase of the presently developed countries — is probably due largely to the lower productivity of the agricultural sector.

We have no direct confirmation at hand, but several items of indirect evidence strongly support this statement. First, and most telling, is the lower supply of agricultural land per worker noted above. Second, cross-section comparisons for recent years indicate that the shortage of per worker income in the agricultural sector relative to that in the nonagricultural sector is negatively associated with real national product per capita or per worker. This association suggests that the shortage of per worker income in the agricultural sector relative to that in the nonagricultural sector in the underdeveloped countries today is greater than it was in the preindustrial phase of presently

---

[3]This statement is based on the long-term rates of growth shown for Russia in my paper, "Quantitative Aspects of the Economic Growth of Nations: I. Levels and Variability of Rates of Growth," *Economic Development and Cultural Change,* V, 1 (October, 1956), Appendix Table 13, p. 81.

[4]See his *Conditions of Economic Progress,* 3d ed. (London, 1957), Table XXXIII, following p. 308.

[5]See his "Population Pressure, Industrialization and Social Mobility," *Population Studies,* XI, No. 2 (November, 1957), Table I, p. 126.

developed countries. Third, the nonagricultural sector in even the underdeveloped countries includes some modern industries that were nonexistent in the mid-ninteenth century or earlier. It may well be that the per worker income in the nonagricultural sector of the underdeveloped countries is today as high as per worker income in the nonagricultural sector in the preindustrialization phase of currently developed countries. On this possibly extreme assumption, per worker income in the agricultural sector in the underdeveloped countries must be one fourth or one third of per worker income in agriculture in the currently developed countries in their preindustrialization phase (much lower than the one third to one half for *total* income per worker).

Inequality in the size distribution of income in the underdeveloped countries today is as wide as, if not wider than, it was in the presently developed countries in their preindustrialization phase.

Here again we have only indirect evidence. First, limited statistical data suggest that today the inequality in income distribution in the underdeveloped countries is distinctly wider than in the developed countries.[6] Although this may be due in part to the reduction in income inequality in the process of growth of the developed countries, there is some indication that with industrialization, inequality first widened and then contracted, so that inequality in the phases *preceding* industrialization may not have been as wide as that during the early phases of industrial growth. Second, the very wide difference suggested earlier between per worker income in the agricultural and nonagricultural sectors in the underdeveloped countries, a difference wider than that in the preindustrialization phase of currently developed countries, also suggests wider inequality in the size distribution of total income.

Even if relative inequality in the size distribution of income in the underdeveloped countries today were no wider than it was in the preindustrialization phase of the currently developed countries, or even if it were slightly narrower, the appreciably lower income per capita in the underdeveloped countries would aggravate the economic and social implications. For if average income per capita is so low, the majority of the population with incomes significantly below the countrywide average must exist at distressingly low standards of living, and the contrast must be striking between, on the one hand, these large masses of agricultural cultivators and of low-paid *lumpen* proletariat in the few cities and, on the other, the small groups that, either by control of property rights or by attachment to a few economically favorable sectors, manage to secure relatively high per capita incomes.

Social and political concomitants of the low-income structure of the underdeveloped countries today appear to constitute more formidable obstacles to

---

[6]See Theodore Morgan, "Distribution of Income in Ceylon, Puerto Rico, the United States and the United Kingdom," *Economic Journal*, XVIII (December, 1953), pp. 821–834, and subsequent discussion by Harry Oshima and Theodore Morgan in *ibid.*, LXVI (March, 1956), pp. 156–164.

economic growth than they did in the preindustrialization phase of presently developed countries.

The vast array of diverse evidence on the point can hardly be summarized here, nor do we claim that these social and political patterns are necessarily consequences of the low-income structure and attributable to it alone. But at the risk of "economocentricity," it can be argued that the low economic base was a factor in producing the social and political results, and a few illustrations will elucidate the point.

First, the crude birth rates in underdeveloped countries even in recent years, are at least 40 per 1,000, and in many cases well above.[7] Rates as high as these or even higher apparently characterized the United States in the early decades of the nineteenth century, possibly Canada, and other "empty" lands overseas. But in the older countries in Western, Central, and Northern Europe, the birth rates in the preindustrialization phase were already down to the middle 30's, and in some cases close to 30 per 1,000. In other words, part of the process of demographic transition had already taken place; birth rates were as high as those in underdeveloped countries today only when the ratio of population to resources was extremely favorable. Obviously, rapid population growth under the conditions prevailing in underdeveloped countries today is an obstacle to accumulation of capital and to economic growth, as it was in the older European countries in their preindustrialization phase.

Second, let us disregard for the moment literacy rates, which are distressingly low in the underdeveloped countries today, and probably well below those in the currently developed countries in their preindustrialization phase. An even more important problem for many is linguistic and cultural disunity, a problem particularly acute for both the large population units like India and China and for the smaller ones in which groups with different antecedents have been brought together. Without claiming that economic factors predominate, one can argue that the persistingly low level of economic performance and, as part and parcel of it, of communication and transportation, has played an important role. No such major problem of linguistic and cultural unity or literacy appears to have plagued the currently developed countries during their preindustrial phase.

Third, a weak political structure is in large measure predetermined by low and unequal incomes, backwardness of transportation and communication, and linguistic and cultural disunity, if by a strong political structure one means a complex of associations culminating in an efficient sovereign government, checked and guided by underlying voluntary organizations. The cleavage between the masses of population struggling for a meager subsistence and the small groups at the top — precluding a widely graded bridge of "middle" classes — certainly militates against a strong political structure and easily

---

[7]See, for example, United Nations, *Report on the World Social Situation* (New York, 1957), particularly pp. 6–10.

leads to dictatorial or oligarchical regimes, which are often unstable and unresponsive to basic economic problems. In all these respects, the situation in the preindustrial phase of the currently developed countries, again with the possible exception of Japan, was far different in the effective interplay between the government and the interests of the population, and in the much greater influence of the various groups in the population upon the basic decisions made by the state in order to facilitate economic growth.

Most underdeveloped countries have attained political independence only recently, after decades of colonial status or political inferiority to the advanced countries that limited their independence. This is not true of the currently developed countries in their preindustrial phase; industrialization followed a long period of political independence.

This statement is a partial explanation of the weaknesses in the social and political structure of underdeveloped countries today and to that extent is a corroboration of the preceding paragraphs. But there is an important additional element in it. Insofar as their political independence has recently been won only after a prolonged struggle — and is thus an outcome of decades of opposition to the advanced countries, viewed as imperialists and aggressors — not only were economic problems neglected but the native leadership was trained in political conflict rather than in economic statesmanship. There was also a negative association between the forms of advanced economic operation, as practiced by the invaders and aggressors, and its products as reflected in a higher material standard of living: the higher standard was favored, but the forms of organization which made it possible were hated. A similar condition may have existed in the development of some of the presently developed countries: for example, a distinctive minority may have been associated with a revolutionary economic process that necessitated disruptive changes and adversely affected established interests. But such an association could not have been so widely and distinctly felt as are those in the underdeveloped countries, which have had a long history as colonies or inferior political units. Neither could the disruptive effects of the advanced elements in the economy have been as great, nor in some respects as painful, as those resulting from the introduction of Western methods and practices into a social and political framework whose historical roots were radically different from those of the West.

The populations in underdeveloped countries today are inheritors of civilizations quite distinctive from and independent of European civilization. Yet it is European civilization that through centuries of geographical, political, and intellectual expansion has provided the matrix of modern economic growth. All presently developed countries, with the exception of Japan, are either old members of the European civilization, its offshoots overseas, or its offshoots on land toward the East.

This statement is again part of the explanation of the weaknesses in the social and political structure of underdeveloped countries today. But it is useful to recall that the European community went through a series of revolutions from the fifteenth century (to set the initial date as late as possible) to the eighteenth, antedating the agricultural and industrial revolutions in eighteenth-century England which ushered in the industrial system, the vehicle of modern economic growth. The intellectual revolution with the introduction of science, the moral revolution with the secularization of Christo-Judaic religions, the geographical revolution with expansion to the East and the West, the political revolution with the formation of national states, all occurred within the context of European civilization, not in Asia, Africa, or the Americas; and they occurred long before the modern industrial system was born. Whether or not these antecedents were indispensable is unimportant here since we are not concerned with a general theory of the causes of modern economic growth. Our point is simply that participation in this long process of change before the emergence of the industrial system meant *gradual* adaptation, an opportunity to develop within the existing social and political framework the new institutions necessary to exploit the potentials provided by these intellectual, moral, geographical, and political revolutions. Thus, when the presently developed countries within the European orbit reached their preindustrialization phase, they already possessed a variety of social, political, and economic institutions, and particularly a prevailing set of views and scale of values that permitted them to make the further adjustments which industrialization brought in its wake or that were essential concomitants.

The present situations in the underdeveloped countries is in sharp contrast. They are the inheritors of different civilizations, the possessors of social, economic, and political institutions with roots that go far back and represent a heritage of adjustment to a different series of historical events, lacking the same kind of geographical, intellectual, and political revolutions, yet possibly containing a wide variety of other marked changes. These changes, however, are *not* the matrix out of which modern economic growth emerges. Consequently, there is no continuity between the adjustments that may have occurred in these underdeveloped areas before their invasion by the aggressive and expanding European civilization and the adjustments that are needed to take advantage of the potentials of modern economic growth. Some of these other civilizations did indeed reach highly impressive levels: after all, China in the seventeenth or early eighteenth century was a political unit that, in size of population and efficiency of administration, dwarfed even the largest European unit of the day; and some of the accomplishments of the native Indian civilizations were far in advance of anything that the European civilizations could produce at the time. But this very success, the specific adaptation of the social and cultural patterns to the potential (e.g., the development in China of the nonphonetic written language to overcome the problem of diversities of spoken languages, or in India of the caste system) becomes a serious obstacle in their response to an entirely different range of technological potentials, calling for a markedly different set of social and cultural behavior patterns.

These brief comments hardly exhaust the important *economic* characteristics of the underdeveloped economies today in comparison with the developed countries in their preindustrial phase. We have made no reference to the division between participation incomes (of employees and self-employed) and property incomes; the savings and capital investment proportions; the spread of the market economy and the availability of credit and financial institutions; the fiscal and tax systems; the dependence upon foreign trade. These aspects are to some degree implicit in the comparisons already made, and for some of them the evidence is yet to be assembled. And our comments on the social and political framework and the differences in historical antecedents are no more than a few broad strokes on a vast canvas, only the barest preliminary sketch.

Yet they should suffice to convey the far-reaching and striking differences between the underdeveloped countries today and the presently developed countries before their industrialization. Furthermore, many of these contrasts would persist even if the dividing line between underdeveloped and developed countries were set at an appreciably higher level of per capita income. Political weaknesses and heritages radically different from the European characterize many Latin American countries — even if their ratios of population to land or population to resources are relatively favorable — and some in the Middle East and Africa.

The Experience of Japan

Before we consider further the significance of the observations just made, a brief aside on Japan is in order. In almost all respects, except perhaps political weakness, Japan before its industrialization appeared to be similar to the populous underdeveloped countries of Asia. Yet it managed to utilize the potentials of modern economic growth and to forge ahead to higher levels of economic performance. Does this mean that the characteristics of underdeveloped countries indicated in the preceding section are not the formidable obstacles to satisfactory economic growth that we have suggested?

The analysis of the growth of Japan in the light of this question can hardly be presented here; and despite much valuable work in the field,[8] the lack of basic data precludes a firm answer. But one point must be stressed: the per capita income of Japan today, about eight decades after the beginning of the industrialization process, is still far lower than that in any other developed country within the orbit of European civilization. According to the United Nations, Japan's per capita income for 1952–54 was somewhat below $200 — lower than that in any European country covered (even Greece and Portugal) or in most of the Latin American countries. True, the comparison cannot be pushed too far, and these postwar estimates may still reflect transient reductions below the secular level. But in 1938, when economic levels elsewhere

---

[8]See particularly W. W. Lockwood, *The Economic Development of Japan* (Princeton, N.J.: Princeton University Press, 1954).

were drastically reduced after the great depression, Japan's per capita income was $86, between one third and one fifth of the per capita income in Western developed countries.[9] These low levels may be due to the limited natural resources of Japan, and cannot be extrapolated directly elsewhere. But unfavorable ratios of population to resources also characterize the populous underdeveloped countries of Asia and the Middle East, and the point to be emphasized is that despite long participation in modern economic growth, Japan does not enjoy adequately high per capita income and still suffers from the pressure of population on limited resources.

Advantages for the Underdeveloped Countries Today

But granted that the characteristics of underdeveloped countries today do constitute obstacles to economic growth that are more formidable than may have been the case in the presently developed countries in their preindustrial phase, are there not, on the other hand, substantial advantages in the very fact that these countries face the task of growth later in history? To state definitively what these advantages are calls for more knowledge than I possess. But clearly there are two major complexes: (1.) the increased stock of knowledge and experience in the fields of technological and social invention and innovation, and (2.) the extension in the number of developed countries and in their economic attainment.

The Increased Stock of Knowledge. It is hardly necessary to emphasize the striking additions that have been made over the last century, and are being made today, to the stock of basic and applied knowledge of natural processes, and of techniques of production that are the substance of much economic activity. Perhaps less obvious but equally important is the wide diversity of social techniques that have evolved. The known potential of technological and social innovations available to the underdeveloped countries today is, therefore, far greater than was that at the disposal of the presently developed countries at the middle or end of the nineteenth century, let alone earlier.

There seems to be no way to gauge the direct value of this greater potential in terms of feasible economic growth, on the one hand, and to compare it with the obstacles to such growth, on the other. But at the risk of playing the role of Devil's Advocate, I would like to stress certain aspects of this increase in the stock of technological and social knowledge that limit its possible value as a tool in the economic growth of the underdeveloped countries of today.

In the first place, most, if not all, such additions to production and social technology originated in the developed countries and were advanced in response to the needs of these economies or were adapted to the patterns of social and economic life peculiar to them. For example, the remarkable technological changes in agriculture seem to emphasize labor- rather than land-sav-

---

[9]See W. S. and E. S. Woytinsky, *World Population and Production* (New York: The Twentieth Century Fund, 1953), Table 185, p. 389.

ing innovations; but land is the more limiting factor of production in the large underdeveloped countries. Likewise, many social inventions, ranging from the more limited types in the field of financial structure or business organization to such major complexes as the planned authoritarian framework of the USSR, were evolved within the contexts of the specific economies, reflecting their distinctive social setting and historical heritage. Some of these technological and social innovations could, of course, be transferred to the underdeveloped economies of today with relatively minor modifications. But others would require major readaptation, for which the material and human resources may not be available; and still others may be so divergent from the historically determined, deep-seated factors in the structure of the underdeveloped economies that their availability in any meaningful sense of the term is questionable.

In the second place, translating any potential of technological and social innovations into reality requires an investment before returns can be expected. This investment can be defined as the input of material resources and social change required for the adoption of the technological or social innovation in more or less the form in which it is known in the developed countries. With costs so defined, this argument becomes a *supplement* to that stated just above as to the "specificity" of much of the invention and innovation that emerged during the last century. If costs are defined more widely, to include also those of readaptation and change necessary to overcome the specificity limitations, the argument would, of course, include much of what has already been said in the preceding paragraph.

If we hold to the narrower definition of costs (which is still wider than the usual one in economic analysis), the argument can be stated simply. From a review of the history of technological and economic changes since the mid-nineteenth century, one gets the impression that the stock of potential technological innovations is large, so large in fact that much of it has been utilized because of limited supplies of capital and of entrepreneurial ability, and because of the resistance of the existing social institutions, even in the most advanced countries of the day. The time span between major innovations — from the stationary steam engine to steam railroads; from steam power to electric power; from electric power to internal-combustion engines and subsequently to nuclear power (to mention only one line of change) — can be understood as largely due to the fact that even the most advanced nations of the day had neither sufficient stocks of skills needed for the adaptations involved in secondary and tertiary inventions, nor sufficient stocks of capital and economic entrepreneurship to be able to handle all these major innovations within a short time after the underlying scientific discoveries had been made. This means that most of the presently developed economies, indeed all but the pioneer in its early phases, had, in their preindustrial phase, a much larger potential of technological (and correspondingly social) changes than of the means needed to apply them. If so, the *larger* potential of technological and social innovations of the underdeveloped countries today may be of little importance in any comparison with the presently developed countries in their preindustrial phase. Such a potential, that is, a stock of tested knowledge, is a permissive necessary condition, but in itself is not *sufficient*. Material resources for capital input and readiness for social change are also essential. And as we mentioned in our comments on the characteristics of the underdeveloped economies today, material resources for capital inputs are exceedingly scarce, and the cost of social change, given the historical heritage, is unusually heavy.

Third, some of the additions to the stock of technological and social inventions during the last century may render the task of economic growth in the underdeveloped countries more rather than less difficult, if growth means simply a sustained rise in per capita product. Two illustrations come readily to mind. The first is the effect that recent discoveries and innovations in medical and public-health technology have made on the death rates. These changes have made possible in the underdeveloped countries of today far more rapid declines in mortality than occurred in the past in the currently developed countries of the West, and at extremely low cost.[10] With these rapid reductions in mortality, which require no substantial rises in economic product per capita, and with birth rates remaining high or rising, the rates of natural increase have risen rapidly to levels far higher than those observed in the preindustrial phase of the older European countries. And the resulting rapid growth of population only complicates the task of attaining higher levels of income per capita. The second illustration is suggested by what has become known in economic discussion as the "demonstration" effect. The impact of technological change during the last century on communication among various parts of the world has been perhaps as great as on any sector of economic and social activity. It brought in its wake a greater awareness in the underdeveloped countries of the higher standards of living in the developed areas, and produced a pressure for higher consumption levels that may have restricted savings and capital accumulation and added to tensions of backwardness, thus making the task of orderly economic growth only more difficult. Both these complexes of technological and social innovations are major contributions to economic product and welfare in the long run, but in the short run they aggravate the economic growth problems in the underdeveloped areas.

The Extension of the Developed Countries. The existence of many developed and advanced economic areas today, which was not the case a century ago or earlier, may be an advantage to underdeveloped countries, and not only because they are the originators and repositories of the stock of technological and social knowledge. More directly, these advanced areas can contribute to the growth of the underdeveloped countries by demand for their

---

[10]See, for example, the incisive summary discussion by George J. Stolnitz in *Trends and Differentials in Mortality,* Proceedings of a Round Table at the 1955 Annual Conference, Milbank Memorial Fund (New York, 1956), pp. 1–9.

products, by capital investment, by grants, and in many other ways by which the resources of one area can be placed at the disposal of another.

There is little question that over the last century, population, per capita income, and total income of the developed areas of the world have grown proportionately more than the corresponding aggregates for the underdeveloped areas, particularly if we confine the underdeveloped areas to the lowest income units in Asia and Africa. If the demand by developed areas for the products of underdeveloped countries could be assumed to be a constant proportion of the total income of the former, the increase in the number of developed areas would provide markets for the underdeveloped units that have increased *relative* to their domestic output. Likewise, if capital flow from advanced to underdeveloped areas were a constant fraction of the total income of the advanced areas, or still better of the disparity between the two groups in per capita income, one could state firmly that such a flow should have increased proportionately to the domestic income of the recipient underdeveloped countries. But no such constant proportions can be assumed, as can clearly be seen from the marked trends in the ratios of imports to domestic output in the developed countries, or from the well-known facts that the United States was a net capital importer during most of the nineteenth century when its per capita income was among the highest in the world, and that today many of the erstwhile international creditors countries in Europe are exporting proportionately less capital than they did before World War I, despite the fact that their per capita incomes are much higher.

A vast literature deals with import and export propensities, largely of developed countries and covering all too short a time span, and with past and current trends in capital movements among developed and underdeveloped countries. It is hardly possible, or necessary, to discuss that question now. No extensive documentation is needed to support the major point here, namely, that the mere rise in number and economic magnitude of developed countries relative to the underdeveloped ones does not necessarily mean greater relative availability of markets or capital supply from abroad. The political conditions in the underdeveloped areas may be unfavorable to foreign capital imports and to the assistance by foreign enterprises in developing and stimulating export potentials. In the large underdeveloped countries, like all large countries, capital imports can contribute only a small fraction of total capital needs. The very increase in technological potentials may have created in the developed countries themselves a backlog of investment opportunities attractive enough to absorb their savings despite the presumably greater marginal yields abroad (except in the restricted cases of capital exports needed to assure the supply of raw materials indispensable in the domestic economy). And finally, the larger number of advanced countries, emerging out of somewhat different historical antecedents and with different complexes of social institutions, has resulted in the intensified international friction and conflict which constitute a major drain upon the surplus resources of the developed areas and lead to a greater dominance of political than of economic considerations in trade and capital flows to the underdeveloped areas.

Conclusions

Two conclusions have been suggested in the preceding discussion. The first points to the major differences between underdeveloped countries today and the presently developed countries in their preindustrial phase, and the much greater obstacles to economic growth in underdeveloped areas that these differences imply. The second questions the advantages of a late start, in the way of a greater potential of new knowledge and a larger group of developed countries to draw upon. Both conclusions are only suggested: they can hardly be demonstrated with the evidence now available. And their bearing is wide, but cannot be sharply defined: discussion has been in terms of the very low income countries of Asia and Africa, but much applies to other underdeveloped countries.

If these conclusions can be accepted, at least as working hypotheses, some implications for economic analysis and policy can be drawn. These will become apparent if we envisage the process of modern economic growth as the spread of the industrial system from its origin in pioneering Great Britain to the United States and other overseas offshoots of England, Western, Central, and Northern Europe, Japan, and most recently Russia. Since this spreading productive system has a common core, both with respect to technology and the structure of human wants, some features of economic growth will be common to all countries in which it may be taking place. An agricultural revolution — a substantial rise in per capita productivity in the agricultural sector at home or an increasing reliance upon such abroad — is one important, and an indispensable, early element. Another is the growth of the nonagricultural commodity-producing and transportation sectors, industrialization in the narrow sense of the term. The growth of cities and all that is implied in modern urban civilization is a third. The shift from small, individually managed, almost family-attached economic units to big, impersonal units, whether big business corporations or state trusts, is a fourth. The number of such trends integral to modern economic growth can be multiplied, even if confined to the purely economic aspects, and there is a host of inevitable concomitants in the demographic and social processes: birth and death rates, internal migration, literacy, skills of the labor force, and so on, ranging to changes in scales of values. These will all be found wherever the industrial system flourishes, whether in the older European countries that still retain large residues of the preindustrial social structure or in the young and initially empty countries overseas; under capitalism or under the state-managed system of the USSR.

Yet this common core of technological and of minimum social changes associated with the industrial system was planted, as it spread from country to country, within units with different antecedents and historical heritage. And some of the social forms in which the system was clothed were quite different. They were different partly because the one central complex was combined with diverse initial conditions in the various countries of adoption; partly because the very fact that one country was the pioneer, others the immediate followers, and others came still later, in itself affected the measures by which growth or "catching up" was attempted, and the very spirit in which they were undertaken. Differences were also imposed by the size of the countries, economic growth in small and large countries being quite different in method, if not in the common aim of using the potential of modern technology to attain higher levels of economic performance.

This general model suggests that the aim of research on economic growth is to establish and measure the common and variant characteristics of the process; to "explain" the interrelations of the common and variant characteristics, that is, to integrate them into a theory of the growth of a country's economy viewed as a system of interdependent parts combined with a theory of the spread and modification of the process of economic growth as it occurs among pioneer and follower nations; large and small units; and so on. Such an attempt has barely begun, partly because interest in economic growth has been revived only in recent decades, after a long lapse since the mid-nineteenth century and partly because the available data are hard to come by, and have not yet been properly organized and examined. Economic analysis alone may not be sufficient for the explanation and elucidation of economic growth and the provision thereby of a sound basis for growth policy. It is clear, however, that the empirical findings that we now have, being based largely on data for a few developed countries for insufficiently long periods, cover too narrow a range; that the functional relations established from them cannot be extrapolated too far in time and in space; that the very conceptual structure of economic analysis, having been geared to the Western economies and to the short-run problems, may need substantial revision before it can effectively explain the past economic growth of the presently developed countries — let alone be applied to the growth problems of underdeveloped countries today. The comments above on some of the distinctive characteristics of these underdeveloped countries only point up how far removed these countries are from the observable and measurable economic experience, which is the raw material of almost all our empirical research and theoretical analysis.

This bears also upon discussion of policy related to growth problems in the underdeveloped countries, whether by professional economists or by laymen who either eventually make the decisions or determine them by their attitudes. Such economic-policy decisions should presumably be based upon tested knowledge of the possible impact of various factors or measures in relation to clearly formulated objectives. That little of such tested knowledge exists can hardly be denied; nor is it surprising that much of the technical discussion of growth policy is based on mechanical analogies, no matter how elaborate; and much of the discussion by laymen, particularly in the developed countries, follows along similar lines expressed in the cruder terms of what was good for us should be good for them.

These remarks are not meant to advocate abandoning all attempts to formulate bases for analysis and for intelligent discussion of policy. Failure to analyze and recommend is in itself a decision to do nothing, a policy that can hardly be defended. The plea here is for greater realization of how little is known and how much there is to be learned, and hence for greater caution in building models and writing prescriptions; for a clearer perception, particularly on the part of policy-makers, that the problems facing the underdeveloped countries are far more difficult than they appear at first sight, and that these countries cannot be expected to follow the patterns of presently developed areas which had entirely different beginnings.

Questions for discussion and analysis pertaining to this article may be found at the end of Article 8.

Bert Hoselitz †

5. SOCIAL IMPLICATIONS OF ECONOMIC GROWTH*

Part I

The widespread political interest in recent years in the conditions and problems of economic development, and in policies designed so far as possible to abolish poverty and want in many parts of the world, has reinforced among economists the study of theoretical problems associated with economic growth. Economists have long been interested in the forces favoring economic progress. As W. W. Rostow recently pointed out, Adam Smith's *Wealth of Nations* gives great weight to the consideration of economic policies most conducive to economic growth, and the subsequent writings of the classical economists were, to a considerable extent, elaborations of some of these points. Smith and his immediate successors wrote at a time when a constant relation between economic theory and economic policy was considered both necessary and obvious. Since the middle of the last century, however, a body of economic theory began to establish itself, which, on the one hand, to an ever-increasing degree was isolated from the immediate policy implications to which it was subject, and on the other, assumed human motivations and the social and cultural environment of economic activity as relatively rigid and unchanging data. In consequence, the further development of the theory of economic growth (with some notable exceptions like the work of Professor Joseph Schumpeter) tended to concentrate almost exclusively on the task of relating purely economic variables to one another and to disregard the political and social changes which accompanied the process of economic growth.

Even in present attempts at restating the basic framework of an economic theory of economic growth, the necessity of relating this theoretical framework to the cultural conditions and political needs of areas undergoing rapid economic change is sometimes underestimated or overlooked. Propositions

†Bert F. Hoselitz, Professor of Social Science and Economics, University of Chicago. Dr. Hoselitz is the Editor of the influential *Economic Development and Cultural Change.*

*From *Economic Weekly* (Annual edition, January, 1959), pp. 181, 183, 185, 187, 188; (February 14), pp. 261–266, and (February 21, 1959), pp. 291–296. Reprinted by permission of the publisher and the author.

which deal with the dependence of economic progress on the nature of income distribution, the relative magnitude of savings, the impact of inflationary pressures, and the state of a country's balance of payments and terms of trade, are clearly relevant, yet it must be recognized that even a knowledge of all these relationships is not enough, but only a beginning, for a theory which realistically deals with all the variables involved in the development process. And if economists specify (as they sometimes do) that, in addition to the various economic adjustments, a change in the social values cherished by a population is necessary, they make a statement which is true, but on this level of generality meaningless, for it cannot be translated into operational terms.

Wanted: A Theory to Relate Economic Development to Cultural Change

What is needed, therefore, is not merely a theory of economic growth in purely economic terms, but a theory relating economic development to cultural change. In view of the great uncertainties in the realm of theory which concerns itself with cultural change in general, it may be premature and, in terms of scholarly resources available, perhaps uneconomical even to attempt the statement of a general theory of economic development and cultural or socio-structural change. We may better begin by developing theoretical models for different types of societies and different types of movements or transitions from "traditional" to more "modern" forms of economic organization. The attempts to develop a general, universally valid theory of economic and cultural change may lead into the impenetrable jungle in which have been lost so many who searched for the way to the formulation of a general theory of history. The attempt to meet a more limited objective, the concentration on situations which are now clamoring for practical solution, may lead to the elaboration of a theoretical framework which may be useful not merely in providing a guide for present policy, but also in enlarging the boundaries of our general theoretical knowledge of social and economic change.

In pursuing this more limited objective one outstanding case presents itself, both because of its contemporary practical significance and its intrinsic theoretical interest. This is the problem of economic growth and associated cultural change in those countries which, in the official language of the United Nations and the United States Department of State, are designated as "underdeveloped." A Committee of Experts of the United Nations has defined such a country as one "in which per capita real income is low when compared with the per capita real income of the United States of America, Canada, Australasia, and Western Europe."

Problem of Transition

This definition not only specifies the variable which is considered most significant in measuring the level of economic advancement, but also classifies a series of countries as advanced and others as underdeveloped. It further suggests that the most important problem for investigation is the transition from a state of "underdevelopment" to one of "development" or "full development," and that other processes of economic change, even if they are associated with an increase of real income (that variable by which the level of development is measured), are not necessarily relevant or may not be subject to the same regularities as the transition from economic backwardness to economic advancement.

If, moreover, instead of regarding this transition as a problem of economic growth in abstract, purely formal economic terms, we center our attention on how underdeveloped, often stagnating, economies reach a form of economic organization which permits them to achieve permanent indigenous economic growth, we are invariably driven to consider (in addition to the formal mechanisms of economic adjustment) the changes in culture and social structure which this transition calls forth.

Instead of being concerned with the problem of economic growth in the most general terms, we are interested in elaborating a theoretical model which permits us to analyze a process of transition from a social system displaying a "traditional" form of economic organization to one displaying a different, presumably "more advanced" economic organization.

This process involves not merely a reshaping of the "economic order" but also a restructuring of social relations in general, or at least of those social relations which are relevant to the performance of the productive and distributive tasks of the society.

In practice, that is, in a situation requiring the elaboration of a development plan for a given country or region, this problem requires for its solution that the plan embrace not only prescriptions for economic adjustments but also for the channeling of associated social and cultural changes.

Variety of Actual Conditions

The United Nations Technical Assistance Administration and other agencies participating in programs evolving development plans are conscious of this need, and technical missions going to underdeveloped countries include, in addition to economists and engineers, specialists in education, social welfare, and sometimes even cultural anthropology. Their task is to advise how economic planning may be directed into channels in which frictions with existing cultural and social forces will be minimized and incentives for the planned changes maximized. Owing to profound differences in the cultures of the various populations participating in economic development plans, a multitude of forms has been found in which cultural or social structural factors do affect economic growth. The very great variety of actual conditions appears to make generalizations impossible, or at least very difficult.

Yet several attempts to generalize have been undertaken. These attempts were not specifically related to the elaboration of a general theory of economic development and cultural change, but rather to the development of a theory of capitalism — a problem which has some similarities to the one under consideration. Such a theory confines itself to propositions on the pattern of economic growth and associated social change under specific historical conditions encountered by the countries of Western Europe and by overseas territories settled by Western Europeans in the last three or four hundred years.

Past Development Unplanned

But the development of capitalist economies in Western Europe consisted of unplanned autonomous movements, whereas the current efforts to induce economic growth are consciously initiated and, as far as possible, carefully planned, at least in their economic aspects. The fundamental difference in developing a theory for past and present economic growth is that the former process is an overall social process in which *a priori* no causal primacy can be assigned to any one or any one set of variables. As concerns present instances of economic development, it is quite proper to regard such factors as accumulation of capital, planned introduction of new skills and new work techniques as the primary variables, and to regard adjustments in the social structure as positive, negative or neutral "responses" to these "stimuli." In other words, the governments of underdeveloped countries are resolved to plan for economic development and to carry out these plans to the extent of their abilities. The impact of social and cultural factors consists, therefore, not in determining whether or not, or even in what form, economic growth is to take place, but how easily and smoothly the objectives of a development plan can be attained and what costs — not all of which are strictly measurable in money or other resources — are involved in reaching the goals.

Thus, apart from the case of autonomous, unplanned economic growth exemplified by Western European capitalism, in which cultural and socio-structural variables may be assumed to have created the conditions for economic change, in all those instances in which economic change is planned, the social structure and the culture impose modifications of, and in some instances, barriers to the process of economic change.

Limitations Largely Non-economic

Although a series of predominantly economic factors may be enumerated which account for some of the limitations and difficulties in the path of economic development, many of them are, in turn, based upon political and socio-structural arrangements. For example, the very poverty of poor countries, the high propensity to consume on the part of a large proportion of their population, the real or alleged low rate of savings, and the tendency of a high birth rate are such barriers. Additional economic barriers of a more specialized kind are difficulties of meeting balance of payments deficits due to capital goods imports which are needed urgently for development, the constant threat of inflationary pressures, inadequate fiscal procedures, misallocation of real savings which are applied to the construction of durable consumers' goods, such as luxury apartment houses, night clubs, and hotels, rather than for industries producing mass consumption goods, unbalanced and frequently overambitious development plans, and the inability to carry through much needed land reforms.

But however real all these difficulties may be, they are grounded in the last resort on the peculiarities of political and social relations of underdeveloped countries rather than on specific economic principles applicable to them. Many of these difficulties are the outflow of perennial poverty and would presumably wholly or partially disappear if the poverty of the less advanced countries could be mitigated. For example, it has been asserted repeatedly that the quasi-Malthusian dilemma which many of these countries face would be eradicated by a rapid increase in average real incomes, and that the attainment of higher incomes in itself would exert a brake on further rapid population growth. Similarly, it may be argued that the "misdirection" of real savings into cash hoards, foreign assets, or durable consumer goods of an obvious luxury type, is an outcome of the wide diversity in wealth, political power, and education between different classes of the society; and that the overemphasis on investment in real estate, which in some countries has led to a relative hyperinflation of land values, is determined in large part by a set of cultural values which are still strongly tainted by traditional attitudes reaching back to an era in which the holding of large landed estates was the most important outward sign of elevated social status.

Equilibrium of Stagnation

The barriers in the path of economic development of underdeveloped countries, whether looked at from a strictly economic or a wider socio-structural viewpoint, appear to be due to two related facts. One is the existence of a situation of relative socio-economic equilibrium which an economically underdeveloped country exhibits, and the other is the abrupt, quasi-explosive character of the transition process from a stage of underdevelopment to a stage of advancement. I wish to discuss these two propositions a little more in detail.

The concept of equilibrium is familiar to social scientists and has been used with good results in several connections. Unfortunately, a state of equilibrium is sometimes confused with a state of perfect immobility. In consequence, social scientists speak of "dynamics" whenever any movement in the social structure they study is discernible. It is clear that the concept of equilibrium is used here not in this narrow sense of frozenness, but rather in the sense in which economists use the concept "stationary" equilibrium. In this meaning we speak of a system in equilibrium if, as a consequence of movement by one variable or one set of variables, a countermovement is released which has the tendency of reestablishing the original situation. Examples of the forces and counterforces which exist in an underdeveloped country are provided by the dilemmas created as a consequence of unbalanced development programs, or the partial implementation and partial non-fulfillment of such programs. The need for consistency in socio-economic plans and the dire results of contradictory targets have been made evident by frequent experiences in the Soviet Union and other countries with rigorous central plans. As I will show later, this kind of imbalance in the implementation of development programs may be an obstacle to economic advancement, especially if various complementary parts of a development program are accomplished with different speeds. I shall show how a health program outran a necessary educational program, and how, through the lagging education of the population concerned, the health program failed in the long run.

Experience of Latin America

It may perhaps sound somewhat absurd to designate a situation of stagnation and persistent poverty as a stage of equilibrium. But how else should we describe a situation in which the various social forces appear to be balanced so neatly, and in which cultural values tend to emphasize so strongly a status quo, that the general framework of social relations has remained essentially unchanged for many generations, in spite of halting and gradual advances in technical skills and slight increases of real income?

The conquest of Latin America by the Spaniards brought a real change in the social relations under which the indigenous population lived, a set of cultural values and socio-political principles was erected which have undergone little if any fundamental change, in spite of the achievement of independence, in spite of the slowly changing ethnic composition of most countries, and in spite of the often rapid succession of short-lived governments. Only Mexico's revolution of 1910 went beyond strictly political limits and took on a social character. But in all other Spanish-American countries — barring Chile and Argentina whose entire settlement patterns and demographic-ethnic composition differed basically from those of the other countries — we witness a tenacious clinging to the social and cultural system introduced by Spain some four hundred years ago.

In spite of the superficially intensely revolutionary history of many of the Latin American countries, few, if any, tendencies making for real social change developed. The high degree of adaptability of the social framework existing in these countries is manifested by the fact that it proved relatively invulnerable against the inroads made in the economy of these countries by large foreign investments. Also, this framework survived almost without change important political changes. For example, in the Republics of Central America, it survived the attainment of political independence, the decomposition of the Federation of Central America, and the formal severance of political ties with the Spanish Empire. I do not wish to discuss the historical determinants of this remarkable degree of stability in the general makeup of the social framework, but no doubt a good deal of weight must be attributed in the explanation of this stability to Dr. Angel Palerm's insistence on the prevalence of medieval-feudal values over those of the nascent Renaissance middle classes in Spain at the time of the conquest of America.

Social Forces in Spain

Of all the dates in Spanish history, the year 1492 stands out. At that moment a task had been achieved which, for centuries, had collected and inspired all the forces Christianity could muster on the Iberian peninsula. The expulsion of the Arabs had taken place under the clear and unmistakable leadership of the Castilian knights. However subject to ridicule and satire might appear the values and social order of Castilian chivalry to Cervantes at the turn of the seventeenth century, less than a hundred and fifty years before the publication of *Don Quixote* these were the values and the social order under whose aegis the most notable achievements of Spanish Christianity had been accomplished. In the process, the merchants of Barcelona, Valencia, and other trading towns had contributed funds and materials without which the task could not have been accomplished. But the leadership was with Castile. Under the overwhelming impact of these events began a period in which all the evolutionary forces of which Spain was capable seemed to blossom out suddenly. The constellation of the social forces, attained at the end of the Arab wars, prevailed for some time, and it was a social framework which stood under the strong influence of Spanish feudal society which became transferred to the newly conquered territories in the New World. The political and economic institutions of the new provinces were created under the impact of strong feudalistic survivals in Spain's social order and, because of the relative isolation from the main arena of social and political development in northwestern Europe — an isolation which the merchantilist policy of Spain enhanced even more — the Spanish colonies in America developed an even stronger attachment to traditional social arrangements than the mother country itself.

By the time the old social order had been replaced in Spain by the more liberal regimes of the last Bourbons, it still flourished in full bloom in Latin America. Whatever other differences there may exist in the endowment with natural resources, conditions of soil, climate, and other environmental factors between the United States and Canada, on the one hand, and Hispanic America on the other, a most plausible case for the difference in economic advancement between Anglo-Saxon and Iberian America can be made by stressing the different social systems under which the exploration and settlement of each of the two areas occurred. Anglo-Saxon America was discovered and settled by a population which adhered fully to the social values of modern capitalism. Indeed, New England Puritanism represents the epitome of the capitalist spirit in the sense in which Max Weber used the term. Ibero-America, on the other hand, was explored and settled under the leadership of a group of men who had experienced the power of feudal institutions and who believed in the hegemony of knighthood and its ideology over the bourgeoisie and its values. The institutionalization of the two sets of cultural value in the regions of overseas settlement by Anglo-Saxons on the one hand and Iberians on the other appears to lend a strong dynamism to one set of societies and a quality of exceedingly stable equilibrium to the other set.

A Quasi-Explosive Process

The corollary to interpreting an underdeveloped economy as being in an equilibrium stage — even though this state is not an enviable one — is the proposition that the transition to a state of economic advancement is an abrupt, or, as I have said earlier, a quasi-explosive process. This process does not merely have a sudden beginning; its main characteristic is its relative shortness and the rapidity with which alterations in the society and economy take place. This aspect of the crucial stage in the process of economic advancement is such an outstanding phenomenon that it is often not especially underlined. For example, Professor Viner in discussing the experience of the western countries which have attained a high level of average output says that "rapid economic progress has come to only a few countries and usually only for limited periods of time." In this passage, he sums up what is called here the transition process in almost epigrammatic form. For although it is not denied that some highly developed societies have experienced periods of rapid economic expansion (for example the United States after 1940), most actual examples of rapid economic progress which would be cited would consist of an enumeration of the "industrial revolutions" which the various advanced countries of the West have passed through.

The conception of the transition stage as a quasi-explosive process of change coincides with some aspects of Professor Schumpeter's view on economic development. As is well known, Schumpeter defines economic development as the carrying out of new combinations, that is, the introduction of innovations. New combinations may be of various kinds. Schumpeter singles out five: the introduction of a new good; of a new method of production; the opening of a new market; the conquest of a new source of supply; and the elaboration and application of a new form of industrial organization. But not all new combinations are genuine economic development, only those which produce breaks or discontinuities. Schumpeter says explicitly that "insofar as the new combination may in time grow out of the old by continuous adjustment in small steps, there is certainly change, possibly growth, but neither a new phenomenon nor development in our sense."

It would be an interesting exercise to investigate in greater detail the difference between continuous and discontinuous change in each of the five sub-classes Schumpeter enumerates. For example, it is difficult to conceive how the conquest of a new source of supply could be anything else but a discontinuous change. On the other hand, it is true that the introduction of a new good or of a new method of production may be slow, gradual processes of change which occur over long periods of time in such a way as to make it impossible in any relatively short interval to measure the degree of change which has occurred.

Discontinuous Changes Are Bunched

Schumpeter does not specify the unit with which he is concerned. When he speaks of the differences between slow, continuous, and discontinuous changes, he does not indicate what social entity he considers undergoing change. From the general context of his discussion, for example, the emphasis on the role of entrepreneurs as the carriers of innovations, it appears that he thinks of a firm or perhaps an industry. However, on the basis of a more general social theory the hypothesis may be stated that discontinuous change, when it occurs, is not likely to be a singular phenomenon, but appears to be bunched. In other words, if we have one instance of discontinuous change, i.e., if we encounter one new combination which represents economic development in Schumpeter's sense, we may expect with a high degree of probability other simultaneous discontinuous changes in the same society. This means nothing else but that a society either shows characteristics of relative stability, i.e., the equilibrium state of underdevelopment, or relative progressiveness.

If the process of the economic advancement of a society were plotted on a Cartesian diagram, and time were measured along the horizontal axis and some index of economic development — say average income — along the vertical axis, this hypothesis would yield a curve resembling a flattened out S. Both tails of the curve would be almost horizontal and the middle part of the curve would be steep. The lower left tail of such a curve represents the stage of economic underdevelopment, and the upper right tail that stage of "economic maturity," if such a stage is ever reached. If we assume the curve to be smooth throughout, the problem of distinguishing between two or more stages of economic development, becomes one of arbitrarily selecting points on the curve, which represent class limits into which countries corresponding to the various stages (for example "underdeveloped," "intermediate," "advanced") are to be placed. But historical evidence would lend plausibility to the statement supported earlier that the curve itself is discontinuous, and that the stage of economic development exhibits, in its initial phase, an "explosive" character.

It is extremely difficult, if not impossible, to adduce incontrovertible historical evidence for this statement, since reliable statistical data in sufficient detail and accuracy for any index of economic development are lacking. But the explosive character of industrialization, wherever it has occurred, has been noted not infrequently. For example, Paul Mantoux writes of the English industrial revolution that it was "the sudden growth and blossoming of seeds which had for many years lain hidden or asleep;" John H. Clapman writes about Germany in the middle 1860's that "all the forces tending towards industrialism and urbanization had struck Germany at once;" and Louis M. Hacker regards the American Civil War as an event which "helped in the maturing of our industrial production and, more particularly, our heavy industries, virtually over night." These are "qualitative" statements, but they are expressed by leading economic historians whose thorough familiarity with the events about which they write cannot be doubted. The overall impression gained from G. C. Allen's discussion of Japanese industry in the early 1930's appears an additional point in fact, and the extremely rapid increase in average output in the Soviet Union under the first three five-year plans provides another example of sudden and rapid economic advance.

Primarily in Industrial Sector

The instances which have been cited have several characteristics in common. At the time the process of rapid advancement set in, the countries already had sizable secondary industries, although in a large proportion the majority of the labor force was still employed in agriculture. The advance was made primarily in the industrial sector, but agriculture participated in the developmental process. After a relatively short time, sometimes not more than two generations, the increase in output rose so much that, in spite of a rapidly growing population, it exerted a noticeable impact upon living standards. And in those cases where this was not true, as in Japan and the Soviet Union, it was due to the deliberate diversion of resources into armament industries and/or the planned accumulation of capital at an exceedingly high rate. Moreover, an important feature of an economy which has passed through the explosive transition stage of development is that at the end further capital expansion can normally be financed out of voluntary net savings, whereas in underdeveloped economies voluntary gross savings often are insufficient to supply funds for replacement and wear and tear of capital equipment. In other words, an underdeveloped economy constantly hangs on the verge of decline, unless it is bolstered up by imports of foreign capital in the form of loans or grants, or by economic or political pressures which force constraints upon domestic consumption standards that would be absent if more reliance could be placed on voluntarism.

Some evidence for this last observation is provided by the experience of countries, notably Taiwan and The Philippines, where after the withdrawal of suzerainty by a colonizing metropolitan power, capital was not only not maintained at a stable level, but the quantity of capital declined even though foreign aid, in some instances on a large scale, was forthcoming. I am not suggesting that some of this decline cannot be ascribed to the war, but from whatever scanty statistical data are available, we can conclude that the loss of capital in the postwar period in these two countries was greater than can be attributed to the destruction of war and subsequent civil strife. I am not suggesting either that societies on a low level of economic development do not undergo changes in their productive structure. Certainly the economic history of the countries of South and East Asia, or of Ibero-America shows that new capital, new industries, and new equipment were installed. But these new installations have left unaffected the overwhelming majority of the countries' producers, and although some installations have been on a considerable scale, they were not large enough to shake up traditional socio-structural relations sufficiently to set in motion a rapid process of development similar to that which occurred in the economically advanced societies of the West.

Part II

The interpretation of the crucial phase of the economic development process as an "explosive process" leads to a series of important considerations. To begin with, it forces us to distinguish neatly between two, and perhaps three different stages in the growth pattern, the stage of "underdevelopment," the stage of "transitional growth," and the stage of "advancement." Most reasoning by economists on economic development has been grounded upon the experiences gained from, or assumed to reign in, advanced societies. If, on the other hand, we distinguish different stages of growth it becomes necessary also to distinguish different degrees of applicability of various economic propositions. For example, the statement that in order to have an increase in output, accumulation of capital is necessary, other things being equal, is applicable to all stages of growth. But the statements that the development of new skills is entirely or predominantly a cost borne by private individuals, i.e., that the investment in "human capital" is a matter of purely private decision making, or that a certain given rate of investment can be attained also on the basis of purely private decisions, may be propositions which are not applicable to all stages of the growth process. This partial inapplicability is not due to their limited economic validity, but to their full or partial incompatibility with structural relations of societies in certain less advanced stages of economic growth.

Growth of Total Real Output

A second consideration is that in appraising the nature of the transition process the customary yardstick of average output may fail us. Although there does not seem to exist any inner necessity for this, historically, economic "revolutions" which coincided with the "explosive" transitional stages have also been periods of rapid population growth. This means that the rate of growth of total real output is usually much faster than the rate of per capita output. For example, on the basis of the data published by Colin Clark, the total real income of Japan more than doubled in the 27 years from 1887 to 1914, whereas real product per man-year only increased by 61 percent in the same period. During the next decade, from 1914 to 1924, total real income again more than doubled, whereas product per man-year increased by just 100 percent. Total real income again more than doubled in the next 13 years, from 1924 to 1937, whereas total real product per man-year increased only by about 80 percent. If the rise in total real output had been compared with per capita real income figures rather than real product per man-year, the discrepancies in growth rates would have been even greater.

Results similar to those for Japan are also obtained from Colin Clark's figures for the chief Western European countries, for example, France, Belgium, Netherlands, Switzerland, Germany, and notably Great Britain. For the latter country Clark's figures show that from 1812 to 1841/47 national income in constant prices rose by 38 percent and that income per head of working population decreased by about 10 percent. This result is difficult to believe. But even if we assume that this result is the outcome of the use of price deflators of somewhat doubtful validity, and that it is based, moreover, on faulty estimates of both the 1812 and 1841/47 income figures, it is not altogether surprising to find that British real incomes per occupied person remained constant or increased only imperceptibly during the 30 years following the end of the Napoleonic wars. Nevertheless, in terms of structural alterations and the introduction of innovations, this period of British economic history was as productive as any other before or after. It was during this time that the first railroads were built, that the influence of bank credit in the financing of industrial enterprises made itself strongly felt for the first time, and that the joint-stock company as a form of organization of industrial (in contrast to commercial or financial) enterprises was inaugurated on a large scale.

Changes in Societal Structure

Thus, the transition period may be said to be characterized by a rapid growth of total real output, rather than average real income and the fruits of economic development in the form of improved living standards (especially mass living standards) may only accrue after the transition process is well under way and, in extreme cases, after this stage has come to an end. But if this is so, the question may be raised in what way can a process of transition from a stage of "underdevelopment" to a stage of "advancement" be distinguished from a process of gradual, slow increase in total income which may be, among other reasons, caused merely by a growth of the number of population? This is a troublesome question, for as Professor Viner has shown, economic growth might be and sometimes is viewed as the "result of growth of a population which was and remains miserably poor, ill fed, ill housed, ill governed, unwashed, untutored, and unhealthy."

It is clear that the purely economic measures do not serve in order to distinguish in such a case. Even the so-called non-monetary measures, such as for example, number of hospital beds per 1000 persons, or illiteracy rates, or consumption of square yards of cloth per person per year, do not help. The only indication of whether we have economic development or not is provided by answering the question whether and to what extent alterations in the overall societal structure have taken place. The process of innovation which economists tend to apply only to economic variables, is one which may also produce social innovations. Only if the economic innovations are of a magnitude or profundity to affect the society as a whole in its internal structural relations can we speak of genuine economic development.

No Rigid Pattern

The third general observation on the nature of the transition process is still necessary. So far the discussion has been kept, at least in its more theoretical portions, on a level of generality which may have given the impression that the development process and, in particular, the transition stage, follow one fairly rigid pattern. This is, of course, by no means the case. I have already pointed out that economic growth is essentially a process which forms part of the history of a society and that more insights may be gained about the nature of the process of economic growth from historical studies than from either generalizations drawn from hypothetical situations resulting in a framework of arbitrary assumptions characteristic of stationary analysis in economics, or from the tacit or explicit assumption that currently underdeveloped countries are in any but the most fundamental socio-cultural aspects the images of earlier historical stages of currently developed countries. But if the study of economic growth can be furthered significantly by concentration on historical patterns of development, we must guard against falling into the other extreme of regarding each process of economic growth as so unique that its study may not yield the recognition of factors which lend themselves to general application.

Four Propositions

One attempt to derive a generally applicable set of propositions from historical study has been undertaken by Professor Simon Kuznets. Among the statements which he believes are generally applicable from his survey of historical development patterns, notably in those countries which now have the highest per capita real incomes, Professor Kuznets stresses especially the following four:

(1.) The main advances in real income were achieved in the last 150 to 200 years. This would lead to the social and economic history of the world of more than 200 years ago or — if we stipulate a more or less long gestation period — of say 300 years ago, and is of little significance for our problem.

(2.) The main advances were made in association with the introduction of industrialism, that is, a "wide application of knowledge, based on empirical science, to the problem of economic and social technology."

(3.) The introduction of a system of industrialism, characterized by these traits requires a "cultural milieu in which existing values do not impede an open-minded view on nature, a dispassionate consideration of empirical findings, and a strong desire to enhance the material welfare of man."

Propositions (2.) and (3.) are most widely accepted and universally agreed upon as conditions and/or results of economic advancement. In fact, the attempts of most underdeveloped countries today are directed toward the acquisition of a sizable sector of industry and one of the chief obstacles which they encounter is the impediment imposed upon this endeavor by the tenacity of traditional so-called "irrational" cultural valuations on the part of many persons in economically little advanced societies. The joint efforts of the technical aid programs of the United Nations, the World Bank, the Food and Agriculture Organization, and other agencies are directed, therefore, toward the provision of improved technologies, while the complementary efforts of Unesco are directed at a simultaneous eradication of illiteracy and the provision of more adequate educational and research services, so as to lay the groundwork for cultural change.

(4.) The last general finding of Professor Kuznets is the proposition that the adoption of a system of industrialism apparently requires a system of private enterprise as the main form of economic organization and democracy (in the Western sense) as the prevalent form of political organization.

Taken together, these propositions amount to stating that the only society which has so far proved to be capable of developing the productive forces of the economy sufficiently to show a sizable gain in real income has been modern Western free enterprise capitalism.

Not Representative Enough

A further task which remains is to determine whether the four factors which were singled out by Kuznets are related to one another in some peculiar fashion, or whether they are, in turn, all dependent in some clearly identifiable way on some other variable not specifically stressed by him. We are here confronted with the problem of developing a theory of capitalist development, a task which has been undertaken by many men of genius, but which has not been crowned with conclusions which find general and undisputed acceptance. All the great theories of capitalist development by men like Malthus and Ricardo, Marx and his disciples, Sombart, Weber, and others, have found more or less convincing critics; and a synthetic theory which would incorporate all that is good in the various "one-sided" theories has not been proposed and may be impossible to develop.

The very procedure chosen by Professor Kuznets, that is, his study of the past growth processes of only those countries which on a cross-sectional basis show the highest per capita incomes is, in part, responsible for this outcome. Although it is plausible to expect that more can be learned about the history of the growth process if the most advanced countries are selected for study, an analysis of the predominant social relations in these advanced countries would have shown that they exhibit similar political and socio-economic foundations, and a generalization of our insights in the development process would have required comparison with countries which, on the one hand, have shown clear signs of economic growth although, on the other, they may not yet have reached a level high enough to be ranked among the approximately 15 countries with the highest per capita incomes.

Japan and Soviet Union

The two countries which have, doubtless, shown signs of rapid growth, although in terms of per capita income they have not caught up yet with Western Europe and North America, are Japan and the Soviet Union. The fact that Japan experienced a period of rapid economic growth following the restoration of the Meiji is generally admitted and clearly appears from the figures which Professor Clark has published and to which reference was made a little earlier. Although on the basis of a measure in the customary per capita income terms, Japan is still below the countries of Western Europe, Anglo-Saxon North America and Australasia, it has attained a level of productivity which is substantially higher than that of any comparable oriental society.

As concerns the Soviet Union there is considerable dispute as to the precise magnitude of economic advancement since the inauguration of the first Five Year Plan. In part, this is due to the scarcity and incompleteness of Russian statistical data, in part to the arbitrary value assigned to the monetary unit, and in part, doubtless, to some bias with which most students approach Soviet data. However, from a neutral and fairly unbiased, as well as rather well-informed source, the Economic Commission for Europe of the United Nations, we may conclude that the Soviet Union has made rapid and impressive economic progress in the last thirty years. Comparing the output of several strategic raw materials and fuels in the Soviet Union and the seven most highly industrialized countries of Western Europe (which, in 1951, had together a population approximately equal to that of the USSR), the Economic Commission for Europe concludes that, in 1951, "the output of coal, electricity and steel in the Soviet Union is about one-half of that in Western Europe and is increasing at a much faster rate than can be expected for

Western Europe," and that "there are indications that, if present rates of expansion are maintained, by the end of this decade the production and consumption of major industrial raw materials in the Soviet Union will be equal or superior to that in the seven most industrialized countries of Western Europe." On the basis of this evidence and the undoubted industrial inferiority of Russia at the time of the Revolution and even thereafter, the fact of rapid economic progress in the Soviet Union cannot be doubted.

If we confine our historical analysis and the attempt to derive generalizations from it is not confined to the few Western countries which had (on the basis of the United States Department of State computations) per capita real incomes of more than $200 in 1939, but includes also the historical analysis of Japanese and Russian development, we may be forced to alter some of the generalizations offered by Professor Kuznets. Economic development, as viewed here, is interpreted as a process exhibiting a noticeable improvement of output achieved ordinarily in a short period of time, whereas, in the view of Kuznets, the additional condition is set that a minimum level of per capita real income be reached or exceeded. A less rigorous definition of economic advancement results in admitting the possibility that certain factors may be operative which may prevent an economy from reaching a certain level of development, although they do not prevent development altogether. For example, on the basis of the data supplied by Colin Clark, the highest figure of Japanese output per man-year ever reached was 649 International Units. This figure, which was obtained in 1943, is roughly six and a half times that of annual output per member of the labor force at the beginning of the Japanese process of growth in 1887. But it remains below the annual product per man-year which in the United States and Great Britain was reached before the middle of the nineteenth century. Moreover past economic progress in the United States and Great Britain has been, and chances for future progress in these countries are much better than in Japan, so that it may justly be doubted whether Japan ever will catch up with the United States and Great Britain.

Coal-Oil-Steel Complex

This last statement rests on an implicit assumption, that is, that future chances of growth are best in those societies which have already made the most rapid and far-reaching progress in the past. Let us recall that the first general proposition cited from Professor Kuznets related to the relative recency of the growth process in the most advanced countries. This clearly establishes its close association with the process of industrialization, but beyond that, with the use of a technology appropriate to the specific resource endowment of the industrially most advanced countries. This can be stated in other words by saying that, on the basis of resources, relatively most abundant in the advanced countries, a technology was developed which tended to be peculiarly suited for the industrial and with it the general economic advancement of these countries. At the same time, and given this technology, the less advanced countries are in a less favorable condition as concerns their chances to reach the level of development of the more favored societies and, indeed, may never catch up with them. Moreover, just as industrialization, by making use of a technology more fully in tune with the resource complex of the developed countries, gave them an impetus which permitted them to outdistance in the last 150 or 200 years the poorer countries, so the continued impact of basically the same technology permits them to further outdistance the poorer countries as time goes on. Although the specific distribution of non-renewable natural resources among presently advanced and underdeveloped countries does not prevent the poorer countries from experiencing economic growth through industrialization and the introduction of western technology, it may put limitations on the eventual level of advancement which these countries can reach, as well as on the speed with which they may reach significantly more elevated levels of output, provided this technology, especially the coal-oil-steel complex, remains the basis of industrial growth. If coal and oil could be replaced by other sources of power, say fissionable materials, and if iron and its derivatives could be replaced by some other basic structural material, which is more generally available in the poorer countries, say aluminium, a technological revolution may take place which might alter the relative chances of ultimate economic progress through industrialization of the poorer countries.

So long as we assume that, in its basic framework, an industrial technology based on coal, oil, and iron as chief raw materials remains dominant, we must conclude that economic growth, though possible as such in all societies, may not enable all of them to reach the same level of advancement (in terms of per capita real output). In the light of this reasoning we can also explain why the Soviet Union appears to have a better prospect of catching up with and perhaps outdistancing some of the Western European countries than Japan, India, or the countries of South East Asia. A similar analysis could also be applied to the spectacular rise of the United States and the somewhat less spectacular rise of Germany. Since it is impossible to predict, within any tolerable limits of accuracy, what would be the eventual prospects of advancement of the various countries if the technological framework of industrialization changed radically, the alternative growth patterns which may be specified are all founded upon accepting the predominant Western technology as given.

Assuming technology to be given, there are two further variables which have a fundamental impact on the specific pattern of economic growth. The first is often loosely stated as relating to the man-land ratio, or the population density per resource unit at the beginning of the growth process, and the other relates to the degree of autonomy and spontaneity with which the growth process is inaugurated. Stated in somewhat different terms, the first set of variables determines whether the growth process is primarily intrinsic, i.e., whether it consists primarily in an intensification of economic activity within a given geographical space, or whether it is primarily expansionist, i.e., whether it consists primarily in an extension of the economic "frontier" and a gradual spatial expansion of the area in which more advanced technology and economic organization are applied.   The process of capitalist development in the Western world, as a whole, exhibits both the intrinsic and the expansionist growth patterns, and I consider it to be the chief merit of W. W. Rostow's recent book, *The Process of Economic Growth,* to have shown not only the existence of these two patterns of economic development, but also to have related them to fluctuations in other variables of great economic significance, such as prices, etc. But if the growth process of Western capitalism as a whole may be said to exhibit both intrinsic and expansionist features, different countries in the Western world show wide variations. In some of them, for example, Germany, or Switzerland, intrinsic patterns are considerably more important than in other countries, such as, for example, the United States or Australia, where an extension of the frontier is a clear characteristic of the development process.

It would, of course, be a mistake to assume that every country or region whose economic history has been surveyed exhibits either an intrinsic or expansionist growth pattern in pure form. The case of Britain is an example where a slim balance between intrinsic and expansionist development prevailed. Although in the older industrial centres — London, Bristol, Sheffield, Birmingham, for example — intrinsic patterns of development preponderated, several expansionist episodes are clearly discernible: the draining of the fens must be regarded as a process of internal colonization and the growth of coal and iron production in South Wales and the north-east of England and Scotland, as well as the development of textile and other industries in the new industrial center of Lancashire and elsewhere, which set in motion such a vast movement of internal migration, must also be considered as an extension of the internal geographical frontier.   Finally, in the nineteenth century, the growth of foreign investment and the impact of the returns from this investment had profound influences upon further British economic growth.

Switzerland and Germany, the Scandinavian countries and Belgium, but also France and even Japan display predominantly intrinsic patterns of growth. Some countries, like Belgium and Denmark and Switzerland had only very limited possibilities of "internal colonization." But even some of the larger countries, such as France, for example, were so evenly settled before the advent of the industrial revolution that relatively few "new" areas within the country's boundaries were opened up in the course of economic progress.   Foreign investment and colonial expansion played a role, but were, on the whole, much more limited in scope than in Britain. To be sure, the acquisition of Korea and Taiwan, and later the domination of Manchuria by Japan, were important events influencing strongly the capacity of economic growth of the center. But the main growth process was concentrated on the homeland. With the exception of Hokkaido whose new fields land-hungry peasants gobbled up during the past century, Japan's farm land has been fully exploited for centuries; and the growth of industry was superimposed upon the earlier domestic commerce and handicrafts of such cities as Tokyo (Edo), Osaka, Kyoto, and others which even before the downfall of the Shogunate had populations of around a million persons.

The Westward Movement

In contrast to these countries, the growth pattern of the United States, Canada, and Australia, is profoundly different. It is not necessary to recount here in any detail the history of the settlement of North America or Australia, but the greatness of the population shifts and associated expansion of settlement may be gauged, if we recall that in 1860 at the eve of the vast industrial upsurge in the United States, Chicago had barely more than 100,000 inhabitants, Minneapolis, Cleveland, and Detroit were little more than villages, and Los Angeles, Denver and Seattle only dots on a map. The importance of this development pattern for our purposes is not so much to point to the addition of vast areas to the economically effective area of a country, nor to derive inspiration from the heroism and romance of the westward movement. It is important rather because it depended on the appearance of a singular mass phenomenon: the willingness and, indeed, the eagerness of entire communities of persons to relinquish the security of familiar surroundings and to settle in the wilderness or almost-wilderness.

To explain the westward movement by population pressure or even by purely economic motives such as looking for an escape from low wages or low agricultural yields must be rejected. To be sure, the westward movement had economic effects for those who took part in it as well as for those who remained behind. For settlement in the West seemed to offer a chance to many who had knowledge of at least the rudiments of agriculture. And although the majority of the migrants were farmers or farmers' sons, the urban workers benefited nevertheless from their movement westwards, because without it they would have swelled the ranks of the urban proletariat in the East. Thus, in contributing to the easing of pressure on wages in the older settled centers and in sustaining the idea that those who moved took a chance, but also might possibly win a new world, the extension of the frontier exerted a strong influence on the old American doctrine of equality of opportunity and strengthened it.

Force of Egalitarian Ideology

But the interaction between the principle of equal opportunity, one of the ideological fundamentals on which American society was built, and the motives which pushed people toward the unknown West was more complex.

It was so generally admitted that everyone could improve his economic position, in the long run, provided he was industrious, honest and frugal, that the doctrine of equal opportunity may be seen to have been at the very core of the expansionist pattern of American economic growth. During more than a century, Americans who could have spent their lives rather comfortably in the familiar surroundings of the friends and acquaintances of long standing, left their towns and villages and went into the new and inhospitable western regions where they often lived in isolation and always had to face a hard struggle with nature, Indians, or pillaging raiders. One may submit that the decision to move west involved hardships and privations, at least for some time, and that whatever "dividends" were gained in the process accrued only rarely to the first settlers, and usually only to their children or grandchildren. Here becomes applicable a German proverb which was usually applied to emigrants: "Der erste hat den Tod, der zweite hat die Not, der dritte hat das Brot." (The first has death, the second has misery, the third has bread.)

From a purely economic viewpoint many of the migrants thus acted very irrationally when they went west. Obviously some went because they felt that their domestic economic situation was hopeless. Others tried to escape a family or other interpersonal relations with which they could not cope. Some ran away from a place where they had been involved in a crime or other dishonest act, and others were religious fanatics or plain adventurers who looked for a free and dangerous life. In the case of many or perhaps all migrants strong personal motives played a role. But the factor which permitted all these widely divergent motives to become translated into externally analogous actions was the force of an egalitarian ideology which had its roots in the social thought evolved prior to and during the American Revolution. In its most general form it was a joining of some parts of the old Puritan doctrine to the newer one of Thomas Jefferson and his circle. In its more specific form it induced the peopling of the West, the search for opportunity and success in that vast empty area to the West towards which Americans felt drawn themselves as if by manifest destiny.

And in the long run this expectation of success was confirmed. The gradual settling of the American West contributed not only to the maintenance and even improvement of relatively elevated real incomes of those who remained behind, but also, in the long run, to the prosperity of those who had travelled West themselves. Many did not live to experience this prosperity, but their children and grandchildren benefited from the endurance of the first settlers and became living proof that this endurance, this abstinence had paid off. By the end of the nineteenth century, much of the early romanticism of the westward movement had disappeared, but so had the worst risks and hardships. In exchange, the grains and meats of the West, its minerals and fruits, had begun to conquer the markets of the world.

In The Soviet Union

I cannot enter into an equally extended discussion of the parallel process in Canada and Australia, but an investigation of the peopling of British North America and the continent of Australia would show the prevalence of factors similar to those operative in the United States. Even the penetration of Siberia in its early stages, during the eighteenth and nineteenth century, seems to have been supported by an egalitarian and libertarian ideology, which was in full contrast to the official Tsarism, and present-day Bolshevism. But the chief expansion into Russian Asia occurred in the last twenty years under Bolshevik rule. There it was carried on not any more by an ideology of freedom and opportunity, but by the compelling power of the state.

But the very fact that the Soviet Union did experience economic growth on the expansionist pattern, and Japan on the intrinsic pattern, is proof that the former is not indispensably bound up with an ideology such as that prevalent in nineteenth century America, or that the latter has as a necessary prerequisite the evolution of a spirit of capitalism. Wherever "autonomous" growth has occurred, there ideologies have had a deep influence and force. But we can also have "induced" development, that is, rather than relying on the unplanned, and as it were, accidental, combination of factors producing a system of social values conducive to development, we may rely on the conscious organization and ordering of the forces and capacities of a society with the aim of economic progress.

Japan as Model

We obtain, therefore, four fundamental patterns of economic development, depending upon whether economic growth is autonomous or induced, and whether it is intrinsic or expansionist. Great Britain and the countries of Western Europe represent the autonomous-intrinsic type of development; the United States, Canada, and Australasia the autonomous-expansionist type; Japan the induced-intrinsic type; and the Soviet Union the induced-expansionist type. We cannot predict with too much accuracy which of these types the various currently underdeveloped countries will follow. But in view of the relatively dense settlement of many underdeveloped countries, and in view of the increasing role which conscious planned economic development plays in them, we may expect to see a prevalence of the induced-intrinsic type of development. This means that the experience of Japan, rather than any other country, will serve as a model for the policies to be followed in presently underdeveloped countries.

Part III

I believe I have shown in the preceding sections that economic development, especially if it involves industrialization, implies a rapid, and in a sense, revolutionary process which, if it is to take root in a society, must penetrate widely and deeply and hence affects the social structural and cultural facets of a society.   In other words, economic development consists not merely in a change of production techniques, but also, in the last resort, in a reorientation of social norms and values.   Any analysis of economic development if it is to be fruitful and complete must include a set of propositions relating changes in production techniques to changes in values.

Oversimplification

Most past attempts at bringing about economic development can be viewed as proceeding from either one of these extremes.   Current proposals, especially those made by some publicists who are well-intentioned but often ill-informed, and even those made by some spokesmen for government agencies or international organizations, appear to be based on notions very close to a theory of economic determinism.   If the underdeveloped countries were only supplied with capital in appropriate form valued at several billion dollars annually, so the argument runs, their economy and presumably their society would be changed drastically.   Even a conservative interpretation of this view comes to the result that economic changes, notably the introduction of new techniques and new capital instruments, are a necessary prerequisite, and indeed the most likely path by which social behavior patterns and cultural norms can be changed.   However, it is doubtful whether the transformation of a society can be explained in such simple fashion and there is no doubt that the obstinacy with which people hold to traditional values, even in the face of a rapidly changing technology and economic organization, may impose obstacles of formidable proportions.

It may be asked whether a more fruitful procedure may not be the attempt to alter values first and to expect that this will create a climate favorable for new economic forms and processes.   But it appears, from theoretical reflection and historical experience, that this method has little chance of success.   We have the testimony of our most distinguished anthropologists who argue that a diffusion of values or value systems is impossible.   The historical experiences, notwithstanding the success of some individual missionaries, confirm this.   In those instances in which religious conversions of whole societies were attempted, as in the case of the Spanish and Portuguese colonies, the long-run effects on social structure and the economy have been small; we also note failure of attempts to remodel only secular values, while leaving the religion undisturbed, as was the case in upper Burma, where the British tried to replace traditional quasi-tribal social relations by a social system based on the free market and the rule of law.   The result was negative; Burma experienced social disorganization on a large scale, culminating in gang warfare and a formidable increase of violent crimes; the expected positive results were not forthcoming.   Although there was great improvement in output, there was little improvement in the level of living of the average Burman and the allocation of developmentally most significant functions continued to be influenced strongly by status considerations rather than considerations of equity and efficiency.

Non-Economic "Factors"

If we try to interpret the aspirations of the presently economically less advanced countries, we find there also a strange ambiguity which appears to be the result of partial unawareness of the close interconnectedness of economic advancement and cultural change. For the spokesmen of the poorer countries most emphatically favor economic progress resulting in an elevation of general levels of living, and blame their poverty on previous colonial status or quasi-colonial imperialistic exploitation. At the same time their rejection of colonialism and imperialism manifests itself in a heightened sense of nationalism, the symbolic expression of which consists in the repudiation of foreign philosophies and external behavior patterns and the reaffirmation of traditionally honored ways of acting and thinking.

For example, the nationalism in Gandhi's independence movement was associated with the return to highly inefficient methods of traditional Indian activity, and in present-day Burma independence is not only accompanied by a resumption of traditional names and dress, but by a strengthening of Buddhism, a religion which reflects an ideology totally opposed to efficient, progressive economic activity. The realization of economic advancement thus meets with numerous obstacles and impediments. Many of these obstacles are in the realm of economic relations; there is scarcity of capital, there is a demand for new skills and new techniques, there is a need for better roads and improved systems of communication, for public utilities and new sources of power. But some of the impediments to economic progress are beyond the area of economic relations. If the observation is made that among the prerequisites of economic development is the growth of a middle class, or the evolution of a spirit of venturesomeness, or the elimination of corruption among officialdom, we are confronted with changes in the social organization and culture of a people rather than its economy. I propose to discuss in the remainder of this paper some of these non-economic "factors" which are yet too little explored, but which appear to exercise a strong negative and positive influence on the attainment of economic betterment.

Introducing Innovation

If we ask how technological or economic innovations are introduced in a society, we immediately encounter two problems. One is the question of which innovations will be adopted with different degrees of ease and which will be rejected, and the other is the question of what person or group of persons performs the tasks of adopting and further spreading the new techniques in a society. Within the context of this paper the first question is of subordinated importance, since we are not dealing with specific innovations but the general problem of development and all underdeveloped countries are eager to accept more modern forms of economic activity, although for diverse reasons some of them may reject one or the other type. For example, though India may reject or hesitate to adopt modern methods of meat packing, it is eager to introduce other industries.

But the second question, who carries the main burden in the process of innovation, is of great interest to us; evidence for this is the fact that in discussing economic development emphasis has so often been placed on the presence or absence of certain social groups exhibiting particular attitudes (e.g., venturesomeness) or performing special roles (e.g., bureaucracy, "middle class"). In somewhat different terms, we may say that economic development requires the formation of a social group which constitutes the spearhead of different kinds of innovations.

Social Mobility

It is plain from these considerations that one of the prerequisites of economic and technical advancement is a high degree of social mobility. If, for whatever reasons, social advancement of people in less privileged ranks in society is made difficult, or if the cleavages in status, power, and wealth between different social groups are great, an impediment to economic development of considerable magnitude is thereby in existence. Very primitive societies apart, the main status-determining factors are wealth, political power, and education. The ideal form of the liberal state is based on the assumption that each of these factors will be in the hands of a different social group or class and that, in addition to the separation of powers in the political field, there will be a "balance" of social power and status. It will be remembered that an important aspect of the Marxian criticism of "bourgeois capitalism" was based on the assertion that this separation did not exist, or existed only in appearance and that, in Engels' words, "the modern state no matter what its form is essentially a capitalist machine, the state of the capitalists."

Now whether or not this statement was true of the nations of nineteenth century Europe, the social situation on which it is based is true of many underdeveloped countries today. In many of the countries of Asia, the Near East and Latin America, wealth, political power, and education are concentrated in a small group of people, and not infrequently the very individuals who control political power are also the richest and best educated in the society. But this very monopoly of status-conferring factors is an impediment to economic development. The gap between the privileged and the masses, between the rulers and the ruled, is immense and there is nothing to fill it. But even to the extent to which this gap is being filled by an incipient middle class consisting chiefly of educators, government officials, and members of the intelligentsia, this group must, in order to assure its maintenance, either align itself with the ruling group or suffer being pushed into positions of harsh antagonism to that group.   Hence, intellectuals often attain positions of leadership among the discontented, the unprivileged, the poor; hence the appeal the communist ideology exerts on intellectuals in underdeveloped countries; hence also the enhanced social cleavage which becomes little, if at all, mitigated by the rise of the middle class.   The cleavage of the world into two antagonistic camps becomes reflected in the political and ideological issues in a developing country and the possibility of evolutionary development towards higher levels of living disappears more and more as a practical third alternative between either the maintenance of social status quo or the revolution which threatens to throw the country into the arms of communism.

Inadequate Knowledge

Another obstacle to economic development which is found in underdeveloped countries is the nature of their aspirations and the form in which the realization of these aspirations is pictured.   In more concrete terms this may be stated by saying that economic development plans are often unrealistic and divorced from the more immediate needs and productive capacities of these countries.   I have drawn attention earlier to the ambiguity of simultaneously aiming at economic progress and the preservation of national and cultural traditions.   But there is also an ambiguity in the thinking of many leaders of underdeveloped countries between the objectives of developmental efforts and practicable attainments.   The point is sometimes stated in a rather drastic form by emphasizing the fact that many development plans fostered by underdeveloped governments give a high priority to the establishment of steel mills and other forms of heavy industry even though such plants may have little justification on the basis of considerations of efficiency and rational allocation of resources.   We may look at this matter from two points of view.   We may either regard the wish for a steel mill as a childish, irrational desire which merits only ridicule.   But we may also regard it as a symbolic expression of the wish for industrialization, and the implicit acknowledgement of the fact that little is known about the priorities and time sequence of such a process.   I would regard it as evidence of the latter alternative, and here the obstacle to fruitful development is founded on defective knowledge and consequent inability to make rational workable plans.

In spite of numerous surveys of natural resources, soil types, and other environmental factors, knowledge of the natural endowment as well as the human resources of most underdeveloped countries is very imperfect.   The United Nations and its specialized agencies have often been confronted by this fact.   A mission of experts sent to Haiti produced a voluminous report on development possibilities in that country.   Yet the chief impression one gains from reading the report of that mission is the frequent repetition of the statement that fruitful recommendations cannot be made because of the absence of reliable information. Similarly, the International Bank for Reconstruction and Development and the Food and Agriculture Organization have been hamstrung in actually carrying through developmental projects for which funds would have been available, simply because workable projects which could withstand the careful scrutiny of experts were not forthcoming.

Lag in Concomitant Adjustments

Ignorance is always an obstacle to rational action. But in the case of economic development it is doubly fatal, because in this case action cannot be postponed for political or moral reasons. The consequence is that on the one hand programs are undertaken in fields where obvious needs for improvement exist (such as public health, for example) which, however, cannot maintain themselves because the necessary concomitant adjustments in the economy lag behind, and on the other hand that short-run programs are initiated which tend to lead to such allocation of resources (and hence to certain new rigidities and vested interests) as to make the attainment of the long-run objective more difficult. Evidence for both contingencies is frequent.

As concerns public health programs, the attempts at control of tropical diseases are very instructive. For example, yaws and malaria are dreaded diseases in Haiti. A campaign to control yaws in the Marbial Valley failed to have lasting results, although inoculation with antibiotics led to temporary relief, because the economic status of the mass of the population was not elevated enough to permit them to meet the most elementary standards of cleanliness. A swamp drainage project designed to eliminate carriers of malaria fell into disrepair after a few years, the drainage canals got choked up and large expenditures turned out to have been in vain. Owing to indifference, corruption, and mismanagement, the project was not kept going properly after its foreign initiators had left.

Short-Run and Long-Run Aims

Examples of the conflict between short-run and long-run aims are also numerous. For many one-crop countries it presents a real dilemma. The long-run objective of economic development programs for these countries is greater diversification of production, to make them less dependent on one or two or three staple exports, the prices of which are determined on the world market, subjecting, in this way, the international accounts of the one-crop country to great uncertainties and often violent fluctuations. At the same time the major export industry deserves full support in the short-run because it is the chief asset producing foreign exchange which, in the absence of generous loans or foreign aid, provides the wherewithal for economic development. The experience with coffee planters in some Latin American countries and rubber planters in some countries of South East Asia shows the restraining influence on long-run plans of economic diversification exercised by vested interests in an important export industry.

Mexican Dilemma

Another instance of conflict between short-run and long-run objectives of economic development plans is reported by Wilbert E. Moore. Moore believes of the Ejido that although it

> alleviated the immediate economic ills of the Mexican rural population . . . did . . . make possible a re-establishment of the partially isolated village, agricultural underemployment, and all the conservative traditions of a land-hungry peasantry . . . . All indirect evidence indicates that in terms of long-run developments the Ejido was a strongly conservative move in the strict sense; that is, the possible increase in market orientation, improved education, and productive technique seems to have been offset by re-establishing the traditional village.

Professor Moore here again points to the fact that the implementation of short-run objectives creates vested interests which impede the full realization of the long-run developmental goals. But the nature of the vested interests in this case is very different from that of the vested interests fostered by the extension of an export crop in a one-crop country. In the latter case these vested interests are based chiefly on the expectation of economic gain, in the former case they consist in the rejuvenation of a traditional way of life which, in many of its aspects, is opposed to economic progress.

I believe that the dilemma found by Professor Moore in Mexico poses a general problem, notably for areas in which an extension of agricultural settlement is still possible. The fact that some underdeveloped countries, in spite of great rural population density in certain localities, have still considerable areas of uncultivated arable land, is often regarded as fortunate. In a country like India or Egypt, where further horizontal expansion of agriculture is virtually impossible, economic development is pushed necessarily into the channels of industrialization accompanied by intensification of agriculture, i.e., the application of policies resulting in higher yields per acre. This process is accompanied in all likelihood by a rapid increase of the population, and, since industrialization is associated with urbanization, by an increase in the required quantity of real output per family or productively employed individual. It is probable that under these conditions increase in agricultural productivity will not be commensurate with increase in demand for products grown on the land (foods, fibers, hides and skins, and chemical raw materials, such as oils and lumber), and the scarcity of economically usable land becomes a serious bottleneck to development. On the other hand, countries in which substantial areas of unused land are still available can syphon off part of the developing population surplus by settling it on new lands, and can simultaneously expand the output of agricultural raw materials with the increasing demand for such materials by developing industry.

Looked at purely from the viewpoint of the strategy of resource allocation planning in the short run, this group of countries (among which belong most countries of South East Asia, the Middle East, and Latin America) is therefore in a position in which rational planning may mitigate the economic sacrifices involved in industrialization. But the existence of an agricultural frontier and the knowledge that such a frontier exists exerts an influence on policies actually made. As Professor Moore has shown in his book, referred to earlier, recruitment of large masses of peasants and primitives for industry is a hard task. Resettlement may not be much easier, but it may be more acceptable to some native peoples than induction into the industrial labor force. To the extent, therefore, to which local population pressure is mitigated by resettlement — as for example by moving people in The Philippines from Luzon to Davao, or in Indonesia from Java to the outer islands — the traditional agricultural way of life with its pre-industrial and non-rational aspects (in Max Weber's sense) is given a new lease of life and industrial progress made more difficult.

Conflict of Values

In essence the conflict between the two ways of life is a conflict of values. Just as Hinayana Buddhism in Burma, with its other-worldly orientation, calls forth a philosophy of life which is not conducive to economic advancement, so the strengthening of traditional methods of small scale agriculture reinforces the system of values which have flowered into great cultural achievements in the past, but which it has been impossible to adapt to rational, efficient economic activity. This conflict in values has sometimes been expressed as the antagonism between city and countryside, the mutual estrangement between the urban and the rural inhabitant. To a contemporary American, and perhaps also to a contemporary European, this distinction may appear spurious. But it is a difference which is obvious to a student of the social structure of oriental societies since it implies a wide difference in ways of life. In Western Europe the transition from one way of life to the other — and the values implied in each of them — took place during three or four hundred years, and was aided by enclosure acts, "Bauern legen," pauperization, the adaptation of the Calvinist ideology to the objectives of the commercial and industrial middle class, and other measures which turned the rolling green hills of Warwickshire and the Tyneside into the "Black Country" and the fields and wastes of Lancashire into the cotton center of the world. I am not expressing nostalgic regrets over the passing of the European Middle Ages, but I am trying to indicate that, parallel with the external change in the landscape, the minds and aspirations of men, the things they valued and were taught to value, changed; and with this in mind it is perhaps not quite wrong to say that the England or

France of the thirteenth century resembled more the present Middle East or South East Asia than the England or France of our day.

As has been pointed out earlier, value systems offer special resistances to change but, without wishing to be dogmatic, I believe it may be stated that their change is facilitated if the material economic environment in which they can flourish is destroyed or weakened. This seems to be the experience of Western European economic development, and it seems to be confirmed by the findings of students of colonial policy and administration, and research results on the impact of industrialization in underdeveloped countries. Economic development plans which combine industrialization with an extension of traditional or near-traditional forms of agriculture are thus creating a dilemma which in the long run may present serious repercussions on the speed and facility with which ultimate objectives can be reached. This does not mean that, wherever this is possible, extension of agricultural production should not be undertaken in combination with industrialization. But rural resettlement should be regarded as a form of industrialization rather than an extension of traditional methods of farming. In view of existing pressures and the absence in almost all underdeveloped countries of an efficient administrative apparatus the difficulties which such a program confronts are obvious.

Acquisition of New Skills

Reference to the experience of the transition from medieval to modern economic organization in Western Europe brings to mind another important factor which may prove to be a serious obstacle to technological advancement. This obstacle is found in the changes required in methods of work and levels of skill which necessarily accompany technical change and alterations in the scope and form of economic activity. Little needs to be said here about these two points since much of the relevant evidence has been collected by Professor Moore in his book. It appears that these obstacles, although real, are less significant than those opposing economic development because of vested interests of an elite, or the vigor of a non-industrial system of values. To a certain extent resistances against new modes of technical and economic processes and changing kinds and levels of skill are specific aspects of the two last-named factors. But since from the socio-psychological point of view economic development may be interpreted above all as a change in the division of social labor, some special attention to skills and modes of work appears to be in order.

Confining ourselves, at first, to a discussion of skills, the first question which might be raised is whether economic development requires a transition from less complex to more complex skills or vice versa. This question is impossible to answer because there exists no generally agreed upon classification of skills in terms of their complexity, and even if it existed the answer would be ambiguous. Certainly the manual skill of a hand loom weaver is superior to that of a man who runs a power loom, but the skill of the mechanic who tends the power loom and keeps it in repair is probably superior to that of the hand loom weaver. In general, it may be said that mechanization, by "putting the skill into the machine" has two opposite effects. It simplifies many manual operations and makes possible the rapid training of large numbers of unskilled or semi-skilled workers. It thus creates a large demand for people whose skill level is indifferent and who can acquire the necessary manipulatory accomplishments by a process of on-the-job training. At the same time it requires the development of a group of men, foremen, engineers, technical maintenance men, petty administrators, and others capable of rendering services which often require not only a high level of dexterity but a considerable variety of aptitudes. The dexterity and ingenuity of the African native mechanic who, in some relatively isolated place in the Sudan, repairs and keeps going with some wire and pieces of sheet metal a model T Ford, which in the United States would be considered fit only for the junk heap, cannot be denied. But men like him belong to the same class as the Chinese ivory worker who produced the most delicately carved decorations on a cigarette-case, and the anonymous medieval stonecutters who chiselled the capitals of the Gothic cathedrals of France.

A Social Problem

It is granted that human capacity for the exercise of highly skilled tasks, human ingenuity, and human intelligence is fairly evenly distributed over the globe. The problem of developing a group of skilled technicians is not a psychological question of the capacity of persons in underdeveloped countries to learn, but a social problem — the creation of attitudes and material and psychological compensations which will make the choice of such careers attractive. In other words, the question we must ask is not: "How can the people of technically less advanced countries learn the modern techniques?" but: "Will they learn them, and how can they be induced to want to learn them?"

It will readily be acknowledged that if the question is put in this form the answer which is suggested involves a whole series of complex social-psychological processes, which may be regarded as special cases of the general problem of the development and institutionalization of culturally deviant behavior. It would go beyond the proper boundaries of this paper to enter into a detailed discussion of the processes which determine the genesis and direction of deviant motivations, but I believe that the identification of the problem area in which the acquisition of new skills and work methods falls indicates the magnitude of the problem and suggests the variety of obstacles which must be overcome to provide for the institutionalization of a new pattern of division of social labor.

Aid from Advanced Countries

Let us now turn to a short consideration of one or two factors having their source in advanced countries which may strongly affect the speed and direction of economic development in the less developed countries. Needless to say that these observations are relevant only if the advanced countries are participating in some fashion, by means of loans, grants, or technical aid in the development of underdeveloped countries. In view of the Point Four program of the United States and the concern of the United Nations and its specialized agencies with technical aid programs, a discussion of these points appears pertinent.

The motives for extending the aid may be mixed; they are in part humanitarian, in part based on the conception that poverty is infectious, or that underdeveloped countries form power vacua and hence invite aggression, and in part on the expectation that the development of less advanced countries by affecting the international specialization of production will have beneficial effects on the foreign trade of advanced countries. Now it is easy to see that in those cases in which foreign aid is tendered by an advanced country with the chief object of building up greater economic or political strength for itself or its side, the advanced country will be more concerned with serving these ends than with policies designed to optimally affect real income levels in an aid-receiving country. It may even grant aid only on condition that the receiving country commits itself to a particular political ideology or joins a defensive alliance.

Tied Aid

This procedure results in "tied" aid. The aid-giving country insists that the developing country meet several objectives at once, of which economic advancement is only one and certain internal and international political goals are others. This situation puts the developing country in a dilemma, since the meeting of the several objectives simultaneously may call for conflicting policies. Even for the countries of Western Europe the need of increased expenditures for defense purposes imposed a serious problem. For they were forced to seriously modify their internal development programs which had been designed to make their economies more viable in the world economic picture, or to depend more heavily on continued American aid, or to drastically lower domestic living standards. Not much argument is needed to show that the last two alternatives are likely to be unpopular both with the peoples and the governments of the countries of Western Europe. Hence the development plans, designed to improve living standards, had to be modified in order to make possible increased efforts of building up armed strength. But the nations of Western Europe belong to the group of economically more advanced countries, and thus a series of alternative steps were open to them which provided them with the possibility of achieving a more or less neat balance between the various policies. In an underdeveloped country this may not be possible, and it may be put before the alternative of either having to abandon virtually all its development plans for the raising of domestic living standards, or to fail in the fulfillment of its international obligations. The former alternative might have disastrous consequences for the government in power in the underdeveloped country and the latter might expose it to criticism and possible discrimination from abroad which also would not be conducive to efficient economic and technical advancement.

This whole set of problems is fully recognized by American policy makers primarily concerned with implementing the Point Four program. The countries with the most uncertain political future are situated along the southern and southeastern rim of Asia. These countries offer the most promising developmental possibilities because they have valuable resources, a relatively dense and intelligent population, and because in most of them the basic forms of capital for development have been provided. These countries have a rudimentary net of communications and transportation, port facilities, and some sources of power. They have some experience with modern forms of government, a small native middle and upper class, and a relatively large number of intellectuals who were educated in European or American universities. At the same time, most of these countries have recently emerged from colonial status, are thoroughly suspicious of, and often even antagonistic to Europeans, and have developed strong sentiments of nationalism with which is intermixed a bias against foreigners, and especially white foreigners.

Political Fears

The result of this situation, however, is that it affects the magnitude and form of American governmental aid and American private investment in these countries. Since there exists the danger that any of these countries may go communist or at least follow the Indian lead of developing a policy of strict neutrality between East and West, any advancement financed by this country may accrue wholly or partially to the Soviet Union and its allies. Similarly, for private investors there exists a risk of expropriation or serious curtailment of freedom of action against which guarantees by present governments are of no avail, for it is feared that a possible future government with different political preferences would not hesitate in renouncing any obligations undertaken by its predecessor.

Thus, the present world political situation operates as a brake on economic development in two ways. Internally, as we have seen before, it imposes a predilection for the status quo and a reluctance to permit deeply penetrating economic and technical changes which would have a tendency to significantly affect the social structure, and externally it leads to timidity and sometimes to the propensity of implementing technical aid programs only slowly and hesitatingly.

A final word of caution remains to be added. Here I have discussed obstacles and impediments to economic advancement, and have not tried to indicate means by which they could be overcome. This does not imply that such means do not exist or could not be devised. Their careful examination would require, however, another paper at least as long as this. But these impediments had to be discussed because they are important factors intervening in development plans.

As has been stated earlier, there exists a strong desire for development in all poorer countries. From the top government officials to the most menial peasants and laborers, aspirations are inculcated and find expression which point to this. Economic development, although endowed with different meanings to members of different societies and different classes of the same society, has become a slogan with formidable powers of attraction. The execution of actual development projects and the attainment of sensibly higher living standards for large masses of peoples is a very great task and certain to lead to many disappointments and disillusionments. In the enthusiasm of regarding economic development as a cure-all, one is wont to overlook or belittle difficulties which might stand in the way of the easy attainment of too frequently all too ambitious targets. An honest and critical evaluation of economic and noneconomic barriers to such development may therefore have the wholesome effect of inducing the drawing of plans which are capable of actual realization and avoid the emergence of unforeseen by-products which may jeopardize the attainment of the objectives of developmental efforts.

Questions for discussion and analysis pertaining to this article may be found at the end of Article 8.

Gottfried Haberler †

6. CRITICAL OBSERVATIONS ON SOME CURRENT NOTIONS IN THE THEORY OF ECONOMIC DEVELOPMENT *

An essay for an issue like the present one should fulfill at least two conditions. First, it should be concerned with a problem which falls within an area of major interest of the eminent scholar who is to be honored. In view of the astounding range of problems to which Professor Papi's writings have made major contributions, this condition is easy to meet. Secondly, however, the quality of the essay should be such as not to be in too great contrast with the work of the great scholar to whom this volume is dedicated. The high standard of scholarship, brilliance and originality set by Professor Papi's writings make it most difficult to meet that condition and I am very conscious that my essay falls short of the desired level.

The content of my paper will be somewhat negative and its tone grumbling, because I find myself out of sympathy with many recent contributions to the theory of economic development. I shall discuss critically four ideas that have played a great role in recent writings on economic development. (1.) The notion of disguised unemployment in underdeveloped countries, (2.) the notion of "balanced growth" or "big push," (3.) the demonstration effect, (4.) the theory of the secular deterioration of the terms of trade for underdeveloped countries.

I do not say that the whole literature on the subject is based on these notions. In fact it would be foolish to say that, if for no other reason than because I know only a small fraction of the immense literature on the subject. But it is safe to say, I believe, that these ideas have played a considerable role in a highly influential part of the literature and they permeate influential official thinking, e.g., many U.N., esp. E.C.E., ECLA and ECAFE publications.

Unemployment in Underdeveloped Countries

In the literature before the Great Depression unemployment was usually regarded as a temporary maladjustment of demand and supply of labor. It

---

†Gottfried Haberler, Galen L. Stone Professor of Economics, Harvard University. Dr. Haberler is the former Editor of the respected *Quarterly Journal of Economics*.
*From *L'Industria*, No. 2 (1957), pp. 3–13. Reprinted by permission of the publisher and the author.

was explained in terms of cyclical or other shifts in demand, low mobility of labor and sluggish price and wage adjustment.

The Great Depression and the Great Keynesian Simplification (of economics) born of the depression experience have made the world employment conscious. Underemployment equilibrium (with or without competition) is regarded as the rule and full employment the rare exception. According to the predominant simpler versions of the new doctrine there is practically always some slack in the economy and this slack is always due to insufficiency of effective demand. The unemployment is either open or disguised. The phrase "disguised unemployment" was coined by Mrs. Robinson and used to designate workers who, having lost well paid positions in industry to which their skill and training entitles them, are doing odd jobs, raking leaves or selling apples to eke out a miserable living.

Keynesian unemployment, open or disguised, was thought to exist only in rich industrial countries. Poor and underdeveloped countries are spared this particular scourge, because they still have plenty of investment opportunities and their poverty keeps the rate of saving low.

According to ultra modern, i.e., Post Keynesian theory, disguised unemployment exists also in underdeveloped countries, typically and chronically (but by no means exclusively) in agriculture. Disguised unemployment is said to be present if a part of the labor force, say 5%, can be removed from the farms without reducing aggregate output; in fact aggregate output may even increase when the input of labor is reduced. It is, in other words, a case of zero (or negative) marginal productivity of labor.

The term "disguised unemployment" is surely not a good one, because most of the writers who believe that such conditions are widespread in the underdeveloped world (e.g., Arthur Lewis, Ragnar Nurkse, Paul Rosenstein-Rodan) do not wish to suggest that disguised unemployment in underdeveloped countries is curable by the same easy methods as disguised and open cyclical or secular unemployment in industrial countries. A mere strengthening of effective demand by means of easy money policy and deficit spending is not only insufficient but positively harmful.

The modern theory of disguised unemployment can be regarded as an extreme version of the well known theory of protection associated with the name Mihail Manoilesco and the theory is, in fact, being utilized for the justification of import restrictions.[1] While Manoilesco only claimed that the marginal

---

[1] For example in numerous publications of ECLA. See esp. *International Cooperation in a Latin American Development Policy* (United Nations, 1954).

It is interesting to note that the originators of the idea (Nurkse and Rosenstein-Rodan) are careful to point out that conditions in the sparsely populated countries in Latin America are not the ones where one would expect disguised chronic unemployment. They refer specifically to old thickly populated countries such as Egypt, India, and South East Europe.

This has not prevented ECLA from embracing the idea wholeheartedly and to make it a cornerstone of its highly protectionist and interventionist policy recommendations.

productivity of labor in agriculture was low compared with other branches of the economy, the modern theory of disguised unemployment goes the whole hog and maintains that it is zero or possibly negative.

To my mind, the claims of the proponents of the theory of widespread disguised unemployment are tremendously exaggerated. I can perhaps better explain what I think is wrong with the theory of disguised unemployment by stating positively what in my opinion is actually true in varying degrees in various countries, not only in underdeveloped but in developed countries as well. If it were possible to improve methods of production in agriculture; *if* the skill of farm laborers is increased; *if* social habits could be changed, a new spirit implanted and the resistance to moving to and living in cities and to working in factories could be overcome; *if* technology in industry could be changed so as to employ unskilled rural workers; *if* capital and other co-operating factors (entrepreneurs, managers, skilled foremen, etc.) could be provided in larger quantities and better quality; *if*, and to the extent that all these things happen or are done, agriculture can release a lot of labor without loss of output and industrial output be stepped up at the same time.

Now there is no doubt that all these things gradually do happen and did happen all the time in developed as well as underdeveloped countries. In fact, economic development largely consists of these changes. Furthermore, few would deny that many of these changes and improvements can be speeded up by appropriate policies (although, if the measures taken are inappropriate or the dosage incorrect the result will be a slow-down rather than a speed-up) and that for some of these changes to happen Government action is indispensable. But it is very misleading to speak of disguised unemployment. In that sense there always was disguised unemployment in developed as well as underdeveloped countries and practically everybody is a disguised unemployed, even in the most highly developed countries, because each of us will produce more ten years hence, when technology has made further progress, skill and training have been further improved, the capital stock increased, etc.

The cases where after removal of a part of the labor force output remains unchanged (or even rises) without capital having been increased, technology improved, social habits changed, etc., or where such changes can be expected to be the automatic and immediate consequence of a prior reduction in labor input, must be comparatively rare and inconsequential compared with the increase in output due to the gradual introduction of all those changes and improvements.

The theory of disguised unemployment is often associated with the proposition that the capital-labor proportion is fixed — forgetting conveniently other productive agents. In other words, production functions (isoquants) are said to have rectangular (or at least angular) shape. In some modern highly mechanized industries, one may sometimes find situations faintly approaching this case. But the assumption that this should be the case in more primitive economies (agriculture) and should be a chronic situation seems to me preposterous.

It is true one can sometimes observe in underdeveloped countries a tendency to introduce a few modern highly mechanized plants with imported machinery, foreign supervisors and mechanics and using very little native labor. But these instances of "show case industrialization"[2] can in no way change the general picture. It should also be observed that they are not instances of the operation of the "Demonstration Effect," but almost always the consequence of faulty policies which artificially foster (e.g., by means of exchange allocation at often fantastically unrealistic rates) the establishment of uneconomic plants and industries.

The Theory of "Balanced Growth" or "Big Push"

This theory asserts that if the typical underdeveloped country wishes to develop, it must push ahead fast and far, all along the line or it will not get anywhere at all. There is no room for slow piecemeal improvements. Owing to the low income and lack of purchasing power the market is too small to permit any one industry to expand unless all others expand at the same time — thus providing a market for each others' wares.

This theory, again, is based on preoccupation with, and exaggeration of the importance of, a few highly mechanized giant plants or industries. These show cases catch the fancy of the onlooker and make him overlook the great mass of small and medium size run-of-the-mill plants and industries which are the backbone even of most highly developed countries.

The theory is contradicted by the patent fact that industrial advance is usually limited by lack of capital, including "social framework investment," insufficient supply of entrepreneurship, of skilled, trained and disciplined labor and not by the insufficient size of the market.

The theory overlooks or discounts the possibility of increasing the size of the market by international trade.

On the basis of this theory, it is impossible to explain why any now developed country ever developed. How conservative and realistic, compared with modern theories, sounds the *Communist Manifesto* where the productive power of the unfettered capitalistic system and its capability of developing and industrializing backward countries is described in truly glowing terms.

The Demonstration Effect

Underdeveloped countries are supposed to be seriously handicapped by the operation of the "demonstration effect." The demonstration effect was introduced into economics by James Duesenberry. He was, however, not speaking of underdeveloped countries and should not be held responsible for its use or abuse in that area.

---

[2]The phrase is W. H. Nichols', "Investment in Agriculture in Underdeveloped Countries," *American Economic Review* (May, 1959).

The "demonstration effect" is supposed to work in the sphere of consumption as well as in that of production.

In our era of improved communication and transportation, of high pressure advertising by means of newspapers, radio, film, etc. consumers in poor countries come into quick and intimate contact with the latest products and gadgets developed and consumed in the richer countries. They try to emulate consumption habits which are beyond their means. This reduces the propensity to save and increases the propensity to import. In the sphere of production, as already noted, the consequence of the demonstration effect is supposed to be that capital intensive and highly mechanized methods of production are adopted which are uneconomical for the resource pattern of the poorer countries.

A similar type of reasoning has been used to explain a high import propensity and the consequent balance of payments troubles ("Dollar shortage") of European countries.

The demonstration effect is best regarded as an explanation, motivation and excuse for inflationary policies. It is doubtful whether it would cause any troubles at all without lax monetary policies. It surely is not specifically related to underdeveloped countries. All of us, even in the most advanced countries, are under constant pressure by high power advertising to live beyond our means. Everywhere we see and read of things we would like to have and cannot afford. Installment credit makes it easy actually to buy things which we should not buy. Some of us actually are tempted into making foolish purchases, which we later regret; but these slips are quickly corrected and no permanent harm results except if and to the extent that installment credit intensifies inflationary expansion during the upgrade and deflationary contraction during the downgrade of the cycle; but this intensification of the cyclical swings is contingent upon the cyclical flexibility of credit in general and could be counteracted by monetary policy.

There is, however, an area in which the demonstration effect really operates and where it causes serious damage to the economies of underdeveloped countries. That is the area of public policy and collective spending.

Many backward countries have adopted and are still in the process of eagerly imitating the latest policies which it took the advanced industrial countries decades or centuries to develop. The latest most up-to-date legislation on social security, regulations of labor, minimum wages, working conditions, channeling of saving through governmental agencies and impounding them for public purposes — all these policies which the developed countries have adopted only in a late stage of their development are often introduced in underdeveloped countries as soon as they are freed from colonial status. Add equalization of income through progressive direct taxation, nationalization of existing enterprises and reservation for the Government of certain industries and you have an economic policy which greatly overtaxes the limited administrative capacities of underdeveloped countries.

There is still another field where the demonstration effect works, namely, the teaching of economics. The latest theoretical innovations — not to say gadgets — such as Keynesian, post-Keynesian and post-post-Keynesian economics exert a strange fascination and are avidly imbibed while the more serviceable types of economics such as Marshallian and other neo-classical analyses are often sadly neglected.

All this sounds exaggerated, and it undoubtedly is. The picture here painted does not apply to all underdeveloped countries and in all of them warning voices can be heard. But in many the demonstration effect works in the areas and ways indicated. Since the Governments can print money and tap other people's income by taxation, this is much more dangerous than its alleged operation in the private sphere.

Terms of Trade

The theory has become so popular that the terms of trade have shown a secular tendency to deteriorate for the underdeveloped countries, the so called "peripheral" world; more precisely for the raw material producing or rather exporting countries.[3] This alleged historical trend is supposed to be the consequence of deepseated factors and hence capable of confident extrapolation into the future.[4]

To my mind the alleged historical facts lack proof, their explanation is faulty, the extrapolation reckless and the policy conclusions irresponsible to put it mildly.

The historical generalization suffers, first of all, from an excessive degree of aggregation. It is improbable in the extreme that it should be possible to make a valid generalization for the very heterogeneous countries which constitute the underdeveloped part of the world. Just to pick a few examples from the Western Hemisphere. Can anyone[5] seriously maintain that the long run[5] change in the terms of trade is the same for (a.) agricultural exporters (Argentina, Uruguay), (b.) mining countries (Bolivia), (c.) coffee exporters (Brazil), (d.) petroleum exporters (Venezuela). Many of these countries have undergone profound changes in their internal economy and trade structure which make long run comparisons extremely hazardous.

If we concentrate on a more homogeneous group of countries whose export trade has not changed much, the fact still remains that the composition of

---

[3]It should not be forgotten that there are some highly developed and industrialized countries, whose exports consist largely of raw materials and foodstuff. To this group belong, for example, Australia and Denmark.

[4]See, e.g., *The Economic Development of Latin America and its Principal Problems* (United Nations, 1950). For a more recent statement see Raul Prebisch, in *National Policy for Economic Welfare*, Columbia University Bicentennial Conference (New York, 1955), pp. 177–280.

[5]During the short run cycle a greater uniformity may be present.

their imports, that is of the exports of the industrial countries has changed profoundly. Scores of new products are being produced and exported and the quality of those that existed 10 or 20 years ago has been improved to such an extent that they are virtually new commodities. No attempt has been made to allow for these quality changes. The above mentioned U.N. report confines itself to the remark: "It is regrettable that the price indexes do not reflect the difference in quality of finished products. For this reason, it was not possible to take them into account."[6] The report then proceeds as if this was a minor, quite unimportant qualification.

There has taken place another far-reaching structural change in world trade, the neglect of which completely vitiates long run comparisons in the terms of trade — namely, the revolution that has occured in transport techniques and transport cost. When in the 1870's and 1880's the American Middle West was opened up and overseas wheat began to flow to Europe, the British terms of trade improved. But obviously that did not mean that the factoral terms of trade of the new exporting regions deteriorated. Agriculture in the old world was indeed hurt but surely not in the underdeveloped "regions of recent settlement" from where the new supplies originated.

In general, as has often been pointed out, if transport costs are reduced it is possible for the commodity terms of trade (exclusive of services) to improve for *both* importing and exporting countries or areas at the same time.

Waiving all these difficulties, or assuming that allowance has been made for them, there still remains the question of productivity changes. In other words, a given deterioration in the commodity terms of trade of a country need not reflect a deterioration of its single or double factoral terms of trade; it may reflect a differential increase in the productivity of the country's export industries.

No attempt has been made by the proponents of the criticized theory to grapple with any of the various defects which I have mentioned.

Suppose, however, we have satisfied ourselves that the terms of trade have in fact deteriorated in the last 100 years for a certain group of countries *posito non concesso*. No policy conclusions could be drawn unless it were possible to advance good reasons for assuming that this deterioration is likely to continue. In order to make such an extrapolation, it would be necessary to attempt an explanation of the alleged trend.

Two reasons are usually given why the terms of trade move against raw material exporters. The first is that prices of finished manufactured goods are bound to be kept high by monopolistic machinations of trade unions and cartels.

This argument, as it is usually presented, rests on a confusion of absolute and relative prices. It is true that industrial progress in the developed countries rarely takes the form of constant money wages and money incomes associated with falling prices, but rather the form of constant (or even rising)

---

[6]*Op. cit.*, p. 6.

prices associated with rising money wages. This may be bad from the point of view of stability and is undoubtedly unjust for fixed income receivers, but there is no evidence that it has changed relative prices as between industry and agriculture or between finished goods and raw materials.

The second reason advanced for the alleged trend is the operation of Engel's law. When incomes rise the world over, demand for foodstuffs and raw materials rises slower than demand for finished industrial products. Hence, the terms of exchange move in favor of the latter against the former.

Engel's law is certainly one of the best established empirical generalizations in economics. But it cannot bear the heavy burden which is placed on it by the theory under review. It applies to food but not to every kind of food. In the case of industrial raw materials, the situation is much more complicated.

The main objection, however, is that the operation of Engel's law is only one factor among many others. The exhaustion of certain raw materials in some of the developed countries (e.g., coal in the U.K; iron ore in the U.S.) which necessitates the massive importation of raw materials is an example of a counteracting tendency.[7]

This development can be regarded as a concrete manifestation of a broad and supposedly all-pervading tendency which has played an important role in classical and neo-classical economics — viz. of the law of diminishing returns.

There is a pessimistic streak — pessimistic from the point of view of the industrial countries, as well as from the point of view of the internal income distribution within each country — going through classical economics from Ricardo and Torrens via J. S. Mill to Keynes (in his debate on the terms of trade with Beveridge) and recently Austin Robinson.[8] It is based on the doctrine that agriculture and extractive industries are subject to diminishing returns while this is not true of manufacturing. Hence, the terms of trade must inexorably turn against the manufacturing industries and industrial countries.

This is evidently the exact opposite of the thesis that Engel's law will turn the terms of trade against the primary producers. We have thus Engel's law pitted against the law of diminishing returns.

Around the turn of the century an influential and vocal group of nationalistic and protectionist German economists (among them A. Wagner and Pohle) warned about the dangers of further industrialization and advocated higher protection for agriculture to arrest or slow down the rapid urbanization and industrialization of Germany which was then at full swing. Their case was partly based on the prediction that the industrial countries would find it

---

[7]There are, of course, examples on the other side, e.g., the substitution of "synthetic" for "natural" materials — which further illustrates the complexity and unpredictability of the board development.

[8]"The Changing Structure of the British Economy," *Economic Journal* (September, 1954).

harder and harder to obtain food and raw materials from abroad, because the food and raw material producing countries, too, would industrialize and use their food and raw materials themselves.[9] Austin Robinson's recent article is reminiscent of those German voices. He reaches the same conclusion for present-day Britain as Wagner and Pohle did for Germany of their time.

Until now these dire predictions have proved entirely wrong. Industrialization and urbanization have proceeded relentlessly everywhere, but the supply of raw materials and foodstuffs have kept pace.

It will perhaps be objected that both parties, the champions of Engel's law and those of the law of diminishing returns, cannot both be wrong simultaneously. For the terms of trade must shift either in favor of one or in favor of the other; it would be a strange coincidence if they did not change at all.

Now, the terms of trade may have shifted back and forth and this is probably what actually happened. But whatever the truth about the terms of trade, both parties can be wrong, and in fact are wrong, in my opinion, in the sense that a deterioration of its terms of trade does not prevent a country from being better off than before (although other things being equal a country would always be better off if foreign demand had been so elastic that a given improvement of technology in a country's export industry had left the commodity terms of trade unchanged instead of producing a deterioration).

Moreover, both parties cannot be right in their respective policy conclusions. For both groups recommend protection for contradictory reasons and purposes; the champions of Engel's law call for more severe import restrictions in underdeveloped countries in order to anticipate a deterioration of the terms of trade *against* the underdeveloped countries; the champions of the law of diminishing returns recommend more protection in the industrial countries in order to anticipate a deterioration of the terms of trade *against* the industrial countries.[10] The terms of trade cannot move in both directions at the same time. In fact, both parties are wrong in their policy recommendations, because it is irrational and irresponsible to base policy on highly uncertain guesses about future developments. Furthermore, even if we were sure that a certain change in the terms of trade was coming, there would be no sense in trying to anticipate it unless it was expected to come so suddenly that it would require a costly and rapid adjustment. In the German discussion 60 years ago, much was made of the argument that industrialization and urbanization was an irreversible process. If by that is meant that once agriculture has been allowed to contract it is difficult to revive agricultural production, wartime experience seems to show that the argument is wrong. It is possible under modern conditions to expand agricultural production fairly quickly when the need arises.

---

[9]See my *Theory of International Trade* (London: Macmillan & Co., Ltd., 1936), p. 285, *et seq.*, for a brief summary and reference to the literature.

[10]It will be observed that the argument in question has nothing to do with the static terms of trade or optimum tariff argument for protection.

Enough has been said, I believe, to demonstrate that the theory of the secular deterioration of the terms of trade for the underdeveloped countries is completely unfounded and the policy recommendations based on it are devoid of any solid basis.

Concluding Remarks

What does it all add up to? We can perhaps say that the four criticized notions and the policy recommendations derived from them are based on three basic convictions.

(1.) A profound distrust of the judgment of individual producers and consumers. The individuals are said to be often irrational and ignorant. The consumer does not know what is good for him. He is typically a spendthrift and is subject to the demonstration effect. Producers are equally irrational and incompetent. They employ workers whose marginal product is zero or negative, they copy methods of production which are unsuited for the resource pattern of underdeveloped countries, they are ignorant of potential external economies and fail to foresee and to anticipate changes in the terms of trade.

(2.) The economists, both native and foreign consultants on their fleeting visits to some backward area, are fully alert and informed about all these things which individual consumers and producers are ignorant of. They foresee changes in the terms of trade, recognize disguised unemployment and external economies and are not subject to the demonstration effect.

(3.) Economists are not only omniscient, but also know what to do to correct the various defects. And there is no doubt about their capability of persuading governments and politicians and of carrying out policies according to the diagnoses and prognoses provided by the economists.

All this sounds fantastic and it is undoubtedly exaggerated, but not to such an extent as to rob the picture that emerges of its relevance for the understanding of actual economic policy in many underdeveloped countries. In almost all backward countries economic policy is highly interventionist and protectionist, verging in some on integrated central planning.

The conclusion I wish to draw is not that an extreme *laissez-faire* policy is most conducive to stimulating economic development. The Government can certainly do much to speed up economic growth and there are many indispensable measures which only the Government can take. My conclusion is rather that by doing too much, by trying to do things that individuals and the market can do better, Governments overtax their limited capacities and are forced to neglect their basic and indispensable functions.

In his keynote talk opening the Columbia University Bicentennial Conference on "National Policy for Economic Welfare at Home and Abroad," an address full of beauty and wisdom, Sir Dennis Robertson asked the question: "What does the economist economize?" His answer was that the economist economizes, or should economize, "that scarce resource, Love" — meaning that they should not act and predicate their recommendations on the assumption that love, goodwill, and cooperative spirit are available in unlimited quantities.

Similarly, on a lower and more pedestrian level, we may say that Governmental know-how, administrative efficiency, and political honesty are a scarce and precious resource, especially scarce in underdeveloped countries. The supply and quality of this resource has improved over the last 150 years in most countries. It can be further increased but only slowly and at a heavy cost in terms of manpower and brain power — another precious and very scarce resource. It cannot be as easily taught or copied and imported from foreign countries as many productive technologies can be. On the other hand, it can be depleted and its quality can be impaired by excessive use and above all it can be misallocated and be spread too thin.

This is what happens in many underdeveloped countries. Prevailing policies misuse and misallocate, spread too thin and deplete and impair the limited supply of Governmental know-how. If Governmental energies and the best brains serving the administrative apparatus are spent on thinking up and operating unworkable and infinitely complex systems of exchange control, rationing of imports, allocation of quotas, nationalizing, expropriating private enterprises, running grossly inefficient public enterprises — if Governments try to do things which private business, native or foreign, can do much more efficiently — it should be no wonder that those services, indispensable for economic growth, which only the Government can perform or which it can perform better, are sadly neglected. Such services and activities are elementary and higher education — if 40% and more of the population are illiterate as is the case, e.g., in most Latin American countries, economic growth must be retarded; public health; basic utilities such as water, communication, postal services, port installations as well as the elementary Governmental services of maintaining law and order. Many or all of these "social overhead investments" are sadly neglected in many or most underdeveloped countries; or they are not developed as fast as they should be in the interest of economic growth, because Governments pour a disproportionate part of their resources into activities, which are either outrightly wasteful or could be performed more efficiently and cheaply by private business, and cause inefficient use of private capital, e.g., by stimulating by all sorts of protectionist devices (including exchange control) of inefficient secondary industries.

Bad economic policies are, of course, not a monopoly of underdeveloped countries. But no doubt there they are especially bad and underdeveloped countries can least afford such waste. Economists in developed countries must take their full share of responsibility for this state of affairs.

Questions for discussion and analysis pertaining to this article may be found at the end of Article 8.

Melvin Blase †

7. THE WORLD FOOD-POPULATION PROBLEM: 1969*

Recently, many have been confused as to whether or not a world food problem exists. A year or two ago a great deal was heard about starvation in India due to drought and other factors. Now it is said that a "Green Revolution" is taking place in Asia and elsewhere. Is there a current problem? If not, how was it solved so quickly?

This article will focus on three things:

(1.) the most recent available statistics concerning the world food-population problem;

(2.) statistics interpreted in terms of human consequences;

(3.) some myths concerning the food-population dilemma.

Food-Population Data

A recent study by staff members of the World Bank provides insights into world *economic* output trends. During the period 1950–1965 world production just about doubled. In per capita terms the increase was more than 50 percent.[1] Consequently, rather than doom and despair, some factors give reason for hope. Further, this suggests development assistance has not been wasted. Clearly, the trends in world output are in the "right" direction. To be sure there were differential rates of growth in various countries.

Agricultural Development

What has happened to agricultural output? Here there are some long term trends and some shorter run data of interest. The U. S. Department of Agriculture has estimated that agricultural output of the world in 1968 was 30 percent greater than the 1957–59 base period. But Table 7-1 on pg. 98 indicates,

†Melvin Blase, Associate Professor of Agricultural Economics, University of Missouri — Columbia.

*From *Business and Government Review*, Vol. 10, No. 3 (May–June, 1969), pp. 20–27. Reprinted by permission of the University of Missouri — Columbia and the author.

[1]John H. Adler, "Poverty Amidst Wealth: Trends in the World's Economy," *Development and Finance,* a publication of the International Monetary Fund and the World Bank Group (Washington, D. C., Quarterly No. 4, 1968).

Table 7-1

Agricultural Production
(Area Per Capita 1957–59 = 100)

Cal. Years	Developed	Less Developed	World[1]
1964	109	102	105
1965	107	102	103
1966	114	97	105
1967	114	102	107
1968	115	102	107

Source: Charles A. Gibbons, "1968 World Agricultural Production Indices," *Foreign Agriculture,* Foreign Agricultural Service, USDA (Washington, D.C.: January 6, 1969), p. 4.
[1]Excludes Communist Asia.

however, that on a per capita basis the increase was only 7 percent. Thus, per capita agricultural production in less developed countries has not displayed a strongly positive trend despite significant aggregate increases. (See Figure 7-1.)

From 1966 to 1967 world food production increased by 3 percent. Since population growth ran at approximately 2.2 percent, some progress was made toward improving per capita supply. Likewise, some progress was made in 1968.[2] However, reason for optimism is rather short lived when the fact is considered that between 1964 and 1965 production per capita had declined.

Consideration of agricultural output by countries and selected regions provides more confusion than insight. In India, for example, the long term trend in food production has been increasing at 3 percent per year, a rate faster than the United States was able to sustain for any extended period. In Latin America, however, between the late 1950's and the mid 1960's there was no change in per capita food production.[3]

Population Trends

Even if agricultural output were increasing rapidly — at a steady rate around the world — there would still be concern. This results from world population trends. In a recent address Robert S. McNamara, President of the World Bank Group, stated:

> I do not need before this audience to deal with the terrifying statistics of population growth as a whole which show that, although world population totaled only one quarter billion in the first century A. D. and required 1650 years to add another quarter billion, it added one billion in the next 200 years; a second billion in the following century and a third

[2]Charles A. Gibbons, "1968 World Agricultural Production Indices," *Foreign Agriculture*, Foreign Agricultural Service, USDA (Washington D. C.: January 6, 1969), p. 4.

[3]*Indices of Agricultural Production for the 29 Latin American Countries (Plus Country Tables for Jamaica and Trinidad and Tabago)*, ERS-Foreign 44, USDA (Washington, D.C.: Revised 1966).

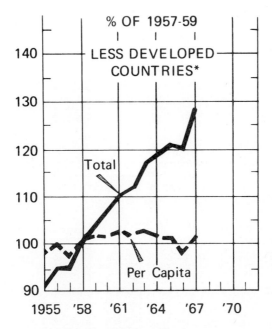

Source: *Handbook of Agricultural Charts 1968,* USDA, Agricultural Handbook No. 359 (GPO, Washington, D.C.: November, 1968), p. 48.
*Latin America, Asia (except Japan and Communist Asia), Africa (except Republic of South Africa).

Figure 7-1

Agricultural Production

Table 7-2
Daily Per Capita Supply
1961–63

| Region | Calories | Protein (grams) | |
		Total	Animal
Undev. countries	2184	55	11
Latin America	2545	65	23
Africa	2209	58	10
Near East	2194	67	15
Asia & Far East	2079	50	8
North America	3090	91	64
Eur. Econ. Comm.	2910	87	46

Source: David R. Wightman, "The Food Problem of Underdeveloped Countries," *Food Aid and Economic Development* (Carnegie Endowment for International Peace in International Conciliation, New York: March, 1968), p. 7.

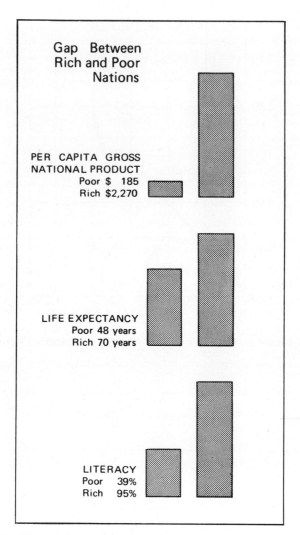

Source: "The Task of Development," *Agency for International Development Proposed Program Fiscal Year 1969*, U.S. Department of State (Washington, D.C.: May, 1968), p. 1.

Figure 7-2

**The Gap
Between the Nations**

billion in the next 30 years. It is now expected to add three more billion by the end of the century. By then, at present rates, it will be increasing one billion each eight years.[4]

---

[4]Robert S. McNamara, Address to the Board of Governors, World Bank Group, Washington, D. C. (September 30, 1968).

Perhaps more disturbing are the statistics of changes within the poor, or less developed, countries. There are approximately one and one-half billion people in those countries now. By the year 2000, three billion are expected to live there. These statistics exclude mainland China for which population data are not available.[5] Thus, population is gaining so rapidly that the world can expect to continue living on the "razor's edge of subsistence."

The Two Worlds

What is the condition today? Several indicators help put world conditions in perspective. In the case of gross national product (GNP), the poor nations have an average per person of $185 v. the rich nations with a group average per capita of $2,270. By comparison the U. S. per capita GNP is approximately $3,900. (See Figure 7-2.)

Another indicator is that life expectancy in the less developed world is 48 years, and in the developed nations 70 years. (One reason for the short life expectancy in the less developed areas is the high rate of infant and child mortality which is discussed subsequently.)

A third indicator is literacy. Approximately 39 percent of people in the less developed countries are literate whereas, in the rich nations 96 percent are considered functionally literate.

How are these conditions manifest in the lives of people? In the less developed world people consume approximately 2000 calories per day, whereas in the U. S. approximately 3000 calories per day are consumed and the diet is of higher quality in terms of protein. (See Table 7-2, pg. 99.)

This is illustrated by the less developed countries consuming 400 pounds of grain per person yearly. Approximately 1600 pounds of grain are used in the U.S. (See Figure 7-3, pg. 102.) Americans enjoy the luxury of a high animal protein diet which requires that large quantities of grain be processed through livestock.

Interpreting the Data

One way of getting the population explosion into perspective is to recognize that nearly as many people have been added to the population of India since 1950 as the entire U.S. population in 1950. As Figure 7-4 (pg. 103) illustrates, relatively few years are required to double a country's population at high percentage annual increases.

Such population growth generates a tremendous drag on an economy. Consider the problem of developing and maintaining educational systems. How does a country build schools, train teachers, and provide books fast enough with a relatively small proportion in the work force?

[5]Adler, *op. cit.*

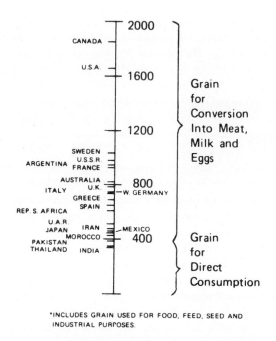

*INCLUDES GRAIN USED FOR FOOD, FEED, SEED AND
INDUSTRIAL PURPOSES.

U.S. DEPARTMENT OF AGRICULTURE   BN 28407

Source: Lester R. Brown, "An Overview of World Food Situation," *International Agricultural Development*, No. 26, USDA (Washington, D.C.: December, 1966), p. 3.

Figure 7-3

Grain Requirements Ladder
(Pounds of grain used per person per year*)

Reproduction Rates

This naturally focuses attention on family planning, which offers a partial long run solution but is plagued with many problems. *First,* the females already exist who will come into child-bearing age during the next 20 years. Consequently, the opportunity for stalling population growth by reducing the number of potentially reproductive members is impossible.

But there is a *second* complication to family planning. In many parts of the world family size is not going to be controlled by the available techniques, whatever they may be.[6] Minimum family size will be determined by the desire to have one male surviving heir to provide the equivalent of social security

---

[6]President's Science Advisory Committee, *The World Food Problem* (GPO, Washington, D.C.: May, 1967), p. 14.

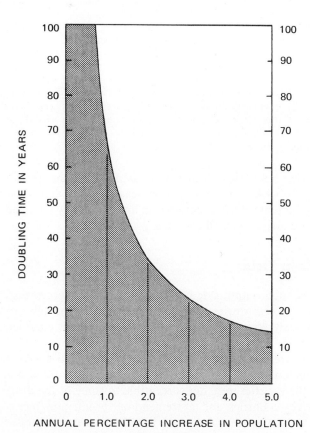

Source: "Population Crisis," *Hearings before Senate Subcommittee on Foreign Aid Expenditures* (GPO, Washington, D.C.: January 31, 1968), p. 470.

Figure 7-4

Population Growth Rates
Number of years to double
at various rates

for the parents. To insure one male heir, on the average, at least four children must be born. This is because the probabilities are approximately 50 percent that a child will be a male and two males are required to insure that one survives.

A *third* quite disturbing dimension involves urgent short range problems. Most pressing is the occurrence of brain damage in infants. Preliminary medical research indicates an association between certain animal protein deficiencies in infant diets and brain damage. Pediatricians Eichenwald and Fry have reported:

In this regard, observations on human infants have shown that inadequate feeding of pyridoxal phosphate, which serves as a coenzyme for most enzymatic reactions of amino acids, results in a series of changes in the physiological function of the brain and in the appearance of clinical symptoms. In the newborn baby, the ingestion of a diet deficient in this substance but otherwise adequate results within 6 weeks in hyperirritability, convulsive seizures, abnormalities in development, and behavioral disorders. If this deficit continues for a sufficiently long period, irreversible alterations of cerebral function will occur, resulting in severe mental retardation.[7]

Consequently, in addition to family planning programs, there must be an adequate nutritional level provided, to increase the probability of survival of a male child so parents will be interested in limiting family size, and to prevent possible brain damage in small children.

Improved Crop Yields

How can the food output side of the coin be made more realistic? One of the spectacular success stories of the century concerns the new crop varieties. For approximately 25 years the Rockefeller Foundation conducted a wheat breeding program in Mexico before its international impact was felt. Even then there was a tremendous risk involved when the varieties were moved from the climatic conditions of Mexico to countries such as India and Pakistan. Fortunately, the varieties were not susceptible to some of the diseases characteristic of Asian countries and a tremendous production increase has occurred. The U. S. Agricultural Attache in India recorded the following in this regard:

In 1964–65 the new short-stem Mexican varieties were grown only at experiment stations. The next year seed multiplication began in earnest. In 1966–67 demand was so great that 18,000 tons of seed were imported from Mexico.

In mid-1967 original plans were to plant 4.6 million acres with high-yielding dwarf Mexican wheat and an outstanding local variety, K-68, grown mostly in Uttar Pradesh, as compared with 1.34 million acres of these varieties in 1966–67. This target was subsequently raised to 6.7 million acres. Actual acreage apparently exceeded even the revised target.

Coverage under the high-yielding varieties of wheat is estimated at 7.0 million to 7.5 million acres, comprising 5.0 million to 5.5 million acres of Mexican wheat and 2.0 million acres of K-68. Average yields from Mexican varieties are expected to be 2 to 3 times higher than from the local traditional varieties, which generally yield 700 pounds per acre on non-irrigated lands and about 1,000 pounds per acre on irrigated land. Many progressive farmers have already harvested or expect to harvest 4,000 to

[7]Heinz F. Eichenwald and Peggy C. Fry, "Nutrition and Learning," *Science,* Washington, D. C., Vol. 163, No. 3868 (February 14, 1969), p. 645.

5,000 pounds per acre from the new high-yielding varieties of wheat this
year. Some will exceed 6,000 pounds (100 bushels) per acre.[8]

It is interesting to find illiterate farmers in various countries adopting these
new varieties. The potential for increased yields is so great that the incentive
of higher income has overcome the obstacles presented by custom. In fact, in
some parts of the world a black market exists in the seed of the new varieties,
produced primarily by U. S. Foundations working not only in Mexico but
also in the Philippines (rice). Just because a farmer is illiterate does not mean
that he cannot "figure."

New Technology

Obviously, for farmers to be able to adopt new varieties they must first be
developed. This is a time consuming process. It requires a sustained commitment of resources for an extended period: some varieties require only about
5 years while others will require up to 25 years. However, past pay-offs have
been very high indeed. But these new varieties are not a panacea, not the solution to all food-population problems, but rather represent a means of *buying time* — approximately 5 to 10 years. During this period the pressure of
starvation will not be upon the world as severely as previously expected. This
"breather" will provide time to launch efforts to develop additional new varieties and other elements of new technology, such as fertilizer programs, irrigation schemes, and some improved management practices such as double
cropping.

Nutrition Problems

Finally, attention is turned to present conditions manifested in this food-
population issue. Perhaps these can be best described by the phrase, "the
children suffer." In some developing countries recommended diets, if used,
would consume the entire income of a typical low income family. This is not
only because the menus are so costly but also because the earning capacity of
the typical wage earner is so low.

In developing countries children are observed with distended stomachs, soft
fat, small bones, and obvious infestations of parasites. Increased energy levels
in these children are obvious as they are rid of parasites, sometimes requiring
as long as 6 months, and their nutritional level improved. Most children never
receive the required medical attention and improved diets, however. A substantial proportion fall victim to the world's largest killer — malnutrition
which frequently is accompanied by green diarrhea.

---

[8]James H. Boulware and V. M. Tandon, "India Harvests Record Wheat Crop,"
Foreign Agriculture, Foreign Agricultural Service, USDA (Washington, D.C.: May 6,
1969), p. 3.

Examining Old Myths

Now attention is turned to some old myths that characterize the food-population problem. There are five that need to be considered.

(1.) The first is "they are lazy," referring to the people in less developed countries. While all generalizations are dangerous, if one is necessary a more accurate statement would be "they are sick and hungry." They are sick in the sense of being infested with parasites, hungry in the sense of being malnourished. True, people in these countries are motivated differently from those in the developed world. Since they live on the fringe of subsistence, this is to be expected.

Behavior patterns in the developed world, too, would change if people had to struggle just to survive. Further, the masses in the less developed countries are caught in a circle of poverty. Low labor productivity means low wages. Because wages are low, income is low; because income is low, savings are low; because savings are low, *investments* are low; because *investments* are low, labor productivity is low — and a full circle has been completed. Determining methods of breaking the circle is challenging some of the world's best minds.

(2.) The second myth is "industry is the answer." In many respects this is the Russian model, but not exclusively. There are industrial fundamentalists in the U. S., also. This approach is well received in many countries because of the world-wide low prestige of agriculture.

Yet, agriculture can also facilitate economic development. It can play a key role by (1.) earning foreign exchange, (2.) providing an internal low cost supply of food, (3.) contributing to capital accumulation, (4.) providing a demand for products of industry, and (5.) gradually releasing a supply of labor as needed in industry. Industry alone is not the answer; industry *and* agriculture can facilitate development.

(3.) The third myth is "let's export our technology." In response, the question should be asked, "How many multilingual rice farmers are there in the United States who are accustomed to producing without mechanization?" More basic than this, however, is the point that much agricultural technology is *location specific*. The example of the new Mexico wheats was the exception rather than the rule, unfortunately. United States agricultural technology is productive because it was developed for a specific ecological environment. Much advanced technology fails when shifted.

While the developed world cannot export its technology in entirety, it can make available the expertise to expand the capability in developing societies to generate the unique technology needed to solve their particular problems. Much of this responsibility has been accepted by U. S. universities. For example, the University of Missouri is undertaking such a program in India and is cooperating with another in Columbia.

The building of indigenous institutions to create technology to solve the agricultural problems of the developing world is time consuming, however.

Nevertheless — if the developed countries are concerned about the problems their children are going to experience in their lifetime — the task, of helping build agricultural research and education institutions in the developing world, will be taken as imperative.

(4.) Closely related to the myth of exporting advanced technology is "we can produce the additional food they need." Reexamination of world population statistics rather well destroys this myth. If some feel it does not, however, they need to consider the question of how will others pay for U. S. agricultural exports? In emergencies some food relief can be justified, but in the long run the task is to foster development world-wide if the circle of poverty is to be broken.

(5.) The fifth myth is "there is no need to care." This is heard in various forms, including some who overlook the efficiency of development programs and say the U. S. should quit throwing its money away.[9] Others say leave foreign policy making to experts — and one result is an alarming militarization of U. S. foreign policy. There is too much at stake in determining foreign policy to leave its determination to the experts alone.

Conclusion

If the developed world turns its back on its responsibilities in the food-population area, further generations will pay. They will pay either in the form of (1.) a tax via higher world-wide food prices, (2.) a tax in the form of providing donations of food for an indefinite period to the developing world, or (3.) future generations will live in a much more politically unstable world.

A final reason for facing the world food-population problem is that ignoring it is inconsistent with the Judeao-Christian tradition that characterizes this country. Foreign policy should not be formulated by policy makers oblivious to the national system of values.

Questions for discussion and analysis pertaining to this article may be found at the end of Article 8.

---

[9]Adler, *op. cit.*

David Kamerschen †

8. FURTHER ANALYSIS OF OVERURBANIZATION*

The Overurbanization Thesis

In recent years the so-called "overurbanization" problem presumably facing the underdeveloped areas of the world has received considerable attention. Janet L. Abu-Lughod describes this phenomenon as follows:

> Many students of urbanization have suggested that countries in the early stages of industrialization suffer an imbalance in both the size and distribution of their urban populations, implying primarily that they have a higher percentage of people living in cities and towns than is "warranted" at their stage of economic development. The term used to describe this phenomenon is "overurbanization," which refers to the end result of excessive migration of un- and underemployed rural folk to the cities in advance of adequate expansion of urban employment opportunities. One consequence of this premature migration is the high rate of unemployment and/or marginal employment in the labor forces of the great cities of Asia and Africa.[1]

The chief proponents of the overurbanization thesis say that Asia, for example, is overurbanized at present in the sense that "at comparable levels of

†David R. Kamerschen, Professor of Economics, University of Missouri — Columbia. The author wishes to thank Howard R. Watts, Supervisor of Statistics, Computer Research Center, University of Missouri, for computational assistance. He would also like to thank W. Whitney Hicks and John C. Murdock for valuable suggestions, without implying that they necessarily agree with the views expressed here. Certain sections of this paper draw on the author's forthcoming book, *Overpopulation and Underdevelopment: Some Common Myths,* to be published by the Asia Publishing House. The research in this paper was supported in part by a summer fellowship from the Research Center of Business and Public Administration at the University of Missouri.

*From *Economic Development and Cultural Change,* Vol. 17 (January, 1969), pp. 235–253. Reprinted by permission of the University of Chicago Press and the author.

[1]Janet L. Abu-Lughod, "Urbanization in Egypt: Present State and Future Prospects," *Economic Development and Cultural Change*, Vol. 13, No. 3 (April, 1965), p. 313. She goes on to add, pp. 313–314, that "Egypt has frequently been cited as an example *par excellence* of an overurbanized country. For example, in 1950, when only 13 percent of the world's population and only 9 percent of the population in underindustrialized regions lived in cities having 100,000 or more persons, almost one-fifth of Egypt's population was to be found in cities of this magnitude. By 1960, the proportion was closer to one in four. Furthermore, in 1947, when only 38 percent of the country's occupied males were engaged in occupations other than farming, some (contd.)

urbanization, the developed countries of today had a correspondingly greater proportion of their labor force engaged in non-agricultural employments."[2] This overurbanization is presumably the result of rural migrants having been "pushed" rather than "pulled" into the urban regions, because of great and increasing population pressures in the rural regions. In short, overurbanization compares a spatial but not an occupational index of the percentage of the population living in urban areas with the occupational but not the spatial index of the distribution of the total labor force in the country as between agricultural and nonagricultural occupations.

As to what should be the normal relationship between the indices, two kinds of norms have been suggested: a cross-sectional analysis of a large number of countries, such as by Davis and Golden using roughly 1950 data, and a historical analogy such as contained in the UNESCO seminar report.

Davis and Golden, using the percentage of active males not engaged in agriculture and the percentage of population in cities of 100,000 and above in a large number of countries (circa 1950), find a zero-order Personian product-moment correlation coefficient of + .86 between the degrees of industrialization and urbanization. Egypt, Greece, Korea, and perhaps Lebanon are off the regression line to a significant extent, suggesting "overurbanization."

The other criterion of overurbanization is based on the historical experience of advanced countries — the U.S., France, Germany, and Canada. The proportions subsisting between urbanization and industrialization at different times in their evolution is used as the norm. For instance, the degree of urbanization in Asia today, one in twelve, is associated with 30 percent of the labor force in nonagricultural activities, whereas at comparable levels of urbanization the above-named advanced countries had roughly 55 percent of their labor force engaged in nonagricultural occupations.[3] Thus Asia, it is claimed,

---

30 percent of the population resided in communities classified as urban. The contention has been that Egypt is too agrarian to support this heavy urban superstructure." Supporters of the Egyptian case include Kingsley Davis and Hilda (Hertz) Golden, "Urbanization and the Development of Preindustrial Areas," *Economic Development and Cultural Change,* Vol. 3, No. 1 (October, 1954), pp. 6–26.

[2]Phillip M. Hauser, rapp., *Urbanization in Asia and the Far East,* Proceedings of the Joint UN/UNESCO Seminar on Urbanization in the ECAFE Region, Bangkok, 8–18 August, 1956 (Calcutta: UNESCO Research Center on the Social Implications of Industrialization in Southern Asia, 1957), p. 8. See also Bert F. Hoselitz, "Urbanization and Economic Growth in Asia," *Economic Development and Cultural Change,* Vol. 6, No. 1 (October, 1957), pp. 42–54; "Indian Cities: The Surveys of Calcutta, Kanpur and Jamshedpur," *The Economic Weekly* (July, 1961), Special Number, pp. 1071–1078; Akin L. Mabogunje, "Urbanization in Nigeria: A Constraint on Economic Development," *Economic Development and Cultural Change,* Vol. 12, No. 4, Part I (July, 1965), pp. 413–438; Gerald Breese, *Urbanization in Newly Developing Countries* (Englewood Cliffs, N.J.: Prentice-Hall, 1966); Kingsley Davis and Hilda (Hertz) Golden, "The World Distribution of Urbanization," *Bulletin of the International Statistical Institute,* Part 4 (1954); and Leo F. Schnore, "The Statistical Measure of Urbanization and Economic Development," *Land Economics,* Vol. 37, No. 3 (August, 1961), pp. 229–245.

[3]UNESCO seminar report, *op. cit.,* p. 138.

is comparatively overurbanized in relation to its degree of economic development.

The purpose of this paper is to critically examine this thesis — with particular reference to the cross-sectional analysis. Thus, this paper shall consist primarily of an empirical extension of the penetrating criticism, briefly described in the following paragraphs.

Sovani's Criticism of the Thesis

Recently, N. V. Sovani questioned the theoretical and empirical foundations of the overurbanization thesis.[4] First, looking at the cross-sectional norm, he argued that the correlation between urbanization and industrialization is only a first approximation. It is also necessary to examine its stability through different stages of industrialization and time in the various countries. The first is done for subgroups of countries in similar stages of industrialization, and the second to determine whether the cross-sectional analysis is supported by the time-series analysis.

Sovani first estimated the simple correlation coefficient r between urbanization and industrialization for countries for which the appropriate data were available. Excluding areas with no cities of 100,000 or more, the 41-country sample had an $r = 0.70$.[5] Then to test how the association works out between highly industrialized countries as against the rest, two subsamples were made — one group consisting of the U.S., Canada, and 15 European countries for which data were available, and another for the remaining 24 countries. The results are somewhat surprising, in that the r between urbanization and industrialization for the group of highly industrialized countries was 0.395 and for the other group 0.85.

> These results indicate that the association between the two variables is much closer in the underdeveloped countries than in the highly industrialized countries or, by implication, that the pace of urbanization in the underdeveloped countries is much more closely dependent on the pace of industrialization than in the highly industrialized areas. This flies in the face of the entire overurbanization thesis, at least in the way it has been formulated up to now.[6]

This result is supported by a similar correlation analysis done for the U.S., Canada, and eleven Western European countries for the year 1891, which yielded $r = 0.84$.[7] The use of occupational data for the entire labor force and

[4]N. V. Sovani, "The Analysis of Overurbanization," *Economic Development and Cultural Change*, Vol. 12, No. 2 (January, 1964), pp. 113–122. See also his *Urbanization and Urban India* (New York: Asia Publishing House, 1966). All subsequent references to Sovani shall concern the first-named work.

[5]Sovani, *op. cit.*, p. 115, note 7, suggests that Davis and Golden might have obtained a higher r because of their use of data for more countries than he had been able to get together. His speculation is verified in our empirical findings discussed below.

[6]*Ibid.*, p. 115.

[7]*Ibid.*, p. 116. Urban population data are from A. Weber, *The Growth of Cities in the Nineteenth Century, A Study in Statistics* (New York: Columbia University, (contd.)

not for males alone as in the more recent data, would suggest that this *r* is slightly smaller than it would be if data for males alone were used. "The indication, however, is clearly that in the earlier stages of industrialization and urbanization in these countries, the correlation was much stronger than now, when both the processes have gone much further."[8]

Further tests were made by studying time series data for these variables in England and Wales, the U.S., Canada, France, and Sweden. Although the sample was small, it gave significant results. The two indices were plotted for each country separately and compared over periods of 80 to 100 years. The two curves were of roughly similar shape but differed considerably in the distance between them at different times, as well as in the way they developed over time. The conclusion emerging from this is that the correlation worked out by Davis and Golden varies at different stages of industrialization and is not stable through time.

Sovani is equally critical of the time-series norm,[9] for this approach, he feels, suggests that the course of development should proceed in all countries as it did in the presently advanced countries.

> The only reason for regarding the situation in a few developed countries as the norm for the rest of the world seems to be nothing better than the fact that they are developed economies. But even if we judge other developed countries at some period of their development, we will find that they did not conform to this standard. For example, when in 1895 the degree of urbanization in Sweden was comparable to that of Asia today (8.2 percent in cities of 100,000 or more), the proportion of the labor force in non-agricultural occupations there was less than 45 percent. Even in 1910, though urbanization had increased slightly to 9.3 percent, this proportion was only 51 percent. Conversely, in Switzerland, though the proportion of the labor force in non-agricultural occupations was 60 percent in 1888, there was no city with a population of 100,000 or more in the entire country at that time. In fact, if we logically pursue the analysis based on this norm, the whole of South and Central America would have to be classified as over-urbanized, and for that matter, the whole of Africa and so too the world! One can turn around and say that, compared to the world outside, these four countries are really overindustrialized or underurbanized with equal justification.[10]

1899). Labor force data are from S. Kuznets, "Quantitative Aspects of the Economic Growth of Nations. II. Industrial Distribution of National Product and Labor Force," *Economic Development and Cultural Change*, Vol. 5, No. 4 Part II (July, 1957).

[8]Sovani, *op. cit.*, p. 116.

[9]Sovani claims the above-mentioned UNESCO figures are wrong for the U.S., 35–46 percent, and France, 48 percent. *Ibid.*, p. 117.

[10]*Ibid.*, p. 117. He goes on to note that the two criteria of overurbanization conflict with each other. "Eight or nine percent of the population living in cities of 100,000 and more will be associated, in the Davis-Golden regression, with 30.5 percent of the labor force engaged in nonagricultural occupations, and not 55 percent as under the second criterion; conversely 50–55 percent of the labor force would be associated with about 18 to 20 percent of the population in cities of 100,000 or more. Several cases can be cited where overurbanization exists according to the second criterion but not according to the first."

Turning from the criteria to the causes of overurbanization, Sovani questions the belief that its main cause is the pressure of population on land in the rural areas "pushing" out people, and not a strong demand for labor from the cities "pulling" them in. According to the overurbanization hypothesis, these migrants are either unemployed or in low-productivity jobs.

Sovani, however, notes that urban employment is found to be, on balance, much more productive than the premigration employment of the in-migrants. Urban per capita incomes are almost always found to be higher than rural per capita incomes in most countries.

In addition, "overurbanization" by either criteria is also found in countries and areas where there is little or no pressure on land in the rural countryside.

> Most of the countries of Central and South America and many in Africa are in this category. There seems to be no invariant correlation between rural pressure and over-urbanization . . . Davis and Golden also did not find any correlation between the degree of urbanization in a country and the average density of population there . . . There is, however, they claim, a negative relationship between urbanization and agricultural density defined as the number of males occupied with agriculture, hunting, and forestry per square mile of cultivated land. *It can be easily seen that this goes against the whole thesis of rural pressure being the main factor bringing about rapid urbanization.*[11]

Finally, in addition to these general criticisms, there have been criticisms by various scholars of particular countries reputed to be overurbanized. For example, Abu-Lughod presents a detailed and empirically based critique of the notion that Egypt is overurbanized.[12] Sovani's regressions also make this presumed classical case of overurbanization suspect. In addition to his general questioning of the hypotheses that rural "push" results in urban growth, Sovani in an earlier article presents a convincing case for the proposition that India has not had rural pressures exploding into urban growth.[13]

Additional Evidence

Simple Correlation Results

Using Norton Ginsburg's fine data, we are able to test at least the cross-sectional aspects of overurbanization in an even more comprehensive manner.[14] In addition to the simple correlation techniques employed by

---

[11]*Ibid.*, p. 118, including note 11 (italics supplied). It should be noted that Davis and Golden are not alone in their "rural pressure" thesis. For instance, Ester Boserup, *The Conditions of Agricultural Growth* (Chicago: Aldine Publishing Co., 1965), p. 71, states: "The preconditions for urbanization . . . are that population density is relatively high."

[12]Abu-Lughod, *op. cit.*

[13]N. V. Sovani, "The Urban Social Situation in India," *Artha Vijnana*, Vol. 3, Part I (July, 1961), pp. 85–103; Part II (September, 1961), pp. 195–222.

[14]Norton Ginsburg, *Atlas of Economic Development* (Chicago: University of Chicago Press, 1961). Most of the data are for the years 1955 and 1956. In a few isolated cases, other sources as well as our own "guesstimates" were used to maintain the 80-country survey.

Sovani, multivariate statistical techniques are employed to assess the importance of the factors affecting urbanization. Our sample consists of 80 countries, including both developed and underdeveloped countries. This larger sample is further divided into two subsamples, on the basis of whether the countries are developed (D) or underdeveloped (U) according to Benjamin Higgins' criterion— "underdeveloped countries . . . are those with per capita incomes less than one-quarter those of the United States"[15] (or here less than $586).

The exact list of variables to be employed in our investigation is presented below:

X_1 = Urbanization 1: percent of population in cities of 20,000 and more;

X_2 = Urbanization 2: a measure of primacy—population of the largest city in each country as a percentage of the total population of the four largest cities;

X_3 = Industrialization: percent of the active population not in agricultural occupations;

X_4 = Total land density: person per square kilometer;

X_5 = Cultivated land density 1: total population per hectare of cultivated land;

X_6 = Cultivated land density 2: agricultural population per hectare of cultivated land;

X_7 = Cultivated land density 3: percent of land area cultivated;

X_8 = Gross national product: U.S. dollars per capita.

Variables X_1 and X_2 are both measures of urbanization. Davis and Golden used a city size of 100,000 instead of 20,000 in their study. However, they claimed there is a regularity about the pyramid of cities by size with the proportion in any major size-class, say 100,000 and above, bearing a systematic relation in the proportion in other size-classes, say above 5,000. Thus, they claim that an index of urbanization is useful, since the proportion of the population in cities above, say 100,000, is roughly similar to the proportion in cities above, say 5,000, from one country to another.[16] X_2 is a different way of measuring urbanization. Many countries have one great city that dominates all others in size of population. It typically also serves as the economic, political, and social center for the nation. X_2 proxies the so-called primate city by showing the population of the largest city as a percentage of the total population. However, to test the overurbanization thesis more in the spirit in which

[15]Benjamin Higgins, *Economic Development* (New York: W. W. Norton, 1959), p. 6. Of course, this arbitrary criterion is subject to all the usual limitations discussed in development texts. It should be mentioned that almost any of the usual definitions of development based on per capita income would not be likely to change the general tenor of our following remarks. For instance, a trial run using 20 percent instead of 25 percent of the U.S. level as the per capita income dividing advanced from underdeveloped countries yielded coefficients that would not change any of our significance levels. These results are available from the author upon written request.

[16]Sovani, *op. cit.*, p. 114, note 4, empirically questions the validity of this proportionality assumption. However, their assumption will be treated as valid for the rest of the paper, in order to demonstrate the serious limitations of their hypotheses even on their own assumptions.

it was formulated, we shall concentrate upon X_1 as the relevant measure of urbanization.

The industrialization proxy variable X_3 — percent of the population *not* in agricultural pursuits — is widely used for this purpose. For land density there are four choices. The X_6 variable is probably the best for testing the rural push hypothesis as it was formulated by the overurbanization proponents. The X_5 and X_7 variables are the next best *for this purpose*. X_4 is the least relevant, in that it relates to total and not to agricultural density.

X_8 will be used as a secondary check on a few things and as an exploratory variable. For shorthand purposes, it will be referred as PCI, for per capita income.

Table 8-1 presents the simple correlation coefficient matrices involving the variables discussed above, separated into three groups: all countries, developed countries, and underdeveloped countries. Although it is difficult to make a strong case for anything on the basis of zero-order correlation analysis, these bits of evidence plus what we know about the overurbanization thesis seem to support the following tentative conclusions.

(1.) The two different measures of urbanization are not significantly related. Overall and for D countries the sign is positive, while for U countries it is negative. Since most of the formulations of the overurbanization hypothesis employ a proxy variable similar to X_1, we shall concentrate upon it.

(2.) Just as Davis and Golden found no significant relationship between the degree of urbanization and the total density in a country, we found very little association. Urbanization measured by either variable is never significantly related to total density at the .01 level for any of the three samples.

(3.) Much more damaging is the relationship between urbanization, X_1 and the three measures of cultivated land density. Although Davis and Golden claim a negative relationship between urbanization and agricultural density, this is not consistent with the rural pressure explanation of rapid urbanization. Therefore, according to the overurbanization thesis, positive and significant coefficients should be found in all three cases, especially for the U countries. However, for all three samples, and for all three measures of density, the coefficients are insignificant. For the variable most relevant for the rural pressure thesis, X_6, we find no significant relationship and "wrong" signs in two of the three samples. The alternative measure of urbanization is generally insignificant, of conflicting signs, and always of higher magnitude for D than U countries — all of which conflict with the rural pressure thesis.

(4.) While this rural pressure argument suggests the undesirablility of urbanization in poor lands, the empirical evidence does not support this. Looking at the association between PCI, X_8, and urbanization, X_1, we find a significant positive coefficient for all countries, and even more damaging the coefficient is significant for U countries at better than the .01 level, while it is insignificant for D countries.[17] This suggests the drive to urbanization in U

[17]Lest a reader think statistical results represented here are inappropriate because of the use of product-moment correlation technique [which assumes, e.g.,   (contd.)

Table 8-1
Simple Correlation Coefficient Matrices

Variable	X_1	X_2	X_3	X_4	X_5	X_6	X_7	X_8
All countries (N = 80)								
X_1	1.00	−.13	.79	.24	.17	.02	.07	.65
X_2		1.00	−.14	−.17	.09	.14	−.07	−.19
X_3			1.00	.31	.12	−.03	.10	.78
X_4				1.00	.10	.10	.51	.06
X_5					1.00	.94	−.14	.19
X_6						1.00	−.16	−.04
X_7							1.00	.00
X_8								1.00
Developed countries (N = 18)								
X_1	1.00	−.19	.59	.22	−.00	−.05	.15	.19
X_2		1.00	−.45	−.21	.39	.42	.26	−.26
X_3			1.00	.40	−.26	−.33	.23	.46
X_4				1.00	−.08	−.14	.63	−.34
X_5					1.00	.99	−.23	−.02
X_6						1.00	−.24	−.02
X_7							1.00	−.19
X_8								1.00
Underdeveloped countries (N = 62)								
X_1	1.00	.02	.67	.17	.17	−.04	.10	.51
X_2		1.00	.10	−.13	−.04	.05	−.18	.10
X_3			1.00	.24	.17	−.04	.15	.63
X_4				1.00	.73	.53	.49	.06
X_5					1.00	.80	−.10	−.12
X_6						1.00	−.11	−.23
X_7							1.00	.30
X_8								1.00

homoscedasticity and a bivariate normal distribution], instead of the less demanding measure of rank correlation, it may be noted that Schnore, *op. cit.*, esp. pp. 234–236, found results similar to those presented here using Spearman rank-correlation coefficients (r_s). For instance, using data *circa* 1950–55, he found the following: (1.) r_s = + .69 (N = 54) between PCI in U.S. dollars, 1949, and "urbanization" (measured as the percent of total population in urban places of 20,000 or more inhabitants), and r_s = + .74 (N = 54) between PCI and "metropolitanization" (measured as the percent of total population in "metropolitan areas"); and (2.) r_s = + .77 (N = 69) between "urbanization" and "industrialization" (measured as the percent of economically active males engaged in nonextractive pursuits, i.e., in other than agriculture, forestry, and fishing, around 1950), and r_s = + .87 (N = 69) between "industrialization" and "metropolitanization."

countries, if it did exist, would not be as damaging as the overurbanization thesis suggests, for PCI levels and urbanization are positively and closely related in such countries.

(5.) Finally, the relationship between industrialization, X_3, and urbanization is contrary to the overurbanization thesis. The association between X_1 and X_3, in this study as in Sovani's, is much closer in the U countries than in the D countries. This implies that the pace of urbanization is much more closely dependent on the pace of industrialization in U than in D countries. This is contrary to the usual formulation of the overurbanization thesis.

Multiple Correlation Results

Within the single-equation least-squares method we have relied on in the present work, the analysis may be extended by employing multivariate statistical techniques.[18] These results are presented in Table 8-2 (pg. 118).

The following tentative conclusions are suggested by Table 8-2.

(1.) The equations involving X_1 as the regressand generally have much more of their variance "explained" than those involving X_2. While this is decidedly so for the D and all-countries samples, it is still true to a considerably lesser extent for the U countries sample. In the U countries when X_2 is the regressand, the multiple correlation coefficients are only slightly different from those involving X_1.

(2.) The industrialization variable is the only variable that is ever significantly different from zero at the .10 or better level. In addition, the coefficient is always positive, *contrary to the overurbanization hypothesis,* for the equations involving X_1 as the dependent variable. This holds for all three samples. While this general result of positive coefficients militates against the overurbanization thesis — in the U countries in particular — it is true that the over-all and the D samples have more (positively) significant coefficients in some cases, as is implied by the thesis. The industrialization coefficients in the equations involving X_2 as the regressand are inconsistent as to sign and are generally not significant.

---

[18]The functions presented here continue to be limited to the linear variety, however. Of course, all the multivariate statistical results must be interpreted in light of any multicollinearity present in the estimating equations. The reader can verify, according to his own standards, in which cases this problem might be serious by comparing the simple correlations between the independent variables given in Table 8-1 with the multiple R in any multivariate equation involving those variables. Equations in which little or no increase in R occurs (and $\bar{R}$ may even fall) as additional explanatory variables as added are also suggestive of a possible collinearity problem.

For a less arbitrary test of multicollinearity that does not involve extensive separate computations, as in factor analysis, but relies entirely on transformations of statistics that are generated routinely during standard multiple regression computations, see Donald E. Farrar and Robert R. Glauber, "Multicollinearity in Regression Analysis: The Problem Revisited," *Review of Economics and Statistics,* Vol. 49, No. 1 (February, 1967), pp. 92–107.

(3.) There is little empirical support for the rural pressure argument of burgeoning urbanization. The variable that is probably the best measure of agricultural density, X_6, is, in all but one case, positively related to urbanization (using either definition) and is never significant. Although Davis and Golden suggested a positive association, this would be contrary to the rural pressure hypothesis. The coefficients for the other three density variables are also insignificant in all equations. While X_5 is like X_6, in that it generally has a positive coefficient, X_3 and X_7 have both positive and negative signs. However, the insignificance of the coefficients makes the signs of very little consequence.

(4.) Because of the high intercorrelation between PCI, X_8, and industrialization, X_3, the addition of the former to the equation adds almost nothing to the percent of the variation "explained."[19] Thus, while either PCI or industrialization alone can "explain" approximately as much as both together in the same equation, the results are shown only for industrialization. This is done since, for this study, industrialization is the more relevant concept and because the simple correlation is slightly higher between industrialization and X_1 than it is for PCI and X_1.

The deviations of the actual from the predicted values, i.e., the "residuals," for the countries in both the U and D groups are presented in the Appendix Table 8-3.[20] This has been done for three separate regressions: the simple case of industrialization on urbanization, and two multiple equations in Table 8-2a (equations 1 and 7). Thus, the interested reader may see in which direction and by how much the individual countries deviate from the "expected." A positive "residual" suggests that the country is relatively overurbanized, and *vice versa* for a negative "residual." In general, the D sample shows a larger percentage of countries with positive residuals than does the U sample. Looking at individual countries (restricting the discussion to the first column in the Appendix Table), the five countries explicitly mentioned as likely to be overurbanized clearly do not conform to their expected pattern. In fact, two of these countries, Korea (− 1) and India (− 1), show negative "residuals," and two have slight positive "residuals," Lebanon (+ 3) and Greece (+ 1). Only Egypt (+ 12) is off the regression line to a significant extent. Restricting the discussion to those countries with deviations of 10 points or more, it can be seen that: (1.) the D countries of Australia, New Zealand, and the U.K. have large positive "residuals," while Belgium and Switzerland have large negative "residuals;" and (2.) the U countries of Argentina, Egypt, Iran, Iraq, Japan, Morocco, Spain, and Syria have large positive deviations, while Ceylon, Cyprus, the Dominican Republic, French Equatorial Africa, Haiti, and the Sudan have large negative deviations.

---

[19]In fact, $\overline{R}$ — the multiple correlation coefficient adjusted for degrees of freedom — fell in many cases as X_8 was added!

[20]I am indebted to an anonymous reader for suggesting that I present the "residuals" for the convenience of the reader. (Table 8-3 begins on pg. 123.)

Table 8-2

Coefficients of Cross-sectional Multiple Regressions
Relating Urbanization (X_1, X_2) to Various Independent Variables

Equation No.	Regressor	Beta coefficients and (t-values) of:					Multiple correlation coefficient adjusted for degrees of freedom $\overline{R}$ and F-statistic
		X_8	X_5	X_7	X_3	X_6	
a. All countries (N = 80)							
1	X_1				.791 (11.356)	.048 (0.690)	.785* (64.549)
2	X_2				-.733 (-1.187)	.141 (1.264)	.117 (1.548)
3	X_1		.072 (1.025)		.781 (11.173)		.787* (65.314)
4	X_2		.104 (0.923)		-.149 (-1.321)		.065 (1.168)
5	X_1			-.004 (-0.052)	.790 (11.259)		.784* (63.920)
6	X_2			-.062 (-0.550)	-.131 (-1.155)		.053 (0.888)
7	X_1	.078 (0.700)			.730 (6.540)	.043 (0.613)	.784* (42.911)
8	X_2	-.239 (-1.345)			.054 (0.302)	.156 (1.400)	.155 (1.646)
9	X_1	.070 (0.624)	.065 (0.918)		.728 (6.561)		.785* (43.327)
10	X_2	-.244 (-1.356)	.127 (1.118)		.037 (0.209)		.122 (1.400)

(continued)

Table 8-2 (continued)

Equation no.	Regressor	X_8	X_5	X_7	X_3	X_6	Multiple correlation coefficient adjusted for degrees of freedom ($\bar{R}$) and F = statistic
		Beta coefficients and (*t*-values) of:					
11	X_1	.086 (0.763)		.002 (0.033)	.723 (6.420)		.782* (42.576)
12	X_2	-.228 (-1.268)		-.078 (-0.691)	.048 (0.266)		.071 (1.133)
b. Developed countries (N = 18)							
1	X_1		.164 (0.778)		.645 (2.984)	.165 (0.765)	.539** (4.478)
2	X_2		.297 (1.315)		-.354 (-1.533)	.302 (1.307)	.437 (3.012)
3	X_1				.634 (2.998)		.540** (4.494)
4	X_2				-.376 (-1.666)		.438 (3.024)
5	X_1			.011 (.052)	.588 (2.749)		.513** (4.031)
6	X_2			.392 (1.834)	-.544 (-2.544)		.514** (4.052)
7	X_1	-.129 (-0.541)			.711 (2.814)	.184 (0.820)	.505** (2.942)
8	X_2	-.120 (-0.470)			-.293 (-1.083)	.319 (1.329)	.383 (1.977)
9	X_1	-.122 (-0.513)	.177 (0.813)		.694 (2.818)		.505*** (2.936)

(continued)

Table 8-2 (continued)

Equation no.	Regressor	Beta coefficients and (t-values) of:					Multiple correlation coefficient adjusted for degrees of freedom ($\bar{R}$) and F = statistic
		X_8	X_5	X_7	X_3	X_6	
10	X_2	-.107 (-0.422)	.308 (1.319)		-.323 (-1.227)		.381 (1.965)
11	X_1	-.108 (-0.420)		-.023 (-0.097)	.646 (2.489)		.470** (2.598)
12	X_2	.090 (0.351)		.421 (1.791)	-.592 (-2.279)		.467** (2.585)
c. Underdeveloped countries (N = 62)							
1	X_1				.667 (6.880)	-.018 (-0.190)	.654* (23.770)
2	X_2				.098 (0.754)	.059 (0.457)	.112† (0.376)
3	X_1		.053 (0.541)		.658 (6.706)		.656* (24.001)
4	X_2		-.056 (-0.426)		.105 (0.800)		.110† (0.362)
5	X_1			.001 (0.015)	.668 (6.806)		.654* (23.738)
6	X_2			-.200 (-1.519)	.125 (0.974)		.118 (1.435)
7	X_1	.160 (1.251)			.568 (4.545)	.015 (.147)	.658* (16.520)
8	X_2	.103 (0.596)			.034 (0.201)	.080 (0.596)	.136† (0.366)
9	X_1	.192 (1.498)	.098 (0.968)		.530 (4.086)		.664* (17.086)

(continued)

Table 8-2 (continued)

Equation no.	Regressor	Beta coefficients and (t-values) of:					Multiple correlation coefficient adjusted for degrees of freedom (R̄) and F = statistic
		X_8	X_5	X_7	X_3	X_6	
10	X_2	.060 (0.343)	−.042 (−0.302)		.065 (0.368)		.119† (0.277)
11	X_1	.168 (1.304)		0.035 (−0.345)	.568 (4.589)		.659* (16.581)
12	X_2	.156 (0.918)		−.229 (−1.711)	.033 (0.201)		.107 (1.235)

Note: The reported coefficients are not the usual regression coefficients, but rather the beta coefficients, which are normalized by adjusting each variable by its standard deviation before estimating the coefficients.
*R is significant at the 1 percent level.
**R is significant at the 5 percent level.
†Since R̄ is quite small, R is shown.

Summary and Conclusions

This paper consists of an empirical extension of some earlier criticisms — especially by N. V. Sovani — of the overurbanization thesis. Through the use of economic analysis, multivariate statistical techniques, and appropriate cross-sectional data, two general conclusions are reached: (1.) there is no invariant (positive) correlation between rural pressure and overurbanization; and (2.) there is no significantly closer (positive) relationship between industrialization and urbanization in all countries, or more especially developed countries, than in the underdeveloped countries. Both of these conclusions are at odds with the usual formulation of the overurbanization hypothesis.

In addition, the argument that rapid urbanization in underdeveloped countries hampers economic growth through the misallocation of scarce capital resources is not convincing. First of all, the simple correlation coefficients between PCI and urbanization, X_1, are much higher for the U countries ($r = .51$) and over-all countries ($r = .65$) than for the D countries ($r = .19$).[21] Furthermore, the multiple correlation coefficients for X_1 and PCI are always positive for U and all countries and always negative for D countries. And the coefficients for the U sample are much closer to being significant at the .10 level than for the other samples. While we do not suggest more rapid urbanization as a panacea to the problems facing the presently underdeveloped countries, the argument regarding the presumed economic burden of rapid urbanization in these areas is clearly suspect.

In short, the definition, existence, causes, and consequences of overurbanization are either unsatisfactory or unsubstantiated. And the conclusions and criticisms of Sovani, *et al.*, are confirmed and, we believe, reinforced.

---

[21]Similarly, for X_2 the coefficients for all, D, and U countries are $r = -.19$, $= -.26$, and $r = +.10$, respectively.

Appendix
Table 8-3

**Comparison of Actual with Predicted Values, i.e., "Residuals," for Each
of the Individual Countries in Each of the Groups**

Country: D = developed U = underdeveloped		(1) "Residuals" from regression of X_3 on X_1	(2) "Residuals" from regression of X_3 and X_6 on X_1	(3) "Residuals" from regression of X_3, X_6 and X_8 on X_1
1. United States	D	6.83	7.15	3.74
2. Canada	D	−9.53	−9.20	−10.88
3. New Zealand	D	11.20	11.39	10.68
4. Switzerland	D	−13.90	−14.00	−14.62
5. Australia	D	12.67	13.00	12.50
6. Luxembourg	D	−6.97	−6.88	−7.85
7. Sweden	D	−7.83	−7.58	−8.24
8. Iceland	D	9.02	3.60	2.74
9. France	D	−7.77	−7.56	−8.15
10. Belgium	D	−13.17	−13.08	−13.00
11. United Kingdom	D	17.93	18.17	18.57
12. Norway	D	−4.87	−4.77	−5.15
13. Finland	D	−4.53	−4.36	−5.51
14. Denmark	D	6.14	6.39	6.22
15. West Germany	D	4.80	4.81	5.10
16. Venezuela	D	2.76	2.99	2.51
17. Netherlands	D	8.43	8.36	8.97
18. U.S.S.R.	D	7.85	8.04	7.39
19. Uruguay	U	−10.00	−9.71	−9.53
20. Czechoslovakia	U	−9.96	−9.84	−9.61
21. Israel	U	9.54	9.73	10.84
22. Austria	U	5.48	5.48	5.00
23. Ireland	U	−1.68	−1.52	−1.29
24. Poland	U	−2.35	−2.22	−2.59
25. Italy	U	−4.56	−4.44	−3.66
26. Hungary	U	3.08	3.23	2.24
27. Union of South Africa	U	4.52	4.85	5.11
28. Argentina	U	10.46	10.50	11.70
29. Cyprus	U	−17.46	−17.18	−16.53
30. Cuba	U	7.61	7.74	8.27
31. Panama	U	−2.15	−1.94	−1.72
32. Colombia	U	0.16	0.16	0.27
33. Rumania	U	5.58	5.42	4.82
34. Costa Rica	U	−6.44	−6.36	−6.22
35. Malaya	U	4.60	4.66	4.78
36. British N. Borneo	U	−5.56	−5.46	−6.55
37. Yugoslavia	U	−2.83	−2.80	−3.13
38. Bulgaria	U	4.86	4.84	4.17
39. Turkey	U	4.60	4.78	4.07

(continued)

Appendix
Table 8-3 (*continued*)

Country: D = developed U = underdeveloped		(1) "Residuals" from regression of X_3 on X_1	(2) "Residuals" from regression of X_3 and X_6 on X_1	(3) "Residuals" from regression of X_3, X_6 and X_8 on X_1
40. Lebanon	U	3.33	3.49	3.55
41. Brazil	U	−0.01	0.07	0.20
42. Spain	U	14.70	14.93	15.44
43. Nicaragua	U	0.41	0.66	0.37
44. El Salvador	U	−4.60	−4.65	−4.67
45. Japan	U	12.58	11.02	12.16
46. Greece	U	1.16	1.32	1.91
47. Dominican Republic	U	−10.20	−10.20	−9.83
48. Ecuador	U	−5.12	−5.13	−4.63
49. Portugal	U	−9.24	−9.08	−8.38
50. Philippines	U	−8.05	−8.08	−7.74
51. Iraq	U	15.87	16.13	15.45
52. Mexico	U	3.79	4.00	4.31
53. Chile	U	5.60	5.89	7.38
54. Guatemala	U	−1.96	−1.97	−2.16
55. Algeria	U	3.11	3.31	2.94
56. Morocco	U	11.04	11.30	11.13
57. Peru	U	−4.14	−4.28	−3.98
58. Honduras	U	0.15	0.26	−0.33
59. Ghana	U	−7.30	−7.22	−7.26
60. Egypt	U	12.69	12.11	12.35
61. Tunisia	U	5.11	5.40	5.43
62. Indonesia	U	−6.77	−6.82	−6.66
63. Ceylon	U	−11.52	−11.67	−10.9
64. Syria	U	25.10	25.27	25.28
65. Paraguay	U	−7.18	−7.06	−6.37
66. Taiwan	U	6.50	5.73	6.16
67. Thailand	U	2.14	1.97	1.42
68. Iran	U	13.32	13.51	13.13
69. Sudan	U	−14.67	−14.51	−14.00
70. Belgian Congo	U	2.44	2.79	2.19
71. South Korea	U	−1.17	−1.01	−0.45
72. Haiti	U	−14.57	−16.11	−15.37
73. India	U	−1.26	−1.12	−1.05
74. Nigeria	U	−9.17	−8.93	−8.36
75. Bolivia	U	6.78	7.00	7.04
76. French West Africa	U	−5.97	−5.79	−6.06
77. French Equatorial Africa	U	−16.57	−16.41	−15.80
78. Pakistan	U	−8.41	−8.41	−8.02
79. China	U	−4.24	−4.57	−4.32
80. Burma	U	−9.67	−9.51	−8.88
Durbin-Watson statistic		2.47	2.44	2.44

(continued)

Appendix
Table 8-3 (*continued*)

Country: D = developed U = underdeveloped	(1) "Residuals" from regression of X_3 on X_1		(2) "Residuals" from regression of X_3 and X_6 on X_1		(3) "Residuals" from regression of X_3, X_6 and X_8 on X_1	
	D	U	D	U	D	U
Total number of countries with positive "residuals"	10	30	10	31	10	30
Percentage	55.6	48.4	55.6	50.0	55.6	48.4
Total number of countries with negative "residuals"	8	32	8	31	8	32
Percentage	44.4	51.6	44.4	50.0	44.4	51.6

Source: The "residuals" are computed using the over-all (N = 80) estimating equations presented in Table 8-2a. The results in column 2 (3) of the present table are related to equation 1 (7) in Table 8-2a.

Questions for Discussion and Analysis

Article 3

1. *Are there large areas in the United States that meet the qualifications of the typical underdeveloped country? How do they meet the qualifications? How is it possible that they can exist within an affluent nation?*
2. *Which of the "Characteristics of Underdeveloped Countries" on Liebenstein's list do you think are subject to debate? Why?*
3. *Would reduction of high mortality rates assist in the development process? Would reduction of high birth rates assist in the development process? Would a simultaneous reduction of both assist in the development process?*
4. *What role, if any, does the form of political organization play in determining the state of development, or, in other words, should the item "form of political organization" appear as a "Cultural and Political" identifying mark of underdeveloped countries?*
5. *The relatively poor soil and other contributing factors do provide relatively low yields per acre in many underdeveloped societies. This is also true in much of the United States. Why can these areas of the United States be classified as developed, whereas countries such as the Sudan, with relatively low yields, are classified as underdeveloped?*

Article 4

6. *Why is the birth rate higher in many underdeveloped countries than in the United States or other developed countries?*
7. *Is Japan a developed or underdeveloped society?*
8. *Is unequal distribution of income necessarily a bad thing if the goal of a country is economic growth?*
9. *Kuznets' sixth comparison between developed and underdeveloped countries focuses around the fact that the latter are more recently independent and hence have greater weaknesses in the social and political structure than do the developed countries. Is this so? Why or why not? How does one measure these "weaknesses?" What are they?*

Article 5

10. *Social values may play some role in determining the economic path of a society. Are these values important enough to consider efforts on the part of developed countries to promote changes in values in the less developed countries?*
11. *Given your opinion expressed in your answer to the preceding question, is there any cost to a society in promoting changes in the social order?*
12. *Is there any real difference between growth on an expansionistic pattern and growth on an intrinsic pattern? Both have the same result, or do they?*

13. *How is it possible in achieving the short range goals in a development program to reduce the possibility of achievement of the longer range goals? Should short term goals then be ignored?*
14. *If skills are available in the typical less developed country, and in many cases they are, why does much of the development effort focus on the generation of skills and problems of the unskilled?*

Article 6

15. *How can the demonstration effect to consumers assist in promoting economic development? How can the demonstration effect to producers assist in impeding economic development?*
16. *Governmental inability to provide services necessary to economic development is frequently cited as one of the weaker links in the chain leading to development. Won't development in the private sector induce the proper governmental activity, allowing further development?*
17. *The underemployment view of the less developed country points out that there is a redundancy of labor in many of these countries, that given the capital stock, not all workers can be employed since there are so many of them, and the marginal product would be less than zero if all were employed. Can this argument be validly applied to employment problems existing today in countries such as the United States? If you think it can, explain how.*
18. *Is the "demonstration effect" the reason that many less developed countries use development funds for building beautiful capital cities, subsidizing nationally owned airlines, or constructing huge hydroelectric projects when there exists no market for the power? If not, what is the reason why decisions might be made to do these things?*
19. *If government loses its control of certain sectors of the economy and allows the private sector of the economy to handle them, how might these sectors grow in a pattern that will not allow for orderly economic development?*

Article 7

20. *If population growth and the rate of growth of the food supply have been approximately equal in the past few years, is there any need to worry about a "razor's edge of subsistence?"*
21. *If a society must devote larger and larger portions of its effort to providing for the food necessary to sustain the population, what will happen to the growth of the capital stock and to per capita income?*
22. *Why might subsistence farmers in underdeveloped countries be very suspicious of new agricultural innovations and refuse to use them?*

23. *The Chinese "great leap forward" of the 1950's was a failure. Efforts to industrialize the mainland in a very short time, with a steel mill in every large town, did not succeed. Why did the desire to move larger percentages of the population into industry from agriculture fail?*

24. *Is agricultural development a necessary prerequisite for industrial development?*

Article 8

25. *Is there typically any relationship between industrialization and the emergence of very large cities in a society? Must this relation hold?*

26. *Does the appearance of large numbers of unemployed in the large cities of underdeveloped societies give any information as to the productivity of workers in the agricultural sector?*

27. *Even with "overurbanization," per capita incomes in cities are found to be significantly higher than in the rural areas. There evidently is no trend toward making these equal. Why might we expect this discrepancy to continue to exist?*

Section III

APPROACHES TO DEVELOPMENT AS AN ANALYTICAL PROBLEM: MEASURES AND MODELS

This section is important first, in that it contains several articles dealing with the crucial measuring problems in economic development, and second, it presents articles dealing with a number of the most popular development models of recent years. These models are associated with such people as Rostow, Hirschman, Lewis, Rosenstein-Rodan, Nurkse, etc., many of whom are discussed at various places in this volume.

Pesek sets the stage for all empirical investigations of economic development by pointing out that there are at least five different methods of calculating rates of growth. What is important is that all five of these are based on a different set of algebraic constraints and hence yield five different rates of growth for one identical stream of output! And yet important policy matters are formulated on the basis of "the" growth rate, with usually little question as to how this rate was computed. The basic requirement in all such calculations is that the actual total output during the period covered be equal to the calculated total output. But that is not enough. All of the methods he surveys vary widely in their reliability, objectivity, and ease of application. Using some criteria that would suit most economists, Pesek offers a new, hopefully superior, method "which rests on a more meaningful set of algebraic restraints, which faithfully reproduces the flow of actual output during the period covered, and which better than other methods resists purely accidental deviations from the long run trend."

Kleiman discusses some further problems associated with the use of national income figures for comparisons of economic welfare. In particular, he shows that the association between the demographic attributes of age composition, size of consumption units, and the level of per capita income leads to an exaggeration of the differences on welfare levels between nations and to a distortion in the size of these levels intertemporally. For instance, he shows that since children need less food than adults, a country with a relatively large number of children — the technical term is a high dependency ratio (DR) where DR measures the ratio of very young and old to the economically productive age group (usually taken to be 15–64) — would have a higher standard of living than one with a smaller DR, *given* the income level. In addition, insofar as there are economies of scale in consumption with respect to family size, the smaller the family is, the higher the per capita income required to provide a given level of living. As an empirical matter, it turns out that the per capita income of some countries would have to be increased by as much as 20 to 40 percent to eliminate the bias resulting from differences in age structure and in size of households in order to make meaningful international comparisons.

The Harberger selection is also concerned with measurement problems. That is, it investigates the way in which different views of the process of economic growth imply different norms for the analyses of benefits and costs of individual projects, and vice versa. The author circumscribes the view that the private sector rate of return should be used as the criterion in the public sector. His point is simple, yet important: benefits to society must be included in cost-benefit analysis. If we regard economic growth as primarily the result of investment, then we must drastically revise our norms. Alternatively, if we wish to accept the norms typically applied in cost-benefit analysis, it is necessary to assume a view of economic growth in which investment is not very crucial. He illustrates his thesis nicely with respect to the Indian economy.

The remaining papers in this section turn to the discussion of various models that have been developed in recent years in an attempt to understand economic development and growth. The study by Kuznets is a critical review of one of the better known of these models — Walter W. Rostow's theory of the stages of the development process. In the process Kuznets presents a terse review of Rostow's thinking. Kuznets first sets out what he thinks are the minimum requirements for any sequence of stages to make sense. Next he criticizes certain aspects of the take-off stage; in particular, the fuzziness in delineating it and in formulating its distinctive characteristics. Finally, he demonstrates the inconsistency between Rostow's model and the empirical data in certain countries.

Myint reviews the interesting theory of economic development which has been proposed by Professor Hirschman. Myint feels Hirschman has done a good job of presenting the case for unbalanced growth and the case for psychological factors in economic development. However, Myint is sharply critical of Hirschman on several counts. Most important, Myint criticizes over-reliance on a pure demand approach to economic development. In attempting to evaluate Hirschman's contribution, Myint, presents a concise but yet understandable explanation of Hirschman's model.

Streeten attempts to present a middle approach to the protracted controversy over "balanced" growth (BG) versus "unbalanced" growth (UG). The former has been most prominently associated with Ragnar Nurkse and Paul Rosenstein-Rodan, whereas UG has been identified with Albert Hirschman. Streeten discusses the merits and faults of both doctrines. Before doing that, he clears the air in regard to what relevance planning (private or governmental), supply limitations, and elasticities have to these doctrines. Followers of either view would do well to consider carefully Streeten's summary of the strengths and shortcomings of each approach.

Enke reviews, amends, and extends the interesting theory of development by W. A. Lewis. His basic amendment to the Lewis thesis is to divide the analysis into three stages instead of two. The first (last) stage involves only capital "widening" ("deepening"), whereas the second stage is both capital "widening" and "deepening." The elasticity of supply of labor (E) in the three stages is as follows: stage 1, $E = +\infty$; stage 2, $0 < E < +\infty$; and stage 3, $E = 0$. He also amends the basic model by noting that the labor supply function may not be continuous and the capitalists saving function may involve different arguments than those suggested by Lewis. The basic extension of the Lewis model offered by Enke includes a diagrammatic representation not found in Lewis. Enke's review of the Lewis model at the beginning of his paper and his list of five amendments and extensions of the Lewis model at the end of his paper are worth perusing.

The final selection in this section reviews the progress that has been made in neoclassical growth models in recent years. Although economic growth occupied a prominent place in the work of the classical economists — especially Adam Smith — rigorous growth models were virtually absent from economics until the Harrod-Domar growth models around the middle of the twentieth century. The really intensive study of neoclassical growth models, both with and without technological advance, can approximately be dated from the path-breaking contributions of Solow and Swan in 1956. Ferguson reviews the one-sector models with both neutral and biased technical progress within the framework of the Golden Age and Golden Rule models that have become so famous in recent years. What is especially noteworthy is that Ferguson's review is in terms of graphs and elementary mathematics, although the existing literature ordinarily employs advanced mathematics. His Table 16-1 contains a compact summary of his results.

In the section entitled "The Cobb-Douglas Case," Ferguson assumes that the implication of a declining share of capital is an eventual situation in which that share must equal zero. This need not be the case. See J. Kirker Stephens, "Comment," *Quarterly Review of Economics and Business,* Vol. 9, (2) (1969), pp. 70–71, for a demonstration of this.

Boris Pesek†

9. ECONOMIC GROWTH AND ITS MEASUREMENT*

Introduction

Aside from the huge shadow cast by what to the ancient Greeks was the smallest imaginable unit of matter, we live in a propitious part of the century. Our progressive fathers fought their conservative opponents by giving the reactionary promise to push the national income back to the 1929 level. Today their conservative sons fight the progressive opponents by making the revolutionary promise to double the present high level of income in some twenty-five years; but the public turns to those who promise to do the same thing in a mere twelve to fifteen years. Today's star witness before a Congressional Committee is not a labor economist measuring unemployment; he is an expert on economic development measuring growth. The rate of economic growth is becoming a major tool for economists and statesmen attempting to evaluate the past and present performance of our economic system and measuring the resources which can be made available by the affluent society for the improvement of the lot of the non-affluent within and beyond its borders. To the poor countries this rate of growth is a matter of vital, almost desperate, interest. Finally, this rate of growth is a key variable in the economic and political competition to which we have been challenged by Premier Khrushchev.

In view of the great importance of the estimates of the rate of economic growth for economists and statesmen alike it seems appropriate to inquire into the methods which are being used to calculate this rate. At present, there exist five different methods of calculating the rate of growth; all five are based on a different set of algebraic restraints and, consequently, all five yield different rates of growth for one, identical, stream of output. For example, the selection of a certain method of calculating the rate of growth of the American gross national product from 1929 to 1959 can lead to a rate as low as 2.9 percent and

†Boris P. Pesek, Professor of Economics, University of Wisconsin — Milwaukee. The author wishes to thank his colleague, Einar Hardin, who read and discussed this article with him in detail. All his suggestions proved to be invaluable. All responsibility must, however, remain the author's.
*From *Economic Development and Cultural Change,* Vol. 9 (April, 1961), pp. 295-315. Reprinted by permission of the University of Chicago Press and the author.

as high as 4.1 percent.[1] In addition, several of the methods currently used are highly sensitive to the selection of the period to be covered and an addition of one or two years can affect the results obtained quite drastically. Again, as an example, I might mention the growth of the American gross national product in the period 1950–57. If we use the method most popular today, the rate of growth will be calculated to amount to 3.6 percent. If we add a year (1958), the rate will drop to 2.9 percent; if we add another year, it will jump up to 3.4 percent.[2]

In some cases the selection of the method of calculation and of the time period covered is discussed by the writer very thoroughly and the reader is made aware of the consequences of these decisions and of the reasons which led the researcher to make them. In other cases, a terse footnote of fifteen words is all the reader is told about the selection of the method used despite the fact that this method is one with which, judging by an informal poll of my colleagues, few are familiar.[3]

In this paper I shall discuss the five methods in current use and attempt to show that all of them make use of algebraic restraints which are not very meaningful for an economist. In addition, I shall show that some of them depend excessively on purely accidental configurations of the pattern of output over time. Consequently, most of them seriously overestimate or underestimate the actual performance of the economies which we want to study. Subsequently, I shall offer a new method which rests on a more meaningful set of algebraic restraints, which faithfully reproduces the flow of actual output during the period covered, and which better than other methods resists purely accidental deviations from the long run trend. In the second, empirical, section of this paper I shall compare this method with the five other methods in current use to enable the reader to judge all of them on the basis of their actual performance.

Methods of Calculating a Rate of Growth

Method I

The simplest and most widely used technique of calculating economic growth is based on the geometric average of the ratios of output during successive time periods:

$$g_1 = \left(\sqrt[n-1]{\frac{P_2}{P_1} \times \frac{P_3}{P_2} \times \ldots \times \frac{P_n}{P_{n-1}}} - 1 \right) \times 100. \qquad (1.)$$

[1]See Table 9-2, column 7.
[2]See Table 9-2, row 1, columns 4, 5, and 6.
[3]Arthur F. Burns devotes a chapter (2) to such a discussion in his *Production Trends in the United States Since 1870* (New York, 1950). William H. Shaw states in his *Value of Commodity Output Since 1869* (New York, 1947), p. 9: "Average annual rates of growth were computed by using Glover's method to fit exponential curves to original data."

where g_1 is the rate of growth based on Method I and P the output in periods $1, 2, 3, \ldots, n$. Since all the terms but two under the root sign cancel out, we need to know only the two terminal outputs P_1 and P_n:

$$g_1 = \left(\sqrt[n-1]{\frac{P_n}{P_1}} - 1 \right) \times 100. \tag{1A.}$$

By this method we can calculate a rate of growth which, if compounded annually over a given period, yields the terminal percentage increase in the variable analyzed. The use of this technique is exceedingly widespread. In the *National Income, 1954 Edition* we find the following statement:

> A simple and meaningful comparison of the long-term rate of growth in national production is provided by the average annual percentage increase in constant-dollar gross national product from 1929 to 1953, which were both years of high utilization of productive resources. According to this calculation, the rate of expansion in the real volume of output has averaged over this 25-year period about 3 percent per year.[4]

If the editors of *National Income, 1954 Edition* intend their rate of growth to measure the past performance of the American economy (and the context suggests that this is the case) then they are clearly not justified in claiming that "the rate of expansion of the real volume of output has averaged. . .about 3 percent per year." Such a claim intimates that the calculated rate simply "averages" or evens out the troughs and peaks in the business cycle and their effects on "the real volume of output." Were this the case, then the total gross national product produced by the economy during this period would have to amount to 5,443.3 billion real dollars: the gross national product of 1929, 149.3 billion real dollars, compounded annually at the rate of growth of 3 percent. The actual output, however, amounted to 4,936.6 billion real dollars. Thus, to use this "average" rate in order to speak about the "expansion of output" is grossly misleading.

What the editors of the *National Income, 1954 Edition* should have said is much more complex and conditional:

> If between 1929 and 1953 the real volume of output had grown at a constant rate, as it did not, then the rate of expansion in the real volume of output would have averaged over this 25-year period about 3 percent per year.

However, even this statement, though now qualified by the denial of the assumption on which it rests, is still not correct. The reason is that the position of the terminal point 1953, on which the calculation of the rate is based, is not independent of the actual past performance of the economic system. If the real volume of output had grown at the constant rate of 3 percent then the

---

[4]United States, Department of Commerce, Office of Business Economics, *National Income, 1954 Edition* (A Supplement to the *Survey of Current Business*) (Washington, 1954), p. 2.

system would have produced during this period additional goods and services worth 507 billion additional real dollars. Since net investment usually amounts to some ten percent of the gross national product, it may be estimated that productive resources available in 1953 would have been higher by some 50 billion dollars. If it still were true that the year 1953 was one marked by "high utilization of productive resources," as the writers of the Department of Commerce specify, then the real volume of output would have been higher. But then the rate of growth with which this circle started would have been higher. An entirely correct statement describing this rate of growth would read:

> If between 1929 and 1953 the real volume of output had grown at a constant rate, and if none of the output lost because the above assumption is incorrect had been devoted to the production of investment goods, then the rate of expansion in the real volume of output would have averaged over this 25-year period about 3 percent per year.

To introduce the statement of the Department of Commerce by these two indispensable qualifications is to make it meaningless.

It might be emphasized that an extreme situation like the Great Depression is not necessary to condemn this method of calculation of the rate of growth. In the recent study of the Joint Economic Committee of the United States Congress, testimony was given comparing Soviet and American economic growth in the period 1950–58; a period distinguished by very mild fluctuations in the American output. Gerhart Colm claims that during the period 1950–57 our rate of growth was 3.6 percent per annum.[5] This rate implies that American output during this period amounted to 2,889 billion dollars of constant purchasing power; the actual output has been 58.2 billion dollars higher. In his calculation the witness threw out the year 1958 as atypical. Another witness has included it.[6] The rate of growth in his testimony consequently fell to 2.9 percent per annum and the implied underestimate of the actually produced output jumped to 130.3 billion real dollars. Somewhat later the Central Intelligence Agency was asked to prepare estimates for the same Committee. The year 1959 could be included; consequently, the rate of growth jumped to 3.4 percent.[7] The resulting implied underestimate of the gross national product dropped back to 62.2 billion real dollars.

To calculate the dollar value of the error caused by the erroneous, or at least superficial, calculation of the rate of growth is not an idle exercise. In the

---

[5]Gerhart Colm, "Evaluation of the Soviet Economic Threat," in United States Congress, Joint Economic Committee, *Comparison of the United States and Soviet Economies* (86th Congress, 1st Session) (Washington, 1960), Part II, p. 534.

[6]Boris Bornstein, "A Comparison of Soviet and United States National Product," *ibid.,* p. 391.

[7]The CIA, working with preliminary estimates, rounded the figure to 3-1/4. Cf. *Comparison of the United States and Soviet Economies,* prepared by the Central Intelligence Agency in cooperation with the Department of State and the Department of Defense for the Joint Economic Committee, United States Congress (Washington, 1960), p. 48.

present situation, in which the public shows awareness that some basic decisions in our society are not being made correctly, it has become customary to argue that no absolute sacrifices are necessary to achieve correction: that it would be enough to make sure that a greater proportion of the annual increment of output will be allocated to "education, urban reconstruction, roads, water development and other forms of social overhead capital on whose adequacy the quality of American society partially depends."[8] This painlessly-disposable increment is bound to be calculated incorrectly if the rate of growth by the use of which it is calculated is biased and misleading. Thus, W. W. Rostow argues that if we could only increase our rate of growth to 4 percent per year, the Soviet threat could "easily be met by a society with over a $500 billion GNP and a more than $20 billion annual increment in GNP."[9] He states that this is "within our grasp if our growth potentials are fully and well used."[10]

How difficult is it, really, to achieve this goal? To decide this issue I took the output assumed by Rostow for the year 1960 (500 billion real dollars) and I assumed that this output will grow in the periods 1960–67, 1960–68, and 1960–69 by the same percentages by which the gross national product of 1950 grew in the periods 1950–57, 1950–58, and 1950–59. Thus, the calculated rate of growth g_1 for 1950–57 must be identical with the rate g_1 for 1960–67, g_1 for 1950–58 identical with g_1 for 1960–68, and g_1 for 1950–59 identical with g_1 for 1960–69. Table 9-1 shows that a simple repetition of our 1950–57 performance during the period 1960–67, with a calculated rate of growth g_1 amounting to 3.6 percent would produce 25 billion real dollars *more* than the increment desired by Rostow and yielded by a constant rate of growth of 4 percent; a rate which he considers challenging enough to require a much better use of our growth potential. An increase of our production by one-half of one percent would be enough to yield an additional 29 billion real dollars and thus enable us to follow the 1950–58 patterns; patterns with the calculated growth rate g_1 of 2.9 percent! Some effort, though still a most modest one, would be required to enable us to produce according to the 1950–59 patterns with a calculated rate g_1 of 3.4 percent and still come up with the painlessly-disposable increment desired by Rostow.

Something is obviously quite seriously wrong with the calculation of the rate of growth if a calculated rate g_1 of 3.6 percent can yield more than an actual compound rate of 4 percent; if a calculated rate g_1 of 2.9 percent can yield negligibly less than an actual compound rate of 4 percent; if a calculated rate g_1 of 3.4 percent can yield as much as an actual compound rate of 3.8 percent. And something is wrong with the calculation of a rate of growth if an economist using it is led to posit what he considers to be a challenging goal but which actually can be reached (as Table 9-1 shows) by a further relaxation of our flabby effort.

[8]W. W. Rostow, "Summary and Policy Implications," in United States Congress, Joint Economic Committee, *op. cit.*, Part III, p. 600.

[9]*Ibid.*, p. 601.

[10]*Ibid.*, p. 601.

Table 9-1
Problems of Growth of GNP, 1960–69

| | | Output implied* | | |
| | | | Growth at rate g_1, 1950's pattern | Growth at compound rate of 4 percent | Sum in (5) less sum in (4) |
Pattern of growth (1)	Rate g_1 for period in cols. (1) and (4) (2)	During period (3)	(billion dollars) (4)	(billion dollars) (5)	(billion dollars) (6)
1. 1950–57	3.6	1960–67	4,632	4,607	−25
2. 1950–58	2.9	1960–68	5,262	5,291	+29
3. 1950–59	3.4	1960–69	5,933	6,003	+70

*As in Rostow's calculations, the gross national product in 1960 is assumed to be 500 billion real dollars.

Method II

If meaningful results are to be obtained, the actual stream of output during the period studied has to be taken into consideration. One technique is based on the calculation of the arithmetic mean of the annual rates of growth:

$$g_2 = \left(\frac{\sum_{t=1}^{n} \frac{P_t}{P_{t-1}}}{n-1} - 1 \right) \times 100. \tag{2.}$$

I was able to discover only one case of use of this method. The shortcomings of this method are serious: more so than those of Method I. Consider an output series 100, 90, 99; output first decreases and then increases by ten percent. Consequently, the rate of growth will be shown to be zero despite the fact that in period two and three output decreased by eleven units. An extension of the above series could drive output to zero and still the calculated rate of growth would not show a negative growth.

A. F. Burns, while giving absolute preference to "a simple exponential curve fitted to a production series" (which shall be discussed later) states that a geometric mean of year-to-year changes is preferable to an arithmetic mean. He writes:

> An arithmetic mean of year-to-year percentage changes is defective because the theoretical scale of percentages is limited at one end but not the other. A geometric mean of percentage changes is preferable to an arithmethic mean since it is based on the logarithms of percentage changes (or rather link ratios), and therefore gives equal weight to changes of equal proportionate magnitude. The geometric mean of percentage changes has nevertheless a serious defect: it is absolutely conditioned by two items, the initial and the final values and these may of course be of "accidental" magnitude. The geometric mean can report what happened from one time unit to another, but not what happened during the period

marked off by them, and is therefore but poorly suited to yield the level
of information about growth that is desired here.[11]

Method III

While Burns' statement rejects the arithmetic mean with arguments of
sufficient strength to eliminate the arithmetic mean from use by all but the least
sophisticated, his conditional argument in favor of the geometric mean (which
he himself does not use) seems to be of questionable validity. The formula for
"the geometric mean of percentage changes" can be written as follows:

$$g_3 = \left(\sqrt[n-1]{\frac{P_2 - P_1}{P_1} \times \frac{P_3 - P_2}{P_2} \times \ldots \times \frac{P_n - P_{n-1}}{P_{n-1}}} \right) \times 100. \tag{3.}$$

This method fails to yield useful results if one of the factors is equal to zero or
if some of the factors have negative signs. A parenthetical statement of A. F.
Burns "(or rather link ratios)" suggests that he really meant Method I.

Method IV

Two other methods of calculating the rate of growth fit exponential growth
curves of the type

$$Y = ab^t \tag{4.}$$

to the values of the variable observed during the period to be analyzed. One
method utilizes the least squares technique to calculate the rate of growth. In
the least squares method the assumptions are made that

$$\sum_{t=1}^{n} {}_e Y_t = \sum_{t=1}^{n} Y_t \tag{5.}$$

and that

$$\sum_{t=1}^{n} \left({}_e Y_t - Y_t \right)^2 = \min., \tag{6.}$$

where ${}_e Y_t$ stands for the estimated value of some variable and Y_t for the actual
value of that variable in time t. However, it is not possible to fit an exponential
curve directly to the actual values of the variable when we use the least squares
method. The curve has to be fitted to the logarithms of the observed values of
the variable.

We obtain

----

[11]Arthur F. Burns, *op. cit.*, p. 35.

$$g_4 = \left(\sqrt[t-1]{\sqrt{\frac{_e P'_t}{a'}}} - 1 \right) \times 100, \tag{7.}$$

in which $_e P'_t$ and a' are calculated by the least squares method on the basis of the requirements that

$$\sum_{t=1}^{n} \log {_e P'_t} = \sum_{t=1}^{n} \log P_t \tag{8.}$$

and that

$$\sum_{t=1}^{n} \left(\log {_e P'_t} - \log P_t \right)^2 = \min. \tag{9.}$$

Thus, the sum of *the logarithms* of the actually observed values is made equal to the sum of *the logarithms* of the estimated values of output.[12] This means this technique makes the product of the actual outputs equal to the product of the estimated outputs. Both these products and their equality are, from the standpoint of economics, meaningless. On the other hand, the economically meaningful requirement that the sum of actual outputs be equal to the sum of the estimated outputs is not satisfied. Despite these conceptual shortcomings this method, as we shall see in the next section, containing a number of empirical comparisons, yields often growth rates which express the "correct" growth rates much better than the rates yielded by one of the three methods just discussed.

Method V

To eliminate this shortcoming James W. Glover[13] developed another technique of fitting an exponential growth curve to serial data.

In his technique

$$g_5 = \left(\sqrt[t]{\frac{_e P''_t}{a''}} - 1 \right) \times 100 \tag{10.}$$

where $_e P''_t$ and a'' are calculated so as to satisfy the requirement that

$$\sum_{t=0}^{n-1} {_e P''_t} = \sum_{t=0}^{n-1} P_t \tag{11.}$$

---

[12]The technique of calculation can be found in any statistical textbook.
[13]James W. Glover, *Tables of Applied Mathematics in Finance, Insurance, Statistics* (Ann Arbor, 1923), p. 468.

and that

$$\sum_{t=0}^{n-1} {}_{e}P''_{t} \, t = \sum_{t=0}^{n-1} P_{t} \, t. \qquad\qquad (12.)$$

Thus, the sum of the actual values of output is made equal to the sum of the estimated values of output; in addition, the sum of the products of the actual values of output and the measure of time is made equal to the sum of the products of the estimated values of output and the measure of time.

I am not sure that James W. Glover intended his technique to be used for the calculation of economic growth: his terse description of his technique covers less than half a page. However, it has been used for this purpose in the past. For instance, William H. Shaw used it in *Value of Commodity Output since 1869* (New York, 1957) and Arthur F. Burns in *Production Trends in the United States since 1870* (New York, 1950). John W. Kendrick used Glover's method to check results reported in his *Productivity Trends in the United States* (National Bureau of Economic Research, 1961).

Glover's technique eliminates the key objection to all the above discussed methods by making the sum of the actually produced output during the period analyzed equal to the sums of the estimated outputs. However, the satisfaction of this criterion, which we consider so important for the judging and comparing of the past performance of economies, can be evaluated only in conjunction with the second restraint (12.) because any rate of growth will satisfy the first restraint (11.): a zero rate of growth with the arithmetic mean of the sum of output, any positive rate with a starting point suitably smaller than the mean of the sum, or any negative rate with a starting point suitably bigger than the mean of the sum.

Glover's second restriction, which is necessary to obtain a unique rate of growth, does not seem to be defensible from the standpoint of economics. First, the requirement that the sum of the products of actual outputs and the set of weights $0, 1, 2, 3, \ldots, n$ be equal to the sum of the products of estimated outputs and the same set of arbitrary weights cannot be given any economic interpretation. Indeed, if we claim that the year 3 is twice as important as the year 2 (weights 2 and 1 respectively), consistency would require that the year 4 be considered twice as important as the year 3: another set of weights 1, 2, 4, 8, $\ldots, n$ would seem at least equally defensible.

Second, this arbitrary set of weights which increase at a decreasing rate and the results obtained by the use of this set will be predicated on the no less arbitrary selection of the point of origin. If the origin is the year 1869, as in Shaw's study, the ratio of weights given to the years 1929 and 1939 will be $\frac{59}{69}$. If the origin is the year 1928, the ratio of weights for the same years 1929 and

1939 will be $\frac{10}{1}$.[14] A bias caused by the selection of an abnormal base year is in many cases easy to detect; a bias caused by selection of a normal year which will yield a biased set of weights for some of the subsequent years is almost impossible to detect without extensive calculations.   Third, it seems desirable to require that any index number measuring the rate of economic growth be able to stand the time reversal test. Glover's method, quite obviously, cannot meet the test. Glover's technique, by giving the overwhelming share of weights to the most recent years might perhaps be profitably used if the goal is not to measure the performance of an economic system in the past, but to predict the likely performance of an economic system in the future. Here, given the customary condition of a fairly "normal" recent past, the assumption is strong that an extrapolation of a recent, normal, past will yield the best prediction of what is likely to happen in the future. This is as far as I shall pursue this topic because the subject of this paper is the problem of best measuring what happened in the past and not the problem of best predicting what is likely to happen in the future.

I would like to offer for consideration and possible use two methods of calculation of the rate of economic growth, both of which seem to me to be superior to the methods used up to now.

---

[14]It should be realized that the arithmetic center of the series (by which I understand a point in time such that any change in output at this point will leave the calculated rate unaffected) is in the case of Glover's method different from the calendar-time center. This fact may, occasionally, affect our interpretation of results obtained. A. F. Burns in *Production Trends* used Glover's method to measure growth rates in overlapping calendar decades. For each calendar decade he selected a working decade in an effort to eliminate cyclical effects: the boundaries of the working decades do not, of course, coincide with the boundaries of their calendar decades. When Burns then assigned the values of the rate of growth during the working decades to the centers of the calendar decades, the failure to take the arithmetic centers into consideration could have led to a quite peculiar results. Because he does not specify his working decades, a hypothetical example must suffice:

Calendar decade	Working decade	Calendar center of calendar decade	Arithmetic center of working decade
1900–1910	1902–1912	1905	1909
1905–1915	1903–1913	1910	1910
1910–1920	1912–1922	1915	1919

a. Burns' rules for selection of working decades are satisfied.

The rules which Burns followed in the selection of working decades (*op. cit.*, p. 39) fail to take into account that the arithmetic center of the working decades is not the calendar center of those decades. While the discrepancy between the calendar centers of the calendar and working decade may be small, the above hypothetical example shows that the discrepancy between the calendar center of the calendar decade and the arithmetic center of the working decade may be substantial.

Method VI

The first method rests on the requirement that

$$\sum_{t=1}^{n} {}_eP_t = \sum_{t=1}^{n} P_t \qquad\qquad (13.)$$

and on the requirement that the estimated output in period 1 be equal to the actual output in period 1; in other words, the base year must be selected in the case of this method:

$${}_eP_1 = P_1. \qquad\qquad (14.)$$

Then an exponential equation

$$P = ab^t$$

can be fitted to the observed values of the output over a period of time so that

$$P_1 + P_1b + P_1b^2 + \ldots + P_1b^{n-1} = P_1 + P_2 + \ldots + P_n. \qquad\qquad (15.)$$

After multiplication, this formula reduces to

$$\frac{b^n - 1}{b - 1} = \frac{\sum_{t=1}^{n} P_t}{P_1} \qquad\qquad (16.)$$

and, of course,

$$g_6 = (b - 1) \times 100. \qquad\qquad (17.)$$

This formula has the advantage not shared by any method discussed previously except Glover's: it assures that the sum of the actual outputs during the period will be equal to the sum of the estimated outputs during the period. It does not suffer from the peculiar weighting procedure which burdens the only other method fulfilling the above requirement. Finally, it is exceedingly easy and fast to calculate. Its disadvantage which it shares with the now commonly used g_1 is that the selection of the base period is arbitrary. (However, in contrast to g_1, this rate reflects the pattern of output during the period analyzed and is not determined by the no less arbitrarily selected terminal point.)[15]

---

[15]The most efficient method of finding the rate of growth g_6 is as follows:

(a.) Calculate

$$\frac{\sum_{t=1}^{n} P_t}{P_1} = x$$

(contd.)

Method VII

This disadvantage can be overcome when we select simultaneously a growth rate *and* a fictitious base year quantity $\hat{P}_1$ such that (a.) the sum of the actual outputs during the period be equal to the sum of the estimated outputs for the same period and that (b.) the sum of the squared absolute deviations between the actual outputs in the various periods and the estimated outputs for the same periods be minimized.

Modify (16.) by substituting $\hat{P}_1$ for P_1 and introduce a requirement that

$$\sum_{t=1}^{n}\left(\hat{P}_1 b^{t-1} - P_t\right)^2 = \text{min.} \tag{18.}$$

Differentiate (18.) with respect to $\hat{P}_1$ and set the derivative equal to zero, which yields

$$\sum_{t=1}^{n} \hat{P}_1 b^{2(t-1)} = \sum_{t=1}^{n} P_t b^{t-1}. \tag{19.}$$

After we solve for $\hat{P}_1$ and substitute in (16.) we get:

$$\frac{b^n + 1}{b + 1} = \frac{\sum\limits_{t=1}^{n} P_t b^{t-1}}{\sum\limits_{t=1}^{n} P_t} \tag{20.}$$

and

$$g_7 = (b - 1) \times 100. \tag{21.}$$

The advantages of this method of calculating the growth rate are substantial: total production during the period is reflected: only g_5 and g_6 share this desirable feature. The rate which one obtains by the application of this method is neither determined by the initial and final values of the time series analyzed (g_1) nor is the rate influenced more by the initial value in the series analyzed than it is by any other value (in contrast to g_6). While the case for the minimization of the squares of the deviations is not as strong as it has been thought in the past, it appears to me substantially stronger than the case for the use of a

---

(b.) find this number x in the body of a table showing amount of 1 Per Annum at Compound Interest ($S_{\overline{n}|} i$) in period n;

(c.) the rate of interest shown by the table for the known x and n is the rate g_6.

set of arbitrary weights employed by the method yielding g_5. A disadvantage of this method is that it requires a fairly substantial computational effort.[16]

Comparison of Performance

To give the reader some tools for judging the relative performance of the various methods discussed and suggested in this paper, I shall present several comparisons. While the selection of the best method of calculating the growth rate must depend on our evaluation of the usefulness and appropriateness of the algebraic restraints on which this method is based, it is surely of substantial importance to see the various competing methods in action: ". . . judgment must always play a dominating role in the choice of statistical technique."[17]

In Table 9-2 I used the American gross national product from 1929 to 1959 to compare the performance of all seven methods. The first three subperiods were selected because of their recently being discussed widely. The next three time periods were selected because all three have been used to compare the relative performance of the American and Soviet economic systems. Finally, the entire period 1929–59 was used as a part of a comparison of the performance of these methods as they might be applied to a fairly long period of time. In the case of the periods 1945–52 and 1946–52 both Methods I and II show extreme sensitivity to economic fluctuations caused by the addition or subtraction of one single year from the group of seven other years. While the exclusion of the year 1945 increases the calculated rate of growth by Methods I and II by 111 and 105 percent respectively, under Method IV this rate increases by only 86 percent and under Methods V and VII by only 55 percent in both cases. In the case of the periods 1950–57, 1950–58, and 1950–59 the same patterns emerge. The addition of one year, 1958, causes the rate of growth calculated by Methods I and II to decrease by 19.5 and 19 percent respectively; the addition of the same year decreases the rates of growth yielded by Methods V and VII by 12 and 15 percent respectively. Addition of another year (1959) leads to an increase in the rate of growth in the case of Methods I and II; it causes either a negligible decrease or no change in the case of Methods V and VII.

---

[16]Union Carbide Corporation prepared in the past and has made available to the profession a splendid set of tables to facilitate the calculation of the rate g_1. This corporation could easily prepare tables containing the tabulation of

$$x = \frac{b^n + 1}{b + 1}.$$

This should substantially diminish the computational effort required. To those who have access to an electronic computer I will be glad to send on request a copy of a program which solves equation (20.) for b. Addendum, 1972: A book of tables based on a slight modification of the above method has been prepared by Dudley J. Cowden and Neville L. Rucker, *Tables for Fitting An Exponential Trend by the Method of Least Squares*, Technical Paper 6, Graduate School of Business, University of North Carolina, Chapel Hill, N.C.

[17]Arthur F. Burns, *op. cit.*, p. 41.

Methods I, II, and IV lead to erroneous estimates of the total output of the economy in all the cases analyzed. In a few instances the error is rather small; in numerous instances it is substantial (lines 11 through 14 in Table 9-2). In the case of Methods V, VI, and VII the error is absent. Perhaps a better way of looking at the same problem is to calculate the actual increment to output during the period under study (line 15). As the four following lines indicate, the error in the estimate of the increment which has been made available to the society through economic growth can be substantial if we use Methods I, II, and IV; it must be zero if we use Methods V, VI, and VII. For the period 1945–52, the increment is overstated by some 30 billion real dollars *per year* by the use of Method I. For all the other periods the error is never smaller than 4 billion real dollars per year and can be as high as 46 billion real dollars per year. For Method IV the average annual error is quite small in some instances (smaller than a billion real dollars in three cases); quite substantial in some others (e. g., over 14 billion real dollars per year for the period 1950–58).

From this it seems to be obvious that Methods V and VII are quite superior in performance to all the other methods. The results of Method V in these seven cases are undistinguishable from those of Method VII, but we shall see in the last comparison that this is not always the case and that, especially in the case of really long periods, Method V will not prove to be a close substitute for Method VII. Method VI, which has been used as a stepping stone to Method VII, yields results which miss by substantial margins the standard represented by Method VII. The reason for this is undoubtedly the excessive dependence of this method upon the (arbitrary) selection of the base year. For this reason Method VI has been eliminated from the comparisons which follow.

In Table 9-3 (Tables 9-2 and 9-3 are presented on these pages, 146-147 and 148-149.) the most commonly used Method I is compared with the suggested Method VII. The comparison is based on data for gross domestic and gross national products of forty-four countries selected by Simon Kuznets.[18] It is apparent that the results yielded by Method I are in many cases rather crude approximations to the more correct results yielded by Method VII. In the case of some countries, the rate of growth rises as a result of the use of Method VII by 74, 49, 24, 22 percent; in other cases, it drops by 94 and 25 percent. As a consequence of the use of Method VII, there are 18 decreases and 24 increases in the rate of growth of the gross domestic product, the average change amounting to 12.7 percent. There are 17 decreases and 27 increases in the case of the gross national product, the average change amounting to 10.6 percent. Table 9-3 well illustrates the reasons why, in my opinion, Method VII is preferable to Method I. For a comparison of a great number of countries it is necessary to select an arbitrary time period common to all and thus give up any attempt to exercise the judgment which is so essential in the case

[18]Simon Kuznets, "Quantitative Aspects of the Economic Growth of Nations," *Economic Development and Cultural Change,* VIII, No. 4 (July, 1960), Part II.

Table 9-2

Comparison of Performance of Various Methods of Calculation of the Rate of Growth, United States Gross National Product,[a] Selected Years

		1945-52 (1)	1946-52 (2)	1953-59[b] (3)	1950-57[c] (4)	1950-58[d] (5)	1950-59 (6)	1929-59 (7)
(1) Rate of Growth	Method I (g_1)	1.8	3.8	3.0	3.6	2.9	3.3	2.9
(2)	Method II (g_2)	1.9	3.9	2.6	3.7	3.0	3.4	3.3
(3)	Method IV (g_4)	2.2	4.1	2.5	3.5	3.0	3.0	4.1
(4)	Method V (g_5)	2.7	4.2	2.5	3.4	3.0	2.9	3.9
(5)	Method VI (g_6)	0.5	3.0	2.2	4.1	3.9	3.7	2.3
(6)	Method VII (g_7)	2.7	4.2	2.4	3.4	2.9	2.9	3.9
(7) Total Output during Period[e] (billions of 1954 dollars)	Method I	2,676.1	2,217.7	2,827.4	2,889.6	3,218.5	3,697.4	8,939.0
(8)	Method II	2,685.5	2,224.5	2,793.4	2,899.9	3,231.6	3,714.5	9,728.9
(9)	Method IV	2,423.9	2,160.2	2,765.2	2,854.0	3,347.3	3,670.5	8,308.2
(10) *Actual* Method V, Method VI, Method VII		2,478.0	2,164.0	2,763.0	2,947.4	3,348.4	3,776.4	8,335.3
(11) Error in Output Estimate[f] (billions of 1954 dollars)	Method I	+198.1	+53.7	+64.4	-57.8	-129.9	-79.0	+603.7
(12)	Method II	+207.5	+60.5	+30.4	-47.5	-116.8	-61.9	+1,393.6
(13)	Method IV	-54.1	-3.8	+2.2	-93.4	+1.1	-105.9	-27.1
(14)	Method V, Method VI, Method VII	0	0	0	0	0	0	0
(15) Actual Increment to Output during Period[g] (billions of 1954 dollars)		-34.0	+186.5	+180.0	+402.6	+485.5	+595.4	+2,699.5

(continued)

Table 9-2 (continued)

(16) Calculated Increment to Output (18) during Period (billions of 1954 dollars) (19)	Method I	+164.1	+240.2	+244.4	+344.8	+355.6	+516.4	+3,303.2
	Method II	+173.5	+247.0	+210.4	+355.1	+368.7	+533.5	+4,093.1
	Method IV	- 88.1	+182.7	+182.2	+309.2	+484.4	+489.5	+2,672.4
	Method V / Method VI / Method VII	- 34.0	+186.5	+180.0	+402.6	+485.5	+595.4	+2,699.5
(20) Annual (21) Error in (22) Increment[h] (billions of (23) 1954 dollars)	Method I	+28.3	+8.9	+9.2	- 8.3	- 16.2	- 8.8	+ 20.1
	Method II	+29.6	+10.1	+4.3	- 6.8	- 14.6	- 6.9	+ 46.4
	Method IV	- 7.7	- 0.6	+0.3	- 13.3	- 0.1	- 11.8	- 0.9
	Method V / Method VI / Method VII	0.0	0.0	0.0	0.0	0.0	0.0	0.0

a. Gross national product in constant (1954) dollars reported in United States Department of Commerce, *United States Income and Output* (1958), pp. 118–119, and *Survey of Current Business* (July, 1960), p. 3.

b. Column (3): Period used by Gerhart Colm, "Evaluation of Soviet Economic Threat," in United States Congress, Joint Economic Committee, *Comparisons of the United States and Soviet Economies* (Washington, 1960), Part II, p. 534.

c. Column (4): Period used by Boris Bornstein, "A Comparison of Soviet and United States National Product," *ibid.*, p. 391.

d. Column (5): Period used by Central Intelligence Agency, *A Comparison of the United States and Soviet Union Economies*, prepared for United States Congress, Joint Economic Committee (Washington, 1960), p. 48.

e. Lines 7, 8, 9, and 10: Sum of base period outputs times

$$\left(\frac{g}{100}+1\right)^{n-1}$$

Actual base period outputs in the case of Methods I, II, and VI; calculated base period outputs in the case of Methods IV, V, and VII.

f. Lines 11, 12, 13, 14: Actual output during period (line 10) minus implied total output during period (lines 7, 8, 9, and 10).

g. Lines 15, 16, 17, 18, and 19: Actual output during period (line 10) minus actual output in base period times number of years covered.

h. Lines 20, 21, 22, and 23: Line 16 minus 15, line 17 minus 15, line 18 minus 15, line 19 minus 15 divided by the number of years following the base year.

Table 9-3

**Comparison of Performance of Methods I and VII, Selected Countries,
Post-World War II Years[c]**

Countries Grouped by Per Capita Product	Method I[a]		Method VII[b]		Correction of Rate of Growth as Percentage of Rate g_1	
	Gross Domestic Product (Rate g_1)	Gross National Product (Rate g_1)	Gross Domestic Product (Rate g_7)	Gross National Product (Rate g_7)	Gross Domestic Product	Gross National Product
	(1)	(2)	(3)	(4)	(5)	(6)
GROUP I						
1. Australia	1.51	1.52	2.63	2.64	+ 74.2	+ 73.7
2. Belgium	2.80	2.86	3.20	3.26	+ 14.2	+ 14.0
3. Canada	4.21	4.19	4.06	4.01	+ 3.6	− 4.3
4. New Zealand	2.83	2.80	3.28	3.27	+ 15.9	+ 16.8
5. Sweden	3.80	3.83	3.97	4.00	+ 4.5	+ 4.4
6. United Kingdom	2.45	2.35	2.80	2.77	+ 14.3	+ 17.9
7. United States	2.94	2.95	2.99	3.01	+ 1.7	+ 2.0
GROUP II						
8. Denmark	2.70	2.72	2.51	2.53	− 7.0	− 7.0
9. Finland	3.48	3.49	3.87	3.89	+ 11.2	+ 11.5
10. France	4.66	4.64	5.77	4.80	+ 23.8	+ 3.4
11. Germany, West	7.50	7.45	7.85	7.77	+ 4.7	+ 4.3
12. Netherlands	5.25	5.23	5.76	5.70	+ 9.7	+ 9.0
13. Norway	3.77	3.70	3.84	3.74	+ 1.9	+ 1.1
14. Venezuela	11.29	11.86	11.58	11.69	+ 2.6	− 0.1
GROUP III						
15. Argentina	1.45	1.47	2.16	2.15	+ 49.0	+ 46.3
16. Austria		5.88		6.45		+ 9.7
17. Chile	2.74	2.68	1.50	1.39	− 45.3	− 48.1
18. Ireland	1.50	1.34	1.30	1.15	− 1.3	− 14.2
19. Israel	8.52	8.46	9.91	9.93	+ 16.3	+ 17.4
20. Puerto Rico	4.02	2.87	4.13	2.55	+ 2.7	− 12.1
GROUP IV						
21. Brazil	4.67	4.67	4.74	4.71	+ 1.5	+ 0.9
22. Colombia	5.01	5.33	5.10	5.26	+ 1.8	− 1.3
23. Costa Rica	6.76	7.05	6.17	6.73	− 8.1	− 4.5
24. Greece	6.57	6.83	7.02	7.25	+ 6.8	+ 6.1
25. Italy	5.35	5.38	5.54	5.56	+ 3.6	+ 3.3
26. Malaya						
27. Mexico		5.94		6.86		+ 15.5
28. Turkey	4.60	4.56	3.95	3.92	− 14.1	− 14.0
29. Union of South Africa		5.44		5.85		+ 7.5
GROUP V						
30. Dominican Rep.		8.90		9.06		+ 1.8
31. Guatemala	5.80	5.53	5.73	5.55	− 1.2	+ 0.4
32. Iraq	11.57	10.20	12.78	11.13	+ 10.5	+ 9.1
33. Jamaica	11.37	11.22	12.16	11.93	+ 6.9	+ 6.3
34. Japan	8.25	8.18	8.07	8.02	− 2.6	+ 6.0
35. Portugal	4.14	4.15	4.03	4.40	− 2.6	+ 6.0

(continued)

Table 9-3 (continued)

	(1)	(2)	(3)	(4)	(5)	(6)
GROUP VI						
36. Bolivia	1.21		0.07		– 94.2	
37. Ceylon	3.32	3.39	2.97	2.91	– 10.5	– 14.2
38. China (Taiwan)	9.44	9.42	8.94	8.93	– 5.3	– 5.2
39. Ecuador	5.50	5.31	5.06	4.98	– 8.0	– 6.2
40. Egypt	5.92		7.25		+ 22.5	
41. Ghana	2.13	2.30	2.22	2.39	+ 4.2	+ 3.9
42. Honduras	3.02	4.25	2.63	3.71	– 13.0	– 12.7
43. Paraguay	12.85		12.84	12.98	– 0.0	
44. Peru		4.62		4.69		+ 1.5
45. Philippines	6.81	6.70	6.58	5.79	– 3.4	– 13.6
46. Rhodesia and Nyasaland						
GROUP VII						
47. Belgian Congo	4.27	3.77	4.46	3.94	+ 4.4	+ 4.5
48. Burma	6.01	6.04	5.77	5.77	– 4.0	– 4.5
49. India						
50. Kenya						
51. Korea, South						
52. Morocco	3.08	3.50	3.05	3.36	– 0.1	– 4.0
53. Nigeria						
54. Pakistan						
55. Uganda						

a. Columns (1) and (2) are reproduced from Simon Kuznets, "Quantitative Aspects of the Economic Growth of Nations," *Economic Development and Cultural Change*, VII, No. 4 (July, 1960). Part II, Appendix Table 3, pp. 84–87.

b. Columns (3) and (4) are based on a recomputation of original data used by Kuznets. Description of sources is given in Kuznets, *op. cit.*, p. 86.

c. Entries are based on constant market price values from 1951 to 1957, unless otherwise indicated.

of Method I. Any attempt to select time periods comparable from the standpoint of the business cycle is bound to bog down in complete arbitrariness and subjectivity of any such decision. The advantages of Method VII, which depends no more on the two terminal years than it depends on all the other years become thus readily apparent.

Finally, in Table 9-4 (pg. 150), I compare Methods I, V, and VII by the use of data covering a very long period of time. On an *a priori* basis we would expect that Method I will yield results highly comparable or identical with the results yielded by Method VII because the period is long enough to eliminate the effects of the cyclical fluctuations which are such an enemy of Method I. Surprisingly enough this expectation fails to be realized. In some cases the rates of growth yielded by Methods I and VII are in reasonable proximity to each other, even though the rate of growth of 3.063 percent and the rate of 2.752 percent (for Consumer Perishables) will yield quite a different stream of output over a period as long as the one under analysis. In other cases the error introduced by Method I is very substantial: Producer Durables are said to grow by 4.249 percent in the case of Method I while they actually grow at the rate of 3.449 percent as indicated by Method VII.

Table 9-4

**Comparison of Performance of Methods I, V, and VII, Value
of Commodity Output, 1879–1939 (Producers' 1913 Prices)**

Commodity Group	Rate of Growth		
	Method I (1)[a]	Method V (2)[b]	Method VII (3)[a]
Consumer Perishable	3.063	2.9	2.752
Consumer Semi-Durable	2.773	2.9	2.770
Consumer Durable	4.503	4.7	4.362
Producer Durable	4.249	3.6	3.449
All Finished Commodities	3.346	3.2	3.079

a. Columns (1) and (3): Data used for calculation found in William Howard Shaw, *Value of Commodity Output Since 1869* (New York, 1947), pp. 70–77.
   b. Column (2): *Ibid.*, Table 2, p. 9.

In the case of this long run comparison a discrepancy appears for the first time between the results yielded by Methods V and VII. Method V persistently overestimates the rate of growth. This is precisely what we would expect from a method in which the more recent years, containing higher absolute increases in output, receive the lion's share of the total weights.

Conclusion

The rate of growth has become in recent years one of the most important magnitudes for economists, statesmen, and the general public. What is the basic purpose of calculations of this rate? In all instances I have encountered the purpose is to measure the average annual increment to output in terms which make this increment comparable for various countries and various time periods. The most convenient method of accomplishing this goal of comparability is to express the average annual increment as a percentage of the total output produced in the preceding year. Therefore a growth rate of, say, two percent means that during a certain period, on the average, two units of output have been added each year to every hundred units of output produced in the preceding year. To make sure that this is indeed the only purpose and the only use of the growth rate, let me recount some of the uses of this rate encountered in preceding discussions. In the study by Simon Kuznets cited earlier the main purpose of calculating the rate of growth is to relate it to the average percentage of output devoted to investment goods: Kuznets calculates the number of units of investment goods which have been necessary to produce one additional unit of output per year. In the case of the Colm-Bornstein estimates, the purpose surely has been to compare the increment to actual outputs of the United States and Russia. In the case of W. W. Rostow the growth rate is explicitly used to calculate the increment to output which we need in order to satisfy certain urgent public needs.[19]

Thus, the term "rate of growth" is but a name given to the average ratio of the annual increments of output to the outputs produced in the preceding years, the average being calculated for a certain period of time. Therefore the minimum requirement which we must impose on any method of calculating the rate of growth must be that it faithfully measure this ratio of *actual* increments to *actual* outputs. If it fails to do so, what does it measure and what does it mean? I submit that in such a case it does not measure anything and means nothing. We have seen that the geometric average of the product of the output ratios (Method I), the arithmetic average of the percentage changes from year to year (Method II), and the least squares method of fitting data to an exponential curve (Method IV) all fail to meet this standard: they often grossly overestimate or grossly underestimate the actual increments to output (Cf. Table 9-2).[20]

While the satisfaction of the requirement that the total actual output during the period covered be equal to the total calculated output is essential if the calculated rate of growth is to be meaningful, it is only the basic requirement.

---

[19]Cf. Kuznets, *op. cit.,* Table 10. He speaks about "the incremental capital-output ratio" and uses the formula

$$\frac{\text{Gross Domestic Capital Formation}}{\text{Gross Domestic (National) Product}}$$

$$\frac{\text{Rise per year, Gross Domestic (National) Product}}{\text{Gross Domestic (National) Product}}$$

[20]The objection could be made that if these three methods correctly measure the average percentage change in output it does not matter if they fail to yield the correct absolute increment: if the slope of the regression line is correct, it makes no difference that we do not know its position. Such an objection cannot be upheld. Suppose that the actual GNP amounts to 500 billion dollars, the (presumably) correct rate amounts to 4 percent, and the incorrect base for this rate is 600 billion dollars. The actual increment then will be 24 billion dollars (4 percent of 600 billions); this is not four but almost five percent of the actual output: *both* the slope and the position of the regression line are necessary.

More concretely: let us take the first country in Table 9-3, Australia. Output in 1951 amounted to 4,707 million (real) pounds; total output during the period 1951–57 amounted to 33,939 million pounds. Had there been a zero rate of growth during the period, output would have amounted to 32,949 million pounds (seven times 4,707 million pounds). Thus, the increment produced during this period amounted to 990 million pounds.

The rate of growth calculated by Method I is 1.51 percent (Cf. Table 9-3). The calculated total output in the period 1951–57 then must be 34,476 million pounds (sum of 4,707 million pounds compounded at 1.51 percent per year). Thus, the total increment yielded by Method I amounts to 1,527 million pounds instead of the actual increment of 990 millions.

Investments represent 27.9 percent of the output during this period (Kuznets, *op. cit.,* p. 77): 8,032 million pounds in the period 1951–56. The ratio of investment goods in 1951–56 to the increment produced in 1952–57 has therefore the value of 8.1; the ratio based on the formula reproduced in footnote 18 and on the rate of growth yielded by Method I has the value of 18.5 (27.9/1.51). It is more than twice as high!

Any rate of growth associated with a suitable base year output will satisfy it: a zero rate of growth with a base year output equal to the average output produced during the period; a negative growth rate associated with a base year output suitably higher than the mean one; a positive growth rate associated with a base year output suitably lower than the mean output. A useful method of calculation of the rate of growth, while satisfying the basic requirement discussed above, should yield a growth rate which best reflects the stream of output during the time period covered by the calculation. The various methods differ widely in their reliability, objectivity, and ease of application. The most widely used method, employing observations from only the initial and terminal periods (Method I) is extremely sensitive to an inevitably arbitrary selection of time periods. A conscientious analyst is compelled to attempt to select those years which he considers least affected by special circumstances, and must base his choice on his detailed knowledge of the economy in question. While, as Arthur F. Burns points out, "judgment must always play a dominating role in the choice of statistical techniques, and the only question that really matters is whether the judgment is 'good' or 'bad,' "[21] judgment should affect the choice of the statistical *method*, not the choice of the *results* yielded by any particular method. The very purpose of a useful statistical method is to limit the scope of judgment as to the kind of results obtained and to extract results of more than subjective validity. The political importance of the calculation of the rate of growth lends further importance to the reliability and objectivity of the method. Method I, because of the extreme sensitivity to the precise time period selected for calculation suffers substantially on this score. Method II, based on the arithmetical average of the percentage changes during the period covered, does not yield results perceptibly superior to those yielded by Method I.

Method VII has the advantage that it takes the entire stream of output during the period covered into account. Method I completely fails to do so and Method II, based on the arithmetic average of percentage changes from year to year, divides the period into a series of unrelated segments of two years duration. Method IV, based on the least squares technique, often yields rates of growth not very different from those yielded by Method VII; however, its use might lead to controversy because it yields erroneous estimates of the total output and of the increments to the original output. The advantages of Method VII over the Glover method (Method V) are marginal if the data cover short periods of time. In case of long periods, the peculiar set of weights employed by the Glover method does affect the results obtained. For all these reasons, Method VII appears to be the most desirable technique of calculating the rate of economic growth.

---

[21]Arthur F. Burns, *op. cit.*, p. 41.

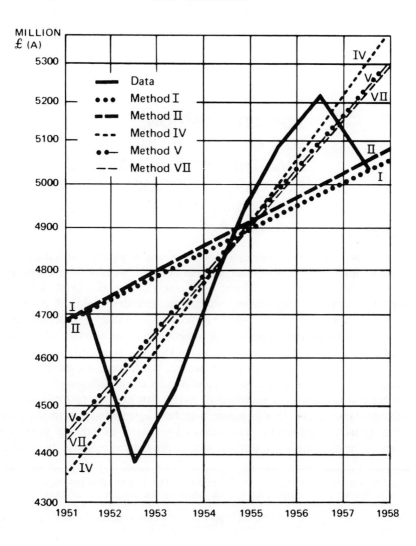

Figure 9-1

**Illustration of the Performance of the
Various Methods: Gross Domestic Product of
Australia in Constant Prices, 1951–57.**

*Questions for discussion and analysis pertaining to this article may be found
at the end of Article 16.*

Ephraim Kleiman †

10. AGE COMPOSITION, SIZE OF HOUSEHOLDS, AND THE INTERPRETATION OF PER CAPITA INCOME*

Introduction

The conceptual problems associated with the use of national income figures for international or intertemporal comparisons of welfare levels are well known. Furthermore, as pointed out by Kuznets,[1] there also exists a systematic downward bias in the income estimates of underdeveloped countries, which results in an exaggeration of the differences in welfare levels implied by international comparisons of per capita income. Even so, for lack of any better measure, per capita income still remains the best standard for summary comparisons of standard of living. However, the income estimates used in such comparisons are often adjusted to eliminate those differences which do not reflect real variations in standard of living, but are due to differences in institutional structures.[2] In this paper, a rather neglected aspect of the interpretation of such comparisons will be raised — that of differences in the age structure of the population[3] and in the size of the consumption units in which

†Ephraim Kleiman, Professor of Economics, The Hebrew University of Jerusalem. The author wishes to thank Dr. N. Liviatan of the Eliezer Kaplan School — The Hebrew University, for explaining to him some of the intricacies of family budget analysis. Addendum, 1972: A reference to an early and ingenious work in this field, Merrill K. Bennett, "International Disparities in Consumption Levels," *American Economic Review*, Vol. 41 (September, 1951), pp. 632-649, was lost in one of the early drafts.

*From *Economic Development and Cultural Change*, Vol. 15, No. 1 (October, 1966), pp. 37-58. Reprinted by permission of the University of Chicago Press and the author.

[1]S. Kuznets, "National Income and Industrial Structure," in *Economic Change* (New York: Norton, 1953), esp. pp. 153-158.

[2]By including estimates of untraded goods and services. See, for example, Phyllis Deane, "Measuring National Income in Colonial Territories," *Studies In Income and Wealth*, VIII (Princeton: National Bureau of Economic Research, 1946), 145-174.

[3]For an attempt to incorporate changes in the age structure in a formal model of economic growth, see Leif Johansen, "Death Rates, Age Distribution and Average Income in Stationary Population," *Population Studies*, XI (1957-58), pp. 64-77. The effects of changes in the age structure on income estimates was also discussed briefly by S. Kuznets in *National Income and Its Composition, 1919-1938* (New York: National Bureau of Economic Research, 1941), pp. 150-155. A counterpart procedure, of weighting different groups in the labor force by their earning, can be found (contd.)

it is organized. In particular, it will be shown that the association between these demographic attributes and the level of per capita income results in the exaggeration of international differentials in welfare levels and in a distortion of the rise of these levels over time.

The Effect of Changes in the Age Composition

Briefly speaking, the argument regarding the effects of the age structure can be illustrated by the following example. Consider two individuals of widely differing physical dimensions, so that providing a suit for one of them requires much more cloth than providing a suit for the other. With the standard of living measured in terms of suits, the same income per capita would provide a lower standard of living for the tall, fat man than for the short, thin one. Of course, with respect to all items consumed, such differences may well cancel each other out; nor need there be any systematic association between them and income. The same cannot, however, be said of the consumption differentials associated with age. To satisfy the same need in food, clothing, etc., a child's requirements are, on the whole, smaller than those of an adult.[4] Consequently, the same *per capita* income represents a higher standard of living for a population consisting largely of children than for one consisting mainly of adults.

Generally speaking, the rise of per capita income over time was accompanied by a decrease in the share of the younger age groups in the population. Similarly, countries characterized by low per capita income also tend toward a higher concentration of population in the younger age brackets than those characterized by higher per capita incomes.[5] This introduces an upward bias in the interpretation of differentials in per capita income as representing those in the standard of living. To eliminate it, changes in the standard of living should be measured not by those in income per capita but, rather, per some standard consumer unit, which would take into account the relevant changes in the age structure of the population.

The connection between the age composition of consumers and standards of living has been treated extensively in family budget studies. Scales for the measurement of young consumers in adult equivalents made their first appearance in Engel's "quets." Some such scales were based on information regarding nutritional requirements at different ages; others were derived by

---

in L. D. Long, *The Labor Force Under Changing Income and Employment* (Princeton: National Bureau of Economic Research, 1958), Appendix C.

[4]This also implies, of course, that "dependency" ratios overestimate the economic burden of supporting a dependent population. These ratios are derived by comparing the sizes of the population below and above working age to that of working age. They implicitly assume that the consumption requirements of children are the same as those of adults and of aged people. I propose to deal with this question explicitly elsewhere.

[5]In part, but, of course, only in part, this phenomenon is self-explanatory. With the same GNP per person engaged, per capita income will be lower the higher the ratio of the dependent population to that engaged in production.

comparing the consumption patterns of families of different age composition. The methodological problems involved in the derivation of such scales are treated by Wold and by Prais and Houthaker.[6] Their economic interpretation is discussed by Woodbury,[7] who also presents the equivalence scales used in, or derived from, a number of different consumption studies. Some additional scales are mentioned by Woytinski.[8] These scales seem to vary considerably one from the other, a phenomenon the possible meaning of which will be discussed later.

For the purpose of the present investigation, two extreme scales will be used, to provide minimum and maximum limits for the probable effect of the age structure on the standard of living. The two scales are shown in Table 10-1. Scale A, which relates to all items of expenditure, is derived from German and Swedish studies of the years 1907–08. It is identical with Wold's "German-Austrian" scale, which he found also was verified by later studies.[9] Scale B is the one established by Prais and Houthaker with respect to expenditure on food, on the basis of two British surveys conducted in 1937–39.[10]

Table 10-1
Equivalent Consumption Scales by Age Groups

Age	Scale A	Scale B
under 1	0.11 ⎱ 0.13	0.37 ⎱ 0.52
1–4	0.14 ⎰	0.55 ⎰
5–9	0.29	0.61
10–14	0.49	0.76
15–19	0.84	0.86
adult	1.00	1.00

It should be mentioned here that the derivation of equivalence scales for non-food items from family budget analysis is considerably complicated by the existence of economies of scale in consumption.[11] Consequently, the equivalence scales for these expenditures are probably less meaningful than those relating to food only. As the Prais and Houthaker food scale ascribes rather high weights to children, we may regard it as providing the upper limit of the range in which the "true" scale for all expenditures lies. In both the scales used here, the unit of measurement was originally the consumption of

[6]H. Wold, *Demand Analysis* (New York: Wiley, 1952); and S. Y. Prais and H. S. Houthaker, *The Analysis of Family Budgets* (Cambridge: Cambridge University Press, 1955).

[7]R. M. Woodbury, "Economic Consumption Scales and Their Uses," *Journal of the American Statistical Association,* XXXIX (1944), pp. 455–468.

[8]W. S. Woytinsky and E. S. Woytinsky, *World Population and Production* (New York: Twentieth Century Fund, 1953).

[9]Wold, *op. cit.*, p. 223; and Prais and Houthaker, *op. cit.*, Table III, p. 462.

[10]*Op. cit.*, p. 141.

[11]These economies of scale will be discussed in the following section.

an "adult" male.[12] For some age groups separate equivalents were for males and females. To simplify matters, it has been assumed here that the population in all age groups is composed equally of both sexes. Following Woytinsky, the unit of measurement was defined as a simple average of the consumption of an adult male and an adult female.[13] Finally, the original scales were adjusted to comply with the age grouping of the available population data.[14]

As can be seen from Table 10-1, the weights attributed to children under Scale A are much lower than those attributed to them under Scale B, the difference between the two decreasing with age. It should be noted that neither scale allows for a decline in consumption equivalents after adulthood has been reached. In fact, some scales ascribe lower weights to persons above a certain age.[15] However, any decrease in the consumption of old people is probably due to the decline, with age, not of consumption requirements, but of income.[16]

To illustrate the extent of the bias introduced by disregarding changes in the age composition of population, two sets of estimates were prepared of the equivalent adult-consumer population of the U. S., 1850 to 1960. These were obtained by applying the scales of Table 10-1 to the age distribution of population, shown in the Appendix. The result, for each scale, was expressed as a ratio of the equivalent adult population to total actual population. As can be seen from Figure 10-1 (pg. 158), these ratios increased throughout most of the period examined here, reaching their highest point in 1940.[17] Thus, the increase in *per capita* income over-estimated the increase in income *per consumer* between 1850 and 1940. The opposite is true of the two decades following 1940, in which changes in the age composition, by themselves, would have caused the living standards to rise more rapidly than suggested by the rise in per capita income.

The use of two extreme equivalence scales makes it possible to determine the limits of the effect of a changing age structure to the standard of living. The percentage changes per decade in the consumers-to-population ratio are presented in columns (1.) and (4.) of Table 10-2 (pg. 159). They show the growth of the equivalent population relative to the total one. Between 1850

---

[12]Adulthood starting at 19, in the former case, and at 18, in the latter.

[13]Woytinsky and Woytinsky, *op. cit.*, p. 273.

[14]Thus, for example, the scale for "under 4" is an average of the scale for "under 1" with the weight of 1 and that for the "1–4" group with the weight of 4. This neglects inequalities in the size of some sub-groups.

[15]Thus, the "ammain" scale attributes to males over 60 only 90 percent of the weight given to those in the 19–60 group. See E. G. Tough and E. L. Kirkpatrick. "Scales for Measuring the Standard of Living," *Journal of the American Statistical Association*, XXVII (1933), pp. 55–63. In the Sydenstricker and King scale, the consumption equivalent reaches its peak between the ages of 23 and 26, then starts to decline monotonically. See Woodbury, *op. cit.*, p. 462.

[16]Or to the relegation of elderly people to positions of secondary importance, insofar as the allocation of consumption within the household is concerned.

[17]With the exception of the 1870–80 decade.

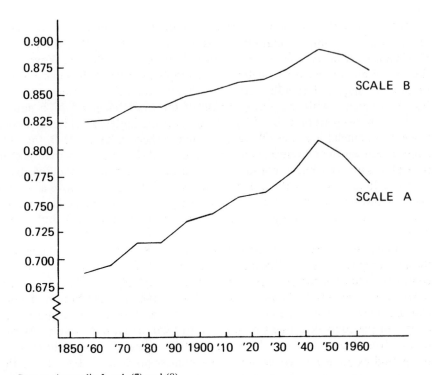

Source: Appendix I, col. (7) and (8).

Figure 10-1

Ratio of Equivalent Adult Consumer Units to Total Population, U. S. 1850–1960

and 1940, this amounted to between 8 and 17.4 percent. In other words, this is the extent to which the rise in per capita income in this period overestimated that in the standard of living.[18]

The Effects of Changes in Size of Households

One of the factors behind the decrease in the share of the younger age groups in the population was the decline in the size of families. This resulted in a decrease in the size of households, which was further enhanced by urbanization and by the increased mobility of labor associated with the rise in incomes. Insofar as there exists economies of scale in consumption with respect to the size of household, the smaller the household, the higher the per capita income

---

[18]An intermediate estimate is obtained by using the rule-of-thumb scale suggested in Woytinsky, *op. cit.*, which attributes to all population under 20 *half* the weight of an adult. This method, however, is not sensitive to changes in the age structure of the lower age groups. Thus, it fails to register the change in the trend after 1940.

Table 10-2

Percentage Changes per Decade in the Age-Composition and the Size-of-Household Effects

Years	Adult Equivalence, Scale A			Adult Equivalence, Scale B			Combined Age and Size Effect			
	Age composition effect	Size of household effect, size factor		Age composition effect	Size of household effect, size factor		Scale A Size factor		Scale B Size factor	
		0.65	0.85		0.65	0.85	0.65	0.85	0.65	0.85
	(1)	(2)	(3)	(4)	(5)	(6)	(7)	(8)	(9)	(10)
1850–60	0.9	1.8	0.6	0.5	2.2	1.4	2.7	1.5	2.7	1.9
1860–70	3.2	–	0.2	1.4	0.3	0.5	3.2	3.4	1.7	0.9
1870–80	-0.3	0.3	0.1	-0.1	0.5	0.2	–	-0.2	0.4	0.1
1880–90	3.1	-0.5	-0.1	1.3	0.3	0.1	2.6	3.0	1.6	1.4
1890–1900	0.8	1.1	0.4	0.5	1.2	0.5	1.9	1.2	1.7	1.0
1900–10	2.2	0.8	0.5	1.0	0.8	0.6	3.0	2.7	1.8	1.6
1910–20	0.7	1.7	0.7	0.3	1.3	0.7	2.4	1.4	1.6	1.0
1920–30	2.4	0.8	0.5	1.0	1.8	0.6	3.2	2.9	2.8	1.6
1930–40	3.5	1.7	0.6	1.8	2.5	1.1	5.3	4.1	4.3	2.9
1940–50	-1.6	3.1	1.3	-0.8	3.1	1.1	1.4	-0.3	2.3	0.3
1950–60	-3.4	3.9	1.5	-1.7	2.7	1.3	0.4	-2.0	1.0	-0.4
1850–1940	17.4	7.8	3.5	8.1	11.4	4.9	26.6	21.5	20.4	13.4
1940–60	-4.8	7.1	2.8	-2.5	5.9	2.4	1.9	-2.3	3.3	-0.1
1850–60	11.6	15.5	6.5	5.4	17.9	7.4	28.9	18.9	24.3	13.2

Col. (1), Col. (4): changes in the ratio of adult equivalents to total population, from Appendix 1.
Col. (2), (3), (5), (6): changes in the ratio of single-consumer equivalent households to the size of households, measured in terms of adult equivalents. Computed, respectively, from columns (8), (10), (9), and (11) of Appendix II.
Col. (7) to (10): Index age composition effect (i.e., rate of change plus 100) *multiplied* by the corresponding index of size-of-households effect, minus 100.

required to provide a given standard of living. Consequently, a decline in the size of households means that part of the rise in incomes is swallowed by the negative effect of the decrease in scale and cannot be used to raise the standard of living. If changes in income are to represent correctly those in living standards, this effect should be taken into consideration.

The economies of scale in consumption received in the past much less attention than the equivalence scales described above. Various methods of estimation, as well as of interpretation, are discussed in the already mentioned study by Prais and Houthaker. Briefly speaking, such economies of scale mean that the same income per person "goes farther" in larger households. The difficulties in estimating them correctly lie in the fact that any savings resulting from them are used to raise the standard of living — i.e., to increase consumption. Furthermore, there exists usually a strong negative association between size of household and income per person. Therefore, as measured in budget studies, the elasticity of family expenditures with respect to size of household combines both scale effects and income elasticities. If economies of scale exist, a household consisting of any given number of consumer units can be regarded, for consumption comparison purposes, as equivalent to some smaller number of single-consumer households. The expenditure of such an equivalent household can be expected to be a function only of its income.[19] By comparing such a formulation with that of the estimation equation actually used, the pure scale effect can be separated from that of income.[20]

---

[19]Abstracting for the time being from the association between the size of households and their age composition, let S be the number of consumer units in a household, and S^{θ} the equivalent number of single consumer households, where $0 < \theta < 1$. The pure scale effect is equal to $(1 - \theta)$. Assuming the consumption function to be of a logarithmic form, and the scale effect to be the same for all items of expenditure,

$$\frac{X}{S^{\theta}} = \left[\frac{Y}{S^{\theta}} \right]^{\alpha}$$

where α is the income elasticity. This equation can be rewritten as either

$$X = Y^{\alpha} S^{\theta(1-\alpha)}$$

or as

$$\frac{X}{S} = \left(\frac{Y}{S} \right)^{\alpha} S^{(1-\theta)(\alpha-1)}$$

[20]The mode of separating the two effects depends on the estimation equation actually used. If this is of the form

$$X = Y^{\alpha} S^{\beta}$$

then, by comparing with the first reformulation of footnote 19, we have

(contd.)

Alternatively, it has been argued that the savings resulting from the economies of scale are used to raise the quality of the goods consumed. Then, the

$$\beta = \theta(1 - \alpha)$$

and

$$\theta = \frac{\beta}{1 - \alpha}$$

By substituting and rearranging, we have

$$\theta_0 = \frac{\sum_i \beta_i \frac{X_i}{Y}}{1 - \sum_i \alpha_i \frac{X_i}{Y}}$$

A similar reformulation can be effected for the per capita type of estimation equations.

If the estimation equation is in per capita terms, i.e.,

$$\frac{X}{S} = \left(\frac{Y}{S}\right)^\alpha S^\lambda$$

the second reformulation should be used, yielding

$$\lambda = (1 - \theta)(\alpha - 1)$$

and

$$\theta = 1 - \frac{\lambda}{\alpha - 1}$$

In fact, the economies of scale may be expected to vary from one item of expenditure to another. The expenditure on any given commodity, i, would then be expressed as

$$\frac{X}{S^{\theta_i}} = \left[\frac{Y}{S^{\theta_0}}\right]^{\alpha_i}$$

where θ_i is the scale factor with respect to consumption of the ith commodity, and θ_0— the scale factor with respect to all expenditures — is approximated by an average of the specific scale factors weighted by the corresponding items' share in total expenditure,

$$\theta_0 = \sum_i \theta_i \frac{X_i}{Y}$$

The above equation can be rewritten as

$$X_i = Y^{\alpha_i} S^{\theta_i - \theta_0 \alpha_i}$$

so that

$$\theta_i = \beta_i - \theta_0 \alpha_i$$

scale effect can be derived from estimates of the elasticity of the dearness of purchases with respect to household size.[21]

Using the latter method, Prais and Houthaker obtained, with respect to expenditure on food, an estimate of an exponential factor of 0.87 for the conversion of households into single-consumer equivalents.[22] This suggests that, as sizes of households vary, the economies of scale amount to 13 percent of the relative change in household size. Strikingly similar results were obtained on the basis of Liviatan's study of consumption patterns in Israel in 1956–57.[23] This yielded estimates of the scale effect in food expenditure of between 14 and 17 percent.[24] However, estimating the scale effect "quality" data "tends to

---

[21]Distinguishing between differently priced varieties of a given commodity, the average price per unit purchased is found to be a function of income and family size. The estimation equations usually used are either

$$P = Y^{\alpha} S^{\beta}$$

or

$$P = \left(\frac{Y}{S}\right)^{\alpha} S^{\lambda}$$

This can be expressed as a function of income per single-consumer equivalent,

$$P = \left(\frac{Y}{S^{\theta}}\right)^{\alpha}$$

which can be rewritten as

$$P = Y^{\alpha} S^{-\theta\alpha}$$

or as

$$P = \left(\frac{Y}{S}\right)^{\alpha} S^{(1-\theta)^{\alpha}}$$

Comparing these formulations with those of the estimation equations actually used, we have in the first case

$$\theta = -\frac{\alpha}{\beta}$$

and in the second

$$\theta = 1 - \frac{\lambda}{\alpha}.$$

[22]*Op. cit.*, 149–150.

[23]N. Liviatan, *Consumption Patterns in Israel* (Jerusalem: Falk Project for Economic Research in Israel, 1964).

[24]Liviatan estimated the elasticity of "quality" with respect to family income and to size of household (*ibid.*, pp. 22–25). Consequently, the scale effect for each of the commodities investigated by him was obtained by dividing the income elasticity by that of size. The resultant scale effects were then weighted by the average shares of the corresponding commodities in consumption. This yielded an over-all scale conversion coefficient of 0.83. The alternative estimate of 0.86 was obtained by dividing by each other similarly weighted average income and size elasticities.

underestimate the *true* increase in the standard of living."[25] Furthermore, it can be argued that the economies of scale in food consumption are probably smaller than in other items of expenditure.[26] Thus, a scale effect of about 15 percent should be regarded as providing the lower limit of the effect of changes in the size of household on standard of living.

Considerably higher estimates of the scale effect are obtained using the alternative method, by which the conversion factor of households into single-consumer equivalents is derived from the elasticities of expenditure with respect to income and to family size.[27] Thus, for example, Liviatan's estimates of these elasticities for all food items together are 0.516 and 0.255, respectively.[28] This yields an exponential conversion factor of 0.6, which indicates that, as the size of household varies economies of scale in the consumption of food amount to as much as 40 percent of the relative change in household size. For other items of expenditure, similarly derived estimates of the economies of scale vary between 60 percent in durables and 50 percent in expenditures on health, education, etc., to 33 percent on such sundries as tobacco, personal services, entertainment, etc.[29]

While the "quality" estimates understate the extent of economies of scale in consumption, the latter estimates probably overstate them. For the purposes of the present investigation, two extreme values of the scale effect were chosen to examine the effects of changes in the size of households on the standard of living. These correspond to exponential conversion factors of household sizes into single-consumer equivalents of 0.65 and 0.85. Applying the lower estimate of the scale effect to the average household size figures for the U. S., we find the 5.55 persons' household of 1850 to have been equivalent to 4.29 single-consumer households, while the equivalent of the 3.30 persons' household of 1960 is 2.76.[30] In other words, in terms of single-consumer equivalents the

---

[25]See Prais and Houthaker, *op. cit.*, p. 150.

[26]Using a somewhat more sophisticated method, Prais and Houthaker estimated the specific economies of scale to be about 20 percent in most food items, 50 percent in fuel, and 67 percent in expenditure on rent. On the other hand, there seemed to be no such economies in clothing and diseconomies in durables. The latter, however, seem to be spurious. See *ibid.*, pp. 150–151.

[27]See note 19 above.

[28]Liviatan, *op. cit.*, Table 1.

[29]No estimates of the scale effect could be derived for household maintenance and for clothing and footwear, as their elasticities with respect to size of household did not differ significantly from zero, nor their income elasticities from 1.

Further estimates of the scale effects were derived from the rough averages of the income and size elasticities obtained in the large number of family expenditure surveys summarized by H. S. Houthaker, "An International Comparison of Household Expenditure Patterns, Commemorating the Centenary of Engel's Law," *Econometrica*, XXV (1957), 532–551. As a general rule of thumb, Houthaker suggests the values of 0.3 and–0.4 for the size elasticities of expenditure on food and on sundries, respectively-and zero for all other items. The corresponding income elasticities are 0.6 and 1.6 — resulting in single-consumer conversion factors of 0.75 and 0.67, respectively.

[30]That is, with economies of scale of 15 percent, the income required to provide a certain standard of living for 5.55 persons living in one household.

population was only 76 percent of the actual one in 1850, as against 84 percent one hundred ten years later. Therefore, to provide the same standard of living per person would have required 10 percent more income in the later year than in the earlier one.[31] Under the higher estimate of the scale effect, the corresponding increase in income requirements amounts to 20 percent.

However, it should be remembered that the scale effect estimates do not take into consideration the tendency of the age composition of households to vary with their size. In general, large households include more children, in proportion to adults, than do small ones. Consequently, estimates of the scale effect contain in them also elements of the previously discussed effects of the age composition. And the association between variations in the age composition and those in size need not be the same over time, as in the cross-section studies from which the present estimates of the scale effect were derived. To eliminate the effects of the age composition, the original household-size figures were transformed into the equivalent members of adults, and the scale effect was then computed for changes in the number of the equivalent adults per household. As has been seen above, the ratio of equivalent adults to total population has been rising for most of the period considered here. Therefore, measured in terms of a constant age composition, the decline in the size of households was not as large as when measured simply in number of persons, regardless of age. Consequently, the diseconomies ensuing from the reduction in the scale of consumption units were also smaller.

These computations, which are shown in Appendix II, were carried out twice for each of the extreme scale-effect values examined here, using alternatively the two equivalency scales of Table 10-1. Thus, four estimates were obtained of changes in the ratio between the equivalent number of single-consumer households and the number of actual households, net of changes in their age composition. The development of this ratio over time is shown in Figure 10-2. It is interesting to note that for a period of about three decades, between 1960 and 1890, it hardly changed. This was due to changes in the age composition almost out-weighing those in size, so that the size of households remained unchanged when measured in terms of equivalent adults, rather than in those of the actual number of persons.[32] In the following decades, however, the decline

---

[31]Let S_0 and S_1 be the actual household sizes in two periods. The increase in the ratio of equivalent to actual population is equal to

$$\frac{S_1^{\theta}}{S_1} \bigg/ \frac{S_0^{\theta}}{S_0} = \left(\frac{S_1}{S_0}\right)^{\theta} \bigg/ \frac{S_1}{S_0} = \left(\frac{S_1}{S_0}\right)^{\theta-1}$$

[32]Let W stand for the ratio of equivalent adults to total population, and S be the number of *persons* per household. Then, the relative change in size of households of standard age composition is $W_1 S_1 / W_0 S_0$. For this to remain unity, then

$$\frac{S_1}{S_0} = \frac{W_0}{W_1}$$

See also col. 2 and 3 of Appendix II.

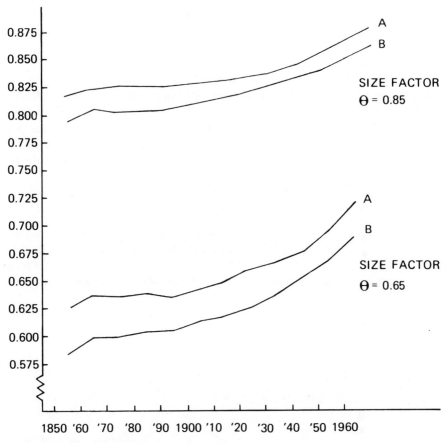

Source: Appendix II, col. 8–11.

Figure 10-2

**Ratio of Single-Consumer-Equivalent Households to the Age-
Standardized Size of Household, U. S., 1850–1960**

in the number of persons per household could not be offset by the increase in
the ratio of equivalent adults to population. The age-adjusted size of households declined, and the ratio of single-consumer households to their actual
number rose. For the whole period 1850 to 1960, assuming a scale effect of
0.35, the decline in the ratio amounted to between 16 and 18 percent. In other
words, because of the diseconomies resulting from the decline in the size of
households (net of changes in their age composition), the same standard of
living would require 16 to 18 percent more income per capita in 1960 than in
1850. With a scale effect of only 0.15, the corresponding diseconomies vary
between 6 and 8 percent. These changes in the economies of scale are summarized in Table 10-2, in the form of percentage changes per decade, together

with the corresponding changes resulting from developments in the age structure. As can be seen both from the table, and by comparing Figures 10-1 and
10-2, during the greater part of period examined here, both effects operated in
the same direction.

In the last two decades, however, the previously operating trend in the age
composition reversed itself. It is interesting to note that — in contrast to the
development observed between 1860 and 1890 — this raised the effects of the
decline in the size of households; not only did the number of persons per
household decrease, but the proportion of children among them rose, resulting
in an even sharper decline in the size of households in terms of adult equivalents.

The Over-All Changes in the Ratio of Consumption Units To Population

The age and size effects were combined to obtain estimates of the over-all
changes in the ratio of standard consumption units to population.[33] The percentage change per decade in this ratio is shown in Table 10-2. As can be seen
from Figure 10-3, the two extreme estimates (not shown in the figure) are much

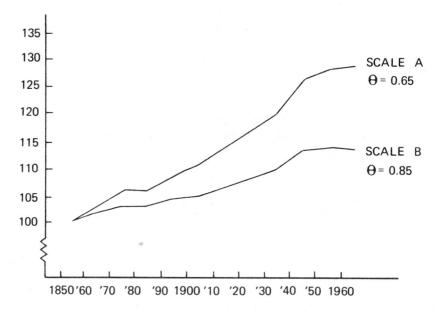

Source: Appendix III, col. 1 and 4.

Figure 10-3

**Growth of Consumer Population Relative to Total Population, U. S.,
1850–1960 (1850 = 100)**

[33]The two effects are multiplicative, not additive.

more narrow: 19 to 24 percent. This means that in estimating changes in the standard of living from income data, the increase in actual population in this period has to be raised by between one-fifth and one-fourth to correct it for changes in age composition and in size of households. Taking into consideration the length of the time period examined here, the resultant adjustment of per capita income figures may seem of small importance. But for some of the sub-periods, this adjustment considerably reduces the estimated rise in standards of living.

The rates of growth per decade in per capita income between 1880 and 1950 are shown in Table 10-3. It can be seen that, even if only the intermediate values of the combined effect are considered, the estimate of the increase in the standard of living per decade is reduced by as much as 20 to 30 percent in the slow growth decades between 1910 and 1940.

Table 10-3
Percentage Changes per Decade in Real Income per Capita and per Consumption Unit, U. S., 1880–1950

	Income per capita	Ratio of consumption units to population	Income per consumption unit
	(1)	(2)	(3)
1880–90	12.6	1.6–3.0	9.3–10.8
1890–1900	23.8	1.2–1.7	21.7–22.3
1900–10	17.6	1.8–2.7	14.5–15.5
1910–20	8.5	1.5	6.9
1920–30	12.7	2.8	9.6
1930–40	16.7	4.2	12.0
1940–50	23.1	−0.3–2.3	20.3–23.5

Sources: col. 1: Computed from S. Kuznets, *Capital in the American Economy* (Princeton: NBER, 1961), Table R-40(a). Rates of change were computed from five-year moving averages of NNP per capita centered on the decennial years.

col. 2: Intermediate estimates, from col. 8 and 9 of Table 10-2. Where the difference between the two estimates was insignificant, their arithmetic average was taken.

col. 3: The relative change in per capita income, divided by the relative change in ratio of consumption units to population.

International Comparisons

In this section an attempt will be made to estimate the effects of differences in age composition and household size on international comparisons of welfare levels. This was limited to 29 selected countries for which the relevant data were available. The percentage distribution of population by age groups for each of these countries is shown in Appendix IV.[34] By applying the equivalency scales described above to these distributions, two alternative estimates were obtained of the ratio of the equivalent adult population to total population. These ratios can be seen to vary considerably among different groups of

---
[34]The data refer to the years 1955–61; see the notes to Appendix IV.

countries. Thus, under the lower scale, A, the equivalent adult population amounted to as much as 84 percent of total population in West Germany and in Sweden, as against only 61 percent in Taiwan, Cambodia, and Iraq. Under the higher B scale, the corresponding figures are 91 and 81 percent, respectively. Thus, because of difference in age composition alone, the per capita income estimates of the latter countries have to be raised by 10 to 20 percent (depending on the equivalence scale used) to make them comparable to those of the former ones.

Considerable difference can be observed also in the average size of households. Among the countries included in the present investigation, the number of persons per household varied from as little as 2.8 in Sweden and 3.0 in Denmark and West Germany to as much as 5.7 in Taiwan, the Philippines, and Turkey.[35] The large-household countries can, therefore, be expected to enjoy larger economies of scale in consumption than do the small-household ones. However, as discussed in the previous section, "Effects of Changes in Size of Households," large households are usually associated with a high share of the younger age groups in the population. To obtain an estimate of the differences in economies of scale, the household size figures have, therefore, to be adjusted for differences in the age composition of the population. By multiplying the number of persons per household by the corresponding ratio of the equivalent adult population to total population, the household size data were expressed in terms of comparable numbers of adults. The results of these computations are shown in Appendix V, for both adult equivalence scales. As could have been expected, thus transformed the differences in household sizes are considerably smaller than in the original data: under scale A the variations in household sizes are reduced to the range between that equivalent to 2.3 adults in Sweden and that equivalent to 4.0 in Turkey. The effects of the economies of scale were then estimated in the manner described in the section mentioned previously; i.e., by computing the ratio between the equivalent number of single-consumer households and the age-standardized household size. This is also the ratio between the income required to provide a certain standard of living to a population organized in households of a given size and that which would have been required to provide it were population organized in single-consumer households. In Appendix V, four estimates of this ratio are presented for each country, using the two alternative adult-equivalence scales and two alternative values of the economies of scale. The lowest ratios were obtained by using the A equivalence scale and a size conversion factor of 0.65. These ranged from 78 percent in Sweden to about 62 percent in Thailand and in Turkey. The highest ratios resulted from the use of Scale B and a conversion factor of 0.85, with a corresponding variation of between 88 and 79 percent. Thus, if the per capita income of data of, for example, Turkey are to be

---

[35]The data refer to private households, defined as "the persons who jointly occupy the whole or part of a housing unit, usually share the principal meals and have common provisions for basic living needs." See UN, *Demographic Yearbook 1962*, p. 36.

made comparable to those of Sweden, then, because of differences in size of households and in the related economies of scale, the Turkish data ought to be raised between 11 and 22 percent — depending on the equivalence scale and the size conversion factor used.

It has been noted before that the association between household size and age composition narrow the international differences in the economies of scale in consumption. However, the variations in the number of persons per household are too large to be wiped out completely when the household size is standardized in terms of equivalent adult consumer. Consequently, large economies of scale are, on the whole, found to exist in those countries which are charaterized by a high share of the younger age groups in their population. Four variants of the combined effect of both the age structure and the size of household are presented in the last four columns of Appendix V. There, the standardized consumption units' equivalent of the population is expressed as a percentage of total population.[36] For the two extreme variants, this ranges between 42 and 66 percent and between 65 and 80 percent, respectively. In other words, in international comparisons of standards of living, the per capita income of certain countries has to be raised by as much as 20 to 40 percent to eliminate the bias resulting from differences in age composition and in size of households.

The two extreme variants of the combined age and size effect were applied to per capita income data to obtain comparable estimates of income per consumption unit. To facilitate comparisons, the three sets of data shown in Table 10-4 (pg. 170) were presented in index form, in which average income for each country was expressed as a percent of the U.S. one. It can be seen that, relative to the U. S., the income per consumption unit in most of the European countries included in the table was lower than income per capita. But the differences between the index of income per capita and that per consumption unit were small. On the other hand, considerable differences can be observed in the case of the Far East and Middle East countries. In all of them the index of income per consumption unit is higher than the one of income per capita, though the extent of this difference varies considerably from one country to another.

The corrections introduced by computing income per consumption unit, rather than per capita, are summarized in Table 10-5 (pg. 171). The divergences of the indices of income per consumption unit from that of income per capita are expressed, for each country, as a percentage of the latter. It can be seen that, while in the case of some countries the correction introduced is rather trivial, in others it is quite considerable. Thus, in comparisons with the U.S., the use of per capita data underestimates the welfare level of, for example, Puerto Rico by between 15 and 25 percent, of Iraq by between 14 and 33 percent, and of Taiwan by as much as between 17 and 37 percent.

---

[36]This equivalent unit is equal to an adult, single-consumer household.

Table 10-4
**Income per Capita and Two Estimates of Income per Consumer Unit,
29 Selected Countries, 1957**

	Income per Capita, 1957		Income per Consumer Unit			
	U. S. Dollars	Index U.S. = 100	U. S.[a] Dollars	Index U.S. = 100	U. S.[b] Dollars	Index U.S. = 100
United States	2,108	100.0	3,718	100.0	2,792	100.0
Canada	1,472	69.8	2,820	75.8	2,067	74.0
Sweden	1,171	55.6	1,788	48.1	1,464	52.4
New Zealand	1,127	53.5	2,068	55.6	1,548	55.4
Australia	1,075	51.0	1,937	52.1	1,455	52.1
Denmark	869	41.2	1,425	38.3	1,139	40.8
Germany (West)	711	33.7	1,183	31.8	920	32.9
Israel	602	28.6	1,190	32.0	833	29.8
Czechoslovakia	580	27.5	1,007	27.1	761	27.3
Puerto Rico	473	22.4	1,037	27.9	718	25.7
Hungary	415	19.7	707	19.0	540	19.3
Argentina	402	19.1	776	20.9	562	20.1
Cyprus	307	18.8	762	20.5	550	19.7
Malaya	313	14.8	715	19.2	469	16.8
Bulgaria	310	14.7	579	15.6	411	14.7
Rumania	305	14.5	542	14.6	410	14.6
Jamaica	272	12.9	553	14.5	388	13.9
Panama	272	12.9	617	16.6	408	14.6
Japan	252	12.0	529	14.2	359	12.9
Yugoslavia	225	10.7	434	11.7	311	11.1
Portugal	197	9.3	377	10.1	264	9.5
The Philippines	194	9.2	466	12.5	298	10.7
Turkey	192	9.1	438	11.8	293	10.5
Iraq	135	6.4	316	8.5	205	7.3
Taiwan	127	6.0	305	8.2	195	7.0
Egypt	118	5.6	267	7.2	178	6.4
Iran	95	4.5	209	5.6	144	5.2
Thailand	88	4.2	206	5.5	132	4.7
Cambodia	87	4.1	197	5.3	133	4.8

Sources: M. Usui and E. E. Hagen, *World Income, 1957* (Center for International Studies, MIT, November 1959).

a. Computed using the *lowest* ratio of standard consumer units to population, shown in Appendix V, col. 9.

b. Computed using the *highest* ratio of standard consumer units to population, shown in Appendix V, col. 9.

It should be noted that while the corrections introduced by computing income per consumption unit are largest, relatively speaking, in low income countries, they are far from being perfectly associated with the level of income.[37] Thus, the ratio of the equivalent population to total population is much higher in certain European countries than in those Asian or American ones characterized by the same level of income per capita: compare Hungary

[37]The coefficients of correlation for the data in Table 10-5 are: –0.643 with respect to the highest estimate of the relative divergence of the income-per-consumer index from the income-per-capita index, and –0.554 with respect to the lowest estimate.

Table 10-5
Ranges of the Relative Divergence of Income per Consumer from Income per Capita Indices, 29 Selected Countries, 1957

	Relative divergence [a] (percent)	Income per capita (U. S. dollars)
Sweden	−5.8 to 13.5	1,171
Germany (West)	−2.4 to 5.8	711
Denmark	−1.0 to 7.0	869
Hungary	−2.0 to 3.6	415
Czechoslovakia	−0.7 to 1.5	580
United States	0	2,108
Rumania	0.7	305
Australia	2.2	1,075
Bulgaria	0 to 6.1	310
New Zealand	3.6 to 3.9	1,127
Portugal	2.2 to 8.6	197
Yugoslavia	3.7 to 9.3	225
Israel	4.2 to 11.9	602
Cyprus	4.8 to 9.0	397
Argentina	5.2 to 9.4	402
Canada	6.0 to 8.6	1,472
Jamaica	7.8 to 12.4	272
Japan	7.5 to 18.3	252
Panama	13.2 to 28.7	272
Malaya	13.5 to 29.7	313
Puerto Rico	14.7 to 24.6	473
Thailand	11.9 to 31.0	88
Egypt	14.3 to 28.6	118
Iraq	14.1 to 32.8	135
Turkey	15.4 to 29.7	192
Iran	15.6 to 24.4	95
The Philippines	16.3 to 35.9	194
Cambodia	17.1 to 29.3	87
Taiwan	16.7 to 36.7	127

Sources: Table 10-4
a. The relative excess of index (to U. S. base) of income per consumer unit from the index of per capita income. Derived by dividing col. 4 and 6 of Table 10-4, respectively, by col. 2 of the same table.

with Argentina or Puerto Rico and Portugal with Turkey and the Philippines. This means that in international comparisons of per capita income, it is impossible to say *a priori* that neglecting differences in the age composition and in the size of households always overestimates the true differences in the standards of living. However, more often than not, this will be the case, particularly when the comparison relates the income levels of underdeveloped countries to those of Europe or of the United States. On the other hand, it might be expected that in the future the decrease in the weight of the younger age groups in the populations, and in the size of households, in the underdeveloped economies will proceed more rapidly than in the highly developed ones. Then, a comparison of the rates of growth of per capita income will overestimate the relative rise of the standard of living in the developing economies.

Some Qualifying Remarks

The object of this paper was to illustrate the effects of differences in age composition and in size of households on the interpretation of intertemporal and international variations of per capita income; and to provide estimates of the ranges within which these effects may fall. The actual findings presented here depend, of course, on the numerical values ascribed to the adult-equivalence scales and to the economies of household scale in consumption. To this extent, they are subject to refinement and revision, should better estimates of those parameters become available. However, the procedure followed here also raises some questions of a more general nature.

The adult-equivalence scale is, probably, in itself a function of the standard of living. It would not be surprising if it were found that at higher income levels the equivalent adult weight of children is larger than at lower ones. This could be explained by the association between income and the number of children per family: the fewer a family's children the more precious each of them becomes to its parents, the allocation of consumption within the family changing correspondingly in their favor. However, even if this is the case, it seems that the same equivalence scale should be used throughout — i.e., for all the periods, or all the countries compared. Changes in the weights ascribed to children reflect those in tastes. In other words, if an increase in income was used only to increase the children's consumption, raising it relatively to that of the adults, this should not be taken to mean that the standard of living has not risen. There still remains the usual question whether the base-period or the end-period weights should be used throughout.

A similar question pertains to the economies of scale. In particular, it can be claimed that, as households decline in size, more provisions were made in the economy to cater to the needs of smaller units, thereby diminishing the extent of the dis-savings involved in this decline.

Finally, it should be remembered that the decline with time in the share of the younger age groups in the population was due not only to that in the size of families, but also to the lengthening of the average life span. The latter development may, of course, be regarded in itself as a rise in the welfare level. It could, therefore, be claimed that the negative effect this has on the standard of living, through the increase in the ratio of adult consumer units to population, is outweighed by the opposite effect of people living longer. But to be consistent, this approach would require that standard of living be measured not by annual income per capita, or per consumer, but rather by income per lifetime. There is, however, no reason why income should provide a measure of the welfare derived from living longer relatively to that resulting from other factors. Consequently, changes in welfare cannot be measured by any one summary measure, and each of the factors contributing towards them has to be evaluated separately. And as regards one of them, income per annum, increased length of life — other things being equal — has to be viewed as decreasing income per consumer unit. (Editor's Note: Appendices I-V follow on pages 174-180).

Questions for discussion and analysis pertaining to this article may be found at the end of Article 16.

Appendix I.

Table 10-6

Changes in the Age Composition and in the Ratio of Equivalent Adult Population to Total Population, U. S., 1850–1960

	Percentage distribution of population by age groups						Ratio of equivalent adult population to total population	
	Under 5 years (1)	5–9 (2)	10–14 (3)	15–19 (4)	Over 19 years (5)	Total (6)	A^a (7)	B^b (8)
1850	15.1	14.0	12.5	10.9	47.5	100.0	.688	.824
1860	15.4	13.3	11.8	10.7	48.8	100.0	.694	.831
1870	13.8	12.1	12.1	10.1	51.9	100.0	.716	.843
1880	13.8	12.9	11.4	10.0	51.9	100.0	.714	.842
1890	12.1	12.0	11.2	10.4	54.3	100.0	.736	.853
1900	12.1	11.7	10.6	9.9	55.7	100.0	.742	.857
1910	11.6	10.6	9.9	9.8	58.1	100.0	.758	.863
1920	10.9	10.8	10.1	8.9	59.3	100.0	.763	.869
1930	9.3	10.3	9.8	9.4	61.2	100.0	.781	.878
1940	8.0	8.1	9.7	9.4	64.8	100.0	.808	.894
1950	10.7	8.8	7.4	7.0	66.1	100.0	.795	.887
1960	11.3	10.4	9.4	7.4	61.5	100.0	.768	.872

Sources: 1850–1950 — U. S. Bureau of the Census, *Historical Statistics of the United States, Colonial Times to 1957* (Washington, 1960). 1960 — *Statistical Abstract of the U.S.*, 1963.

a. Sum of col. 1 to 5, weighted by scale A of Table 10-1.
b. Sum of col. 1 to 5, weighted by scale B of Table 10-1.

Appendix II.
Table 10-7

Size of Households and Its Single-Consumer Equivalent, U. S., 1850–1960

	Size of households (persons)	Household size standardized in adult equivalents[a]		Single-consumer equivalent of standardized size of households[b]				Ratio of single-consumer equivalent to age-standardized size of households[c]			
				Size factor of 0.65		Size factor of 0.85		Size factor of 0.65		Size factor of 0.85	
		Scale A	Scale B	Scale A	Scale B	Scale A	Scale B	Scale A	Scale B	Scale A	Scale B
	(1)	(2)	(3)	(4)	(5)	(6)	(7)	(8)	(9)	(10)	(11)
1850	5.55	3.82	4.59	2.39	2.69	3.12	3.65	.626	.586	.817	.795
1860	5.28	3.66	4.39	2.33	2.63	3.01	3.54	.637	.599	.872	.806
1870	5.09	3.64	4.29	2.32	2.58	3.00	3.44	.637	.601	.824	.802
1880	5.04	3.60	4.24	2.30	2.56	2.97	3.41	.639	.604	.825	.804
1890	4.93	3.63	4.21	2.31	2.55	2.99	3.39	.636	.606	.824	.805
1900	4.76	3.53	4.08	2.27	2.50	2.92	3.30	.643	.613	.827	.809
1910	4.54	3.44	3.93	2.23	2.43	2.86	3.20	.648	.618	.831	.814
1920	4.34	3.31	3.77	2.18	2.36	2.77	3.09	.659	.626	.837	.820
1930	4.11	3.21	3.61	2.13	2.30	2.70	2.98	.664	.637	.841	.825
1940	3.77	3.05	3.37	2.06	2.20	2.58	2.81	.675	.653	.846	.834
1950	3.52	2.80	3.12	1.95	2.10	2.40	2.63	.696	.673	.857	.843
1960	3.30	2.53	2.88	1.83	1.99	2.20	2.46	.723	.691	.870	.854

Sources: Col. 1: 1850 to 1950 — U.S. Bureau of the Census, *Historical Statistics of the United States from Colonial Times to 1957* (Washington, 1960). 1960, UN *Demographic Yearbook*, 1962.
a. Col. 1 multiplied, respectively, by col. 7 and 8 of Appendix 1.
b. Col. 2 and 3 raised to the powers of 0.65 and 0.85.
c. Col. 4 and 5 divided, respectively, by col. 2 and 3; and col. 6 and 7 divided also, respectively, by col. 2 and 3.

Appendix III.

Table 10-8

Ratio of the Equivalent Adult Single-Consumer Population to Total Population, U. S., 1850–1960

	Scale A Size factor		Scale B Size factor	
	0.65	0.85	0.65	0.85
	(1)	(2)	(3)	(4)
1850	.431	.562	.485	.657
1860	.442	.570	.498	.670
1870	.456	.590	.507	.676
1880	.456	.589	.508	.677
1890	.458	.606	.517	.687
1900	.477	.614	.525	.693
1910	.491	.630	.535	.705
1920	.503	.639	.544	.713
1930	.519	.657	.559	.724
1940	.545	.684	.584	.746
1950	.553	.681	.597	.748
1960	.555	.668	.603	.745

Col. 1 and 2 equal to col. 7 of Appendix I multiplied, respectively, by col. 8 and 10 of Appendix II.

Col. 3 and 4 equal to col. 8 of Appendix I multiplied, respectively, by col. 9 and 11 of Appendix II.

Appendix IV.

Table 10-9

The Percentage Distribution of Population by Age Groups and the Ratio of the Equivalent Adult Population to Total Population, 29 Selected Countries, 1955–61

| | Year | Under 1 | 1–4 | 5–9 | 10–14 | 15–19 | Over 19 | Total[a] | Ratio of equivalent adult population to total population[b] | |
									Scale A	Scale B
	(1)	(2)	(3)	(4)	(5)	(6)	(7)	(8)	(9)	(10)
United States	1960	2.3	9.0	10.4	9.4	7.4	61.5	100.0	76.8	87.2
Canada	1956	2.6	9.8	11.2	8.9	7.2	60.3	100.0	75.6	86.4
Argentina	1961	10.4		10.1	9.3	8.4	61.8	100.0	77.6	87.6
Jamaica	1960	3.6	13.0	13.7	10.8	9.0	49.9	100.0	68.9	82.7
Panama	1960	3.6	13.3	14.5	12.1	9.9	46.6	100.0	67.3	81.8
Puerto Rico	1960	3.2	11.9	14.0	13.6	10.5	46.8	100.0	68.4	82.4
Bulgaria	1956	1.8	7.2	9.3	8.2	7.5	66.0	100.0	80.2	89.0
Czechoslovakia	1961	1.6	6.8	9.5	9.4	7.7	65.0	100.0	80.0	88.9
Denmark	1960	1.6	6.4	8.1	9.1	8.3	66.5	100.0	81.3	89.6
Germany (West)	1960	1.7	6.3	7.2	6.5	7.3	71.0	100.0	83.5	90.7
Hungary	1961	1.4	6.1	9.3	8.3	7.4	67.4	100.0	81.5	89.7
Portugal	1960	2.2	8.0	9.6	9.2	8.2	62.8	100.0	78.3	87.9
Rumania	1956	2.2	8.3	9.3	7.6	9.0	63.5	100.0	78.9	88.1
Sweden	1960	1.1	5.6	7.1	8.1	7.9	70.1	100.0	83.7	90.9
Yugoslavia	1961	10.9		10.8	9.7	7.4	61.2	100.0	76.7	87.2
Cyprus	1960	13.1		11.8	11.7	8.4	55.0	100.0	73.0	85.2
Egypt	1960	2.9	13.0	14.6	12.2	8.3	49.0	100.0	68.3	82.5
Iran	1956	3.4	14.2	14.9	9.6	7.5	50.5	100.0	68.2	82.5
Iraq	1957	3.3	16.0	15.2	10.3	7.9	47.3	100.0	66.0	81.2
Israel	1961	2.5	9.7	12.4	11.5	8.2	55.7	100.0	73.4	85.3
Turkey	1955	3.1	13.0	13.4	9.9	9.7	50.9	100.0	70.0	83.2

(continued)

Appendix IV.

Table 10-9 (continued)

The Percentage Distribution of Population by Age Groups and the Ratio of the Equivalent Adult Population to Total Population, 29 Selected Countries, 1955–61

	Year	Age group						Total[a]	Ratio of equivalent adult population to total population[b]	
		Under 1	1-4	5-9	10-14	15-19	Over 19		Scale A	Scale B
	(1)	(2)	(3)	(4)	(5)	(6)	(7)	(8)	(9)	(10)
Cambodia	1959		18.5	14.5	11.6	9.8	45.6	100.0	66.1	81.3
Japan	1955	1.9	8.4	12.4	10.6	9.7	57.0	100.0	75.3	86.3
Malaya	1957	3.6	14.2	15.2	10.8	9.7	46.4	100.0	66.7	81.4
The Philippines	1960	2.9	14.0	16.1	12.7	10.4	43.9	100.0	65.8	80.8
Taiwan	1956	4.4	15.4	14.4	9.9	10.2	45.7	100.0	65.9	80.8
Thailand	1956	2.4	12.4	14.4	11.4	10.8	48.6	100.0	69.4	83.0
Australia	1960	2.2	8.4	9.9	9.5	7.5	62.4	100.0	77.7	87.6
New Zealand	1956	2.5	9.3	11.1	8.5	7.2	61.4	100.0	76.4	86.8

Source: UN *Demographic Yearbook, 1962.*
a. Discrepancies in totals are due to rounding.
b. Computed by weighting the percentage shares of the different age groups by the equivalence scales of Table 10-1. The ratios were computed from the original population data.

Appendix V.

Table 10-10

Size of Households in Actual Numbers of Persons and in Adult Equivalent, the Economies of Scale Effect and the Combined Age and Household Size Effect, 29 Selected Countries, 1955–61

	Year	Size of Households			Ratio of single-consumer equivalents to number of equivalent adults per household[a] (percent)				Ratio of adult, single-consumer equivalents to total population (percent)			
		Number of persons	Number of equivalent adults		θ=0.65		θ=0.85		Scale A		Scale B	
			Scale A	Scale B	A	B	A	B	θ=0.65	θ=0.85	θ=0.65	θ=0.85
	(1)	(2)	(3)	(4)	(5)	(6)	(7)	(8)	(9)	(10)	(11)	(12)
United States	1960	3.3	2.6	2.9	73.1	69.0	88.5	86.2	56.7	68.7	60.4	75.5
Canada	1956	3.9	2.9	3.4	69.0	64.7	86.2	82.4	52.2	65.2	55.9	71.2
Argentina	1960b	4.3	3.3	3.8	66.7	63.2	84.8	81.6	51.8	65.8	55.4	71.5
Jamaica	1960	4.0	2.8	3.2	71.4	66.7	85.7	84.8	49.2	59.0	55.2	70.1
Panama	1960	4.7	3.2	3.8	65.6	63.2	84.4	81.6	44.1	56.8	51.7	66.7
Puerto Rico	1960	4.8	3.3	4.0	66.7	62.5	84.8	80.0	45.6	58.0	51.5	65.9
Bulgaria	1956	3.7	3.0	3.3	66.7	66.7	83.3	84.8	53.5	66.8	59.4	75.5
Czechoslovakia	1961	3.1	2.5	2.8	72.0	71.4	88.0	85.7	57.6	70.4	63.5	76.2
Denmark	1955b	3.0	2.4	2.7	75.0	70.4	87.5	85.2	61.0	71.1	63.1	76.3
Germany (West)	1957b	3.0	2.5	2.7	72.0	70.4	88.0	85.2	60.1	73.5	63.8	77.3
Hungary	1960b	3.1	2.5	2.8	72.0	71.4	88.0	85.7	58.7	71.7	64.0	76.9
Portugal	1960	3.8	3.0	3.3	66.7	66.7	83.3	84.8	52.2	65.2	58.6	74.5
Rumania	1956	3.6	2.8	3.2	71.4	65.6	85.6	85.7	56.3	67.6	57.8	74.4
Sweden	1961	2.8	2.3	2.5	78.3	72.0	87.0	88.0	65.5	72.8	65.4	80.0
Yugoslavia	1961	4.0	3.1	3.5	67.7	65.7	83.9	82.9	51.9	64.4	57.3	72.3
Cyprus	1960	3.9	2.8	3.3	71.4	66.7	85.7	84.8	52.1	62.6	56.8	72.2
Egypt	1960	5.0	3.4	4.1	64.7	61.0	84.8	80.5	44.1	56.0	49.6	65.4
Iran	1956	4.8	3.3	4.0	66.7	62.5	84.8	80.0	45.5	57.8	51.6	66.0
Iraq	1957	5.2	3.4	4.2	64.7	59.5	82.4	81.0	42.7	54.4	48.3	65.8
Israel	1961	3.9	2.9	3.3	69.0	66.7	86.2	84.8	50.6	63.3	56.9	72.3
Turkey	1955	5.7	4.0	4.7	62.5	57.4	80.0	78.7	43.8	56.0	47.8	65.5

(continued)

Appendix V.

Table 10-10 (continued)

Size of Households in Actual Numbers of Persons and in Adult Equivalent, the Economies of Scale Effect and the Combined Age and Household Size Effect, 29 Selected Countries, 1955–61

| | | Size of Households Number of equivalent adults | | Ratio of single-consumer equivalents to number of equivalent adults per household[a] (percent) | | | | Ratio of adult, single-consumer equivalents to total population (percent) | | | |
| | Number of persons | Scale A | Scale B | θ=0.65 A | θ=0.65 B | θ=0.85 A | θ=0.85 B | Scale A θ=0.65 | Scale A θ=0.85 | Scale B θ=0.65 | Scale B θ=0.85 |
Year (1)	(2)	(3)	(4)	(5)	(6)	(7)	(8)	(9)	(10)	(11)	(12)
Cambodia 1958b	5.0	3.3	4.1	66.7	61.0	84.8	80.5	44.1	56.0	49.6	65.4
Japan 1955	5.0	3.8	4.3	63.2	60.5	81.6	81.4	47.6	61.4	52.2	70.2
Malaya 1957	4.8	3.2	3.9	65.6	61.5	84.4	82.0	43.8	56.3	50.1	66.7
The Philippines 1957b	5.7	3.8	4.6	63.2	58.7	81.6	80.4	41.6	53.7	47.6	65.2
Taiwan 1956	5.7	3.8	4.6	63.2	58.7	81.6	80.4	41.6	53.8	47.4	65.0
Thailand 1960b	5.6	3.9	4.6	61.5	58.7	82.0	80.4	42.7	56.9	48.7	66.7
Australia 1960c	3.6c	2.8	3.2	71.4	65.6	85.7	84.4	55.5	66.6	57.5	73.9
New Zealand 1956	3.6	2.8	3.1	71.4	67.7	85.7	83.9	54.5	65.5	58.8	72.8

Source: UN *Demographic Yearbook, 1955 and 1962; Israel Statistical Abstract 1963.*
a. See footnote 28 in text.
b. Household-size data refer occasionally to a different year than those regarding age composition. As can be seen by comparing with Appendix IV, only rarely does the difference exceed a period of three years.
c. Extrapolated on the basis of 1947 data.

Arnold Harberger †

11. ON DISCOUNT RATES FOR COST-BENEFIT ANALYSIS*

Introduction

This paper is concerned with the choice of the appropriate rate of discount for use in cost-benefit analysis and project appraisal. In particular, attention is focused on the manner in which the appropriate discount rate depends upon the conditions prevailing in the labor market of the economy in question. Where labor is genuinely in excess supply, to the point where all workers to be employed in the operation of a project can be assumed to be drawn from a large pool of unemployed, the wages to be paid to labor should not be counted as an economic cost, and should therefore not be deducted from the gross benefit stemming from the investment in the project. The consequence of this procedure is to produce high estimated returns to investment, and consequently high discount rate for cost-benefit work. For India in particular, the assumption of a superabundant labor supply, in the sense just mentioned, would appear to require that a discount rate of over 30 percent be used in cost-benefit analysis.

When, on the other hand, the labor market of an economy is functioning well, and is expected to produce relatively full employment in future years, the wage payments involved in the operation of a project should normally be counted as true economic costs of that project, and should therefore be deducted, along with costs of materials, etc., from the gross benefits of the project before arriving at its expected net benefit stream. This more traditional approach leads to an estimated discount rate far lower than that obtained on the assumption of truly superabundant labor, but even so the resulting rate for India appears to be well in excess of ten percent per annum — a figure substantially above the rates used in official Indian project evaluation procedures.

Between the extremes of superabundant labor on the one hand and a "tight" labor market on the other lie a whole continuum of possible "hybrid"

†Arnold C. Harberger, Professor of Economics, University of Chicago.
*From *Trabajos Sobre Desarrallo Economico, 1966-67* (Economic Development Institute of the World Bank, 1967). Reprinted by permission of the author.

situations, in which part but not all of the wage bill should be treated as a project cost. Associated with these intermediate situations are discount rates for cost-benefit analysis that are higher, the lower the fraction of the wage bill that is considered to be a true economic cost of the project's operation. These rates for India would range from something above 10 to something above 30 percent as one reduced from 100 to zero percent the fraction of the wages bill assigned as project cost.

The Relevance of the Marginal Productivity of Capital in the Private Sector

In the calculation of the appropriate rate of discount to be applied in India under any given set of assumptions, I have tried to estimate what would be the marginal productivity of capital in the private sector of the Indian economy under these assumptions.

I justify this approach by noting that if a government wishes to use a certain amount of its financial resources to provide benefits (via investment) for future generations, among the avenues open to it are investments in industrial establishments similar in nature to those already existing in the private sector. Such investments could be made directly in government-owned establishments, or indirectly by providing equity and debt financing for the establishment or expansion of basically private enterprises. It should be noted here that many precedents exist for both of these ways of using public sector funds. Many countries (and particularly India) have established government-owned firms in areas traditionally served by the private sector, and the mixed corporation (owned partly by government and partly by individuals) is a familiar element on the economic landscape of a number of countries.

Two important caveats must be borne in mind in using the private-sector rate of return as the criterion for public sector projects. The first is that, in measuring the private sector rate of return, social benefits which do not accrue to the private investors themselves but are attributable to their investments must be counted as part of the return to capital. This simply reflects the fact that government decisions on the uses of public funds within the public sector can (and should) be governed by weighing against their costs the total benefits produced by such projects; thus in order to place private-sector investments on a comparable basis the same procedure should be used. This entails attributing as benefits (a.) such taxes as are paid out of the income generated by investments, (b.) any net increment to consumer surplus that would result from a typical marginal investment in the private sector, (c.) any excess of wages paid over the alternative earnings of the workers employed, and (d.) any external benefits associated with private sector investments.

The second caveat concerns the use of the observed average "social" rate of return on private investments rather than the expected future "social" rate of return on such investments. Obviously, when we consider the various possible uses of today's investible funds, what we should compare are the future rates of return that are expected to accrue from investments in alternative projects. The rate of return that is observed today on past investments in the private sector can therefore be no more than a guide to the probable outcome of new investments in this area. It is likely to be a better guide if it has maintained its level over a relatively long period than if it has shown a significant upward or downward trend, but even so it is still only a guide. Particular care must be taken to avoid using the private-sector rate of return in a particular narrow class of investments as the criterion rate for social projects, if it is felt that any significant expansion of the capital stock in that private-sector activity would have the effect of significantly reducing the rate of return.

If, on the other hand, a fairly broad class of private sector activities is considered as the alternative outlet for public-sector investible funds, and if these are activities for which demand is likely to grow significantly in the future, then the likelihood is strong that these activities will be able to absorb substantial amounts of public sector funds, without a significant reduction in their rate of return, and the use of their currently-measured rate of return as the criterion-rate for public sector projects is more readily justified.

Thus, if one can demonstrate the existence of ample investment opportunities in the private sector having "social" marginal productivities of, say, 15 percent per annum or more, we cannot in the face of this evidence justify public sector investments promising a "social" yield of only 10 percent. The ideal investment policy would strive to equalize the "social" marginal productivity of capital in all lines of activity. But even a less-than-ideal policy — one recognizing the existence of numerous market and other imperfections — would nonetheless require that public sector projects produce an expected yield equal to the average "social" rate of marginal productivity in the private sector of the economy or in a relevant subsegment thereof. Particularly in India, where the public sector has invested in a wide range of activities that in many other countries remain in private hands, one of the reasonable alternatives to doing any given public sector project would be to invest in one or more lines of activity now dominated by the private sector. The rates of return obtainable on such investments thus become directly meaningful for decisions on the allocation of the investible resources of the public sector, and investment of substantial funds at expected rates of social return significantly below those obtainable within the private sector would appear to reflect poor decision-making and/or implementation. If policies can be pursued, and funds mobilized to drive the social rate of return down to 10 percent everywhere, well and good; but in the meantime the social rate of return in the private sector represents a challenge that public sector projects should be called upon to meet. If not enough public sector projects can be found that meet this challenge, the surplus investible funds of the public sector should be channeled, directly or indirectly, into the (presently private sector) activities of highest yield.

Measuring the Social Yield of Private Investments
Assuming a "Shadow Wage" of Zero

In this section I shall outline the procedures followed and summarize the results obtained in calculations designed to estimate the social rate of marginal productivity of capital in the "modern" private sector of the Indian economy, on the assumption that the "shadow wage" is zero. This last assumption reflects a belief that is widespread in the literature on underdeveloped countries in general and especially on India. I shall not for the moment attempt to argue the merits on this assumption, but simply follow through its logical consequences in the field of project evaluation. Operating on this assumption, we must attribute the full value added of an operation to the capital invested therein: the rate of return of capital becomes, in effect, the value-added/capital ratio. Since we are concerned with social rather than private benefits, value added should be calculated gross of taxes — both direct and indirect — paid by the enterprise in question. The resulting sum of private net-of-tax return to capital plus wage bill plus tax payments is our estimate of social net income attributable to the capital invested in an enterprise, when a zero shadow wage is assumed.

Our estimates were designed to measure the rate of productivity of capital invested in physical assets. Hence, the capital stock figures for an enterprise or activity should represent net fixed assets plus inventory holdings. However, most firms hold significant amounts of financial assets (cash, securities, receivables), at least some of which generate interest or dividend income for the firm. It would obviously be improper to attribute income generated by financial assets to the physical assets owned by the firm. Hence, we deducted from social net income as defined above an amount equal to ten percent of the excess of financial assets over short-term financial liabilities (principally accounts payable). This procedure undoubtedly overstates the actual earnings on financial assets, hence leads to an understatement of the social net income attributable to physical assets.

Both the figures on social net income attributable to physical assets and the figures on the value of the stock of physical assets were then expressed in 1955 prices, so as to value both income and capital in units of constant purchasing power. The deflation procedures were crude, owing to the fact that only price indexes of rather broad coverage are available for India. To offset to some extent the crudeness of the deflating indexes, procedures were consciously adopted that would tend to overstate the value of physical assets in 1955 prices while understating the amount of income — also in 1955 prices — attributable to these assets.[1] Thus, at a second point in the estimation

---

[1]These procedures are discussed in detail in Arnold C. Harberger, "Investment in Man vs. Investment in Machines: The Case of India," in C. A. Anderson and M. J. Bowman, eds., *Education and Economic Development* (Chicago: Aldine Press, 1965). The procedures were applied there to estimate the global rate of return to investment in physical capital in Indian industry; in the present paper they are applied to obtain estimates of rates of return by industry class.

procedure, the estimates were biased in the direction of understating the desired rate of return.

Additional biases in the same direction were introduced to take account of the tendency of business firms to overstate depreciation whenever possible in order to enjoy the maximum possible tax advantage. A number of alternative methods for doing this were outlined in the paper just cited, but two of them proved to be uniformly the most conservative; i.e., to produce the lowest estimates of the rate of return to physical capital. The first of these (Method A) operates on the identities:

True Net Income = Gross Income — True Depreciation Allowance

True Net Assets ≡ Gross Assets — True Accumulated Depreciation

From these it follows that

$$\frac{TNI}{TNA} \gtrless \frac{GI}{GA} \quad \text{as} \quad \frac{TDA}{TAD} \lessgtr \frac{GI}{GA}$$

using the obvious initials as symbols. Now even though tax considerations make actual depreciation allowances exceed the "true" (i.e., economically appropriate) allowance, and to make the actual accumulated depreciation exceed its "true" counterpart, there is no presumption that the ratio of actual depreciation allowances to actual accumulated depreciation will be similarly strongly biased as an estimate of the true ratio. Hence, when the ratio of ADA/AAD is less than the ratio of gross income to gross assets, Method A uses (GI/GA) as an *under*estimate of the (TNI/TNA). This, for the data examined, is typically the case. In the infrequent cases where (ADA/AAD) exceeded (GI/GA), the ratio of net income to net assets derived from the books of the enterprises (with, of course, all the adjustments previously discussed) was used as the estimate of (TNI/TNA) in Method A.

Method B is based on the modern approach to capital budgeting in that it calculates internal rates of return on a cash-flow basis. The annual cash flow associated with the physical assets of an enterprise is estimated by taking the difference between gross income attributable to physical assets and the outlay on new physical assets. Neither of these figures is influenced by arbitrary depreciation procedures. Having calculated the normal cash flows for a series of years on this basis, the initial cash flow (i.e., the amount "invested") is taken to be the gross assets of the firm prior to first year of normal cash flows, and the final cash flow (i.e., the "final repayment" on the investment) is taken to be the gross assets of the firm at the end of the last year for which normal cash flows were measured. A typical pattern of cash flows would, for example be: −136,000, + 2994, + 3383, + 4709, + 5649, + 19933. The first figure in this sequence represents gross assets at the end of 1955, the subsequent four figures represent net cash flows during the years 1956 through 1959, and the final figure represents gross assets at the end of 1959 — all, of course, expressed in 1955 prices. The internal rate of return implied by the above series — dating the initial and terminal flows at December 31, and the intermediate flows at June 30 of the corresponding years — is 38.5 percent per annum.

The data underlying Table 11-1 are produced by a survey of 1001 companies, regularly conducted by the Reserve Bank of India.[2] The sample is large and well representative of the "modern" private sector in India. In fact, the 1001 companies, taken together, regularly account for more than two-thirds of all corporate investment in India. The Reserve Bank of India consolidates the accounts of reporting companies on an industry and sector basis, as well as for the sample as a whole. It is these consolidated figures that were used in making the computations lying behind Table 11-1. In the case of Method A, rates of return for each industry were calculated separately for each of the years 1955 through 1959, and the resulting estimates were then averaged to yield the figure reported in the table.

It is important to realize that, in spite of the high estimates emerging from the table, there is a strong presumption that they understate the correct figures. First, the estimating procedures were consciously biased to produce underestimates. Second, no account was taken of consumers' surplus in developing the estimates. Third, the procedures used develop estimates of the marginal productivity of capital on the basis of the observed average rate of return (adjusted as indicated above) in each line of activity. Where the relevant production function is characterized by constant returns to scale, the marginal productivity of capital will tend to equal the average rate of return, but where increasing returns to scale are present; as may be the case in several of the covered industries, the marginal productivity of capital will tend to exceed the average rate of return on which our estimates were based.

By and large, the highest estimated rates of return in Table 11-1 are those affected by indirect taxes. The third column of the table presents estimates in which indirect taxes are not incorporated in the social return to capital; it can be compared with column (1) to indicate the importance of indirect taxes in any sector. Nonetheless, not much relevance should be attributed to column (3), since, in general, the taxes generated by a new investment should be considered as part of the benefit it produces.

Implications and Relevance of a Zero Shadow Wage

Table 11-1 shows clearly that there are many lines of activity in the private sector of the Indian economy in which the social marginal productivity of capital would exceed 30 percent per annum if the shadow wage were indeed equal to zero. In fact, 2/3 of the listed industries fall into this category when Method A is used, and nearly 3/4 when Method B is used. For the total sample, Method A yields an estimated overall marginal productivity of capital of 33.6 percent, and Method B produces an estimate of 38.5 percent per year.

---

[2]See *Reserve Bank of India Bulletin* (September, 1961), pp. 1403–1457; (October, 1961), pp. 1752–1776.

Table 11-1

**Estimates of the Social Rate of Return to Capital in Indian Industry,
Assuming a Shadow Wage of Zero
(Based on Data from Reserve Bank of India Survey of 1001 Companies, 1955–59)
[Percent per Year]**

Industry	Method A	Method B	Method A (excluding indirect taxes)
Total	33.6	38.5	27.4
Tobacco Manufactures	110.3	101.0	41.1
Rubber and Rubber Mfgrs.	50.1	62.0	32.6
Mining and Quarrying	47.0	58.5	46.8
Cotton Textiles	41.2	47.5	33.8
Sugar	40.7	61.5	19.5
Processing of Grains and Pulses	40.5	47.5	34.5
Mineral Oils	39.9	49.5	23.8
Coffee Plantations	38.9	47.5	38.8
Tea Plantations	38.7	45.5	38.4
Trading	38.3	39.5	38.2
Edible Oils	36.2	39.0	24.8
Machinery (exc. Transp. and Elec.)	35.9	42.5	35.6
Pottery, China, Earthenware	34.8	42.0	34.8
Electrical Machinery	34.7	39.5	33.6
Medicines and Pharmaceuticals	34.2	39.0	32.4
Rubber Plantations	32.9	37.5	32.2
Processing and Manufacturing, n. e. c.	32.3	38.0	23.7
Construction	31.7	35.0	31.7
Chemical Products, n. e. c.	31.5	35.5	29.8
Paper and Paper Products	30.6	36.0	23.1
Cement	27.8	32.0	20.0
Jute Textiles	27.1	28.0	27.1
Hotels, Restaurants, Eating Houses	25.0	27.0	24.5
Iron and Steel	23.9	25.5	22.2
Transportation Equip.	22.2	23.5	22.0
Silk and Woolen Textiles	21.3	24.5	19.5
Aluminum	20.5	23.5	20.5
Basic Industrial Chemicals	17.0	19.0	16.8
Shipping	13.1	16.0	13.1
Elec. Generation and Supply	11.1	11.5	11.1

Other lines of approach tend to confirm this conclusion. If labor is so abundant that its scarcity value is zero, then the whole output of the economy must be attributed to capital (broadly defined so as to include land, etc.). The social rate of return on capital for the economy as a whole then becomes the ratio of net national product to the capital stock. Even though we have no good estimates of the capital stock of India, there are no grounds to presume that it exceeds 3 times the net national product. Thus, it must be presumed that an exercise similar to the present one, carried out for the whole

Indian economy, would produce an estimated social marginal productivity of capital of 33 1/3 or more percent per annum.

It thus appears that if the hypothesis of a zero shadow wage is correct, Indian planners should be using a discount rate of at least 30 percent in evaluating the alternative projects confronting them. This high rate is counter-balanced, so to speak, by the fact that the assumption of a zero shadow wage permits one to include the entire wages bill to be generated once a project gets into operation as a part of the yield of the capital invested in that project. In the net, the use of a zero shadow wage will substantially benefit labor-intensive activities, and will weigh heavily against capital-intensive activities, as a glance at Table 11-1, in which the industries are arranged in descending order of social rate of return (under Method A), will verify.

Not only does a high discount rate weigh against capital-intensive projects, it also discriminates strongly against projects with long gestation periods and/or with long economic lives. At a 30 percent rate of return, an invested sum should more than double in 3 years, and should multiply by nearly five in six years. An investment of 100 today in a project with a six-year gestation period must produce, starting with the seventh year, an *annual* yield of 145 in order to pay off at 30 percent. By the same token the present value of 100 six years hence is only around 20, evaluated at a discount rate of 30 percent per year, and the present value of 100 twelve years hence is only a little over 4.

These simple relationships have tremendous implications as to the sorts of projects that would be acceptable when high discount rates are used. Large irrigation projects would have to be tremendously productive in order to justify their long gestation periods. Investments with long lives, such as houses and roads, would benefit little from their longevity — the "economic" annual rental of a house, for example, would be a third or more of its value, if a 30 percent discount rate were used.

In the long run, if the policy implications of a zero shadow wage were followed through consistently, there would have to be a massive readjustment of relative prices in the economy. By concentrating investment in those lines with the highest ratios of value added (gross of indirect taxes) to capital and short gestation periods, the prices of their products would tend to be driven down while increasing scarcity would drive up the prices of products produced in lines with low ratios of value added to capital and/or long gestation periods. By such a process of price adjustment, projects of types initially neglected because their ratios of value added to capital were too low would ultimately become acceptable. Indeed, if a 30 percent discount rate were applied consistently throughout the economy for a sufficiently long period, the ratios of value added to capital-at-charge would tend toward equality at approximately 30 percent in all lines of activity. (Capital-at-charge is obtained by accumulating past capital outlays at the critical discount rate — here

30 percent — and of course adjusting the capital-at-charge for depreciation during each year of its use.)

The implications of a zero shadow wage, sketched briefly above, suggest very different directions for Indian economic planning than have in fact been followed. Should we therefore conclude that Indian planning has been grossly wrong? I think not, at least not on the basis of the evidence and arguments presented, for up to now we have been operating on the assumption that the shadow wage is in fact zero. In point of fact, there is substantial evidence suggesting that this assumption is quite inappropriate for India, and it is to this evidence that we now turn.

The idea that labor is so superabundant in India that its shadow price should be zero is deeply rooted in the situation of Indian agriculture — a sector employing some 70 percent of the Indian labor force. Here, it is said, one confronts an enormous pool of labor, whose marginal productivity is (virtually) zero. Large quantities of this labor could be withdrawn from Indian agriculture, the argument goes, without occasioning any significant reduction in agricultural output.

There is considerable and good evidence that weighs against this argument. More than a quarter of the Indian agricultural labor force works for wages, which are voluntarily paid to the workers by their employers. It is to be presumed that these employers are getting, in return, a marginal product per worker that is at least equal to the wage being paid. If the marginal productivity of labor were below the wage paid, the first to suffer would be the wage laborers who would then be put out of work. Yet the average adult male wage-laborer in Indian agriculture worked, in 1956-57, over 250 full-time equivalent days per year at wages averaging 1 rupee or more per day. The average agricultural labor household in India had an income of nearly Rs. 400 per year, while even the landless, casual-labor households had an average income of over Rs. 335 per year.[3] When agricultural households are classified according to their per-capita consumer expenditures in 1956-57, the lowest 28 percent of the households had per-capita expenditures averaging 71 rupees and per-household expenditures of some 380 rupees per year.[4]

The high number of days worked by adult male laborers in Indian agriculture is in part explained by the fact that there are typically two plantings and two harvests per year, and partly by the fact that the seasonal peaks of employment in agriculture are filled by women and children entering the work force at such times, and by a seasonal reflux of some male workers from the cities.

---

[3]See Government of India: The Cabinet Secretariat, *The National Sample Survey, No. 33: Wages, Employment, Income and Indebtedness of Agricultural Labor Households in Rural Areas* (Delhi: 1960), pp. 18, 23, 61.

[4]See Government of India: The Cabinet Secretariat, *The National Sample Survey, No. 46: Consumer Expenditure of Agricultural Labor Households in Rural Areas* (Delhi: 1961), pp. 31, 37.

The important conclusions that follow from this evidence are (a.) that even the most disadvantaged groups of agricultural workers in India work more days per year than is common for farmers in most advanced countries and (b.) that they earn incomes-per-worker in excess of the national per-capita income, which was 292 rupees at the time to which the data cited above apply. An Indian income of Rs. 335 per year, in 1956–57, would correspond to a U.S. income of nearly $3,000 per year in 1964, when both are expressed relative to the respective per capita national incomes. Yet the average member of the U.S. agricultural labour force did not obtain in 1964, significantly more than $3,000 of personal income from all sources. We obviously do not conclude that labor has a zero marginal productivity in U.S. agriculture, and by the same token I fail to see how we can reach this conclusion for the Indian labor forces in the face of the relationships just indicated.

Further evidence strongly suggesting that the marginal productivity of labor in agriculture is not zero in the Indian economy has recently been assembled by Professor T. W. Schultz.[5] Schultz analyzes the effects of the influenza epidemic of 1918–19 on agricultural production in India. This epidemic cost the lives of millions of people throughout India, and struck at different rates in different areas. Comparing periods of similar climatic conditions prior to and subsequent to the year of the epidemic itself, Schultz obtained a high correlation between the percentage drop in population in an area, on the one hand, and the percentage fall in agricultural output on the other, between the "before" and "after" years. Moreover, the elasticity of output with respect to changes in labor force, implied by Schultz's data, suggest that the marginal productivity of labor in Indian agriculture is approximately equal to the average wage. Schultz's test of the hypothesis of zero marginal productivity is a direct one, and its results are powerful. Its only weakness is that it refers to the India of some 45 years ago — but it is well to recall that India was commonly regarded as overpopulated then, and that its per capita income was then undoubtedly somewhat lower than it is now. It should be added that in spite of the substantial difference in time, the results of Schultz's test lead to the same general conclusions as the National Sample Survey evidence presented above.

A final piece of evidence negating the idea of a zero marginal productivity of labor in Indian agriculture comes from Professor K. N. Raj's study of the great Bhakra Nangal Dam project.[6] In discussing the recruitment of labor for this project, Professor Raj states:

> It is a common assumption to make, on theoretical analyses, that the supply of unskilled labor in under-developed countries is almost infinitely elastic. This, obviously, is not always true. For instance, the additional demand for unskilled labor created by the Bhakra Nangal project, even at the peak level of activity during the construction of the canals, cannot

[5]See T. W. Schultz, *Transforming Traditional Agriculture* (New Haven: Yale University Press, 1964), pp. 53–70.

[6]K. N. Raj, *Economic Aspects of the Bhakra Nangal Project* (Bombay: Asia Publishing House, 1960).

be regarded as very large, when considered with reference to the investment undertaken or the area (and population) over which the construction
work was spread. Yet the supply of unskilled labor from the areas adjoining the work proved hardly adequate. In March 1954, when the total
number employed on the Bhakra Canals was around 100,000, it would
appear that as much as 60 percent of the labor required had to be imported from other States.[7]

This result was observed in spite of the fact that the wages paid were good
(typically Rs. 2 per day plus free housing). It is obviously hardly consistent
with the notion of a large pool of labor having zero marginal productivity,
which can readily be drawn upon to meet additional labor requirements.

I believe that the evidence cited above warrants our rejecting the hypothesis
of zero marginal productivity of labor in Indian agriculture, and with it the
hypothesis of a zero shadow wage for the labor used in Indian industry. We
can, however, attempt to estimate at this point what would be the minimum
shadow wage for the labor used in the modern industrial sector of India. We
have seen that the average casual laborer in Indian agriculture earns over Rs.
300 per year. Yet such workers will not willingly present themselves for work in
a typical industrial establishment for Rs. 300 a year. By and large, modern
industrial establishments are located in the urban sector, where the real costs
of housing, food, transportation to and from work, etc. are significantly greater
than they are in the villages of rural India. Moreover, there are other "costs"
associated with the migration of rural labor to urban areas, notably the transportation costs that many workers feel impelled to bear in order to maintain
periodic contacts with their native villages. (Many urban workers in fact leave
their families in the village, returning there as often as they can, providing maintenance for their families, and, of course for their own separate maintenance
in the city. It is factors like these, on the labor supply side, that explain why
even the lowest-paid of urban workers obtain incomes substantially in excess
of those earned by their rural counterparts. These factors need not always
be operative — i.e., if the pattern of economic development required a migration flow, in the net, from city to country, some of the forces listed above
might even work to produce a differentially higher wage in agriculture. But
in the Indian context the forces of economic development are in fact drawing
population to the urban areas, and to do this urban wages must be sufficient
to attract the required flow.)

In point of fact, the lowest paid urban workers — household sweepers,
ricksha drivers, casual construction laborers, for example, appear to earn
approximately Rs. 2 per day (including some income in kind in the case of
sweepers). These occupations are unorganized, have completely free entry,
and are subject to no legal minimum wages; thus no "artificial" forces are at
work to press their wage levels above. Moreover, these occupations do not
require any special skills, and in fact are often entered by rural-urban migrants.

---

[7]*Ibid.*, pp. 77–78.

It is reasonable, under these circumstances, to interpret the differential between wages in these occupations and the wages of casual rural laborers as reflecting the premium needed to elicit the required amount of migration. This being the case, we can consider the wage of Rs. 2 per day, or roughly Rs. 600 per year, to be the effective shadow price of completely unskilled labor in the cities. This judgment is confirmed by data from the National Sample Survey. In 1957–58, for example, the 26 percent of the urban population with lowest per capita incomes lived in households in which per household consumption expenditures were over Rs. 720 per year.[8] This amount is roughly consistent with the figure of Rs. 600 of income per worker, as some of the households in this category had more than one income-earner.

Measuring the Social Yield of Private Investments on the Assumption that Shadow Wages Equal Actual Wages

This section presents estimates of the social yield of capital in Indian industry, based on the assumption that the shadow wage is equal to the actual wage paid in each line of activity. This means, of course, that the shadow wage is not the same as among industries and activities, but it is quite appropriate that the shadow wage should vary with the skill of labor and with the region. The assumption that the shadow wage everywhere equals the actual wage in effect attributes all variations in wages to factors like skill and region, and leaves no room for "artificial" factors — such as legal minimum wages in given lines of activity — to explain wage differentials. As was the case with the assumption of a zero shadow wage, we shall examine the implications of the assumption that shadow wages equal actual wages without for the moment inquiring into its validity. This is done in Table 11-2. The concept of social return to capital used in Table 11-2 is similar to that underlying Table 11-1, except for two adjustments. In the first place, the wage bill is not imputed as part of the return to capital here, since we are treating wages as a true economic cost. In the second place, only a part of indirect taxes is imputed to capital: namely, that fraction which the net income from capital bears to value added in the activity in question.[9] Thus, "capital's share" of indirect taxes is assigned as part of the social return to capital, a procedure consistent with that underlying Table 11-1 because the assumptions behind Table 11-1 assigned 100 percent of value added as return to capital.

The full costing of labor has a dramatic effect upon the rate of return to capital. Whereas in Table 11-1, two-thirds of the industries covered had

---

[8]Indian Statistical Institute, *The National Sample Survey, No. 80; Tables with Notes on Consumer Expenditure* (Calcutta: Indian Statistical Institute, 1961), Tables 2.3.0 and 2.5.0.

[9]For a justification of this procedure see my paper, "The Measurement of Waste," *American Economic Review,* LIV, No. 3 (May, 1964), p. 65.

Table 11-2

Estimates of the Social Rate of Return to Capital in Indian Industry, Assuming Shadow Wages = Actual Wages
(Based on Data from Reserve Bank of India Survey of 1001 Companies, 1955–59)
[Percent per year]

	Method A	Method B	Method A (exc. indirect taxes)
Total	13.2	13.0	10.9
Tobacco	44.6	47.5	15.5
Mineral Oils	32.4	39.5	18.8
Processing of Grains and Pulses	26.1	28.5	22.3
Sugar	21.7	23.0	11.1
Rubber and Rubber Manufactures	21.2	23.0	14.1
Processing and Manufacturing, n. e. c.	19.2	21.0	14.0
Coffee Plantations	18.1	19.0	18.1
Electrical Machinery	17.6	17.0	17.1
Paper and Paper Products	16.9	18.5	12.9
Cement	15.8	16.5	11.0
Rubber Plantations	15.7	16.0	15.4
Machinery (exc. Transp. and Elec.)	15.1	15.0	15.1
Pottery, China, and Earthenware	14.8	15.5	14.8
Construction	13.2	12.5	13.2
Chemical Products, n. e. c.	12.7	13.5	11.9
Tea Plantations	12.6	12.5	12.5
Iron and Steel	12.2	12.0	11.2
Medicines and Pharmaceuticals	12.1	12.0	11.5
Silk and Woolen Textiles	12.0	16.0	11.0
Trading	11.6	9.5	11.6
Edible Oils	11.5	10.0	8.1
Aluminum	10.2	12.0	10.2
Transportation Equipment	10.2	11.0	10.1
Cotton Textiles	9.7	8.0	8.2
Mining and Quarrying	9.5	9.0	9.5
Electricity Generation and Supply	7.7	8.0	7.7
Basic Industrial Chemicals	7.5	9.5	7.4
Hotels, Restaurants, and Eating Houses	6.4	5.5	6.2
Shipping	5.3	9.5	5.3
Jute Textiles	5.1	5.0	5.1

social rates of return to capital above 30 percent, and the over-all rate for the total sample was above 33 percent, here, in Table 11-2, slightly over a third of the industries covered have rates of return below 12 percent, and the average for the total sample is only about 13 percent.

Column 3 of Table 11-2 excludes capital's share of indirect taxes and thus shows the gross-of-income-tax rate of return to physical capital in the covered industries. It is notable that this series shows a marked central tendency — half the industries covered had rates of return between 10 and 15 percent, and three quarters between 7 and 17 percent.

In spite of the fact that the rates of return estimated in Table 11-2 are low when compared with Table 11-1, they are quite high when compared to the rates of return (3–5 percent) commonly used for cost-benefit analysis in India. And it should be emphasized that Table 11-2 is based on extremely conservative assumptions. Not only does the estimation procedure contain a downward bias, but also a very narrow concept of social benefit is used. In fact, the only element of non-private benefit entering into a return to capital measured in Table 11-2 consists of taxes. The results therefore strongly suggest a drastic upward revision of the discount rate used for project evaluation in India.

Measuring the Social Yield of Capital on "Intermediate" Assumptions

We now inquire into the validity of the assumption that the actual wage and the shadow wage are equal. We take as the point of departure the conclusion — reached in the section entitled, Implications and Relevance of a Zero Shadow Wage — that the minimum plausible value of the shadow wage for unskilled workers in urban employments in India was around Rs. 600 per year. Now although we do not have direct data on the wages per man-year paid by the 1001 companies in the Reserve Bank of India Survey, we do know that in modern factory establishments in India the average annual earnings per worker averaged between Rs. 1000 and Rs. 1200 per year in 1956–58.[10] These earnings obviously apply to the average of the skill-mix of workers used in factory establishments, and not just to unskilled labor. Clearly the shadow wage for this skill-mix will substantially exceed the minimum Rs. 600 figure that was estimated for the least skilled class of workers. But granting that the shadow wage relevant for the companies in the Reserve Bank survey is higher than Rs. 600, the key question is by how much. Most employers undoubtedly do try to obtain labor of a given quality at the minimum possible cost — a policy which tends to produce a situation in which actual wages and shadow wages are the same. On the other hand, not all employers succeed in this aim — union pressure and government policy being the principal forces leading to wage rates above the supply price of labor — and some employers appear to pursue a conscious policy of paying wage rates that are somewhat above the going market. In any event, regardless of why wages are higher than required, we can be quite sure that they sometimes are so in fact. This is demonstrated by the fact that some industrial enterprises — particularly the larger and more modern ones — have long waiting lists of qualified applicants for work, who are ready and willing to work at the wages these enterprises pay, but who must typically settle for jobs in other lines of activity which pay less.

---

[10]Government of India, Ministry of Information and Broadcasting, *India, 1961* (Delhi: 1961), p. 377.

Table 11-3

**Estimates of the Social Rate of Return to Capital in Indian Industry, Assuming
Shadow Wages = Eighty Percent of Actual Wages**
(Based on Data from Reserve Bank of India Survey of 1001 Companies, 1955–59)
[Percent per year]

	Method A	Method B	Method A (excluding indirect taxes)
Total	17.3	17.5	14.3
Tobacco	57.7	66.0	20.9
Sugar	36.2	39.0	24.8
Mineral Oils	33.9	41.5	19.8
Processing of Grains and Pulses	29.0	32.0	24.7
Rubber and Rubber Manufactures	27.0	30.5	17.8
Coffee Plantations	22.3	24.5	22.3
Processing and Mfg., n. e. c.	21.8	24.0	16.2
Electrical Machinery	21.0	21.5	20.4
Paper and Paper Products	19.6	22.0	15.1
Machinery (exc. Transp. and Elec.)	19.3	20.0	19.2
Rubber Plantations	19.2	20.0	18.8
Pottery, China, and Earthenware	18.8	20.5	18.8
Cement	18.2	19.5	13.0
Tea Plantations	17.9	18.5	17.7
Trading	17.2	15.0	17.1
Construction	17.1	16.5	17.1
Mining and Quarrying	17.0	18.0	16.9
Chemical Products, n. e. c.	16.9	18.0	16.0
Medicines and Pharmaceuticals	16.5	17.0	15.7
Edible Oils	16.5	15.0	11.8
Cotton Textiles	16.2	15.0	13.6
Iron and Steel	14.6	14.5	13.5
Silk and Woolen Textiles	13.9	17.5	12.7
Transportation Equipment	12.8	13.5	12.7
Aluminum	12.6	14.0	12.6
Hotels, Restaurants, and Eating Houses	10.1	9.5	9.9
Jute Textiles	9.9	9.0	9.9
Basic Industrial Chemicals	9.5	11.5	9.3
Electricity Generation and Supply	8.5	9.0	8.5
Shipping	6.8	10.5	6.8

Thus, particularly when we look at the combined group of 1001 companies in the Reserve Bank survey, we should properly allow for some excess of actual wages over shadow wages. It is the size of this excess rather than its existence which is open to doubt. Some observers of the Indian scene feel that the excess is so small that it can be neglected for practical purposes; these people would consider the results of Table 11-2 to be sufficiently accurate to serve as a reasonable guide for setting the rate of discount to be used in cost-benefit work. Other observers, however, feel that the excess of actual over shadow wages in the modern industrial sector may be quite large — perhaps as high as 15 or 20 percent. Table 11-3 is presented as illustrative of the sort of measure of the social rate of return to capital that these people would regard as relevant.

Table 11-3 is similar to Tables 11-1 and 11-2, except that here 80 percent of the wage bill has been treated as a cost and the remaining 20 percent has been assigned as part of the social return to capital. In allocating indirect taxes, capital was assigned that fraction of indirect taxes which the adjusted return to capital (i.e., including 20 percent of the wage bill) bears to value added in each industry.

Obviously, a careful effort to measure the social rate of return to capital in any industry would properly entail an investigation into the various types of labor used by that industry, and into their likely employment alternatives and/or supply prices. One would presumably arrive at a different ratio of shadow to actual wages for each category of labor. The relevant ratio for the industry as a whole would be the weighted average of these separate ratios for each class of labor. Similarly, the relevant industry-ratios would surely differ from industry to industry; this is why Table 11-3 should be regarded as merely illustrative. Nonetheless, if the weighted average of the respective industry ratios of shadow to actual wages were .8, the figures given in Table 11-3 for all 1001 companies taken together would be appropriate measures of the social rate of return to capital for the overall-group, subject of course to the downward biases mentioned earlier.

Comparing the results of Tables 11-2 and 11-3 for the overall sample, we conclude that the social rate of return to capital in Indian industry is either somewhat in excess of 13 percent (Table 11-2) or somewhat in excess of 17 percent (Table 11-3). The importance of this difference should, however, not be exaggerated, for if we were to use the 13 percent rate to evaluate a project, we should not assign any of the wage bill as part of the return to capital, while if we were to use the 17 percent rate, we would presumably have to assign a portion of the wage bill—a proportion which would equal 20 percent of the difference between actual and shadow wages in the project being evaluated was representative of the corresponding difference assumed for the 1001 companies in the construction of Table 11-3. Although a 17 percent rate is itself harder to achieve than a 13 percent rate, the assignment of a portion of wages to the return to capital eases the task, particularly for relatively labor-intensive activities.

The differences in the assumptions underlying Tables 11-2 and 11-3 roughly reflect, I believe, our present degree of uncertainty. We cannot be sure that the shadow wage equals 100 percent of the actual wage, nor can we be sure that it equals 80 percent of the actual wage. We can be reasonably certain that it lies somewhere in between. Given this range of uncertainty it is comforting to know that it does not create any very serious problems for cost-benefit analysis. Many projects that pass a 13 percent rate-of-return test when wages are counted as social benefits will also pass a 17 percent rate-of-return test when 20 percent of wages are counted as social benefits. Likewise, many projects that pass a 17 percent test when 20 percent of wages are counted as benefits will also pass a 13 percent test when no wages are counted. This, of course, does not say that the two sets of criteria will always lead to the same decision in respect of a project — the 17 percent test is biased, relatively, in favor of labor intensive projects, and the 13 percent in favor of capital intensive projects. These differences can be perceived in the relative rankings of the different industries in Tables 11-2 and 11-3. Mining and quarrying — a labor intensive industry in India — ranks much higher in Table 11-3 than in Table 11-2, and jute textiles and trading, also labor-intensive industries, rank somewhat higher.

In spite of the differences in concept underlying the two tables, however, there is a striking degree of correspondence in their rankings of the industries by rate of return. For example, the top 9 industries in Table 11-2 are also the top 9 in Table 11-3, and the bottom 5 industries are also the same in both tables. Moreover, very few of the industries changed their ranking by more than two or three places as between Tables 11-2 and 11-3. This correspondence reflects the fact that the two sets of criteria are not really very different, and suggests that project evaluation under either set would not lead us into gross errors of judgment.

Summary and Conclusions

One way of viewing the intent of this paper is to juxtapose, initially, conventional project evaluation procedures with those implied by the hypothesis of zero marginal productivity of labor. The conventional procedures use rates of discount of 3 to 5 percent and consider all labor costs as true social costs. The zero marginal productivity of labor hypothesis, on the other hand, appears to require, for India, the use of a rate of discount well above 30 percent per annum, and would consider no labor costs as true social costs. These two sets of criteria have vastly different implications as to which projects should be accepted and which rejected.

The evidence presented in this paper, however, leads to the rejection of both of the extreme positions just outlined. Even if one follows convention in counting all wages as social costs, the data on India suggest that the social rate of return to capital is near 13 percent rather than 3–5 percent. On the other hand, the data lead to the rejection of the hypothesis underlying a zero shadow wage, and suggest that the maximum plausible allowance for an excess of private over social cost of labor would, for Indian industry, be something like 20 percent of the wage bill. When this allowance is made in calculating the social rate of return to capital in Indian industry, the resulting estimate is somewhat over 17 percent per annum, but far below the over-30 percent figure that was implied by the hypothesis of a zero shadow wage. With the narrowing of the range of uncertainty with respect to the discount rate from 3–30 percent to 13–17 percent, one obtains a great reduction in the degree of divergence of the implications of alternative criteria within the uncertain range. Thus, even though, for lack of adequately precise data, we may have to live with some uncertainty with respect to the relationships between actual and shadow wages for some time to come, this uncertainty does not appear to be so great as to stand in the way of a very substantial improvement of present project evaluation criteria.

Appendix

A Note on the Social Cost of Labor Used in Investment Projects

Where, in this paper, we have taken the shadow wage to be different from the actual wage, we have permitted this assumption to be reflected in a reallocation of the value added produced by a project, once in operation. We have not permitted it to be reflected in the capital cost of the investment itself. Thus, a zero shadow wage for textile operatives led to an upward adjustment of the social return to capital in the textile industry, but it did not lead to a downward adjustment of the value of the capital employed in the textile industry, to reflect the fact that some labor was used in the making of that capital equipment. How can this apparent asymmetry of treatment be justified?

The answer lies in the fact that the investible surplus of the Indian economy (represented by both private and public savings) is for various reasons, social and political as well as economic, rather stringently limited. Assume, for simplicity, that in a given period it is strictly given. Then the question of promoting maximal growth amounts to getting the most out of a given sum of available savings. The investible funds are just as much "spent" when they are paid out for labor services as when they are paid out for machinery or for capital services. Maximizing the rate of growth from a given investible surplus therefore entails getting the most per rupee of investible funds paid out, regardless of whether the payment is made for the services of labor or for those of capital. Thus, if one accepts the commonly-held (and I believe correct) view that the investible surplus in India is very hard to expand, and if one is interested in maximizing the net increment to output that can be generated by this surplus, one cannot escape valuing capital expenditures at, so to speak, their full cash cost, as we have done in this paper.

Questions for discussion and analysis pertaining to this article may be found at the end of Article 16.

Simon Kuznets †

12. NOTES ON THE TAKE-OFF *

Requirements for a Theory of Stages

The sequence of stages, of which the take-off is one, is offered by Professor W. W. Rostow as a scheme for viewing and interpreting modern economic development. It is, therefore, a gloss on the major distinction between modern and nonmodern (traditional) types of growth; I regret that in offering his scheme, Professor Rostow does not spell out the characteristics inherent in modern economic growth that distinguish it from the traditional and other types. Many come easily to mind: a high and sustained rate of increase in real product per capita, accompanied usually by a high and sustained rate of increase in population; major shifts in the industrial structure of product and labor force, and in the location of the population, commonly referred to as industrialization and urbanization; changes in the organizational units under whose auspices and guidance economic activity takes place; a rise in the proportion of capital formation to national product; shifts in the structure of consumer expenditures, accompanying urbanization and higher income per capita; changes in the character and magnitudes of international economic flows; and others could be added. Underlying all this are the increasing stock of useful knowledge derived from modern science and the capacity of society, under the spur of modern ideology, to evolve institutions which permit the exploitation of the growth potential provided by that increasing stock of knowledge.

The distinction between modern economic growth and other types, and our concentration on the former, are justified by a basic working assumption that we can study the characteristics of such growth most effectively if it is not merged with the evolution of economics before the eighteenth century or with the growth of those parts of the world that have not yet begun to tap the

†Simon Kuznets, Professor of Economics, Harvard University.
*From *The Economics of Take-Off in Sustained Growth,* Proceedings of the Conference of the International Economic Association (London: Macmillan & Co., 1963); reprinted in Simon Kuznets, *Economic Growth and Structure* (New York: W. W. Norton & Co. Inc., 1965), pp. 213–235. Reprinted by permission of the publisher and the author.

sources of modern technology. If we assume that modern economic growth is different from other types and affected by new and different factors, we would only confuse matters and face an impossible task in treating the growth of Germany in the second half of the nineteenth century and that of France in the thirteenth century, for example, as members of the same family of economic growth processes. In short, although allowing for historical continuity, we recognize modern economic growth as something quite new; and in order to observe it clearly, perceive its mechanism, and understand its driving forces, we must distinguish it from other types and study it by itself.

Distinguishing stages within modern economic growth is an operation similar to that which distinguishes modern from nonmodern economic growth, and the basic assumption that justifies the former parallels the one that justifies the latter. By claiming that stage *A* is distinct from stage *B*, we are saying that the characteristics commonly found in stage *A* are so distinct from those in stage *B* that it is methodologically improper to treat the two indiscriminately. Stages within an economic epoch or some such general construct, like the constructs themselves, are a classificatory device, governed by the hypothesis that the generality of observation and invariance of analytical relations secured thereby are maximized.

An adequate test of such a hypothesis comes at the end, not at the beginning, of a long period of study. But this does not mean that we need take seriously every suggestion of stages or other dividing lines within the sequence of modern economic growth, particularly if we recognize the major differences between it and nonmodern growth. For if these differences are recognized, and the cumulative character of growth is a matter of definition, it is all too easy to suggest stages. Since modern economic growth presumably has roots in the past, a nonmodern economy stage and a stage of preparation are readily suggested, and we can divide the latter into several phases: initial preparatory phase, middle preparatory phase, and final preparatory phase. Then, since, again by definition, modern economic growth is not attained in a few years, we can discuss the early or emergence period, the middle stage, maturity (biological analogy), postmaturity, and so on. The very ease with which separate segments can be distinguished in the historical movement from nonmodern economic growth and within the long span of the latter should warn us that any sequence of stages, even if offered only as a suggestive, not a substantive, scheme must meet some minimum requirements.

(1.) A specific stage must display empirically testable characteristics, common to all or to an important group of units experiencing modern economic growth. This means the specification of modern economic growth, identification of the units that have manifested such growth, and establishment of the empirically testable characteristics claimed to be common to these units at the given stage.

(2.) The characteristics of a specific stage must be distinctive in that, not necessarily singly but in combination, they are unique to that stage. Mere precedence (or succession) in time does not suffice: given the unidirectional character of growth (by definition) any period is characterized by larger economic magnitudes than earlier ones and by the structural shifts that accompany such larger magnitudes (particularly a rise in per capita income). Stages are presumably something more than successive ordinates in the steadily climbing curve of growth. They are segments of that curve with properties so distinct that separate study of each segment seems warranted.

(3.) The analytical relation to the preceding stage must be indicated. This involves more than saying that the preceding stage is one of preparation for the given stage. More specifically, we need to identify (again in empirically testable terms) the major processes in the preceding stage that terminate it, and, with the usual qualifications for exogenous factors, make the next (our given) stage highly probable. Optimally, this would permit us to diagnose the preceding stage *before* the given stage is upon us, and thus would impart predictive value to the whole sequence. But even short of this aim, it means specifying the minimum that must happen in the preceding stage to allow the given stage to emerge.

(4.) The analytical relation to the succeeding stage must be indicated. Here, too, a clear notion (again in empirically testable terms) must be given of the occurrences in the given stage that bring it to a close, aside from mere passage of time. Optimally, such knowledge would permit us to predict, *before* the given stage is finished, how long it still has to run. But even short of such precision, we should know the essentials that occur during a given stage to bring about its end and clear the ground for the next stage.

(5.) These four requirements relate to the common and distinctive characteristics of a specific stage in an analytical (and chronological) sequence that links successive stages. However, these common and distinctive characteristics may differ among important groups of units undergoing modern economic growth. Consequently, the fifth requirement is for a delineation of the universe for which the generality of common and distinctive characteristics is claimed, and for which the analytical relations of a given stage with the preceding and succeeding ones are being formulated.

Characteristics of the Take-Off

Against the background of the requirements just stated, we may consider Professor Rostow's discussion of the common and distinctive characteristics of the take-off stage and the relations between it and the contiguous stages.

The three common characteristics explicitly listed by Professor Rostow are:

> (1.) a rise in the rate of productive investment from (say) 5 percent or less to over 10 percent of national income (or net national product); (2.) the development of one or more substantial manufacturing sectors with a high rate of growth; (3.) the existence or quick emergence of a political,

social and institutional framework which exploits the impulses to expansion in the modern sector and the potential external economy effects of the take-off and gives to growth an ongoing character.[1]

To these we add three more characteristics implicit or explicit in Professor Rostow's discussion.

(4.) A marked rise in the rate of growth of national income (or net national product) and of per capita income, in constant prices. This follows directly from the rise in the proportion of investment listed under (1.), and Professor Rostow's discussion of the "Prima Facie Case" (Rostow I, p. 34), which assumes no rise in the marginal capital-output ratio. The rate of growth of real income per capita rises from close to zero to about 2 percent per year.

(5.) The leading sectors in the take-off have ranged historically "from cotton textiles, through heavy-industry complexes based on railroads and military end-products, to timber, pulp, dairy products and finally a wide variety of consumer goods" (Rostow I, p. 46). But these sectors were leading because of the enlarged demand for their products brought about by appropriate transfers of income, capital imports, etc.; because of their new production functions; because of their profitability and inducement to entrepreneurs to plow back profits; and because of the expansion and technical transformation in other parts of the economy effected by their expansion.

(6.) The take-off is a relatively short period: in many of the countries identified by Professor Rostow it is appreciably less than thirty years and in most of these it is little more than twenty.

How distinctive are these characteristics? Do they occur in combination only in the take-off stage and in no other stage, particularly the preceding transition, or pre-conditions, stage and the succeeding self-sustained growth, or drive to maturity stage? Professor Rostow is not explicit on this point. Presumably a rise in the investment proportion from 5 to 10 percent or more does not occur in the transition stage. Yet much of what Professor Rostow would attribute to the take-off has already occurred in the pre-conditions stage.[2] Thus, the agricultural revolution assigned to the pre-conditions stage "must supply expanded food, expanded markets, and an expanded supply of loanable funds to the modern sector" (Rostow II, p. 24); much of social overhead capital is already invested in transport and other outlays in the pre-conditions stage (Rostow II, p. 24); and, in general, "the essence of the transition can be described legitimately as a rise in the rate of investment to a level which regularly, substantially and perceptibly outstrips population growth" (Rostow II, p. 21). In short, one wonders whether the three specifically stated characteristics of take-off could not be found in the pre-conditions stage unless explicit qualifications are attached: for example, the investment proportion in

---

[1]W. W. Rostow, "The Take-Off into Self-Sustained Growth," *The Economic Journal*, LXVI, 261 (March, 1956), p. 32. Referred to henceforth as Rostow I.

[2]W. W. Rostow, *The Stages of Economic Growth* (Cambridge, Mass.: Harvard University Press, 1960), Ch. 3, pp. 17-35. Referred to henceforth as Rostow II.

that earlier stage must stay below 5 percent; the marked agricultural revolution does not immediately call for, and in fact is possible without, a contemporaneous rapid growth in some manufacturing sector; and investment in overhead capital in transport and other areas is not necessarily accompanied by a rapid growth of one or more modern manufacturing sectors. Finally, one should note that characteristic (3.) of the take-off mentions both the *existence* and the *quick emergence* of the political, social, and institutional framework favorable to exploiting "the impulses to expansion in the modern sector" as admissible alternatives. But if that framework already exists at the beginning of the take-off, its emergence must be assigned to the pre-conditions stage. How then does the latter differ from the take-off in which the framework emerges?

The line of division between the take-off and the following stage of self-sustained growth or drive to maturity is also blurred. Presumably the later stage is marked by the existence of the proper social and institutional framework, which also exists during the take-off. Presumably this later stage also witnesses the rapid growth of one or more modern manufacturing sectors. Indeed, the only characteristics that are distinctly appropriate to the take-off and not to the next stage are the rise in the rate of productive investment to over 10 percent of national income and the implicit rise in the rate of growth of total and per capita income. But are we to assume that both the rate of investment and the rate of growth of product (total and per capita) level off at the high values attained at the end of the take-off stage? And is it this cessation of the rise in the rate of investment and in the rate of growth that terminates the take-off stage? No explicit statement is made by Professor Rostow; Chapter 5 in Rostow II contains a list of dates when "maturity" was reached in a number of countries but there is little discussion of what took place between the end of the take-off stage and the end of the next stage.

Given this fuzziness in delimiting the take-off stage and in formulating its distinctive characteristics, and given the distinctiveness only in the level of the rate of productive investment (and the implicit rate of growth), there is no solid ground upon which to discuss Professor Rostow's view of the analytical relation between the take-off stage and the preceding and succeeding stages. At any rate, the brief comments that can be made within the scope of this paper will follow the review of the empirical evidence.

To what universe do the common characteristics claimed for the take-off period apply? In his most recent presentation, Professor Rostow distinguishes the "general" case of a traditional society from that of the small group of nations (the United States, Australia, New Zealand, Canada, and "perhaps a few others") "born free" (Rostow II, pp. 6 and 17-18). The distinction is particularly important in the analysis of the pre-conditions stage, and Professor Rostow does not indicate whether the characteristics of the take-off stage in the originally traditional societies are different from those in the countries "born free." The distinction made in the discussion of pre-conditions is not repeated in the discussion of the take-off, unless the qualification about the rates of investment higher than 5 percent in some countries (Canada and Argentina) before the take-off stage, necessitated by heavy overhead social capital needs (see Rostow II, p. 8) can be interpreted as such. But this qualification does not stress the distinction between traditional and free-born countries: overhead social capital needs were presumably heavy in Russia and for that matter, on a relative scale, in Switzerland. We may therefore infer that Professor Rostow, who includes the dates of the take-off period for both types of economy in the same list, assumes that the characteristics of the take-off are broadly the same for all countries undergoing modern economic growth.

Empirical Evidence on the Take-Off

In dealing with the empirical evidence on the take-off, I am impeded by three difficulties. First, much of the specific evidence on the take-off period will presumably be presented in the individual country papers, and I am neither competent to assemble it nor eager to duplicate it. Second, quantitative evidence, and much of it must be quantitative, is not available for some of the take-off periods suggested by Professor Rostow. Third, as already indicated, Professor Rostow's discussion does not yield a description of take-off characteristics sufficiently specific to define the relevant empirical evidence.

Thus, I do not know what "a political, social and institutional framework which exploits the impulses to expansion in the modern sector, etc." is; or how to identify such a framework except by hindsight and conjecture; or how to specify the empirical evidence needed to ascertain whether such a framework is in "existence or in quick emergence." It seems to me that Professor Rostow, in the passage cited, defines these social phenomena as a complex that produces the effect he wishes to explain, and then treats this definition as if it were a meaningful identification.

It is easier to define the characteristic that specifies "the development of one or more substantial manufacturing sectors with a high rate of growth" once high is explained. But a review of empirical evidence on this point holds little interest if I am correct in assuming that the major distinctive characteristic of the take-off is a marked rise in the rate of growth of per capita and hence of total income. If the rate of growth does accelerate, some sectors are bound to grow more rapidly than others, as has been demonstrated in Arthur F. Burns' and my own work on production trends, partly in response to the differential impact of technological opportunities (including raw material supplies) and partly in response to the different income elasticities of the demand for various goods. Under these conditions, one or more manufacturing sectors, and one or more sectors of agriculture, transportation, services, etc. are bound to show high rates of growth. The pertinent question is why manufacturing and not agriculture, transport, or any other rapidly growing industry should be specified as the leading sector.

In considering this question, we must keep in mind the two essentials of a leading sector. First, sector A leads, if it moves independently of sectors B, C, D, etc., within the country but under the impact of factors which for the given national economy may be considered autonomous. These may be technological changes embodying some new inventions; changes in the resource base resulting from new discoveries; changes in foreign demand, which are external to the given economy; and breaks in social structure (political revolution, agrarian reform, and the like), which could be viewed as changes exogenous to economic processes proper. The point to be noted is that the autonomous nature of this characteristic, relative to the given national economy, rests upon the stimulus, not upon the response. The response may reflect many other factors besides the stimulus which are part and parcel of the economy and society.

This brings us to the second essential of a leading sector, the magnitude of its effects, or more specifically, the magnitude of its contribution to a country's economic growth. Sector A may be responding to an autonomous stimulus, but unless its contribution to the country's economic growth is substantial, it does not lead the country's economic growth, no matter how high its own rate of growth. After all, a thousandfold rise in the production of paper napkins over a decade does not make it a leading industry.

The lower limit to a significant contribution can be set only in terms of empirical analysis. We must distinguish the direct contribution to the growth of the economy, total and per capita, of sector A — the product of its weight in the economy and its percentage rate of growth — from its indirect contribution, through its backward and forward linkages with sectors B, C, D, etc.; and from its contribution, again indirect, through its effects on social structure and qualities of the population (e.g., urbanization, organizational form of the economic unit, education, and the like), which in turn affect a country's economic growth in a variety of ways. The magnitude and particularly the timing of these direct and indirect effects differ. A sector's direct and indirect contributions in a given period may be quite small, although its own rate of growth is high and the novelty of its technology makes it the cynosure of the eyes of its contemporaries and of latter-day historians; whereas in a later period its contributions may be far greater, although its rate of growth has declined and the bloom of its novelty faded.

To establish these leadership characteristics of sectors — the autonomous character of the impulse and the timing and magnitude of their direct and indirect contributions to a country's economic growth — involves intensive study, not only of the leading sectors but also of those affected by them, extending into the quantitative framework of the whole economy. Leadership of sectors, or any other element in the acceleration of the rate of growth, can be established only by careful analysis of the particular circumstances preceding and during the period of acceleration, country by country, and by the application of statistical, theoretical, and other tools to the historical evidence.

This type of analysis is lacking in Professor Rostow's discussion and is beyond my powers here.

I therefore turn to the purely statistical characteristics claimed for the take-off stage; but even here I find it difficult to specify Professor Rostow's meaning. I assume from the context that "rate of productive investment" refers to *net,* rather than *gross,* capital formation, and that the adjective "productive" means the inclusion of all components of the presently accepted definition of capital formation. But does he mean net *domestic* capital formation, that is, all net additions to the stock of reproducible material capital within the country, whether financed by domestic savings or by capital imports (and excluding capital exports, when such occur), or net *national* capital formation (usually referred to as net capital formation without further qualification), that is, only net additions to reproducible stock within the country financed by domestic savings plus capital exports, if any? Professor Rostow emphasizes changes within the country (under characteristic (3.) mentioned earlier) that should help mobilize domestic savings, and much of his discussion is in terms of maximizing domestic savings, that is, in terms of the net national capital formation proportion to national income. This emphasis is corroborated by the use of national income as denominator, since the proper denominator for net domestic capital formation is net domestic product (although for most countries the two totals are numerically close). Yet in the analysis of capital-output relations, the appropriate ratio, particularly for a capital importing country, is that of net domestic capital formation to net domestic product. Professor Rostow cites long-term data for Sweden and Canada, and for one he uses the domestic capital formation proportion and for the other the national capital formation proportion. There is the further question whether the ratios of capital formation to national product should be based on totals in current or in constant prices: the former are more appropriate to the view of the proportion as a savings rate, the latter to the view of the proportion as affecting output.

Before presenting the statistical results, I shall attempt to resolve these doubts and define the measures more precisely. For a capital-exporting country we may use the ratio net national capital formation to net national product; for a capital-importing country we should use both net national and net domestic capital formation, as proportions of net national and net domestic product, respectively. Further, we use ratios based on current price totals, partly because the available price indexes are crude and partly because in most cases the differences in long-term movement between the capital formation proportions based on current and on constant price totals are not appreciable. We can then ask whether in the periods of take-off dated by Professor Rostow the rises in these capital formation proportions are of the magnitude he suggests. I shall deal here with four countries, all included in Professor Rostow's "general" category: Great Britain, Germany, Sweden, and Japan.

Four Countries

For Great Britain, Phyllis Deane and W. A. Cole have recently completed a major study. Their results indicate a net national capital formation proportion of about 6.5 percent for England and Wales in 1770–1880, a period close to Professor Rostow's dates of 1783–1802, compared with about 5 percent indicated by Gregory King at the end of the eighteenth century. The Deane-Cole estimates, which thenceforth apply to the United Kingdom, suggest a climb to about 9 percent for the period from the 1820's to the 1850's, and a further rise to a pre-World War I peak of 14 percent in 1905–14. The picture is thus one of a slow and relatively steady, rather than sudden and rapid, acceleration. The rate of growth of national income (in constant prices) follows the same general pattern. For England and Wales, the annual rate of growth for 1770–1800 is 1.5 percent, compared with 0.9 percent for 1740–70 and 0.3 percent for 1700–40. Then the rate of growth for the United Kingdom rises to well over 2.5 percent per year in the last quarter of the nineteenth century.

For Germany (the territory of the German Reich in 1913) we have the studies by Professor Walther Hoffmann of net capital formation and by Professors Hoffmann and J. Heinz Müller of national income for the period back to 1851. For 1850–73, the period dated by Professor Rostow as the take-off, we have the following proportions of net capital formation to national income (in current market prices): about 8.5 percent for the 1850's, 9.75 percent for the 1860's, 13.5 percent for the 1870's. The rise is appreciable, but is due in part to the favorable business cycle of the 1870's, and in the 1880's the net capital formation proportion is still below 14 percent. Then the proportion rises to a peak of 16.5 percent in 1901–13. Here the net capital formation proportion increases only about 60 percent in the twenty-odd years dated as the take-off, and doubles only after a steady and sustained climb for about six decades. This steady rise in the net capital formation proportion is accompanied by a relatively stable rate of growth of net national product: about 2.5 percent per year for the entire period, somewhat more in the decades from 1851 to 1880, and somewhat less in the decades from 1880 to 1913.

For Sweden the most recent estimates, by Dr. Osten Johansson, currently at the University of Stockholm, are a revision of the older series which I used in my earlier paper and which Professor Rostow cites in his discussion. The major correction was for the understatement of construction in the early decades.

The directly available estimates yield a *gross* domestic capital formation proportion (to gross domestic product) of somewhat over 9 percent in 1861–70. On the assumption of a ratio of capital consumption to gross domestic capital formation of about 0.4, the net domestic capital formation proportion is almost 6 percent. The gross domestic capital formation proportion climbs, somewhat unsteadily, to 13.5 percent in 1901–10, and the implied net capital formation proportion to over 8 percent. The rise continues to reach a peak in

1941 — 50 of 21 percent gross, and roughly 13 percent net. Thus, the net domestic capital formation proportion rises gradually, and doubles only after almost eight decades, not just two or three.

The *national* capital formation proportions present about the same picture, except that the steady climb begins after the 1880's. From an average of about 9.5 percent in 1861–80, the gross capital formation proportion rises to 11 percent in 1891–1910, to over 14 percent in 1911–20, and to 20.5 percent in 1941–50. The corresponding net national capital formation proportion would be somewhat less than 6 percent in 1861–90, almost 7 percent in 1891–1910, and slightly over 12 percent in 1941–50.

The rate of growth of total product is also gradual. Although it ranges from 1.8 to 5.4 percent per year for decadal periods (the high rate being for 1941–50), the average for 1871–80 (Professor Rostow's take-off dates are 1868–90) is about 2.3 percent per year, compared with 3.2 percent for the 1860's and 3.4 percent for 1891–1910. The averages for the longer periods suggest a perceptible although gradual acceleration in the rate of growth, from 2.6 percent for 1861–90 to 2.9 percent for 1891–1920, to 3.8 percent for 1921–50.

For Japan, the recent and only acceptable estimates of capital formation (by Professor Henry Rosovsky of the University of California) begin in 1888 and therefore include only part of 1878–1900, the take-off period dated by Professor Rostow. The *gross* domestic capital formation proportion excluding military investments (which were large in Japan) was between 10 and 11 percent in 1888–97, and the gross national proportion was slightly higher. On the assumption that capital consumption was about 0.4 of gross domestic capital formation, the corresponding net capital formation proportions were between 6 and 7 percent, and there is no ground for assuming that they were significantly lower in the preceding decade. Subsequently, the domestic capital formation proportion fluctuated around the same level until World War I, and it was only after that war that it rose significantly, to between 16 and 17 percent on a gross basis and to between 10 and 11 percent on a net basis. The *national* capital formation proportion moved somewhat more erratically, with substantial capital imports in 1900–10, and 1920–30, but the broad secular trend was the same. Not until four or five decades later were the capital formation proportions twice their initial size.

There is no evidence of a perceptible acceleration in the rate of growth of either total or per capita income. From 1878 to 1902 the average rate of growth of total income was about 4.9 percent per year; from 1893 to 1917 it was 3.2 percent; from 1908 to 1932, 4.9 percent; from 1918 to 1942, 4.9 percent.[3] The average rate of growth of income per member of the gainfully occupied population for the same four long periods was: 1878–1902, 3.7 percent per year; 1893–1917, 2.6 percent; 1908–32, 4.3 percent; 1918–42, 4.0 percent.

---

[3]These and the following rates are from Kazushi Ohkawa *et al., The Growth Rate of the Japanese Economy since 1878* (Tokyo: 1957), Table 6, p. 21 and Table 7, p. 24.

A Summary for Twelve Countries

Two or three other countries for which Professor Rostow suggests tentative dates for the take-off period could be added. But the presentation of all the statistical evidence, even for a few countries, would far transcend the limits of this paper, and summaries like those above are barely adequate. We now have long-term records on capital formation and national product for twelve countries, excluding those in the Communist bloc, and a detailed discussion of these is now available.[4] Here I only summarize the evidence for the few countries in Professor Rostow's list and consider its bearing on his assumptions concerning the movement of the capital-investment proportions and the implicit movement of total product during what he defines as the take-off period. Unfortunately, I do not now have adequate estimates for France, Belgium, and Russia, additional countries in Professor Rostow's list.

In a number of countries, the net capital formation proportions, particularly domestic, are substantially higher than "5 percent or less" at the beginning of the take-off periods. This is certainly true of Germany; of the United States, where the estimates by Professor Robert Gallman for the 1840's and the 1850's suggest a gross domestic capital formation proportion of between 15 and 20 percent; of Canada where Dr. O. J. Firestone's estimates indicate gross domestic capital formation proportions of 15 percent in 1870, 15.5 percent in 1890, and 13.5 percent in 1900. Also, if net rates of 6 to 7 percent may be considered significantly higher than those of "5 percent or less," this is true of Great Britain, Sweden, and Japan.

In no case does the net domestic capital formation proportion even approach twice its initial size in the two or three decades dated as the take-off; and although the movements of the net *national* capital formation proportions are more erratic, they too fall far short of doubling during the take-off periods.

There is no evidence to support the assumption of a marginal net domestic (or national) capital-output ratio of 3.5 to 1. The ratio is neither the same for different countries nor stable over time. For the United Kingdom, the marginal net national capital-output ratio at the beginning of the nineteenth century was about 3 (it was about 4 for England and Wales in 1770–1800, if the crude data can be trusted). In Germany in the 1850's the net national capital-output ratio was between 3 and 3.5; in Sweden in 1881–90, on a *gross* basis, the ratio was between 3 and 4, but on a net basis it would have been between 2 and 3.5; in Japan in 1888–97, the gross domestic capital-output ratio was about 3, and the net somewhat less than 2. Moreover, in many countries the the net capital-output ratios show a marked trend over time. For example, in

---

[4]See "Quantitative Aspects of the Economic Growth of Nations: VI. Long-Term Trends in Capital Formation Proportions," *Economic Development and Cultural Change,* IX, 4, Part II (July, 1961). Paper V, dealing with the international comparison of capital formation proportions for recent, post-World War II years, appeared in *ibid.,* VIII, 4, Part II (July, 1960). Since the detailed statistical data and sources are cited in these two papers, they will not be repeated here.

the United Kingdom, the marginal net national capital-output ratio, which was 3 in the first part of the nineteenth century, rose to almost 6 in the period from 1880–89 to 1910–13; and even the net *domestic* capital-output ratio rose from about 3 before the middle of the nineteenth century to 3.7 in the three decades before World War I. The net national capital-output ratio for Germany rose from between 3 and 3.5 in the 1850's to about 5.5 for the decades from 1891 to 1913.

In no case do we find during the take-off periods the acceleration in the rate of growth of national product implied in Professor Rostow's assumptions of a doubling (or more) in the net capital formation proportion and of a constant marginal capital-output ratio. The capital formation proportions, if they rise, climb at a sustained rate and for a much longer period than the two or three decades of take-off. Rates of growth of total product, if they show any long-term acceleration (and those for only a few countries do within the period beginning with the take-off stage) increase slowly, and certainly over a longer period than the short span of the take-off.

The summary above relates to a few countries, none of which is in the Communist bloc, and is based upon crude estimates. But the data are firm enough to suggest rough orders of magnitude, and they bear directly upon what seem to be the essential statistical characteristics of the take-off period as Professor Rostow identifies them. Unless I have completely misunderstood Professor Rostow's definition of take-off and its statistical characteristics, I can only conclude that the available evidence lends no support to his suggestions.

The Distinctiveness and Generality of the Take-Off Stage

The failure of aggregative data to reveal the characteristics claimed by Professor Rostow as typical of the take-off stage, at least in countries that did not experience the drastic and forced transformation associated with Communist revolutions, is disturbing. It casts serious doubt on the validity of the definition of the take-off as a general stage of modern economic growth, distinct from what Professor Rostow calls the pre-conditions, or transition, stage preceding it and the self-sustained-growth stage following it. The doubt is only reinforced by some more general questions concerning Professor Rostow's over-all scheme. These questions can be discussed under three heads: (1.) the meaning of pre-conditions; (2.) the effects of the widely diverse historical heritages of premodern economics on the characteristics of their transition to modern economic growth; (3.) the meaning of self-sustained growth.

The Pre-Conditions Stage

Professor Rostow treats the pre-conditions stage and much of the sequence as analogous to a mechanical, or more specifically, an aeronautical process, despite his several references to economic growth as essentially "biological." The picture suggested is that of the sequence involved in putting an airplane (or a glider) into flight. First there are the checking and fueling, which provide the pre-conditions, then there is the relatively brief take-off, when the driving force is accelerated to produce the upward movement, and finally there is the levelling-off into self-sustained flight. This analogy, perhaps unfair to Professor Rostow's stage sequence, is useful because it pinpoints the basic question in connection with the whole pre-conditions stage: can such pre-conditions be created without *at the same time* producing changes throughout the economy that, in and of themselves, initiate modern economic growth, that is, a higher rate of increase of total product, a higher rate of capital formation, growth of one or several modern productive sectors, and so on? To put it differently, is it realistic to talk of the pre-conditions created in one time span and of the initiation of modern economic growth in another span chronologically distinct?

The answer to this question depends upon the pre-conditions. Since modern developed economies make effective use of a wide variety of technical and social inventions, many of which date back to a time far earlier than the initiation of modern economic growth, pre-conditions whose creation is chronologically distinct from the early periods of modern economic growth can be found. Thus, many current commercial instruments, maritime laws, and monetary practices originated, in much the same form, long before the second half of the eighteenth century, which may be taken as the date of the beginning of modern economic growth. But for the pre-conditions that Professor Rostow emphasizes in his discussion (Rostow II, Ch. 3) — transformation of agriculture and overhead capital investments — the answer is, to my mind, quite different. I do not see how, particularly in the "general" traditional society not "born free," a major change in agricultural productivity that provides more food per capita and more savings can be achieved without a rapid growth of some manufacturing and other sectors not only to provide employment for the displaced agricultural population but also to supply the producer and consumer goods required by the higher agricultural productivity and by the people who share in its benefits. And the production relations associated with increased overhead capital investments should bring about similar concomitant changes. Indeed much of what Professor Rostow says in Chapter 4 about income shifts and income flows in the process of take-off (particularly about agricultural incomes in Rostow II, pp. 46–47) is equally relevant to the discussion of pre-conditions in his Chapter 3.

Perhaps by further specification one could distinguish clearly, and in chronological sequence, some phases of the agricultural revolution and of increased capital investments that precede the distinctive changes that can be established for the take-off stage, but I doubt that this is possible. For any significant transformation of agriculture in the crowded traditional societies and any marked rise in overhead capital investment are, to my mind, already part and parcel of modern economic growth; and, given the technological, economic, and social interrelations within the economy, they can hardly occur unless *accompanied* by the changes that Professor Rostow assigns to the take-off stage. In short, the case for separation between the rather vaguely defined pre-conditions stage and the apparently more sharply defined take-off stage presented by Professor Rostow seems to me extremely weak. And Professor Rostow's casual reference to the duration of the pre-conditions — "a long period up to a century or, conceivably, more" (Rostow I, p. 27) — does not make the case stronger.

Past History and the Nature of Transition

In his recent book, Professor Rostow treats traditional economy as a single stage in a sequence of five stages and, as already indicated, draws only one relevant distinction, that between the small group of nations "born free" and all others in the single category of traditional economies. Thus, the latter includes the Western European countries, whose civilization was in many ways the cradle of modern economic society and which, during the epoch of merchant capitalism, were on the "taking" side vis-à-vis the rest of the world. It also includes the old Asian countries with their different history and endowments, the African societies with their specific heritage and culture, and many countries in the Western Hemisphere which are not among the "free-born." The inclusion of all these countries in one group implies that the stages of pre-conditions and take-off in all of them are characterized by basically the same important features. And we disregard for the present a major question of the legitimacy of characterizing all premodern economies as a stage.

To say that this is a heroic oversimplification is not to condemn the scheme out of hand. After all, modern economic growth, when and where it occurs, does have distinctive characteristics, not merely by definition but because it draws upon a transnational stock of useful knowledge and of social invention and is powered by human views and desires that have many similar features the world over. Yet it is fair to argue that the stocks of knowledge and social inventions themselves change over time, and that the modern economic growth of different countries is a process of combining the different complexes of historical heritage with the common requirements of the modern "industrial system." The parameters of the combination are likely, therefore, to differ from country to country, depending upon their specific historical heritages, upon the time when they enter modern economic growth, and upon their relations with other countries, particularly those already developed. The proper analysis of the process of modern economic growth in individual countries requires, therefore, a far more meaningful typology of "traditionalism" (or, to use another term, "underdevelopment") than is provided by Professor Rostow. Nor can we disregard the timing of the process in relation to other countries, an aspect that plays such an important role in Professor Gerschenkron's intriguing hypothesis of the increasing "strain of backwardness" and the association between the degree of backwardness and the characteristics of the transition to modern economic growth.

The point is that it is in the *early phases* of a country's modern economic growth particularly that these distinct peculiarities of historical heritage, position in the sequence of spread of the industrial system, and relation to other already developed countries put their impress upon a country's growth. After 70 to 100 years of modern economic growth, one developed country would conceivably be similar in its characteristics to others despite differences in initial position. (Even this comment has limited validity: compare Japan today, after eight decades of rapid economic growth, with, say, Germany or France after a century of it.) However, in the early phase the differences in pattern of growth are likely to stand out most clearly, for at that point the diverse historical heritages have not yet been overlaid with the similarities imposed by sustained modern economic growth. And since the take-off stage, which to my mind overlaps with much of the pre-conditions stage, is an early phase of modern economic growth, the differences among countries in the parameters of the take-off are likely to be more notable than those in growth at later stages. An adequate stage theory or any other analytical scheme for studying economic growth, should point out not only the similarities but also the major differences, which reflect observable differences in historical antecedents, timing of entry into the process of modern economic growth, and other relevant factors. Professor Rostow's disregard of the major sources of differences in the early phases of modern economic growth among the developed "traditional" countries imposes severe limits on his claims to generality.

The Meaning of Self-Sustained Growth

The self-sustained growth that is supposed to occur in the stage following take-off is somewhat of a puzzle. Is it self-sustained in a sense in which it is *not* during the take-off and/or any earlier phase? If the reference is to the higher per capita income attained at the end of the take-off, which permits higher savings and capital formation proportions, which, in turn, permit higher rates of growth (assuming the marginal capital-output ratio is constant) — then one can argue that the same automatic mechanism operates during the take-off, once a significant increase in per capita income occurs, which presumably happens at the beginning of the take-off stage. If the reference is to the existence of favorable social institutions, these must also have existed through most of the take-off stage. Furthermore, many institutional changes are gradual, and if they have continually improved during take-off or earlier, their effects on the rate of growth should have been continuous. Consequently, since both income increases and institutional improvements abounded, it is difficult to accept the suggestion that growth was not self-sustained before the end of the take-off stage, but acquired that property only during the succeeding stage.

Obviously, the term is an analogy rather than a clearly specified characteristic, and for this reason alone it should be avoided. In one sense any growth is self-sustained: it means an irreversible rise to a higher level of economic performance that may facilitate the accumulation of reserves for further growth, whether these are funds for capital investment, greater efficiency of the labor force supplied with more consumption goods, economies of large scale, or other uses. In another sense any growth is self-limiting: the rise to a higher level may mean a reduction in incentive, pressure upon scarce irreproducible resources, and, perhaps most important, the strengthening of entrenched interests that may resist growth in competing sectors. And, indeed, the analysis of any widely and broadly conceived process of economic growth must reveal these and many more self-sustaining and self-limiting impacts of growth. If then Professor Rostow characterizes one stage of growth as self-sustained and others, by inference, as not, he must mean that in the latter stages the obstacles generated by past and current growth outweigh the self-sustaining impacts, whereas in the former stage the self-sustaining impacts outweigh the self-limiting ones. Obviously, both sets of impacts need documentation, both need to be weighed in terms of empirical evidence, far more than Professor Rostow provides in his casual characterization. Given the two sets of impacts of economic growth, the outcome is uncertain, and the process can never be *purely* self-sustained since it always generates *some* self-limiting effects. In this sense, economic growth is always a struggle; it is misleading to convey an impression of easy automaticity, a kind of soaring euphoria of self-sustained flight to higher economic levels.

Concluding Comments

The gist of our discussion can be given in a few brief propositions.

(1.) Leadership of a sector depends upon the origin of its growth in an autonomous impulse, not in response to other sectors in the country, and upon the magnitude of its direct and indirect contributions to the country's economic growth. The autonomous impulse and the various types of contribution to growth differ in timing, and the identification and chronology of leading sectors requires specification and evidence lacking in Professor Rostow's discussion.

(2.) The doubling of capital investment proportions and the implicit sharp acceleration in the rate of growth of national product, claimed by Professor Rostow as characterizing his take-off periods, are not confirmed by the statistical evidence for those countries on his list for which we have data.

(3.) There is no clear distinction between the pre-conditions and the take-off stages. On the contrary, given the pre-conditions emphasized by Professor Rostow — transformation of agriculture and overhead capital investments — there is a *prima facie* case for expecting the pre-conditions and the take-off stages to overlap.

(4.) The analysis of the take-off and pre-conditions stages neglects the effect of historical heritage, time of entry into the process of modern economic growth, degree of backwardness, and other relevant factors on the characteristics of the early phases of modern economic growth in the different traditional countries.

(5.) The concept (and stage) of self-sustained growth is a misleading oversimplification. No growth is purely self-sustaining or purely self-limiting. The characterization of one stage of growth as self-sustained, and of others, by implication, as lacking that property, requires substantive evidence not provided in Professor Rostow's discussion.

A few comments may help to put these conclusions into proper perspective.

First, the evidence used to test Professor Rostow's scheme is not conclusive. Some non-Communist countries for which we have no data may have experienced a period of growth conforming with Professor Rostow's take-off stage. Also, his scheme may fit the Communist "take-offs," but my knowledge of them is inadequate for checking. All that is claimed here is that aggregative data for several countries do not support Professor Rostow's distinction and characterization of the take-off stage. On the other hand, the fact that the evidence is confined to aggregative data does not limit their bearing. Economic growth is an aggregative process; sectoral changes are interrelated with aggregative changes, and can be properly weighed only after they have been incorporated into the aggregative framework; and the absence of required aggregative changes severely limits the likelihood of the implicit strategic sectoral changes.

Second, although we concentrated on the take-off stage, and the two contiguous stages — pre-conditions and self-sustained growth — much of what was said applies by inference to other stages in Professor Rostow's scheme. Moreover, the characterization of the traditional economy as a stage raises numerous questions. But an explicit discussion of the rest of the scheme would take us too far afield.

Third, my disagreement with Professor Rostow is *not* on the value and legitimacy of an attempt to suggest some pattern of order in the modern economic growth experience of different countries. On the contrary, I fully share what I take to be his view on the need to go beyond qualitative and quantitative description to the use of the evidence for a large number of countries and long periods, in combination with analytical tools and imaginative hypothesis, to suggest and explain not only some common patterns but also, I would add, the major deviations from them. However, for reasons indicated above, I disagree with the sequence of stages he suggests.

If we cannot accept Professor Rostow's sequence of stages, particularly his notion of a distinct and commonly found take-off stage, what are we left with?

Let us begin by agreeing that modern economic growth displays certain observable and measurable characteristics which in combination are distinctive to it, that is, were not evident in earlier economic epochs; and that these characteristics can, in principle, be established with the help of quantitative and other data whenever such growth occurs. What these characteristics are is a matter for discussion; but I believe that agreement could easily be reached on some of them, for example, those relating to rates of growth of national product, total and per capita, and to structural shifts that commonly accompany them. Let us assume for purposes of illustration that such growth requires a minimum rise in per capita income sustained over a period of at least two or three decades, a minimum shift away from agriculture, and any other identifiable indispensable components of modern economic growth that we may specify.

With this specification of modern economic growth, it becomes possible, given the data, to place its beginning in the various countries in which it occurred. The date of inception need not be a year, or even a quinquennium; it may be a band of some width, but still narrow enough to permit us to say that the two or three decades following it are the early phases of modern economic growth and the two or three decades before it are those directly preceding the beginning of modern economic growth — without missing much in between. If, then, we consider it important to study only the early decades of modern economic growth, those immediately preceding it, or both, in the hope of establishing characteristics and relations that would permit us to construct an adequate theoretical scheme, we may want to call the first two or three decades following the initiation of modern economic growth the "early growth phase" and the two or three decades preceding it the "late premodern phase."

Obviously, the two or three decades are only illustrative, and the length of the period may vary from country to country: the phase selected for concentrated study would have to be defined in terms of some reasonably realistic preliminary notions concerning the length of time during which the distinctive characteristics of early growth persist or during which the immediate antecedents must be studied. The firm point in this approach is the feasibility of dating the beginning of modern economic growth by some "hard" data, relating to one or several characteristics inherent in modern economic growth. In doing this, all that we specify is the *early* phase of the segment of the long record of modern economic growth on which we wish to concentrate. The termination of the period is then to be set on the basis of any substantive hypotheses concerning the distinctive characteristics of the early phase, although one would assume that since the span of modern economic growth in most countries is not much over a hundred years, there are narrow limits to the length of the early growth phase that an economist *of today* can set.

The term "early phase" of modern growth is far less appealing than "takeoff": it does not carry the suggestive connotation of the latter. And the same is true of "late premodern period" compared with "pre-conditions," and of "middle growth period" compared with "self-sustained growth." But the appealing terms employing mechanical or biological metaphors carry the danger of misleading us into believing that the suggested connotations are relevant to observable reality. It is my conviction that at the present stage of our knowledge (and ignorance), it is the better part of valor to link the constraining influence of phase distinction to the bare lines of observable and measurable growth processes: and to concentrate discussion on the early decades of modern economic growth in those countries for which we can identify its beginning, with excursions into the premodern growth past and the post-early decades of modern growth when they seem warranted.

Questions for discussion and analysis pertaining to this article may be found at the end of Article 16.

Hla Myint †

13. THE DEMAND APPROACH TO ECONOMIC DEVELOPMENT*

Most of the thinking on the underdeveloped countries is concerned with the *supply* side of their problem: with their lack of capital, technical knowledge and entrepreneurship. Thus, it is generally accepted (1.) that, to make up for the lack of private entrepreneurs in these countries, their governments should undertake overall economic development plans; (2.) that outside capital and technical aid should be injected into these countries in sufficiently large amounts to jerk them out of their underdevelopment equilibrium; and (3.) that these large-scale investment programs should be planned on the principle of "Balanced Growth." Except for the criticism of a few laissez-faire minded economists, this may be fairly described as "the new orthodoxy" in the subject. Professor Albert O. Hirschman's book on *The Strategy of Economic Development*[1] is a stimulating and instructive reaction against all this. But unlike the laissez-faire economists he does not call for a lessening of state interference but rather for a different type of state interference. In the place of an overall development plan on all fronts based on the doctrine of balanced growth, he advocates a policy of starting from certain strategic sectors of the economy and inducing *unbalanced* growth through deliberately engineered pressures of excess demand and bottlenecks. Thus, his Demand Approach stands out in sharp contrast with the usual Supply Approach to economic development. In section I of this paper, we shall summarize some of his arguments, and in section II we shall show where they have been vitiated by his excessive reaction against orthodoxy and reliance on the purely Demand Approach.

I

Hirschman starts from the position that most underdeveloped countries possess a considerable amount of unused resources of all kinds: underemployed

†Hla Myint, Senior Lecturer in Economic Development of Underdeveloped Countries, Oxford University.

*From *Review of Economic Studies,* Vol. 27 (February, 1960), pp. 124–132. Reprinted by permission of the publisher and the author.

[1]Editor's note: future page references are to this edition of Hirschman's book, *The Strategy of Economic Development* (New Haven: Yale University Press, 1958).

agricultural labour, misdirected entrepreneurship and potential saving capacity frittered away in hoarding and conspicuous consumption — not to mention the modern industrial techniques that are waiting to be transferred from the advanced countries. Moreover, once the development process gets started it will set into motion powerful "feed-back" mechanisms which will elicit further supplies of the required resources. He therefore maintains that the problem of economic development should not be approached in terms of a "missing component" such as capital, technical knowledge and entrepreneurship. Rather it would be approached in terms of an overall "binding agent" which will bring together and make use of these scattered and unused resources. The creation of this "binding agent" according to Hirschman is not a matter of physical shortage of any type of resources, not even entrepreneurship. It essentially consists in breaking down the psychological and sociological factors which are inhibiting the underdeveloped countries' will and ability to mobilize their unused resources (pp. 6–7). But these factors creating resistance to economic change are, however, more complicated than suggested by the usual "Sociological" explanation of economic backwardness, such as the dead-weight of tradition and customs suppressing individual initiative, lack of a "protestant ethic," etc. Rather they are made up of contradictory desires resulting from an odd mixture of an excessive enthusiasm for economic development and exaggerated expectations from modern technology on the one hand, and an almost sub-conscious resistance to the necessary changes amounting to a creation of artificial obstacles on the other (pp. 138–139; 185–186). Nor is it always true to say that the economic development of the underdeveloped countries is inhibited by an excessive group-mindedness. People living in a stagnant society where the total social product has long been stationary may get into the habit of thinking that individual improvement can take place only at the expense of somebody else and that therefore no economic change should be permitted unless it benefits every member of society equally and at the same time. But the same stagnant conditions may equally give rise to the opposite reaction of excessive individualism and the habit of thinking that it is not possible to move and improve society as a whole so that the best thing is to cut oneself adrift from the dead weight of society and ruthlessly pursue selfish and short-term gains. Now Hirschman believes that this excessive individualism is as much responsible for inhibiting economic growth in underdeveloped countries as excessive group-mindedness. Thus, excessive individualism is responsible for typical misdirection of entrepreneurial ability in these countries such as excessive liquidity preference and hoarding, undue preference for speculative and trading ability and "wholesale and hasty abandonment of ongoing ventures and forms of production in favor of some new 'get rich quickly' activity" (p. 20). The creation of a favourable mental climate for economic development is therefore not merely a matter of removing obstacles to individual enterprise. It must aim at resolving the contradictory psychological drives into a more harmonious mixture of group- and individual-minded attitudes to change so that the individual can feel that he is advancing at his own rate in an economically expanding framework while society can feel that individual gains are not necessarily predatory but may add to the total social product. This need for a harmonious mixture between two extreme attitudes has been obscured by the traditional one-sided concept of the Schumpeterian entrepreneur as a rugged individualist and the rebel against society. In point of fact in order to initiate economic development successfully in underdeveloped countries this "individualistic aspect has to be balanced with the equally vital co-operative" aspect of entrepreneurship such as the ability to engineer agreements among all interested parties, to inspire loyalty and co-operation and to maintain good relationships with labour, government departments and the public in general (p. 17). This "co-operative" aspect of entrepreneurship is what the underdeveloped countries lack even more than the "individualist" aspect.

Must we then wait patiently for the mental habits and attitudes to change and for a harmonious mixture of group- and individual-mindedness to develop slowly on its own accord? Hirschman feels we cannot afford to wait because the same psychological forces which have created the impasse have also built up a "grand tension," a highly explosive mixture of hopes and fear which is too big and complex to be resolved at one go. The solution he suggests is to break up this grand tension into a series of smaller and more manageable tensions and challenges which the underdeveloped countries can hope to resolve more successfully (p. 209). Hirschman's "development strategy" is therefore designed to set up tensions, pressures and pacing devices in selected sectors of the economy which will give very clear signals and induce or compel both the state and the private entrepreneurs of these countries to take further "easy-to-take" investment decisions. Formally this boils down to a policy of choosing certain strategic "autonomous" investments which will maximize "induced" investment. But Hirschman is really aiming at a school of entrepreneurs using not only market forces, but "non-market" or political and psychological forces as educational aids (p. 64).[2]

Given this approach, Hirschman rejects the doctrine of "Balanced Growth" for at least two reasons. (1.) It requires the simultaneous setting up of a large number of industries to create demand for each others' products and external economies for each other. But this requirement would raise an impossibly

[2]For instance Hirschman suggests that the underdeveloped countries should be made to learn the need for regular maintenance and servicing of their durable capital equipment by adopting industries and processes for which lack of maintenance results in a complete disruption of production instead of slow deterioration. He believes that they can meet this challenge judging from the fact that underdeveloped countries do manage to run reasonably efficient air lines where the penalty of neglect is immediate and obvious whereas they generally let their road system run down badly. On the same basis, he feels that the government of the underdeveloped countries should be allowed to invest in "show pieces" like large hydro-electric and steel mills because a strong compulsion to "deliver the goods" here could compel greater efficiency than the same amount of investment scattered over a number of small scale projects (pp. 142–144).

difficult challenge. If the underdeveloped countries already possess a sufficient amount of entrepreneurial and managerial resources to set up a whole flock of industries at the same time, they would not have remained underdeveloped in the first instance. (2.) However, the more serious objection to the doctrine of "Balanced Growth" lies in its basic logic of trying to attain balance itself. This is really not more than an exercise in comparative statics, focusing attention first on the initial underdevelopment equilibrium and next on the balanced growth equilibrium after it has been fully attained. It leaves out the path from one position to another which is necessarily made up of a series of unbalanced adjustments and disturbances by which growth is communicated from leading sectors of the economy to others, from one industry to another and from one firm to another. Further, once we have attained the plateau of balanced growth, the very fact that it is an equilibrium position means that there would be no more tensions and pressures for further growth. Thus, development strategy should aim at keeping alive the disequilibrium process as long as possible by a judiciously selected series of autonomous investments and disturbances creating further imbalances (pp. 62–66).

Granted this, we still have to choose between two types of imbalances. (a.) We may start with an autonomous investment which will induce further investments through the pressure of excess demand: i.e., the outputs of the induced industries are the inputs of the autonomous industry. (This is what Hirschman calls the "Backward-Linkage" effect, backward or away from the final consumers' demand.) (b.) Or we may start from an autonomous investment which induces further investments by providing an excess supply of its produce: here the output of the autonomous industry is the input of the induced industries (the Forward-Linkage effect). Ideally of course we should start with investment in an industry which is capable of generating induced investments in both backward and forward directions. But if such an ideal industry is not available, Hirschman strongly feels that we should start by generating the pressure of excess demand because he thinks that it is altogether a more powerful, reliable and calculable method of stimulating economic development. Excess supply alone is somewhat of a broken reed — like a lowering of the rate of interest to stimulate investment at the bottom of a slump.

Hirschman then applies his excess demand approach to the two chief problems of investment criterion for economic development.

Social Overhead Capital v. Directly Productive Activities

While admitting that a minimum of social overhead capital is necessary for economic development, he believes that the underdeveloped countries tend to invest too much in transport systems and power stations ahead of demand and too little in directly productive activities, and that this is the chief factor aggravating their endemic inflation. To create excess capacity in public utilities is only a permissive method of stimulating economic development. If we like a really compulsive method of development we should start at the other end by building factories and let the pressure of excess demand and public opinion break the bottlenecks in public utilities (p. 63).

Forcing Domestic Industrial Development

In contrast to the usual view of imports as "leakages" and the chief destroyer of domestic industries, Hirschman emphasises the creative and dynamic role of imports in creating new wants and building up a potential domestic market for new products. Using an input-output model with fixed technical coefficients and foreign trade, he treats the growth in the total volume of imports of an under-developed country as an autonomous variable which induces investment in a new domestic or import substitute industry as soon as the import demand for a particular commodity crosses the threshold of the minimum economic size of the industry required to produce it. Once established this new industry will exert the pressure of excess demand on other domestic industries whose outputs form its inputs. The probability of induced investment taking place in any of these latter industries depends on the ratio of the amount of excess demand created and its own minimum economic size of production (pp. 113–116). To begin with, in most underdeveloped countries, this induced investment mechanism will be rather weak so that it gives rise to what Hirschman calls the "Import Enclave" industries. These are the typical light consumer goods of those countries which import not only machinery but also processed or almost finished materials and are concerned only with giving "final touches" to the new commodities. Gradually however the stimulus of excess demand will work its way through the "backward linkage" effect to the rest of the industrial structure (pp. 112–113). But although this process is capable of stimulating significant economic growth, Hirschman feels that it may be excessively gradual. The domestic net value added consists mainly of the wages of the operators in the final stage of production and the pressure of expansion if demand tends to leak out in further imports of the required processed materials and machinery. So Hirschman suggests that the underdeveloped countries might hasten the process and try to bite off "as large pieces of value added at a time as they can chew." This may be done by searching for and investing in some "intermediate" or "basic" industry whose products are distributed as inputs through industrial sectors besides also going to final consumers' demand. At this point, Hirschman's argument becomes indistinguishable from the more familiar arguments of setting up heavy and/or capital goods industries instead of consumers' goods industries in the underdeveloped countries.

II

We may now criticize some of Professor Hirschman's arguments.

The first thing that we should question is his excessive reaction against the whole of the supply approach, particularly the "missing components" approach to the underdeveloped countries. The cruder versions of the missing component view embodied in naive proposals to make massive injections of outside capital and technical aid to "finish the job" in the underdeveloped countries admittedly deserve the short-shrift Hirschman has given them. But what he fails to realize is that, if properly interpreted, the missing component view whether with respect to capital or to entrepreneurship, far from conflicting with his unbalanced growth approach is really complementary to it. In fact, as we shall see, in spite of his attempt to shut it out, it is continually creeping back into his argument through the back door.

Consider, for instance, the relationship between capital scarcity and the limits to the pursuit of unbalanced growth. Let us take an example[3] of an underdeveloped country which has a given supply of saving with which it can build either ten small factories producing different products or one large factory producing a single product. The advantage of building ten small factories is not only balanced growth and having a variety of products, but also that all these products will be available within a short time. The advantage of building one large factory is it enjoys the economies of large-scale production and modern technology; but it will have a big excess capacity with the existing demand for its product. But if the country goes on using its entire annual saving to build one such large factory each year, at the end of, say, ten years it would end up with ten large-scale technically efficient factories capable of producing more than the hundred small factories it would have had by keeping to the balanced growth path every year.

In this example, the country's capacity to go on building only one large factory each year clearly depends on its time-preference and willingness to put up with the shortages of those commodities which have to wait their turn to be produced. In other words, the limits to the pursuit of unbalanced growth are determined by the supply of saving. Hirschman might argue that this result is obtained by taking an unfair example of unbalanced growth via excess supply. But this is not so. In the first two or three years it is true that a few big factories which have been built will have excess capacity: but in the later years when let us say seven or eight out of ten factories have been completed, they would be exerting the pressure of excess demand on the output of the unfinished factories. To use Hirschman's analogy, we are now left with a few missing pieces in the jigsaw which can be easily filled in. But even if we start with Hirschman's brand of unbalanced growth via excess demand, a supply of saving is still necessary to bridge the gap of time between the generation of excess demand and the response of induced supply. Thus, while the industries exerting the pressure of excess demand are waiting for the bottlenecks elsewhere to be broken, they would be incurring higher costs and wastage of resources which would have to be met with saving and sacrifice from somewhere. The truth of the matter is that any departure from the equilibrium or balanced growth path, whether via excess demand or excess supply, for the sake of a higher rate of growth necessarily entails a

---

[3]I owe this numerical example to Mr. P. P. Streeten.

sacrifice of some present income for the sake of a greater future income. Hirschman came near to it when he speaks of foreign aid providing "a margin of manoeuver" (p. 208) but in general by his excessive reaction against the shortage of capital approach he has failed to appreciate the full implications of his own unbalanced growth approach.

Our example also shows that a ruthless policy of the unbalanced growth is likely to be carried out more successfully by a totalitarian government which can enforce its own priorities and preferences ignoring the pressure of public opinion or what Hirschman calls the "automatic non-market force." In this connection, his analysis of the politics and the government of the underdeveloped countries is surely too flimsy to sustain his statement: *"It is our contention that nonmarket forces are not necessarily less 'automatic' than market forces"* (p. 63; Italics in the original). Consider his argument that the governments of the underdeveloped countries should start by investing more in factories than in public utilities. He begins by ignoring the established views that while the economies of scale are very pronounced in most types of public utilities, it is very costly to extend their capacity once they have been built. He then relies heavily on the argument that once there are bottlenecks in public utilities "strong pressures are felt by public authorities 'to do something,' and since the desire for political survival is at least as strong a motive as the desire to realize a profit, we may ordinarily expect some corrective action to be taken" (p. 64). This is a very impressionist way of treating political factors, He himself later argues that too much has already been invested in public utilities precisely due to political beliefs concerning the proper division of spheres between public and private enterprises and due to the desire of governments to invest in politically convenient ventures. He ends by giving Japan, Turkey and U.S.S.R. as examples of countries which had economic development via bottlenecks in public utilities. One would have thought that none of these countries were notably susceptible to the correcting pressure of public opinion during that phase of their development (pp. 93–94).

Let us now consider the next "missing component" — entrepreneurship. Given Hirschman's lack of concern over the shortage of capital, his attitude towards entrepreneurship is different from those who would look upon its growth in the underdeveloped countries as a major capital-saving factor adapting modern technology to conditions where labour is cheap and capital scarce. Hirschman works in terms of a model where traditional products produced by traditional methods are left by themselves in a sort of economic reserve, while the growth of new wants leads to the production of new commodities by a direct adoption of modern technology. Thus, while he broadens the concept of entrepreneurship in one direction by stressing its "co-operative" functions, he narrows it in another by postulating the "process-centred" automatic type of modern technology which virtually runs not only itself but also the entrepreneur (pp. 129–131). But in spite of this difference it is nevertheless, true to say that Hirschman's approach is essentially a variant of the missing component approach in terms of entrepreneurship. As we have seen, one of his main arguments against the balanced growth doctrine is that there would not be a sufficient number of entrepreneurs in the underdeveloped countries to run a whole flock of new industries at the same time. He also makes repeated statements such as "we have identified the ability to make such (investment) decisions as the scarce resource which conditions all other scarcities and difficulties in the underdeveloped countries" (p. 27); or "we have identified one force that by itself would make for steady growth: the ability to invest" (p. 49).

It is therefore unfortunate that in his excessive reaction against the missing component approach, Hirschman should insist on trying to distinguish his own theory from the entrepreneur shortage theory by using such vague and unhelpful terms as "growth perspective" and "binding agent." Once we have penetrated this thin disguise, a number of points become clearer. First, if we are willing to define entrepreneurship reasonably broadly, we can subsume the shortage of capital, technical knowledge and even of entrepreneurship under this single missing component. Thus, provided we have clever enough entrepreneurs to begin with they will be able to mobilize the necessary domestic savings and raise the necessary supply of indigenous technicians. If one of the most important aspects of entrepreneurship is to choose the right men to delegate power to, even the supply of entrepreneurship could be expanded quickly once we have the initial nucleus of entrepreneurs. This is really what Hirschman seems to be driving at most of the time when he makes the rather dramatic statement that the underdeveloped countries are not held back by a shortage of supply in resources. If this is so, the difference between him and the other writers boils down to the difference in the degree of optimism with which they regard the possibility of raising this initial nucleus of entrepreneurs. Here it seems that Hirschman occupies a peculiar middle position between the laissez-faire and the anti-laissez-faire economists. The laissez-faire economists would argue that the initial crop of entrepreneurs in the underdeveloped countries can be raised by removing various institutional obstacles to economic individualism and by the automatic working of a free enterprise system offering adequate rewards for risk-taking and initiative. Hirschman rejects this partly because he feels that the entrepreneurs in the underdeveloped countries are already too individualistic and partly because he believes that the signals for profitable investment opportunities should be spelled out in larger letters than under laissez-faire for the novice entrepreneurs of the underdeveloped countries to respond successfully: hence his development strategy. On the other hand, Hirschman is not as pessimistic as those who believe that the free play of economic forces will cumulatively tend to widen the gap in business experience and financial strength between the foreign and the idigenous entrepreneurs in the underdeveloped countries so that various countervailing forces should be set up to give the latter a chance. It may be that Hirschman is right in holding on to his peculiar middle position but he has not satisfactorily answered a number of objections which can be raised against it from both sides. Thus, the laissez-faire economists can say his strategy of generating excess demand exaggerating sectional price rises will aggravate the inflation which the underdeveloped countries are already suffering and that the misdirection of entrepreneurship in the underdeveloped countries into speculative and other get-rich-quickly activities is the result not of excess individualism but of excessive inflation. On the other hand, those who believe that the entrepreneurs in the underdeveloped countries require a whole range of countervailing forces to help them can ask Hirschman why he confines himself only to the exaggeration of market signals without making use of other devices such as cheap credit facilities, dissemination of technical knowledge, etc. Finally we may also add the query how the "co-operative" aspects of entrepreneurship which Hirschman regards as essential are supposed to be developed by his strategy of excess demand.

We may now pass on[4] to the third missing component which Hirschman barely mentions: natural resources. It is, however, clear that with his Latin American background he is mostly thinking in terms of an underdeveloped country which still has a considerable amount of unused land and other natural resources (e.g., p. 112). Now there is nothing wrong with this assumption which has relevance to other parts of the underdeveloped world such as certain countries in South East Asia and West Africa. But the trouble is that Hirschman uses this assumption implicitly and therefore extends it to all types of underdeveloped countries at all stages of development.[5] In particular, he is too cavalier in treating overpopulation simply as another of his excess demand factors which will somehow or other stimulate the underdeveloped country to reorganize itself and increase productivity at least enough to maintain its customary standard of living. Here one cannot help feeling that Duesenberry's "fundamental psychological postulate" is a somewhat inadequate make-weight against Malthus (pp. 176–182). Further, if we grant Hirschman his assumption of unused land and natural resources, the classical method of exploiting these resources is by investing in transport and communications which again damages his argument for government investment in directly productive activities instead of in social overhead capital.

Let us now turn to Hirschman's attempt to extend his excess demand approach to the problem of setting up domestic or import-substitute industries in the underdeveloped countries. As we have seen, he uses an input-output model with fixed technical coefficients and treats the growth in the total volume

---

[4] I pass over technical knowledge as a missing component because I substantially agree with Hirschman that once there is an organized effective demand and attractive salaries, the supply of indigenous skilled labor and technicians is more responsive and elastic than generally assumed. See H. Myint, "An Interpretation of Economic Backwardness," *Oxford Economic Papers* (June, 1954), p. 141.

[5] For a more cautious formulation of the "unused resources" argument based on this assumption, see H. Myint, "The 'Classical Theory' of International Trade and the Underdeveloped Countries," *Economic Journal* (June, 1958), pp. 317–337.

of imports as an autonomous variable which induces investment in a domestic industry as soon as the import demand for its produce crosses the "threshold" marked by its minimum economic size. There seem to be three unresolved conflicts in Hirschman's argument here.

(1.) First, there is the conflict between the technical and the economic concepts of the minimum size of domestic production of a commodity which determines its "threshold." Now this idea of the threshold is suggested to Hirschman by an input-output table (on p. 113) which is "disaggregated" for imports so that the total demand for each of them M_1, M_2 ... M_k is clearly shown. Given this, it was an easy step to postulate the minimum production size for each T_1, T_2 ... T_k so that the first import-substitute industry will come to be set up as soon as M_1 is equal to T_1 and so on down the line. In order to obtain such a clear-cut threshold however we must treat the minimum size of production say T_1 as a technical minimum representing the output capacity of the smallest sized plant required to produce commodity 1 by modern techniques similar to those employed by the foreign suppliers of the commodity. But Hirschman insists that his concept of minimum is not technical but economic. He defines it as "the size at which the domestic firm will be able both to secure normal profits and to compete with existing foreign suppliers, taking into account locational advantages as well as disadvantages, as well as perhaps some infant industry protection" (p. 101). But if we take into account all the variables relevant for the determination of a genuine economic minimum we are back in the familiar untidy world where it will be very difficult to derive a clear cut threshold merely by inspecting whether or not the total import demand M_1 has reached a certain minimum size T_1. Given favourable domestic conditions, it may be possible to set up a competitive import-substitute industry before the demand has any where near approached Hirschman's minimum. This may be done either by using small-scale cottage industry methods instead of a modern factory or by setting up a modern factory with some surplus output capacity. Provided there are other favourable cost-reducing domestic factors to counteract this disadvantage the factory might succeed in spite of the smallness of the market. On the other hand the mere fact that the total demand has reached T_1 does not ensure that the new industry will be competitive and earn normal profits. It is also doubtful, in the real world of technical advances, whether T_1 is in fact a stable and constant magnitude. Finally, the new domestic industries to be established in Hirschman's model are all single firm industries and he has not told us how "normal profits" will be determined and the dynamism generated in this world of monopolies.

(2.) The second conflict is between the Induced-Investment creating capacity and the Comparative Costs. Although Hirschman claims that his analysis "automatically" takes account of comparative costs, the conflict between the two divergent criteria is never squarely faced. For instance, using the table of intersectoral relations for Italy, Japan and U.S.A. calculated by H. B.

Chenery and T. Wantabe, Hirschman points out that "the industry with the highest combined linkage score is iron and steel." He goes on to say: "Perhaps the underdeveloped countries are not so foolish and so exclusively prestige-motivated in attributing prime importance to this industry" (p. 108). But he does not quite have the courage of his convictions and whenever he feels that he has pushed the Induced-Investment criterion too far, he tends to cover himself by saying, "if at all economically feasible" (e.g., p. 118). What we would like to know is how far he would pursue the Induced-Investment criterion if it is *not* for the time being economically feasible and conflicts with existing comparative costs.

(3.) The third conflict arises from the fact that while Hirschman treats the growth of imports of new commodities as the prime mover of the industrialization process of the underdeveloped countries creating a ready-made demand for their new domestic industries, he skates very lightly over the snag that at present these imports will have to be financed mainly by the expansion of primary exports. Here again we would like to have a clearer statement of how far Hirschman is willing either to expand or contract the production of these primary exports to promote industrialization, failing luck in having surplus capacity to produce an export commodity which happens to have a very elastic demand at the time (p. 172).

In fact Hirschman's whole treatment of the balance-of-payments problem of the underdeveloped countries is unsatisfactory and eccentric. Other economists may worry about the fluctuation in the prices of primary products, but to Hirschman the balance-of-payments problem of the underdeveloped countries is yet merely another of the excess demand pressures which would stimulate their economic development provided they do not aggravate their inflation by investing too much in social overhead capital. For instance, what is one to make out of his argument that the balance-of-payment difficulties of these countries are not due to an excess of total demand over available resources but merely due to a certain growth sequence which leads to expansion of those sectors whose output has low "exportability" (p. 169)? On the subject of outside aid to ease the balance-of-payments difficulties of the underdeveloped countries, Hirschman again tries to sustain his view that what they really need is not a "supplement of real resources" or general investible funds but merely specific additional imports and speaks favourably of the barter agreement negotiated by Russia with a number of underdeveloped countries (p. 172). Thus, he ends up by advocating tied aid or investment in its narrowest form! He obviously has no experience of the practical difficulties which the "specificness" of the imports creates for the underdeveloped countries which have entered into such barter agreements.

To sum up: (1.) Hirschman has successfully established the case for unbalanced growth: but his argument has been vitiated because he has unnecessarily and excessively tied it up with a pure Demand Approach to economic development. (2.) He has also done real service by stressing the psychological factors of economic backwardness in opposition to the usual concern only with the physical supply of resources. But by his somewhat optimistic belief in the pressure of excess demand to overcome all physical shortages of resources, by his over-tender attitude towards inflation and balance-of-payments deficits and by his outright rationalization of the underdeveloped countries' fondness for prestige-creating large scale industries and modern technology, Hirschman reminds us of the psychiatrist who claims to cure his patients by humoring them in their wilder fancies instead of telling them a few hard facts of life. In the end we are left with the doubt whether even such a persuasive exponent of this technique as Professor Hirschman can really talk himself out of the frequently dismal and negative task of the economist in the underdeveloped countries of pointing out the need to husband scarce resources and to make painful choices.

Questions for discussion and analysis pertaining to this article may be found at the end of Article 16.

Paul Streeten †

14. BALANCED VERSUS UNBALANCED GROWTH *

The main weakness of the doctrine of Unbalanced Growth (UG) is that, for countries embarking on development, unbalance is inevitable. No admonition is needed. The crucial question is where to unbalance and how much. A second defect is its concentration on stimuli to expansion and its neglect of resistances caused by UG. Its merit, on the other hand, is the inclusion of attitudes and institutions among the dependent variables of the model and in particular its discussion of linkages. The main weakness of the doctrine of Balanced Growth (BG) is that the creation of final markets is rarely a serious obstacle. They can easily be created by import restrictions. Its merit is stress of coordination and the investment package. But investment is not the only component of policies which should be coordinated. In the BG vs. UG controversy the role of government planning has not been brought out clearly. It is argued that both presuppose (a different kind of) planning, for they are both concerned with lumpiness and complementarities.

Another unclarified issue is that of supply limitations. If BG stresses markets as the limiting factor, UG stresses decisions. Both, and particularly UG, have been criticized for neglecting the "ceiling." It is argued below that the distinction between resources, markets and decisions is misleading and that the relevant lines run across these categories. For some countries the assumption of high supply elasticities of resources is justified. Finally, the relation between the BG-UG controversy and others, such as concentration *versus* dispersal, center *versus* periphery, is briefly examined. The theory of BG and the notion of the Ideal Plan are contrasted with approaches that contain attitudes and institutions among their variables and in which the objectives are themselves changed in the process of development.

In this article we shall attempt to show that the questions posed by the controversy over balanced *versus* unbalanced growth have not been very

†Paul P. Streeten, Warden, Queen Elizabeth House, Director, Institute of Commonwealth Studies, Oxford, Fellow Bailol College. The author wishes to thank Gunnar Myrdal for his help on this article which is a by-product of collaboration with Professor Myrdal on a Twentieth Century Fund Study of development in South Asia.
*From the *Economic Weekly* (April 20, 1963), pp. 669–671, 673-674. Reprinted by permission of the publisher and the author.

fruitful, although each doctrine contains some valuable insights.   Before we enter upon discussion of the merits and faults of the doctrines of balanced growth (BG) and of unbalanced growth (UG), it is necessary to clarify two questions to which the contributors to the debate have not given clear and satisfactory answers.   The first question, most relevant in the present context of our discussion, concerns the role of planning; the second question the role of supply limitations and supply inelasticities.

The Role of Planning

In the controversy the role of government (or for that matter private) planning has not always been brought out clearly.   In particular, it is not always clear whether the question under consideration relates to planning, or whether it relates to an attempt to explain development that takes place without planning, or with only an initial impulse of planning in the form of an investment project, while things are thereafter left to take their own course with market forces responding to demand and supply.

Nurkse thought that BG is relevant primarily to a private enterprise economy.[1] It is (he argued) private investment that needs market inducements. In this doctrine, the choice between public and private investment and between direct controls and market incentives is mainly a matter of administrative expediency. But he seems to be wrong in this.   The indivisibilities assumed in BG imply the need for coordination, i.e., planning, although it would, in principle, be possible to have either private or public coordination.

UG as propounded by Hirschman is consistent with, but does not require, initial *and* continued planning.   His state administrators are — or should be — subject to the same kind of pressures as private entrepreneurs.   The role of the state is both to induce and to repair disequilibria. Thus, state action becomes a dependent, as well as an independent, variable.[2] But again, on closer inspection it would seem that UG, to be most effective, does require planning and preferably state planning, because no private firm may want or be able to carry the surplus capacity and the losses, and because private horizons are too narrow.

Complementarities and Indivisibilities

It is not surprising that both BG and UG should, to be most effective, presuppose each (a different kind of) planning, for they are both concerned with lumpy investments and complementarities.   Coordination is needed in order both to get things done that otherwise would not be done, and in order to reap the rewards of complementarities.   Market forces look best

---

[1]Ragnar Nurkse, *Equilibrium and Growth in the World Economy* (Cambridge, Mass.: Harvard University Press, 1961), pp. 249–250 and p. 280.

[2]Albert O. Hirschman, *The Strategy of Economic Development* (New Haven: Yale, 1958), pp. 65, 202.

after adjustments that can be made in infinitesimally small steps. This is why the concept "marginal" plays such an important part in neo-classical Western economic theory. It is also one of the important differences between developed and underdeveloped countries. In the former a new profitable investment project is normally small relative to the size of existing capital equipment (however measured), relatively to new investment, and relatively to the hinterland of facilities on which it can draw. In underdeveloped countries indivisibilities are more prominent and marginal adjustments rarer for at least four reasons.

First, both the existing stock of equipment and the additions to it are small compared with those in advanced countries with comparable populations. Since plant and equipment often have to be of a minimum size for technical reasons, the addition of a plant or of a piece of equipment makes a greater proportionate difference both to the stock of capital and to total investment.

Second, economic development is usually directed at moving people from agriculture to industrial enterprises. This normally implies an increase in the number of indivisible units.

Third, the necessary social overhead capital and the basic structure of industry (power, steel, transport, housing, government buildings) consist of large indivisible units.

Fourth, complementarities between enterprises and activities are likely to be more important in the meager economies of underdeveloped countries, so that a given investment is more liable to require complementary and supplementary investments. Both BG and UG give rise to external economies. A cost incurred by A creates profit opportunities for B. If steps are taken to seize these opportunities at once and in one type of sequence (BG), the results will be different than if they are seized later and in a different type of sequence (UG). But there is no guarantee that A will be induced by market forces to incur these costs, indeed there is a presumption that he will not be so induced.

The Role of Supply Limitations

We next turn to the role of supply limitations and supply inelasticities in the controversy. Nurkse explicitly confined his discussion to the demand side. He assumed supplies to be available and asked what would investment have to be like to justify them? He wrote:

> There is no suggestion here that, by taking care of the demand side alone, any country could, as it were, lift itself up by its boot-straps. We have been considering one particular facet of our subject. The more fundamental difficulties that lie on the supply side have so far been kept off-stage for the sake of orderly discussion.[3]

---

[3]Ragnar Nurkse, *Problems of Capital Formation In Underdeveloped Countries* (Fairlawn: Oxford University Press, 1953), pp. 30–31.

Nevertheless, the position of this chapter in his book and the emphasis laid on it have led to misinterpretations. If BG stresses *markets* as the main limitation on growth, UG in the Hirschman version stresses *decisions*. The implication of Hirschman's theory is that supplies will be forthcoming with relative ease if only the lack of decision-taking can be overcome. This shift of emphasis to an attitude, usually assumed either constant or automatically adjusted to precisely the required extent, should be welcomed. Hirschman has been charged with excessive preoccupation with *investment* decisions.[4] Much of his book indeed focuses attention on them, but it is clear that he had a wider concept in mind, as is shown by his use of the terms "development decisions" and "developmental tasks."[5]

Careless Use of Western Concepts

Insofar as BG is concerned with the creation of markets through complementary investment projects and the inducement to invest by providing complementary markets for final goods, it stresses a problem which is rarely serious in the countries of the region. Final markets can often quite easily be created without recourse to BG, by import restrictions and, less easily, by export expansion.

On the other hand, although UG is correct in pointing to the scarcity of decision-taking in some countries,[6] it should not be contrasted, but it should be combined with the provision of more supplies. The contrast drawn by UG between scarcity of physical resources and scarcity of decision-taking can be misleading. Those who stress resources say that decisions will be taken as soon as resources are available; those who stress decision-taking say that resources will flow freely as soon as adequate inducements to take decisions are provided. The former group of experts go out on missions and advocate high taxation in order to "set resources free," the latter recommend low taxation in order to "encourage enterprise."

Both views reflect misplaced aggregation and illegitimate isolation, two types of bias introduced by the careless use of Western concepts and models. No general formula will serve. The correct division often cuts across these categories. The question is what combination of resource policy, reform of attitudes (including 'incentives') and of legal, social and cultural institutions, is necessary in a particular situation.

---

[4]"Hirschman, on the other hand, might find it more difficult to support, by reference to the Burmese experience, his thesis that development strategy should be directed at maximizing investment (which he equates with development) decisions. Decision-making was indeed a critical factor in this experience. But the decisions which were most needed and most lacking were not investment decisions, but administrative, managerial and policy decisions." — Louis J. Walinsky, *Economic Development in Burma 1951-1960* (New York: Twentieth Century Fund, 1962), p. 593.

[5]Hirschman, *op. cit.*, p. 25.

[6]Though not in all: there is, for example, too much enterprise in Malaya.

Entirely Different Problems

Moreover, the tendency of both BG and UG to underplay supply limitations diverts attention from the fact that planning must be directed as much at restricting supplies in certain directions as at *expanding* them in others. The policy package presupposes a choice of allocating limited supplies, i.e., supplies growing at a limited rate, and in response to certain stimuli, to the most important uses, combined with inducements to decisions of all kinds (not only investment decisions). These supply limitations are considerably less important in advanced industrial countries now and were less important in the early developing phase of many now advanced countries, like Sweden or the regions of recent settlement. These countries had almost unlimited access to capital at low interest rates, a reserve of skilled labour and plentiful natural resources. Again, certain underdeveloped regions in advanced countries (Southern Italy, the South of the USA) can draw on supplies but lack development decisions.

The models developed in the BG v UG controversy seem to have drawn on this kind of experience from "ceilingless economies" which is relevant to South America but not to the entirely different problems of South Asia. The two important differences between, on the one hand, advanced countries now and in their development phase, and, on the other hand, the underdeveloped countries of South Asia are:

(1.) that investments in advanced countries can more often be treated as marginal than in underdeveloped countries, and;

(2.) that advanced countries are and were high supply-elasticity economies with responses and institutions already adapted to economic growth.

The Questions Posed

Both doctrines have certain faults. The trouble with advocating UG is that, for countries embarking on development, unbalance is inevitable, whether they want it or not; and governments and planners do not need the admonitions of theoreticians. All investment creates unbalances because of rigidities, indivisibilities, sluggishness of response both of supply and of demand in these low-elasticity economies and because of miscalculations.[7] There will be, in any case, plenty of difficulties in meeting many urgent requirements, whether of workers, technicians, managers, machines, semimanufactured products, raw materials or power and transport facilities and in finding markets

---

[7]There is, indeed, a danger that planners turn necessity into virtue as the following euphemistic passage from India's Second Five-Year Plan shows:
"There cannot be a complete balance between developments in each five year plan; to some extent, a measure of imbalance — seeming over-expansion in some lines and under-expansion in others — may facilitate more rapid and better-balanced development over a period. Considerations of this kind apply particularly to sectors like development of power, transport and basic industries where investments are by nature 'lumpy.' " — Government of India, *Second Five Year Plan* (Delhi: Planning Commission, 1956), p. 17.

permitting full utilization of equipment. Market forces will be too weak or powerless to bring about the required adjustments and unless coordinated planning of much more than investment is carried out, the investment projects will turn out to be wasteful and will be abandoned.

Insofar as unbalance does create desirable attitudes, the crucial question is not whether to create unbalance, but *what* is the *optimum* degree of unbalance, *where* to unbalance and *how much*, in order to accelerate growth; which are the "growing points," where should the spearheads be thrust, on which slope would snowballs grow into avalanches? Although nobody just said "create any old unbalance," insufficient attention has been paid to its precise composition, direction and timing.[8]

The second weakness of UG is that the theory concentrates on stimuli to *expansion*, and tends to neglect or minimize *resistances* caused by UG. UG argues that the active sectors pull the others with them, BG that the passive sectors drag the active ones back. While the former is relevant to South America, the latter is relevant to South Asia. It would, of course, be better, as Nurkse would have liked it, if *all* sectors were active, and the wish may have been father of the thought behind these models. But the problem is how to activate them. Activation measures must take the form both of positive inducements and of resistances to resistances.

The UG model in the Hirschman version has the great merit, in comparison with many other models, of including attitudes and institutions, and in particular investment incentives, normally assumed fully adjusted to requirements, and of turning them from independent variables or constants into dependent variables. In particular Hirschman's discussion of forward and backward linkages is provocative and fruitful. It brings out the previously neglected effects of one investment on investment at earlier and later stages of production. But the doctrine underplays obstacles and resistances (also in attitudes) called into being by imbalance.[9] Shortages create vested interests; they give rise to monopoly gains; people may get their fingers burnt by malinvestments and may get frightened by the growth of competition. The attitudes and institutions evolving through development will arouse opposition and hostility. Some of these resistances may be overcome only by state compulsion, but the governments of the "soft states" are reluctant to use force and the threat of force. Once again, the absence of this type of reaction from the models is both appropriate for Western countries and is opportune to the planners in South Asia, but in introduces a systematic bias and neglects some of the most important issues.

---

[8]This accounts for remarks such as the following:

"To those not readily enchanted by the paradoxical, the Hirschman strategy may seem to resemble that incorporated in such statements as 'The most efficient way to walk a tightrope is to advance, swaying precariously first to one side then to the other,' *op. cit.,* or 'To teach your child to conduct himself safely in traffic, set him off to cross Times Square against the traffic light' " — Louis J. Walinsky, *op. cit.,* p. 594.

[9]My own previous presentation shared these defects. Cf. *Economic Integration,* Second Edition (Leiden: A. W. Sythoff, 1964), Chapter 5.

Lack of Markets Not Main Obstacle

Turning now to BG, we have seen that its main weakness is that it is concerned with the creation of complementary domestic markets as an inducement to invest, whereas markets in the countries of the region can usually be created by import restrictions, and, where possible, export expansion. This relates to final goods and principally to consumers' goods. As far as intermediate markets are concerned, Nurkse came out in favour of UG (vertical imbalance) in his second Istanbul Lecture.[10] Social overhead investment provides the conditions and inducements for consequential direct productive investment. As for horizontal balance, he believed that the case "rests on the need for a 'balanced diet'."[11] But he later drew a distinction between BG as a method and BG as an outcome or objective.[12] What remains of the doctrine is the emphasis on the complementarity of markets for final goods as an ultimate objective for investment incentives. But not only is absence of markets not normally a serious obstacle to development; even where it is, it is by no means the main obstacle and, in any case, balanced growth cannot always remove it.

What is sound in BG is the stress on the investment package, on the need for coordination, on the structure of an investment complex. But investment is not the only component in this package: and there is too much stress on the complementarity of final markets. What is needed is a package of policy measures containing:

(1.) complementary investments;

(2.) actions to reform attitudes and institutions, including the desire to invest, but also the ability and willingness to work, (which may involve raising *consumption*), to organize and manage and in particular to administer politically;

(3.) a carefully thought-out time-table showing the sequence of the various measures which would be determined by technological, political and sociological factors;

(4.) controls checking undesirable or less desirable investments; and

---

[10]R. Nurkse, *Equilibrium and Growth in the World Economy, op. cit.*, pp. 259–278.

[11]"The difficulty caused by the small size of the market relates to individual investment incentives in any single line of production taken by itself. At least in principle, the difficulty vanishes in the case of a more or less synchronized application of capital to a wide range of different industries. Here is an escape from the deadlock; here the result is an over-all enlargement of the market. People working with more and better tools in a number of complementary projects become each others' customers. Most industries catering for mass consumption are complementary in the sense that they provide a market for, and thus support, each other. This basic complementarity stems, in the last analysis, from the diversity of human wants. The case for 'balanced growth' rests on the need for a 'balanced diet.' " — Ragnar Nurkse, *Problems of Capital Formation in Underdeveloped Countries* (New York: Oxford University Press, 1953), pp. 11ff.

[12]Ragnar Nurkse, *Equilibrium and Growth in the World Economy, op. cit.*, p. 279.

(5.) policies designed to weaken or eliminate obstacles and inhibitions to development, including resistances induced by measures (1.) to (4.).

Related Issues

The BG v UG discussion is related to a wider and more fundamental dilemma. If it is stipulated that several things be attempted (e.g., a series of mutually supporting investment projects, dispersal over a wide region, encouragement of small-scale enterprise) either each is so small in itself and in its effects that the total result is negligible, or nothing is done at all. On the other hand, if efforts are concentrated on a "leading" sector or on a growing region or on a large-scale project, absence of supporting projects may mean waste or at best the further advance of an enclave.[13]

Dispersal Versus Concentration

Is it better to achieve nothing because efforts are too widely dispersed or because concentration means sacrificing complementary measures? Should the butter be spread so thinly that it cannot be tasted or put on in a lump with the risk that it might drop off the bread altogether? Should all the eggs be put into one basket or distributed over many? Dissipation through dispersal or neglect through concentration? Less pessimistically: is it preferable to

---

[13]J. K. Galbraith in a mimeographed and undated note on Pakistan's Second Plan Outline, pp. 17ff, argues against "the inclusion of all good things in the Plan" and gives an example of the usefulness of concentration:

"In the late eighteenth and early nineteenth centuries the accessible agricultural area of the United States — that between the Appalachian Plateau and the sea — was relatively small and there were occasional food shortages in the sense that grain had to be imported from Europe. The solution was to drive a canal to provide access to the abundant and rich lands of the Ohio Valley. No other way of increasing production was so important; it was obviously worthwhile at this stage of development to concentrate on this one thing alone. This in effect was done. After the Erie Canal was opened in the eighteen-twenties food became abundant and cheap along the eastern seaboard. Had a modern agricultural mission set about increasing food production in the early nineteenth century, and in the light of modern technology and organization, it would have urged the establishment of experiment stations, proposed an extension service, suggested the development and adoption of new varieties of grain, advocated supervised credit, proposed more attention to marketing services, and quite possibly have used the occasion to stress the importance of starting work in home economics, farm management, rural health and rural sociology. The canal would have been only one among all of these good ideas and would probably not have been built. And all the rest being of far less immediate effect, the food imports would have continued. At a later stage it is worthwhile in a country such as the United States to devote itself to ways by which production can be made more efficient. But this is after the central opportunities are exploited. It is not a pattern to be applied to countries where concentration on essentials is still the urgent requirement."

Galbraith's moral may not be applicable to South Asia. Even were there similar big ventures to be undertaken, their spread effects would be unlike those that followed historically in the U.S.A., where the government, at the same time, did a number of other things, including some of those mentioned by Galbraith.

waste efforts by spreading them thinly or to neglect important areas in favour of development within a self-contained already more advanced region?

A priori considerations can be advanced on either side. On the one hand, economies of scale, indivisibilities, the need for a "big push" and the presence of thresholds point to concentration. On the other hand, the necessity to change many things simultaneously and to coordinate action in various fields points to attack on a broad front. In practice the problem appears in such forms as: should the Indians spread their efforts to start community development and agricultural extention works over the 500,000 villages clamouring for them, thus running the risk that nothing will change, or should they concentrate on a few selected villages; should they rely on programmes raising yields while leaving aside numerous other desirable objectives, or should they combine these policies with others, directed at education, irrigation, public works, etc., each of which would have to be decimated?

The dilemma is made more complex because it contains three distinct choices: first, the conflict between efficiency and other goals such as equity, justice, political strategy, preservation of communities and their way of life, etc.; secondly, the choices imposed by the requirements of efficiency; and, thirdly, the intertemporal solution of the conflicts between efficiency and other goals. Thus, more redistribution in favour of the poor or backward regions may be possible in the longer run if strong emphasis is placed on efficiency, at the cost of sacrificing redistribution in the short run. To spread efforts widely merely for the sake of equality now, or because of political pressures, may mean less equality in the long run, whereas giving unto those who have may be the best way of lifting up those who have not.

Nature of Spread Effects

The question turns on the nature of the spread effects which may be market-induced or policy induced. It is permissible to let the center grow at the expense of the periphery, if an efficient tax system can redistribute some of the benefits to the periphery. Such spreading of benefits may occur even without policy intervention if the center demanded factors or products from the periphery, or supplied capital and enterprise to it. But the conditions for such automatic spread, viz., a high degree of mobility, competition and divisibility, are not likely to be fulfilled. Not only may there be absence of spread effects or simply polarization within enclaves, but the presence of back-wash effects would actually harm the periphery. Growth there may be retarded by the growth in the center. Finally, the spread effects may be weakened or annulled by resistance effects. By these is meant the growth of anti-development forces induced by the process of growth itself. A policy of resistance to resistance effects must then accompany the development effort.

Such abstract categorizing yields no general formula which would solve the dilemma between concentration and dispersal. The circular interdependence of the relevant conditions will differ in different circumstances. Political facts, such as the demand to cover the whole Indian countryside with an agriculture extension service, cannot be evaded.

The notion of an Ideal Plan in which a set of objectives is contrasted with a realm of policies,[14] and the notion of Balanced Growth show certain affinities. In both there is a strict and permanent division between a set of ends and a set of "neutral" means; "efficiency" is served by adapting the means in an optimal fashion to the ends. Both methods of solving problems assume a finished and completed system and rational conduct as an adaptation to this system. But in fact, such systems are never complete. Neither ends nor means nor "other things," normally assumed separate and constant, can be regarded as "given." Psychological, sociological, cultural and institutional limitations and the valuations which they produce are just as real as physical limitations, though both types can be overcome by appropriate policies.

The Ideal Plan — a Myth

The point is that the system of values and ends changes in the process of development. There is no Ideal Plan, but an unfolding vision in which valuations initially constitute obstacles, but policies to remove these obstacles change the values. The dispute between concentrate! and disperse!, which often neglects political pressures and the inhibitions of planners, is inspired by the same type of model as that used in abstract welfare economics. To render this model an appropriate guide to decision-taking, one would have to do the following things:

(1.) muster evidence about consequences which may not be available or which may be extremely costly;

(2.) know the objectives of policy and the solution of conflicts between objectives, which may not be known but open to exploration as a result of trial and error;

(3.) reduce the complexity of objectives to a simple index, which may be impossible;

(4.) reach agreement between different social groups and regions on the objectives of policy, whilst in fact there will be disagreement, compromise, persuasion or struggle;

(5.) isolate a sphere of "pure" policy which contains only neutral means, whereas in fact whole means-ends sequences may be valued, so that decisions are simply of the type: do this! or do that!

Since none of these conditions is likely to be met, and certainly not all, no general model can be used to decide, even in principle, let alone in any particular instance on the correct answer. Each decision will have to be taken on its merits. By a process of learning, evidence will be accumulated, the ends

[14]See Paul Streeten, "Programmes and Prognoses" in Gunnar Myrdal, *Value in Social Theory* (London: Routledge and K. Paul, 1958).

will be clarified, the complexity possibly simplified, social divergence may be reduced and a growing area of "neutral" means may be reclaimed from the initial morass of all-pervading valuation.

Questions for discussion and analysis pertaining to this article may be found at the end of Article 16.

Stephen Enke †

15. ECONOMIC DEVELOPMENT WITH UNLIMITED AND LIMITED SUPPLIES OF LABOUR*

Among the most important articles on economic development to have appeared during the past decade must be included those by Professor Arthur Lewis on the significance of capitalistic growth with "unlimited" supplies of labour.[1] Few people are able to combine economic theory and realistic detail so remarkably. And yet attempts to restate his "system" in geometry or algebra suggest a number of inconsistencies. Some of these are sufficiently fundamental to indicate amendments to his theory. And a novel policy implication is revealed on how to "capitalize" an economy.

The Lewis Model

The parts of the Lewis model of concern here are the following. There is a country that includes initially a large "subsistence" sector and a small "capitalistic" sector. The essence of early economic development is the transfer of labour from the former to the latter during a so-called first stage. The marginal product of labour in the subsistence sector is negligible, zero, or negative. The subsistence output is supposedly constant, however.

During the first stage there is an "unlimited" supply of labour to the capitalistic sector — i.e. the labour supply is infinitely elastic for all practical purposes — at a wage based on the product per worker in the subsistence sector.[2] During this period, extra capital from whatever source is used in the modern sector for capital "widening" rather than "deepening," the capital to labour ratio remaining constant. Hence, the number of workers employed in the capitalistic sector is a function of total capital accumulation, and

†Dr. Stephen Enke, Manager — Economics Development Programs, General Electric TEMPO, Center for Advanced Studies. The author acknowledges his indebtedness to his graduate students at Duke University, and to Professor O. P. F. Horwood of the University of Natal, whose questions and comments instigated this paper.
*From *Oxford Economic Papers,* N.S., Vol. 14, No. 2 (June, 1962), pp. 158–172. Reprinted by permission of the Clarendon Press, Oxford, and the author.
[1]W. A. Lewis, "Economic Development with Unlimited Supplies of Labour," *The Manchester School of Economic and Social Studies* (May, 1954); also "Unlimited Labour: Further Notes," *ibid.* (June, 1958).
[2]Which may include implicit rent if peasant cultivators own their own land.

more investment means more labour drawn proportionately from the subsistence sector. During this first stage it is the product per worker in the traditional sector that determines wage rates in the capitalist sector, which in turn determines capital to labour ratios employed there. Output per worker in the capitalist sector is higher than wages per worker, for labour is joined with capital, and so entrepreneurs enjoy a surplus from which they can save and invest. Any technological improvements accrue to the capitalists because wage rates cannot rise so long as there is "unlimited" labour supply. Lewis also holds that the ratio of profits to national income must rise and therefore that the percentage of annual income that is invested must rise also. In all essential respects the first stage is a "classical" model of growth.

The peculiarities of the second stage, which distinguish it from the first stage, are various and not entirely unambiguous. On the one hand, the second stage is characterized by higher wage rates, higher ratios of capital to labour employed in the modern economy, and a total capital stock that accumulates faster than the hired labour force so long as the capitalist sector grows. On the other hand, the second stage is described as being "neo-classical," which presumably means that profit and wage rates are determined *by* the relative marginal productivities of the aggregate stock of capital and labour in the modern sector, and not conversely. Capital catches up with the labour supply. The wage of labour to capitalists is no longer determined by workers' alternatives in the subsistence sector. This last seems to imply a final absorption of the subsistence sector and a zero wage elasticity of labour supply.

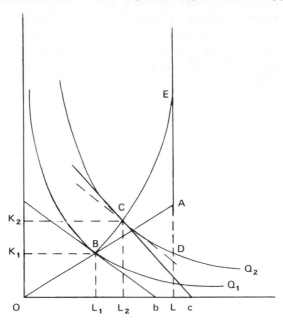

Figure 15-1

The first diagram, 15-1, not offered by Lewis however, illustrates his thesis perhaps.[3] The production isoquants refer to the capitalistic sector only, the output of the subsistence sector not being shown. OL is the total labour force in the country, OL_1 indicates the modern sector's employment, and population is assumed constant for simplicity's sake. There is OK_1 capital in the nation, all in the capitalistic economy, and as capital is saved from profits there is a movement during the first stage away from O. The capital to labour ratio remains unchanged during this first period. The parallel tangents drawn to the output isoquants, assuming wage rates unchanged, confirm that profit rates of return on invested capital are constant also. At A the country *must* move from the first stage into another stage, if not before. The argument is not really affected if a given residual quantity of subsistence labour refuses ever to migrate for some reason. The capitalist sector, if not the whole economy, expands output, in the last of all stages by reason of capital accumulation and not extra labour. The marginal productivity of labour must increase as the capital to labour ratio must increase. Real wage rates rise and the profit rate on invested capital falls. Investment may cease if a point is reached where those who save would rather invest abroad. During the first stage the workers do not benefit directly from development, but they do during the second, the first stage being necessary to attain the second.[4]

From this description it is evident that most really poor and backward countries are still in Lewis' first stage. The theorem asserts that almost anything that increases a country's stock of capital, and so causes a transfer of workers to more productive employment in the capitalist sector, is indirectly or directly beneficial to labour. Anything that increases the cost of labour to capitalists will reduce profits and so slow capital accumulation.

The following analysis will suggest a number of amendments to the Lewis model, however. Using the same basic assumptions, three distinct stages can be distinguished, which will be designated 1, 2, and 3, and be explained below. It can be shown that during stage 2, while capital to labour ratios in the modern capitalist sector are still determined in part by the productivity of subsistence workers, there will be some capital widening *and* deepening, and that profits will be declining relative to national income. This might arrest the development process. It depends rather on the savings function that is assumed for capitalists. More important probably, as an incentive to continued investment than the ratio of aggregate profits to national income, are the profit return on invested capital and wealth per capitalist. Another complication is that the importance and duration of stage 2, relative to that of stage 1,

---

[3]I.e. Fig. 15-1; this has been the subject of correspondence between Lewis and the author.

[4]One might ask why K_1 capital is not combined with L labour at D, thereby spreading the capital more uniformly and thinly throughout the economy, and attaining a higher isoquant at D. But this would involve a real wage rate, given interest rates, below output per worker in the subsistence sector. Either these workers would have to labour for a lower wage or capitalist employers would have to pay a wage above labour's marginal product when combined with capital in modern processes.

depends upon whether accumulations are used to subtract workers from the subsistence sector (which is the way Lewis often reads) or to add capital to the labour and land already employed in agriculture (thereby deferring a wage rate increase until stage 3).

Definition of Sectors

The validity of the model depends partly upon the concept of "capitalist" and "subsistence" sectors, partly upon assumptions regarding labour productivity and family sharing of output within the traditional sector, and partly upon the savings function of capitalists. These matters help to determine whether the first stage terminates when the supply price of labour to capitalist employers rises — a large subsistence sector remaining — or when the wage in the capitalist sector ceases to be based on subsistence alternatives and is determined by marginal productivities in the capital sector above. We shall first consider the definition of the two sectors.

Lewis does not make the common error, sometimes ascribed to him by popularizers, of supposing that a capitalistic sector is exclusively an industrial one. Mention is made of capitalistic plantation agriculture for instance. He realizes, too, that "if the capitalist sector produces no food, its expansion increases the demand for food, raises the price of food in terms of capitalist products, and so reduces profits."[5] He is perfectly aware that industrialization depends upon agricultural improvement. Accordingly, his capitalist sector is simply defined as one that "uses reproducible capital, and pays capitalists for the use thereof."[6]

The concept of a subsistence sector is equally clear. Lewis defines it as the non-capitalist sector, not using reproducible capital, and not paying capitalists for its use.[7] So it includes artisan manufacturers — in the original sense of the word — as well as traditional agriculture. The subsistence sector is not limited to agriculturalists who consume only their own output.

Each sector may produce both food and non-food and both may include agriculture. Nevertheless, at least initially, it is evident that most of the agricultural land is in the subsistence economy. And all industrial output is from the capitalist sector.

Lewis states at one point that the subsistence output is constant[8] — which would imply a zero marginal product of labour in one sense — whereas at other places he states that subsistence labour has a negligible, zero, or even negative marginal product.[9] This apparent inconsistency can be reconciled often by assuming that hours worked annually per adult in the subsistence

---

[5]*Op. cit.,* 1954, p. 173.
[6]*Op. cit.,* 1954, p. 146.
[7]*Ibid.,* p. 147.
[8]*Ibid.,* p. 157.
[9]*Ibid.,* pp. 142, 189.

sector vary inversely with the subsistence labour force. Therefore, the marginal product of an *hour* of work might be positive but the marginal product of a subsistence sector *worker* might be zero for the time being. But it is obvious that, long before the subsistence economy is absorbed, its output must decline. The last subsistence workers, with plenty of land to use, must have a distinctly positive marginal product.

Lewis seems to feel that the average product of subsistence labour is very "low" because it has not been fructified with capital. However, as labour migrates to the modern capitalistic sector, the relative attractiveness of the subsistence sector to workers may increase. The reason that Lewis gives is that there will be fewer people remaining to share its food and other output.[10] Actually, as we shall see, the real reason is likely to be another one. And by stressing capitalization of agriculture, rather than industry, it can be postponed by an open economy.

Labour Supply to Capitalists of Subsistence Families

The location of the boundary between stages 1 and 2 is very sensitive to assumptions made regarding economic incentives and output sharing within extended families of the subsistence economy. Lewis usually assumes that the supply price of subsistence labour to the capitalist sector is subsistence output per subsistence worker. But this is not entirely logical.[11]

From the outset it is necessary within the subsistence sector to distinguish between (1.) a·worker's average product, (2.) consumption per head, (3.) a worker's marginal product, (4.) hours worked per labourer annually, and (5.) an hour's marginal product.[12]

It is obvious that most adult male villagers are working not only for themselves but for many dependants. The ratio of dependants to adult working males may typically be about 3 to 1. Thus, a worker's average product is about three times, say, his consumption per head. Lewis seems to assume that the marginal product of a worker is zero — for subsistence output during stage 1 is supposedly unchanged when workers emigrate — the remaining labourers possibly working a little more each to compensate. Under these circumstances

---

[10]". . . if capital accumulation . . . is reducing absolutely the number of people in the subsistence sector, the average product per man in that sector rises automatically, not because production alters, but because there are fewer mouths to share the product." *Ibid.*, p. 172.

[11]Lewis states (*op. cit.,* 1954, pp. 148–149): ". . . in economies where the majority of people are peasant farmers, working on their own land, we have a far more objective index, for the minimum at which labour can be had is now set by the average product of the farmer; men will not leave the family farm to seek employment if the wage is worth less than they would be able to consume if they remained at home." But *output per worker* is not the same as *consumption per head.* There are other dependent people in the family. The quoted sentence contradicts itself.

[12]In what follows, it is supposed that family consumption equals family output in value, there being no saving.

the supply price of subsistence labour to the other sector — temporarily neglecting special living costs there — should be *consumption per head* and not *product per worker*. Moreover, as workers' mouths are not the only ones that have to be fed in the subsistence family, an emigration of workers should have a relatively small effect on *per capita* availability of food and other goods. And in fact, once it is admitted that *workers* have a positive though low marginal product, the departure of adult males from the subsistence family might leave consumption per head a little lower or higher but practically *constant*. Here, perhaps, is the true explanation of "unlimited" labour supply during Lewis' stage 1.

But rural adult males must be assessed as producers as well as consumers. The product of an extra hour's labour is very low in many poor and over-populated countries: presumably it is barely sufficient to provide the extra food calories required for extra energy used and to compensate for the dis-utility of work. The marginal product of a worker relative to his average product may be very low, even lower than the ratio of a labour hour's marginal to average product, because of an inverse relation between number of workers and hours worked by each labourer. However, as more subsistence sector workers emigrate, it becomes increasingly impossible for remaining workers to labour more hours each. Moreover, the ratio of land resources to subsistence workers is increasing, so that the marginal product of a worker must increase also.

Continual emigration must eventually result in a worker's marginal product exceeding consumption per head. A subsistence worker, by staying with his family, is then adding more output than he is subtracting as consumption. It would disadvantage the family for him to leave for the capitalist sector unless the net wage there, after deducting special living costs away from home, equals or exceeds his marginal subsistence product as a worker. Some of the excess he can remit home in money form. Thus, the supply price of subsistence labour to the capitalist sector, as migration continues, is based upon the subsistence worker's marginal product as stage 2 begins.

Table 15-1

Consumption and Marginal Product of Workers

(1) Workers	(2) Output	(3) Family Size	(4) Output Per Head	(5) Workers Marginal Product
1	80	9	8.9	70
2	150	10	15.0	55
3	205	11	18.7	35
4	240	12	20.0	20
5	260	13	20.0	10
6	270	14	19.4	5
7	275	15	18.3	..

The relations involved are represented in Table 15-1 and in Figure 15-2. There is a village family of 8 dependants plus from 1 to 5 adult male workers. As the number of workers varies (col. 1), there is a change in total output (col. 2), a change in number of family members (col. 3), a change in consumption per family member (col. 4), and a change in worker marginal product (col. 5). This allows for the possibility that each worker may labour more hours a year if there are fewer of them. The point of the table is that consumption per head varies hardly at all over the range of 7 to 3 workers. When these relations are charted the segment of the output per head marked ST is perhaps Lewis' "unlimited" supply of labour. But, as labour is withdrawn so that 3 or fewer men remain, the capitalist employers in the modern sector must pay a wage based on the SR segment of the workers' marginal product curve.[13]

It remains to explain the discontinuity involved in having consumption per head establish the supply price of labour, when it exceeds worker marginal product, and yet have marginal product be determining when it exceeds consumption per head. In the abstract, a subsistence worker should always migrate *whenever* the capitalist sector can pay him more than his marginal product at home, even though this is less than domestic consumption per head. But there is a practical problem. Domestic consumption per head may approximate some minimum of existence. And even if the capitalists' wage offer is sufficient to live on, the worker himself may not want to accept less for paid work than he consumes at home, despite family loyalties. But most important, it is usually difficult or impossible for rural families to send food or other support to relatives in the capitalist sector, although urban relatives can always remit money home. It is this last asymmetry that logically explains the discontinuity in labour supply schedules to the modern economy of subsistence families.

Special living costs in the capitalist sector have the effect of extending the portion of the over-all labour supply schedule that is based on consumption per head and curtailing that based on worker marginal product.[14] This is especially so if workers take dependants to live with them. The theoretical conclusion is that the supply price of subsistence labour to the capitalist sector

---

[13]In the diagram the horizontal axis represents the number of adult males more or less gainfully occupied in a family enterprise. The vertical axis represents either physical output or its money equivalent. The AP curve is the output per worker. The MP is related marginal product curve of a worker. The AC curve is average consumption, being output divided by all resident family members including 8 dependants. The MP' curve shows what the marginal product of workers *would* be if

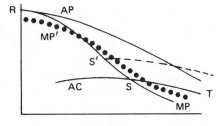

Figure 15-2

each laboured say a standard 2,000 hours annually. It is assumed — *vide MP* as compared with MP' — that workers labour more hours when there are fewer of them.

[14]Diagrammatically, this is shown by the dotted curve, terminating at S'.

is the *higher* of (1.) domestic consumption per head plus special living costs if any, *or* (2.) a worker's subsistence marginal product.

Stages 1, 2, and 3

All this suggests that there are really three distinct stages and not merely two.

The peculiarity of stage 1 is that there is an "unlimited" supply of labour from the subsistence sector at a constant supply price approximating consumption per head plus any special costs of living in the capitalist sector. Hence, labour to capital ratios are constant. Profits are a constant fraction of the capital sector's value of output assuming no technological change. The expansion path is shown by *OB* in Figure 15-3. Growth does not benefit the workers but only capitalists if population is stationary. This is clearly Lewis' first stage.

The peculiarity of stage 2 is that, although a considerable subsistence sector remains to be absorbed, the price of labour to the capital sector is rising. It is now based on marginal labour product in both sectors. The altering ratios in which labour is combined with capital in the modern sector, and hence the relative marginal products of these two factors, is partly determined by workers' marginal alternatives in the subsistence sector. Extra sector output is partly contributed by extra employed labour. The expansion path is *BCE* in the diagram.

The peculiarity of stage 3 is that no subsistence sector remains. The relative marginal productivities of labour and capital in the modern sector depend upon its production function and the relative quantities of labour and capital in the economy. The direction of causation has been reversed. Only extra capital — or improved technology — can augment output. The expansion path is vertical in the diagram.

Both stages 2 and 3, as defined here, seem on occasion to fit Lewis' descriptions of his second stage. In both cases wage rates are rising, capital to labour combinations are increasing, and the profit rate of return on invested capital is declining. This squeeze on profits may terminate capital accumulation and growth.

It is exactly this danger that makes the distinction between stages 2 and 3 so important. Growth during stage 3 inevitably means higher wage rates that slow capital accumulation. There is no more labour to be had.[15] But during stage 2 there is more subsistence labour available. The crucial question is how much higher wages have to be paid to obtain it for use with extra capital. Certainly this is the case if labour is subtracted from subsistence agriculture and employed in capitalistic industry. Fortunately, an alternative exists as we shall see (in section after next), and that is to add capital to rural labour and land to establish a modern agricultural sector. For an open economy, there

---

[15]International immigration and "labour-saving" innovations are ignored.

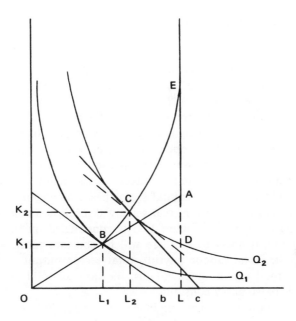

Figure 15-3

is hence an opportunity to convert a potential stage 2 into an actual stage 1, thereby postponing an increase in wages. But stage 3 can never be transformed into stage 1 because the subsistence economy has been absorbed.

Capitalists' Savings and Profit Levels

Continual output expansion of the modern sector requires continuing accumulations of capital whatever the stage of growth. The capitalists do practically all the saving by the economy from their profits. In fact, Lewis almost seems to assume that aggregate annual savings and profits are identical. Consumption of capitalists is apparently zero or constant. Accordingly, he is confident of accelerating investment during stage 1. But profits may be "squeezed" during stage 2, and *a fortiori* during stage 3, so that growth may be slowed or arrested. It will be useful to explore his reasoning on profit levels and capitalists' savings.

Stage 1 Profits

Capital accumulates supposedly at an accelerating pace because profits are increasing. As Lewis writes:

> So long as unlimited labour is available at a fixed real wage, the share of profits in the national income will increase. There are two reasons for this. First, the share of profits in the capitalist sector may increase. And

secondly the capitalist sector will expand relatively to the national income.[16]

But there are several difficulties.

First, if it is profits *per se* that matter why bother about the relation between capital sector output and *national* income, the latter including as it does the *subsistence* sector's output?

Second, should one consider the *ratio* of profits to the capital sector's output relevant, this is *not* increasing during the first stage if one abstracts from innovations. If the country is an open economy as regards capital movements, interest rates may be an exogenous determination by the outside world, and so the ratio of interest (or profits) to wages is presumably constant too. If the economy is closed, and the capital sector has a homogenous first degree function of production, a constant real wage will result in a constant residual profit return on investment. Figure 15-3 is constructed on the assumption that, in expanding from O to B, there will be constant ratios among total capitalists' profits, total labour payroll, total sector output, total workers employed, and total capital stock. Thus, the ratio of total profits to total sector output is presumably constant.

Third, annual total investment might be determined by the rate of return on investment, and at times one infers Lewis assumes that even without technological improvements this will increase during stage 1.[17] However, if there are constant returns to scale in the capitalist sector, the profit return on invested capital will be constant.[18]

---

[16]*Op. cit.,* 1958, p. 8.

[17]*Vide* the diagram on p. 152 of the 1954 article; and in the 1958 article (p. 26) describing entry into stage 2, he writes: ". . . and the profit margin (now) does not necessarily increase all the time."

[18]Lewis seems to have been led astray, and into assuming an increasing ratio of profits to capital sector output, by his two-dimensional diagram as reproduced here (*op. cit.,* 1954, p. 152). The horizontal axis represents quantity of labour employed in the capitalist sector and the vertical measures in money the wage and marginal value product of labour in the capital sector. The wage is W and constant. As capitalists make more investments, the marginal value product of any *given* ordered unit of labour increases. The area above the wage line but below labour's marginal product curve can be integrated to represent total profits. Suppose V_1 is the marginal value product curve of labour with \$$x$ of capital. If the capital stock is doubled, and assuming constant returns to scale so as to exhaust the product according to neo-classical distribution principles, the marginal product that was previously the lth labourer's will now be that of the $2l$th labourer. Thus V'_2 (dotted)

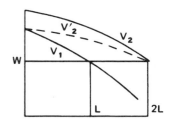

Figure 15-4

results. But Lewis assumed a curve such as V_2. Hence, he supposed the total area under the marginal product curve increases proportionately more than the rectangular payroll area as capital and labour are increased by the same percentage. But using continuous curves, and assuming constant returns to scale, the point is that the second worker with double capital is the equivalent of the first worker before, the   (contd.)

Stage 2 Profits

How will aggregate profits be affected by capital accumulation in stage 2? Assuming some savings, such as an increase in total capital stock from say K_1 to K_2 in Figure 15-3, rival capitalists will seek to add labour drawn from the subsistence economy. For reasons given, to all workers they will have to pay a higher wage per worker, and they will add labour until its marginal value product is equal to its increased average cost. Perhaps the new equilibrium is at C on Q_2 with L_2 labour employed in the modern sector. Wages per worker in the capitalist economy were OL_1/Ob of Q_1 and they are now OL_2/Oc of Q_2. If there are constant returns to scale in the modern sector,[19] the residual profits of capitalists will equal the marginal product of capital times total capital employed, and the reward per unit of labour will be higher and that of capital will be lower than before. Profits become a smaller fraction of sector output.[20]

Why Capitalists Save

In any event, not very much is known about what makes really wealthy capitalists save, in contrast, say, to what makes professional salary earners save. It is a very middle-class view, suitable perhaps for advanced countries, that people consume and so save as a function of their income. In undeveloped countries, the vast majority of the population either cannot or will not save, and it is the wealthy who do most of the saving without much difficulty.[21]

One peculiarity of wealthy families is probably that they consume what constitutes a regressive fraction of owned asset values. They do not alter their way of living from year to year as incomes fluctuate. Given their position, both financially and socially, they have a more or less customary expenditure pattern. An extra dollar on consumption adds little satisfaction and decreasing utility returns. But an extra dollar saved may give increasing returns as

---

second quarter worker afterwards has the same product as the first quarter worker before, and so on, the two marginal product curves (e.g. V_1 and V'_2) properly having the same vertical axis intercept.

[19]Figure 15-3 is drawn on the assumption that a doubling of K and L will result in double output, so that, if Q_2 is twice the Q_1 output, any ray from the origin will intersect Q_2 at twice the distance as Q_1 from O.

[20]It is fortunate for society that capitalists do not operate as a monopolistic conspiracy, basing their savings decisions on the relation of *changes* in profits to *changes* in total capital stock. A slight increment in capital, used to transfer workers at a slightly higher wage, increases the total sector *payroll* by a greater percentage than the wage increase. The extra payroll is offset by reduced total profits. Hence, the rate of return on the last dollar of investment may be negative. However, most investors see only the ratio of total profits to total capital, and this average rate of return (being positive) may provide enough incentive to continue them saving.

[21]The importance of the middle class for economic development lies not in their savings — which in the aggregate are small relative to those of the wealthy — but to their services as managers, engineers, biologists, doctors, teachers, etc.

regards family status and power. The number of rival families diminishes very rapidly in a small country as family wealth accumulates.

One could very reasonably assert that the savings of wealthy capitalist families are the residual that remains after asset determined consumption has been deducted. For example, an individual capitalist's savings may follow the rule:

$$\Delta K_i = K_i r - C \cdot K_i^{\alpha},$$

where K_i is his wealth in millions of dollars, r the annual rate of return on assets, C is the dollars spent on consumption per million dollars' worth of capital assets, and the α exponent is less than unity.[22]

The above formulation means that capitalists collectively consume less if a given national asset stock is owned by a few capitalists rather than many. But the distribution of produced wealth does not alter capitalists' profit income. Hence, aggregate annual savings vary inversely with the number of capitalists, other things equal. If all real capital assets were owned by ten families, the rate of saving from profits would presumably be greater than if equal value assets were owned by a million families, not because the ten families' individual *incomes* would be larger but just because they would have more *wealth* on an average. All this suggests that aggregate savings of an economy depend only in part on total national profits and not at all on the ratio of profits to national income.

If savings are partly determined by wealth per capitalist, it becomes important to consider the rate at which capital as contrasted with capitalists is increasing annually — something that is hardly mentioned in economic development literature. If capitalists are increasing at the same rate as most undeveloped countries' populations, which is about 2 to 2.5 percent a year, they are doubling their numbers every thirty-five to thirty years approximately. This means that their aggregate consumption may be doubling every thirty-odd years. *Ceteris paribus,* if annual investment per capitalist family is to be maintained, total capital stocks must be doubling every thirty-odd years also. If capital stocks double sooner, the more rapid increase in individual family assets will in turn increase annual savings, and this recursive element (or "feedback") may be an important growth factor.

The question remains as to whether capital accumulation may be brought to a halt during stage 2. As explained already, an increment of capital "seeking" an immigrant worker will probably raise wages, which higher wages must be paid to all capitalist sector workers. Hence, the rate of return on capital (r) will fall. The danger is that an increment of capital may decrease r proportionately by more than K increases proportionately. The reduced profits, further offset by increased consumption, must then occasion smaller annual total savings. Additions to the stock of capital might even cease.

---

[22]As r is a variable (see below), the above equation is not tantamount to defining consumption in terms of income; in addition, even capitalists may have some earned income, but if so the incentive to work is not usually the salary.

Hence, it is important to consider ways in which extra capital might otherwise be employed without unduly raising wages during the second stage.

Capitalizing Agriculture Necessary

The reason that wages rise during stage 2 is that the subsistence marginal products of remaining rural workers increase as others transfer to the capitalist sector. This is inevitable, if many were but are no longer engaged in agriculture, and usable land is a scarce good. The ratio of land to labour will then be increased by workers' emigration and any remaining labourer becomes a substitute at the margin for more acres.

This would not occur, however, if extra capital could be employed in a manner that would not alter the labour to land ratio in subsistence agriculture. In other words, wages might not rise relative to profits if land and labour could be transferred into the capitalist sector at "equal" rates.[23] As land is immobile physically, this means that capital must come to it, rather than labour migrating to capital.

As indicated before, the subsistence sector is not entirely agricultural, nor is the capitalist sector entirely industrial. Rural labour does not have to leave the rural land in order to work with expensive produced means of production. Capital does not have to be combined with labour to the exclusion of land. So one way to ensure an "unlimited" supply of labour at a fixed real wage during the early stage would be, not only to subtract subsistence labour for capitalist sector employment, but also to add capital to the labour and land of the subsistence sector. Obviously this latter capital addition would enforce a revolution in agricultural practices. Modernization and capitalization of agriculture would have to go hand in hand.[24]

There are other potent reasons why there will have to be a certain amount of capitalizing of agriculture anyway. When labour migrates from the subsistence sector, there is a tendency for those who remain behind to eat much of the previous share of the departed relatives, so that there must be an increased food availability in the nation when population shifts to urban industry.[25] Moreover, if the capitalist sector is almost entirely industrial and the economy is closed, the desire of capitalist sector workers to eat will increase the real income per head within the subsistence economy and shift the terms of trade against the industrial capitalist sector.[26]

---

[23]I.e., the quantity of land transferred, as a percentage of total land in the subsistence sector, must equal the percentage of subsistence labour transferred.

[24]If these innovations are "land-saving," raising the marginal productivity of land relative to labour, so much the better.

[25]See Enke, S., "Food Constraints on Industrial Development in Poor Countries," *Southern Economic Journal* (April, 1961).

[26]See Gutman, G. O., and J. Black, "A Note on Economic Development with Subsistence Agriculture," *Oxford Economic Papers* (October, 1957); Ranis, G. and J. C. H. Fei, "A Theory of Economic Development," *American Economic Review* (September, 1961); also Enke, S., "Industrialization through Greater Productivity in Agriculture," *Review of Economics and Statistics* (February, 1962).

A final question is whether stage 2 can be eliminated entirely, with the whole early stage being like stage one, as Lewis describes it. This seems possible if the land and labour resources remaining in the subsistence sector are maintained in the same proportions. This would require no combination of capital with labour that was not accompanied by its traditional amount of land.

Practically, this means less stress on industrialization, and concentrating instead on modernizing and capitalizing agriculture. The higher *per capita* incomes that result will naturally occasion a demand for industrial products that may be imported in exchange for agricultural exports. A very open economy, with extensive participation in foreign trade, then becomes a condition of national economic development. This was the imperial prescription for colonial growth and there are many examples of its moderate success. However, rightly or wrongly, such development policies are politically unacceptable in most independent backward countries.

Conclusions

The extraordinarily important analysis and conclusions of Lewis might usefully be amended or supplemented in at least five significant respects.

First, there are three distinct stages in the capital sector's output growth, the first involving only capital "widening," the second entailing both capital "widening" and "deepening," and the third occasioning capital "deepening" only. The boundary between the first and second stage is marked by a change from an infinitely elastic to a less than infinitely elastic labour supply to the capital sector. The boundary between the second and third stage is marked by a change from a positive to a zero elasticity of labour supply.

Second, the labour supply by subsistence families to the capitalist sector is not a continuous function. The supply price, assuming extended family sharing of food and other output, is the higher of consumption per head or worker marginal product. The asymmetry is caused by the ability of urbanized workers to remit funds to rural relatives and the inability of subsistence families to support relatives employed in the capital sector.

Third, although nothing conclusive can be asserted, it seems possible that aggregate annual saving by capitalists depends upon their total profit income and individual capitalists' wealth. There seems no special reason for assuming that annual accumulations are determined by the ratio of profits to national income. Unequally owned assets may contribute something to growth.

Fourth, the raising of wages in the capitalist sector might be lessened (increasing accumulation and sector growth), if increments of capital were combined with rural land and labour in modern agriculture. The alternative of transferring labour from subsistence agriculture to capitalized industry, raising the ratio of land to labour in the subsistence economy, must raise the marginal product of a subsistence worker. This is of special significance where limited land resources occasion markedly increasing returns to workers in subsistence agriculture when other workers emigrate.

Fifth, a development plan that stresses "capitalistic" agriculture is probably impossible in a closed economy. The resultant "unbalance" of output would swing the terms of trade against a capital sector that was almost entirely agricultural. The policy choice is between accepting higher real wages during stage 2 *or* postponing stage 2 indefinitely but accepting open trade with the world economy.

Questions for discussion and analysis pertaining to this article may be found at the end of Article 16.

Charles Ferguson†

16. THE SIMPLE ANALYTICS OF NEOCLASSICAL GROWTH THEORY*

The neoclassical theory of growth, with or without technical progress, has been the subject of intense research since the appearance of Solow's and Swan's original papers.[1] If the saving ratio is constant and technical progress is not included in the model, it is easy to show that the natural rate of growth is equal to the warranted rate and that this rate is constant and stable. Further, the rate is the same for output, consumption, capital, investment, and saving. The natural rate in this model is determined by and is equal to the *one* relevant parameter: the exogenously determined rate of growth of the labor force. This variant of the neoclassical model truly represents a Golden Age model, and it has been shown to represent a Golden Rule model as well.[2]

When technical progress is introduced, matters become somewhat more complicated because capital, labor, and output cannot all grow at the same constant rate. One way to handle the matter is to introduce an arbitrary definition of the "natural rate." The definition commonly employed is as follows: the natural rate of income growth is that rate which, while maintaining full employment, causes the capital-output ratio to remain constant.[3] That is to say, one *defines* the natural rate as that rate which prevails when technical progress

---

†Charles E. Ferguson, Professor of Economics, Texas A & M University. The research embodied in this paper was undertaken while the author held a fellowship from the Social Science Research Council, Auxiliary Research Award. The usual caveat applies.

*From the *Quarterly Review of Economics and Business* (Spring, 1968), pp. 69–83. Reprinted by permission of the publisher and the author.

[1]Solow [31] and Swan [32]. For an interesting precursor, see Tobin [34]. Bracketed numbers refer to sources listed at the end of the article.

[2]A Golden Age model is one in which all variables change at a constant relative rate. See Robinson [28]. A Golden Rule model is a Golden Age model in which the path of consumption is uniformly higher than that derived from an other Golden Age model. See Meade [25], Phelps [26], and Robinson [29].

[3]The origin of this definition is not clear. Green [14] attributes it to Harrod, although it is not the definition given by Harrod on page 87 of [16]. In an entirely different setting, the definition appeared as early as 1957 in Kaldor [23]. For other examples of growth models based upon this definition, see Amano [1], Brems [3], Ferguson [12] and [13], Hahn [15], Inada [18], and Marty [24].

is Harrod-neutral. Alternatively, one may deduce this as a theorem pertaining to the stability of the model.[4]

In either case, when technical progress enters the model, the natural rate may be a variable rate, or at least only asymptotically constant; and the elasticity of substitution, the bias of technical progress, and the rate of change of the saving ratio, as well as the rate of growth of the labor force, enter as determining influences.[5] The model with technical progress may be a Golden Age model, but it can be a Golden Rule model only under very special circumstances.[6]

The object of this paper is to present a comprehensive analysis of the one-sector, neoclassical theory of growth under conditions of neutral and biased technical progress.[7] The model of growth and technical progress presented here is a synthesis of models developed by many writers. Originality lies chiefly in the interpretive and expository aspects of the paper and possibly in the approach to stability conditions.[8] The analysis relies upon a simple graphical device and upon two elementary mathematical relations. It is hoped that the paper presents a graphical technique by which neoclassical growth models can be analyzed.

Notation

The notation used throughout is standard and largely mnemonic; however, it is convenient to set out all symbols in catalogue form:

Y = national income or output measured in units of the single output produced by the economy;

K = either the stock of homogeneous capital or the flow of homogeneous capital services measured in units of the single output which, in one-sector models, must be both a consumption and a capital good;

L = quantity of homogeneous labor employed;

I = investment, measured in units of the single output;

S = savings, measured in units of output;

A = production function constant;

T = rate of technical progress;

H = measure of Hicks-biased technical progress;

$G_x{}^a$ = actual rate of growth of any variable x, i.e., $G_x{}^a = \dfrac{\dot{x}}{x}$, where a superior

---

[4]For examples, see Smithies [30], Uzawa [36], and Vanek [39] and [40].

[5]See Ferguson [13].

[6]See Phelps [27].

[7]Most of the literature deals with the case of neutral technical progress. Biased progress has been studied chiefly in connection with two-sector models. See, for examples, Diamond [6], Fei and Ranis [9] and [10], and Takayama [33]. An exception for one-sector models is Amano [1]. Also, biased progress in a one-sector model was treated tangentially by Smithies [30].

[8]In each section there are footnotes to indicate: (a.) the models upon which the synthesis is based, and (b.) what is thought to be original and what is a summary and restatement of existing work.

dot indicates the operator $\dfrac{d}{dt}$;

$G_x{}^n =$ natural rate of growth of x;

$n =$ rate of growth of the labor force;

$w =$ real wage rate of labor;

$r =$ real rate of return on capital;

$s =$ savings ratio;

$t =$ time;

$y =$ output-labor ratio;

$k =$ capital-labor ratio;

$\sigma =$ elasticity of substitution;

$\pi =$ ratio of the relative share of labor to the relative share of capital;

$\alpha =$ relative share of capital;

$\lambda =$ rate of Hicks-neutral technical progress; and

$\eta, \theta =$ variable production function coefficients of capital and labor respectively.

Assumptions

The analysis depends upon five general assumptions and a variety of special assumptions that are introduced from time to time. The latter are noted explicitly when relevant; the general assumptions are stated now and are not repeated.

A.1. The economy produces a single output (Y) by utilizing two inputs, capital (K) and labor (L). Each of the inputs is homogeneous within itself.

A.2. Output is produced according to the neoclassical production function

(1.) $Y = F(K, L, t).$

The production function is continuous and twice differentiable. The marginal products (F_K and F_L) are continuous, positive, and declining over the relevant range; that is,

$$F_K > 0, \ F_L > 0, \ F_{KK} < 0, \ F_{LL} < 0.$$

A.3. The production function is homogeneous of degree one in K and L. Thus (1.) may also be written:

(2.) $y = f(k, t).$

A.4. The economy maintains a position of competitive equilibrium, which implies that inputs are rewarded according to competitive imputations; that is,

(3.) $r = F_K = f'(k); \ w = F_L = f(k) - kf'(k).$

A.5. The labor force is always fully employed and grows at the constant rate n; that is,

(4.) $L(t) = L(0)e^{nt},$

so

(5.) $$G_L{}^a = G_L{}^n = n.$$

Geometry

The conventional isoquant map is of little use in portraying growth because it is cumbersome to construct growth paths. A slight modification, however, permits one to do this readily. First, note that an isoquant is obtained from (1.) by setting

(6.) $$dY = F_K dK + F_L dL = 0.$$

The slope of the isoquant is

(7.) $$-\frac{dK}{dL} = \frac{F_L}{F_K},$$

or the marginal rate of technical substitution. By A.2., the isoquant is negatively sloped and concave from above.

The isoquant so obtained is plotted in the K-L space. To permit easy representation of growth rates, plot the isoquant in the log K-log L space. The only problem is to determine the shape of the isoquant; its slope must be negative since capital and labor are assumed to be substitutable. Consider the expression for the slope of the isoquant plotted in the log K-log L space:

(8.) $$-\frac{d \log K}{d \log L} = -\frac{\dfrac{dK}{K}}{\dfrac{dL}{L}}$$

$$= -\frac{dK}{dL} \frac{L}{K},$$

which, from (7.) and A.4, is

(9.) $$-\frac{d \log K}{d \log L} = \frac{F_L L}{F_K K} = \frac{wL}{rK} = \pi.$$

The slope of the isoquant is, therefore, the ratio of relative shares. Consequently, the curvature of the isoquant depends entirely upon the elasticity of substitution at any instant of time. This property is illustrated in Figure 16-1. Panel a shows two isoquants for the Cobb-Douglas function, that is, $\sigma = 1$. Relative shares are constant, and the isoquants must accordingly be parallel straight lines. (See pg. 260 for Figure 16-1.)

Panels b and c depict isoquants representing inelastic and elastic substitutability respectively. First consider Panel b and the isoquant Y_0. Since $\sigma < 1$,

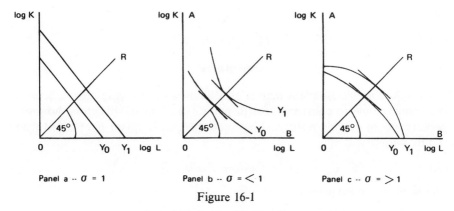

Figure 16-1

Isoquants in Double Log Space

an increase in the capital-labor ratio from any initial level must cause an increase in the relative share of labor. For movements downward and to the right, the isoquant must become progressively flatter. Hence overall, the isoquant must be concave from above when the elasticity of substitution is less than unity.

Next, consider a level of output greater than Y_0, say Y_1. The line OR is the 45° line, along which capital and labor grow at the same rate. Movement along the ray OR accordingly implies a constant capital-labor ratio and, consequently, constant relative shares. Hence, the slopes of Y_1 and Y_0 must be the same at the points where they are cut by OR. Along any ray whose slope is greater than OR, capital grows more rapidly than labor. Thus the capital-labor ratio increases, accompanied by an increase in the relative share of labor. Accordingly, given any ray properly within the open cone AOR, the slopes of the successive isoquants must be progressively greater at the points where they are intersected by the ray. The reverse argument applies to any ray properly within the open cone ROB. Hence, Y_0 and Y_1 in Panel b indicate the general appearance of the isoquant map when the elasticity of substitution is less than unity. It should be clear that exactly analogous arguments show that the isoquants are concave from below when the elasticity of substitution is greater than unity and that they shift in the manner shown in Panel c, Figure 16-1.

Finally, it is possible to indicate the way in which the isoquants shift in most instances of neutral and biased technical progress.[9] The Hicks definition is adopted throughout: technical progress is labor using, neutral, or capital using according as the ratio of relative shares (π) increases, remains unchanged, or decreases for a given capital-labor ratio. Since neutral technical progress does not affect relative shares, Y_0 and Y_1 in Figure 16-1 actually represent neutral

---

[9]It is subsequently shown that the isoquant shifts are indeterminate when (a.) $\sigma < 1$ and technical progress is capital using, and when (b.) $\sigma > 1$ and technical progress is labor using. These cases are immaterial, however, inasmuch as the results of the neoclassical model are also indeterminate.

technical progress.[10] In most cases, labor-using technical progress is represented by progressively steeper isoquants and capital-using technical progress by progressively flatter isoquants.

The Neoclassical Theory of Growth [11]

From (1.) the actual rate of income growth is

(10.) $$G_Y^a = \alpha G_K + (1 - \alpha)G_L + T,$$

where

$$T = \frac{F_t}{F}.$$

According to the definition introduced previously, the natural rate of income growth is that rate which preserves full employment while maintaining a constant capital-output ratio. Thus along the natural path,

(11.) $$G_L = n \text{ and } G_Y = G_K.$$

Using (11.) in (10.), the natural path of income growth is given by

(12.) $$G_Y^n = n + \frac{T}{1 - \alpha}.$$

The conditions of macroeconomic equilibrium impose an additional restriction: saving must equal investment, or

(13.) $$S = I,$$

where

(14.) $$S = sY,$$

and

(15.) $$I = \dot{K}.$$

Equations (13.), (14.), and (15.) together imply

(16.) $$G_I = \frac{\dot{I}}{I} = \frac{\ddot{K}}{\dot{K}} = G_S + G_Y.$$

---

[10]One normally depicts technical progress by a uniform shift of the isoquant toward the origin. This movement shows that the same output may be obtained from smaller input combinations. The isoquants here are shown as moving outward because full employment of the constantly growing inputs is assumed.

[11]The model developed in this section is intended to be a general representation of the one-sector, neoclassical model. It differs from the conventional form only in the way in which the stability conditions are analyzed. For similar general models, see Amano [1], Drandakis and Phelps [8], Ferguson [12] and [13], Green [14], Inada [18], Jones [22], Swan [32], and Uzawa [38]. For similar models in which technical progress is purely factor augmenting, see David and van de Klundert [5], Ferguson [11], and Phelps [27]. For the special cases of Cobb-Douglas production function, but otherwise similar, see Brems [3], Hahn [15], Smithies [30], and Solow [31].

Two important questions concerning growth equilibrium immediately arise: (1.) Can the natural rate be a *constant* rate, either permanently or asymtotically? and (2.) Is the existence of a natural path of any kind consistent with a constant saving ratio? Attention is first directed to the latter question.

If the saving ratio is constant, $G_s = 0$ and (16.) becomes, along the natural path,

(17.) $$G_I{}^n = \frac{\ddot{K}}{\dot{K}} = G_Y{}^n.$$

At an initial point on the natural path, providing it exists, $G_K{}^n = G_Y{}^n$. Hence, the rate of acceleration of capital from an initial equilibrium on the natural path is

(18.) $$\frac{d\left(\dfrac{\dot{K}}{K}\right)}{dt} \frac{K}{\dot{K}} = \frac{\ddot{K}}{\dot{K}} - \frac{\dot{K}}{K} = \frac{K}{\dot{K}} \frac{d}{dt}\left(n + \frac{T}{1 - \alpha}\right).$$

From (18.):

(19.) $$\lim_{t \to \infty}\left[\frac{\ddot{K}}{\dot{K}} - \frac{\dot{K}}{K}\right] = \frac{K}{\dot{K}} \lim_{t \to \infty} \frac{d}{dt}\left(n + \frac{T}{1 - \alpha}\right).$$

The last expression is crucially important. If $G_Y{}^n = n + \dfrac{T}{1 - \alpha}$ is a constant, $\dfrac{d}{dt}\left(n + \dfrac{T}{1 - \alpha}\right) = 0$. The rate of growth of capital is always equal to the rate of growth of saving, investment, and income. Similarly, if

(20.) $$\lim_{t \to \infty} \frac{d}{dt}\left(n + \frac{T}{1 - \alpha}\right) \to 0,$$

the natural path is asymptotically constant and stable. The rate of growth of capital approaches the rate of growth of investment which, by (17.), must equal the rate of growth of income. On the other hand, if the limit in (20.) is not zero, the rate of growth of capital is different from the rate of growth of investment. Since the latter necessarily equals the rate of growth of income when the saving ratio is constant, the natural path cannot exist (or is unstable) when the saving ratio is constant.

The question whether the natural rate can be a constant rate is dealt with in the remainder of the paper.

The Cobb-Douglas Case ($\sigma = 1$)

Neutral Technical Progress [12]

The case of neutral technical progress and unit elasticity of substitution is the one yielding the most direct and conclusive answers. The production function

---

[12]For almost identical models, see Brems [3], Hahn [15], Smithies [30], and Solow [31].

becomes

(21.) $$Y = Ae^{\lambda t}K^{\alpha}L^{1-\alpha}, \quad \lambda \geqq 0;$$

and the expression for the natural rate of growth is

(22.) $$G_Y{}^n = G_K{}^n = n + \frac{\lambda}{1-\alpha} > n = G_L.$$

Since n, λ, and α are constants, the rate of growth of capital equals the rate of growth of investment. The natural path exists with a constant saving ratio and it is globally stable. The situation is illustrated in Panel a, Figure 16-2.

The arrow labeled $n + \dfrac{\lambda}{1-\alpha}$ represents the constant rates of growth of output, capital, investment, and saving. Thus, the rates of growth of the output-labor and capital-labor ratios are $\dfrac{\lambda}{1-\alpha}$. If the initial capital-labor ratio is such as to place the economy at point 1, all variables will always grow at their constant rates, including relative shares (i.e., $G_\pi = 0$). If the initial endowment ratio is not the equilibrium ratio, the rate of investment adjusts so that the economy rapidly converges to the equilibrium path.

Consider the original endowment represented by point 2. At this point, the output-capital ratio $\left(\dfrac{Y}{K}\right)^0$ is greater than the equilibrium ratio at point 1, $\left(\dfrac{Y}{K}\right)^*$. The actual rate of investment is thus greater than the natural rate:

(23.) $$\left(\frac{I}{K}\right)^0 = s\left(\frac{Y}{K}\right)^0 > s\left(\frac{Y}{K}\right)^* = \left(\frac{I}{K}\right)^*$$

Capital and the capital-labor ratio accordingly grow more rapidly than the natural rate, as indicated by the dashed path. Since the actual capital-labor ratio grows more rapidly than the equilibrium capital-labor ratio, the actual output-capital ratio must eventually equal the equilibrium output-capital ratio, so that

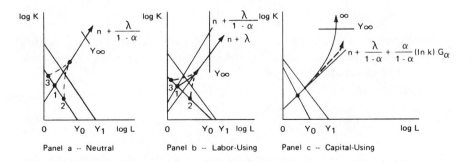

Panel a -- Neutral   Panel b -- Labor-Using   Panel c -- Capital-Using

Figure 16-2

The Natural Path with Unit Elasticity of Substitution

the actual and natural rates of investment are equal. The inequality in (23.) is removed, and the economy proceeds along the natural path. By an analogous argument one may prove that an initial endowment ratio greater than the equilibrium ratio (such as point 3) sets in motion forces that cause an adjustment to equilibrium.

The moving equilibrium established by neutral technological progress and unit elasticity of substitution truly represents a Golden Age path. Every variable grows at a constant rate, including the rate of return on capital. Indeed, it is easy to prove that the variables of interest grow at the following rates:

$$G_Y = G_K = G_I = G_S = n + \frac{\lambda}{1 - \alpha},$$

(24.)
$$G_k = G_w = \frac{\lambda}{1 - \alpha},$$

$$G_s = G_\pi = G_r = 0.$$

Biased Technical Progress [13]

Biased technical progress can be introduced into the Cobb-Douglas function only by allowing the exponents to become functions of time, that is, $\alpha = \alpha(t)$. The production function is now written

(25.)
$$Y = Ae^{\lambda t}K^{\alpha(t)}L^{1-\alpha(t)},$$

where technical progress is labor using, neutral, or capital using according as $\dot\alpha \lessgtr 0$. Obviously, if $\dot\alpha < 0$, $\alpha \to 0$ as $t \to \infty$; if $\dot\alpha > 0$, $\alpha \to 1$ as $t \to \infty$. The asymptotically stable case in which technical progress is labor using, that is, $\dot\alpha < 0$, is considered first.

At any instant of time, the natural rate of growth of income is

(26.)
$$G_Y{}^n = n + \frac{\lambda}{1 - \alpha} + \frac{\alpha}{1 - \alpha}(\ln k)\, G_\alpha.$$

However,

(27.)
$$\lim_{t \to \infty} G_Y{}^n = n + \lambda,$$

a constant rate. Therefore a constant natural path will be consistent with a constant saving ratio if the rate of growth of capital is asymptotically the same as the rate of growth of investment.

From (26.), the counterpart of (19.) is

(28.)
$$\lim_{\substack{t \to \infty \\ \alpha \to 0}} \left[\frac{\ddot K}{K} - \frac{\dot K}{K} \right] = \lim_{\substack{t \to \infty \\ \alpha \to 0}} \frac{K}{\dot K} \left[\frac{\lambda \dot\alpha}{(1 - \alpha)^2} \right] = 0,$$

---

[13]To my knowledge, this special case of the general biased progress model has never appeared previously in the literature.

since $\dot{\alpha} \to 0$ as $\alpha \to 0$. Thus, the rates of growth of capital and investment are ultimately equal and equal to the natural rate of income growth. This is illustrated by Panel b, Figure 16-2. Suppose the initial capital-labor ratio is the equilibrium ratio, so movement begins from point 1 on Y_0. The initial rate of growth of output and investment is $n + \dfrac{\lambda}{1 - \alpha}$. These variables experience a decline as α becomes less and less, ultimately approaching the equilibrium path $n + \lambda$, as indicated by the solid arrow. Now, as t increases, the presence of labor-using technical progress causes the isoquant to shift, becoming progressively steeper (as illustrated by the slopes of Y_0, Y_1, ..., Y_∞). Thus, the graph also shows that ultimately the share of labor approaches unity and the share of capital approaches zero.

Along the way, the actual rates of growth of capital and of the capital-labor ratio exceed the equilibrium rates:

$$(29.) \qquad G_K{}^a = \frac{\dot{K}}{K} = \frac{\lambda}{1 - \alpha} + n - \frac{\lambda \dot{\alpha}}{(1 - \alpha)^2} > G_Y{}^n,$$

since $\dot{\alpha} < 0$. Thus the actual path lies above the equilibrium path, but it approaches the natural path as $t \to \infty$. The asymptotic equilibrium is shown schematically by the vertical isoquant Y_∞. Ultimately, capital, output, saving, and investment all grow at the rate $n + \lambda$. The solution, however, is not particularly appealing because $r \to 0$ as $t \to \infty$ and the rate of growth of the wage rate increases without bound, since $\log {}_e k$ increases without bound.

In summary, labor-using technical progress and unit elasticity of substitution establish an asymptotically constant and stable natural path. The natural path does not represent a Golden Age because some variables change at variable rates; and the natural rate is unrealistic, even for "unrealistic" models, because the rate of return on capital approaches zero.[14]

The case of capital-using technical progress is of even less interest and will be treated summarily (see Panel c, Figure 16-2). The initial natural rate is given by (26.); however, since $\alpha \to 1$, $(1 - \alpha) \to 0$ and

$$(30.) \qquad \lim_{t \to \infty} G_Y{}^n = \infty.$$

The natural path is a variable path, and it is also unstable with a constant saving ratio. This may readily be seen by noting that

---

[14]The reader may easily prove for himself that initial endowments such as points 2 and 3 ultimately lead to the equilibrium path. For example, at point 2, the actual output-capital ratio is greater than the equilibrium ratio (since K at 2 is less than K at 1 and Y is the same, both points being on the isoquant Y_0). Thus, the actual rate of investment is greater than the natural rate, and capital and the capital-labor ratio accordingly grow at a rate greater than the natural rate. Hence, the actual output-capital ratio must decline and eventually equal the equilibrium ratio.

(31.) $$\frac{\ddot{K}}{\dot{K}} - \frac{\dot{K}}{K} = \frac{K}{\dot{K}} \frac{d}{dt} \left[n + \frac{\lambda}{1-\alpha} + \frac{\alpha}{1-\alpha} (\ln k) \, G_\alpha \right].$$

Taking the derivative on the right-hand side and applying L'Hospital's rule, one sees that there is ultimately an infinite divergence between the rate of growth of investment and the rate of growth of the capital stock. Thus the natural path does not exist, since the rate of growth of capital cannot equal the rate of growth of income when the saving ratio is constant. A variable saving ratio is required to establish a natural path; but even then the natural path is a variable path, and the relative share of labor goes to zero, as indicated by the horizontal isoquant Y_∞.[15] Finally, as indicated by the dashed line, capital and the capital-labor ratio always grow more slowly than required by the natural rate, and the output-capital ratio is always too high.

Neutral Technical Progress and Non-Unit Elasticity [16]

The Cobb-Douglas case makes for simple analysis because biased technical progress is the only force that can cause a change in relative shares. Neutral progress with non-unit elasticity of substitution is equally simple because a change in the capital-labor ratio is the only force that can cause a change in relative shares. In this section inelastic and elastic substitutability are analyzed by means of Panel a, Figures 16-3 and 16-4, respectively.

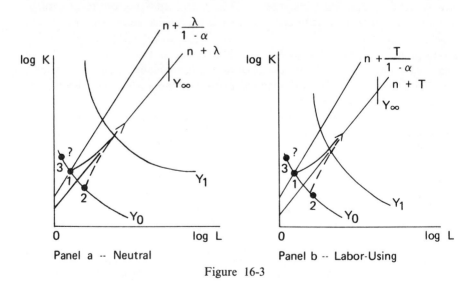

Panel a -- Neutral   Panel b -- Labor-Using

Figure 16-3

The Natural Path with Inelastic Substitution

---

[15]For more detail on the variable saving ratio, see Ferguson [13].
[16]The results presented in this section, though implicit in several models, are believed to be original.

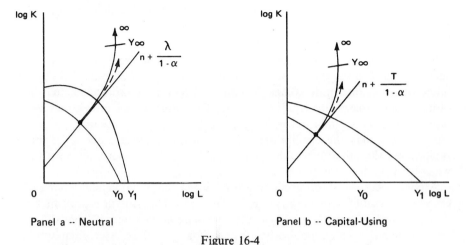

Panel a -- Neutral   Panel b -- Capital-Using

Figure 16-4

The Natural Path with Elastic Substitution

Inelastic Substitution

For neutral technical progress at a constant rate, the production function becomes

(32.) $$Y = e^{\lambda t}F(K, L),$$

and the natural rate of growth is

(33.) $$G_Y{}^n = n + \frac{\lambda}{1 - \alpha} > n.$$

Starting from the equilibrium endowment at point 1 (Panel a, Figure 16-3), the capital stock grows more rapidly than the labor force, thus causing the capital-labor ratio to increase. The increase in the capital-labor ratio causes an increase in the marginal rate of technical substitution which, by the equilibrium assumption, implies that $dw > dr$. Given $\sigma < 1$, $dw > dr$ implies $\dot{\alpha} < 0$.

Thus,

(34.) $$\lim_{t \to \infty} G_Y{}^n = \lim_{t \to \infty} n + \frac{\lambda}{1 - \alpha} = n + \lambda.$$

The natural path is asymptotically constant, as shown by the heavy arrow in Panel a. The natural path is also stable (that is, it exists) because the rates of growth of capital and investment are asymptotically identical:

(35.) $$\lim_{t \to \infty} \left[\frac{\ddot{K}}{\dot{K}} - \frac{\dot{K}}{K} \right] = \lim_{t \to \infty} \frac{K}{\dot{K}} \left[\frac{\lambda \dot{\alpha}}{(1 - \alpha)^2} \right] = 0,$$

since $\dot\alpha \to 0$ as $\alpha \to 0$. In transition to equilibrium, capital and the capital-labor ratio grow somewhat more rapidly than output and the output-labor ratio respectively. But asymptotically they merge.

Starting from an initial endowment ratio smaller than the equilibrium ratio, such as point 2 in Panel a, causes a rapid convergence to equilibrium. Since the initial output-capital ratio is greater than the equilibrium ratio, the actual rate of investment exceeds the equilibrium rate. The capital-labor ratio grows more rapidly than the equilibrium ratio, and the share of labor accordingly grows more rapidly than the equilibrium rate. Thus, convergence tends to be more rapid when the initial capital-labor ratio is below the equilibrium ratio than when it equals the equilibrium ratio.

A convergence problem arises, however, when the initial capital-labor ratio exceeds the equilibrium ratio (point 3, Panel a). This situation presented no difficulty in the Cobb-Douglas case because the relative share of labor did not depend upon the capital-labor ratio. In this situation it does. The initial output-capital ratio is less than the equilibrium ratio, which implies that the actual rate of investment is less than the equilibrium rate. Thus, the actual rate of growth of capital is less than the equilibrium rate. The equilibrium rate exceeds the rate of growth of the labor force (see (33.)). However, the actual rate of growth of capital could be less than the rate of growth of the labor force. In that event the capital-labor ratio would decrease and the relative share of capital would increase. The exact behavior is indeterminate.

For most initial endowments, nonetheless, the natural rate exists and is asymptotically constant. It has a further interesting property. Though labor's relative share continually increases and approaches unity as $t \to \infty$, the rate of return on capital may remain constant or even increase in the short run. Of course it must ultimately approach zero.

From (32.) and the assumption of competitive imputations,

(36.)
$$G_r = \frac{\dot r}{r} = \frac{\dot F_K}{F_K} = \lambda - \sigma_{KK}G_k,$$

where

$$\sigma_{KK} = -\frac{KF_{KK}}{F_K} = \frac{LF_{KL}}{F_K}.$$

Obviously, the rate of return increases, remains unchanged, or diminishes according as $\lambda \gtreqless \sigma_{KK}G_k$. The rate of growth of the wage rate is always positive and is given by

(37.)
$$G_w = \lambda + \sigma_{LL}G_k,$$

where

$$\sigma_{LL} = \frac{KF_{LK}}{F_L} = -\frac{LF_{LL}}{F_L}.$$

Finally, the wage-rate of return ratio, or the marginal rate of technical substitution, always increases, as shown by subtracting (36.) from (37.):

(38.) $$G_w - G_r = \frac{1}{\sigma} G_k,$$

since $\sigma_{KK} + \sigma_{LL} = \frac{1}{\sigma}$ by the latter's definition.[17]

Elastic Substitution

The case of elastic substitution with neutral technical progress and a constant saving ratio may quickly be shown to be uninteresting (see Panel a, Figure 16-4). With $\sigma > 1$ and $G_k > 0$, $\dot{\alpha} > 0$ and $\alpha \to 1$ as $t \to \infty$. Thus (34.) is changed to

(39.) $$\lim_{t \to \infty} G_Y{}^n = \lim_{t \to \infty} n + \frac{\lambda}{1 - \alpha} = \infty.$$

The natural path, if it exists, is a variable path; but it does not exist because there is always a divergence between the rates of growth of capital and of investment, which may easily be seen by applying L'Hospital's rule to the analogue of (35.). Thus, the rate of growth of capital cannot equal the rate of growth of income. The natural path does not exist when the saving ratio is constant. Further, the output-capital ratio is always too high and the rates of growth of capital and the capital-labor ratio too low.

Non-Unitary Substitution and Biased Technical Progress [18]

With non-unitary substitution and biased progress the general form of the production function is that shown in (1.) and repeated here as

(40.) $$Y = F(K, L, t).$$

The natural rate of growth is thus

(41.) $$G_Y{}^n = n + \frac{T}{1 - \alpha},$$

where $$T = \frac{F_t}{F}.$$

Before examining the various cases it is helpful to consider the general expression for the rate of growth of the ratio of relative shares $\left(\pi = \frac{wL}{rK} \right)$. The calculus of growth immediately yields

---

[17]That is, for functions homogeneous of degree one, $\sigma = \dfrac{F_K F_L}{F F_{KL}}$

[18]The general model of technical progress presented here is well established in the literature. See Amano [1], Bardhan [2], Diamond [6], Drandakis and Phelps [8], Fei and Ranis [9] and [10], and Jones [22]. Certain interpretative results and the treatment of the stability conditions are believed to be original.

(42.) $$G_\pi = (G_w - G_r) - G_k.$$

From (40.) one obtains

(43.) $$G_w = \frac{F_{Lt}}{F_L} + \sigma_{LL} G_k,$$

and

(44.) $$G_r = \frac{F_{Kt}}{F_K} - \sigma_{KK} G_k.$$

Subtracting (44.) from (43.) yields

(45.) $$G_w - G_r = H + \frac{1}{\sigma} G_k,$$

where

$$H = \frac{F_{Lt}}{F_L} - \frac{F_{Kt}}{F_K}.$$

Obviously, technical progress is (Hicks) labor using, neutral, or capital using according as $H \gtreqless 0$.

Substituting (45.) in (42.), one obtains

(46.) $$G_r = H + \left(\frac{1 - \sigma}{\sigma}\right) G_k.$$

By definition of the growth path, $G_k > 0$. Thus

$$\left(\frac{1 - \sigma}{\sigma}\right) G_k \gtreqless 0 \text{ according as } \sigma \lesseqgtr 1.$$

In two instances opposing forces are encountered. If the elasticity of substitution is less than one, the second term on the right in (46.) tends to augment π. However, if technical progress is capital using, the first term tends to reduce π. A priori, the case of capital-using technical progress coupled with inelastic substitutability is indeterminate. By analogous reasoning, labor-using technical progress and elastic substitutability lead to an indeterminate model. There are thus only two cases to consider, illustrated by Panel b, Figures 16-3 and 16-4.

Inelastic Substitution and Labor-Using Technical Progress

With $\sigma < 1$ and $H > 0$, both terms in (46.) augment π; hence $\dot\alpha < 0$. Therefore

(47.) $$\lim_{t \to \infty} G_Y^n = \lim_{t \to \infty} n + \frac{T}{1 - \alpha} = n + T.$$

The natural path is asymptotically constant if it exists. The crucial consideration for the existence of the natural path is the asymptotic difference between the rates of growth of investment and of the capital stock:

$$(48.) \qquad \lim_{t \to \infty} \left[\frac{\ddot{K}}{\dot{K}} - \frac{\dot{K}}{K} \right] = \lim_{t \to \infty} \frac{K}{\dot{K}} \left[\frac{(1 - \alpha)\dot{T} + T\dot{\alpha}}{(1 - \alpha)^2} \right].$$

Presumably $\dot{\alpha} \to 0$ as $\alpha \to 0$. If the rate of technical progress T is constant or declining, $\dot{T}$ will equal or approach zero. However, if $\dot{T} > 0$, the natural path will not exist. $\dot{T} > 0$ is not itself very plausible; hence it does not seem unreasonable to believe that the growth path exists and is asymptotically constant.

As in the case of neutral progress with inelastic substitutability, there is some question as to convergence when the initial capital-labor ratio is greater than the equilibrium ratio (point 3, Panel b, Figure 16-3). In this instance, convergence is more likely because $H > 0$ tends to augment π irrespective of the actual G_k. Thus, even if $G_k{}^a < 0$, $\pi > 0$ is not precluded, and this is all that is needed for ultimate convergence.

Elastic Substitution and Capital-Using Technical Progress

The last case may be disposed of quickly. With $H < 0$ and $\sigma > 1$, both terms in (46.) work to decrease π. Hence $\dot{\alpha} > 0$ and $\alpha \to 1$ as $t \to \infty$. Accordingly

$$(49.) \qquad \lim_{t \to \infty} G_Y{}^n = \lim_{t \to \infty} n + \frac{T}{1 - \alpha} = \infty.$$

The natural path is not constant even if it exists. Using L'Hospital's rule, it is also easy to show that it does not exist if the saving ratio is constant.

Taxonomy of Growth Models

From the preceding discussion it is clear that there are three crucial elements in the general neoclassical theory of growth: the nature of technical progress, the value of the elasticity of substitution, and the behavior of the saving ratio. If one assumes that the saving ratio is constant, as I have done throughout, these factors reduce to two. From the foregoing results, Table 16-1 may be prepared.

Table 16-1

The Taxonomy of Growth Models

Elasticity of substitution	Nature of technical progress		
	Neutral	Labor using	Capital using
$\sigma = 1$	Stable, constant	Stable, constant	Unstable, variable
$\sigma < 1$	Stable, constant	Stable, constant	Indeterminate
$\sigma > 1$	Unstable, variable	Indeterminate	Unstable, variable

Three comments seem in order. First, any combination involving elastic substitutability or capital-using technical progress is academically uninteresting so long as one holds to a constant saving ratio.[19] Second, within the upper left 2 x 2 of interesting cases, only neutral progress and unit elasticity provide a

---

[19]Further comments on this point are made in my conclusions.

permanently constant natural path. The other three cases involve only asymptotic constancy. Third, the four stable cases are readily seen to involve Harrod-neutral technical progress. Thus, whether one begins with the definition of the natural path as the Harrod-neutral path, as I have done, or whether he deduces it as a stability condition, the results are the same.

Purely Factor-Augmenting Technical Progress

An interesting specialization of the production function in equation (40.) occurs when one postulates that technical progress is purely factor augmenting. On the one hand, this specialization permits empirical implementation of the model;[20] on the other, it is useful in theoretical studies of the turnpike and the "golden rule."[21] Under the assumption of strictly factor-augmenting technical progress, the production function may be written as

$$(50.) \qquad\qquad Y = F[\eta(t)K, \; \theta(t)L].$$

When the production function has the form shown in (50.), H takes the following form:

$$(51.) \qquad H = \left[\frac{F_{Lt}}{F_L} - \frac{F_{Kt}}{F_K} \right] = \left[\frac{\dot{\theta}}{\theta} - \frac{\dot{\eta}}{\eta} \right]\left[1 - \frac{1}{\sigma} \right].$$

Many economists apparently believe that the "efficiency growth" of labor has exceeded that of capital.[22] If this is a plausible assumption,

$$\frac{\dot{\theta}}{\theta} - \frac{\dot{\eta}}{\eta} > 0,$$

and the first term on the right in (51.) is positive. In this special case, the *bias* of technical progress depends entirely upon the *magnitude* of the elasticity of substitution. In particular,

$$(52.) \qquad\qquad H \gtreqless 0 \text{ according as } \sigma \gtreqless 1.$$

Thus, if the elasticity of substitution exceeds unity, technical progress must be labor using; and, contrariwise, if the elasticity of substitution is less than unity, technical progress must be capital using.

Consequently, if the rate of labor augmentation exceeds the rate of capital augmentation, only *a priori indeterminate* situations can materialize unless $H = 0$.[23]

---

[20]See David and van de Klundert [5] and Ferguson [11].

[21]See Phelps [27].

[22]See especially David and van de Klundert [5].

[23]It is interesting to note that the empirical results, though different in most respects, point to indeterminacy. David and van de Klundert [5] found inelastic substitutability and capital-using technical progress. Ferguson [11] found elastic substitutability and labor-using technical progress. Needless to say, these empirical studies do not measure an economy moving along an equilibrium path of exponential growth. In a different connection, Phelps [27] has shown that a Golden Rule path exists if, and only if, the model is characterized by Harrod-neutral progress, which is represented by purely labor-augmenting technical progress.

Conclusion

The morals to be got from this piece of taxonomy seem to emerge clearly. They are now listed, not necessarily in order of importance.

(1.) The *nature* of technical progress, the *magnitude* of the elasticity of substitution, and the *behavior* of the saving ratio are the three crucial elements in the neoclassical theory of economic growth. This, of course, presumes the assumptions introduced earlier. These may be changed and they may be criticized. One may use a two-sector model, which gains realism at the sacrifice of simplicity. Yet much the same conclusions emerge.[24] Next, if a one-sector model is used, and if the spirit of the neoclassical theory is retained, I see no alternative to assumptions A.2, A.3, and A.4. In principle, one could sacrifice the assumption of constant labor force growth without doing extreme violence to neoclassical theory. Yet empirically, the rate of growth of the labor force has been secularly constant over an extraordinarily long period of time. Thus, little by way of realism could be gained by dropping A.5. Hence, it seems that if one is to deal with single-sector, neoclassical models, there are only three factors of basic interest.

(2.) If theory is to be a guide to empirical research, emphasis must be placed upon purely factor-augmenting technical progress. For one reason, this comprises the only class of empirically feasible production functions. More importantly, perhaps, this is also the only class for which both the elasticity of substitution and the bias of technical progress are uniquely identified.[25] At the same time, this is theoretically less satisfying than the more general model.

(3.) It seems reasonably well established that the aggregate elasticity of substitution is unity or less; or at least, further studies are likely to produce elasticity coefficients lying within the existing disparate bounds. What does become important is the relative rates of "efficiency growth" of capital and labor (see (51.)).

(4.) Finally, the item I have so far ignored demands attention. The saving ratio may not be a constant; it may be a stabilizing variable susceptible of policy control; and policy control may be very important if short-run disequilibria are to be kept consistent with long-run equilibrium conditions.

---

[24]See, for example, Corden [4], Inada [17], [19], and [20], Jones [21], Takayama [33], Uzawa [35] and [37], and Vanek [39].
[25]See Diamond, McFadden, and Rodriguez [7].

Bibliography

[1] Akihiro Amano. "Biased Technical Progress and a Neoclassical Theory of Growth." *Quarterly Journal of Economics,* Vol. 78, No. 1 (February, 1964), pp. 129–138.

[2] Pranab Bardhan. "On Factor-Biased Technical Progress and International Trade." *Journal of Political Economy,* Vol. 73, No. 4 (August, 1965), pp. 396–398.

[3] Hans Brems. "Growth, Distribution, Productivities, and Thrift in Cobb-Douglas Models." *Southern Economic Journal,* Vol. 29, No. 3 (January, 1963), pp. 181–188.

[4] W. M. Corden. "The Two-Sector Growth Model with Fixed Coefficients." *Review of Economic Studies,* Vol. 33, No. 95 (July, 1966), pp. 253–262.

[5] P. A. David and Theo van de Klundert. "Biased Efficiency Growth and Capital-Labor Substitution in the U. S., 1899–1960." *American Economic Review,* Vol. 55, No. 3 (June, 1965), pp. 357–394.

[6] Peter A. Diamond. "Disembodied Technical Change in a Two-Sector Model." *Review of Economic Studies,* Vol. 32, No. 90 (April, 1965), pp. 161–168.

[7] _____, Daniel McFadden, and Miguel Rodriguez. "Identification of the Elasticity of Substitution and the Bias of Technical Change." mimeographed manuscript.

[8] E. M. Drandakis and Edmund S. Phelps. "A Model of Induced Invention, Growth, and Distribution." *Economic Journal,* Vol. 76, No. 304 (December, 1966), pp. 823–840.

[9] John C. H. Fei and Gustav Ranis. "Innovation, Capital Accumulation and Economic Development." *American Economic Review,* Vol. 53, No. 3 (June, 1963), pp. 283–313.

[10] _____. "Innovational Intensity and Factor Bias in the Theory of Growth." *International Economic Review,* Vol. 6, No. 2 (May, 1965), pp. 182–198.

[11] C. E. Ferguson. "Substitution, Technical Progress, and Returns to Scale." *American Economic Review, Papers and Proceedings,* Vol. 55, No. 2 (May, 1965), pp. 296–305.

[12] _____. "Savings and the Capital-Output Ratio in the Neoclassical Theory of Growth." *Quarterly Review of Economics and Business,* Vol. 5, No. 2 (Summer, 1965), pp. 53–63.

[13] _____. "The Elasticity of Substitution and the Savings Ratio in the Neoclassical Theory of Growth." *Quarterly Journal of Economics,* Vol. 79, No. 3 (August, 1965), pp. 465–471.

[14] H. A. John Green. "Growth Models, Capital, and Stability." *Economic Journal,* Vol. 70, No. 277 (March, 1960), pp. 57–73.

[15] F. H. Hahn. "The Stability of Growth Equilibrium." *Quarterly Journal of Economics,* Vol. 74, No. 2 (May, 1960), pp. 206–226.

[16] R. F. Harrod. *Towards a Dynamic Economics.* London: Macmillan, 1948.

[17] K. I. Inada. "On a Two-Sector Model of Economic Growth: Comments and a Generalization." *Review of Economic Studies,* Vol. 30, No. 83 (June, 1963), pp. 119–127.

[18] –_____ "Economic Growth Under Neutral Technical Progress." *Econometrica,* Vol. 32, No. 1–2 (January–April, 1964), pp. 101–21.

[19] _____. "On the Stability of Growth Equilibria in Two-Sector Models." *Review of Economic Studies,* Vol. 31, No. 86 (April, 1964), pp. 127–142.

[20] _____. "On Neoclassical Models of Economic Growth." *Review of Economic Studies,* Vol. 32, No. 90 (April, 1965), pp. 151–160.

[21] Ronald W. Jones. "The Structure of Simple General Equilibrium Models." *Journal of Political Economy,* Vol. 73, No. 6 (December, 1965), pp. 557–572.

[22] _____. " 'Neutral' Technological Change and the Isoquant Map." *American Economic Review,* Vol. 55, No. 4 (September, 1965), pp. 848–855.

[23] Nicholas Kaldor. "A Model of Economic Growth." *Economic Journal.* Vol. 67, No. 267 (September, 1957), pp. 591–624.

[24] A. L. Marty. "The Neoclassical Theorem." *American Economic Review.* Vol. 54, No. 6 (December, 1964), pp. 1026–1029.

[25] J. E. Meade. "The Effect of Savings on Consumption in a State of Steady Growth." *Review of Economic Studies,* Vol. 29, No. 80 (June, 1962), pp. 227–234.

[26] Edmund S. Phelps. "The Golden Rule of Accumulation: A Fable for Growthmen." *American Economic Review,* Vol. 51, No. 4 (September, 1961), pp. 638–643.

[27] _____. "Second Essay on the Golden Rule of Accumulation." *American Economic Review,* Vol. 55, No. 4 (September, 1965), pp. 793–814.

[28] Joan Robinson. *The Accumulation of Capital.* London: Macmillan, 1956.

[29] _____. "A Neo-Classical Theorem." *Review of Economic Studies,* Vol. 29, No. 80 (June, 1962), pp. 219–226.

[30] Arthur Smithies. "Productivity, Real Wages, and Economic Growth." *Quarterly Journal of Economics,* Vol. 74, No. 2 (May, 1960), pp. 189–205.

[31] R. M. Solow. "A Contribution to the Theory of Economic Growth." *Quarterly Journal of Economics,* Vol. 70, No. 1 (February, 1956), pp. 65–94.

[32] T. W. Swan. "Economic Growth and Capital Accumulation." *Economic Record,* Vol. 32, No. 63 (November, 1956), pp. 334–361.

[33] Akira Takayama. "On a Two-Sector Model of Economic Growth with Technological Progress." *Review of Economic Studies,* Vol. 32, No. 91 (July, 1965), pp. 251–262.

[34] James Tobin. "A Dynamic Aggregative Model." *Journal of Political Economy,* Vol. 63, No. 2 (April, 1955), pp. 103–115.

[35] Hirofumi Uzawa. "On a Two-Sector Model of Economic Growth, I." *Review of Economic Studies,* Vol. 29, No. 78 (October, 1961), pp. 40–47.

[36] ———. "Neutral Inventions and the Stability of Growth Equilibrium." *Review of Economic Studies,* Vol. 28, No. 76 (February, 1961), pp. 117–124.

[37] ———. "On a Two-Sector Model of Economic Growth, II." *Review of Economic Studies,* Vol. 30, No. 83 (June, 1963), pp. 105–118.

[38] ———. "Optimal Technical Change in an Aggregative Model of Economic Growth." *International Economic Review,* Vol. 6, No. 1 (January, 1965), pp. 18–31.

[39] Jaroslav Vanek. "Towards a More General Theory of Growth with Technological Change." *Economic Journal,* Vol. 76, No. 304 (December, 1966), pp. 841–854.

[40] ———. "A Theory of Growth with Technological Change." *American Economic Review,* Vol. 57, No. 1 (March, 1967), pp. 73–89.

Questions for Discussion and Analysis

Article 9

1. *"The question of the calculation of the rate of growth is not important as long as everyone understands what decisions were made in choosing one of the alternative methods and precisely what method was chosen."* Comment.

2. How does Pesek's new method for measuring economic growth differ from the five methods previously in use?

3. Pesek claims that his new method for measuring economic growth *"rests on a more meaningful set of algebraic restraints, which faithfully reproduces the flow of actual output during the period covered, and which better than other methods resists purely accidental deviations from the long run trend."* Explain.

Article 10

4. Is it reasonable to make scales of equivalent consumption by age and then apply these to long run data series on the economy to produce equivalent per capita data? What are the assumptions necessary to do this, and are these assumptions realistic?

5. If something like zero population growth is achieved for the United States, the age composition of the population will shift in favor of the adults. What will be the effect on equivalent per capita income?

6. What is an "economy of scale in consumption?" What will happen to economies of scale in consumption if a reduced population growth in the United States takes place (or with zero population growth)?

7. Would income per consumer unit change more for the United States or more for India if the growth rate of the population were to change? Which country would find the greatest impact on consumption?

Article 11

8. What is an appropriate rate of interest for use in cost-benefit analysis if we consider Indian projects? What is an appropriate rate for the United States? How do you reconcile the difference between the two rates you have quoted?

9. Given the social rates of return shown in Harberger's Table 11-1, why would India be interested in heavy industry, since these industries evidently have lower than average rates of return?

10. Why does a high rate of discount militate against long term projects? (Hint: Try, for a project of five years with income of $10,000 per annum, a five percent discount rate and compute the present discounted value of the income for each of the years. Now do the same thing with a fifteen percent discount rate. Compare, year by year, the present value of the future returns.)

Article 12

11. *If investment equal to 10 percent of GNP is required for a country to take-off, and it is very difficult to get to this figure without the aid of the developed countries, how did the first country become developed?*
12. *What is "self-sustained" growth?*
13. *Criticize the characteristics and pre-conditions to "take-off."*

Article 13

14. *Unbalanced growth requires transmission of stimuli throughout an economy. What are the linkages necessary to assure that unbalanced growth will actually work?*
15. *Myint makes a case that unbalanced growth will require "guidance" from the government. Is this actually the case?*
16. *Unbalanced growth provides signals through increased prices in various sectors in the economy in which expansion is profitable. Increases in prices may well force a deterioration in the balance of payments. Does this matter? How might such an effect be minimized?*
17. *Could the theory of unbalanced growth be applied to underdeveloped areas in the United States in order to determine why they are yet underdeveloped and provide some guidance as to how development might take place?*
18. *Should a country such as India invest in steel mills? Should Burma? Should Hong Kong? Kenya? Australia? New Zealand?*

Article 14

19. *Unbalanced economic growth allows for the fact that there are linkages in the economy that induce growth in other sectors once one sector begins to develop. If there is a rapid expansion of agricultural output, perhaps some milling expansion, there will be induced some improvements in the transportation system, and so forth. Is economic planning consistent with a policy of unbalanced growth?*
20. *Why does Streeten make the statement that in South America the active, developing sectors pull the others with them, whereas in South Asia the passive sectors hold the active sectors back? What assumptions are necessary to justify this statement?*
21. *Balanced growth requires a "package" of development projects carried out simultaneously in order to provide for the interdependence of firms and of sectors. What are the necessary conditions for preparation of such a group of projects? Are these things available in Botswana or Nepal or Malawi or Honduras?*
22. *Does the "take-off" thesis of Rostow presume unbalanced or balanced growth?*

Article 15

23. Why does Enke recommend the addition of capital to the labor and land of the subsistence sector in order to assure the "unlimited" supply of labor at a fixed real wage?
24. Is the distinction between "capital widening" and "capital deepening" a useful one for purposes of economic development?
25. Enke asserts that saving by capitalists depends on total profits and assets, as opposed to saving being determined by the ratio of profit to national income (see his third "conclusion"). Which is the better determinant? Why? Under what circumstances would you reverse your view?

Article 16

26. Is there a difference between the study of economic growth by looking at the problems of development of Africa and Asia and looking at development as presented in neoclassical growth theory?
27. Can models of capital accumulation and a dynamic growing economy assist in planning for the economic development of countries?
28. According to C. E. Ferguson: "The nature of technical progress, the magnitude of the elasticity of substitution, and the behavior of the saving ratio are the three crucial elements in the neoclassical theory of economic growth." Explain.

Section IV

THE INGREDIENTS OF DEVELOPMENT (THE SUPPLY SIDE)

The articles in this section deal with the role of supply factors in economic development. And since labor is the major factor of production, it receives most of the attention. In addition, one selection reviews the role of capital accumulation in economic development, while still another article looks at the entire production process with special emphasis on Asian agriculture.

Enke estimates the returns from reducing the growth rate in population. As he points out, the increased importance of such exercises is brought out by the fact that the United States now grants technical assistance on birth reduction methods, and at least six countries have explicitly put contraception into their development plans. Even the Roman Catholic Church is at least taking a second look at its negative stand on birth control. He goes on to give a sophisticated treatment of the relative merits of the various methods available to prevent births. Here we see where economic and technological efficiency differ. Withdrawal, one of the least effective methods physiologically, turns out to be one of the most effective methods from an economic viewpoint, whereas contraceptive pills, one of the most effective methods physiologically, turn out to be one of the least effective methods from an economic standpoint. Of course, the "best" method from society's point of view must take into account the tastes and preferences of the public — e.g., Catholics currently are for the most part restricted by their faith to the rhythm method. Enke's primary conclusion is startling and worth quoting, "If economic resources of a given value were devoted to retarding population growth, rather than accelerating production growth, the former resources could be 100 or so times more effective in raising *per capita* incomes in many L.D.C.s [Less Developed Countries]." He also discusses the various financial incentives that might be used to encourage family planning.

Enke emphasizes that much of the success of his programs depends upon devoting sufficient resources for education. Schultz, the foremost expositor of the theory of human capital, discusses the advantages of education and investment in human capital in poor countries. He disposes of most of the naive arguments as to why poor, largely unindustralized countries cannot benefit substantially from such investments. What is needed is proper balance between investment in human and nonhuman capital. He goes on to show that many of the paradoxes and puzzles about economic growth in developing countries can be resolved by recognizing the importance of human capital. An imbalance between the two distinctly different types of investment helps explain such things as the so-called Leontief paradox, the poor results of foreign aid programs, the limited capital absorptive capacity of poor countries, and the apparent inconsistency of having "disguised unemployment," in the rural sector concomitant with a shortage of agricultural workers.

It is on this last point regarding "disguised unemployment" that the selection by Kao, Anschel, and Eicher focuses. They present a comprehensive and lucid survey article on the much discussed phenomenon of underemployment. They argue that the presence or absence of "disguised unemployment" is largely an issue of definition and the assumptions about the institutional factors involved. Probably most, but not all, writers define "disguised unemployment" in terms of a zero marginal product of labor and the condition of *ceteris paribus* (i.e., no other changes occur). Using this definition, Kao, Anschel, and Eicher examine the theoretical foundations of "disguised unemployment." They show how various writers have answered the three basic questions that can explain the existence of this phenomenon. Next, they demonstrate that a good part of the reason for the high estimate of "disguised unemployment" in developing countries is that the tests were "poorly conceived." They suggest that there is no hard evidence to suggest that "disguised unemployment" in underdeveloped countries is more than 5 percent of the labor force.

Typical of the studies that support the "capital-is-not-important" theory is the selection by Theodore Morgan. In this paper Morgan is concerned with the analytical and empirical relation of investment to economic growth. Specifically, he examines and rejects the view that economic growth depends primarily on investment, and its corollary that investment necessarily leads to economic growth. In fact, he shows under what fairly general conditions investment can be a positive burden to achieving economic growth. Morgan also asks: "What is capital and what is investment?" He shows the powerful impact that this taxonomy can and does have in shaping policy in both rich and poor countries alike. Morgan concludes that the traditional model of economic growth in which nonhuman material capital formation is taken up as the central issue, with qualification entered for other influences, is un-· satisfactory. Moreover, Morgan does more than merely state that a more coherent and general model of growth is needed, he tries to provide one.

Schatz's article attempts to re-establish the crucial importance of capital formation in the growth process in backward countries. We have reviewed some of the "capital-is-not-important approaches" in Section III, in Morgan's article, and elsewhere. Briefly, other authors have tried to establish the importance of the supply of some other factor such as entrepreneurial ability, technical progress, proper preconditions, large markets, etc., as the vital element. Schatz tries to redress what he regards as an imbalance by restating the importance of capital in the growth process. In fact, he takes the strong position that a high rate of capital accumulation is both a *necessary* and a (nearly) *sufficient* condition for rapid growth. The foundation for his "primacy-of-capital" position depends heavily on the importance of the external effects of investment. (In this sense he is in the balanced school; see Streeten's article in Section III.) Schatz is less sure on the issue of political feasibility.

In the final selection in this section, T. W. Schultz presents, in a previously unpublished paper, his ideas on Asian agricultural production functions. He first demonstrates the usefulness of certain empirical findings, such as declining income elasticities with opulence, high returns to technology, declining productivity of land with opulence, etc., in analyzing Asian agriculture. His discussion of "disguised unemployment," population, and investment in human capital tie in with some of the other papers in this section. While Schultz reviews the sources for future profitable opportunities in Asia, he recognizes there are still some key unsettled economic problems in Asian agriculture relating to: (1.) the supply of innovative skills; (2.) the timing of institutional reforms; (3.) the supply of inventive skills; (4.) the supply of agricultural inputs, especially fertilizer and water; and (5.) the size of the food grain market. Finally, he discusses what problems will still be present even if the modernization of Asian agriculture is successful — an analysis of how success as well as failure can have its problems.

Stephen Enke †

17. THE ECONOMIC ASPECTS OF SLOWING POPULATION GROWTH*

Introduction

The past decade of planned economic development has been a disappointing experience for many aspiring peoples and their governments. National domestic production in most Less Developed Countries (L.D.C.s) has grown faster than population by only one or two percentage points annually. It is no wonder that the United States will now grant technical assistance to reduce births on request,[1] that half a dozen countries have incorporated contraception in their development programmes[2] and that the Catholic Church is reconsidering its position on certain birth-control methods other than "rhythm."[3]

Why High Birth-Rates Matter

Reasoned economic concern over high birth-rates in L.D.C.s — usually 40 per thousand a year and higher — has little to do with theories of optimum and static population size. First, high birth-rates cause a natural rate of population increase that is almost too fast to maintain *per capita* output in some countries. Second, high birth-rates mean a high ratio of dependent children, unable to produce but always consuming.

(1.) With crude birth-rates continuing at 40 plus per thousand a year, and crude death-rates continuing to fall, many nations' population at present

†Stephen Enke, Manager — Economics Development Programs, General Electric TEMPO, Center for Advanced Studies.
*From the *Economic Journal,* Vol. LXXV (March, 1966), pp. 44–56. Reprinted by permission of the publisher and the author.
[1]The Agency for International Development, following President Johnson's 1965 State of the Union pledge to "seek new ways to use our knowledge to help deal with the explosion in world population," instructed its United States A.I.D. missions abroad to henceforth consider requests for assistance in family planning (with two practically unimportant exceptions).

[2]India, Pakistan, Taiwan, Korea, Ceylon and Turkey.

[3]Involving a consistent reinterpretation of natural law in the light of change circumstances and new methods having novel or uncertain mechanisms of contraception.

rates of natural increase will double every 25 to 35 years. Perhaps the employed labour force can double as fast. But natural resources cannot increase by definition. And many poor countries cannot save and invest enough yearly to double their stock of capital in, say, 30 years. Therefore, unless innovations increase final output to factor input rates rather more rapidly than now seems the case, aggregate output *per capita* may barely increase. Most of these countries cannot both have natural increases in population of from 2 to 3% annually and increases in *per capita* income of 3% a year or better. Even in the most advanced nation, there is an inverse relation between annual rate of increase in population and in output per head.[4]

(2.) The fraction of population under 15 years of age is highly dependent on age-specific birth-rates, and increases with it. Very approximately indeed, and the interactions are complicated, a country with crude birth-rates of 40 per thousand a year could have as high as 40% of its population under 15 years of age. This percentage might be as low as 20 for a country with an annual crude birth-rate of 20 per thousand. Children under 15 are not significant producers, but only consumers. Lower birth-rates, reducing the relative burden of infant dependency, would "release" consumption to others. Additionally, depending on private saving propensities and government fiscal policies, perhaps a third of such released consumption could be diverted into useful investment.

Both these ideas are expanded below. Thus, the present discounted value of released consumption — several times the *per capita* income in many countries — provides the bases for several estimates of the economic worth of preventing a birth. And examination of the relative growth rates of output and population leads to the startling conclusion that resources used to retard population growth can contribute perhaps a hundred times more to higher incomes per head than resources used to accelerate output growth.

Superior Effectiveness of Investment in Reducing Births

Output per head (V/P) can be increased by investing resources in making the output numerator larger or the population denominator smaller than they would otherwise be in, say, 1975.

---

[4]Consider a modified Cobb-Douglas approach to this problem. Assume $\%\Delta V = (l \cdot \%\Delta L) + (k \cdot \%\Delta K) + \phi$, where V is national gross value added, L is number of persons in the labour force, K is the value of the aggregate capital stock, ϕ is increase in productivity due to innovations, l is the share of national output paid to labour and k that to capitalists. Suppose l is 0.5 and k is 0.2, these summing to less than unity, indicating diminishing returns due to scarce natural resources. Over 5 years population (P) increases, say, 12%, and also L, the P/L ratio being constant. Perhaps K increases 30% during these same 5 years. Then there is a 0.5 times 0.12 (*i.e.*, 6%) increase in output attributable to extra labour force. And there is a 0.2 times 0.30 increase in output (*i.e.*, 6%) attributable to capital stock increase. Summing, unless ϕ contributes, there is 12% more output for 12% more people.

Suppose $0.5 million worth of resources are invested every year in industrial plants to raise national output. The rate of return on these investments is 15% a year. After 10 years $5.0 million has been invested, and the annual output increase (ΔV) attributable to it is $0.75 million a year. Perhaps national output (V) at the start in 1965 was $500 million. Then the proportionate change in yearly national output ($\Delta V/V$) due to this $5.0 million investment is 0.0015.

Now suppose $0.5 million of resources — but medical and contraceptive resources this time — are invested each year in a birth-reduction programme that stresses the use of intra-uterine devices (I.U.D.s). The cost per participant each year is about $1, so there are 500,000 participants on an average each year during the 1965–75 time period. And perhaps the live births fertility of a typical woman participant is 0.15 infants a year. Thus, the reduction in births (ΔP) over 10 years is 0.75 million infants. Perhaps national population at the start in 1965 was 5.0 millions.[5] Then the proportionate change in national population ($\Delta P/P$) due to this investment is 0.15.

If $5.0 million over 10 years gives a $\Delta P/P$ of 0.15 when used to retard population growth, and a $\Delta V/V$ of 0.0015 when invested to accelerate output growth, the superior effectiveness ratio of birth reduction over output expansion ($V\Delta P/P\Delta V$) is 100 times.[6]

This ratio of superiority varies proportionately with assumed rates of fertility of women practicing contraception (f), and inversely both with returns to capital (r) and with cost of programme per participant. Table 17-1 gives examples. It is staggering to encounter such ratios when comparing different economic policies.

Table 17-1

Superior Effectiveness Ratio ($\Delta VP/P\Delta V$)
(Sensitivity to f and r)

r \ f	0.10	0.15	0.20	0.25
0.20	50	75	100	125
0.15	67	100	133	167
0.10	100	150	200	250

It does not follow, though, that conventional development investments (e.g., power dams and cement plants) should be terminated in favour of birth-reduction programmes. At most, these latter programmes could never usefully cost more than perhaps $\frac{1}{25}$ of the formers' budgets. And, in free societies,

---

[5] V/P in this example is accordingly $100/year.

[6] A rather similar estimate was expressed by President Johnson in his speech before the commemorative meeting of the U.N. General Assembly in San Francisco in 1965, where he stated: "Let us act on the fact that less than $5 invested in birth control is worth $100 invested in economic development."

the State can only use resources to slow population growth to the extent that adults want fewer children, and so voluntarily participate in birth-reduction programmes.[7]

Value of Preventing a Birth

What is the "worth" of preventing a birth from the viewpoint of a government that is seeking to increase outputs disposable in future to those alive today? What does a typical infant ultimately cost its society, in this sense, measured at time of birth? What does it mean to "prevent a birth?"

Fifteen-year Estimates

Not many Heads of Government look beyond 15 years. Any birth prevented between 1965 and 1980 affects *consumption* immediately, but cannot affect *output* significantly during that time. Everyone who can become 15 years old during this period is born already.

The present discounted value of the consumption "released" if a country does not have 1,000 infants born this year, representative as regards sex and other attributes, can be estimated after a fashion. It is necessary to assume survival expectancies through each year. Typical consumption values by age are needed. And there must be agreement on a discount rate that reflects time preferences and capital productivity in the country.

For a country with a *per capita* income, V/P, of $100 yearly, from which 10% is saved, the present value of preventing a birth in the sense of released consumption over 15 years is $280 at an interest rate of 15%. At 10% it is $384. And at 20% it is $212.

Such estimates scale approximately with V/P, from $100 up to $500 perhaps, so in a country with an output per head of $250 annually these "worths" for 10%, 15% and 20% would roughly be $960, $700 and $530, respectively.

Total Life Estimates

Theoretically, the present discounted value of typical infants' consumption (negative) *and* production (positive) *after* 15 years should be included. Roughly, in a "V/P equals 100" country a typical undiscounted net surplus during 15–55 years of age is perhaps no more than $840. Practically, at 15% return, the present value of this $840 is an insignificant $17 at date of birth. This gives a net $263 at 15% for a country with a V/P of $100. Accordingly, very generally stated, the "worth" of preventing a birth in a typical L.D.C. is about 2.6 times the output per head.[8]

---

[7]This paper does *not* consider the relative worth of improving population *quality* through expenditures on health and education.

[8]As a standard, per 1,000 population, 400 are under and 600 are over 15 years. If (contd.)

Meaning of Prevention and Postponement

What does it mean to "prevent a birth?"

The above "worths" are the values to society of "permanently" preventing a birth some woman would definitely have otherwise had this year. The probability of the birth this year must be 1.0 without contraception and 0.0 with birth control. Moreover, whatever the probabilities had been of her giving birth next year and in future years, these must remain unchanged. This is an extreme case, admittedly rather unrealistic, and estimates of the "worth of prevention" made on this basis are not directly relevant to birth-reduction programmes. However, this case needs to be calculated initially, because other important "estimates of worth" are derived from it.

Most realistic probably is the case of birth *postponement*. This calculation depends on the fertility rate of exposed and fertile women considering only "pregnable" women, and excluding those who are already pregnant or have not resumed *menses* following childbirth. Perhaps this rate (f) is 0.25 for such women in their twenties. Effective contraceptive practice during a year, assuming the value of f in immediately following years is not altered, then "prevents" 0.25 of an infant during the current year. Thus, if the value of "permanently" preventing a birth is $260 the value of postponing it one year is 0.25 of $260, or $65. This value declines as women age and f falls. Such a calculation of the yearly postponement worth of contraception is especially significant in primitive societies, where women take no precaution against conception at any time.

Sterilization is the only birth-control method where, assuming "faithful" wives, "probable" births are completely prevented. If a married man has a vasectomy the present discounted value of the probable future children his wife would otherwise have can be estimated. This in turn should be multiplied by the value of "permanently" preventing a birth. As estimated above, for a country where V/P is $100, this may be about $260. Then, taking some typical fertility rates, the present discounted value of a vasectomy is roughly $275 when the wife is 25 years old, $193 when she is 30 and $148 at 35 years.

The practical importance of these "worths" is that they form a basis for determining the maximum cost in resources a government can incur to postpone or "prevent" a birth. Thus, if three-fifths of all pregnancies result in live births the value of postponing a conception is three-fifths the value of postponing a birth.[9] Specifically, if the value of postponing a birth one year is

output per head is $100 yearly, and consumption 90, the under-15s may be consuming $70 on an average or $28,000 worth. The over-15s are then consuming $62,000 worth or $104 each. Output per head for the over-15s is then $167. But perhaps 0.25 of this is attributable to capital and land. Thus, over-15s each add $125 to output each year as workers and consume $104. Their net contribution is then $21 a year as workers. Discounted at 0.15, by years from birth, this is about $17.

[9]The biological distinction between conception and pregnancy is ignored here.

$65, Government should then use less than $39 worth of resources to prevent a pregnancy through birth-control measures.[10]

Economic Cost of Reducing Births

The resource cost of reducing births is extraordinarily low relative to the apparent economic worth. Estimates of this cost vary, of course, depending on the mix of methods used. For a major national programme stressing a reasonable mix of methods, but with emphasis upon intra-uterine devices (I.U.D.s), over 5 years the annual cost per participant is under $1 and the cost per birth prevented during this half decade is probably $5.

Costs of Methods

Certain methods have a fixed "starting" cost for initial training, devices, etc., with very low or zero recurrent "operating" costs thereafter: examples are withdrawal, rhythm, diaphragm, I.U.D. and vasectomy. Other methods have low or zero "starting" cost but relatively high recurrent costs: examples are condoms, foam tablets and especially pills. Recurrent costs vary with frequency of coitus in the case of condoms and tablets, but not for contraceptive pills.

Table 17-2, Column 1, estimates crudely the cost for each participant over 5 years, depending upon method. It is assumed that both withdrawal and rhythm require some initial instruction (as noted above). The cost of pills is extremely high compared to other methods. The I.U.D. cost estimate assumes a single insertion and one recheck by a paramedic. The vasectomy cost per year varies inversely with the length of the period considered.

These estimates are of resource costs, assume that participants volunteer without expensive propaganda campaigns, and are independent of whether Government or acceptor pays varying fractions of these costs.

Cost Effectiveness Comparisons

Within broad limits it is possible to make cost-effectiveness comparisons of alternative birth-control methods. Rough cost estimates (Col. 1) must be compared with estimates of effectiveness (Col. 2). Different methods can be ranked accordingly when the constraint is defined.

A distinction must be made between the *idealized* effectiveness and the *operational* effectiveness of different methods. Some methods that are effective if a couple practices them faithfully as instructed, and notably rhythm,

---

[10]This assumed pregnancy wastage of two-fifths does not distinguish between involuntary and induced abortions. Wastage rates in L.D.C.s seem to be much higher than in advanced countries, and certainly higher than reported. Better health measures would reduce mortality at birth, and so raise the worth of preventing or postponing a pregnancy.

Table 17-2

Hypothetical Costs and Effectiveness of Alternative Contraceptive Measures During a 5-year Programme

	(1) Cost/user (5 years)	(2) Pregnancies prevented (5 years)	(3) Cost each pregnancy prevented	(4) Cost each birth prevented	(5) Births prevented per $1 million, 000	(6) "Acceptors" per $1 million, 000
0. Zero control	0	0	0	—	—	—
1. Withdrawal	0.25	1.25	0.20	0.33	3,000	4,000
2. Rhythm	0.50	1.0	0.50	0.83	1,200	2,000
3. Condom	12.00	1.2	10.00	16.7	60	83
4. Foam tablet	12.00	1.0	12.00	20.00	50	83
5. Diaphragm	4.50	1.5	3.00	5.00	200	222
6. Pills	90.00	1.7	52.90	88.60	11	11
7. I.U.D.s	2.00	1.8	1.11	1.85	540	500
8. Vasectomy	3.00	1.9	1.57	2.62	381	333

N.B. These magnitudes are good at best to one significant digit. The variable costs assume about 50 exposures a year. No account is taken of possible deaths or reconsorting during the year. Two-fifths of all conceptions are assumed to result in early miscarriages, abortions or neo-natal deaths. No allowance is made for drop-outs.

are relatively ineffective where sustained motivation, dependable supply sources or household utilities are lacking. Failure rates for any of the *traditional* methods seem to be higher with poor Asian villagers than with educated and prosperous Westerners. This is not at all true of I.U.D.s and vasectomies, however. Otherwise, lacking good data from primitive cultures, the estimates of Col. 2 can be little more than intelligent guesses for these methods.[11]

The 5-year costs of Col. 1, divided by the 5-year effectiveness (pregnancies prevented) estimates of Col. 2, give the 5-year costs per pregnancy prevented of Col. 3. These are multiplied by 1.67, allowing for miscarriages, abortions, stillbirths and fatalities shortly after birth, to give the 5-year costs per birth prevented of Col. 4.

Withdrawal, one of the least effective methods biologically, has supposedly the highest effectiveness per unit cost, because it can be readily explained and involves no purchases or medical treatment. The contraceptive pill, among the most effective methods physiologically, is the worst from an economic viewpoint. As these cost-effectiveness ratios tentatively vary by a factor of 250 times between the most and least costly, and perhaps by a factor of 20 even between rhythm and condom, the choice of a method to stress is important.

What is the Best Method?

What is the best method depends upon whether the effective constraint of a birth-reduction programme is *budget* or *participants*. Suppose, for example, that the costs and effectiveness of the various methods are again as set out in Table 17-2. Also assume that the maximum *potential* "acceptors" in a country is 10 million cohabiting women or men.

If acceptors are not the constraint, *i.e.*, the budget is the limitation, the "best" method is that which prevents the most pregnancies per unit cost. Suppose only $1 million is available over 5 years. According to Table 17-2, Col. 5, withdrawal is then preferable to all other methods, because 3 million births (5 million pregnancies) are prevented. And the 4 million actual participants shown in Col. 6 are less than the potential of 10 million.

However, if the budget exceeds $2.5 million over 5 years in this instance the effective constraint will be participants and not funds. Given 10 million actual rather than potential acceptors regardless of method, for each alternative budget over $2.5 million there is a "best" method that maximizes births prevented. However, at successively higher budgets above $2.5 million the best method in each case will have a lower effectiveness to cost ratio. Hence, the truly best method is that associated with the best budget. And the best of all budgets is that which equates the cost and worth of preventing births at the margin.

---

[11]The absolute values of Col. 2, but not the ranking of methods, are based on the assumption that participants, exposed, pregnable and of representative ages, will have an average fertility of 0.24 a year, allowing for a 0.4 pregnancy and peri-natal wastage.

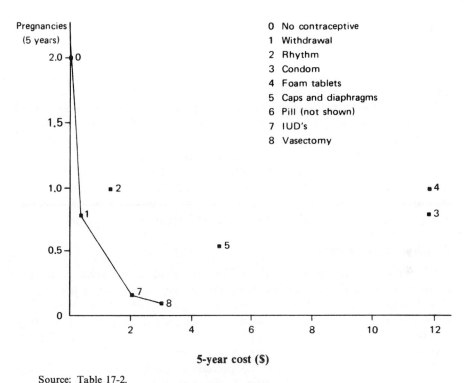

Source: Table 17-2.

Figure 17-1
**Hypothetical Pregnancy Reductions and Costs Associated with Different
Contraceptive Methods per Acceptor (5-year Programme).**

Figure 17-1 explains this optimization. The vertical axis gives expected
pregnancies and the horizontal axis expected costs over 5 years. The scatter
points represent the data of Cols. 1 and 2 of Table 17-2.[12] Noteworthy is the
envelope of efficient methods, linking points representing Zero Control, Withdrawal, I.U.D. and Vasectomy. The inefficient methods, with higher costs or
more expected pregnancies, are Rhythm, Diaphragm, Condoms and Tablets,
while the Pill is so costly it cannot be plotted. Considering efficient points, in
cost-effectiveness terms, Method 7 (I.U.D.) is inferior to Method 1 (Withdrawal), and Method 8 (Vasectomy) is in turn inferior to Method 7, as indicated by the slopes of imaginary rays from the zero point (of no contracep-
tives) to these scatter points.

But which method is best in marginal terms?

A shift to I.U.D.s from Withdrawal means an extra cost of $1.75 per ac-
ceptor, and an extra pregnancy prevention of 0.55 over 5 years, for a *marginal*

---

[12]Except that Col. 2 gives expected pregnancies *prevented,* so this value must be
subtracted from 2.0 (the number of pregnancies expected with *no* birth-control practices) to obtain the ordinate value.

cost per pregancy prevented of $3.17. Adoption of vasectomy, instead of I.U.D., means an extra cost of $1 per participant and an extra 0.1 pregnancy prevented, for a marginal cost of $10. The question is whether $3.17 or $10 best reflects the economic worth of preventing a pregnancy, in the sense of at least postponing it for an average period of 5 years?

Considering even a low-income country with a V/P of $100 a year, where the value of preventing a birth permanently is around $250 to $300, the worth of postponing a pregnancy among participants for 5 years on an average is worth almost $200.[13] Accordingly, Government would be justified in using $30 million worth of resources on vasectomies for 10 million men over 5 years, reducing pregnancies by 19 millions during this period. This would be better than spending $20 million on I.U.D.s, reducing pregnancies by 18 millions, given the assumption of 10 million "acceptors" regardless of method.

Preferences of Public

Of course, fecund and exposed couples who want to postpone or prevent children are not really indifferent as regards method. Catholics at present are prohibited from any method other than rhythm. Otherwise, often not realizing how much contraceptive effectiveness varies among methods, couples who want fewer children will usually prefer the method that "costs" them least in money, inconvenience and embarrassment.[14]

Thus, Government may have one preference ranking of methods while couples wanting fewer children have differing ranking systems of their own. Politically, Government must usually offer all methods, but this need not preclude it from subsidizing one method as against another. Were Government to insert I.U.D.s free, but charge the full price for contraceptive pills, for instance, few participants would use the latter.

The art for Government is only to discourage inefficient methods for which practitioners do not have a strong preference, while encouraging efficient methods for which those who want fewer children do not have a strong revulsion.

Costs of Different Mixes of Methods

The sensitivity of programme costs to different mixes of methods used is indicated by Table 17-3. The increasing use of I.U.D.'s instead of foams by women, and of vasectomies instead of condoms by men, increases contraceptive effectiveness and reduces costs. There will hopefully be a gradual substitution of "once-for-all" methods, although requiring individual medical

---

[13]Assuming $263 as the worth of permanent prevention, a fertility rate of 0.24 a year for participants, a 0.6 birth-to-pregnancy ratio and an average postponement of 5 years, then $263 × 0.24 × 0.6 × 5 gives $189.

[14]Some primitive women do not like to see a male doctor; some couples living with parents do not want them to know contraception is being practiced; and poor families may not buy enough birth-control materials in advance.

attention, in the place of devices that must be repeatedly supplied and depend for effective use on sustained motivation.

Table 17-3

Effect of Method Mix on Pregnancies Reduced and Costs

Method mix	A	B	C
No. Acceptors, %			
Condoms — Foams	70	28	10
I.U.D.s	20	50	60
Vasectomies	10	22	30
Reduced pregnancies, 5 years	132	163	176
Cost, 5 years per 100	$910	$502	$330
Cost/acceptor/year	1.82	1.0	.66
Cost/reduced pregnancy	$6.90	$3.08	$1.88

Source: Costs and effectiveness are based on Table 17-2.

Magnitude and Cost of Programmes

The magnitude and cost of a birth-reduction programme will depend, of course, upon goals established by Government. Japan halved its birth-rate in 10 years after the Second World War, from 34 to 17 per thousand annually, abortion being widely and openly used; but that nation cannot be considered typical of under-developed countries in Asia or elsewhere. A more probable contraceptive goal might be a one-third reduction in crude birth-rates during a decade.

Achievement of such a goal requires that about half the couples in the procreative age groups, couples over 25 years old being represented somewhat disproportionately, must be effectively practicing one or other method of control at any one time.

A typical L.D.C. comprises about 16 men and 16 women per 100 population who are fecund and exposed. Some of these 16 women will not be pregnable in any month, because of pregnancy, or post-partem amenorrhoea. Another substantial fraction will be young couples who want their first boy or girl. If these women who *cannot* conceive or *want* to conceive are deducted, perhaps 8 women (or their partners) per 100 population are "eligible" in any one month to practice birth control.

Realistically, there will be some rotation of participants among this group, so that perhaps 10% of the population are involved in any year. The cost per "acceptor" a year varies with the mix of contraceptive methods used, but with Mix B (see Table 17-3) this is $1. It follows arithmetically that the cost of the national programme per head of population is 10 cents a year.

An annual cost of 10 cents per head means government budgets, assuming all the programme is financed through the State, that are typically about 1% of the economic development programmes in many L.D.C.s.   Table 17-4 gives selected examples.   It is astounding to realise that resources having a value of 1% of all those used for development, assuming sufficient participants, could be as effective in raising *per capita* income as the other 99%.[15]

Table 17-4

Estimated Annual Costs of Birth-reduction Programmes Relative to National Development Budgets for Ten Selected Countries

Country	(1) Population, 000,000	(2) Estimated cost family planning programme, 000,000 year, $	(3) Total cost development programme, 000,000 year, $	(4) Relative cost of programme to reduce births, %
Brazil	80	8.0	2,043	0.4
Colombia	16	1.6	334	0.5
India	470	47.0	3,921	1.2
Korea	28	2.8	105	2.7
Mexico	40	4.0	412	1.0
Nigeria	42	4.2	227	1.9
Pakistan	107	10.7	1,064	1.0
Taiwan	13	1.3	149	0.9
Tunisia	5	0.5	200	0.2
Turkey	30	3.0	538	0.4

Col. 1. 1964 estimates.
Col. 2. Population × 10 cents.
Col. 3. Includes United States assistance, country's own contribution and expenditures from other external aid sources expected in financial year 1965.
Col. 4. Col. 2 divided by Col. 3.

Using Resources and Bonuses To Increase Participation

None of the L.D.C.s currently have 8 women (or their partners) per 100 population practicing effective birth control. The number is often not a tenth as large. Sooner or later, as government planners realize how great are the economic advantages to the nation of reducing births, there will be a greater willingness, however, to use resources for public education on contraception. The granting of bonuses to families that practice contraception effectively, or to men who volunteer for a vasectomy, will also become more widespread. It is important also to recognize, in making this choice between education and bonuses, that the latter are transfer payments and have no opportunity production cost.

---

[15]This excludes possible transfer payment bonuses (see p. 295).

Resources for Education

Various surveys indicate that many simple peoples understand very little about why reproduction occurs and how it can be prevented. The most effective and recent methods of birth control — notably the I.U.D. but also vasectomy — are known but vaguely to a few. Some of this ignorance can be remedied by direct education in secondary schools, to men and women in the civil and military services, and indirectly through radio and movies. However, even if the cost per acceptor a year was thereby *tripled* the annual programme cost would typically be only 3% of all resources used for economic development in a country, and the superior effectiveness ratio could be around 33.

Bonuses to Participants

It is really much cheaper in terms of resources for Government to encourage participation through offering bonuses that are transfer payments. There is then a transfer of purchasing power from tax-payers to acceptors. Couples who limit births are rewarded by Government in the name of society for behaving more than others in conformity with the public interest.

Such bonuses can be large enough to be influential.

Thus, if the worth of postponing a pregnancy one year is about $39 in a country where V/P is $100 (see p. 287) and the resource cost of a reasonable method mix is $1 per acceptor a year (see Table 17-3), Government could afford to pay over $30 a year bonus to women who remain non-pregnant. Practically, each participating woman would have to register with a clinic and be superficially examined there each 17 weeks, receiving $10 on each visit if she did not miss her last examination and is again found to be not pregnant.[16] How this woman remains non-pregnant is her own affair, but she might well ask for an I.U.D. at the clinic when registering there. And the $30 a year is to her the equivalent of 4 months' *per capita* consumption in her country.

Considerably higher bonuses could be granted to vasectomy volunteers, varying from $260 to $148 (see p. 287) in a country where *per capita* income is $100. This could be analogous to a bonus approaching $10,000 in the United States. While the fraction of eligible men who would volunteer as a result might not be high, so large a sum ensures that its availability will be publicized.[17]

---

[16]For details of this scheme see *Economics for Development* (Prentice Hall, 1963), pp. 377 *et seq.*

[17]The bonus-vasectomy programmes in Madras and other Indian States ordinarily require consent of spouse, two surviving children and a waiting period for reconsideration. Vasectomy should not be confused with castration. It affects fertility but not virility, and the operation can be performed without hospitalization and with a local anaesthetic. (See *Economics for Development*, pp. 379 *et seq.*)

Government, representing all tax-payers, has an interest in making these bonuses less than the full reservation price to the economy. As acceptance of birth reductions became more widespread, these bonus rates could presumably be reduced, sharing more of the gain with society at large. If this shifting "supply" schedule of participants is relatively elastic, so that the ratio of marginal cost to average cost does not greatly exceed unity, a given budget for these payments will be more effective.[18]

Other Financial Incentives

There are other ways in which Government can use funds to extend a birth-reduction programme that partly involve extra resources but also provide generous suppliers' surpluses.

It can offer private doctors generous fees for vasectomies and the insertion of I.U.D.s. It can offer generous fees to midwives and others who "introduce" new acceptors to the clinics. And it can distribute condoms, etc., free to stores and midwives to retail at a generous profit margin.

All such arrangements increase the cost per acceptor, but they also increase the number of participants, and each extra couple reducing births means an extra net product for the economy.

Conclusions

The main conclusions are important for policy-makers. (1.) If economic resources of given value were devoted to retarding population growth, rather than accelerating production growth, the former resources could be 100 or so times more effective in raising *per capita* incomes in many L.D.C.s. (2.) An adequate birth-control programme in these countries might cost as little as 10 cents *per capita* yearly, equivalent to about 1% of the cost of current development programmes. (3.) The possible use of bonuses to encourage family planning, whether paid in cash or kind, is obvious in countries where the "worth" of permanently preventing a birth is roughly twice the income per head. Economists can make a major contribution to economic development by refining and explaining such estimates for particular nations.[19]

---

[18]It is in the best Pigovian and libertarian tradition that Government should induce individuals to behave socially, whether in the matter of abating smoke nuisances or having fewer children, through the use of special taxes or subsidies.

[19]A fair question is whether these same arguments, applied above to L.D.C.s, do not apply equally to More Developed Countries. It is almost certain that *per capita* income would rise faster in the United States if the rate of population increase were lower. But otherwise there are many dissimilarities. First, the burdensome child-dependency ratio is very much a function of the birth-rate, which is much lower in the United States the productive contributions of adults are discounted less drastically to productive adulthood in the United States. Third, if interest rates are lower in the United States the productive contributions of adults are discounted less drastically to time of birth. Fourth, additional natural resources are available in the United States (contd.)

Bibliography

[1] Berelson, B. "National Family Planning Programmes: A Guide." *Studies in Family Planning,* No. 5 (December, 1964).

[2] Calderone, Mary S. *Manual of Contraceptive Practice.* Baltimore: Williams & Wilkins, 1964.

[3] Cox, Peter R. *Demography.* Cambridge: Cambridge University Press, 1950.

[4] Enke, S. *Economics for Development.* New York: Prentice Hall, 1963, Part IV.

[5] International Planned Parenthood Federation. *Medical Handbook.* 1964.

[6] Perrin, E. B. and M. C. Sheps. "Human Reproduction: A Stochastic Process." *International Statistical Institute* (August, 1963).

[7] Taeuber, Irene B. "Asian Populations: The Critical Decades." *World Academy of Arts and Sciences* (Den Haag, 1964).

[8] Tietze, C. "Pregnancy Rates and Birth Rates." *Population Studies* (July, 1962).

Questions for discussion and analysis pertaining to this article may be found at the end of Article 22.

---

at relatively slight increases in cost of use. Fifth, the United States population is doubling more slowly than in L.D.C.s, giving more time for capital stocks to double and innovations to be made. Sixth, innovations that increase output-to-input ratios seem to be made more rapidly in More Developed Countries. Seventh, and often overlooked, it is mostly the poor and ignorant who have large families and contribute to birth-rates in the U.S.; but they comprise a *minority* of the population instead of the majority (as in L.D.C.s). *They* may need assistance of the kind described in this paper.

Theodore Schultz †

18. INVESTMENT IN HUMAN CAPITAL IN POOR COUNTRIES*

Investment in human capital is a distinctive and important feature of the economy of high income countries.[1] These investments have become large and recognition of the capital that is thus created is clearly fundamental to an understanding of the economic growth of these countries. But it is not obvious that poor countries can benefit substantially from such investments until they have achieved a large measure of industrialization. The opportunities for a high rate of return on investments in man may not exist for them. Many believe such investments unwarranted during the early stages of industrialization.

My plan is first to examine the basis on which these beliefs rest and the underlying issues which would have to be resolved in putting them to a test. I plan, next, to show that there are important puzzles about the economic behavior and performance of poor countries that can be resolved by introducing human capital into the analysis. My third step is to present a set of propositions about the role of human capital in poor countries that are testable, although the task of testing them will not be easy and must await further work.

Beliefs Opposing Any Substantial Investments

Let us consider, first, the order in which things should be done in entering upon industrialization. If a poor country were to spend more of its resources on education, for example, it would have fewer resources to invest in new plants, equipment, and inventories. Therefore, it is argued, there is a kind of natural order in first developing a more productive plant and then, out of the increase in national income, spending more on education. Proceeding

†Theodore W. Schultz, Charles S. Hutchinson Distinguished Service Professor, University of Chicago.

*From *Foreign Trade and Human Capital*, edited by P. D. Zook (Dallas: SMU Press, 1962), pp. 3–15. Reprinted by permission of the publisher and the author.

[1]Theordore W. Schultz, "Investment in Human Capital," *American Economic Review*, Vol. LI (March, 1961), pp. 1–17.

thus, a country keeps the horse ahead of the cart. Much history can be cited in support of this sequence. During the early industrialization in Western Europe, plant and equipment came first and welfare expenditures followed with a long lag. Governments and the rising business people of that period are not renowned for their concern about welfare measures. Labor was abundant and cheap; it was mainly illiterate and unskilled, and did mostly manual work that required chiefly brute force. Incidentally, this capacity to do manual work is the classical concept of labor to which much of economics is still tied, although it is patently wrong. Nevertheless, it is true that programs to improve the skills and knowledge and health of workers generally were not a prerequisite to the advances that were made during this phase of the industrial revolution. Why, then, should welfare programs be essential for poor countries today? The issue to ponder here lies in the fact that poor countries now entering upon industrialization are not employing the simple, primitive machinery and equipment of that period, and they are not adopting techniques of production of a century or two ago. Nor could they do so even if they wished to, because such equipment and techniques have become collectors' items for our museums.

Another view frequently expressed is based on the belief that a poor country can employ only a handful of skilled people because it, as a rule, is predominantly agricultural, agriculture is backward, and a backward agriculture does not employ highly trained people. Thus, although new skills and knowledge are useful and valuable in high income countries, they are thought to be redundant in poor countries. The issue here can be restricted to agriculture. Suppose a country endeavors to win a substantial part of its economic growth out of agriculture. Is it possible to do this without raising the level of skills and knowledge of cultivators?

A substantial literature exists which claims that there are many "unemployed intellectuals" in most poor countries; and this literature goes on to emphasize the social stresses and political dangers inherent in increasing the number who are so unemployed. Clearly, there also are some students who, upon their return from their studies abroad, find it hard to obtain work that will put their new skills and knowledge to good use. Education in this context, so it is argued, is a luxury that a poor country can ill afford. The real issue underlying these situations would appear to be whether the skills and knowledge that these intellectuals and returning students possess are the type that are useful in economic endeavor and appropriate to the economic circumstances of these countries.

Still another belief about when to invest in people goes back to the uses that were made of the large movements of capital from western countries to less developed countries. This capital was used to build harbors, ports, railroads, textile mills, and some factories and to develop many plantations. It was not used to build and operate schools. It is clear, however, that this capital as a rule increased production substantially. Are there any reasons why imported capital used for similar purposes today will not give fully satisfactory results? The central issue here turns on who is to run these new establishments once they have been constructed. In general, competent European personnel accompanied these earlier capital exports and proceeded to run the enterprises that emerged. This arrangement is now unacceptable to most of the poor nations acquiring capital from abroad. Who, then, will step in and run these new port authorities, power installations, railroads and, above all, the many plants equipped with modern machinery? The lesson to be drawn from recent experiences clearly indicates that it is much easier to build and construct than it is to develop qualified people to operate and manage such establishments.

No doubt, wherever one turns a critical factor in the economic growth of poor countries is the relative shortage of capital. It is axiomatic that poor countries are in this sense "starved" for capital. But this proposition does not tell us whether too much or too little is being invested in human capital relative to that invested in nonhuman capital on the assumption that some education, on-the-job training, and some health facilities and services are in substance a form of capital.

Puzzles About Economic Growth in Poor Countries

There are paradoxes and puzzles about the way the economies of poor countries perform that can be resolved once human investment is taken into account.[2]

Clearly, our economic aid to poor countries has been much less effective than that to Western European countries after the war. The postwar recovery and subsequent economic growth of Western Europe has exceeded our expectations by a wide margin, whereas the economic growth of virtually every poor country receiving economic assistance from us has failed to come even near to what had been expected. Economists, as I have noted in some detail in another paper,[3] in assessing the implications of the heavy wartime losses in plant and equipment both from bombing and from wear and tear during the war, very much overrated the retarding effects of these losses on recovery. The prospects for recovery and growth were *underestimated* because in identifying and measuring productive capacity no account was taken of the human capital that had survived the battles and the ravages of the war and the important part that such capital plays in production in a modern economy. On the other hand, the economic growth potentials of poor countries were *overestimated* and for the same basic reason, namely, the omission of human capital as a critical factor in growth. As a consequence, altogether too much was expected from the additions of physical (nonhuman) capital only, given the low level of human capital. The mistaken assessments in both of these instances are a

---

[2]The counterpart of these perplexing situations for high income countries is discussed in *ibid.*, pp. 3–7.

[3]*Ibid.*, pp. 6–7.

result of relying upon a partial concept of capital instead of using an all-inclusive concept of capital.

Another aspect of the same basic question, which admits of the same resolution, is the apparent low rate at which poor countries can put new foreign capital to good use. The judgment is expressed repeatedly by those who have a responsibility for making such capital available to poor countries that it can be absorbed at best only "slowly and gradually." But this experience is at variance with the widely held impression that these countries are poor fundamentally because they have so little capital and that additional capital is truly the key to their more rapid economic growth. Here, again, the reconciliation is to be found in shifting from a partial to an all-inclusive concept of capital. The new capital available to poor countries from outside goes as a rule into the formation of equipment and structures. But it is not available for additional investment in man. Consequently, human capabilities do not stay abreast of physical capital and these capabilities become limiting factors in economic growth. It should come as no surprise, therefore, that the absorption rate of capital to augment only particular nonhuman resources is necessarily low.[4]

Although poor countries have an abundance of cheap labor and little capital relative to the United States, a study by Leontief concludes that the participation of the United States in the international division of labor is based on her specialization on labor intensive rather than capital intensive lines of production.[5] Thus the United States, which is rich in capital and in which labor is dear, resorts, according to Leontief, to foreign trade in order to economize on her capital and to dispose of her labor, rather than the other way around. The counterpart of this result is that poor countries use their foreign trade with us to economize on their labor and to dispose of their capital, through the export of commodities that are relatively capital intensive. This paradox could arise if the United States were to achieve a comparative advantage in lines of production which required mainly the abilities of engineers, chemists, and other technically trained workers. The value productivity of these particular forms of human capital could exceed that of physical (nonhuman) capital if it were employed to produce the capital intensive goods that we import.

Much has been written in recent years about "disguised unemployment" in poor countries which, it is presumed, includes many workers in agriculture whose marginal productivity is zero. Yet, there are not enough workers in agriculture during harvest and other peak seasons without many women, old people, and children entering the fields to work. The seasonality of agriculture is not the villain of this inconsistency. The production activities in agriculture, whether the income of a country is low or high, are necessarily such

---

[4]*Ibid.*, p. 7.

[5]Wassily Leontief, "Domestic Production and Foreign Trade: The American Trade Position Re-examined," *Proceedings of the American Philosophical Society*, Vol. XCVIII (September, 1953).

that labor requirements in producing crops are seasonal. The widely held belief that a substantial fraction of the labor in agriculture in poor countries has an annual marginal productivity of zero is, I am sure, contrary to fact. Although it is obvious that the productivity and earnings of agricultural labor in poor countries are unbelievably low by western standards, it is not obvious that they are low because the workers are in agriculture and because of the seasonality of agriculture. A plausible explanation is to be found in the poor quality of the resources employed, not least of which are the poor skills and lack of useful knowledge of those who till the soil.

In this connection, let me direct attention to some of the perplexing cross-currents in world agricultural production. Take, first, the Asian scene. India, notwithstanding her many efforts to increase food production, is not doing well; and China, despite her massive and radical programs, is in real trouble. Yet Japan, with two or three times as dense a population and with much poorer natural resources for growing food, is expanding her food production rapidly.[6] Japan became self-sufficient in rice in 1960. The plausible explanation is that Japan has acquired the skills and knowledge that are required for a modern agriculture, whereas India and China have not. In Latin America, the countries with the best agricultural areas—Argentina, Chile, and Uruguay, for example—have been doing badly, whereas "poor" Mexico has more than doubled her agricultural production since World War II. Agricultural production in Mexico has risen at higher rates than that of industry, which also has done remarkably well. Mexico, too, has been developing a modern agriculture and at an impressive rate in cotton, wheat, and other crops.

Western Europe is also perplexing on this score because the increases in agricultural production have been unexpectedly large. These old, crowded, industrial workshops with a population density substantially greater than that of Asia and with poor agricultural land generally, have increased their agricultural production 35 percent and per capita production 13 percent compared to the prewar figures. Israel, which is also European, along with a population density fully that of Europe, has increased her agricultural production about 60 percent during six recent years. How have these European countries and Israel managed all of this? The key factor has not been new land or land that is superior for agriculture, nor has it been mainly the addition of more reproducible capital, although new and better forms of such capital have played a part. This European and Israeli agricultural transformation is based predominantly upon new skills and useful knowledge required to develop a modern agriculture.[7]

[6]The production of rice rose from 10.9 million metric tons of brown rice in 1956 to 12.9 million tons in 1960. Acreage increased only 2 percent, whereas production rose 18 percent. Rice imports have declined rapidly from their record postwar high of 1.4 million tons to .16 million tons in 1960. During 1935–39 the annual average rice imports for a much smaller population were 1.9 million tons. U.S.D.A., *Foreign Crops and Markets* (April 3, 1961), p. 9.

[7]Theodore W. Schultz, "A New Era for Agriculture in Economic Growth," (contd.)

The Role of Human Capital in Poor Countries

In the remainder of this paper I can do no more than to attempt to discern the more important connections between human capital and economic growth in particular types of poor countries and to formulate these in such a way that the knowledge that we obtain from experience can be used to test whether these formulations are correct.

(1.) A poor community that has been approximately stationary for decades, except for a slow increase in population and a commensurate increase in reproducible capital, is likely to be close to equilibrium in the way the resources of the community are allocated. Experience gained by trial and error will have provided a useful body of information about the available techniques of production and the marginal contributions to be had from each of the available resources in production. Meanwhile, within this community, it is assumed, there have been no appreciable changes in techniques or in other variables affecting production, consumption, and savings. Thus, there will have been enough time to adjust consumption and savings to preferences and capital formation and the allocation of resources in production with a close regard for marginal considerations. Therefore, given the people and their preferences and the resources they possess, this community will be performing close to its economic optimum. Are there any poor communities like this? My guess is there still are many with these characteristics. Economists miss seeing them because such communities are swamped in national estimates. Anthropologists, however, do find them: Sol Tax,[8] for example, who based his *Penny Capitalism* on a small community in Guatemala, and David Hopper,[9] whose Ph.D. dissertation was based on field work in Senapur, India.

Let me point out several implications based on this economic conception of a poor community. First, it is not possible to increase appreciably the stream of income of such a community by proposals only to reallocate the existing resources of the community regardless of how much farm management or production economics a competent outside adviser may bring to bear. What this means is that there are few, if any, gains to be had from merely shifting a few resources from wells in order to improve irrigation ditches, or from these to add a few water buffaloes for field work, or to decrease the acreage planted to one crop so as to increase another, or to do with a few less individuals who dig and repair wells in order to add to the number of workers to do other tasks. A second implication is that the rates of return to each of the various forms of the reproducible capital and to the value placed on land are

International Farmers' Convention in Israel 1959 (Jerusalem: Government Press at Achva Coop. Printing Press Ltd. 1959).

[8]Sol Tax, *Penny Capitalism: A Guatemalan Indian Community*, Smithsonian Institution, Institute of Social Anthropology No. 16 (Washington, D. C.: Government Printing Office, 1953).

[9]W. David Hopper, "The Economic Organization of a Village in North India" (Doctoral dissertation, Cornell University, June, 1957).

approximately equal once account is taken of differences in risk and uncertainty that are associated with each productive asset. Moreover, after
adjusting for risk and uncertainty, it is likely that the level of these rates is
relatively low. Thus, if some foreign capital were to become available to
this community for a few more wells, irrigation ditches, and water buffaloes,
and for apprenticeship to train a few more well diggers and ditch repair men,
the rate of return at the margin in each case is likely to be relatively low. The
third implication is that the incentive to save and invest is small because of the
low rate of return; and the gains to be had from bringing in some outside
capital would also be small if such capital were to be used only to augment
somewhat the stock of existing resources.

(2.) The critical question becomes, is it possible for a poor community with
the above characteristics to free itself from the very unproductive equilibrium
in which it is caught? If it is to break out of this low income trap, the community must turn to more productive resources than those it is employing.
Such superior resources do exist. Accordingly, although the opportunity
for economic growth from any reallocation of resources that presently exist
in a poor community or from increasing the stock of these existing resources
is very small, the opportunity for economic growth from the much superior
resources to be had from the advanced countries is very large. In this sense,
there exists a major disequilibrium between poor communities and advanced
countries which have developed vastly superior resources. These superior
inputs do not consist of land or other natural resources. In part they are embodied in particular forms of reproducible (nonhuman) capital, namely, in
equipment and structures, seeds, insecticides, fertilizer, and the like. In
large part, however, they consist of skills and knowledge not only for using
the better forms of nonhuman capital but also as productive inputs in their
own right. It is easy to be misled by the apparent sequence in which nonhuman capital and human capital were added during the early period of industrialization. At that time the gap between new, superior resources and the
old, traditional resources was small, whereas today the gap between the superior resources developed over many decades in the advanced countries
and the primitive, obsolete resources in poor countries has become extraordinarily large. To bridge this gap, that is to take advantage of the real opportunity it affords for growth to poor countries, requires a relatively high
level of skill and much knowledge far beyond what was needed during the
early phases of the industrial revolution in Western Europe.

(3.) There is another class of low income communities represented by countries that are, in fact, winning for themselves considerable economic growth by
introducing and adding some of these superior resources. These countries,
with some notable exceptions, are caught in an imbalance in the way they
allocate their funds among these superior resources. Their objective is to
industrialize, and for them steel mills are the real symbol of industrialization.
Thus, they concentrate their investments upon new equipment and structures

and neglect the required skills and knowledge. This one-sided effort is under way in all too many of these countries in spite of the fact that the skill and knowledge required to take on and use efficiently the superior techniques of production, one of the most valuable resources that they can obtain from advanced countries, is in very short supply in these less developed countries. Some growth, as a rule, can be had from more equipment and structure even though the labor available is lacking both in skill and knowledge. But the rate of growth is seriously limited by this imbalance in investment between human and nonhuman capital in such countries. The Horvat[10] formulation of the optimum rate of investment which treats knowledge and skill as a critical investment variable in determining an optimum rate of economic growth is both relevant and important.

This formulation implies that those countries which avoid this imbalance between human and nonhuman investment in acquiring and adapting such superior resources will realize, to that extent, a higher rate of economic growth. It is very plausible that a substantial part of the unusual success achieved in this respect by a number of countries can be explained on these grounds: for example, Mexico since 1940, Israel during the fifties, Puerto Rico since 1940, U.S.S.R. especially since World War II, Denmark from 1870 to 1900, Germany from 1870 to World War I, and Japan from 1890 also to World War I and again following that war.

(4.) It is no longer efficient for any country to rely upon a system of apprenticeship to develop the skills that are required for industrialization and for developing a modern agriculture. Schools are more efficient, and in the case of agriculture an organized extension service has many advantages in this respect.

(5.) As low income countries make some progress in acquiring and adopting the superior resources so abundantly available in the advanced countries, the difference in wages and salaries between skilled and unskilled workers will be relatively larger in the low than in the high income countries. This proposition excludes poor communities considered under (1.) above, for it is restricted to low income countries that are in the process of modernizing their agriculture and industry. In this class of countries, therefore, if this formulation of relative earnings of skilled and unskilled workers is consistent with the facts, there is a clear presumption that there is underinvestment in skills, given certain plausible beliefs about the real costs of developing these skills.

Conclusion

It is doubtful that the circumstances that characterized the early industrial revolution of Western Europe have their counterpart in poor countries today.

---

[10]B. Horvat, "The Optimum Rate of Investment," *Economic Journal,* LXVIII (December, 1958), pp. 747–767.

Conceivably it may have been "efficient" at that time to have delayed making substantial investments to improve the skills and knowledge of a people. Under existing circumstances, however, it is likely to be very inefficient for poor countries to do as Europe did two or more centuries ago. The argument that a backward agriculture does not demand these skills is relevant only if a country is resigned to its lot. A modern agriculture can be had by each and all, but to develop such an agriculture requires a transformation from what the country has to a vast array of superior resources which entail many skills and much new knowledge on the part of those who farm. The so-called unemployed intellectuals and some of the returning students represent individuals who simply are not prepared to do the kind of skilled work that is required, either because of the education they have received or because of their preferences. Although foreign capital during earlier periods was seldom used to build and operate schools, it did bring with it competent personnel to run and manage the new plants and installations that were made possible by this capital.

Many a major puzzle about economic growth in poor countries can be resolved by taking human capital into account. A discernible imbalance between the investment in human and nonhuman capital is the key, whether it be the poor results from our economic aid to low income countries, or the very slow rate at which these countries, although they are starved for capital, can absorb additional amounts of foreign capital, or the so-called Leontief paradox, as the apparent inconsistency between disguised unemployment in agriculture and the shortage of agricultural workers, or the perplexing cross-currents in present world agricultural production.

A poor community can be close to an optimum in consumption, in savings, and in the way the resources under its control are allocated, including the formation of capital. The rate of return to additional investments simply to increase the stock of any of the reproducible resources being employed and to develop skills of the kind that exist in such a community is likely to be relatively low when adjustments are made for differences in risk and uncertainly that impinge on each set of these resources. To escape such a low return and low income trap, the community must acquire and learn how to use effectively some of the superior resources that have been developed by the advanced countries. The gap between these primitive and the superior resources in what they will produce for a given investment is exceedingly large. The size of this gap is a measure of the opportunity for economic growth open to such communities.

When poor countries, however, enter upon the process of developing a modern agriculture and industry, with some notable exceptions they invest too little in human capital relative to what they invest in nonhuman capital; skills and knowledge useful in their economic endeavor are neglected as they concentrate on new plants and equipment. Thus, an imbalance arises and as a consequence they fail, often by a wide margin, to attain their optimum rate of economic growth.

Questions for discussion and analysis pertaining to this article may be found at the end of Article 22.

Charles Kao, Kurt Anschel,
and Carl Eicher †

**19. DISGUISED UNEMPLOYMENT
IN AGRICULTURE:
A SURVEY***

Introduction

One of the recurring concepts in the postwar economic development literature is that of disguised unemployment—that is, the case in which the marginal product of labor is zero or negative. Although much has been written about
this topic, the literature is widely scattered and often inaccessible. Moreover,
the articles and papers reprinted seem to assume an implicit knowledge about
the evolution of the concept of disguised unemployment, the theoretical un-
derpinnings of the concepts, and the present status of empirical studies of the
issue. Therefore, the modest objective of this survey paper is to review the
literature on disguised unemployment.

This paper is divided into three sections. In the first, disguised unemployment is discussed in historical perspective. The second examines the theoretical foundation of disguised unemployment with special references to contributions by Nurkse [34], Lewis [25], Eckaus [8], Leibenstein [22, 23], and
Mellor [30]. Since the presence or absence of disguised unemployment is an
empirical issue, the final section examines recent empirical studies to appraise
methodological advances in measuring disguised unemployment in less developed countries.

Disguised Unemployment in Historical Perspective

Joan Robinson coined the words "disguised unemployment" in 1936 to
describe workers in developed countries who accepted inferior occupations as
a result of being laid off from industries suffering from a lack of effective demand [44, 45]. She was referring to workers having a low rather than a zero
marginal product of labor.

---

†Charles H. Kao, Professor of Economics, Wisconsin State University — River
Falls; Kurt R. Anschel, Associate Professor of Agricultural Economics, University
of Kentucky; and Carl K. Eicher, Associate Professor of Agricultural Economics,
Michigan State University.
*From *Agriculture in Economic Development,* edited by Carl K. Eicher and Lawrence
Witt (New York: McGraw-Hill Book Company, 1964), pp. 129–144. Reprinted by
permission of the McGraw-Hill Book Company and the authors.

Studies by Buck [2], Warriner [56], and Rosenstein-Rodan [46], in the 1930s and 1940s in less developed countries presented statistical data for China and Southeastern Europe to suggest that a large percentage of agricultural labor was idle for substantial periods of the year. In fact, Buck collected data on over 15,000 farms in China during the years 1929–1933 which revealed that only 35 percent of the men between fifteen and sixty years of age had full-time jobs. Buck's labor utilization approach [2], of course, did not reveal anything about the marginal product of labor. Doreen Warriner followed in 1939 with a widely quoted study [56], which revealed that before World War II in "Eastern Europe as a whole, one-quarter to one-third of the farm population is surplus . . ." [56, p. 68]. Next, in 1943, Rosenstein-Rodan [46], wrote that twenty to twenty-five million of the 100 to 110 million people in Eastern and Southeastern Europe were either wholly or partially unemployed [46, p. 202]. In 1945, Mandelbaum [27] estimated that from 20 to 27 percent of the active rural workers in Greece, Yugoslavia, Poland, Hungary, Rumania, and Bulgaria were redundant; he presented a "mechanical" model of planned industrialization to absorb the surplus labor within one generation. The studies cited so far all measured labor utilization in agriculture in many countries in the 1930s and 1940s and are widely cited as support for the existence of disguised unemployment in agriculture. In fact, the widely quoted 1951 United Nations report [54], by a group of experts including W. Arthur Lewis, T. W. Schultz, and D. R. Gadgil, cited these studies and added that it seems "safe to assume that for many regions of India and Pakistan, and for certain parts of the Philippines and Indonesia, the surplus (rural population) cannot be less than the prewar average for the East European Region" [54, p. 9]. The experts advanced this definition of disguised unemployment: zero marginal product of agricultural labor and the condition of *ceteris paribus,* which has been adopted by Leibenstein [22, 23], Viner [55], Rosenstein-Rodan [46], and many others.

The presence or absence of disguised unemployment is partly an issue of definition. While the writers mentioned above accept a zero marginal product of labor and the condition of *ceteris paribus,* Navarrete and Navarrete in a 1951 article [33] relaxed the *ceteris paribus* assumption and included the introduction of some capital into the production function in their definition of underemployment. Obviously the greater the reorganization of agriculture and the greater the introduction of capital, the larger the volume of workers who can be transferred out of agriculture without affecting agricultural output.

In 1953, Nurkse [34] introduced a theory of economic development on the assumption that disguised unemployment was present over a wide portion of Asia. Nurkse stated that development could be initiated and accelerated in these countries, by forming capital through the employment of redundant rural labor. Farm output does not fall, in the Nurkse schema, when workers are shifted to nonfarm tasks, because he relaxes the static assumptions slightly to permit better organization through "consolidation of scattered strips and plots of land" [34, p. 33]. The Egyptian economist Koestner was among the first to criticize the disguised unemployment doctrine when, in an article written in 1953 [21], he strongly criticized Nurkse's position.

Lewis presented another version of disguised unemployment in 1954, when he introduced a model of capital formation and development in which the capitalist sector grew by drawing on cheap rural labor without any significant reduction in agricultural output [25, 26]. This is discussed in more detail in the next section of this paper. Next, Eckaus explained the existence of disguised unemployment by limited technical substitutability of factors of production in agriculture [8].

Concentrated opposition to disguised unemployment came from Warriner in 1955 [58] and Schultz in 1955 and 1956 [48, 49]. Warriner reversed her earlier position in *Land and Poverty in the Middle East* [57] in which she showed that 50 percent of the Egyptian rural population was surplus by noting that she had omitted the labor requirement for capital maintenance in agriculture [57, p. 26]. Schultz [48] wrote that "all too much attention is being directed to taking up the existing slack in countries that now have a poor collection of resources on the assumption that there are many underemployed resources readily available for economic growth" [48, p. 373]. While Schultz cited examples in Latin American countries where the removal of agricultural labor resulted in a decline in agricultural output [48], he argued on a broader scale and wrote,

> I know of no evidence for any poor country anywhere that would even suggest that a transfer of some small fraction, say, 5 percent, of the existing labor force out of agriculture, with other things equal, could be made without reducing its [agricultural] production [48, p. 375].

Viner was the next strong opponent of disguised unemployment [55]. Writing in 1957, he criticized writers such as Eckaus [8] who contended that disguised unemployment could exist in agriculture because of limited technical substitutability of factors of production, by noting:

> I find it impossible to conceive a farm of any kind on which, other factors of production being held constant in quantity, and even in form as well, it would not be possible, by known methods, to obtain some addition to the crop by using additional labor in more careful selection and planting of the seed, more intensive weeding, cultivation, thinning, and mulching, more painstaking harvesting, gleaning and cleaning of the crop [55, p. 347].

In an unpublished dissertation in 1957, Kenadjian reviewed a wide range of studies of disguised unemployment and concluded:

> ... that almost invariably the estimates of surplus labor have been inflated and the opinions about the extent of redundance in a particular country have contained elements of gross exaggeration in all the countries about which quantitative information can be found to any significant extent. In particular, assertions that disguised unemployment exists in proportions as high as 25 to 30 percent of the labor force in any sector of the

economy of even the most overpopulated countries of the world appear to be entirely without foundation [19, p. 259].

Harberler joined the attack in 1957 [13] and 1959 [14] and criticized disguised unemployment, basing his reasoning on the propositions earlier advanced by Schultz and Viner.

Our discussion so far has summarized the important literature in the disguised unemployment debate, with the exception of theoretical developments by Eckaus, Leibenstin, Lewis, Nurkse, Georgescu-Roegen and Mellor, which are inspected more fully in the next section. Five empirical studies will be discussed in detail in the final section.

The Theoretical Foundation of Disguised Unemployment

This section will examine the assumptions and theoretical foundation underlying the concept of disguised unemployment. Almost all economists define disguised unemployment as the existence of a portion of the labor force which can be removed without reducing output. Most also assume that no other changes occur (*ceteris paribus*). The theoreticians must suggest answers to the following questions if they are to explain why disguised unemployment exists contrary to the expectations of orthodox theory. First, if labor is unemployed or otherwise wasted, why are techniques not introduced which use less land and capital relative to labor? Second, with given technology (fixed capital-land-labor ratios), why is labor used to the point where no returns are forthcoming? Employers of hired labor lose money when they pay a wage to labor whose product is zero or negligible. The self-employed who produce nothing would do better to hire out their surplus labor for a wage. Third, why are wages higher than the marginal product? If large numbers of people produce nothing or very little, wages normally would be bid down to the marginal product of labor.

We will attempt to outline how several economists deal with one or more of the above questions. Eckaus [8] discusses only the first; Lewis [25], Georgescu -Roegen [12], Leibenstein [22, 23], and Nurkse [34] propose solutions to the second and third. Mellor [30], on the other hand, pursues a different path by arguing that unemployment may be related to a deficiency of demand.

Eckaus, writing in 1955 [8], is the only one who systematically analyzes the technological restraints which might lead to disguised unemployment. He says that disguised unemployment exists when "with agricultural techniques remaining unchanged, withdrawal of farm labor would not reduce output" [8, p. 545]. He then asks why, if labor is in surplus, more labor-intensive techniques are not in use. He believes that even the most labor-intensive agricultural process requires some minimum amount of capital per unit of labor; there is some minimum ratio of capital to labor, but many underdeveloped nations have less capital than is required to utilize their whole labor force. Hence, a portion of the available supply is unused. Eckaus left it to others to explain why labor is used until its marginal product is zero, but continues to be paid a positive wage.

Lewis, in his well-known article [25] "Economic Development with Unlimited Supplies of Labor," analyzes the relationship between the subsistence and capitalist sector of an underdeveloped country.[1] In his model, surplus labor is available in both rural and urban areas. The rural labor surplus is disguised in the sense that everyone is working, but if some portion is withdrawn output will not fall; the remaining workers will just work harder. The urban surplus labor is openly unemployed; porters waiting for the next ship to come in, retail traders waiting for a customer, messengers sitting in the courtyard. Workers, rural and urban, do not receive their marginal product, but a higher traditional wage. Lewis suggests that the average product per worker in agriculture determines the traditional wage. Labor employed in the capitalist sector will also be paid the traditional wage as long as there is a surplus of labor in the subsistence sector. The low and constant wages permit large profits for potential reinvestment in the capitalist sector. The economy grows at a faster rate, because profits grow relative to the size of the capitalist sector and an increasing proportion of national income is reinvested.

In this article, Lewis' chief contribution to the concept of disguised unemployment is his explanation of the existence of a greater than zero wage when the marginal product of labor is zero. He explains by tradition and lack of alternatives the existence of self-employed labor which receives a positive wage, but whose marginal product is negligible. In peasant agriculture, each family member receives the family's average product regardless of contribution. Since there are no opportunities for receiving a wage higher than the average product on the family's farm, there is no motivation to leave the farm and the average product will be greater than the marginal product.

Georgescu-Roegen [6, Selection 8], provides an alternative explanation of zero marginal product of agricultural labor [12]. Georgescu-Roegen contends that neither capitalism nor socialism is an efficient form of organizing agriculture in an overpopulated country. Under capitalism, labor will not be employed beyond the point where its marginal product equals the wage rate and, as a result, a portion of the labor force will remain idle and the total agricultural output will not be maximized. Feudalism, as Georgescu-Roegen points out, provided such an institutional framework because the family maximized employment beyond the point where its marginal product equaled wages. Today feudalism has been replaced by individual peasant holdings and the total agricultural output is still maximized because the employment of the peasant family is governed by maximizing total family output rather than by the principle of marginal productivity. Hence, marginal product is zero when the total output of the family farm is maximized.[2]

---

[1]For amendments to the Lewis model, see the articles by Ranis and Fei [6, Selection 10], [42], Barber [1], and Enke [7].

[2]Dandekar, [6, Selection 9] disagrees with Georgescu-Roegen's analysis.

Leibenstein provides another explanation of a greater than zero wage rate. When labor is unemployed and the labor market is competitive, wages would be bid down to very low levels. He explains the phenomenon of greater than zero wages through an interaction between labor productivity and wage rates. Since output per man increases due to improved nutrition when wage rates increase, landlords find it profitable to hire all available labor to prevent wage rates being bid down, poor nutrition, and the resulting small output per man. Although net revenue would be higher if only a portion of the labor force were utilized, wages would fall, causing productivity to decline.[3]

Nurkse defines disguised unemployment as zero marginal product of labor when some organizational changes are introduced. If minor changes such as consolidation of landholdings are permitted, then a substantial amount of agricultural labor can be used in other pursuits, such as building dams and rural roads, without reducing agricultural output. Nurkse explains that labor is used until no more output is forthcoming, because family labor is not paid. He assumes a freeholding peasant agriculture in which food is shared among all family members. Nurkse does not believe that significant savings of labor can be made through the reduction of leisure time or through the exertion of greater effort by the remaining workers, but must be obtained through better use of labor time. Owing to poor organization, much time is spent on essentially inefficient tasks, such as walking from place to place, transporting materials and products, and organizing and supervising other workers. He suggests that through reorganization enough labor time can be saved to make feasible the utilization of labor in other capacities.

Nurkse's early optimism for releasing surplus labor through changes in agricultural organization was qualified somewhat in 1958 [36] when he wrote that such changes in agricultural organization "are a major undertaking and cannot be lightly taken for granted" [36, p. 262].

The last approach to disguised unemployment to be discussed assumes a deficiency of demand. Mellor [30] is the chief proponent of this position. He argues that the peasant in the underdeveloped country works hard to achieve some traditionally determined minimum standard of living, but has no motivation for increasing his income above that level because of tradition-bound consumption patterns.

Mellor's deficient demand approach is similar to the concept of unemployment advanced by Joan Robinson in her demand deficiency theory. There are few empirical data to support Mellor's position. For a survey of literature rejecting the notion of tradition-bound peasants consumption patterns in Africa, for example, see the recent article by Jones [18].

Empirical Studies of Disguised Unemployment

Five empirical studies of disguised unemployment in Thailand, India, Italy,

[3]Criticisms and amendments to Leibenstein's propositions are found in [37, 10, 28, and 59].

and Greece are examined in this section [31, 32, 41, 47 and 50].[4] Three are on the micro level. Two are on the macro level. Discussion will center on two aspects: the methodology adopted in these studies and their empirical results.

Generally speaking, two methods are available to measure disguised unemployment. The first is the direct method, which is based upon a sample survey. This method uses the labor utilization and the labor productivity approaches. The labor utilization approach presents an inventory of what labor is used in the field or in other farm tasks as a percentage of the available supply. The labor productivity approach goes a step further and examines the relationship between the quantity of labor used and/or available and the level of production [30].

The indirect method, which relies on secondary data, is the second method of measuring disguised unemployment. The three variants of this method measure (1.) the difference between the number of labor hours required to produce a given output and the number of labor hours available from the active agrarian population, (2.) the difference between the density of population deemed adequate for a given type of cultivation and the actual density of population, and (3.) the difference between the number of acres or hectares required under a given type of cultivation to provide one person with a "standard income," in contrast to the number of available acres or hectares and available agrarian population. (See [47, p. 2].)

Mellor and Stevens' Study in Thailand

Mellor and Stevens undertook a study of the average and marginal product of farm labor in Thailand, which was based on labor income records obtained by personal interviews in 104 rice farms at Band Chan, Thailand, and published in 1956 [31]. All farms were assumed to have a similar rice production function. The total output of rice was estimated with a high degree of accuracy because most of the rice was taken to the local miller for polishing. Labor inputs were measured in terms of man equivalents on the basis of interviews concerning the number of persons available for farm work on each farm. In their analysis, Mellor and Stevens [31] said:

> ... labor that is available for farm work but is doing no work is counted as part of labor input. Labor that is actually on the field but contributing no increment in output through its efforts is not treated differently from labor that is not working but is available for such work [31, p. 785].

To estimate the productivity of labor they used a least-square linear regression equation. The equation is $Y = 30.4 + 13.5X$ (Y = total product, X = man equivalent). The b (slope) value in the equation of 13.5 tang (which is equal to approximately 24 pounds or 0.54 bushel) is not significantly different from zero at the 5 percent level of significance. They write [31], "This is consistent with

---

[4]Other empirical studies of disguised unemployment are in [5, 19, 39, and 40]. Oshima also mentions some additional empirical studies in [37].

the hypothesis that in this type of area, the marginal product of labor will be zero or close to zero" [31, p. 987]. Thus, disguised unemployment existed in this area. More recently, Mellor [30] commented on this village study and stated that the data were inadequate for more than a rough approximation of disguised unemployment [30, p. 3]. Given the assumptions of labor homogeneity and a uniform production function, this study represents a valid method of measuring marginal labor productivity.

Harry T. Oshima, commenting recently on the Mellor and Stevens' study, (See [6], Selection 11), stated:

> There is one empirical study, . . . of 104 farms in one Thai village. In this pioneer study, the conclusion is reached that there is substantial zero MPP farm workers. I feel it is hazardous to regard this study as conclusive for either theoretical or policy use. The spread of the data in the scatter diagram relating rice yields to labor input for each of the 104 farms suggests to me, not a linear regression line as it does to the authors, but inadequate data and/or dubious assumptions. For example, they assume that rice production functions for each of the 104 farms were the same. In estimating labor input, the authors exclude working children under 15 years old and include all persons 15 years and above, whether working or not [38, p. 450].

Mujumdar's Study in India

In a recent book, Mujumdar studies two facets of underemployment in agriculture, namely, disguised and seasonal unemployment [32]. Attention here is given to the empirical results of disguised unemployment.

Field investigation covering three months in 1954–1955 was conducted in nine selected villages of the Bombay Karnatak region to measure the degree of disguised unemployment. The author interviewed village officers and studied village records to determine the population, occupations, land use, number of livestock, labor movements, work schedule, and standard cultivated holdings in each village. Also, twenty-five families in each village were intensively interviewed to determine family size, occupation, sources of income, size of holdings, and annual work schedule.

The author uses the standard cultivated holding as his most important tool in estimating underemployment. He defines it as "the area of land which is sufficient to absorb, in given conditions of techniques and type of farming, the labour of an average farm family working with a pair of bullocks" [32, pp. 83–84]. Unfortunately, Mujumdar does not tell us how he determined the standard holding. He simply states:

> When once the standard holding is defined for a village or area, the intensity of employment can be measured against the standard so determined. The ideal case being that of full employment when the cultivated holding is of the size of the standard unit or above. All other cases come under disguised unemployment . . . [32, p. 202].

Mujumdar finds in his nine-village study of small farmers that "roughly about 71 percent of the farmers are affected by disguised unemployment" [32, p. 208]. Thus, this figure, "in spite of all the limitation, present(s) in concrete terms the alarming proportions which the phenomenon of disguised unemployment has assumed" [32, p. 208].

There are at least three shortcomings of Mujumdar's methodology. First, the standard holding is essentially an arbitrary unit. It assumes that bullocks are used in producing all crops and allows no alternative production techniques. Nor does it recognize the possibility that bullocks may be labor-replacing, and hence uneconomical, on farms with large amounts of available family labor relative to land. In addition, Mujumdar makes no adjustments for differences in capital, land fertility, and irrigation on each farm. Second, Mujumdar makes no special attempt to quantify the labor input and include it in his analysis. He assumes that all farms are using the most labor-intensive techniques available. Yet, this, he admits, is not true of India. Third, Mujumdar, like many other economists, fails to relate his empirical definition to his theoretical definition of disguised unemployment which is defined as:

> taking the size of labour force as given, disguised unemployment may be described as a situation in which the withdrawal of a certain quantity of the factor labour to other uses, will not diminish the total output of the sector from which it is withdrawn, *given* a measure of reorganization in the sector [32, p. 39].

Mujumdar's empirical definition classifies any worker on a farm of less than the standard holding as underemployed; he sees no need to estimate his productivity or the productivity of the group. Using the standard holding rather than the marginal productivity technique, Mujumdar arrives at the dubious conclusion that more than 70 percent of the agricultural population are affected by disguised unemployment.

Rosenstein-Rodan's Study in Southern Italy

In 1957, Rosenstein-Rodan [47] wrote that it was his firm belief that disguised unemployment of more than 5 percent exists in many — though not all — underdeveloped countries; he supported this belief by measuring disguised unemployment in southern Italy [47, p. 1]. He used the static concept of disguised unemployment.[5]

The following major assumptions and criteria were used:[6] (1.) Only agricultural small holdings of peasant owners and tenants were included. (2.) The active population was assumed to be between fourteen and sixty-five years of age. Coefficients of labor efficiency of men, women, and children were used

---

[5]The static concept refers to the amount of population in agriculture which can be removed without any change in the method of cultivation and without leading to any reduction in output. Hence, the marginal product of labor is zero. (See [47], p. 1.)

[6]Only the six most relevant considerations are listed here.

for each type of cultivation. (3.) Surplus workers were assumed to be involuntarily unemployed. (4.) Labor hours required for each type of cultivation over the whole year, month by month, were counted and compared with available labor hours. An average of 270 available workdays per year was assumed. (5.) A distinction was made between (a.) removable disguised underemployment or disguised unemployment, (b.) disguised fractional underemployment, that is, labor hours not used throughout the whole year which do not add up to an entire labor unit (persons in this category cannot be moved out of agriculture), and (c.) seasonal underemployment due to climatic factors. These distinctions were taken into account in calculating the number of laborers, affected by disguised unemployment. (6.) A slight deviation from the static concept was allowed in the analysis. The author used the direct method of questionnaires to distinguish different types of cultivation, different sizes and forms of property, the composition of the labor force, and the number of labor hours required and supplied.

Rosenstein-Rodan [47] found that "more than 10 percent of the active labor force in southern Italian agriculture is surplus . . ." [47, p. 4]. Later, however, Kenadjian [19] discussed this matter with Rosenstein-Rodan and reported:

> When Rosenstein-Rodan observes that in southern Italy around 10 to 12 percent of the actual population in agriculture are removable, he is including among the removable surplus the individuals who are needed for 50 days or less. If the more rigid definition, which is also the more sensible one, is adopted, the removable surplus is reduced to 5 percent [19, p. 250].

This clearly illustrates that a careful appraisal of the definition is necessary before one so blindly accepts an author's statement that 10, 20 or 70 percent of the labor is redundant in agriculture.

Schultz's Study in India

As was pointed out earlier, T. W. Schultz supported the validity of the disguised unemployment concept in the United Nations report [54] in 1951 [54, p. 9] and later rejected the existence of disguised unemployment in publications in 1956 [48, 49]. In *Transforming Traditional Agriculture*, he reinforced this position by turning to the influenza epidemic of 1918–1919 in India to test the hypothesis that the marginal product of a part of the labor force in agriculture was zero [50]. This incident was used because the epidemic struck suddenly; the death rate reached a peak within weeks and then diminished rapidly. Those who survived were not debilitated for very long. Schultz estimated the existence of disguised unemployment by comparing the reduction in acreage sown with the reduction in the labor force. Such a comparison assumes that if any disguised unemployment exists, the acreage sown will not be reduced as a result of a sudden reduction in labor force. The rationale for such a comparison is [50] "where there are many people relative to land and much land is cultivated intensively, the expectation would be that acreage sown would be less sensitive to a decrease in the labor force than total yield" [50, p. 65]. Therefore, the acreage sown "would be a more decisive test than . . . a reduction of the same percentage in agricultural production" [50, p. 66]. Schultz found that the agricultural labor force in India was reduced by about 9 percent, while:

> The area sown in 1919–20 was, however, 10 million acres below, or 3.8 percent less than that of the base year 1916–17. In general, the provinces of India that had the highest death rates attributed to the epidemic also had the largest percentage decline in acreage sown to crops. It would be hard to find any support in these data for the doctrine that a part of the labor force in agriculture in India at the time of the epidemic had a marginal product of zero [50, p. 67].

The influenza epidemic test was a unique laboratory technique to use in measuring disguised unemployment. An advantage of this approach was that the influenza epidemic did not directly affect animals, and therefore the only change in the factors of production was in the number of workers. Since India's population grew 44 percent from 1921 to 1951 as compared with 5 percent from 1894 to 1921,[7] the population pressures in India today are much different from those of the period studied by Schultz. Therefore, one wonders whether Schultz needs more observations from India in the post-1920 period and from other countries in the 1960s before he can conclude "a part of the labor working in agriculture in poor countries [today] has a marginal productivity of zero . . . is a false doctrine" [50, p. 70].

Pepelasis and Yotopoulos' Study in Greece

Pepelasis and Yotopoulos [41] recently published a macro level study which was designed to measure the volume of removable surplus labor as well as that seasonal surplus labor in Greek agriculture for the period from 1953 to 1960. Removable (chronic) surplus labor was defined as the amount of labor which could be removed for at least one year without any change in the quantities of other factors of production and without leading to any reduction in output [41, p. 86]. The authors measured surplus labor by comparing the labor available with the labor required for a given volume of output within the agriculture sector. The indirect method, using secondary data, was employed to derive estimates of labor availability and labor requirements.

The labor available was calculated from the total size of the agricultural population from fifteen to sixty-nine years old, as measured by the Census. This estimate was converted into a labor potential and into homogeneous

[7]See A. Coale and E. Hoover, *Population Growth and Economic Development in Low-income Countries: A Case Study of India's Prospects* (Princeton, N.J.: Princeton University Press, 1958).

Man Productive Units on the basis of conversion coefficients measuring the workday of an adult male farm worker. Finally the Man Productive Units were converted into Man Productive Days available during the period from 1953 to 1960 [41, Chapter 4].

Separate estimates of the annual agricultural labor requirements for farming, husbandry, forestry, fishing, and agricultural transport were computed. Given each year's agricultural activities, Pepelasis and Yotopoulos derived annual labor requirements by product by applying a "labor-intensity coefficient," that is, a labor/land and/or a capital output ratio. The labor coefficients were "expressed in terms of man and supplementary . . . nine-hour workdays estimated to be used per *stremma* of animal or unit of output to produce the given volume of agricultural output of the year" [41, p. 108]. The authors found that "chronic surplus labor in Greek agriculture is virtually nonexistent. From the eight years of our series, it existed only in 1953 and 1954 to a degree of 3.5 and 2.3 respectively. The other years of the period are marked by a seasonal shortage of labor" [41, p. 136]. The authors commented on the feasibility of removing the chronically unemployed by noting "if in one village of 100 working agricultural population the surplus labor is 2 percent, this does not imply that we can remove for a whole year two workers without decreasing the total output of the village" [41, p. 138]. This is so because that labor is not divisible, for both physical and institutional reasons. The 2 percent, for example, may consist of fractions of labor in surplus spread among a number of families; therefore, "we cannot exactly determine how much chronic surplus labor it is feasible to remove. . . . Its size can only be determined through a *disaggregative microeconomic investigation based on the direct method of studying a sample of farm households*" [41, p. 138]. The important point of this study is the nonexistence of disguised unemployment in Greek agriculture since 1954.

Summary

We have pointed out that the existence of disguised unemployment is largely a matter of definition and the assumptions about the institutional forces involved. Nevertheless, some writers agreed upon the zero product of labor definition in the early 1950s, and it is an understatement to say that the development literature in this period was optimistic about development through the transfer of redundant agricultural labor to other occupations. We have shown that the empirical studies supporting this optimism were often poorly conceived. In addition, we have noted that by considering temporary rather than permanent labor transfers and by allowing some reorganization of production, various writers have arrived at a high percentage of disguised unemployment. To date, there is little reliable empirical evidence to support the existence of more than token — 5 percent — disguised unemployment in underdeveloped countries as defined by a zero marginal product of labor and the condition of *ceteris paribus.*

Questions for discussion and analysis pertaining to this article may be found at the end of Article 22.

Bibliography

[1] Barber, William J. "Disguised Unemployment in Underdeveloped Economies." *Oxford Economic Papers,* Vol. 13 (February, 1961), pp. 103–115.

[2] Buck, John Lossings. *Chinese Farm Economy.* Chicago: The University of Chicago Press, 1930.

[3] —— *Land Utilization in China.* Chicago: The University of Chicago Press, 1937.

[4] Cho, Yong Sam. *Disguised Unemployment in South Korean Agriculture.* Berkeley: University of California, 1963.

[5] Dandekar, V. N. "Economic Theory and Agrarian Reform." *Oxford Economic Papers,* Vol. 14 (February, 1962), pp. 69–80.

[6] Eicher, Carl K., and Lawrence Witt. *Agriculture in Economic Development.* New York: McGraw-Hill Book Co., 1964. (Editor's Note: Reference inserted for clarification purposes.)

[7] Enke, Stephen. "Economic Development with Unlimited and Limited Supplies of Labor." *Oxford Economic Papers,* Vol. 14 (June, 1962), pp. 158–172.

[8] Eckaus, Richard S. "Factor Proportions in Underdeveloped Countries." *American Economic Review,* Vol. 45 (September, 1955), pp. 539–565.

[9] Ezekiel, Hannan. "An Application of Leibenstein's Theory of Underemployment." *Journal of Political Economy,* Vol. 68 (October, 1960), pp. 511–517.

[10] Fei, John C. H. and Gustav Ranis. "Capital Accumulation and Economic Development." *American Economic Review,* Vol. 53 (June, 1963), pp. 283–313.

[11] Frankel, S. Herbert. *The Economic Impact on Under-developed Societies.* Oxford: Basil Blackwell & E. Mott, Ltd., 1953.

[12] Georgescu-Roegen, N. "Economic Theory and Agrarian Economics." *Oxford Economic Papers,* Vol. 12 (February, 1960), pp. 1–40.

[13] Haberler, Gottfried. "Critical Observations on Some Current Notions in the Theory of Economic Development." *L'Industria,* No. 2 (1957), pp. 3–13.

[14] ——. "International Trade and Economic Development." Fiftieth Anniversary Commemoration Lectures, Lecture III, National Bank of Egypt, Cairo, 1959.

[15] Hsieh, Chiang. "Underemployment in Asia: Nature and Extent." *International Labor Review,* Vol. 55 (January–June, 1952), pp. 703–725.

[16] ——. "Underemployment in Asia: Its Relation to Investment Policy." *International Labor Review,* Vol. 56 (July–December, 1952), pp. 30–39.

[17] International Labor Office. *Measurement of Underemployment.* Geneva: 1957.

[18] Jones, William O. "Economic Man in Africa." *Food Research Institute Studies,* Vol. 1 (May, 1960), pp. 107–134.

[19] Kenadjian, Berdj. "Disguised Unemployment in Underdeveloped Countries." Unpublished doctoral dissertation, Harvard University, 1957.

[20] Khan, Nasir Ahmad. *Problems of Growth of an Underdeveloped Economy — India.* New York: Asia Publishing House, 1961. Especially Chapter VII.

[21] Koestner, N. "Comments on Professor Nurkse's Capital Accumulation in Underdeveloped Countries." *L'Egypte Contemporaine,* Vol. 44 (April, 1953), pp. 1-8.

[22] Leibenstein, Harvey. "The Theory of Underemployment in Backward Economies." *Journal of Political Economy,* Vol. 65 (April, 1957), pp. 91-103.

[23] _____. *Economic Backwardness and Economic Growth.* New York: John Wiley and Sons, Inc., 1957.

[24] _____. "Underemployment in Backward Economies: Some Additional Notes." *Journal of Political Economy,* Vol. 66 (June, 1958), pp. 256-258.

[25] Lewis, W. Arthur. "Economic Development with Unlimited Supplies of Labour." *Manchester School of Economic and Social Studies* (May, 1954), pp. 139-192.

[26] _____. *The Theory of Economic Growth.* London: George Allen & Unwin, Ltd., 1955.

[27] Mandelbaum, K. *The Industrialization of Backward Areas.* Oxford: Basil Blackwell & Mott, Ltd., 1945.

[28] Mazumdar, Dipak. "The Marginal Productivity Theory of Wages and Disguised Unemployment." *Review of Economic Studies,* Vol. 26 (June, 1959), pp. 190-197.

[29] _____. "Underemployment in Agriculture and the Industrial Wage Rate." *Economica,* Vol. 26 (November, 1959), pp. 328-340.

[30] Mellor, John W. "The Use and Productivity of Farm Family Labor in Early Stages of Agricultural Development." *Journal of Farm Economics,* Vol. 45 (August, 1963), pp. 517-534.

[31] Mellor, John W. and Robert D. Stevens. "The Average and Marginal Product of Farm Labor in Underdeveloped Economies." *Journal of Farm Economics,* Vol. 38 (August, 1956), pp. 780-791.

[32] Mujumdar, N. A. *Some Problems of Underemployment.* Bombay: Popular Book Depot, 1961.

[33] Navarrette, Alfredo, Jr. and Ifigenia M. Navarrette. "Underemployment in Underdeveloped Economies." *International Economic Papers,* No. 3 (1953), pp. 235-239. Translated from *El Trimestre Economico,* Vol. 17, No. 4 (October-December, 1951).

[34] Nurkse, Ragnar. *Problems of Capital Formation in Underdeveloped Countries.* Fair Lawn, N. J.: Oxford University Press, 1953.

[35] _____. "Excess Population and Capital Construction." *Malayan Economic Review,* Vol. 2 (October, 1957), pp. 1-11.

[36] _____. "Trade Fluctuations and Buffer Policies of Low Income Countries." *Kyklos,* Vol. 11, fase. 2 (1958), pp. 141-154; 244-265.

[37] Oshima, Harry T. "Underemployment in Backward Economies: An Empirical Comment." *Journal of Political Economy,* Vol. 66 (June, 1958), pp. 259–264.

[38] _____. "The Ranis-Fei Model of Economic Development: Comment." *American Economic Review,* Vol. 53 (June, 1963), pp. 448–452.

[39] Parthasaratry, Gogula. "Underemployment and Indian Agriculture." Unpublished doctoral dissertation, University of Wisconsin, 1957.

[40] Patel, K. R. "The Nature and Extent of Under-Employment of the Self-Employed Cultivators." Unpublished doctoral dissertation, University of Bombay, India, 1962.

[41] Pepelasis, Adam A. and Pan A. Yotopoulos. *Surplus Labor in Greek Agriculture, 1953–1960.* Athens, Greece: Center of Economic Research, Research Monograph Series 2, 1962.

[42] Ranis, Gustav and John C. H. Fei. "A Theory of Economic Development." *American Economic Review,* Vol. 51 (September, 1961), pp. 553–558.

[43] _____. "The Ranis-Fei Model of Economic Development: Reply." *American Economic Review,* Vol. 53 (June, 1963), pp. 452–454.

[44] Robinson, Joan. "Disguised Unemployment." *Economic Journal,* Vol. 46 (June, 1936), pp. 225–237.

[45] _____. *Essays in the Theory of Employment.* London: Oxford University Press, 1947.

[46] Rosenstein-Rodan, Paul N. "Problems of Industrialization of Eastern and South-Eastern Europe." *Economic Journal,* Vol. 53 (June–September, 1943), pp. 202–211.

[47] _____. "Disguised Unemployment and Underemployment in Agriculture." *Monthly Bulletin of Agricultural Economics and Statistics,* Vol. 6 (July–August, 1957), pp. 1–7.

[48] Schultz, Theodore W. "The Role of Government in Promoting Economic Growth." In *The State of the Social Sciences,* Leonard D. White, editor. Chicago: University of Chicago Press, 1956.

[49] _____. *The Economic Test in Latin America.* New York State School of Industrial and Labor Relations Bulletin 35, Cornell University, Ithaca (August, 1956), pp. 14–15.

[50] _____. "The Doctrine of Agricultural Labor of Zero Value." In *Transforming Traditional Agriculture.* New Haven, Conn.: Yale University Press, 1964.

[51] Sen, A. K. *Choice of Techniques.* Oxford: Basil Blackwell & Mott, Ltd., 1960.

[52] Singh, Tarlok. *Poverty and Social Change.* London: Longmans, Green & Co., Ltd., 1945.

[53] Sovani, N. V. "Underemployment, Micro and Macro, and Development Planning." *Indian Economic Journal,* Vol. 2, No. 4 (April, 1955), pp. 301–310.

[54] United Nations. *Measures for the Economic Development of Underdeveloped Countries.* New York: Department of Economic and Social Affairs, 1951.

[55] Viner, Jacob. "Some Reflections on the Concept of Disguised Unemployment." *Contribucões a Analise do Desenvolvimento Economico.* Livraria Ager, Editora, Rio de Janeiro, 1957. Reprinted under the same title in *Indian Journal of Economics*, Vol. 38 (July, 1957), pp. 17–23.

[56] Warriner, Doreen. *Economics of Peasant Farming.* London: Oxford University Press, 1939.

[57] ———— *Land and Poverty in the Middle East.* London: Royal Institute of International Affairs, 1948.

[58] ———— "Land Reform and Economic Development." Fiftieth Anniversary Commemoration Lectures, National Bank of Egypt, Cairo, 1955.

[59] Wonnacott, Paul. "Disguised and Overt Unemployment in Underdeveloped Economies." *Quarterly Journal of Economics*, Vol. 76 (May, 1962), pp. 279–297.

Theodore Morgan †

20. INVESTMENT VERSUS ECONOMIC GROWTH*

I

In classical economic thinking labor was considered a factor of production whose productive powers can be increased primarily through specialization and the use of more capital, rather than through an increase in labor's own capacity and incentives. Labor was looked on as undifferentiated work power; conspicuous socioeconomic classes received income flows that could be roughly identified with wages, profits, and rents.

The traditional emphasis is represented today in variants on the form $P = f(T,L,K)$, where T is a measure of productivity of all inputs, L is quantity of labor, and K quantity of capital. Natural resources (the classical "land") are taken for granted or included in capital. Variants on the model introduce time lags, divide capital and labor into their varieties, reason about substitution possibilities, and analyze dynamic sequences. The focus of attention remains on increasing one or more of these three determinants of production, among them especially capital, seen as more amenable to policy influences than the others. Growth in production is often visualized as the outcome of a saving rate and a fairly stable aggregate capital-output ratio.

The prominence of the orthodox growth analysis has been supported and increased in the past thirty years by underemployment analyses, Keynesian and variants, that determine the level of employment through savings-investment interactions, and by their evolution into Harrod-Domar growth theory. The traditional savings-tangible-investment growth model seems clearly dominant today, despite minority views. A survey of the journals published by the two largest professional economic associations, the *American Economic Review* and the *Economic Journal,* for their twelve regular issues of 1964,

†Theodore Morgan, Professor of Economics, University of Wisconsin — Madison. The author is grateful for research support during the writing of this paper to the Agency for International Development and to the Graduate School of the University of Wisconsin, and for assistance from Nawal Fag el Noor at Wisconsin and from Betty Leong, Yap Choo Lian, and Catherine Dragon of the Economic Research Centre of the University of Singapore.

*From *Economic Development and Cultural Change*, Vol. 17, No. 3 (April, 1969), pp. 392–414. Reprinted by permission of the University of Chicago Press and the author.

1965, and 1966, finds that 40 out of 64 articles, notes, and communications dealing with economic growth, or nearly two-thirds, follow this line of reasoning.[1] In the Abramovitz survey of the "Economics of Growth" for the American Economic Association Anthology of 1952,[2] almost two-thirds of the total space is given over to capital formation as a cause of economic growth.[3] Capital is usually defined in physical terms, with social factors entered as influences on the rate of accumulation of such capital and the efficiency of its use. In the remarkable survey by Hahn and Matthews, "The Theory of Economic Growth,"[4] 43 of 72 relevant pages, or over half, are devoted to savings-investment causes of income change.

The traditional and dominant view is currently being subjected to considerable criticism. As an interpretation of English economic growth of a century to two centuries ago, the theory can be charged with misleading plausibility in presenting labor as a homogeneous resource over a time when labor differentiation was rapidly increasing, and with misleading exclusion of borderline economic and noneconomic changes that may have been crucial. As an interpretation of present-day less developed countries' growth problems and experience, the qualifications and criticism take on a pragmatic and urgent note. Much of their force comes from doubt on the emphasis in traditional theory on savings-tangible investment as the central cause of economic growth.[5] Hahn and Matthews, at the end of their survey, suggest that refined

---

[1]

Table 20-1

	AER	EJ	Total
Total of articles, notes, and communications published in 1964, 1965, and 1966	146	146	292
Of these, on growth economies	19	45	64
Of these, investment-as-a-cause-of-growth approaches	14	26	40
Other approaches	5	19	24

Growth economics took up a smaller proportion of the *AER*'s total than of the *EJ*'s — 13 percent, as compared to 31 percent; but of these, investment-as-a-cause-of-growth took up a larger proportion — 74 percent, as compared to 58 percent.

There were in both journals borderline approaches hard to classify. Minor comments and replies were excluded from the count of both journals. The *Proceedings* of the American Economic Association were also excluded.

[2]Abramovitz, M., "Economics of Growth," Vol. 2, of *A Survey of Contemporary Economics*, B. F. Haley, ed. (Homewood: Richard Irwin, 1952), pp. 132–178.

[3]Even though Harrod-Domar theories are excluded as making no assertion about the probable actual development of an economy over time, p. 170n.

[4]*Economic Journal* (December, 1964), pp. 779–902.

[5]For example, Robert Solow generalizes, after exploring one standard kind of model: "Investment is at best a necessary condition for growth, surely not a sufficient condition. Recent study has indicated the importance of such activities as research, education, and public health." "Technical Progress, Capital Formation, and Economic Growth," *American Economic Review, Papers and Proceedings* (May, 1962), p. 86.

analysis of an economic system in which one of the inputs is durable capital goods:

> [may have reached] the point of diminishing returns. Nothing is easier than to ring the changes on more and more complicated models, without bringing in any really new ideas and without bringing the theory any nearer to casting light on the causes of the wealth of nations. . . . It is essentially a frivolous occupation to take a chain with links of very uneven strength, and devote one's energies to strengthening and polishing the links that are already relatively strong.[6]

[6]*Op. cit., p. 890.* They recommend two lines of inquiry for more attention in the future: the motivations of economic agents, avoiding the "twin dangers of empty formalism and inconclusive anecdote;" and the concept of "the world as a whole as an underdeveloped economy" (pp. 890–891).

Among economists concerned mainly with growth problems of less developed countries, the traditional model is well represented. Nurkse's position was nearly unqualified: "The country's incremental saving ratio . . . is the crucial determinant of growth." *Problems of Capital Formation in Underdeveloped Countries* (New York: Oxford Press, 1953), p. 142. The United Nations ECAFE experts in their 1960 Report on *Programming Techniques for Economic Development* judge "The final goal of development planning is . . . to find the best way of breaking the vicious circle between capital shortage and underdevelopment and to design the most efficient and optimum rate of capital accumulation. Capital accumulation may very well be regarded as the core process. . . ." E/CN.11/535, p. 8 Gunnar Myrdal, often unconventional, recommends for development "a policy of the utmost austerity . . . to hold down the level of consumption in the degree necessary for rapid development." *Economic Theory and the Underdeveloped Regions* (London: Methuen, 1957), pp. 82–83.

Rostow presents as a necessary but not sufficient condition for take-off the rise of the share of net investment in national income "from (say) 5 percent to over 10 percent." *The Stages of Economic Growth* (Cambridge: Cambridge Press, 1964), p. 37. Chenery and Strout use an intermediate, flexible model, in which deficiency of domestic saving and investment (by national income definition) *may* limit economic growth. But supply of skills and organizational ability (whose quantity may be increased without conventional investment) and supply of imports can also limit economic growth. H. Chenery and A. M. Strout, "Foreign Assistance and Economic Development," *American Economic Review* (September, 1966), pp. 679–733.

In contrast: Arthur Lewis disavows (in conversation) savings and investment as holding the critical place in economic growth, though his writings often seem to give strong support to the conventional analysis. Bauer and Yamey write, "It is often nearer the truth to say that capital is created in the process of development than that development is a function of capital accumulation." *The Economics of Underdeveloped Countries* (Cambridge: Nisbet and Cambridge, 1957), p. 127. Myint emphasizes the complex of factors that limit the capacity of a country to invest its saving productively. *The Economics of the Developing Countries* (London: Hutchinson, 1964), pp. 15–17. Lauchlin Currie enters a vigorous dissent to the preoccupation with investment as a priority condition for economic advance. *Accelerating Development* (New York: McGraw-Hill, 1966). A. K. Cairncross, in several papers, notably "The Place of Capital in Economic Progress," in his *Factors in Economic Development* (London: Allen and Unwin, 1962), questions the priority of capital as a cause of national growth. S. Herbert Frankel analyzes the constraints on the possible contributions of capital. *The Economic Impact of Under-Developed Societies* (New York: Oxford University Press, 1953), pp. 67–79. See section IV.

V. K. R. V. Rao, Director of the Institute of Economic Growth in New Delhi, is a spokesman in the less developed world for the traditional austerity-investment road to growth. He brings together data from the U. K., the U. S., and other present high-income countries, on their past experience of a high proportion of women and children in the factories, a long work week, repression of unions, and denial of vote to labor. He (contd. on next page)

The preoccupation of the economics profession with nonhuman material capital as the critical determinant of economic growth has had its influence on policy. Development planners in less developed countries have been encouraged to focus their attention on investment for capital goods, and as the best proxy for that, on expenditure targets for investment. The practical developers of the International Bank complain:

> Because some governments consider investment virtually synonymous with development, they have emphasized the fulfillment of the financial investment targets in their plans rather than the physical output targets that the investments are aimed at achieving. They have sometimes seemed to act as though the attainment of production targets follows automatically, or with minor additional effort, the realization of financial investment targets.[7]

If qualifications on the capital goods approach to economic growth are modest, then that approach is justified, and economic analysis can seek efficiently to integrate the basic model with the qualifications. But if the qualifications dominate the set of causes, then traditional analysis is misleading, and policy prescriptions may be perverse. Perhaps one should *not* follow the recommendation from classical theory to check consumption increases or even cut consumption, in order to raise the supply of capital goods. Perhaps certain kinds of consumption should be expanded — those that promise the optimum combination of present satisfaction with promise of future productivity rise through effects favorable to health and energy, skills and incentives, and improved organization.

---

judges that political democracy is the enemy of economic growth: if the worker had won political freedom earlier, he could have prevented economic development either from taking place at all, or certainly from taking place at his expense. Similarly, Asoka Mehta of the Indian Planning Commission visualizes the major issue for labor unions in poor countries as that of subordinating wage gains to the development of the country. "The Mediating Role of the Trade Union in Underdeveloped Countries," *Economic Development and Cultural Change* (October, 1957), pp. 16–23. Robert M. Hutchins presents a simplified version of the doctrine in U. S. newspapers: "Since the worker will spend any money he can lay his hands on, whereas the employer, whether he is a capitalist or the Communist Party, will save and invest, the thing to do is to use cheap labor, work it long and hard, and deprive it of any considerable share of the fruits of economic advance." Column of July 1, 1966.

[7]Albert Waterson, *Development Planning: Lessons of Experience* (Baltimore: Johns Hopkins Press, 1965), p. 299.

Reddaway reminds Indian planners: "Capital expenditures are a very important means of helping to attain these outputs but they are not an objective in themselves. If some other plan of raising output could be discovered during the plan period (e.g., by the use of better seeds instead of costly irrigation schemes), then the essence of the plan would be fulfilled even if the capital expenditures were far below the original figures." W. B. Reddaway, "Importance of Time Lags for Economic Planning," *Economic Weekly* (Bombay, January, 1960), p. 227; in Waterston, *op. cit.,* p. 299. Galbraith also complains of a mistaken emphasis on nonhuman material investment as synonymous with development: ". . . [steel mills, dams, and fertilizers factories] get the discussion, the money, the visitors, the glow of pride." J. K. Galbraith, *Economic Development in Perspective* (Cambridge: Harvard University Press, 1962), pp. 51–52.

This paper is concerned with the empirical and logical relation of investment to income changes. Section II, following, considers definitions of investment; Section III, empirical evidence on the correlation of investment with income changes, Section IV, investment-income growth relationships, including the extent to which investment by any definition is not a contributor to income growth, but is instead a burden on, or a result of, changes in production; and consumption rise or organization changes the cause of growth. Section V is the conclusion.

II

A

One can define any activity that adds to tomorrow's potential income as investment, and the product of such activity, whether material or nonmaterial, as capital. So Schultz, among others, adds to traditional capital concepts that of "Investment in Human Capital."[8] Part of such investment is what would ordinarily be called consumption.

This most general definition is tautologous: it cannot possibly be wrong. But it will often be misunderstood to refer to things traditionally called capital: that is, only to nonhuman material capital.

Acceptance of a general concept of capital implies that in addition to material capital, (1.) the traditional capital goods, and (2.) the newer human capital, there is also nonmaterial capital, embodied currently neither in things nor in people: (3a.) nonmaterial producers' capital, the social organization for developing and maintaining the conditions for effective production, including law and order, the discovery and dissemination of technical knowledge, and the maturing of social values congenial to efficient production; and (3b.) nonmaterial consumers' capital, the social relationships that give meaning and satisfaction to many kinds of consumption and in some measure to all consumption.[9]

---

[8]"Investment in human capital is probably the major explanation for growth in national output. Much of what we call consumption constitutes investment in human capital. Direct expenditures on education, health, and internal migration to take advantage of better job opportunities are clear examples. Earnings foregone by mature students attending school and by workers acquiring on-the-job training are equally clear examples. . . . The use of leisure time to improve skills and knowledge is widespread, and it too is unrecorded." Theodore Schultz, Presidential Address at the American Economic Association Meeting, December 28, 1960, in the *American Economic Review* (March, 1961), pp. 1–15.

John Vaizey, commenting on "the present apparent imbalance in economic theory," asks whether we are moving "towards a new political economy," emphasizing human resource problems. *The Residual Factor and Economic Growth* (Paris: OECD, 1964), p. 201.

[9]Harry Johnson suggests that nonmaterial capital, embodied in neither human nor nonhuman forms, consists of "the state of the arts (the intellectual production capital of society) and the state of the culture (the intellectual consumption capital of society)." *The Residual Factor. . . .op. cit.,* pp. 219–225. This division seems awkward, in that (contd. on next page)

The generalized notion of capital inherits a respectable minority tradition in economic thought. Irving Fisher developed such a concept in detail,[10] winning Marshall completely to it from the abstract and mathematical point of view. It lost out, thought Marshall, only because it was not "in touch with the language of the market."[11] Knight was sympathetic to the abstract concept, emphasizing both heterogeneity within conventional factor categories and substitutibility across the boundaries.[12] Schultz, Becker, Sjaastad, Mushkin, and others have shown the fruitfulness of the generalized approach in human capital analysis.[13]

B

In contrast, Hicks defines a person's income, and according to Samuelson properly does so, as the maximum he can consume without shrinking his future consumption. The definition is usually interpreted — and Hicks himself did so — as meaning that income is consumption plus capital accumulation. The definition also implies that only capital accumulation contributes to potential income growth.[14]

---

the state of the arts and of culture must be embodied in either human beings or in recorded materials. And yet there is a nonmaterial background and requisite for production and consumption. The above is an attempt at separating it out.

Pigou emphasized the "current stock of ideas" as occupying a dominant place among productive resources. A. C. Pigou, *Income* (London: Macmillan, 1949), p. 19. Slichter, like other writers, depicted knowledge embodied in increased energy availability, improved arts of management, and technological research as a fundamental cause of economic growth. Sumner H. Slichter, *Economic Growth in the United States* (New Orleans: Louisiana State University Press, 1961), pp. 74–83.

[10]In his fullest statement, he defined wealth as "material objects owned by human beings" (which consists of land, land improvements, and commodities), plus human beings (freemen who possess their own productive capacity). His earlier articles in the *Economic Journal* and the *Quarterly Journal of Economics* are summarized and developed in *The Nature of Capital and Income* (New York: Macmillan, 1927).

[11]*Principles of Economics,* 8th ed. (London: Macmillan, 1936), pp. 787, 788. Marshall's objection has less force if the aim is not, as his was, to explain "mankind in the ordinary business of life," but to explore the conditions for economic advance. Fisher took issue with Marshall on his own ground; *op. cit.,* pp. 61–64.

[12]Frank H. Knight, *Risk, Uncertainty and Profit* (Boston: Houghton Mifflin, 1921), pp. 123–140.

[13]Theodore W. Schultz *et al.,* "Investment in Human Beings," *Journal of Political Economy,* Supplement (October, 1962). Knight goes to some pains to argue against "commonly assumed grounds of distinction between labor and property services;" *op. cit.,* pp. 126–129.

[14]J. R. Hicks, *Value and Capital* (Oxford: Oxford University Press, 1939), pp. 171–184, esp. pp. 176–177. P. A. Samuelson, *Foundations of Economic Analysis* (Cambridge: Harvard University Press, 1948), pp. 353–354; Solow, *op. cit.,* p. 43. Hicks did not much like even the best qualified version of his definition: "We shall be well advised to eschew income and savings in economic dynamics." His objectives were technical ones: the difficulty of measuring real income over time, the complications introduced by durable consumer goods, the incommensurability of choices made at the beginning of one week with those made at the beginning of the next, and inconsistency in people's expectations and plans. He finally came to an *ex post* kind of (contd.)

But if other kinds of capital than material capital goods are important and may be of major importance, as many growth economists are convinced, then the theoretical boxes should take account of the possibility or the fact; and conventional divisions of income, consumption, and investment become still more awkward than Hicks saw them.

Ex post, the produced heap of income can always be divided into two piles, labeled "consumption" and "investment" (or capital formation, and identical with real savings), whose sum equals the original total. But suppose instead we follow fairly conventional concepts: income is consumption plus investment: consumption is what gives satisfaction (by some definition) to people; investment is what contributes to their future potential income. Then income is made up of piles that must be double-counted: (a.) simple consumption, (b.) consumption that is also investment, and (c.) nonhuman material capital formation and nonmaterial investment. Consumption is a plus b; investment is b plus c. The total of consumption plus investment $(a + b + b + c)$ is greater than income. The total of simple consumption and simple investment $(a + c)$ is less than income.[15]

Simple and convenient points of logic, like the statement that "An economy whose consumption is rising cannot be consuming all its income,"[16] become, in this more realistic framework, simply wrong.

C

The low-brow and practical definitions, which automatically come to mind, are the national accounts concepts. The national accounts have three purposes: to classify final product meaningfully, to explain changes in total demand, and to interpret economic growth. There is no reason to assume that a classification ideal for one purpose is also ideal for others.[17]

In the standard national accounts, income is consumption (including a portion of government real outlay) plus investment. Gross investment is, following fairly standard definitions: (a.) newly produced durable goods (those with an average life exceeding one year) acquired by their ultimate business

income ("consumption plus capital accumulation") which satisfied him for limited purposes, only by explicitly leaving out the accumulation or dissipation of human capital (pp. 178–179).

Hicks continues to differentiate his growth theory from economic development, concluding firmly in his recent *Capital and Growth* that they have nothing to do with each other (Oxford University Press, 1965), pp. 3, 4.

[15]Or else consumption and saving add to greater than income, if by main force and some illogic, b is called saving as well as consumption.

[16]Solow, *op. cit.*, p. 43. This frequent view can also be in error for a second reason. Suppose a country has zero net savings year after year, but that the flow of durable consumer goods into use exceeds their rate of depreciation. Then, though measured national income is constant, the actual standard of living is rising. Cf. Harry G. Johnson, "The Political Economy of Opulence," in *Money, Trade and Economic Growth* (Cambridge: Harvard University Press, 1962), p. 171.

[17]Cf. Bonner, J. and D. S. Lees, "Consumption and Investment," *Journal of Political Economy* (February, 1963), pp. 64–75.

users, including new residence construction (since home-owning is treated as a business); plus (b.) change in business inventories valued at current replacement cost. (c.) Government investment is often estimated separately. The total of *a, b,* and *c* is domestic investment. There may be some convenience from adding in (d.) foreign investment, which is the excess of exports of goods and services (domestic output sold abroad and production abroad for which payments are due to domestic-owned resources) over imports (domestic purchases of foreign output, domestic production for which payments are due to foreign-owned resources, and net private cash gifts to abroad). If one is courageous, he may subtract an estimate for depreciation to get net measures of investment and of income.

Keynes was unworried about the division in the national accounts between consumption and investment because he was concerned with the motives of groups of spenders: "Any reasonable definition of the line between consumer-purchasers and investor-purchasers will serve us equally well provided it is consistently applied."[18]   But Keynes' lighthearted view is inappropriate if one's aim is to analyze the process of economic growth. In its continuing effort to improve the usefulness of national accounts, the National Bureau of Economic Research has been experimenting with redefining U.S. national accounts categories so that they interpret growth more effectively. John Kendrick of the Bureau adds to conventional investment other uses of resources that increase productive capacity.   Part of these are purchases of durable goods plus inventory change of consumers and of government. The rest consists of intangible outlays: (1.) education and training, (2.) medical and health outlays, (3.) research and development, (4.) mobility costs, and perhaps — an optional item — (5.) costs of rearing children to working age. Much under these headings is usually classified as "consumption." (He does not include, but raises the question of including, non-economic-resource inputs that raise productive capacity.)

Kendrick's total investment turns out to diverge widely from official investment estimates. His total investment is much larger; its share of GNP has grown as GNP has grown; and it is more stable cyclically. In 1965 his total investment is $422 billion,[19] or 381 percent above the official (gross) investment figure of $111 billion.

---

[18]*General Theory* (London: Macmillan, 1960), p. 61.

[19]Excluding rearing costs. If they are included, total investment is $476 billion. In the present official estimates, gross investment is 16 percent of GNP: Kendrick's total investment is 47 or 53 percent of adjusted GNP, depending on whether rearing costs are excluded or included.

Total investment as a share of "adjusted GNP" has risen from 38 percent in 1929 to 47 percent in 1965. The contrast suggests, reasonably enough, that the share of income a society devotes to future growth rises when income rises.

Adjusted GNP includes imputations needed for consistency with total investment estimates. Official GNP in 1965 is $681 billion: official imputations for space rental value, financial services, farm consumption, and payments in kind total $39 billion. Adjusted GNP in 1965 is $892 billion, or 31 percent higher. It includes additional (contd.)

Kendrick's work is a major advance toward shaping national accounts so that they interpret better the process of economic growth.[20] Meanwhile, we still have, in less developed as in more developed countries, the standard national income measures of consumption and investment and their elements, gradually being refined in detail.

What is the usual practice on the above definitions? Often the practical man, and economists too, mix together definitions *B* and *C*. Income is consumption and investment: investment contributes to future potential income, whereas consumption does not (definition *B*): and for purpose of practical policy, investment and consumption are identified with the national income concepts *C*. But definition *B* is inaccurate, and the identification of *B* and *C* is misleading.

III

A number of studies of aggregative input-output relationships in the United States and the United Kingdom attest to a dominant proportion of changes in output in excess of changes in input of the total quantity of capital and labor.[21]

---

imputations of $210 billion for business investments charged to current expense, student compensation, and rentals on capital goods.

If imputations are added for housewife services, volunteer labor, and consumption charged to business expense, GNP rises to well over one trillion dollars. Some further imputations are also plausible.

A summary of this experiment-in-progress is given in John W. Kendrick, "Studies in the National Income Accounts," *Forty-seventh Annual Report* (National Bureau of Economic Research, June, 1967), pp. 9–15. See also his "Restructuring the National Income Accounts for Investment and Growth Analysis," *Statistick Tidschrift,* No. 5 (1966), p. 353–365.

[20]But even the improved figures suffer, for growth analysis purposes, from three weaknesses. (1.) There is the standard trouble and taxonomy. Items are put into one box or another through decisions that are uncertain at the margin; sometimes an item plausibly belongs in two boxes, like activities raising output capacity (investment?) that also provide current utility (consumption?) *a* + *b*, p. 395; and "noneconomic activities," completely thrown out, often fit the definition of investment. (2.) The degree of fulfillment of a given criterion is a variable. "Total investment" is a box holding activities that less or more efficiently fulfill the criterion of raising productive capacity. (3.) Nonexhaustive inputs (like the productive use of previous leisure time) are omitted.

[21]Schmookler finds an average rise of 1.4 percent per year in output per unit of input, 1904–13 to 1929–38. Jacob Schmookler, "The Changing Efficiency of the American Economy," *Review of Economics and Statistics* (August, 1952), pp. 214–231. Valavanis-Vail finds a shift upward of about 3/4 percent a year, 1869/1948, in the production function from given inputs. Stephen Valavanis-Vail, "An Econometric Model of Growth: USA 1869–1953," *American Economic Review, Proceedings and Papers* (May, 1955), pp. 208–221. Fabricant estimates that 90 percent of the rise in U.S. output per capita is due to "technical progress" rather than to rises in inputs. S. Fabricant, *Economic Progress and Economic Change* (New York: NBER 34th Annual Report, 1954). Abramovitz, partly drawing on Kendrick, finds that in the 75 years 1869–78 to 1944–53, U.S. inputs into production per capita rose only 14 percent, while productivity per capita rose 248 percent, a ratio of 1 to 18. M. Abramovitz. "Resource and (contd. on next page)

These studies measure technical progress as a residual: the difference between growth rates of production and of inputs of labor and material capital, the latter measured as real inputs weighted by base period wage rates and capital earnings taken as measures of marginal products. The studies suffer from the large amount of aggregation required in the calculations — both capital and labor are highly heterogeneous[22] — and from the assumption that factors are paid their marginal products, that is, that the factor markets are

Output Trends in the United States since 1870," *American Economic Review, Proceedings* (May, 1956), pp. 5ff. Solow, in an aggregative econometric study for the U.S. covering 1909–48, which makes the data less heterogeneous by omitting agriculture and government, and which assumes that technical and organizational advance must be embodied in new capital equipment, finds that 90 percent of the rise in gross output per manhour is *not* accounted for by changed inputs of land and capital. R. M. Solow, "Technical Change and the Aggregate Production Function," *Review of Economics and Statistics* (August, 1957), pp. 312–320; corrected later for a computing error, *op. cit.* (November, 1958). Massell, using the same procedure on U.S. manufacturing 1919–57, comes out with an identical figure. *Op. cit.* (May, 1960), pp. 182–188. Denison, making courageous estimates of the constituents of the "residual" not explained by quantitative inputs, shows changes in real U.S. income 1919–57 originated as follows:

Increase in labor hours	27 percent	
Increase in capital	15 percent	
Total increase in real inputs		42 percent
Improvement in labor quality	26 percent	
Technical and organization advances	32 percent	
Total productivity increase		58 percent
Total		100 percent

E. F. Denison, *The Sources of Economic Growth in the United States, etc.* (New York: CED Supplementary Paper 13, 1962), p. 266. For an earlier period, 1909–29, Denison's procedure finds inputs accounting for more than the above (57 percent) and productivity increases for less (43 percent). Reddaway and Smith, in a study of British manufacturing, 1948–54, find a bit over half of growth resulting from capital and labor inputs and almost half (46.7 percent) from increased productivity. W. B Reddaway and A. D. Smith, "Progress in British Manufacturing Industries in the Period 1948–54," *Economic Journal* (March, 1960), pp. 17–37. Table 1, p. 26. Aukrust finds, from an econometric study for Norway, 1900–55, that normal improvement in organization and techniques leads to a 1.8 percent rise in national product a year. A large increment in real capital (9 percent) is needed to raise output as much; or a considerable rise in employment (2.5 percent). The rate of growth of the economy was not very sensitive to changes in the amount of investment. Odd Aukrust, "Investment and Economic Growth," *Productivity Measurement Review* (February, 1959), pp. 35–53. A study by Niitamo for Finland gives similar results. Olavi Niitamo, "Development of Productivity in Finnish Industry, 1925–52," *op. cit.* (November, 1958).

On the other hand, Griliches finds that "residual" causes of output increases can, in a sample study, be explained by wrong specification, measurement, or weighting of inputs, plus economies of scale. "Wrong specification" includes neglect of quality improvement of labor inputs. Zvi Griliches, "The Sources of Measured Productivity Growth: United States Agriculture, 1940–60," *Journal of Political Economy* (August, 1963), pp. 331–346.

[22]"There is no reason to suppose that any single object called 'capital' can be defined to sum up in one number a whole range of facts about time lags, gestation periods, inventories of materials, goods in process, and finished commodities, old and new machines of varying durability, and more or less permanent improvements to land." Solow, *op. cit.*, pp. 13–14.

perfectly competitive or behave as if they were.[23] They do suggest that the contribution of capital to increased output in these economies is likely to be some 10 to 30 percent of total contributions, with the lower part of the range more probable.

The international correlation of national income measures of investment and measured growth has been explored for a number of countries over certain post-World War II years, by Hill and by his critics Johnson and Chiu. All three find the correlation to be poor:

> the relation between growth and one kind of investment cannot be the same as that between growth and another kind. . . . In so far as any general association exists between growth and investment, it is largely due to investment in machinery and equipment. This is especially the case for growth in GNP per person employed, where all of the correlations, excepting that with machinery and equipment, are quite trivial.[24]

There is some indication in their studies that a high rate of investment may be a necessary condition for growth, though it is clearly not a sufficient condition.[25] The more northern countries tend to have high investment rates without particularly rapid growth, interpreted by Hill as due to the demands of their geography and climate for a large volume of construction, which has little effect on measured income increases.[26] Smaller and lower income countries typically show less relationship between investment and income than holds for the five major countries.

---

[23]Other implied assumptions in the approaches are considered in Hahn and Matthews, *op. cit.,* pp. 833–853.

[24]T. P. Hill, "Growth and Investment according to International Comparisons," *Economic Journal* (June, 1964), pp. 297–298. The last two sentences are repeated for emphasis in the later "Reply," *Economic Journal* (September, 1965), p. 631, to a "Comment" by D. W. Johnson and J .S. Chiu in the same issue. Hill does find a strong correlation between gross investment and GNP growth for the U. S. and the U. K., France, Italy, and Germany 1954–62, but the association weakens when employment is allowed for and smaller countries are included. There might possibly be better correlation if a longer time period were allowed for investment effects to work themselves out.

[25]Johnson and Chiu, *op. cit.,* p. 269; Hill, *op. cit.,* p. 165. This accords with the cautious view of Solow as given in *American Economic Review, Proceedings* (May, 1962), p. 86.

[26]"The demolition of some dismal nineteenth century school and its replacement by a modern, well-designed, and well-equipped building should lead to a real improvement in the quality of education, but the flow of educational services included in GNP is unchanged in these circumstances." Hill, *op. cit.,* p. 299. Professor David Granick suggests that critical periods in the growth process are likely to be characterized by large shifts in the proportion of measured to unmeasured outputs and also in the proportion of measured to unmeasured inputs; so that conventional preoccupation with measured inputs and outputs can readily lose the central significance of what is going on.

Hill suggests: "There is a tendency for construction to be more closely associated with the provision of services than with the production of goods; and vice versa . . . for machinery. This fact, in conjunction with the known tendency for the growth of output per person in services, especially as conventionally measured, to be much slower than
(contd. on next page)

The Secretariat of the Economic Commission for Europe has explored the relation between conventional capital inputs and growth rates for 22 Western countries in the 1950's. They conclude there is "practically no correlation." Morss has studied the same relationship for 46 less developed countries 1960 to 1965. He regressed average annual growth in real output on the ratio of national-income investment to GNP: R^2 came out as 0.009. Morss concludes that present classification practices for investment and consumption "are not useful as a predictor of growth differences among developing countries."[27]

Low correlation does not disprove the existence of causation, nor would high correlation prove it. What is proved is that any causation between conventional investment and measured income growth was (in these countries, for these periods of time, and granting the data are reasonably accurate) unimportant compared to other influences.

in the production of goods, is probably the basic explanation underlying many of the results of this paper" (p. 303).

As to the relationship Hill suspects is critical, the share of GNP going to machinery and equipment as compared to the share going to construction: there is no correlation between the two for his sample countries and period, no matter whether residential construction is included or excluded (pp. 296, 320).

[27]The ECE study was published in United Nations, *Some Factors in European Economic Growth during the 1950's* (Geneva, 1964). For all 22 countries, the correlation coefficient is 0.2. When, for more homogeneity, they select out the 13 most industrialized countries, the correlation coefficient is nearly as low. If Norway, an extreme deviant, is also omitted, it rises to 0.69. Investment ratios and growth rates are average annual figures for 1949–59. Four low-growth-rate countries (Denmark, Norway, Sweden, and the U.S., at about 3½ percent a year) have a wide range of investment ratios, including the highest. Four high-growth-rate countries (Austria, Greece, Italy, and Turkey, at about 6 percent) have relatively low (15 to 23 percent) investment ratios (p. 18).

The second study is Elliot R. Morss, "Fiscal Policy, Savings, and Economic Growth in Developing Countries: An Empirical Study" (July, 1968, unpublished).

Suits has attempted unsuccessfully to relate conventional investment to growth in Greece. Daniel B. Suits, *An Econometric Model of the Greek Economy* (Athens: Center of Economic Research, 1965).

Patel has related annual growth rates in real domestic product to investment as a percent of GDP for 37 less developed countries, 1953–54 to 1962–63. The countries are placed in six groups, from the slowest growing (+ 1 percent a year) to the fastest growing (+ 7 to + 11 percent a year). The investment ratios vary mildly in the same direction, from 15 to 21 percent. S. J. Patel, "A Note on the Incremental Capital-Output Ratio and Rates of Economic Growth in the Developing Countries," *Kyklos*, Vol. 21 (1968 Fasc. 1), pp. 147–150.

As to empirical judgments on the growth experience of particular countries, the range is between the unqualified statement of Chenery and Strout: "In the past decade . . . [in] Greece, Israel, Taiwan, and the Philippines . . . a substantial increase in investment . . . led to rapid growth of GNP," and the complex judgments of Kuznets, and also of Habakkuk: "The factors favorable to development are so varied and have historically combined in so many different ways that I see no possibility of isolating a small number of crucial variables." See Chenery and Strout, *op. cit.*, pp. 679–680; Simon Kuznets in, for example, *Modern Economic Growth* (New Haven: Yale University Press, 1966), esp. Chap. 9; and H. J. Habakkuk, "Historical Experience of Economic Development," in E. A. G. Robinson, ed., *Problems in Economic Development* (London: Macmillan, 1965), p. 119.

In the special form of the marginal-capital-output-ratio (dk/dO, or $MKOR$), the relationship of (net or gross) material investment to production changes has had much attention. $MKOR$'s cannot be used for setting priorities, since they take account neither of the durability of the capital used, nor of the complementary inputs required of labor and supplies. But they can be useful for estimating conventional capital requirements.

The dk-to-dO ratios will vary by level of technology and by resource price variations, which means from one economy to another (within a range[28] of at least 4 to 1); from one industry to another within an economy (within a range of 100 to 1 or more); and in consequence of these causes, from one period of time to another (by decade averages, within a range of 2½ to 1 or more).

IV

This section consists, first, of an analysis of the implications of empirical marginal capital/output ratios, and then of a fairly concrete listing of cases in which the conventional argument that nonhuman material investment causes income changes fails and in which other causes of income changes are central.

A

The case for income changes caused by such investment is straightforward: the underemployment investment multiplier is irrelevant to it. Production rises (dO) because of improved proportions (dK) in the production mix, or because better performance is embodied in the replaced or added capital. On the dK-to-dO relationship a vast and subtle literature is based, much of it surveyed up to recently in the Hahn and Matthews article.[29]

Empirical $MKOR$'s (marginal capital/output ratios) have been supposed to measure this causation. But it turns out that they do not do so, even in theory. If other than conventional capital inputs normally dominate the causes of income change, for which the evidence is overwhelming, then empirical $MKOR$'s are an inverse function of the rate of growth (and not a measure of the contribution of capital to growth). We modify slightly Leibenstein's demonstration of the relationship: take a standard Cobb-Douglas production function in which nonhuman and nonmaterial inputs are explicit:

$$dO' = a + b\,dK' + c(dH',\, dN')$$

[28]Simon Kuznets, "Capital Formation Proportions, etc.," *Economic Development and Cultural Change* (July, 1960), Part II, pp. 43–68. U. S. Department of State, "Intelligence Report No. 7670" (Washington, 1958).

[29]*Op. cit.*

and

$$MKOR \text{ or } \frac{dK}{dO} = \frac{\text{antilog } [dK']}{\text{antilog } [a + b\,dK' + c(dH', dN')]}$$

The log increment in output is dO', that of capital is dK', and dH' and dN' are log increments in human and nonhuman nonmaterial capital, respectively. Qualitative changes in inputs and organization are measured by the log of a. Elasticities of output with respect to factor inputs are measured by b and c.

Given such an equation, $MKOR$ carries its traditional meaning only if dk causes of growth are large compared with the total of other causes. If not, changes in output will have a low correlation with changes in capital inputs: that is, the ratio of dK to dO will usually fall when dO rises, and *vice versa*; $MKOR$'s will be inversely correlated with the rate of growth.

The presumption that other inputs than conventional capital are dominant, and that in consequence $MKOR$-output change correlations are negative, is supported with nearly total regularity in Leibenstein's empirical tests: in 129 out of 134 observations, Patel's findings are also consistent with that presumption: in his study of 37 less developed countries grouped by growth rates 1953–54 to 1962–63, $MKOR$'s vary without exception inversely with the growth rates[30]

Aside from the empirical relationship of dK/dO to dO, there is also that of dK to dO. Causation between the two runs in both directions: a rise in production, whatever its cause, will normally result in a rise in conventional capital formation. Suppose that a country's real income rises. We can perhaps attribute this autonomous rise, to borrow Cairncross' hypothesis for the Victorian era, to a compound of technological change, growth of markets, and entrepreneurial zeal and effectiveness. Then a linkage effect will be at work: more warehousing is needed: more transportation, including road, railway, and/or air equipment; more distribution facilities; and for some products more intermediate or final processing and adapting. And the government out of rising revenues is likely to spend more on building and equipment. In each case investment rises, but as a result of the initial increased production.

There is also the effect on consumer's capital. If population is not growing as fast as production grows, average real income is rising. Among the things consumers will spend their larger incomes on is housing.[31] The housing portion of gross fixed investment is considerable: the 1953–61 average for 16 higher-income countries ranges from one-sixth to one-third.[32] In addition, acceleration effects from any rise in consumer spending proliferate through an economy and swell investment outlays — but as effects, not causes, of the initial production increase. In these cases, investment is needed during the

[30]Harvey Leibenstein, "Incremental Capital-Output Ratios and Growth Rates in the Short Run," *Review of Economics and Statistics* (February, 1966), pp. 20–27. Patel, *op. cit.,* p. 149.

[31]Cairncross, *op. cit.,* p. 100.

[32]From data collected by Hill, *op. cit.,* p. 290.

growth process, but to avoid supply-demand distortions and so facilitate continuation of growth, rather than as the initiating force.

Empirical *MKOR*'s therefore measure jointly: (1.) the inverse of the rate of growth of production due to noncapital-input causes; (2.) consumer income-elasticity of demand for housing; and (3.) acceleration effects from other consumer spending — these in addition to what *MKOR*'s are conventionally supposed to measure: (4.) the effect of added capital toward increasing production.

B

There are several capital-output relationships that permit major increases in production without increases in the quantity or quality of capital, and perhaps even with a decrease. The reasoning below can apply to a given industry, without any technological change taking place.

(1.) Income can obviously rise from increased utilization of existing capital. In many a country, holidays are numerous: religious holidays compound with patriotic ones to cut the work year. Colombia's normal 220 days a year could be increased by 22 percent through adoption of a 5½ day week with a modest six holidays a year and two-weeks vacation pattern. To have people willing to get along on fewer holidays turns on stronger incentives, possibly better health, and simple willingness to make a change.

Similarly, equipment and buildings can be used two or three shifts a day, with some time down for repairs and maintenance, rather than one shift only. Equipment can be run nearly 24 hours a day. Buildings need not stand empty and idle most of the time: evenings, nights, mornings, and weekends can be exploited. If labor and supplies are available, and there is willingness to adjust habits and organization, then output can rise from this cause by a factor of 100 to near 200 percent from the same capital stock.[33]

Also, there can be fuller use of overbuilt capacity. Cairncross points out that railway building in North America and Europe absorbed during the late nineteenth century a smaller amount of total national investment, but railroads nonetheless increase rapidly their hauling of freight and passengers.[34] Overbuilding can in special areas permit a highly variable increment to production, complementary resources being available.

Capital often stands idle for lack of demand and effective organization — a cause that sometimes overlaps the three phenomena listed above. In many

---

[33]Lauchlin Currie, *Accelerating Economic Growth* (New York: McGraw-Hill, 1965), p. 54. He estimates that in Latin America generally, even where industrial equipment is fully utilized during working hours, the combination of frequent holidays plus normal one-shift operation means such equipment is in use no more than 20 percent of the year. That is, a near-five-times rise in industrial production is possible, given adequate supplies of complementary factors.

[34]A. K. Cairncross, "Reflections on the Growth of Capital and Income," *Scottish Journal of Political Economy* (June, 1959); reprinted as Chap. 6 in *Factors in Economic Development* (London: Allen and Unwin, 1962), p. 103.

a poor country, and sometimes in richer ones also, equipment and structures are underutilized because of the throttling effects on domestic manufactures of a syndrome of over-valued exchange rates, protectionism causing price hikes for intermediate goods inputs, and high urban wage rates sustained by government edict and union pressures. These can more than offset the stimulus to production from inflating domestic demand, protectionism on final products, and specific schemes attempting to expand exports. In India, for example, manufacturing production has in recent years run much below its potential.[35] In Indonesia, an extreme case, the utilization of equipment has recently been, by crude estimate, at 15 percent of capacity. The priority issue, when production is running sharply below capacity, is not more capital, but better utilization of what capital there is.

(2.) Another reason why national production can often be raised without changing the existing quantity of capital is implied in the rising share of government in economic decisions. Government direction of resource flows is, for right reasons and wrong, relied on much more than it was in the past; and this reliance has its implications. In the nineteenth century and before, merchandising, craft production, and even factory-type production were often started up in a corner of the house or in the barn; and so also private schools and hospitals. But under the aegis of government, insitutions must have a dignity suited to that of the State. The inefficiency may go deeper than this tendency; in many a country showpieces swallow up a good part of government investment outlays: a new airport to take the newest jets, a new highway to the capital from the airport, national monuments, even statutes of the President.[36]

On the average, less of prudent economic calculation is in many a country going into government expenditure decisions than have gone and go into the agonizing appraisals and reappraisals of businessmen hazarding their own money. If there is more of politically explained misuse of resources than existed in the past,[37] then the importance of a simple increase in quantity of

---

[35]"The Ministry of Commerce and Industry takes the view that the extent of under-utilization of industrial capacity is of the order of 15 to 20 percent." *Report of the Import and Export Policy Committee* (New Delhi: Ministry of Commerce and Industry, 1962), p. 10.

[36]Arthur Lewis comments on public investment in less developed countries: "Public factories, schools, hospitals, and other structures are nearly always colossal, striking and expensive, built to the glory of their architects and their supporting politicians." "Unemployment in Development Countries," Lecture at the Midwest Research Conference, Chicago, October, 1964, p. 16. "I would give high marks to a development programme in which only 10 percent of the expenditures was in nonsense of this kind." *Economic Bulletin of the Economic Society of Ghana* (May-June, 1959).

[37]Clair Wilcox, in his excellent study of the subject, concluded that economic development has not been the central concern of any government in Southeast Asia. "The Planning and Execution of Economic Development in Southeast Asia," Occasional Paper 10, Center for International Affairs, Harvard University, 1965, p. 35. Despite their mixed purposes, these governments are more involved in economic policy decisions than ever before.

capital is lessened, and the problems of strategy in improving the economic efficiency of political decisions — reform-mongering[38] — gain higher priority.

(3.) Sometimes income rises *because* of using a decreased amount of capital. In recent years, rice cultivation in Ceylon used, following traditional procedure, excessive quantities of irrigation water. Soil nutrients were leached away. Less water and smaller irrigation works could have raised rice production.

Many a technical advance diminishes capital needs: the telegraph and wireless replace the pony express and railroad communications. The implied priority problem is what innovations, which may be capital-saving, can be efficiently adapted into a particular region, given its economic, social, and political conditions.

C

It has become commonplace to evaluate the human factor — health, energy, technical skills, habits of regularity, and responsible helpfulness — as a major determinant of economic advance. Health and energy require, among other things, adequate nutrition, sanitary habits and facilities, and medical care. Formal education, beyond a point, seems to be thought less important for productive efficiency than it was considered a few years ago, and training in practical skills near the point of use, and on-the-job training, more important.[39] Also critical is the cultivation of responsibility, concern, and willing cooperation toward productive goals. The use of leisure time for self-improvement can be highly productive. Finally, one of the simplest ways of raising productivity is to have people move from places and jobs where they are less productive to where they are more so.

Added real outlays are not always needed to achieve these improvements in human productivity. Where they are, some would be classified as conventional investment: others would usually be listed as consumption.

There is striking contrast between the trivial estimated loss to GNP found in a number of empirical studies from wrong allocation of resources (in seven different studies of four countries and two regions, between 0.01 and 1 percent) and the wide efficiency gains rewarding better motivation and organization (for example, as a result of 27 ILO productivity missions, a median rise

---

[38]As Albert Hirschman calls it. See *Journeys toward Progress* (New York: Twentieth Century Fund, 1963).

[39]In an experimental study in India, Harberger's data suggest that marginal returns on education are somewhat lower than those on investment in physical capital. Arnold C. Harberger, "Investment in Men versus Investment in Machines: The Case of India," in C. Arnold Anderson and Mary Jane Bowman, eds., *Education and Economic Development* (Chicago: Aldine, 1965), p. 29. Myint states firmly: "The educational effect of apprenticeship and promotion to skilled grades in ordinary economic life is more far-reaching than huge sums of money spent on educational institutions." H. Myint, "An Interpretation of Economic Backwardness," *Oxford Economic Papers* (June, 1954), pp. 132–163.

in work productivity of 41 percent).[40] The seven studies showing trivial loss from wrong resource allocation seem too few and specialized to justify taking them as proving what is true generally: conspicuous examples of serious waste are easy to find. But the evidence for wide gains from better motivation and organization is impressive. Leibenstein considers the explanation of those gains to be that:

> the relation between inputs and outputs is not a determinate one . . . (a.) contracts for labor are incomplete, (b.) the production function is not completely specified or known, and (c.) not all inputs are marketed, or if marketed, are not available on equal terms to all buyers.[41]

Most people and organizations are working well within their production capacities. The critical problem of raising production seems often that of diminishing the gap: of enabling and persuading them to work more productively.

The conventional savings-investment model checks consumption growth or cuts consumption, so that maximum savings flow into capital goods creation. But: (a.) even in the highest income societies, some proportion of the population is living at levels of consumption of food, clothing, medical and sanitary services, and other social services (plus housing classified as investment) that are correlated with their ability to produce; in lower income societies the proportion can become the great majority. The peasant of China, India, and Guatemala is said to know for how many hours of digging on his land a handful of rice or corn will provide energy, or for how many miles it will enable him to carry a burden. As for health, little work can come from people weakened by malnutrition from lack of calories or protective foods, or debilitated by malaria, filaria, tuberculosis, intestinal parasites, and other diseases.

Barely to exist requires a considerable consumption intake. The marginal cost of raising consumption to enable six or eight hours of work to be done can offer a good bargain to a society. In a partly theoretical, partly empirical study of the relation of production to calorie intake, Carl Shoup concludes that there is a range of consumption where the ratio of marginal products to increased consumption reaches the order of from 20-to-1 to 80-to-1. High returns from increased consumption are apt to be found, he judges, where absenteeism from illness is due to too little consumption and where children's low consumption is a burden on their future productivity.[42]

(b.) Furthermore, incentives are crucial. Among the most solid and least subject to erosion by cynicism are the incentives of obtaining more of the

[40]Harvey Leibenstein, "Allocative Efficiency versus 'X Efficiency,'" *American Economic Review* (June, 1966), pp. 393, 400.

[41]*Ibid.*, pp. 407, 412.

[42]Looking to food only, suppose that to keep a person alive with minimum activity requires 1500 calories a day, and that to work takes an added 300 calories per hour; then zero work costs 1500 calories (unless the person is let starve); four hours work costs 2700 calories, or 675 an hour; and eight hours work costs 3900 calories, or 488 an hour. (contd.)

goods and services people want. To the extent that this diagnosis deserves priority in a given area, the most incentive-carrying consumer goods and services are what are needed. Wristwatches, transistor radios, fountain pens, sarees, and bicycles can be more useful toward higher incomes than generators, drill presses, lathes, and locomotives. A conventional policy of raising taxes or raising consumer goods prices and making them more scarce, with the intention of raising the saving rate and so the rate of accumulation of capital goods, can have the perverse effect of actually cutting the capital goods supply, if a discouraged and enfeebled work force lowers its input of effort sufficiently.[43]

Some light on the practical question of priorities is found in the judgments of the 24 country missions sent out by the International Bank for Reconstruction and Development, 1949 to 1961. The missions generally gave highest priority to increased output of essential consumption goods, especially agricultural products; second priority to the tertiary sector, especially transportation; and third place to education. These priority goals are partly intermediate (the means to growth) and partly ultimate (the purpose and definition of growth); and they are achieved by real outlays that would be classed conventionally both as investment and consumption.[44]

D

Economic advisers often come back from less developed areas impressed by the crucial influence on growth possibilities of institutional or organization changes. Some resource flows to improve institutions or organizations can be classed as traditional investment (nonhuman material capital formation); some cannot.

V

The implication of this paper is that the traditional model of economic growth, in which nonhuman material capital formation is taken as the central issue, with qualification entered for other influences, is unsatisfactory. It is awkward in theory and has probably been on occasion perversely misleading

---

Many writers have touched on this relationship. Kuznets, generalizing from his statistical inquiries, is emphatic about its significance: "The low level of consumption may be as important in explaining the low productivity in the underdeveloped countries as the low level of capital stock or material capital formation." S. Kuznets, *Modern Economic Growth, op. cit.,* p. 506. Cf. Carl S. Shoup, "Production from Consumption," *Public Finance,* Vol. 20, No. 1–2 (1965), pp. 173–202. Shoup gives a bibliography on pp. 173–174 of studies relevant to the productivity of consumption.

[43]Arthur Smithies, "Rising Expectations and Economic Development," *Economic Journal* (June, 1961), p. 269. Smithies develops the case for economic growth set in motion by rising expectations for consumer supplies.

[44]Dorra H. Alwan, *An Analysis of Investment Criteria in Mission Reports of the International Bank,* unpublished Doctoral dissertation, University of Wisconsin, Appendix II, B, "Priorities."

in practice. Its deficiencies are peculiarly great with respect to the growth problems of less developed areas.

A more coherent and general model of growth is very much needed. The logic of policy for economic growth is, irrespective of conventional or national income divisions between consumption and investment, to set up a hierarchy of uses for resource units, from those whose social returns are highest to those that are lowest. The hierarchy is determined by as detailed cost-benefits analyses as are feasible. The total resources to be made available for development — which determines the cut-off point in the hierarchy, between projects that will and will not be undertaken — are a variable whose quantity is in part determined by the marginal development promise of those resources. For any given place and time it is unlikely that a perfectly wise policy board will find a gap in the hierarchy, with "investment" above and "consumption" below. Those outlays will probably be intermingled along the scale; some conventional "consumption" uses of resources may be at or near the very peak.

To apply the term "investment" to a higher range of the scale, or to all resource uses that raise future potential consumption, has the advantage of avoiding a change of language. But it will mislead every hearer who has not forcibly dug his way out from the traditional meaning. It seems more accurate in analyses of growth problems, and in practice less likely to mislead, simply to speak of the hierarchy of resource uses, and within that hierarchy, to evaluate items without prejudice or favor because of their belonging to a conventional "consumption" or "investment" classification.

Questions for discussion and analysis pertaining to this article may be found at the end of Article 22.

Sayre Schatz †

21. THE ROLE OF CAPITAL ACCUMULATION IN ECONOMIC DEVELOPMENT *

There are fashions in economics. Capital formation was once seen as the crucial element in the development of underdeveloped economies but the trend has been running against this view. Instead of capital the key importance of the necessary preconditions,[1] the supply of other factors of production such as entrepreneurship,[2] or other requisites of economic development such as widening of markets or technological progress are stressed.[3] The leading textbooks on economic development are skeptical about the central role of capital accumulation.[4] In view of this trend, this note restates the case for the primacy of capital formation, and attempts to pinpoint the specific areas of disagreement between those who emphasize capital and those who view it more modestly. The article also suggests that the controversy has an ideological aspect.

The position presented here is that a high rate of capital accumulation is necessary and (nearly) sufficient for rapid economic development, that it is economically feasible, but that the issue of political feasibility (which is related to the ideological aspect of the controversy) is in doubt. Despite the emphasis of some economists on the capital economizing nature of growth through technological progress,[5] it is widely agreed that the large amounts of capital are

†Sayre P. Schatz, Professor of Economics, Temple University. The author wishes to thank the students in his graduate colloquium in the economic development of Africa at Columbia University, Spring, 1967, for their helpful comments.
*From *Journal of Development Studies,* Vol. 5 (1) (October, 1968), pp. 39–43. Reprinted by permission of the author and the publisher.
[1]See, e.g., W. W. Rostow, *The Stages of Economic Growth* (Cambridge: Cambridge University Press, 1960).
[2]See, e.g., E. E. Hagen, *On the Theory of Social Change: How Economic Growth Begins* (Homewood, Illinois: Dorsey Press, 1962), and David C. McClelland, *The Achieving Society* (Princeton, N.J.: Van Nostrand, 1961). [This writer has criticized the latter in "Achievement and Economic Growth: A Critique," *Quarterly Journal of Economics* (May, 1965)].
[3]See, e.g., A. K. Cairncross, "The Place of Capital in Economic Progress," in L. H. Dupriez, ed., *Economic Progress* (Louvain: Institut de Recherches Economiques et Sociales, 1955).
[4]See, e.g., Charles P. Kindleberger, *Economic Development* (2nd ed., N.Y.: McGraw-Hill Book Co., 1965), Chap. 5, and Gerald M. Meier, *Leading Issues in Development Economics* (N.Y.: Oxford University Press, 1964). Chap. 3.
[5]See, e.g., Cairncross, *op. cit.*

necessary in the underdeveloped economies for capital deepening and widening. Already known production methods of high capital intensity replace backward methods requiring little capital in the market economy and the scope of the market sector broadens at the expense of the subsistence sector.

On the sufficiency issue, the position that a high rate of investment is just one of many requisites for accelerating growth certainly appears to be a strong one. If additional capital is to have its full effect, one can hardly deny that it must be accompanied by additional inputs of other factors of production, improvements in technology and other improvements in the economic environment. However, a reasonable statement of the capital-emphasis view need not be so simplistic as to overlook these requirements. The question is not one of the historical causes of development in the presently advanced economies. The issue is one of development strategy in contemporary underdeveloped economies — where a vast backlog of technological development already exists (although the problem of adaptation cannot be shrugged off), and where economic growth is already an overriding national concern. Under these circumstances, the primacy-of-investment position maintains, the accumulation of capital is the most effective way to *create* the other conditions required for economic growth; these requisites are created concurrently with and primarily by a high rate of capital formation.

This contention is based upon a broad conception and high estimate of the external effects of investment.[6] Such investment creates the scarce factors of production. Labour becomes skilled, disciplined, accustomed to the routine and regularity of modern productive processes, and responsible in handling expensive equipment through experience. Invaluable managerial and entrepreneurial skills are created in the same ways.[7] With a growing capital stock and with the upgrading of labour and entrepreneurship, real incomes increase. The enlarged markets that result induce greater effort and greater production by the peasantry.[8] Given the advanced level of technology already extant in

[6]This refers to the external effects of investments in the directly productive sector as well as the infrastructure. The thesis of the article refers to capital in the traditional sense. If investment in human capital were included, the thesis would win wider agreement but would be less specific and less interesting.

[7]Most industrial as well as commercial entrepreneurs in Nigeria, for example, acquired the necessary knowledge and skills by working in large enterprises. E. K. Hawkins has pointed this out [E. K. Hawkins, *Road Transport in Nigeria* (London: Oxford University Press, 1958), p. 94] and my own studies indicate the same thing. Managerial and entrepreneurial skills are also created outside the investing enterprise through a powerful "emulation effect"; small businessmen emulate the production standards and methods of the larger firms. E.g., Calloway finds that the "intense capacity" of small businessmen in Ibadan, Nigeria, to emulate larger firms with higher standards is one of the major factors explaining the success of many of these small operators. (Archibald Calloway, "Crafts and Industries," paper prepared for Seminar on Ibadan in the Changing Nigerian Scene, University of Ibadan, 1964).

[8]Substantial increases in production have occurred through greater peasant effort. For descriptions of the importance of this process in two African countries, see, e.g., Robert E. Baldwin, *Economic Development and Export Growth: A Study of Northern Rhodesia, 1920-1960* (Berkeley and Los Angeles: University of California Press, 1966), (contd.)

the developed economies, capital accumulation is inevitably the bearer of technological progress. Investment helps to generate many other tangible improvements in the economic environment.[9] And there are the broad intangible effects of capital accumulation about which the economist has little to say, but which are nevertheless exceedingly important.[10] The higher the rate of investment, it is maintained, the more rapid will be the entire process of sociological, technical, attitudinal, psychological and economic change, i.e., the entire process of modernization.

The primacy-of-capital position (as stated here), stands or falls on the importance of the external effects of investment. Thus, the pivotal difference between the capital-emphasizers and the capital-deprecators on the "sufficiency" of capital issue lies in their judgment of this slippery empirical question. The controversy cannot easily be settled because the external effects of investment are exceedingly difficult even to specify fully, let alone measure. Consequently, neither side can unequivocally be declared the victor.[11]

Even if the capital accumulation boosters should be right about the near-sufficiency of investment, it may be objected that a high rate of investment is not economically feasible in most underdeveloped economies. The limited absorptive capacity thesis maintains that most of these economies today cannot absorb, i.e., cannot find rewarding uses for, a large flow of capital. The

pp. 64–65 and 144–164 *passim* Gerald K. Helleiner, *Peasant Agriculture, Government and Economic Growth in Nigeria* (Homewood, Illinois: Richard D. Irwin, Inc., 1966), Chap. 1.

It might be pointed out here that the external benefits investment (i.e. the degree to which social benefits may exceed private) are broader than those which are encompassed in the usual definitions of technological plus pecuniary external economies.

[9]With the establishment of an increasing number of productive enterprises the conditions are created for improvements in the deliveries of capital equipment, spare parts, raw materials and other inputs, reducing expensive interruptions of production caused by delays in the receipt of these items. Facilities emerge for more knowledgeable ordering and more efficient and economical installation of equipment. With a higher concentration of enterprises the economy generates better repair services, better and more knowledgeable consultants, money-saving specialists and subsidiary services of all kinds. Widened markets resulting from expanded real income encourage larger scale and more efficient production techniques. New enterprises may ameliorate the restrictive effects of monopoly. Investments provide linkage effects that stimulate other investments in new undertakings.

[10]An economist as much concerned with measurement as Tinbergen believes that the "almost invisible influences" of investment may be of decisive importance. Jan Tinbergen, "The Relevance of Theoretical Criteria in the Selection of Investment Plans," in *Investment Criteria and Economic Growth*, papers presented at a conference, October 15–17, 1954 (Cambridge, Mass.: Center for International Studies, 1955), pp. 9–12.

[11]Those who simply dismiss the external effects of investment because they are too intangible and unmeasurable to work with are (illegitimately) making the implicit assumption that these effects balance out to zero. Economists are frequently reluctant to accept the major importance of external economies and dis-economies because we have a vested interest in upholding the validity of the price system signals. If external effects are highly important, the precision and elegance of price theory — the core and showpiece of "economic science" — suffers diminished relevance because it overlooks a major portion of the real-world effects of economic activity.

less developed economies, it is maintained, simply cannot generate enough investment projects with attractive pay-offs to enable a country to carry out a high investment strategy.[12]

However, this challenge to the capital-emphasis point of view is met like the previous challenge, i.e., by reference to the external effects of investment. The argument is as follows. The limited absorptive capacity thesis is based on the monetary returns to investment; the thesis refers to the limited number of *profitable* investments in the developing economy.[13] If the external effects of investment are important, however, then it is simply not true that there are few productive investment opportunities. At any given time, there are many pecuniarily unattractive projects, both in the directly productive sector and in the infrastructure, which nevertheless have high *social* marginal productivities.[14]

Investment in such projects, the argument continues, also adds to the country's real absorptive capacity in *subsequent* periods. A large portion of the indirect benefits of investment have precisely the effect of developing additional absorptive capacity. The creation of skilled and responsible labour, management and enterprise, the introduction of more advanced technology, and the many other tangible and intangible improvements in the economic environment sketched in notes 7–10 all help to make further investments economically possible and productive. The investment process feeds on itself; it is self-generating and cumulative.

In sum, the argument is that economic feasibility is in a sense not really a separate issue. If the capital-emphasis thesis passes the sufficiency test because of the external effects of investment, it also passes the economic feasibility test for the same reasons.

There is, finally, the issue of political feasibility. It may be said that one cannot realistically expect the governments in most underdeveloped countries to carry out the vigorous measures necessary for a sharp increase in the rate of investment. These governments have neither the will nor the ability to impose the required level of taxation, particularly on the more affluent classes, or to take other necessary, opposition-arousing steps. Neither would the governing groups have the understanding or resolution to carry through a robust investment programme based on social marginal productivity of capital despite pecuniary unprofitability. (Nor, for that matter, would the Western aid-giving nations have the understanding or inclination to support such programmes.)

---

[12]This writer has himself argued in this way about *profitable* investment opportunities. "The Capital Shortage Illusion: Government Lending in Nigeria," *Oxford Economic Papers* (July, 1965).

[13]Of course, the absorptive capacity thesis *need* not be based on monetary returns. Like other concepts, it could be modified to take into account the divergences between the private and the social effects of economic activity. It would then refer to the social rather than the private marginal productivity of capital.

[14]See, e.g., this writer's "The American Approach to Foreign Aid and the Thesis of Low Absorptive Capacity," *The Quarterly Review of Economics and Business* (November, 1961).

At this point the ideological aspect of the dispute emerges — though the sides seem mixed up. Generally it appears that more radical economists have been identified with the primacy of capital position[15] while the de-emphasis of capital accumulation has been a "mainstream" trend. Surprisingly, it thus seems that the mainstream economists insist upon the need for more or less thoroughgoing changes in the nature of society while the radicals stand relatively pat and state that only an increase in the rate of investment is needed.

However, this anomaly in the position of the radicals stressing capital formation is only apparent. The radicals do not dispute the importance of the shortcomings-of-government challenge to the political feasibility of a high rate of investment (as they disputed other objections raised by the capital deprecators). On the contrary, they *stress* the importance of the failings of government; these constitute the chief obstacle to accelerated development. Thus, the basic need is for a fundamental change in government.[16] Here then we do have a real pre-condition for rapid economic growth.

Thus, the capital emphasis position formulated here is that a general (though not universal) pre-condition for accelerated growth is a government that is dedicated to development, ready to invest on the basis of a comprehensive conception of the social productivity of capital, and willing and able to take the steps necessary to mobilize the required financial and real resources. Given such a government, a substantial increase in the rate of capital formation is necessary and (nearly) sufficient for a substantial acceleration of economic development and is economically and politically feasible.

Questions for discussion and analysis pertaining to this article may be found at the end of Article 22.

---

[15]Oskar Lange asserts: "The most important means of achieving economic development is undoubtedly productive investment." He later says that "essential of planning economic development . . . consists in assuring an amount of productive investment which is sufficient to provide for a rise of national income substantially in excess of the rise in population, so that per capita income increases. The strategic factor is investment . . ." [Oskar Lange, *Economic Development, Planning and International Cooperation* (Cairo: Central Bank of Egypt, 1961), pp. 3 and 10]. The major thrust of Paul Baran's analysis of underdeveloped economies is the crucial importance of capital accumulation and of the removal of political obstacles to an enhanced rate of investment. He brushes aside, considering them of secondary importance, all obstacles to economic development other than the nature of the regime [Paul Baran, *The Political Economy of Growth* (N.Y.: Monthly Review Press, 1957)]. See also Maurice Dobb, *Economic Growth and Underdeveloped Countries* (London: Lawrence and Wishart, 1963), pp. 35–44.

[16]A great many radicals hold that the change need not be revolutionary. Soviet theorists, for example, have been discussing at length various non-revolutionary courses of development towards "scientific socialism." [See, e.g., Thomas P. Thornton, *The Third World in Soviet Perspective* (Princeton, N.J.: Princeton University Press, 1964).]

Theodore Schultz †

22. PRODUCTION OPPORTUNITIES IN ASIAN AGRICULTURE: AN ECONOMIST'S AGENDA*

Agricultural production in many parts of Asia, leaving China aside for lack of information, has taken a marked turn for the better, for reasons that are becoming clear. The Asian Development Bank has completed a timely survey and has issued a useful, two-volume report under the title, *Asian Agricultural Survey*.[1] So let us take stock and see what accounts for this forward thrust of Asian agriculture and what it implies for the future. My purpose is to clarify the economic problems that will now require attention. To this end, I am placing four topics on the agenda.

(I.) Valid empirical economic knowledge pertaining to agriculture.

(II.) Controversial issues of the last two decades that are now substantially settled.

(III.) Sources of profitable opportunities in agriculture that are accessible to Asian countries.

(IV.) Key, unsettled, economic problems pertaining to Asian agriculture that now await solution.

Valid Empirical Economic Knowledge

Despite the involvement of economists in empirical analysis and the progress that has been made, the view persists that theoretical work is highbrow economics whereas empirical contributions are lowbrow. Empirical findings are rated as inferior because of a widely-held view that they have little or no universal applicability and that they have a very short life even for the limited circumstances to which they apply. It is, however, a mistaken view because

†Theodore W. Schultz, Charles S. Hutchinson Distinguished Service Professor, University of Chicago. The author wishes to acknowledge that in revising the first draft of this paper, he has benefited much from the critical comments of Jere R. Behrman, University of Pennsylvania, George K. Brinegar, University of Illinois, Steven N. S. Cheung, University of Bombay, Walter P. Falcon and Carl H. Gotsch, Harvard University, John P. Lewis, USAID, India, Gustav Ranis, Yale University, Vernon W. Ruttan, University of Minnesota, and S. Takahashi, International Bank for Reconstruction and Development. Needless to say, none are responsible for any of the shortcomings of this paper.

*An unpublished manuscript. Reprinted by permission of the author.

[1]Asian Development Bank, *Asian Agricultural Survey, Vol. I, Regional Report; Vol. II, Sectional Reports* (Manila, Philippines: March, 1968).

the advance in economic knowledge is fundamentally a joint product of theoretical and empirical analyses. I now turn to four such products, each of which is empirically grounded and valid for a wide range of economic activity the world over.

(1.) It is well established that the income elasticity of the demand for the farm-produced components in food declines as per capita income rises and that this elasticity approaches zero when people become as affluent as they are generally in the United States. But throughout Asia, except for Japan, this income elasticity is still high, although it is substantially less than 1.0. More important it will not decline much in the near future simply because per capita incomes will rise slowly.

(2.) The rate of return to investment in scientific and technical knowledge that enters into agricultural production activities, investment in its creation, adaptation, and dissemination, is high relative to that from most other investment opportunities. Looking ahead, we find no indications that returns to this class of investment will be diminishing during that part of the future that is relevant for economic planning decisions.[2] In priorities established by relative rates of return to alternative investment opportunities, the rate of return to this class of investment pertaining to Asian agriculture is higher than that from this source in the technically advanced countries. It is one advantage in entering late upon the process of modernizing agriculture.

(3.) The value productivity of land declines relative to that of non-land inputs as a consequence of modernization. The process of modernization is made possible by the advance in scientific and technical knowledge; this knowledge is the source of the new inputs and the value productivity of these inputs increases relative to that of land. In this process, new varieties of wheat and rice along with chemical fertilizer are, over time, substitutes for land.

(4.) Cheap food policies imposed by governments, policies that aim to hold the price of food grains to consumers below the marginal cost of producing food grains, become untenable as a consequence of internal supply and demand forces, provided that the country has no agricultural surplus and that there is no foreign food aid. The validity of this economic fact is not dependent upon the form of government, judging from post WW II economic history.

Controversial Economic Issues Pertaining to Agriculture That Are Now Substantially Settled

The controversy over the relevance of economics in explaining the behavior of Asian farmers as producers and consumers is becoming passé. It is increasingly clear that the theoretical and empirical analysis appropriate in explaining

[2]Frank Knight, despite his strong belief that the empirical findings of economists add ever so little to economic knowledge, has presented cogently this fundamental economic fact in "Diminishing Returns from Investment," *Journal of Political Economy*, 52 (March, 1944), pp. 26–47.

such behavior of farmers in Iowa is, also, appropriate in analyzing the economic behavior of farmers in Taiwan, Thailand, the Philippines, Pakistan, and India. In this respect, let me comment on some specific issues.

(1.) The responses of farmers in Asia to improvements in economic opportunities are rational in economic terms. Their responses to changes in product and factor prices are significantly positive. Moreover, the observed lags in these responses are closely akin to the observed lags by farmers in, for example, the United States. Although there are still some intellectuals, very few are economists, who despite the growing body of evidence against them, remain committed to their anti-economic analysis. The elegant prose of a Kusum Nair, enriched by travel over India, the United States, and Japan, has farmers saying, "Economics is dead." But for all that, it is no longer necessary to spend more time testing the proposition that farmers in Asia are indifferent to economic incentives; competent studies now available leave little room for doubt that this is a false proposition.

(2.) Farmers in Asia who are bound by the conditions that characterize traditional agriculture are not significantly inefficient in the allocation of the agricultural resources at their disposal. They approach an economic equilibrium; thus, the production behavior observed comes close to exhausting the economic opportunities open to them. The counterpart of this proposition is that under the dynamic conditions of economic growth now evident in many parts of Asian agriculture there are disequilibria and observable lags in adjustments. These disequilibria represent allocative inefficiencies, and by reducing these lags additional agricultural production can be had.

(3.) The controversy over disguised unemployment in Asian agriculture or over a zero marginal product of a significant part of the labor force in Asian agriculture is now an oddity for the historians of economic thought to ponder. On this issue also, the appeal to data competently analyzed leaves little room for doubt that the marginal product of this labor is positive and not zero and that the earnings of this labor are approximately equal to its marginal product. It is also true, of course, that farmers and farm laborers dependent upon these earnings for their income are very poor because the marginal product of work in Asian agriculture generally is very small.

(4.) Under the conditions of traditional agriculture, the prevailing arrangements determining landowner-tenant shares are not a significant source of inefficiency in the allocation of resources in Asian agriculture. Share tenancy reforms, including land reforms, however desirable as political and welfare goals, will not, in most parts of Asian agriculture under these conditions, result in a substantial increase in agricultural production. But this inference about production effects does not support the view that these reforms are not necessary for political and welfare reasons. Moreover, the dynamics of economic growth now underway in Asian agriculture will require substantially more flexibility in landowner-tenant arrangements and a larger roll for resident farm owners, who are the ones best situated to make entrepreneurial decisions under these dynamic conditions.

(5.) The controversy over the *farm price effects* in countries importing P.L. 480 farm products is, also, virtually settled. No Asian country has sufficient public administrative capability to manage an internal system of two prices that would fully offset the price depressing effects on farm product prices of such P. L. 480 imports. I am aware that P. L. 480 raises several issues in addition to that of the farm price effects, issues that are not as yet adequately clarified. Nor do I want to imply that a settlement of the farm price issue will suffice to keep the government of the United States from, once again, engaging in dumping farm surpluses into poor countries under arrangements akin to those of P. L. 480.

Sources of Profitable Opportunities in Asian Agriculture

This topic is beset with trouble both in thinking about agricultural production and in planning for it. If Asian farmers are, in general, efficient in using the agricultural resources that they have and if Asian agriculture remains traditional, the opportunities would be meager. If there are a dozen or more *necessary conditions*, all of which must be satisfied simultaneously in order to bring about the modernization of agriculture, it would be impossible for any country, rich or poor, to achieve this goal. If planning for industrialization and its implementation is concealing the profitable opportunities in Asian agriculture, it would be difficult, indeed, to discover these opportunities. But, fortunately, recent developments have been dispelling these troubles as they pertain to Asian agriculture. Let me identify some of these developments.

(1.) Food grain prices in Asian countries generally have broken through the constraints of the cheap food policy. Cheap food became untenable because of the inadequate supply, and food grain prices rose sharply. In many parts of Asia they are presently above "normal" for the prospective supply. But, meanwhile, the shock of food shortages has dominated, and the favorable farm price effects has set the stage for the forward thrust in agricultural production.

(2.) It is, also, increasingly clear that not all of the many conditions that agricultural development experts deem "necessary" to get the modernization process underway are, in fact, necessary for this purpose. Even analytically it would require a highly complicated, and, as yet, far from operational, systems analysis to cope with all of these necessary conditions, leaving aside the impossibility of any given government's having the capability of doing everything at once. It has meant, if we take the recommendations on this issue seriously, undertaking all of the following simultaneously: rural community development, land reform, new laws governing landlord-tenancy arrangements, farm cooperatives, farm credit reforms, overhauling market facilities, additional roads and transport, soil and hydrological analyses, irrigation and drainage structures, an agricultural extension service, modern farm machinery, tractors to replace bullocks, organized agricultural research (experiment stations), fertilizer, new varieties that are fertilizer responsive, pesticides, and more still. No doubt each of these has some relevance, but the question that matters, to which I shall return in considering topic IV, is that of determining priorities and the sequence in which these conditions are best satisfied.

(3.) The forward thrust in production in Asian agriculture, weather aside, represents in large part the combined effects of three developments: (a.) favorable farm prices, (b.) new varieties of grains with a biological capacity to utilize additional fertilizer efficiently, and (c.) increases in the supply of fertilizer at prices lower than those formerly charged.

(4.) The biological advance is the pay-off on organized agricultural research; the superior new varieties of wheat were developed predominantly in Mexico, the rice varieties mainly at Los Banos in the Philippines and in Taiwan, and corn, millet, and jowar varieties especially suited to India were developed there. (Corn for Thailand and elsewhere are parts of this picture.)

(5.) Back of the decline in the price of fertilizer are the gains in productivity in the production of fertilizer.[3] These gains, which have come, in large part, from advances in (industrial) technical knowledge, have made lower prices possible. The post-World War II period is of two parts, namely, prior to 1964 –65 and since then. The following price data show that in the United States fertilizer declined by one-half relative to farm products during the decade from 1939–40 to 1950.

Table 22-1

**U. S. Fertilizer Prices Relative to Prices
Received by Farmers for Farm Products**

1939–40	100
1945	62
1950	50
1955	52
1960	49

This decline in fertilizer prices occurred somewhat later in Western Europe and Japan. The response of farmers who have had access to the cheaper fertilizer has been, in large part, to increase their agricultural production. But throughout Asia, except for Japan, Taiwan, and a few local areas, the decline in fertilizer prices underway prior to 1964–65, did not reach the majority of Asian farmers. Meanwhile, since 1964–65, the cost of producing nitrogen has declined once again, and markedly so, as a consequence of an extraordinary technical advance. Furthermore, the cost of producing potash has also declined sharply as the production of potash has shifted to Canada. Now, belatedly, many more farmers in Asia are obtaining access to some fertilizer at

---

[3]For an economic analysis of the gains in productivity in producing fertilizer, see Gian S. Sahota's Ph.D. research at the University of Chicago, "An Analysis of the Causes of the Secular Decline in the Relative Price of Fertilizer," February, 1965; and his book, *Fertilizer in Economic Development* (New York: Frederick A. Praeger, Inc., 1968).

prices that, compared with the price of food grains, make it profitable for them to use fertilizer, especially so where the new fertilizer-responsive varieties of food grains are at hand. *But this process of benefiting from cheap fertilizer has barely begun; it will take decades to exhaust the agricultural production opportunities from this source.*

Key Unsettled Economic Problems Pertaining to Asian Agriculture

In planning for economic development and the contributions that agriculture can make to it throughout Asia, a number of problems that I listed under topic II should be placed on the back burner so that we can get on with those awaiting analysis. Among the problems that should be placed aside are the following: whether or not farmers respond to changes in price, the extent to which the existing agricultural resources are allocated efficiently under conditions of traditional agriculture, closely related, the extent of surplus farm labor under these conditions, the farm price effects in the country receiving P. L. 480 imports, and whether to start with an agricultural extension service or with organized agricultural research in modernizing agriculture.

Turning now to new analytical business, we observe that Asian agriculture is entering upon a secular production boom. Let us assume that the governments of these countries will not return to a cheap urban food policy and that there are no sudden widespread outbreaks of plant diseases that will seriously impair new, highly productive varieties. This secular agricultural production boom will be dependent primarily during the next five to ten years upon increases in supplies of cheap fertilizer, new varieties of food and other grains that are fertilizer-responsive, and installations to control and increase the supply of water (especially those that can be set up in a short period of time, such as tube wells), other water lifting equipment, and improvement of major existing irrigation systems. Thus, back of this agricultural boom, there will be three *agricultural input booms*, i.e., fertilizer, new varieties, and tube wells, and closely related investments to improve the supply of water and do so fairly rapidly. On these assumptions, let me turn to the key unsettled economic problems that, in my view, should be on our research agenda. In approaching these problems, I shall also advance a number of hypotheses.

Supply of Entrepreneurial Skills

For traditional agriculture, we have an economic equilibrium model from which we derive the hypothesis that there is no entrepreneurial supply problem. But the economic dynamics in agricultural production upon which Asian agriculture is entering alter this picture. From the disequilibria associated with this process, we derive two sets of hypotheses: (1.) for relatively simple changes, such as replacing traditional food grain varieties with new, superior varieties, applying some fertilizer, and even joining with neighbors to put down a tube well, the entrepreneurial skills of Asian farmers are not in short supply; and (2.) for the more complicated changes that are also becoming necessary, for example, the efficient use of pesticides and of chemicals to control weeds, the use of mechanical power and other purchased inputs, the use of much more credit in financing the purchase of these inputs, coping with the implied financial risk and with more flexible landlord-tenants arrangements, and acquiring the advantages of owner-operatorship in adjusting to these dynamic developments — all of these and more call for improvements in the quality of the supply of entrepreneurial skills. Schooling becomes increasingly important as a consequence. The hypotheses here advanced are testable. If they are supported, we turn to extension activities, on-the-job-farming experience, and schooling as the means of increasing the quality of this component.

The Timing of Institutional Reforms

The question here is the optimum sequence in undertaking such reforms. In planning for the modernization of Asian agriculture, there has been much controversy over this issue. There is the view that major institutional reforms are a pre-condition and that these reforms are sources of considerable additional agricultural production. The small increases in production and weak dynamics associated with institutional reforms that have been undertaken would appear not to support this view. Nevertheless, the established institutions of traditional agriculture in Asia and elsewhere are not adequate in terms of economic efficiency once modernization is underway. Accordingly, the modernization process gives rise to a demand for institutional changes, and the institutional lags can be observed. Therefore, in view of the agricultural dynamics in many parts of Asia brought about by the availability of new varieties of grains, relatively cheap fertilizer, and tube wells, I would advance the following hypotheses. (1.) Whereas Asian farmers have shown little interest in credit reforms, they will now demand a larger supply of credit including credit that is timely and on better terms than they have had; and they will demand where these reforms do not already exist, legal authorization and technical assistance to help them organize cooperatives for this purpose. (2.) They will demand more flexible tenancy contracts. (3.) They will cooperate among themselves to acquire tube wells and to undertake minor investments to improve the supply of water. (4.) They will also use whatever political influence they have to induce the government to provide more and better large scale irrigation and drainage facilities. (5.) They are likely to be slow in seeing the inadequacies in the markets of agricultural inputs and of the products they sell. These are all testable propositions.[4]

---

[4]I am indebted here to W. David Hopper and his treatment of these issues in "Regional Economic Report on Agriculture," Vol. I, Section III, *Asian Agriculture Survey* (Manila: Asian Development Bank, 1968).

Supply of Scientific and Technical Skills

In allocating their resources, Asian countries, except for Japan, have grossly neglected these skills. They have under-invested in organized agricultural research and, especially, in bringing the advances in modern biology to bear on their agriculture. They have relied quite heavily upon the resources of the Rockefeller and Ford Foundations and upon foreign aid and technical assistance for this purpose. But these resources will no longer suffice. The development process now underway will require new regional research enterprises and many additional research programs to stay abreast. Since I have examined this problem with care elsewhere,[5] I shall do no more than call attention to it here.

Supply of Fertilizer for Asian Farmers

In the United States, agricultural economists have made literally hundreds of studies to determine the agricultural production possibilities of using more fertilizer with profit. But they have not analyzed the production and distribution of fertilizers to explain the decline in fertilizer prices to farmers. They have taken all this for granted. Sahota's study, already referred to, is the exception. But when we turn to Asia, the key problem that governments must solve is that of importing, or producing, and of distributing to farmers fertilizers at prices that are consistent with the prices that now prevail in world trade. The analytical problem awaiting solution in this area is of many parts. It would require a major paper to clarify and formulate the technical development that has occurred since 1964–65 in producing nitrogen and has radically reduced the cost of producing it; the optimum scale of the plant, i.e., 1,000 tons per day, and its implications; the developments bringing down the price of potash; the gains from scale in producing phosphates offset presently by the world shortage of sulphur, soon to be reduced by the large increases in the sulphur from gas that is entering the market; what is a country like India to do in terms of economic efficiency in view of her many outdated fertilizer plants; and, not least, the possibilities of more efficient facilities within Asian countries to transport and distribute fertilizer to farmers and to handle it on farms and apply it to field crops.

Supply of Water for Asian Farmers

In climate, much of Asian agriculture has a marked comparative advantage over agriculture in the temperate parts of the world because Asia's climate permits the growing of two and more crops per year. Then, too, if there is water, the dry season crops produced a substantially higher yield than the

---

[5]"Efficient Allocation of Brains in Modernizing World Agriculture," *Journal of Farm Economics*, Vol. 49, No. 5 (December, 1967), pp. 1071–1082.

crops grown during the wet season. But the economics of water for Asian agriculture is still in its infancy, despite the long history of investment in irrigation and drainage in populous parts of Asia. The economic record of the agricultural production of the large, very expensive irrigation systems installed since World War II, has, in general, been very poor. There are strong reasons for using a different approach to an economic solution of a large part of this water problem. The price of additional capital is high, and it is hard to come upon new large irrigation installation opportunities that will earn upward of ten percent returns. Meanwhile, the technical advance in tube wells and related equipment to lift water has reduced their cost; moreover, the time required to install them is much less than that of the large irrigation systems; thus, the pay-off is not so long delayed. Undoubtedly, the conditions of the physical water supply in the better parts of India and Pakistan are especially favorable at this juncture for additional water by means of tube wells and associated equipment. It also is true that some additional investment to "complete" some of the large irrigation systems recently installed to bring this water to farms and to make it available when it is required in quantities sufficient to make the crop successful would pay off handsomely.

Increasing the Market for Food Grains Within Asia

On the assumption that the production of food grains in much of Asia will increase as a consequence of the modernization of agriculture now underway at a higher rate than the rate of increase in population, will the market demand increase accordingly? The solution to this problem on the demand side is not in any large increases in exports, although countries that have been dependent upon some food grain imports may shift to home-produced food grains in replacing such imports. Better transportation facilities can play a part. In general, the critical problem is that of enlarging the extent of the domestic market. In solving it, the question is: how best to strengthen the economic tendency of the additional agricultural production creating its own demand? The success of Mexico on this score should be highly instructive in analyzing this problem.

Effects of the Modernization of Agriculture

Lastly, the query: What happens if the modernization of agriculture succeeds? Assume, also, that birth rates decline and populations level off. There are three economic consequences of the modernization of agriculture that can be anticipated: (1.) a consumer surplus, (2.) a decline in the Ricardian rent in agriculture, and (3.) a shift in the comparative advantage of the agricultural areas within the country. The consumer surplus concept is old hat in economic theory, but the effects on the personal distribution of income of this surplus have major welfare implications. In the train of the decline in rent, there are important social and political adjustments related to the income from land-ownership. But the gradual shift in the comparative advantage of agricultural areas within the country will set the stage for very serious problems unless they are averted by appropriate policy as modernization occurs. But this raises the question: is there a policy approach that would spare Asian countries from depressed areas within agriculture? Western countries have not been spared; on this score, except for a few small countries, e.g., Denmark, they have all done badly. But parts of agriculture in Italy and France are seriously depressed. The U.S.S.R. is not spared and the depressed Appalachia is testimony of the very uneven agricultural development in the United States. Japan, however, has a better record in averting this problem than that of major Western countries. Consider India: the comparative advantage is shifting as a consequence of agricultural modernization to the northern parts (Ganges plains) and to the major "rice bowls" of the southern parts. A very large triangle in central India is losing out competitively. Millions of people who are dependent upon agriculture reside in this large area that will be left behind. It would be hard to overstate the analytical challenge of discovering policy approaches to cope with this problem that would stand the test of economic efficiency and that would be manageable in planning for the economic development of India.

But these gains in Asian agriculture will be like reaching for the pot of gold at the end of the rainbow unless the opportunities for family planning, are, also, much improved.

Questions for Discussion and Analysis

Article 17

1. *How can it be that a country could find it economically advantageous to prevent a birth? How would the calculations be made in order to determine if it would be worthwhile to pay people to prevent births? Would it be appropriate to include the psychic utility of extra children into your hedonistic calculus?*
2. *It seems rather grisly to compare the various methods of birth control on a basis of comparing economic benefits of reducing births to the costs of implementing the program. Should such comparisons be made, in that the program represents real interference into the personal lives of people? Moreover, even if such an Orwellian approach — i.e., the government assessing the value of infants in terms of discounted costs and revenues — is possible, can you think of any reason why it would not be useful?*
3. *How can high birth rates produce a society which has a relatively high ratio of those who only consume to those who both consume and produce?*
4. *Many societies find their population growth rapid, due to the fact that institutions in the society are geared to high birth rates and high death rates. But the death rate has fallen in the twentieth century, whereas the high birth rate continues. Might there be methods of changing the institutions in a society to allow for a rapid drop in the birth rate?*
5. *Comparisons of different birth control methods using cost benefit analysis allows for the choice of a program or group of programs which give the maximum benefit to society per dollar invested in the program. Does this mean that this method of population control should be instituted? (Hint: Society has other things in the development budget besides birth control programs.)*

Article 18

6. *Given that land, non-human capital, and human capital are needed to produce in a society, how should one go about determining which of these factors of production should receive development?*
7. *The development of human capital is apparently a good thing. Education of the population in usable skills increases the caliber of the labor force. Yet, there are relatively well educated people that are unemployed in many of the less developed countries. How, then, can a case be made for continued generation of human capital?*

8. *Why do countries receiving foreign capital equipment (whether in foreign aid or through purchase) demand that nationals operate the equipment rather than well trained aliens? It would appear that use of these aliens would actually represent an addition of talent to a country's pool of human capital, and that the less developed country should actually demand that foreign talent accompany the capital equipment. (Don't be taken in by the last statement! It ignores a number of important considerations.)*

9. *Schultz supposes "a country endeavors to win a substantial part of its economic growth out of agriculture." He then asks, "Is it possible to do this without raising the level of skills and knowledge of the cultivators?" Show how it might be possible. A more reasonable question on his part might have been, "Might it not be reasonable to assume that one of the more productive uses of resources available for development would be in raising the levels of skills and knowledge of the cultivators, including those in the subsistance sector?" How is that question answered?*

10. *What is the Leontief paradox, and how does it apply to the United States of America? to India?*

Article 19

11. *Is the marginal product of labor zero in less developed countries? How would this be determined?*

12. *Is it proper to define "disguised unemployment" as the case where the marginal product of labor is zero? Are there other cases that might be reasonably described as "disguised unemployment?"*

13. *Suppose that there are one million workers, each of whom is idle six consecutive months of the year, due to the seasonality of the agricultural sector, where they work as farmers. There are therefore five hundred thousand equivalent workers in disguised unemployment. Should these workers be employed? How?*

Article 20

14. *"One can define any activity that adds to tomorrow's potential income as investment, and the product of such activity, whether material or non-material, as capital." (Morgan) It is strange to think of intangible things as capital. Should they be so classified?*

15. *In the treatment of investment, one of the components used in the national income accounts along with plant and equipment is residential housing. Why has residential housing been picked*

for special treatment, and included in investment, while other consumer durables, such as automobiles, are treated as consumption in the current time period?

16. *Should a high rate of economic growth be associated with a high rate of investment?*

17. *Greater utilization rates of idle capital (or partially idle capital) would, assuming that the productivity of capital is positive, result in increases in income. Why, then, is capital, which is very scarce, idle in less developed countries?*

Article 21

18. *Comment pro and con on Schatz's hypothesis that a high rate of capital accumulation is both a <u>necessary</u> and a (nearly) <u>sufficient</u> condition for economic growth. What do externalities have to do with Schatz's thesis?*

19. *How would you classify Schatz in terms of the balanced versus unbalanced growth debate? Why?*

20. *Capital formation is undoubtedly helpful in the development process, yet many countries object to influxes of foreign capital used, for instance, to develop natural resources. Why do they object?*

21. *Is it necessary that the government take a positive role in capital formation? Must the government actually undertake investment projects?*

22. *What is the "social productivity of capital" referred to in the last paragraph of Schatz's article?*

Article 22

23. *In a country that has no agricultural surplus and has a large segment of the economy living at a subsistence level, is it in the best interest of society to set maximum prices on basic foodstuffs in order to keep the cost of food down for the bulk of the populace?*

24. *What is the case for land reform as a means of increasing agricultural productivity?*

25. *Should development of the agricultural sector come prior to, along with, or after development in the industrial sector?*

Section V

APPROACHES TO DEVELOPMENT AS A POLICY PROBLEM: METHODS AND INSTRUMENTS (THE DEMAND SIDE)

Governmental assistance to economic development is limited to the extent that governmental revenues are limited. Aside from the fact that per capita income is low, and on the average, taxation of the mass of the population is difficult, there are other considerations that must be taken into account when considering the tax problems peculiar to developing economies. In addition to being equitable, taxes must be certain; that is, the tax must be known in amount and the amount of payment understood by the individual upon whom the tax is levied. The tax must also be convenient if compliance is to be expected. Convenience implies that the individual paying the tax can do so without considerable imposition. Lastly, the tax must be relatively inexpensive to collect. If a tax costs as much to collect as it yields, the tax has provided nothing to society aside from providing employment for a number of tax collectors and thus reducing unemployment. U Tan Wai outlines the ways that the tax systems of the developing economies differ from those of the more developed countries. A much smaller reliance on direct taxes and the income tax in particular appears to be typical of the less developed country. One of the principal reasons for the relatively less frequent use of the income tax is that the cost of collection of taxation of the bulk of society would be greater than the revenues generated. Taxes can be levied upon these individuals, however, through the use of excise taxes and through the use of taxes on imports. Assuming few ports of entry, customs duties can be collected relatively easily and can serve the dual purpose of providing governmental revenues and providing a tariff umbrella for domestic industry. The same argument can be made for the marketing boards for domestic products. Not only are the citizens protected from price instability, but the taxation of these exports provides revenues (which may vary significantly over time) at a relatively low cost. The comments at the conclusion of the article relative to improved collection (or, in the framework mentioned above, improved certainty) are particularly important in considering the problems of countries that feel a need to increase revenues, but find the current system of taxation broad enough at the moment. An increase of the tax base through enforcement of existing legislation and existing rates may provide considerable revenue.

One of the methods of achieving the goal of economic development is through the use of an economic plan, a plan which will show the current position of the economy and provide for orderly progress, given the resources available, to a goal. The plan is used to provide for progress toward that goal. Planning is used in some form in most large organizations and considerable effort has been put into planning for the United States through the implementation of a "planning-programming-budgeting" system in the Executive branch of the Federal Government.

If planning is such a panacea for economic ills, it stands to reason that the countries feeling these ills most acutely, the underdeveloped areas of the world, would have made extensive use of planning and would have pulled themselves forward perceptibly with the device. This has not been the case.

Watson and Dirlam, in their finely annotated study of planning, point out that there is a large difference between planning in theory and planning in fact, when the planning is to be done in an underdeveloped society. The mere fact of underdevelopment makes planning a very difficult process indeed. Assuming that trained manpower and a statistical base were available, which they are probably not, the implementation of a plan given political upheaval and the mobility of trained manpower is something that the planners cannot guarantee. Project selection is based on sketchy information, probably biased by political considerations, and the meshing of development projects is only poorly done, if at all. The result is that the optimistic estimates of the impact on the society of a given package of development projects are not borne out in fact. Their principal observation is that the allocation of resources within development projects has been carried on long enough with rudimentary planning procedures, and that the history of planning efforts and failures is now long enough that we should begin to profit by the mistakes made in the past so today's planners need not fall into the same pits which trapped planners of some years ago in another society. Demonstration of the errors made in the past will not insure good planning, however. What it will do is reduce the number of "wrong" solutions open to the decision makers in a society when considering the implementation of a planning effort, and that is a worthwhile exercise.

Relations between the developed and underdeveloped countries in international trade has been a subject of intensive investigation by economists. The role of staple commodities in the promotion of development has received consideration, and the stabilization of prices for basic commodities in countries where exports of one or two commodities represent the bulk of foreign exchange earnings has been the subject of investigation. Raul Prebisch has pointed out, however, that there must be a secular decline in the competitive position of the "periphery" of less developed countries in relation to the well developed center: technological progress is not passed on to the periphery from the center due to wage and price rigidities, and the income elasticity of imports is higher for the periphery than for the center. Flanders shows that both of these assumptions are highly questionable. In doing so, she weakens considerably the thesis of the inevitable deterioration of the terms of trade for the periphery, and hence weakens the arguments supporting high protective tariffs for the countries of the periphery.

Prebisch, as Flanders points out, makes certain assumptions as to the income elasticity of imports. There are, of course, alternative assumptions that might be made about the elasticity of imports and exports, the types of technological change that will occur, population change and so forth. Harry Johnson catalogues these changes, and shows what will happen to the role of exports and imports within the national product under varying assumptions. This, then, would also lend credence to the view that Prebisch has a very special case under consideration.

International trade, as can be seen in the earlier articles in this section, has an important place in the theory of development, but its importance in the "staple" theory is central. The argument, originally based on Canadian economic history, is that new countries possess relatively high land/labor ratios and hence, are relatively rich in the primary products of the land. These can be exported, thus providing foreign exchange. Further, through the relationship of the producing industry (say timber, for instance) with other industries (shipbuilding, woodcutting, etc), industries linked to the export industry will be induced. This process of induction is very similar to that described by Hirschman. The principal characteristic separating the staple theory from Hirschman is the central thesis that the leading industry providing the base from which the linkages begins is a "staple" industry. Melville Watkins presents a review of the theory and of its critics. But he does not ask the most pertinent question: Is the staple theory a true "theory?" Is it an analytical frame or a part of an analytical frame?

U Tun Wai†

23. TAXATION PROBLEMS AND POLICIES OF UNDERDEVELOPED COUNTRIES*

In underdeveloped countries the government sector is usually more important than other sectors, not only in those countries where governments have taken upon themselves the task of increasing productive capacity, but also in those where the private sector is relied upon to insure economic growth.[1] In practically all underdeveloped countries it is now customary to have a development program, and fiscal policy is the kingpin in determining the total level of investment. Within fiscal policy, expenditure policies are important; but if tax receipts are not sufficient, governments cannot invest directly or lend to the private sector without resort to deficit financing.

Economic problems in underdeveloped countries are similar to those in developed countries, but there are differences in emphasis and in importance. This is also true of taxation policies, which have slightly different objectives and relatively greater importance in underdeveloped countries. Generally speaking, in developed countries taxation policies, and tax revenues, are geared to cover the amount of socially desired expenditures. Government expenditures are not determined by the amount of revenue. On the other hand, the underdeveloped countries find it difficult to increase the level of taxation and the amount of revenues collected. Therefore, governments desiring to promote economic growth and simultaneously to maintain financial stability have been forced to limit much-needed development expenditures.

The function of tax revenue in relation to the business cycle differs between developed and underdeveloped countries. In both types of economies, tax revenue is dependent on the level of business activity and fluctuates with the business cycle. But only in the developed countries is the amplitude of business fluctuations dampened through changes in government revenues resulting from built-in stabilizers, such as the income tax. Developed countries

†U Tun Wai, Senior Advisor, African Department, International Monetary Fund.
*From the *International Monetary Fund Staff Papers,* Vol. 8 (November, 1962), pp. 428–445. Reprinted by permission of the International Monetary Fund and the author.
[1]This paper was presented on April 9, 1962, at the Institute for International Development, School of Advanced International Studies, the Johns Hopkins University.

also use tax measures, such as depreciation allowances, tax holidays, etc., to influence the business cycle. But this is not possible in underdeveloped countries, because changes in final demand originate from the industrial countries and rarely from domestic sources.

Existing Tax System in Underdeveloped Countries

Tax Revenue

A major characteristic of the tax system in underdeveloped countries is that it does not provide governments with much revenue; this is true not only of actual amounts but also of tax revenue in relation to national income. As shown by Table 23-1 (p. 368), which presents countries according to per capita incomes — high, medium, and low — central government revenue as a percentage of national income varies greatly even between countries in the same range of per capita income. However, the figures in the table provide only orders of magnitude, especially since local governments, which are not included in the table, may be an important part of the government sector in some countries and not in others. Thus, if local governments were included, the revenue collected by the government sector in Belgium, Canada, and the United States would be in the range of one fourth to one third of their national income instead of between 17 percent and 18 percent; in India, it would be double the percentage shown in Table 23-1. However, it is clear that the median percentage is highest for the high income countries and lowest for the low income countries. This suggests some relationship between levels of national income and taxes collected. The reason is that most governments are of the opinion that when per capita income is low, and especially when it is near starvation level, it is not desirable to tax the masses. This has led to extensive exemptions from payment of income tax.

Another important factor that causes low tax yields in underdeveloped countries is that the size of the money (or market) sector is much smaller than in developed economies. It is easier to levy taxes in an economy with monetary or market transactions than in a barter economy, because of difficulties of assessing real income in the latter. As Mr. Richard Goode has said:

> Even highly skilled administrators have made little progress toward including the value of home-produced and consumed foods in the taxable income of farmers. In many underdeveloped countries these products and others obtained by barter make up a major fraction of the total real income of large segments of the population.[2]

There are a number of other reasons, such as illiteracy, lack of systematic

---

[2]From an address by Mr. Goode on "Reconstruction of Foreign Tax Systems," before the Forty-Fourth Annual Conference of the National Tax Association, 1951, published in the *Proceedings* of that Conference, pp. 213–214.

Table 23-1

High, Medium, and Low Income Countries: Central Government Revenue[1] as Percentage of National Income, 1959

High Income Countries (above $500 per capita per annum)[2]		Medium Income Countries ($200–500 per capita per annum)[2]		Low Income Countries (below $200 per capita per annum)[2]	
Austria	32.9	Ireland	26.1	United Arab Republic[3]	23.7
New Zealand	31.4	Italy	22.7	Ceylon	22.4
United Kingdom	30.8	Chile	21.9	Burma	20.6
Finland	29.6	Greece	20.9	Iraq[3]	19.8
Venezuela	27.1	South Africa	18.8	Peru	19.3
Israel	26.6	Malaya	18.7	Korea	16.7
Netherlands	25.8	Costa Rica	16.2	Syrian Arab Republic[4]	16.1
France	25.4	Portugal[5]	15.7	Guatemala	15.9
Norway	25.0	Panama	14.8	Ghana	13.9
Australia	24.0	Lebanon	14.7	Ecuador	13.7
Germany	23.2	Spain	13.2	El Savador	13.6
Sweden	22.9	Japan	12.9	Thailand	12.9
Denmark	20.6	Argentina	11.1	Honduras	12.1
Belgium	17.7	Brazil	10.1	Pakistan	11.6
Canada	17.6	Colombia	8.3	Philippines	10.5
United States	17.1	Mexico	8.1	Indonesia	10.4
Switzerland	8.1			Haiti[6]	9.9
				Turkey	9.9
				India	7.7
Median	25.0	Median	15.2	Median	13.7

Sources: Based on data from United Nations, *Statistical Yearbook* and *Monthly Bulletin of Statistics.*

[1]Government revenue is defined as in the United Nations, *Statistical Yearbook* and includes all taxes, current transfers, sales and charges, surplus of government trading enterprises, interest and dividends received, sales of assets, repayments of loans granted, and capital transfers.

[2]The classification of countries into high income, medium income, and low income groups is based on the 1957 per capita income groupings as computed by Mikoto Usui and E. E. Hagen in *World Income, 1957* (Center for International Studies, Massachusetts Institute of Technology, Cambridge, Massachusetts).

[3]1956 data.
[4]1957 data.
[5]1958 data.
[6]1955 data.

accounting, inefficient tax administration, tax evasion and avoidance,[3] social codes of behavior not requiring voluntary compliance, political influence, etc.

The relation of government revenue to national income often depends on the economic philosophy of the country and upon its type of economy. Thus Mexico, with a higher per capita income than either Burma or Ceylon, collects

[3]An estimate made in 1956 by Mr. Nicholas Kaldor indicates that in India in the assessment year 1953–54 evasion and avoidance of income tax caused a loss of Rs 2,000–3,000 million in revenues from that source. (See *Report of the Direct Taxes Administration Enquiry Committee, 1958–59*, New Delhi, p. 148.) This may be compared with actual tax receipts of Rs 1,300 million in that year.

taxes equivalent only to 8.1 percent of income, in contrast to 20.6 percent for Burma and 22.4 percent for Ceylon, because Mexico is basically a free enterprise economy relying on the private sector for investment and economic growth. But if the government in a private enterprise economy wishes to use fiscal policy to promote economic development, it must be able to obtain its revenues — even though the amount need not be as large as in a socialist economy. In an underdeveloped country, a budget surplus for this purpose is the more necessary because savings and investment in such a country are much smaller than in a developed economy.

Proportion of Revenue from Direct Taxes

A second characteristic of the tax system in underdeveloped countries is the small proportion of total revenue raised by direct taxation.[4] This is indicated by the data in Table 23-2 (p. 370), which show that the median for direct tax revenue as a percentage of total revenue in the high per capita income countries is 43, while that in the low per capita income countries is 20. There are a number of reasons for this. In particular, underdeveloped countries have found that it is easier to collect indirect taxes (e.g., customs duties) than direct taxes, especially when proper records are not kept by small businessmen and professional people. Also, the rate of total taxation has been lower in the underdeveloped than in the developed countries, both in relation to absolute incomes and in relation to per capita income.

Shown in Table 23-3 (p. 371), the rate of personal income taxes on incomes up to £5,000 ($14,000) a year (which is a significant sum in underdeveloped countries) for a married man with two children is somewhat lower in the underdeveloped than in the developed countries. But comparisons of rates on absolute incomes, though meaningful, are not as significant as the rate of taxation in relation to per capita income, shown in Table 23-4. The first point indicated by Table 23-4 is that the tax base is much smaller in underdeveloped than in developed countries because, relative to per capita income, the income which is exempt from tax is much higher in the underdeveloped countries. For example, in the Philippines a married couple with three children is not subject to any income tax unless their income is about 16 times the average per capita income, while in Canada, the United Kingdom, France, and Germany, a married couple is subject to income tax if their income is no more than about twice the average per capita income.

Table 23-3 shows that at high absolute incomes, say £10,000 ($28,000), the rate of taxation is about the same in developed and in underdeveloped countries; but Table 23-4 shows that when expressed as multiples of per capita income the rates of taxation are definitely lower in underdeveloped economies.

---

[4]Direct taxes are those borne by the person or institution responsible for paying the tax — for example, income tax, property tax, capital gains tax, etc. Indirect taxes, on the other hand, are taxes which are shiftable, either forward or backward, in the process of production.

Table 23-2

High, Medium, and Low Income Countries: Direct Tax Revenue[1]
As Percentage of Total Central Government Revenue, 1959

High Income Countries (above $500 per capita per annum)		Medium Income Countries ($200– 500 per capita per annum)		Low Income Countries (below $200 per capita per annum)	
United States	80	South Africa	50	Syrian Arab Republic	33
Venezuela	63	Japan	47	Turkey	27
Netherlands	61	Colombia	42	Burma	25
Australia	59	Spain	40	Pakistan	24
Canada	56	Mexico	35	Peru	23
United Kingdom	51	Brazil	34	Korea	22
New Zealand	51	Chile	32	Honduras	21
Sweden	49	Portugal	31	Thailand	21
Denmark	43	Ireland	26	Ceylon	20
Belgium	40	Panama	25	United Arab Republic	20
Israel	35	Argentina	23	Indonesia	18
Austria	33	Italy	22	India	17
France	29	Greece	20	Ecuador	16
Switzerland	27	Lebanon	18	Philippines	13
Norway	27	Costa Rica	17	El Salvador	12
Finland	23	Malaya	15	Iraq	10
Germany	20			Ghana	10
				Haiti	8
				Guatemala	7
Median	43	Median	29	Median	20

Sources: See Table 23-1.

[1]Direct tax revenue comprises taxes on income and wealth, i.e., income taxes on individuals, corporate income taxes, capital gains taxes, property taxes, death and gift duties, etc. Oil royalties (Venezuela) and profits from state-managed boards (Burma) are also included.

For the seven underdeveloped countries included in Table 23-4, the tax on incomes equal to 50 times per capita national income averaged only 12 percent in 1958–60, while for the seven developed countries included in the table, it averaged 47 percent. (See p. 372 for Table 23-4.)

A tax system based on direct taxes which are graduated in a progressive manner is important both for financing economic development and for controlling inflation. Economic development raises per capita income and money income (as well as real income), and the whole population moves up in the income scale. Those who were paying taxes earlier will pay larger taxes, and some of those who were below the exemption limit will start to pay taxes. The direct tax system thus has a built-in structure for giving governments larger revenues from growth without changing the level of taxation.

Table 23-3

**Selected Underdeveloped and Developed Countries: Central
Government Personal Income Tax, 1958, for
Married Man with Two Children**

| | Income in Pounds Sterling Per Annum | | | | | | | | | |
	1,000	2,000	3,000	4,000	5,000	6,000	7,000	8,000	9,000	10,000
	Tax as Percentage of Income									
Underdeveloped Countries										
Philippines	1.2	5.9	11.0	14.2	17.0	19.2	21.5	23.3	25.2	26.8
Ghana	1.0	5.0	8.8	12.2	15.8	19.9	23.5	26.2	28.3	30.0
Ceylon	4.8	12.6	19.5	25.5	31.7	36.6	41.3	45.7	49.5	52.7
Burma	5.7	15.7	27.1	34.9	40.5	45.1	48.7	51.7	54.1	56.5
Pakistan	5.7	15.2	26.0	32.5	38.2	43.1	47.3	51.1	54.5	57.2
India	6.5	16.2	26.1	34.4	40.6	45.9	49.8	53.0	55.7	57.8
Average	4.2	11.8	19.8	25.6	30.6	35.0	38.7	41.8	44.6	46.8
Developed Countries										
United States	2.9	11.9	14.8	16.8	18.7	20.5	22.1	23.6	25.2	26.7
Canada	3.5	10.5	13.9	17.0	20.3	23.4	26.2	28.3	30.0	31.7
Germany	15.8	24.8	30.5	34.4	36.9	38.8	40.5	41.9	43.1	44.2
Australia	8.3	18.4	25.7	31.1	35.9	39.6	42.3	44.6	46.6	48.3
United Kingdom	6.8	19.6	26.6	32.2	37.5	41.9	45.7	48.8	51.6	54.0
Japan	26.6	37.3	42.9	46.9	49.6	52.0	53.9	55.2	56.3	57.2
Average	10.7	20.4	25.7	29.7	33.2	36.0	38.5	40.4	42.1	43.7

Source: J. Harvey Perry, *Taxation and Economic Development of Ghana* (prepared for the Government of Ghana, United Nations Report No. TAO/GHA/4, Rev. 1, July 1, 1959).

The progressive direct tax system also provides governments with built-in protection against inflation. When prices rise, money incomes increase, and the tax system causes government revenues to increase at least *pari passu* with national income, and very rapidly if the system is sufficiently progressive. On the other hand, if indirect taxes are a large component of revenue, government revenues will lag behind the increases in money income and prices. And if, as in most underdeveloped countries, expenditures increase with rising prices, the budget deficit grows rapidly, adding to the total excess demand and inflationary pressures.

Dependence on Taxes on Foreign Trade

Thirdly, the tax structure in most underdeveloped countries relies heavily on taxes on foreign trade (import duties, export duties, and exchange taxes); in many countries this category accounts for a quarter to a half of the total revenues. A comparison of tax revenues from foreign trade with total revenue (Table 23-5, p. 373) shows a rough relationship between low per capita incomes and dependence on taxes on foreign trade. The reason for this relationship is not obvious until one equates the level of per capita income with an ability to devise alternative forms of taxation. It is easy to understand why, in the absence of knowledge and willingness to rely on other tax measures, most underdeveloped countries have used taxes on foreign trade as an important source of revenue.

Table 23-4

**Selected Underdeveloped and Developed Countries: Burden
of Income Taxes Paid by a Married Couple with Three Children
in Relation to National Per Capita Income, 1958–60[1]**

	Level of Income up to Which No Tax Is Paid (in multiples of national per capita income)	Taxes Paid as Per Cent of Earned Income (at various multiples of national per capita income)			
		10 times	20 times	50 times	100 times
Underdeveloped Countries					
Mexico	1.9	2	4	9	17
Argentina	7.7	3	16	34	43
Malaya	9.8	—	4	12	21
India	11.5	—	2	8	21
Ceylon	12.5	—	2	9	23
Philippines	15.6	—	1	10	19
Burma	19.0	—	—	4	11
Average	11.1	—	4	12	22
Developed Countries					
Australia	0.7	30	43	55	59
United States	1.3	23	35	54	69
Canada	1.9	19	32	45	55
United Kingdom	1.9	28	44	67	78
France	2.1	13	23	35	45
Germany	2.2	20	28	39	46
Japan	3.4	11	19	31	39
Average	1.9	21	32	47	56

Source: United Nations, *Economic Survey of Asia and the Far East,* 1960, p. 94.
[1]Reference years: for per capita national income — fiscal year 1956 for Burma, 1957 for Federation of Malaya, 1958 for Argentina, Canada, France, Mexico, and the Philippines, 1959 for Ceylon, the Federal Republic of Germany, Japan, India, and the United Kingdom, and 1960 for Australia and the United States; for tax laws — fiscal year 1956 for Burma, 1959 for France, Japan, Federation of Malaya, Mexico, and the Philippines, and 1960 for Argentina, Australia, Canada, Ceylon, the Federal Republic of Germany, India, the United Kingdom, and the United States.

In the majority of these countries, international trade is large in relation to national income and therefore constitutes a substantial proportion of total transactions in the market. On the other hand, foreign trade is conducted only through a few seaports or points of entry. Therefore, the imposition of taxes on foreign trade enables governments to collect revenues efficiently and cheaply. And, except in the island countries, such as Indonesia and the Philippines, it is not easy to smuggle goods and thus to evade the payment of customs duties. The policy implications and other consequences of relying on taxes on foreign trade are considered below, in the discussion of individual taxes.

Table 23-5

**High, Medium, and Low Income Countries: Central Government
Taxes on Foreign Trade as Percentage of Total
Government Revenue, 1959**

High Income Countries (above $500 per capita per annum)		Medium Income Countries ($200–500 per capita per annum)		Low Income Countries (below $200 per capita per annum)	
Switzerland	30	Costa Rica	59	Ghana	63
Israel	25	Malaya	53	Haiti	60
Venezuela	22	Lebanon	35	Ceylon	55
New Zealand[1]	14	Colombia	34	Honduras	49
Finland	13	Panama	33	Guatemala	43
Canada	10	Greece	29	Ecuador	40
Netherlands[2]	9	Mexico	23	El Salvador	37
Austria	7	Portugal	23	India	36
Norway	7	Italy[1]	22	Sudan	35
Australia	6	Chile	20	Indonesia[3]	30
Sweden	5	Brazil[4]	15	Thailand	30
Belgium	4	South Africa	15	Korea[3]	28
United States	2	Spain	8	Burma	28
		Japan	6	Philippines[3]	25
		Argentina[4]	5	Iran	24
				Pakistan	24
				Iraq	22
				Peru	18
				Syria	18
				Turkey	12
Median	9	Median	23	Median	30

Sources: See Table 23-1.
[1]Excise duties included.
[2]Import duties only.
[3]Exchange taxes included.
[4]Large and important exchange taxes included.

Direct Taxes

Taxation of Personal Income

There are two basic methods of levying the personal income tax. One is
the schedular method, which is used in a number of Latin American countries, such as Argentina, Brazil, Chile, Peru, and Venezuela; in Asia it is used
in Viet-Nam. The second is the unitary system, which is used in most countries
in Asia, in Colombia, and in the Central American countries.

Under the unitary system, the tax is levied on the total income from all sources, at a progressive rate related to the size of income. Under the schedular system, income is differentiated between sources, and the rate levied varies according to the source of the income, without reference to the size of total income. For example, in Venezuela in 1956, income from personal property was taxed at 5 percent, profits from industrial, commercial, mining, and petroleum enterprises at 2½ percent, profits from agriculture at 2 percent, income from professional work at 2 percent (for nonresidents 7 percent), wages and pensions at 1 percent, capital gains on real property at 3 percent, and unauthorized earnings, e.g., from lotteries, horse racing, etc., at 10 percent. Income from real property was taxed at 2½ percent, but deductions were allowed for (a.) interest on mortgages, (b.) taxes levied on the property, (c.) administrative expenses, and (d.) actual maintenance up to 15 percent of gross income.

The main argument for the unitary system is that it levies taxes according to ability to pay. The main argument for the schedular system is that it is an administratively easier method of collecting taxes. The correct amount of taxes can be withheld in each business without reference to the total income of the person assessed, and the government officials allocated to each type of business are better qualified, because of specialization, to assess and levy taxes on incomes earned. A second argument is that different rates can be levied according to the source and nature of the income. The reasons for wishing to make this distinction are many and include the view that wages are "earned" while profits are "unearned," and that windfall profits should be taxed at a higher rate than wages; that government servants receive lower remuneration than workers in private enterprise and therefore should be taxed at a lower rate; and that a distinction is needed between nonresidents (or foreigners) and citizens.

On the other hand, the millionaire (or, for that matter, the civil servant) with incomes from many different sources is taxed very lightly. Furthermore, since underdeveloped countries need to increase savings and investment, it is inappropriate to penalize profits as is done under the schedular system; if part of the profits are windfalls arising from increases in prices, the solution should be to levy taxes on capital gains.

In actual practice, the two systems have moved toward one another. The unitary system, which provides allowances for certain business expenses, makes business income taxable at a different rate from wages and salaries. Furthermore, self-employed wage earners are not effectively assessed, so that this sector as a whole is taxed at a different rate from others. The schedular system generally incorporates an additional levy on over-all income, which tends to make it approach the unitary system. Thus, the Venezuelan system of 1956 included a supplementary tax levy, which on incomes up to 10,000 bolivares ($3,000) was 1½ percent; on incomes of 64,000 bolivares, 3 percent; and on incomes of 1 million bolivares, 9 percent.

Taxation on Incomes of Corporations and Other Businesses

Basic pattern

The method of taxing the incomes of corporations and other businesses is basically the same in the underdeveloped countries as in the developed countries. But naturally there are differences between countries, depending in part on whether the tax laws have been modeled after the U. K., French, or U. S. system of taxation. These differences concern in particular, technical details, such as the carry-over of losses from earlier years, depreciation allowances, and the double taxation of profits.

Companies with limited liability are usually taxed more heavily than unincorporated enterprises or private partnerships. This may seem justifiable on the grounds that the larger the business, the easier it is to earn income. But in order to promote investment and to create capital markets, it is desirable that preference be given to the corporate form of enterprise. One of the difficulties in raising the level of private investment in underdeveloped countries is that even the rich do not have sufficient funds to establish industries using modern methods of production. This difficulty can be overcome only by encouraging large numbers of investors to pool their financial resources.

The basic level of taxation on companies in underdeveloped countries is generally lower than in the developed countries (Table 23-6, p. 376). Among underdeveloped countries, it is lowest in South America and highest in the Middle and Far East, except in a few countries, such as Thailand, where it is low. Generally speaking, at least in the former colonies of the British Empire, companies have to pay an excess profits tax, defined in varying ways, in addition to the basic rate.

Encouragement of investment

One tax feature widely used by underdeveloped countries is a direct tax concession given for about 5 years to pioneer industries. (In some countries it is given for as few as 3 years, and in others for as many as 25 years.) In Africa, concessions are in force in Gambia, Ghana, Nigeria, and the former French West African countries; in the Middle East — in Iraq, Israel, Jordan, Lebanon, the Sudan, and the United Arab Republic; in Asia — in Burma, Ceylon, India, Pakistan, and the Philippines; and in Latin America — in Bolivia, Chile, Colombia, Cuba, the Dominican Republic, El Savador, Guatemala, Panama, and Puerto Rico.

The concessions take the form of exempting companies operating in designated industries from paying part or all of their income tax. In some countries — for example, El Salvador — there is an additional stipulation that at least one half the capital must be domestically owned; in others — for example, Colombia and Guatemala — there is a condition that local raw materials and other natural resources must be used.

Table 23-6

**Underdeveloped and Developed Countries: Basic Rates
of Taxes on Profits of Corporations, 1958[1]**

(As percentage of taxable income)

Underdeveloped Countries

Middle and Far East		Africa		South America	
Burma	56.6	Ghana	45.0	Jamaica	40.0
Israel	53.7	Sierra Leone	45.0	Mexico	4–33
Indonesia	52.5	Gambia	45.0	Chile	30.7
Ceylon	51.8	Nigeria	45.0	Dominican Republic	7–30
India	51.5	Sudan	12–40	Venezuela	4–28
Iran	4–50	Rhodesia	37.5	Peru	10–20
Pakistan	49.0	Kenya	25.0	Puerto Rico	5–20
Lebanon	5–42	Uganda	25.0		
Malaya	30	Tanganyika[3]	25.0		
Iraq	10–30	Liberia	5–25		
Philippines	28	Fr. W. Africa[4]	22.5		
Turkey	23.5				
Thailand	10–20				
Median	30[2]	Median	25.0[2]	Median	18[2]

Over-All Median 25[1]

Developed Countries

North America		Europe		Other	
United States	52.0	Norway	63.0	Japan	52.0
Canada	45.0	Austria	59.0	New Zealand	50.8
		Sweden	56.0	Australia	40.0
		Germany	55.0	South Africa	30.0
		Italy	48.0		
		United Kingdom	45.5		
		Netherlands	43.0		
		France	41.8		
		Belgium	32.4		
		Switzerland	30.0		
		Over-All Median	47[2]		

Source: J. Harvey Perry, *Taxation and Economic Development of Ghana* (prepared for the Government of Ghana, United Nations Report No. TAO/GHA/4, Rev. 1, July 1, 1959).

[1]A number of countries have excess profits tax as well.

[2]Approximate.

[3]The mainland portion of what is now Tanzania. Tanganyika and Zanzibar form Tanzania. (Editor's note.)

[4]Under independence, French West Africa became the independent republics of Dahomey, Guinea, Ivory Coast, Mali, Mauritania, Niger, Senegal, Togo, and Upper Volta. (Editor's note.)

In addition to concessions on direct taxes, most of the countries mentioned give indirect tax concessions; the one most widely used is exemption for

5 to 10 years from customs duties on the import of capital goods and raw materials. Occasionally, there are other concessions, such as exemptions from real estate and turnover taxes (as in the former French West African countries), from property tax (in Israel), and from business and other internal indirect taxes (in Thailand). Governments which give such exemptions are eager to extend industrialization in order to raise the standard of living. But some of their good intentions are vitiated by the stipulation of elaborate procedures, which have to be observed before a company can benefit from them.

Exemption from taxation, however, is only one factor in promoting industrialization. For example, even in Puerto Rico, which is often cited as an example of rapid industrialization owing to tax concessions, the really important factors have been exemption from U. S. federal income tax (rather than concessions given in Puerto Rico), cheap labor, and the protected market in the United States.[5]

Taxes on Capital Gains and Net Worth

Generally speaking, taxes on capital gains and on net worth are not used widely in the developed countries. They are, however, beginning to be used in underdeveloped countries, for example, in Brazil, Colombia, Guatemala, Honduras, and India. These taxes are justified as a means of transferring windfall profits from private individuals and businesses to the government. They are also justified on grounds of equity when the capital gains arise from communal investment or a general increase in prices rather than from direct investment by the owner of the property.

The principal argument against levying taxes on capital gains and on net worth is that it might discourage saving and encourage spending. Secondly, capital gains are not always the result of communal action; they may stem from the effort of the individual concerned. Furthermore, insofar as a capital gain reflects the expectation of future income, it will be reached by the regular income tax at a later date. Finally, these taxes are most difficult to administer. For a long time to come, they will not be an important source of revenue in underdeveloped countries.

Land Tax [6]

The land tax has been used in most underdeveloped countries, but not as widely as might have been expected in economies where there is little wealth

---

[5]For a detailed analysis, see Milton C. Taylor, *Industrial Tax Exemption in Puerto Rico* (Madison, Wisconsin: 1956).

[6]For a most interesting and useful collection of papers on this subject, see *Papers and Proceedings of the Conference on Agricultural Taxation and Economic Development,* Haskell P. Wald, ed. (Cambridge, Massachusetts: 1954). See also Haskell P. Wald, *Taxation of Agricultural Land in Underdeveloped Economies: A Survey and Guide to Policy* (Cambridge, Massachusetts: 1959).

other than land and where the major part of national income originates from agriculture. For example, Ceylon and Malaya do not have land taxes, but they levy export duties on the principal export crops.

Land taxes are, on the whole, levied in cash rather than in kind. In some countries (Burma, Cuba, India, Indonesia, Iran, Lebanon, Pakistan, the Syrian Arab Republic, and the United Arab Republic) they are based on the value of the annual yield of the crops, and in others (Bolivia, Chile, Costa Rica, El Salvador, Guatemala, Israel, Mexico, and Nicaragua) on the capital value of the land. In Argentina and Brazil they are based on both criteria.

Before World War II, land taxes were relatively more important than they are at present. In some countries — for example, Burma, Egypt, India, Pakistan, and Syria — they constituted between one fifth and one fourth of total central government revenues. In postwar years, land taxes have declined greatly in importance, and in many countries they now represent about 5 percent of total revenues. In a few countries, such as India and the Syrian Arab Republic, they constitute about 10 percent.

There are three main reasons for the decline in importance of the land tax. First, the amount of the tax was fixed originally in relation to the yield per acre when the surveys were made, and this yield may have increased later. Secondly, while the general price level, including that of agricultural products, has risen, the rate of tax charged has increased to a smaller extent. Thirdly, increases in the value of land have been limited because land reforms have decreased the attractiveness of land as a means of investment.

To remedy such defects, and also to reduce the regressive nature of the land tax, many writers have suggested the introduction of a separate income tax on agriculture. This has, in fact, been tried in a number of provinces in India and Pakistan, with limited success. Many Latin American countries (Argentina, Brazil, Chile, and Mexico) include such a tax as part of their schedular system of taxing income. Important drawbacks to obtaining large revenues by taxing agricultural income have been the difficulty of computing income and the fact that the exemption levels have been higher than the income of the average farmer.

Indirect Taxes

Sales Tax or Turnover Tax

The sales tax or turnover tax is used in a number of countries, for example, Argentina, Brazil, India, and Pakistan. Although it is generally very regressive, it has many attractive features for underdeveloped countries, where lack of proper accounting records makes it difficult to determine an individual's income.

However, the sales tax has not been an important source of revenue because, in order to reduce its regressiveness and to prevent a wage-price spiral, most governments have exempted food and other essential items from the tax. Moreover, governments have found it difficult to levy sales taxes in rural areas and have generally confined them to a few major cities.

Excise Taxes

Excise taxes are widely used in underdeveloped countries. They yield large revenues because they are levied on such commodities as tobacco, cigarettes, alcoholic beverages, matches, and petroleum and its derivatives, for which the demand is generally inelastic. They are also easy to administer, as the commodities are channeled through a few points. If the goods are domestically manufactured, the tax is levied at the manufacturing stage; if they are imported (as, for example, gasoline), the tax may be levied at the time of distribution.

Export and Import Duties

Of all the indirect taxes, those on foreign trade are the most widely used; they yield even larger revenues than excise taxes. While it is usual to think only of customs duties as taxes on foreign trade, there are also exchange taxes in countries with multiple exchange rates. Many governments have, at one time or another, made large profits from exchange taxes; in Latin America, this has been true in Argentina, Brazil, Chile, and Uruguay; and in Asia, in Indonesia, the Philippines, Thailand, and Viet-Nam. These profits are not always channeled through government budget accounts; quite often they accrue to the central bank, which subsequently transfers them to the government. Basically, exchange profits are made by the government or the central bank buying foreign exchange from exporters at a low rate and selling it to importers and those needing to make foreign payments at a higher rate. Sometimes the profit is made by selling or auctioning permits to buy foreign exchange from sellers in the market.

Although both export duties and import duties are generally regarded as regressive, the latter are probably less regressive than the former in most underdeveloped countries. The reason is that import duties on luxuries, such as automobiles and cosmetics, are higher than those on food grains and cheap textiles. Export duties are regressive because they are levied on the commodity (e.g., coffee and rubber), are usually specific, and are borne by the grower. Therefore, the burden for the small grower is the same as that for big plantations.

Export duties, especially when they are ad valorem, are useful as a contracyclical fiscal device in underdeveloped economies. During the Korean war boom, beginning in 1950, a number of countries in Asia (Ceylon, Indonesia, Malaya, and Thailand) raised export duties on rubber and tin so that part of the windfall profits from higher export prices accrued to the government. In some instances, the higher the price of the commodity, the higher was the duty, and the lower the price, the lower the duty.[7]

During that boom period, many of these governments had involuntary budget surpluses to which the export duty contributed; these surpluses were effective in preventing domestic money incomes from rising as fast as export prices. The foreign exchange accumulated during the boom was used to finance imports when the boom collapsed and the governments began to have budget deficits. Thus, in the recession, domestic money incomes did not fall as much as they otherwise would have done. Deficit financing during a recession following a boom period, when foreign exchange has been accumulated through budget surpluses, is a mechanism that enables governments in underdeveloped countries to follow a contracyclical fiscal policy, such as that recommended by the Ceylon Taxation Commission.[8]

Marketing Boards

A device which has effects (including possibilities for contracyclical policies) similar to those of export duties is the marketing board. This device has been used in Burma and Thailand for rice, in Ghana and Nigeria for cocoa, and in Indonesia for copra. It has been most effective in Burma and Thailand.

The basis of the system is that the government makes large profits out of its monopoly of the export of the commodity under control. The domestic purchasing price paid by the marketing board is kept more or less unchanged, and well below the minimum international price. The government then obtains the full windfall profits arising from a rise in the latter; similarly, when international prices fall, government profits, rather than the domestic money incomes of exporters and growers, decline.

The use of marketing boards makes it possible for governments to mobilize easily resources to finance economic development. In Burma and Thailand, resources thus obtained have ranged from one fourth to about two fifths of government revenues. Domestic prices have remained unchanged in Burma since 1948, but in the Thailand they have been raised several times.

Adoption of the marketing board device may not be feasible for some countries because of political and economic difficulties. Yet the failure of the

---

[7]In Malaya, the export duty on rubber is levied in four parts, two of which are on the basis of a sliding scale. The sliding scale which yields most of the duties collected on rubber is based on the formula $\dfrac{1.55\ P - 63\ \text{cents}}{10}$, where P is the price in cents notified weekly by the government for duty purposes. The formula comes into operation when the price of rubber exceeds M$0.60 a pound, and it then replaces the ad valorem duty of 5 percent. See United Nations, *Economic Survey of Asia and the Far East, 1957*, p. 157.

[8]See U Tun Wai, "Report of the Ceylon Taxation Commission," *Public Finance* (Haarlem, Netherlands), Vol. XII, No. 2 (1957), pp. 122–144.

Indonesian Copra Fund to provide profits for government illustrates this point. When the international price of copra was much above the domestically fixed price, the Copra Fund had difficulty in procuring supplies because of smuggling; therefore, its profits were low in boom years. On the other hand, when the international price was below the domestic price the Copra Fund experienced large losses. If a marketing board system is to be successful, it must be started when international prices are low, and the political and social control of the private business sector must be effective enough to prevent smuggling.

Price Policy for Government Enterprises

A correct price policy for government enterprises in underdeveloped countries is absolutely essential; otherwise the resources of the government will be frittered away and there will not be sufficient funds for investment. An ideal course for setting a price policy would be to classify the enterprises into three types: (1.) subsidized enterprises, whose prices would not cover fixed costs and perhaps not even operating costs; (2.) normal business enterprise, whose prices would cover all costs, including amortization of fixed costs at replacement values; and (3.) monopolies, which would provide large profits for the government to finance development projects.

In practice, governments of the underdeveloped countries have, without any proper analysis, usually allowed utilities and transport facilities to fall into the subsidized category. It is true that cheap fuel, power, and transportation are necessary to promote economic development, and it is therefore possible to make a case for subsidies to such industries. However, it is preferable to grant subsidies in such forms as tax concessions rather than through a price policy. The latter is apt to conceal the inefficient operations of industries owned and managed by the government.

The case for full cost pricing is very strong. If prices (e.g., passenger fares, utility rates, etc.) of government-owned enterprises are barely sufficient to cover variable costs, the government budget, rather than the enterprises' own funds, has to bear the cost of replacing worn-out equipment. This has caused considerable financial difficulty at one time or another in a number of countries, including Argentina and Turkey. In Bolivia and Ceylon, uneconomic enterprises were closed down as part of the remedy to decrease the strain on the government budget.

The case for monopoly pricing rests on the need for financing economic development, as this technique (like the institution of marketing boards for external trade) enables governments to derive revenue quite easily. A drawback is that there is no market test of whether the enterprise is being run efficiently and, therefore, other criteria have to be established for judging efficiency.

Conclusions

That government revenues in underdeveloped economies are woefully inadequate is clear, but the method by which they can be increased rapidly is not so obvious. Particular tax devices which work successfully in one country (e.g., a marketing board in Burma) may not be appropriate in another. However, there are three fronts along which governments could advance, namely, tax principles, tax administration, and the social and political will to succeed.

It is true that refined knowledge is often lacking about the kinds of taxes which will yield most revenues with the least amount of economic, and perhaps political, disturbance. But when one looks at the impressive array of tax studies undertaken in many countries by government inquiry commissions, private individuals, and the United Nations,[9] one is forced to conclude that knowledge, though useful, is only a small part of the basic problem.

Better tax administration and improved collection methods within the existing structure will produce results, and they are certainly important as a means of increasing government revenues. In most countries, the staff of the tax collecting departments is inadequate. For example, in Japan, where the size of the staff is more adequate than in other Asian countries, there were 65,000 tax collecting employees in 1958 for a population of about 90 million, while Viet-Nam with a population of 12–13 million people had only 1,150 tax collecting employees. If Viet-Nam had the same ratio of tax collecting staff to population as in Japan, the number of collectors would be about 8,500. Other factors for improving the work of tax administrators include higher wages, security of tenure, and better training in accounting and in methods of making assessments.

It has been shown again and again that political indecision has prevented good tax measures from being adopted. Although the Ceylon Taxation Commission in 1955 made 56 recommendations, only a few were adopted by the Government. The same holds true for the recommendations of various Tax Commissions in India and of reports by the United Nations. On the other hand, it has been shown (for example, in Bolivia and El Salvador in recent years) that, when a government makes a determined effort to improve collections, government revenues increase markedly.

Tax reforms, as mentioned above, can be made only slowly; they depend not only on good laws but also on how the laws are implemented. If the tax

---

[9]In the decade from 1945 to 1954 there were 43 official (including UN) and private technical assistance missions in the field of public finance to 27 underdeveloped countries: Afghanistan, Bolivia, Burma, Ceylon, Chile, Colombia, Cuba, Ecuador, El Salvador, Guatemala, Haiti, Honduras, Indonesia, Iran, Iraq, Israel, Japan, Korea, Libya, Mexico, Nicaragua, Panama, the Philippines, Puerto Rico, Thailand, Turkey, and the United Arab Republic. See United Nations, *Taxes and Fiscal Policy in Underdeveloped Countries* (New York: 1954), pp. 111–118, for details. Since then, there have been many more missions, including a number of inquiry commissions, as in Ceylon and India.

systems are judged by the amount of revenue collected in relation to gross national product, some improvement has occurred in postwar years in a number of countries: those in Asia include Burma, India, Korea, and the Philippines, and those in Latin America include Chile, Costa Rica, Ecuador, Honduras, and Venezuela. In the majority of underdeveloped countries, however, there has been very little or no change in the ratio. When tax systems are judged by the proportion of direct taxes to total tax revenue, improvement since the war is indicated for only a few countries: Burma, Ceylon, Costa Rica, El Salvador, Guatemala, Honduras, India, and Mexico.

Questions for discussion and analysis pertaining to this article may be found at the end of Article 27.

Andrew Watson and Joel Dirlam †

24. THE IMPACT OF UNDERDEVELOPMENT ON ECONOMIC PLANNING*

One of the cruel ironies of economic life is that the societies that most want comprehensive economic planning are those least prepared to benefit from it. The economic planner carries with him a bag of sophisticated tricks invented (but seldom tested) in the most advanced countries of the world. He encounters in the backward society attitudes, institutions, shortages of crucial skills, and a lack of information that continually thwart him in his work. Instead of being able to use his techniques to elaborate and realize a grand design, he is time and again forced into awkward and professionally humiliating compromises. Often the most that he is able to say with any integrity is that some courses of action seem more (or less) desirable than others. But since no one dares take the responsibility for inaction, over-all plans continue to emerge. These plans are concocted by methods which bear little scrutiny, and which are, in fact almost never discussed in the literature of economic development.[1] That they often achieve little, and are sometimes harmful, is scarcely surprising.

†Andrew M. Watson, Professor of Political Economy, University of Toronto, and Joel B. Dirlam, Professor of Economics, University of Rhode Island. The authors would like to gratefully acknowledge the helpful suggestions received from C. A. Ashley, Ralph Campbell, B. Fishman, S. Kannapan, M. Singer, P. W. Strassmann, M. Taylor, and H. J. Thorkelson, some of whom dissent from our conclusions.

*From *Quarterly Journal of Economics,* Vol. 79 (May, 1965), pp. 305–326. Reprinted by permission of the authors and the publisher.

[1]The process of making plans, as distinct from the principles of planning, has not been regarded as an important area of study. In selecting materials for his encyclopaedic compendium, *Leading Issues in Development Economics* (New York: Oxford, 1964), Professor Gerald Meier has scoured a large number of published and fugitive sources. Yet his section on "Development Planning in Practice" accounts for only 44 out of 567 text pages, and of these only a quotation from John P. Lewis' book on India comes close to analyzing how a plan is actually put together. The contributors to Professor E. E. Hagen's book, *Planning Economic Development* (Homewood, Ill.: Irwin, 1963), concern themselves in part with this problem, but they lack the elbowroom for grubby but essential details. Albert Waterston's monographs for the IBRD's (International Bank for Reconstruction and Development) Economic Development Institute on Jugoslavian, Pakistani and Moroccan planning have useful sections on the planning process, and certain other publications of the IBRD contain brief discussions of planning administration. With these exceptions, however, the shelves are (contd.)

It is our thesis that the handicaps which appear universally to afflict the planner in an underdeveloped country have been insufficiently considered in setting the goals of, and establishing the institutions for, planning. To support this view, we shall (1.) show by an exercise in synthetic history how rising expectations have come to burden the planning process with unreasonably heavy responsibilities, (2.) indicate the consequences of attempting comprehensive planning against the background of underdevelopment, and (3.) suggest how shifts in emphasis might produce better results. It will not be possible to offer any magic formula for improvement. But if a higher quantum of realism is injected into the discussion, planners will be able to use the resources at hand to greater effect. They will also be able to set a level of expectations for planning that is more in keeping with what is possible.[2]

The Background to Planning: Development in the Preplanning Period

We shall begin by looking at the way in which important economic decisions are taken in an underdeveloped country which has not yet espoused planning. We shall then be able to see why discontent with these decisions arises, why planning is deemed necessary, and in what circumstances planning commences. The difficulties which the planner faces will then emerge more clearly.

Typically, the preplanning government has no independent budgetary agency along the lines of the U. S. Bureau of the Budget. Instead, all funds — those for development as well as those for routine activities — are allocated among competing ministries and agencies by a Ministry of Finance.[3] This Ministry may also be responsible for taxation and the raising of funds from other sources. Decisions about the use of funds intended for economic development are made on an annual basis and usually in a haphazard fashion. There is little long-range thinking and virtually no effort to coordinate one program with another.[4]

---

bare. A publication of the Department of Economic and Social Affairs of the United Nations, *Planning for Economic Development* (New York: United Nations, 1963) is of little value. Its discussion of the formulation of plans offers only well-worn platitudes. The section on implementation is equally unhelpful.

[2]Throughout this paper generalizations will be ventured which, it is believed, apply to most, if not all, underdeveloped countries. Exceptions there must be; but the experience, independent inquiry, and research of the writers suggest that the exceptions are not of sufficient importance to invalidate their conclusions.

[3]The key role of the Ministry of Finance has persisted even into the planning period, particularly in former British colonies, which have modeled their administrations on that of the United Kingdom. See L. Walinsky, "Burma" in Hagen, *op. cit.*, pp. 42–43, and A. Waterston, *Planning in Pakistan* (Baltimore: Johns Hopkins Press, 1963), pp. 53–54.

[4]Disabilities of control by a Ministry of Finance are cogently summarized in A. Waterson, "Administrative Obstacles to Planning," *Economia Latinoamericana, I* (July, 1964), pp. 324–327. See also L. Walinsky, *Economic Development in Burma* (New York: Twentieth Century Fund, 1962), pp. 432–447.

The improvised character of budgeting for economic development allows a diffusion of participation — to a degree that the uninitiated sometimes find astonishing — in decision-making. In time-honored fashion, local interests muster support for local projects. Ambitious ministries and ministers elbow less aggressive competitors out of the way. Experts with foreign training and foreign consultants may ride their own hobby horses. If there is a monarch, or all-powerful prime minister or president, those who can get his ear are instrumental: these intimate advisers may be reinforced by powerful families. Some projects, for political or other reasons, may have high prestige (they may appear to help politically powerful refugees, create an image of industrialization, or cater to an important religious group). Such pressures, of course, are not peculiar to underdeveloped areas. But they are stronger where governments and civil services are weak. They are at once a reason for, and an obstacle to, economic planning.

Compounding the confusion in recent years have been the ubiquitous, world-traveling salesmen of industrial engineering and construction firms. Allying themselves with power groups in the underdeveloped country, they corrupt, overtly or subtly, the government's decision-making process. Venal or deluded politicians plead their cause, and oftentimes succeed in committing slender surpluses to investments of marginal or no value.

At this stage, the private sector is sometimes thought of as relatively unimportant in decision-making: largely agricultural, with a slight admixture of petty trade. Yet in many underdeveloped areas there are large foreign-owned companies that can make extremely important development decisions. Even where there are no known oil fields, a large exploration program can give an appreciable impetus to the economy. A local mine denied foreign partners may be doomed to ineffectiveness. Decisions of airlines, or even hotel companies, often of strategic significance, are usually made in isolation and without full consideration either by the decision-makers or the country itself of the long-run consequences of the moves.

Finally, foreign-aid donors have their own projects and special interests. While local governments may be consulted, the ultimate decisions rest with the givers (who themselves have usually had little experience with planning). There is seldom a chance for the recipients to take the initiative, even if they have the technical capability to do so. Certain funds become available suddenly and unpredictably, as a result of the budgeting vagaries of the donors, and may have to be spent quickly. In an effort to justify appropriations, short-run pay-outs are often given primary emphasis, or, more objectionable still, the spectacular or superficially attractive project receives top priority. Something in concrete is likely to take precedence over something intangible, such as a farm-loan or marketing program. Projects which aim at long-term human development are found to be difficult to justify. With a rapid turnover of supervisory aid officials, responsibility is diminished, and there is a corresponding propensity to initiate ill-conceived projects that are not carried to fruition. Worthwhile schemes may wither, forgotten.

Establishing a "Development Board": The Centralization of Aid Negotiation

As governments become aware of the deficiencies in the use of investment capital, they attempt to correct matters by setting up an agency which is supposed to monopolize decisions concerning development projects. This body may be called a Development Board or something similar. The hope is that the Board will improve the quality of decisions which bear on economic development, partly by carrying out studies which will permit more enlightened choice, and partly by constituting a countervailing center of power more able to resist the pressures to which the Ministry of Finance was subject. Though the move to set up a Development Board is generally taken by the government itself, the final impetus may come from a World Bank report, or from the impatience of the donor countries with the multiplicity of officials with whom they have to deal.[5]

The Development Board may find time to promulgate a few goals that stir popular enthusiasm; in the hurly-burly of administration and negotiation, however, any semblance of organized planning toward these goals, or observing any sort of priority in project selection, disappears. The overriding aim of the Board — and of some well-meaning officials in the aid-giving organizations — is to keep the level of assistance as high as possible, regardless of the sometimes crippling contribution of personnel and funds which has to be made by the recipient. There is sporadic reliance on foreign experts and engineering firms which prepare feasibility studies for various projects, or on economists who appear at research institutes, deliver lectures, or prepare reports. These reports are used on a hit-or-miss basis by the Development Board to make points with the aid donors.

Though for many countries at this stage a blueprint for economic development is available in the form of a report by the World Bank, the usually reasonable and well-considered recommendations of these reports are more often than not ignored. Projects continue to be chosen in much the same way as in the preplanning stage: for personal, political, or religious reasons, with economic justification usually provided after the fact.[6] If an aid recipient feels

---

[5]British and French colonies drew up investment plans pursuant to the requirements of the Colonial Office and the Commissariat au Plan, respectively, during the preindependence period. Representative experiences of the organizations responsible for securing funds in this fashion are reviewed in S. Schatz, "The Influence of Planning on Development: The Nigerian Experience," *Social Research,* XXVII (Winter, 1960), pp. 451–468, and A. Waterston, *Planning in Morocco, Organization and Implementation* (Washington: Economic Development Institute, 1962). See also D. G. M. Dosser, "The Formulation of Development Plans in the British Colonies," *Economic Journal,* LXIX (June, 1959), pp. 255–266. The origin and history of the Jordanian Development Board are summarized in IBRD, *The Economic Development of Jordan* (Baltimore: Johns Hopkins Press, 1957), pp. 425–429.

[6]For numerous illustrations of such projects in Burma, selected even after planning (or at least after the hiring of a consulting agency for planning), see Walinsky, *Economic Development in Burma, op. cit.* The rehabilitation of the Hedjaz Railway may also be mentioned.

strongly enough that it needs a steel mill or an oil refinery, it may at this stage be able to squeeze it out of reluctant donors. P.L. 480 funds are channeled to access highways to politically favored cities, regardless of the already excessive burden of highway maintenance; small towns and villages get little or nothing. Perhaps most important of all, the big-ticket projects continue to be favored by both donors and recipients, even if premature or for other reasons unsuitable.[7]

In such a climate, the Development Board does almost no planning even in the sense of applying a system of priorities. To some extent its impotence is intentional: those already in control have no wish to surrender power to a body which might become semi-autonomous. As a result, the Board is often completely by-passed on the important decisions, and the head of state or a minister negotiates directly with aid sources. Ministries without technical assistants are impatient and skeptical of planning. Other ministries do not cooperate in their assigned responsibilities; they cannot be coerced by an institution whose governing body itself consists of ministers, and whose director has a lower rank. The most competent, and perhaps the most powerful, figures in the development organization tend to be the accountants and auditors, since the primary function of the Board remains that of showing the aid donors that funds have been used more or less for the intended purpose.

The second stage of the preplanning period, then, witnesses the establishment of an organization which is conscious of the importance of development expenditures, and attempts to consolidate negotiations for development projects. Although there are gestures toward longer-range coordination of development projects, there is little or no attempt to establish goals and priorities. Development still lives from hand to mouth.

Pressure for More Planning

The failure of individual project negotiation to achieve even the vaguely formulated goals for the underdeveloped country leads inevitably to mounting pressure for more and better planning. Those officials who know how the development program is arrived at are aware of the shortcomings of annual negotiation and budgeting. They press for longer-term commitments. They are eager to fit development activities, including those of both the ministries and the proliferating independent agencies, into the framework of a plan. They want to adopt targets, balance needs and resources, and appraise projects by applying rational priorities. Their dissatisfaction is legitimate, and can lead to constructive changes.

---

[7]"Officials tended to overemphasize big projects . . . In part this could be attributed to the preference of foreign lending and donor agencies for large projects. . . ." Waterston, *Planning in Pakistan, op. cit.,* p. 61. Egypt appears to have extracted the Aswan Dam funds from donors without any conclusive demonstration that the project's return justified the expenditure. An internal report of the IBRD was unfavorable to the project.

There are, however, other elements which urge more ambitious planning. The special interests that had not hesitated to claim available funds for their pet projects (e.g., hotels in the capital city, awarding of construction contracts to affiliated foreign firms) see that as long as the economy stagnates, their projects may not be profitable. They, too, become concerned about the economy's rate of growth. They are troubled by its failure to exhibit anything other than passive response to successive injections of funds. Again, those businessmen who did not pull any plums out of the pie will also usually favor growth, in the hope that future pickings will be better. Even the ruling political group is usually able to see the weaknesses of an economy which cannot move under its own steam. It, too, may anxiously be looking for a short-cut to growth (though the more farsighted of its members may also see that the social change entailed by growth will undermine its power).

There is also popular support for more ambitious planning. Not only is there a rapidly spreading belief amongst common people the world over that their material lot can, and should, be greatly improved in a short time-span; there is also a growing conviction that economic planning can bring about this betterment. This faith derives partly from the unscrupulous propaganda of other underdeveloped countries reporting the "achievements" of their latest plan, which they compare with the alleged "stagnation" of unplanned economies. Here, too, the quest for social justice joins hands with a longing for rapid growth. Again, partly because of propaganda from planned economies, it is widely believed that planning will equitably redistribute income, raise consumption levels, and prevent the enrichment of a few businessmen, particularly foreign ones.[8]

Finally, the aid-givers, including the United Nations and the World Bank, have become convinced that more ambitious planning is essential. The donors have become restive. Alarmed at the results of nonplanning, they want to look forward to a period when aid will taper off. The United States, in a complete reversal of the Point Four philosophy, has shifted its support from technical assistance to planning.[9] Under the Alliance for Progress, the formulation and adoption of a comprehensive development program have been made conditions of receiving aid. The openly expressed hope is that the plans will result in relieving the U.S. taxpayer of the burden of aid (though the recipient

---

[8]Although the rate of growth of per capita income in Egypt is probably lower than that of any other Arab country, there is a widespread belief through the Arab world (outside of Egypt) that the Egyptian economy is growing rapidly, that the lot of the common Egyptian is greatly improved, and that success has been largely due to planning. The broadcasts of Radio Cairo, beamed at the whole Arab world and much of Africa south of the Sahara, have been mainly responsible for spreading this fiction. See, e.g., Jacques Baulin, *The Arab Role in Africa* (Harmondsworth, England: Penguin, 1962), pp. 46–49.

[9]For Point Four policy, see J. B. Bingham, *Shirt-Sleeve Diplomacy* (New York: John Day, 1954), Chaps. 1–2. A comprehensive critique of the current doctrine appears in A. L. Camargo, "The Alliance for Progress: Aims, Distortions, Obstacles," *Foreign Affairs,* XLII (October, 1963), pp. 25–37.

country may be given the impression that *more* funds will be available if projects are fitted into a plan).

Paradoxically, the application of pressures for planning as a means of reducing dependence upon foreign aid often occurs after the recipient's economy has been adjusted to a minimum level of assistance, and secondary industries depending on the income generated by continuing aid have become rooted. Any hope that assistance can actually be reduced in the immediate future because of planning is therefore likely to be illusory, since the planners can scarcely begin by destroying part of the economy already established.

The Planner's Dilemma: Long-Range Planning or Implementation?

The planning organization often starts out in life a step-child, or even a changeling, without official status. Perhaps, it is an autonomous unit of the Development Board or an *ad hoc* committee reporting to the prime minister. Initially, it is badly understaffed and may have no authority. Its director may have a job with an official title that has nothing to do with planning.

These difficulties are, however, gradually overcome. Foreign advisers are imported to strengthen the staff and train the junior members.[10] An effort may be made, by bypassing civil service regulations, to secure especially competent younger people. Eventually, it is recognized that the planning organization experts are probably more able, even in the operational field, than the civil servants in the ministries with which they deal.

At this point, however, the planning organization approaches an important turning point in its career. Because it works closely with the ministries in reviewing projects, urging the adoption of measures of feasibility and performance, and to some extent determining the deployment of ministry personnel, it inevitably begins to mix in the day-to-day activities of the ministries. The problem then arises of how deeply it should become involved in operations. The planning organization is faced with a choice of taking over much of the work pertaining to development previously carried out by the ministries and other agencies of the government, or restricting itself to something else — which, for lack of a better word, we shall call planning.[11]

---

[10]Foreign advisers have drawn up the Nigerian, Pakistani, Iranian, Jordanian and Burmese plans, to name only a few. With the recent emphasis on planning as a condition of aid, planners have been supplied under contract for many Latin American and Asian countries. Nominally, the planners are in some way attached to the administration of the planning country; in most cases, however, they are financed either by a foreign government or by a philanthropic foundation.

[11]On the other hand, mobile planning teams will not be troubled by their day-to-day relations with other governmental branches because their tenure is only a matter of weeks or months, at most. High-powered economists prepared a development plan for one small Latin American country in six weeks and then departed for other assignments.

The planning organization *may* become a state within a state wielding power far in excess of that of the conventional ministries.[12] But when it manages to grab, or has conveyed to it, such power, it fails to perform its own functions properly. It becomes involved in operations, and its energies are consumed in carrying out the details of the development projects. The members of the planning organization become identified with and favor pet projects. Planning, in the sense of coordination and impartial evaluation of projects, or long-range thinking, is relegated to the background.

Yet the process by which planning shifts insensibly to operations is traceable to the underdevelopment that called forth planning in the first place. A wide-awake and conscientious planning group *can* avoid this slippery path by constantly exercising self-control. But it must be prepared to see those who are in charge delay and repeat mistakes. It must refrain from substituting for the inferior techniques of other officials the obviously superior skills of the planning experts. In the face of continual pressure from all sides, it must put long-run benefits, in the shape of development of self-reliant civil servants and ministries, ahead of short-run gains.

Yet the ideal course is far from clear. Where planning is wholly divorced from operations, nothing tangible appears to come of attempts to plan.[13] The gap between the level of competence in the planning organization and that in the operational organizations may be such that no projects are devised that can conscientiously be included in a plan. Or, if projects and programs

---

[12]The planning organization in Iran evidently enjoyed such power at one time, or so it was alleged when A. H. Ebtehaj, its ex-chief, was arrested. *New York Times,* November 12, 1961, 40:4.

Cf. the (temporary) success of the Klein-Saks mission to Chile in 1955 which did not resign itself to the somewhat frustrating task of "writing a comprehensive report," but instead "in effect usurped the role of policy maker." A. O. Hirschman, *Journeys Toward Progress* (New York: Twentieth Century Fund, 1963), p. 207. In contrast, however, is the situation described in a letter from an economist on a mission in Venezuela. "The best of the Latin American plans by general agreement is right here. But what it is, really, is a collection of all the projects that a normally active and exceptionally well-heeled government has thought up for the next four years, fitted to the indubitable proposition that 20% unemployment and 3% annual population increase imply about a 7% GNP growth rate if improvement is desired . . . Now 7% becomes a 'target' and everything else . . . must be 'quantified in line with national targets,' never mind whether external markets, labor costs, cost-price trends or simple engineering technology would permit such an overall rate. At the other end of the process, the operating agencies go their merry way implementing the decisions which their *jefe* has taken without regard to [the planning organization's] estimates. In short, planning is done by an agency which has no power, and power is exercised by agencies which have no plan." This same correspondent felt, however, that we had overemphasized the defects of planning administration.

[13]In the Philippines, a large number of plans have been prepared, but no effort was made to carry them out. See F. Golay, *The Philippines: Public Policy and National Economic Development* (Ithaca: Cornell University Press, 1961), *passim.* The Burmese experience was similar. The first Jordanian Five-Year Plan, completed in 1961, was held in abeyance and then subsequently revised in a Seven-Year Plan, which remains unpublished. The Nigerian Five-Year Plan has been similarly pigeonholed.

are submitted in reasonably useful form (as a result of assistance from foreign experts or planning officials), they are simply not carried out after incorporation in the plan.

The appropriate extent of control over operations by the planning organization cannot very well be determined on an a priori basis, and the question is seldom permanently settled. It would be tedious to recall how in one country after another the seat of power has shifted from one part of the administration to another, and how the planning organization has swung back and forth between operations and advice, reflecting political changes or the emergence of strong personalities. Almost inevitably, the planner's dilemma is resolved by a power struggle, and not by the adoption of principles of good administration.[14]

Constraints on Planning

Once "planning" is initiated, regardless of its extent, the limitations on what can be achieved soon become apparent (though they are seldom openly admitted). On every side, the planner's freedom of maneuver seems to be restricted.

For one thing, the weight of history is heavy. The range of choice open to the planner is drastically reduced by hand-me-down projects which are already under way, or for which commitments have been made. The marginal benefits of continuing those projects already started may be greater than the marginal costs, even though the project would not be selected *de novo*, and may actually distort the pattern of future development.

The legacy of institutions and personnel is perhaps even harder to reject. An investment bank may have been corruptly or sloppily administered; changing its top officials may be all that is needed to make it efficient. Yet the change may bring all of its activities to a halt. When the aid-dispensing agencies have had a hand in setting up institutions associated with projects — community development organizations, for instance — not only do the planners have to compromise with their principles to please those who pay the shot, but they will usually find, even when the form of the organization has been changed, that the same individuals reappear in strategic positions.

Once planning has begun, moreover, the problem of political interference may become more, rather than less, acute. As the planning organization gains in prestige, it can less readily insulate itself from the needs of the group in power: dissident groups are always ready to seize any stick to attack the ruling

---

[14]A similar problem may be expected to arise in the matter of budgeting. Because the development budget may well represent a substantial part of the total budget, and because development expenditures may in some sense take priority over other expenditures, the role which the planning authority is to play in drawing up the national budget — or even that part of the budget allocated to what are considered development expenditures — has to be defined. Unless a satisfactory working relationship can be reached by the planning division with the budget agency (or the Ministry of Finance), the cabinet, and the individual ministries, a free-for-all may ensue.

party and the planning group itself. The planners must balance short- against long-run considerations in selecting projects. In publicizing what they have done or hope to do, they cannot forget the fate of the Iraq Development Board and the mutilated body of Nuri As-Sa'id. Thus, there remains the temptation to spend funds on make-work schemes or to choose spectacular projects of the capital-intensive type. If the long-run results of such opportunism are disappointing, the politicians are not much concerned with the long-run. In the short run they may be dead.[15]

There is also pressure to include social gains in the plan: unemployment insurance, free medical care, better housing for the poor, higher pensions, and reduction or elimination of child labor. These "gains" usually precede the achievement of a high rate of growth. Sometimes they have been legislated into existence before the appearance of the planning organization. They can seldom be modified or curtailed.

Finally, there will be pressure to set unrealistic targets: to promise rates of growth which could never, even in the most favorable of circumstances, be achieved.[16] Of course, a case can be made for aiming high — the Russians have made much of this technique. Even if the targets cannot be reached, it is argued, people will work harder and achieve more than they would without them. The danger is that the unattainability of the targets will soon become evident and, by emphasizing the impotence of the government, lead to discouragement and dissidence. More important, perhaps, an insistence on high goals that cannot be achieved distorts the whole framework of the plan. It may lead to serious maladjustments in the rates of growth of different sectors to excessive use of foreign exchange and eventually to exchange controls, to excess capacity in heavy industry, and to neglect of basic sectors such as agriculture for which it is more difficult to program a rapid advance.[17]

Tying the plan to unrealistic targets has other objectionable consequences for feasibility studies and other planning in the private sector, unless the forecasts used reject the officially announced rates of growth. Perhaps the solution to this problem is for planners, like businessmen, to keep two sets of books . . .

---

[15]W. B. Reddaway, who is favorably inclined toward Indian planning, points out that the First Indian Plan neglected to initiate schemes that required a long time to complete. *The Development of the Indian Economy* (Homewood, Ill.: Irwin, 1962), p. 192. Cf. the shift in Iranian planning from the large projects of the Second Plan to the small ones of the Third.

[16]The Pakistan First Five-Year Plan was a "disastrous" failure, particularly in agriculture. C. Wilcox, "Pakistan," in Hagen, *op. cit.*, pp. 64–66. The factual justification for the targets of the Second Plan was "only slightly stronger than that of the first." *Ibid.*, p. 71. The Second Indian Five-Year Plan, as is well known, ran into a foreign-exchange crisis, and growth was substantially below expectations. See the informative chart in I. M. D. Little, "A Critical Appraisal of India's Third Five-Year Plan," *Oxford Economic Papers*, XIV (February, 1962), p. 2.

[17]For a sober examination of the consequences of permitting industrialization to take precedence over the raising of agricultural productivity, see J. H. Power, "Industrialization in Pakistan: A Case Study of Frustrated Take-off," *The Pakistan Development Review*, III (Summer, 1963), pp. 191–207.

The Scope of Development Plans

Plans as Statements of Goals

Underdevelopment shows itself not only in the way the work of the planning organization is carried on, but also in the content of plans. The earliest "plans" generally do little more than establish certain over-all objectives (a specific increase in national income over a given period, a specific reduction in unemployment and in the deficit in the balance of payments, etc.). They may also make broad allocations of the funds likely to be available for development (so much for highways, so much for education, and so forth). How these figures are arrived at is seldom made clear. As many countries, at this stage of their planning experience, have not yet carried out a population census or made a thorough study of national income, it can be imagined that the preparation of the plan resembles more a choose-a-number game than a scientific undertaking.

Even in countries where more information *is* available, the planning organization has usually not had time to decide how the funds allocated to each sector are to be spent, or even whether the funds *can* be effectively spent in the time-period of the plan. Nor is it at all clear whether the investment plan, if followed, would result in the achievement of the goals established: the goals are little more than pious hopes, made to seem reasonable by having been uttered by government spokesmen and economists.

In a more developed country, such a document might serve the useful purpose of defining the *grandes options* and thus indicate to the responsible ministries the tentative framework within which they are to work up a more detailed strategy. Elsewhere, however, this early type of plan contributes little or nothing to economic development. As markets are rudimentary and entrepreneurial talent is in short supply, there is little hope of manipulating the private sector of the economy by using the standard controls and incentives.[18] The desired response will not be forthcoming unless a specific course of action is laid down and people are goaded into following it. Even in the government sector, action cannot be expected to issue from the mere statement of objectives. Neither the planning division nor the operating agencies will have the highly qualified personnel necessary for translating the general objectives of the plan into specific projects. The operating agencies may not even subscribe to the general goals. In the end, therefore, such a plan comes to nothing. At most, it has served a political or psychological purpose.[19]

---

[18]The Jugoslavian planning experience may constitute an exception. But the means by which general planning goals have been reached by the efforts of individual Jugoslavian enterprises have never been adequately discussed.

[19]In retrospect, planners who have participated in the preparation of even more comprehensive documents see their major virtue as psychological, in changing attitudes of civil servants and businessmen. See Wilcox, *op. cit.,* p. 78.

Planning as Project Selection

The realization sooner or later dawns that, to bring results, a plan for an underdeveloped nation must identify specific projects for implementation, and these must be broken down into small, manageable units for which responsibility is assigned. The "take-off," if it can be induced at all in such an environment, is seen to be attainable only if someone (probably the planners) is continuously shoving. There is nothing of the Saturn rocket in it.[20]

Unfortunately, when planning begins to concern itself with the selection of projects, underdevelopment again rears its head. The "shelf" is found to be almost bare of projects worked out in sufficient detail to permit rational selection or rejection. For a few projects, it is true, immensely costly and perhaps duplicating engineering studies have sometimes been prepared. Even though they may not be keyed to the long-run objectives of the plan, these projects may be selected for implementation just because the relevant information *is* available. The direction of the plan has thus been swayed by earlier decisions about how the limited funds available for feasibility studies should be used. Other projects, such as the location of ground water or afforestation, are usually not worked up to the point where costs, not to mention benefits, can be estimated. The most rewarding investments may therefore be neglected merely because the studies needed are not ready.[21]

Much of the work of preparing a plan under such conditions will consist in fleshing out projects which at the outset are little more than ideas. This work will probably be done by personnel in both the line organizations and the planning division. But as the planning division is clearly unable to do more than a fraction of the work, and lacks much of the necessary expertise, those operating ministries which have a staff sufficiently skilled to elaborate projects will in the end get a larger share of the funds for development.

When all the projects which are to be considered for inclusion have been worked up as far as has been possible in the time available, they should,

[20]See S. Kuznets, "Notes on the Take-off," in W. Rostow, ed., *The Economics of Take-off into Sustained Growth* (New York: St. Martin's Press, 1963).

[21]See B. Olsen and P. Rasmussen, "An Attempt at Planning in a Traditional State: Iran," in Hagen, *op. cit.,* pp. 224, 237. The Pakistani planners did not apparently feel handicapped by the absence of well-prepared projects for the First Five-Year Plan, and "for large-scale industry the plan went into elaborate detail, specifying how many plants were to be built, how large they were to be, and what materials they were to employ." (See Wilcox, "Pakistan," in Hagen, *op. cit.*, p. 63.) The investment was not carried out, however, and was rescheduled for the Second Five-Year Plan. *Ibid.,* p. 73. Whether the Second Plan has been successful in the large-scale industry area is not clear. A survey of experience under the Alliance for Progress concludes: "The plans already prepared resembled formal shopping lists more than they resembled an outline of priorities within the fiscal discipline which a plan properly conceived requires." S. G. Hanson, "The Alliance for Progress: The Second Year," *Inter-American Economic Affairs,* XVII (Winter, 1963), p. 90. According to R. Vernon, the plans drawn up in response to the requirements of the Alliance for Progress have been "sterile quantitative exercises." *The Dilemma of Mexico's Development* (Cambridge: Harvard University Press, 1963), p. 8.

ideally, be ranked in some order of priority to permit selection. Those selected should then be "meshed" with one another to ensure that advance in one area will not be slowed down by a failure to move ahead elsewhere. In reality, however, neither of these tasks is done well, if at all. Shortages of time, personnel, and information all conspire to make a mockery of both jobs.

Of course, a full-scale cost and benefit study for each project is out of the question. Even simplified techniques of appraisal, in spite of their superficial attractiveness, are not much more useful in practice.[22] Some of these systems *do* have the merit of permitting comparison between those projects which have been studied in detail and those which are little more than a gleam in a minister's eye. They also offer a rough-and-ready way of reducing different categories of benefits — increase in national income, decrease in unemployment, or decrease in foreign exchange requirements — to a common scale of measurement. But they seldom work well when applied. Estimates of costs are unreliable, particularly for projects which have not been studied in detail. And when cost calculations have been made, however shaky, other problems appear: how should the initial investment and the continuing costs be lumped together in one figure? And what part of the required additions to infrastructure should be charged to the project in question? Benefits are even more difficult to assess. For projects which are expected to have important secondary effects, estimating benefits is almost impossible; even when such projects are in operation, quantitative assessment of their effectiveness is extremely tricky. The planners themselves may therefore be in considerable doubt about how to rank a project, and the scope for political interference remains large. In this regard, the coming of "planning" may have made little difference.

When the projects for inclusion have been selected, whatever may have been the process of selection, and when some attempt has been made to dovetail them, the planners should determine whether the implementation of the projects (and the general growth to be expected in the private sector) will in fact achieve whatever broad goals the planning organization has adopted. Should there be a discrepancy, as there almost certainly will be, it behooves the planners to make adjustments: to shuttle back and forth between goals and specific projects until the two are brought into line. For reasons already

---

[22]The authors speak here from their own experience. Expenditures on agricultural research, education, health, and highways cannot be weighed on the same scale as investment in industry. Allocations between the former and the latter cannot be made to depend upon calculation of cost-benefit ratios. See Wilcox, "Pakistan," *op. cit.,* p. 58, and Little, *op. cit.* In "Methods of Economic Programming and Analysis in the Plan," *The Nigerian Journal of Economics and Social Studies,* IV (July, 1962), pp. 92–109, L. M. Hansen illustrates the computation of the return for one project for which data were available. The project was admittedly exceptional. In fact, there seems to be general agreement that there are no uniform criteria that can be adopted by planning boards in selecting projects. See D. Dosser, "General Investment Criteria for Less Developed Countries: A Post-Mortem," *Scottish Journal of Political Economy,* IX (June, 1962), pp. 85–98. The UN *Manual on Economic Development Projects* (New York: United Nations, 1958) is of little use.

outlined, this operation is usually done only in a haphazard fashion and is sometimes not even attempted. Even in France, where the concept of the *navette* has been most elegantly elaborated, and where more information and expertise are available to planners, the actual practice appears to be rather sketchy. Small wonder that in less developed nations the task is seldom taken seriously, and that over-all targets generally have little touch with reality.[23]

In summary, then, underdevelopment makes it necessary to have plans based on projects which are spelled out in some detail, but it also puts obstacles in the way of making such plans. Clearly, the inventing of projects that can be confidently plugged into a plan that has to achieve an over-all balance of both inputs and outputs is far from an easy task, even in optimum conditions. In practice, the best that can usually be done is to decide what are the most limiting constraints (shortages of foreign exchange, lack of skilled manpower, administrative incapacity, poor transportation, political unrest, etc.) and then to tailor the plan to avoid these constraints or, where possible, to remove or weaken them. Thus, import-substitute industries may be favored, or make-work projects, or projects using relatively few college graduates. But the preceding discussion should have demonstrated that the real problem is *not* the one on which economists have lavished so much attention — that of ranking and selecting investment outlets — but rather finding projects that are both well enough worked up and sufficiently suitable that they can, with any integrity, be included in a development plan.[24]

---

[23]See Pierre Masse, "French Methods of Planning," *Journal of Industrial Economics,* XI (November, 1962), pp. 1–17. J. Hackett and A. M. Hackett, *Economic Planning in France* (London: Allen and Unwin, 1963) covers the governmental procedures in some detail. But the crucial questions posed by F. Perroux in *Le IVeme Plan Francais* (Paris: Presses Universitaires de France, 1963) are still not answered. In particular, the mechanism of the transition from demand to investment in specific industries remains unexplained. See the review by M. V. Posner, *Economic Journal,* LXXIV (June, 1964), pp. 420–433.

[24]There are, of course, a number of degrees of refinement possible in attempting to achieve some sort of "balance." In what seems to the writers to be the most reasonable approach — and the one which appears to have been used in the more carefully prepared plans — the planners make a thorough check of three main categories of requirements: foreign exchange (with allowance made not only for the direct requirements but also for increases that will result from changes in the level and distribution of income), savings and investment and key domestic services (to ensure, for instance, that there will be sufficient transport for the planned increase in the output of a mine, or enough electricity generated to provide for all the anticipated increase in consumption). These calculations require forecasts of population changes; of productivity; of export, import and domestic prices; and of savings, taxes, and other fiscal receipts. Without such data, and they are almost invariably absent, less refined techniques must be used. See D. Seers, "Economic Programming in a Country Newly Independent," *Social and Economic Studies,* XI (March, 1962), pp. 34–43, and W. F. Stolper, "Comprehensive Development Planning," a paper prepared for the Economic Commission of Africa Working Party in Addis Ababa, January, 1962, reprinted in Meier, *op. cit.,* pp. 491–496.

More elaborate techniques are precluded because lack of data and expertise do not permit their use. Thus, although a foreign consulting firm had prepared input-output matrices for the Moroccan economy as of 1958, 1960 and 1965, they were not
(contd. on next page.)

In the end, plans are usually plans for the sector most able to work up presentable projects, which is to say the government sector, and are biased in favor of those areas of the government which are best able to produce supporting documents for projects. For the private sector, specific projects will be largely those which the government sponsors or participates in.[25]

Implementation

Having a plan based in greater or lesser measure on specific projects, however, is no guarantee of implementation. Though there is a greater likelihood that *some* results will be obtained, there is still, between conception and realization, many a slip.

In spite of the efforts of the planners, many projects included in the plan will still be vague. Even for projects which are worked out in detail, the civil service will almost certainly be short of administrators able and willing to carry out the recommendations of the plan. Though attempts may be made to strengthen staff in crucial areas, these will almost inevitably be inadequate. Of course, planners should, and usually do, make some allowance for administrative incapacity, and attempt to modify their cost estimates and their targets accordingly. But it seems to be almost a law of nature that they should remain overly optimistic about what can be achieved.[26]

employed; the Ministry of National Economy and Finance did not have personnel qualified to interpret and apply the formulations. A. Waterston, *Planning in Morocco, Organization and Implementation, op. cit.,* p. 33. The Jugoslavs apparently do use linear programming, but only to test the consistency of long-run goals for investment with projected consumption patterns. Indian planning "states its ultimate objectives in very broad terms — e.g., growth of income per head — and then makes a rather uneasy transition to the very specific targets for the *output* of individual items which do not cover the whole field, and are a mixture of final and intermediate products, and which gives no systematic picture of consumption and other end-uses." W. B. Reddaway, *op. cit.,* p. 87. According to Reddaway, who worked closely with the Indians who were preparing the Third Five-Year Plan, there was no reliance on a detailed input-output table. *Ibid.,* p. 86, and "The Development of the Indian Economy: the Objects of the Exercise Restated," *Oxford Economic Papers,* XV (November, 1963), pp. 319, 331. J. P. Lewis believes final-demand models were used. See *The Quiet Crisis in India* (Washington: Brookings Institution, 1963), pp. 125–126. W. Malenbaum suggests that the Indian plan, comprehensive though it may be, is actually little more than a scheme for (1.) making projections about the economy that are not realized in practice, (2.) determining the amount of government investment, and (3.) arriving at a basis for negotiating loans to fill programmed foreign exchange gaps. *Prospects for Indian Development* (New York: Free Press, 1962), Chapter X. See also the chart in Little, *op. cit.,* pp. 16–17.

[25]"In a mixed economy, the hard core of a development program is a program of public expenditures. . ." J. H. Adler, "Public Expenditures and Economic Development," mimeo. (Santiago: Organization of American States, 1962), p. 8. Thus, in India, although the government apparently generates something less than 10 percent of the total product, more than half of the new investment planned is in the public sector.

[26]See H. J. Briton, "Review of Three Books on India," *Economic Development and Cultural Change,* XII (July, 1964), p. 430. "No one seems to have given much thought to the question of ways of modifying the plan to impose less demands on (contd.)

If the planning division is to resist the temptation to get involved in implementation, the normal procedure will be to assign responsibility for governmental projects to the proper authorities in the ministries concerned. Normally, responsibility runs from those directly involved in the project to the ministers, and then to the planning organization. If the projects are designated as development projects, there will perhaps be an attempt to short-circuit the bureaucratic hierarchy; but this is not inevitable, and may even be frowned upon by those persons who wish to establish a smooth-running governmental organization, following the best principles of public administration.[27]

To focus attention on individual projects, one procedure has been to establish interministerial committees specially charged with implementation. The shortcomings of this method, however, are obvious. The officials on the committees may be powerful, but in this case they have little time to spare for the committee. If they are underlings, they are unable to exert the pressure often necessary to spring loose critical barriers. Moreover, the number of committees required, if such a procedure is followed, will be so great that the planning division will not be able to send a representative to every meeting. As record-keeping tends at the best of times to be sketchy — the oral tradition prevails everywhere in underdeveloped countries — there is often no feedback to the planners themselves.[28]

The planning organization may thus launch a plan but remain ignorant of its progress. It is unable to participate in decisions which may be crucial in keeping projects on schedule, and cannot, because of its isolation, quickly intervene to help a project which is in difficulty. When a project goes astray, the planners may not be informed for some time; they are thus unable to make the adjustments necessary to keep the plan truly flexible.

Normal experience seems to be that matters drift until it is too late, and whatever internal consistency a plan once had is lost. Certain projects which have been moving ahead satisfactorily may be slowed down because of the

---

this highly strategic input, or even of ways of specifically adding to her [India's] implementing capacity."

Development plans, in their agricultural chapters, list the various ways in which agricultural output is to be increased — expanded acreage, use of more fertilizer, better varieties of seeds, weed and pest controls — but rarely show how these techniques are to be carried to the individual farmer. Hence, it is not surprising that development plans usually fall far short of realizing their agricultural targets. See J. H. Snyder, "Problems and Possibilities in Planning for Agricultural Development," *Economic Development and Cultural Change,* XII (January, 1964), pp. 123–138.

[27]In Persia, a period in which the Plan Organization apparently had very strong power was followed by an arrangement that made all development projects the direct responsibility of cabinet ministers. *New York Times,* September 14, 1962, 3:5.

[28]In the First Five-Year Plan for Jordan, some sixty committees were charged with responsibilities for making studies or supervising projects. No other procedure, however, could have provided for initiating and checking on the projects. Thus, as a planning "exercise," the establishment of these committees was superior to a mere listing of projects; but in view of the scarcity of trained personnel the government could hope to bring only a tiny fraction of projects to fruition. In Ecuador, there were at least 800 autonomous agencies. Alder, *op. cit.*

failure of complementary projects. The advance of a whole sector may be impeded by the inability of other sectors to produce on schedule. Though for a time the government may remain committed to the goals of the plan, and the plan itself may thus still serve to call forth greater efforts, eventually it is so out of kilter with reality that it ceases to be of any value. At this point, the government may choose to stumble through the remaining period as best it can. Or it may decide to prepare a new plan to come into effect before the time-period intended for the old plan has elapsed.[29]

The new plan, when it does appear, may embody some wisdom acquired during the lifetime of its predecessor; but in all likelihood many mistakes will be repeated, and the new plan may well run aground on the same hazards as the old. The cycle thus repeats itself, though perhaps in a somewhat altered context.

Major Obstacles Resulting from Underdevelopment

We are now in a position to recapitulate, calling attention to those aspects of underdevelopment that are strategic in limiting the scope of planning, undermining the implementation of plans, and slowing down remedial action. Once these obstacles are recognized, and fully taken into account, it may be possible to establish more effective procedures for planning and to set more realistic goals for development.

We shall not dwell at length on the importance of the ideological climate in which the planner must work — the complex of attitudes shared to varying degrees by both the leaders and the public of the underdeveloped country, as well as by officials of the aid-giving organizations. The far-reaching effects of this factor have already been sufficiently stressed. Nor need we insist further on the organizational weaknesses which allow these attitudes to loom large in decision-making. Instead, in this section we shall focus attention on certain key shortages, or constraints, which tend to defeat the planner's efforts and to inhibit growth. The existence of these shortages in less developed regions has been noted by other writers, but only in passing. In most cases, they have been regarded — wrongly — as peripheral aberrations, temporary and capable of being surmounted if planners are aware of them, and if a

---

[29]"The outcome of the comprehensive approach to development planning (in Persia) over the last two to three years has been an economic plan which cannot possibly be carried out by a plan organization." Olsen and Rasmussen, *op. cit.,* p. 246.

The difficulties faced by a planning organization attempting to implement a comprehensive, many-project plan are set forth in some detail in Waterston, *Planning in Pakistan, op. cit.,* pp. 78–80. At one time a Projects Division was established in the Pakistani Planning Commission, which had executive and advisory responsibility. Finally, these functions, plus "progressing" (checking up), were shifted to the Provincial Planning and Development Departments, with evaluation remaining in the Planning Commission. When the latter is unable to fill one-third of its vacancies, the provincial departments are unlikely to be able to assume effective responsibility for the projects. See also Wilcox, *op. cit.,* p. 76.

"sense of crisis" is present. Therefore in reality, they are the essence of underdevelopment.[30]

Lack of Information

Under this heading may be included a multitude of evils, one or other of which will dog the planner all along the way — in preparing the plan, in implementing it, and in revising it through its lifetime. Most crucial, at the outset, will be the lack of statistics. Even the most advanced countries may lack many of the statistical series which planners require, but the shortage is much more serious in an underdeveloped nation: some countries attempt comprehensive plans without even tolerably reliable estimates of population or national income, and no information on their past rates of growth. Other fundamental series, concerning cost of living, agricultural prices, indebtedness, land tenure, and so on, will almost certainly be lacking.[31] On occasion, important data in the possession of other agencies will not be furnished to the planners.

In searching for other kinds of information the planner will find that library facilities are inadequate and works he wishes to consult cannot be obtained. This is one of several reasons why there is so little effective pooling

---

[30]See Hagen, *op. cit.,* p. 362. Hagen quite carefully pulls together what he calls the "difficulties" revealed by his case studies, but does not appear to regard them as much more than incidental obstacles, mostly capable of being overcome by good "planning organization" (principles for which he briefly lists in *ibid.,* pp. 333–335). In his view they do not seem to call for shrinking the area of the economy to be planned or lowering targets. On the contrary, he proposes that in spite of their conspicuous success in developing their economies, the Mexicans and Japanese should change over to hortatory and comprehensive development programs. *Ibid.,* p. 360, Cf. Vernon, *op. cit., passim.,* where no credit is given to economic planning.

Again, Walinsky, in his full-dress review of the experience of the Nathan consultants in Burma (Economic Development in Burma, *op. cit.,*), quotes with approval the significant warning of the report which preceded the participation of the consultants in the planning process: "Success of the development program hinges more on this (adequate manpower) than any other single factor." Yet after hundreds of pages of confirmation of this very point, showing the impossibility of implementing a plan in the face of incompetence, dogmatism and corruption he manages to remain optimistic about what can be done: "To a far greater extent than in the more advanced democratic societies, governments in underdeveloped countries must take major responsibility for initiating and carrying through accelerated economic development." *Ibid.,* p. 586.

[31]A notorious example is the Nigerian population figure. After the first "complete" census, there was not agreement on whether the population was 41.4 or 53.2 million. See W. G. Stolper, "Economic Development in Nigeria," *Journal of Economic History,* XXIII (December, 1963), p. 386. The Third Indian Plan was severely distorted by the planners' ignorance, until very late in the planning process, of the rapid increase in population that had taken place during the period of the Second Plan. See Lewis, *op. cit.,* p. 24. The latest Turkish plan, according to one observer, is a workmanlike job, complete with intersectoral input-output tables. But it has one defect: the underlying statistics are either unreliable or absent. See J. K. Eastham, "The Turkish Development Plan: The First Five Years," *Economic Journal,* LXXIV (March, 1964), pp. 132–136.

of the experience of underdeveloped countries with similar problems. Even reports made by visiting experts a few years earlier may have vanished. Files and other records may have been lost. When projects get under way, the planner may be in the dark about their progress, there being no regular machinery for collecting and feeding back information.[32]

Lack of Suitable Projects Ready for Implementation

Perhaps a special case of the lack of information, this constraint deserves special mention on account of its importance. Because enough projects have not been prepared in sufficient detail, much of the time and the staff of the planning division will be occupied in working up more projects. Nevertheless, the plan, when it emerges, may be less specific than desired, and it may include some projects of questionable value merely because these *had* been prepared in detail.

In certain areas, the plan may have to be kept deliberately vague, since the desirable course of action will not be known until the results of a feasibility study or a resource survey are available; estimating the required investment or setting goals for output is not possible in such areas, and another element of uncertainty creeps into the whole plan. Again, if additional funds for development become available, and for budgetary reasons have to be appropriated quickly, it will sometimes be discovered that no suitable projects are ready. The funds may go begging, or will be applied to hastily conceived schemes on which they and other scarce resources are wasted.

Lack of Qualified Personnel

The lack of skilled human resources is generally more serious than any other resource lack, and is at the root of all the other main shortages characteristic of underdevelopment. To glimpse its importance, we need only imagine the effect of transferring populations from developed to underdeveloped nations.

High administrative officials attend to petty details. This practice occurs partly because of a shortage of trained and trustworthy assistants, and partly because of an inability to delegate power. The consequence is a minor vicious circle: underlings are not trained to accept responsibility, and their superiors neglect the most important work.[33] The few able people at the lower levels

---

[32]According to Lewis, projections of specific industry growth used in the Indian Third Five-Year Plan were not based on actual accomplishments under the Second Five-Year Plan, *op. cit.,* pp. 125–126. Malenbaum states that in India material for studying outputs and operational behavior is "elusive at best." *Op. cit.,* p. 63.

[33]Cf. Olsen and Rasmussen, in Hagen, *op. cit.,* p. 237. The Burmese Economic and Social Board, whose membership included ministers concerned with economic activities, did not meet frequently, did not delegate responsibility, and was so concerned with the operating function that it could not plan development, or even review and appraise performance. A board of enquiry to improve implementation was composed of key civil servants who already had full-time jobs. Walinsky, "Burma," *op. cit.,* pp. 47–48. See other illustrations in Waterston, "Administrative Obstacles to Planning," *op. cit.,* pp. 310–312.

of the civil service are often less effective than they could be, owing to incompetent superiors or colleagues, or because of unwieldy procedures (sometimes left over from colonial days).

The results are everywhere apparent. Schedules for such relatively simple tasks as committee reports cannot be followed. Projects do not produce according to plan. The potential output of a mine, for instance, cannot be realized, because the acceleration of production presents a series of interrelated problems that defy solution. (These may range from the unwarranted interference of directors in matters of office routine to the selection of new sites for exploitation.) Similarly, a potential increase in agricultural output from irrigation remains potential, because, even if the necessary construction is completed, it is a difficult and time-consuming process to work out and get accepted the most desirable live-stock and cropping patterns.[34]

Large-scale projects, unless carried out by foreign personnel, can seldom be incorporated with assurance in a plan. This fact is sometimes temporarily obscured by the letting of major construction projects to foreign concerns, and by the underplaying of projects which make heavy demands on local administrative talent. All too often, the really difficult, *but strategic,* programs which promise to establish bases for continuing growth — community development, the organization of agricultural cooperatives, the creation of agricultural extension and research stations in effective concert, the training of technicians and administrators, and the like — are sacrificed to projects such as highways and dams that can be built under contract with foreign firms.[35]

Attempts to move ahead intensify shortages in personnel. Agencies expand and proliferate, there are frequent changes in jobs, and people shift so often that they fail to acquire a knowledge of their jobs. Able civil servants move up to head ministries, and with a change in the party in power move out of government, never to return (since they cannot re-enter as juniors). Changes in foreign personnel, who are frequently in key positions, aggravate the problem.[36] Foreigners who first conceive the ideas for programs are seldom

[34]In northeast Brazil the construction of numerous large dams over a period of years has been unattended by the development of argiculture. See the summary in Hirschman, *op. cit.,* pp. 43 and 76. In Iraq, according to one well-informed writer, the building of irrigation works became an end in itself, with little attention being paid to subsequent agricultural development. See M. Ionides, *Divide and Lose* (London: Geoffrey Bles, 1960), Chap. 15.

[35]The problem of establishing an effective community development project is perhaps typical. In most countries where the program has been attempted, it has been impossible to train a sufficient number of dedicated and capable persons, to keep them in the villages, and to overcome the hostility of the older and more specialized branches of the civil service to what is regarded as encroachment. See e.g., H. Tinker, "The Village in the Framework of Development," in R. Brabanti and J. Spengler, *Administration and Economic Development in India* (Durham: Duke University Press, 1963), pp. 94–133.

[36]Even staunch supporters of the U.S. foreign-aid program have been disturbed by the rapid turnover of personnel. See *Personnel Administration and Operations of Agency for International Development. Report of Senator Gale W. McGee*, Senate Doc. No. 57, 88th Congress, 2d Session (1963), *passim.* According to Senator Hubert (contd. on next page.)

around when they finally take shape; and those who start projects off have been posted thousands of miles away by the time they are in full-scale operation (if the project is not abandoned before this point has been reached). Since the chances are that one will not be around to be taxed with their failure, there is a temptation to plump for schemes on very short-run grounds.

The "solutions" which have been devised for overcoming shortages of personnel have not been conspicuous for their success; each tactic, if it does not fail utterly, at least has serious drawbacks. In the case of projects which require prolonged experience of local conditions, contracting projects or parts of projects to foreign firms adds greatly to the cost without ensuring that the work will be well done. When the foreigners withdraw on the expiration of their contract, the residue of local training will be minimal and, after the initial thrust by the foreigners, local follow-through may not be forthcoming. The importation of foreign experts to work alongside local personnel may overcome some of these disadvantages, but much will depend on the quality of these "experts" and the duration of their stay.[37] Those whose expertise is confined to a knowledge of how things are done in an advanced country, those who do not easily adapt themselves to the conditions of the underdeveloped country, and those who stay only a short time will contribute little. Those who stay only long enough to make recommendations, and do not remain to see to the establishment of an organization to implement these recommendations, will not have much effect, even where there existed a prior determination to carry out reform. On the other hand, if experts *are* able to get results, there are other dangers: lacking a sense of economic timing, they may try to do too much, and draw too much money and manpower into their own sphere. Other areas, perhaps even more important, but lacking an expert, may be neglected.

Nor, in our opinion, is the training of local personnel abroad (known in the trade as the "Holiday on Ice") often a satisfactory solution.[38] Inevitably, a trip abroad is regarded as a prize in itself: it is a chance to leave a dirty, hot, culturally backward area for New York, London, or Paris, with the additional

---

Humphrey, the job cannot be done with two-year personnel who leave the program six months after they have learned their job. "Two-thirds of the loan officers experienced in Latin-American affairs who were with the Development Loan Fund at the time it was absorbed into AID in November, 1961, have now left the Agency and those who left were among the ablest. . . ." *A Report on the Alliance for Progress,* 1963, Senate Doc. No. 13, 88th Congress, 1st Session (1963), p. 11.

[37]To give only one example, the French government has found that newly independent nations in what was formerly French Africa are unwilling to accept technicians who had African experience during the colonial period. It has therefore been necessary to send experts with no previous African experience, and the result, according to one writer, has been the repetition of many old mistakes. See E. Bonnefous, *Les milliards qui s'envolent* (Paris: Fayard, 1963), p. 188. See also Dudley Seers' "Why Visiting Economists Fail," *Journal of Political Economy,* LXX (August, 1962), pp. 325–338, which aptly pinpoints the difficulties facing foreign advisers and experts.

[38]Cf. R. Brabanti, "Reflections on Bureaucratic Reform in India," in Brabanti and Spengler, *op. cit.,* pp. 50 and 59.

lure of a faintly possible permanent residency abroad. Selection is frequently made on the basis of the political connections of the candidates, not their ability. The people chosen, if competent, are desperately needed on the job. It seems unlikely that the marginal social benefit of a Ph.D. for a geologist with an M.A. who knows the local conditions exceeds the cost of waiting another two years to locate water-bearing strata for 100 villages. But U. S. AID officials do not make their selections on such bases. Very often, the training received is of little value in the context of the underdeveloped nation and may actually disorient the trainee. Or if the training has some application, it may not be used: on his return the trainee is given another job, either through bureaucratic inefficiency or jealousy.[39]

In most cases, it seems best to train on the job, with whatever local teachers can be recruited and foreigners where they are really needed. Such training can sometimes be effectively supplemented by short study trips to countries which are just one notch up the scale in development and have made conspicuous progress with the very problems with which the trainee will be dealing. Short-term, practically oriented courses in regional training centers can also yield good results, but until now this kind of training (which for many kinds of work could be organized at a fraction of the cost of scholarships to the United States) has been little used.[40]

Regardless of what "solutions" are used, however, only limited progress can be expected in overcoming this crucial shortage.[41] While a country is underdeveloped, the shortage of competent personnel will remain a persistent, hard-core problem to which all attempts to accelerate growth will be vulnerable. This obstacle will not disappear until the larger problem, of which it is a part, has been solved.

Conclusion: The Orientation of Planning

Economic, administrative, and statistical underdevelopment constitutes a syndrome, and as development proceeds these symptons will clear up. While

[39]The writers are acquainted with an individual who was regarded as the most highly trained tannery manager in the world. He had studied for several years in the United States, Germany, France, England and Jugoslavia, while waiting for a tannery to be approved, financed and built. When it was finally completed and ready to go into production, he was fired by the directors in a trivial dispute. In another case the director of an agricultural research station and his chief assistant, both highly competent men with M. A.'s, were sent to the United States for a three-year Ph.D. program. The work of the station, which had previously been the only station carrying out important research, came to a standstill.

[40]A good example of a successful venture of this kind is the British Forestry Training Centre in Cyprus to which civil servants from a number of Eastern Mediterranean countries are sent for short-term courses. As the conditions in Cyprus, unlike those found in most parts of the United States, are similar to those in the trainee's homeland, the chances that the training will be transferable are greater.

[41]It cannot be overcome simply by more education *per se*. Middle Eastern countries are today afflicted by unemployment of high school and university graduates who have concentrated on arts courses.

a country remains in an underdeveloped condition, however, the difficulties which confront the planner — the ideological climate, organizational weaknesses, the lack of information and projects, and the shortage of competent personnel — are not merely symptoms of the underlying condition: *they are also crucial obstacles to changing that condition.* Indeed, we venture to suggest that in the great majority of underdeveloped nations today the operative constraints on development are not, as is widely held, the shortage of capital or foreign exchange or natural resources, but rather these other obstacles. It is these others which slow down the rate of growth and limit the capacity to absorb increments in foreign aid. And it is these which should be the focus of the planner's attention.

We are led to conclude that in most underdeveloped nations the orientation of planning — and of all attempts to develop economically — should be changed so that a far greater part of the total development effort is directed to removing, or at least weakening, these constraints. In particular, we feel that projects of the following kinds merit far more attention: the development of essential statistical series and the making of reasonable projections; the survey of essential resources such as minerals, ground water and soils; the study, evaluation and, where suitable, detailed programming of the widest possible range of projects (including those for legal, fiscal and administrative reform); and, *above all,* the development of a more enlightened and capable labor force at all levels, for both the government and the private sectors. Tall orders these, which cannot be filled overnight. But everything suggests that in most underdeveloped nations these are the areas where the long-term yields from investment will be greatest. Without a strenuous effort in this direction, it will be on precisely these obstacles that efforts to speed up growth will flounder.[42]

What cannot be easily removed, however, must be lived with and should be taken into full account. As long as these *are* the operative constraints on growth, it is a costly error to pretend that they do not exist. Effective planning will tailor the program of development to achieve the most that is possible within the limitations beyond the planner's control. Broadly speaking, this means scaling down the program for the public sector so that the energies of capable civil servants are not spread too thinly over a large number of projects, but rather concentrated on essential projects which *collectively* are both strategic and within the realm of the possible.

Ordinarily, there will be a few significant outlets for funds which no one doubts will be beneficial, given the population and geography, no matter what

---

[42]Donald Wilhelm Jr. concludes that "the experience in Burma suggests the need for nothing less than a wholesale revision of the priorities of technical assistance. . . . There emerges a strong case for placing administrative training and improvement near the top of, instead of, as in Burma, toward the bottom of any list of urgent technical measures." "The Place of Public Administration in Overseas Technical Assistance Programs," in C. J. Friedrich and J. K. Galbraith, editor, *Public Policy* (Cambridge: Harvard University Press, 1955), Chap. VI, p. 208.

is to be the ultimate industrial pattern: the linking of portions of infrastructure, such as highways and ports; basic water supply; loans to new business ventures that promise to pay off; loans to farmers who qualify under terms of sound agricultural credit; education, geared to the needs of the economy; and so forth. These can be safely pursued, and can, if it is desired, be articulated into a "plan."[43] If more can be achieved, other projects may be added. But care should be exercised to ensure that the country's capabilities are not so overburdened that ultimately less is achieved than was possible.

Politicians, untutored in the harsh realities of economic life, and dissatisfied with such modest goals, may, if they belong to one end of the political spectrum, be consoled to learn that more *can* be achieved if the government creates conditions which will encourage maximum activity in the private sector — that is, if the greatest possible amount of talent and capital, which for one reason or another lie beyond the government's direct control, is mobilized. To obtain such increments, however, the government may have to be content to lose much control over the economy. It may even have to reconcile itself to a considerable measure of foreign domination of economic life, to seeing some of the most important decisions being made by the "neocolonial" or "imperialist" sector. But it may be this or nothing. Unfortunately, this sad fact is obscured by the propaganda of both aid-givers and aid-receivers which makes excessive claims for what has been achieved. Failures, which might be more instructive, are never mentioned.

The generally prevailing overoptimism indicates that much more pooling of experience is needed, particularly of unsuccessful experience. Economists in both donor and recipient countries would profit greatly from detailed and critical appraisals of what has and what has not been achieved by planning in underdeveloped nations, by aid-giving programs, and by other attempts to force growth. At present, few such studies are available, and the hazards are not well understood. For the politicians of the underdeveloped nation, we should like to organize an educational Cook's tour which would take in such noteworthy archaeological sites as completed factories which have never produced, housing projects which are uninhabited, unfinished water-spreading dams whose initial purpose and design have been forgotten, tracts of virgin soil cleared and now reverting to waste, superhighways used mainly by donkeys and mules, and the countless villages untouched by developmental efforts and in full decay. Wishful it is, no doubt, to imagine that such an itinerary could ever be arranged. But if a concerted attempt is not made to disabuse

---

[43]This is the type of planning, we take it, that is envisaged by A. G. Papandraeou in *A Strategy for Greek Economic Development* (Athens: Center for Economic Research, 1962), Chap. 2. It may be the type of planning that is carried on in Israel; it has been argued, however, that planning in Israel amounts to little more than subsidization of consumption and agriculture by capital imports. S. Riemer, "Israel: Ten Years of Economic Dependence," *Oxford Economic Papers,* Vol. 12 (June, 1960), p. 141, and A. J. Meyer, "The Economic Problems of Israel," *Economic Development and Cultural Change,* X (April, 1962), pp. 331–333.

the decision-makers of their more fanciful notions, we shall be condemned to watching history needlessly repeat itself.

Questions for discussion and analysis pertaining to this article may be found at the end of Article 27.

M. June Flanders †

25. PREBISCH ON PROTECTIONISM: AN EVALUATION*

In the area of international trade and payments theories, one of the most important issues today, from the point of view of relevance to contemporary world problems and application to policy-making decision, is that of determining the optimum commercial policy of underdeveloped or, more euphemistically, "developing" countries. Specifically, there has in recent years been much discussion of the desirability of such countries adopting a policy of protecting and/or subsidising domestic industry, substituting home production for imports of at least some manufactured goods. The importance of the question and the way in which it is ultimately resolved is fairly obvious,[1] and it is not surprising that the debate has been lively; nor is it surprising that the discussion has acquired, at times, ideological overtones, involving issues of planning *vs.* the market mechanism, and social justice, colonialism, unintentional "neo-colonialism" and the like. Many professional economists have addressed themselves to this problem, but none seems to have attracted as much attention among his colleagues nor have had so widespread an influence on thinking outside the profession as Professor Raul Prebisch, until recently the Executive Secretary of the United Nations Economic Commission for

†M. June Flanders, Associate Professor of Economics, Purdue University (on leave) and Associate Professor of Economics at the University of Tel Aviv. The author wishes to thank the following people for helpful comments and suggestions, but absolves them from all responsibility: Irma Adelman, Nathan Rosenberg, Vernon Ruttan, and Rubin Saposnik.
*From the *Economic Journal,* Vol. 74 (June, 1964), pp. 305–326. Reprinted by permission of the publisher and the author.

[1]Interest in the issue has been growing; one sees increasingly frequent reference to it in elementary text-books and semi-popular books in economics written "for the intelligent layman." *Vide, e.g.*, Benjamin Higgins, *United Nations and U.S. Foreign Economic Policy* (Homewood: Richard D. Irwin, 1962), pp. 38 ff. At the same time there has been increasing discussion and recognition of the problem among policy-makers and their advisors. For one example (from a large and rapidly growing host of studies and reports) see United States Congress, *Economic Development in South America*, a Report of the subcommittee on Inter-American Economic Relationships of the Joint Economic Committee (Washington: July, 1962), especially Chapter VII, "The Dilemma Presented by Dependence upon Limited Export Commodities."

Latin America and presently Secretary-General of the United Nations Conference on Trade and Development. Because of the interest which his pronouncements have evoked, it is worth some time and effort to examine his arguments more thoroughly than has heretofore been done; for, interestingly enough, though his writings have been much discussed, most of this discussion revolves around only one part of his multi-faceted argument, and much of it stems from a misinterpretation of even that one part. In what follows we propose to discuss his work and to show that there is not one single "Prebisch thesis" or model, but many, and that it is by no means obvious that they are consistent with one another.

It is usual to begin a critical evaluation of a writer's work by summarising it, but one of the implications of our contention that there are a number of "Prebisch theses" is that his work, by its very nature, defies any attempt to present a single, simple, summary statement of it. There have, indeed, been many exegeses of his text, but in the main these have involved emphasis on one or two aspects of his argument, ignoring the others. It is necessary, therefore, to consider his arguments one by one. The discussion that follows will be based on the two well-known and oft-cited essays, which will be referred to as Prebisch I[2] and Prebisch II[3] respectively.

The most frequently heard view of Prebisch's thesis is that peripheral countries have experienced (and presumably will continue to experience) long-run deterioration in their terms of trade with the centre and that they should counteract this by imposing tariffs on industrial imports. Much of the discussion,[4] therefore, has dealt with the questions of whether in fact the terms of trade of the periphery did fall; and if they fell, what were the reasons for the decline (alleged differences in market structure between peripheral and central countries being the most oft-mentioned issue here). It should be noted, incidentally, that a careful reading of Prebisch shows him to be much less of an "autarkist" than either his detractors or his supporters seem to think.[5]

[2]*The Economic Development of Latin America and Its Principal Problems*, Economic Commission for Latin American (Lake Success, New York: United Nations, Department of Economic Affairs, 1950).

[3]"Commercial Policy in the Underdeveloped Countries," *American Economic Review, Papers and Proceedings*, Vol. XLIV (May, 1959), pp. 251–273.

[4]*Vide, e.g.*, Gottfried Haberler, "Terms of Trade and Economic Development," in *Economic Development for Latin America*, Howard S. Ellis, Ed. (London: Macmillan, 1961), pp. 275–297; Paul T. Ellsworth, "The Terms of Trade between Primary Producing and Industrial Countries," *Inter-American Economic Affairs*, Vol. X (Summer, 1956); Werner Baer, "The Economics of Prebisch and ECLA," *Economic Development and Cultural Change*, Vol. X (January, 1962), pp. 169–182, and also a "Comment" by M. June Flanders, *Economic Development and Cultural Change*, Vol. XII (April, 1964), pp. 312–314.

[5]Chapter VI of Prebisch I is entitled "The Limits of Industrialization." On pp. 45 and 46 particularly he warns of the danger of ". . . sacrificing part of [Latin America's] exports in order to increase industrial production as a substitute for imports." And again: "Nevertheless, exports can be sacrificed to an illusory increase in real income long before the possibilities of intensifying productivity or of utilizing all the manpower available have been exhausted." In Prebisch II he speaks of the need for ". . . a definite (contd.)

One of our purposes here is to discover what in the Prebisch model(s) would tend to cause a deterioration in the periphery's terms of trade. Another is to find the connection between the declining terms of trade and the protectionism he proposes. In other words, what precisely are the benefits which the periphery can be expected to reap from protectionism? In broad categories, there are three types of benefits which Prebisch seems to expect.

One is the "rationing" effect, noted in footnote 5 on p. 410. In Prebisch I this is closely tied in with the world-wide "dollar shortage," so that tariffs are simply one method of rationing limited supplies of United States dollars (Prebisch I, p. 3; Chapter III; Chapter IV). In 1950, of course, Prebisch was not the only economist who was misled into expecting the dollar shortage to continue for ever — or at least for a very long time. By Prebisch II the dollar shortage has dropped from the discussion, but he is still disturbed by the low import coefficient of the United States (Prebisch II, p. 266) and the low capacity to import, because of inadequate foreign-exchange earnings, of the Latin American countries (Prebisch II, p. 267). The high income elasticity of demand for imports into the periphery combined with low income elasticity of demand for imports into the centre will force the periphery to achieve balance-of-payments equilibrium by either of the unattractive alternatives of growing more slowly than the centre, or of restraining its demand for imports, preferably by imposing tariffs. Now, the latter alternative may well be the less unpleasant of the two, but a tariff system designed to ration scarce foreign exchange, not to decrease the total demand for imports, cannot be expected to cause an improvement in the terms of trade. At best it might slow down future deterioration in the terms of trade.[6]

readjustment of commercial policy based on the clear recognition that, instead of trying to crystallize the existing pattern of peripheral imports, an effort should be made to help promote these *changes in composition* which are indispensable for fostering the rate of economic development." (p. 265. Italics added.) "Imports from the centers will continue to depend on Latin American exports to them — a clearly passive situation. The only changes — and these will be very important indeed — will take place in *import composition*, and through them countries will specialize in industrial products as well as agricultural ones. Without the [Latin American] common market, there will be a continued tendency by each country to try to produce everything — say from automobiles to machinery — under the sheltering wing of very high protection." (p. 268. Italics added.) There are many more statements to the same effect, but those cited above are sufficient to show that Prebisch's protectionism is tempered by a sincere concern with allocative efficiency and that (at least part of the time) he views tariffs as primarily a device to allocate scarce earnings of foreign exchange, not as a means for altering the level of trade. This second point is very important, and we shall return to it later.

[6]This would be the case if the imposition of tariffs, by preventing the demand for imports from rising as much as it otherwise would, discouraged the tendency for the periphery's exports to increase, causing a decline in the price of exports. This, as we shall see, rests not on the assumption of price inelasticity of demand for peripheral exports, but rather on the reasonable assumption that the periphery as a whole is a monopolist in the world market for its exports, so that larger quantities of exports can be sold only at declining prices. Prebisch states, laudably, that he is interested only in what happened to all the peripheral countries as a group (Prebisch II, p. 260), but the clarity of his analytical discussion is frequently marred by his failure to specify when he is referring to a single country or considering the total periphery as a unit.

This brings us to Prebisch's second type of benefit from protectionism, that of preventing further deterioration in the terms of trade (or reversing past losses?) by "countervailance."[7] As we shall see, this raises a number of highly complicated issues regarding what Prebisch is really assuming as to market structure, income distribution and wage-rate determination in the periphery and the centre respectively. But there are also some "macro" problems involved. The usual "monopoly" argument for tariffs[8] is presented in terms of a two-country model. Now, even if we assume, with Prebisch, that there is only one centre country and one peripheral country, and even if we assume that they are of roughly comparable economic size, we must recognize that in fact the centre's biggest customer is itself, not the periphery. That is, if we think of two "countries," the centre and the periphery, "domestic" demand will have a greater influence on the prices of export goods, relatively to foreign demand, in the centre than it will in the periphery. Hence, protection in the periphery cannot be expected to cause a significant reduction in the prices of its imports.[9] Furthermore, Prebisch insists that protection should be highly "selective" (Prebisch II, p. 257). But then the industrial product (or products) to be protected will be different in each peripheral country. Thus the "countervailing" effects of the tariffs will be diffused among many industries in many countries of the centre, and will thus be even less likely to influence the prices of industrial imports.[10]

There is one further difficulty with the "countervailance" argument, in terms of consistency with other parts of the model. The past deterioration of the terms of trade of the periphery is attributed in large measure to the downward inflexibility of prices and wages in the centre as contrasted with the periphery.[11]

---

[7]Cf. Werner Baer, *op. cit.*

[8]*Vide, e.g.*, the now classic discussion by Tibor Scitovsky, "A Re-consideration of the Theory of Tariffs," *The Review of Economic Studies*, Vol. IX (Summer, 1942), pp. 89–110.

[9]This point has nothing to do with differences in income elasticity or price elasticity of demand for primary products as compared with industrial products. It is analogous to an attempt by a group of, say, a few hundred automotive engineers to raise their real wages by buying fewer automobiles in the hope that this will lead to a decline in automobile prices.

[10]Prebisch I is specifically concerned only with Latin America. Prebisch II purports to embrace the whole world (p. 251), but many of his arguments are relevant only to Latin America, and at least implicitly he is apparently thinking primarily of Latin America *vis-a-vis* the United States. Within this framework his countervailance argument is stronger, as far as the importance of the peripheral country, both as a buyer and as a seller, is concerned. However, since Prebisch himself does not restrict the applicability of his arguments to the Western Hemisphere, and since commentators generally assume that his proposals are meant to be valid and useful on a global scale, it is reasonable to assess them on that basis.

[11]Prebisch I, Chapter II. It is interesting that this particular argument does not reappear in Prebisch II. This may be due to a decline in its importance, in Prebisch's view, or else to the brevity of the second paper. In any case, it is an important part of the argument in Prebisch I; and the attention it has received in the commentaries justifies our consideration of it here.

If this is so, a downward shift in the periphery's demand function for centre exports will result in making the centre worse off, through unemployment, without making the periphery better off through improvement in the terms of trade. (We need not delve into the subtle and esoteric question of the disutility of envy — or the utility to be derived from seeing one's neighbour worse off than before. There is absolutely no indication that Prebisch would regard such a situation as an improvement from the point of view of the periphery.) In fact, by lowering the income and employment levels in the centre this would actually hurt the periphery by reducing the demand for its exports; however small the income elasticity of demand for imports in the centre may be, there is no reason to expect it to be negative.

The third category of benefits from protection, according to Prebisch, is an "allocative" one. This, like the first, is only indirectly associated with the simple terms of trade argument, and it will be discussed more fully when we examine the formal model(s) in detail.

There is one important expected benefit from protection which Prebisch does not discuss systematically; however, he mentions it at several points, though only incidentally. This is the whole class of benefits that may accrue to a country which is industrialized — the changes in economic "structure," the flexibility, vitality, the changes in social structure and "personality" of a country that many people are convinced comes with, and only with, an increase in the proportion of industrial production to total output of a country. There has been much written on this subject, and many of the arguments are highly plausible. Those who advocate protectionism for this type of reason might well be right. But it is important to note and remember that this is independent of, and very different from, any of the arguments Prebisch advances.[12]

As suggested above, only a part of Prebisch's argument in favour of some protection in the periphery devolves on the assertion that ". . . the great industrial centres not only keep for themselves the benefit of the use of new techniques in their own economy, but are in a favourable position to obtain a share of that deriving from the technical progress of the periphery" (Prebisch

---

[12]The name of Hans W. Singer is frequently joined with that of Prebisch in discussion of the issue. In his paper "The Distribution of Gains between Investing and Borrowing Countries," *American Economic Review, Papers and Proceedings*, Vol. XL (May, 1950), pp. 473–485, he does enunciate what is commonly referred to as "the Prebisch thesis." But he also stresses, and elaborates on, the importance, in a dynamic context, of industrialization *per se*. He argues, for example, that ". . . the most important contribution of an industry is not its immediate product . . . and not even its effects on other industries and immediate social benefits . . . but perhaps even further its effect on the general level of education, skill, way of life, inventiveness, habits, store of technology, creations of new demand, etc. And this is perhaps precisely the reason why manufacturing industries are so universally desired by underdeveloped countries; namely, that they provide the growing points for increased technical knowledge, urban education, the dynamism and resilience that goes with urban civilization, as well as the direct Marshallian external economies. No doubt under different circumstances commerce, farming, and plantation agriculture have proved capable of being such 'growing points,' but manufacturing industry is unmatched in our present age" (pp. 476–477).

I, p. 14). We shall argue that the validity of this assertion is not necessary as a support of his policy recommendations. Nevertheless, this notion is worth examining carefully, for two reasons. First, because this is the part of his analysis that has attracted the most attention and the greatest amount of comment, both critical and favourable. It seems to many writers, and apparently to Prebisch himself, to be the main line of his argument, upon which the validity of everything else he says depends. And secondly, it is that part of his argument which elicits the most emotional response, again both from critics and supporters.[13] The notion that, whether deliberately or not, the developed countries have "exploited" the periphery and will, unless counteracting measures are taken, continue to do so, is not one to be passed over lightly.

Let us examine first the argument presented in Prebisch I (pp. 8-14). Table 2 (Prebisch I, p. 11) is a hypothetical illustration of both the actual and the "ideal". . .

> . . . distribution of the benefits of technical progress between the centre and the periphery, . . . in which it is assumed that the indexes of productivity, per man, are greater [rise more] in industry than in primary production. For the sake of simplification, both are supposed to make an equal contribution to the finished product.

(This last assumption is difficult to interpret in the light of differential rates of productivity change in the two kinds of activity.) In the illustration, productivity *per man* in primary production increases by 20% as a result of technical progress. In the centre technical progress in industrial production raises productivity by 60%. Since industry and primary production contribute equally to the value of the final product, productivity per man, in world output of finished products, rises by 40%. Now, he says, if all productivity changes are reflected in declining prices, and (money?) income does not rise at all, primary producers experience an increase purchasing power of 16.7% per unit of primary product. Since, with a given work force, they can produce 20% more output, their total buying power of finished goods, that is, their total real income, has risen by 40%. In the centre, on the other hand, the purchasing power of a unit of output has fallen to 87.5% of its original value. But since a given number of workers can now produce 60% more than previously, the total real income of the centre has risen by 40%, and the centre and the periphery have shared equally the fruits of the technical progress.

> The benefits of technical progress would thus have been distributed alike throughout the world, *in accordance with the implicit premise of the schema of the international division of labour*, and Latin America would have had no economic advantage in industrializing. On the contrary, the

---

[13]Note, for example, the very angry tone of Gunnar Myrdal's exposition of this view, in *An International Economy, Problems and Prospects* (New York: Harper and Brothers, 1956), pp. 230 ff., esp. p. 235, where he goes so far as to attribute to Prebisch ". . . a sort of 'good loser's' gallantry which is scarcely representative." It should be noted, however, that Myrdal's own defense of protectionism also appeals, more coolly, to considerations of rationing scarce foreign exchange and the like.

region would have suffered a definite loss, until it had achieved the same productive efficiency as the industrial countries.[14]

This argument seems to be based on the factor-price equalization theorem, but is a fallacious and naive interpretation. Quite apart from the many well-known restrictions to any *practical* application of that theorem to the "real world."[15] Prebisch's hypothetical example involves a mis-application of the results of that theorem. As he does elsewhere, he seems to be identifying wages with personal income, that is, assuming that there is only one factor of production in the world, labour. If that is the case, however, the factor-price equalization theorem is not relevant[16] and the equalization of income throughout the world is not an ". . . implicit premise of the schema of the international division of labour." Alternatively, if there are two factors of production the theorem is valid only when both countries produce both commodities. This is a difficult assumption to make when one country is the periphery and the other is the centre; in any case, Prebisch, in the example we are discussing, specifically assumes that there is complete specialization.

Prebisch seems to be arguing here: (1.) that "technical progress," defined by him as an increase in productivity per man, just "happens" and is not the result of an increase in any other input; the benefit derived from such progress, then, is presumably analogous to "unearned" land rent; and (2.) that from the point of view of justice and equity in distribution, such "unearned" benefits should be distributed equally throughout the world. Both of these propositions are highly questionable. The opportunity cost of technical progress is by no means negligible, even if we include only the direct outlay for research and

[14]Prebisch I, p. 8. Italics added. The last sentence in the quotation is hard to understand in view of the benefits which would have accrued to the periphery from the technical progress of the centre.

[15]*Vide, e.g.*, Paul Samuelson, "International Factor Price Equalization Once Again," *Economic Journal*, Vol. LIX (June, 1949), pp. 193–197; for a more detailed discussion see James E. Meade, *Trade and Welfare* (London: Oxford University Press, 1955), Chap. 5. XXI, XXII, XXIII.

[16]If there is only one factor of production, then one of the following must be true: (a.) There is something called "atmosphere," "conditions of production," "climate" or "state of technology," which is not an economic factor because it is free, but which differs between one country and another. In that case there is no reason why wages or — what is the same thing in this situation — *per capita* income should be equal. The single factor, "labour," will be more productive in the country with favourable "atmosphere" than in the other. (b.) There is no difference between countries in "atmosphere," "state of technology," etc. In this case there could never be any difference in factor returns, even if there were no trade. (It may be, in fact, that this is really what Prebisch has in mind, since, as we shall see below, his argument implies that technical progress is a costless activity and its benefits should be distributed equally throughout the world.) In fact, in such a case there is little reason for international trade to exist at all. Leontief has shown that trade will take place even when costs are identical, if tastes are different. But his argument rests on the concavity of the production possibilities curve, which in turn requires either that there be two factors of production or that both goods be produced under conditions of decreasing returns (to scale), which is difficult to imagine in a one-factor world. See Wassily W. Leontief, "The Use of Indifference Curves in the Analysis of Foreign Trade," *Quarterly Journal of Economics*, Vol. XLVII (May, 1933), pp. 493–503.

development made by private business in the countries of the centre. Nor should one ignore the benefits of the centre's progress which accrue to the periphery by means other than the decline in the prices of final products which Prebisch argues should have taken place; the opportunity for peripheral countries to exploit such natural resources as rubber, for example, grew in the first place out of the development in the centre of industries requiring such primary products as inputs.[17] In any case, however, neither of the propositions stated above follows naturally, as Prebisch argues, from the traditional theory of comparative advantage and international specialization.

Having contrasted what he thinks "should" have happened with what in fact, he asserts, did happen, namely the movement of the terms of trade against, rather than in favour of, the periphery, Prebisch goes on to explain the mechanism by which this took place.

> The existence of this phenomenon cannot be understood, except in relation to trade cycles and the way in which they occur in the centres and at the periphery, since the cycle is the characteristic form of growth of capitalist economy, and increased productivity is one of the main factors of that growth (Prebisch I, p. 12).

At this point profits come into the picture, not, however, as a return to a factor of production, but rather as a windfall due to temporary emergence of excess demand.

> As prices rise, profits are transferred from the entrepreneurs at the centre to the primary producers of the periphery. The greater the competition and the longer the time required to increase primary production in relation to the time needed for the other stages of production, and the smaller the stocks, the greater the proportion of profits transferred to the periphery. Hence, follows a typical characteristic of the cyclical upswing; prices of primary products tend to rise more sharply than those of finished goods, by reason of the high proportion of profits transferred to the periphery.
>
> If this be so, what is the explanation of the fact that, with the passage of time and throughout the cycles, income has increased more at the centre than at the periphery?
>
> There is no contradiction whatsoever between the two phenomena. The prices of primary products rise more rapidly than industrial prices in the upswing, but also they fall more in the downswing, so that in the course of the cycles the gap between prices of the two is progressively widened (Prebisch I, p. 13).

What he must mean here, though not explicitly stated, is that the fall in prices in the downswing (in the periphery as compared with the centre) is greater than the relative rise in the upswing (in the centre as compared with the periphery). Otherwise there would not be the long-run ratchet effect that he

---

[17]Prebisch himself makes this point, but dismisses it. "The increased productivity of the industrial countries certainly stimulated the demand for primary products and thus constituted a dynamic factor of the utmost importance in the development of Latin America. That, however, is distinct from the question discussed below." Prebisch I, p. 8. We would willingly agree that it is distinct, but not that it is therefore irrelevant.

speaks of. This is subsequently explained in terms of the wage mechanism at the centre. Some of the rising profits in the upswing are mopped up by higher wages;[18] in the downswing wages are rigid, however, so that prices of raw materials are forced down by more than the previous rise. But greater price-wage rigidity at the periphery would not alleviate the difficulty; it would, in fact, intensify it,

> . . . since, when profits in the periphery did not decrease sufficiently to offset the inequality between supply and demand in the cyclical centres, stocks would accumulate in the latter, industrial production contract, and with it the demand for primary products. Demand would then fall to the extent required to achieve the necessary reduction in income in the primary producing sector (Prebisch I, pp. 13–14).

There is a peculiar asymmetry here. The rigidity of wages in the periphery, if it existed, would result in a decline in employment, presumably, as demand for primary products decreased. Thus, income would be decreased in the periphery by means of unemployment rather than by means of lower prices and real wages. This reasoning is unobjectionable, but surely it should be applied also to the centre. It is not, however. In the centre, *per capita* income is identified, apparently, with wages and the terms of trade, that is, with real wages, and no allowance is made for the declining income *per capita* which is the obvious concomitant of mass unemployment (Prebisch I, p. 13).

In Prebisch II (pp. 258–261) the ". . . process of transfer of real income through the deterioration in the terms of trade" (Prebisch II, p. 258) is explained in terms of "productivity ratios" and "technological densities" rather than differences in market structure between the periphery and the centre. The basic concept involved here stems from Graham's[19] notion of a list of products, ranked in order of the degree of comparative advantage, the commodity at the top of the list being that in which the country has the greatest comparative advantage. Prebisch applies this by comparing the "productivity ratio [which] expresses the relationship of physical productivity per man between the periphery and the centre" with the wage ratio (Prebisch II, p. 258). There is, of course, only one wage ratio[20] and there are as many productivity

[18]"During the upswing, part of the profits are absorbed by an increase in wages, occasioned by competition between entrepreneurs and by the pressure of trade unions. When profits have to be reduced during the downswing, the part that had been absorbed by wage increases loses its fluidity, at the centre, by reason of the well-known resistance to a lowering of wages." Is it generally accepted that this "well-known resistance" existed throughout the period he refers to, from the 1870s to the 1930s? (Prebisch I, p. 13).

[19]Frank D. Graham, "The Theory of International Values Re-examined," *Quarterly Journal of Economics*, Vol. XXVIII (November, 1923), pp. 54–86.

[20]Prebisch does not, in his formal analysis, make use of the notion of "dualism" in the economy of the periphery, in the sense of non-competing groups in the labour market. He does make reference to "low productivity domestic services," which seem to be the source of the indefinitely large reserve of redundant man-power, but the existence of this group does not prevent him from speaking throughout a single wage-rate. For a further discussion of this problem see p. 424.

ratios as there are commodities. A commodity will be exported by the periphery only if the productivity ratio is equal to or greater than the wage ratio. In order for it to export (or stop importing) a commodity for which the productivity ratio is less than the wage ratio wages must fall. However, Prebisch goes on to argue that the difference in productivity between the "best" and the "marginal" export good is transferred "to the centre through the free play of market forces" (Prebisch II, pp. 258–259). But this assertion is valid only under highly restrictive assumptions. To determine the gains from trade by comparing wage ratios with ratios of physical productivity per man is possible only if labour is the sole factor of production and wage costs, therefore, the total cost of production. The parenthetical comment (Prebisch II, p. 259) that land rental is excluded "to avoid complications . . . since it cannot be transferred" is, to say the least, ingenuous. Economists make simplifying assumptions all the time, of course, but this one is analogous to "simplifying" a study of oligopoly by assuming that there is only one firm! A comparison of wage ratios and productivity ratios might be admissible as a rough index of comparative advantage if: (a.) both countries produced the goods that entered into trade, and (b.) if they produced them with roughly the same combinations of labour with other inputs. (Even this is questionable in this instance, since Prebisch himself, as we have noted previously, argues that there is a significant "profit" element included in wages in the centre but not in the periphery.)[21] Thus, it is impossible to say that the productivity of labour (or of anything else) in coffee production is four times as high in Brazil as in Canada, because nobody knows what the productivity of labour in coffee production is in Canada. Furthermore, it would be wrong to say that if productivity per man in beef production in Argentina is three times as high as in the United Kingdom and wages in Argentina are half as high as in the United Kingdom, then beef must cost one-sixth as much in Argentina as in the United Kindgom. It would be wrong, because we know from this nothing about the relative amounts (and costs) of non-labour inputs — land, feed, shelter, etc., involved in beef production in the two countries. In fact, in such a case one could not even say with certainty that Argentina would export beef to the United Kingdom. Furthermore, if the world did indeed have only one factor of production, then the situation would be symmetrical, and the centre would also be transferring to the periphery its differential productivity for all exports for which the productivity ratio is higher than the wage ratio. In order, then, for the periphery to be at a disadvantage in this respect if would then be

[21]This is implicitly the assumption involved in Sir Donald McDougall's study, but he was comparing exports from the United Kingdom and the United States to third countries. This is quite a different matter. In the first place he was by definition confining himself to commodities produced in both countries. Secondly, productive techniques in the United Kingdom and the United States are likely to be more similar than in the United Kingdom and Brazil, for example. See G. D. A. MacDougall, "British and American Exports: A Study Suggested by the Theory of Comparative Costs," *Economic Journal*, Vol. LXI (December, 1951), pp. 697–724; Vol. LXII (September, 1952), pp. 487–521.

necessary to show either, *only* at the periphery are there no factors of production other than labour or else that there is a systematic tendency for the periphery to have a greater "productivity surplus" than the centre over and above the productivity in the last, infra-marginal export commodity. This is an empirical question, but apparently it is Prebisch's belief that there is in fact a tendency for the periphery to have a greater "productivity surplus" than the centre. This is clearly what he means when he talks about "disparities in technological densities" (Prebisch II, p. 262).

This can best be explained by supposing that there are ten commodities, $A \ldots J$, such that the ratio of Country P's productivity to Country C's productivity is highest for commodity A and lowest for commodity J. Then Graham's conclusions are: (1.) that country P is better off in trade the smaller the number of commodities (in addition to A) that it actually exports, that is, the less far down the list it has to go in exporting in order to pay for its imports; but (2.) *ceteris paribus*, P is better off the closer together the internal productivity ratios, A/B, B/C, C/D, etc. The closer together the productivities (in Prebisch's terminology, the more dense the technology), the less deterioration in its terms of trade a country will have to suffer in response to an increase in its demand for imports or a decrease in foreign demand for its current exports.

Suppose P is exporting A and B and importing commodities C through J. Now as productivity (in general?) in the periphery increases and growth occurs, there is surplus man-power in the periphery which must be employed by producing C domestically. Real wages must drop accordingly to maintain the equality of the wage ratio with the (marginal) productivity ratio. Since P's technology is sparse (*i.e.*, not "dense"), the decline in productivity as it moves to producing C is large. Since wages constitute the only cost of production, according to Prebisch, the price in terms of foreign currency of all exports must fall proportionately, and the "differential productivity" of labour in the production of A and B is transferred abroad. But protection of C, the marginal industry, will not cure the transfer abroad of the productivity differential of A as compared to B which had been taking place all along. Furthermore, protection of this type is not only necessarily permanent, as Prebisch recognizes it to be, it is also self-propagating. If P imposes a tarrif on the import of C, Prebisch argues, then if productivity in the production of commodity C increases and protection is maintained, P can raise wages throughout. But if this is done, then B can no longer be exported without protection or subsidization. So that protection, far from being temporary, must increase over time. Presumably Prebisch would argue that this would not be the case because productivity would also increase in B. But if that were the case, then wages could have been raised without the protection. This may be impossible, however, because of the surplus man-power (which, we shall argue, is the real villain of the piece); but then the increase of productivity in C will also generate surplus man-power, and it will be necessary to extend protection to D, and so on.

As noted, the real problem seems to lie with the surplus man-power; Prebisch seems to be thinking of an indefinitely large and growing population, with no relation whatever (even, apparently, at "subsistence" wages) between the wage-rate and the supply of labour. It is possible to make a strong case for protection in such a situation in order to stimulate, or at least permit, industrialization, because of the beneficial social effects (and social external economies), including amelioration of the tendency towards population explosions. But this has nothing to do with the transfer-of-income argument.

Furthermore, it is not obvious why the surplus man-power should not be successfully utilized in the production of goods which are likely to be domestic goods regardless of the terms of trade (within any reasonably expected limits to the terms of trade) because of high transport costs: construction of all sorts, including that of social overhead capital, or various types of services.[22] Nor is it obvious why there should not be an increase in agricultural production for domestic consumption, since poor nutrition and near-starvation are ubiquitous problems in peripheral countries. One is tempted to speculate that the objection to both of these alternatives would be in terms of the desirability of industrialization as such. And again, it should be emphasized that the desire for industrialization is a respectable motive for protection, but is quite independent of the arguments Prebisch employs.

Thus far we have discussed essentially two versions of Prebisch's argument, both dealing with the notion that the periphery transfers abroad the fruits of its technological progress through deterioration in its terms of trade. In one instance this is due to the fact that prices and wages are flexible upward in the centre but not in the periphery; in the other case it is due to the "technological density" of the centre as compared with the periphery. There is yet a third branch of the argument[23] which is stated in Prebisch II (pp. 252–260). Assume that the centre and the periphery are growing at the same rate — presumably *per capita* income is increasing at the same annual rate in both. Then, at a given set of price levels and exchange rates, the periphery will tend to develop a balance-of-payments deficit because its marginal propensity to import is higher than the centre. It is therefore necessary to effect import substitution, which is ". . . defined here as an increase in the proportion of goods that is supplied from domestic sources and not necessarily as a reduction in the ratio of imports to total income" (Prebisch II, p. 153). (It is difficult to comprehend this definition.) One fairly obvious way to achieve this is through devaluation, which Prebisch discusses at some length. The "usual" type of objection to devaluation in such a system would be to argue that it would fail to increase

---

[22]Surely there is no need for services to be confined to the "low productivity domestic services" with which Prebisch is justifiably concerned. Education, for example, is one obvious alternative.

[23]There are others, but these are mentioned in passing, somewhat sporadically, rather than developed systematically. It should be noted that many of Prebisch's "asides" are extremely perceptive, thought-provoking and, in our opinion, more useful and relevant to the problem than much of the "formal" analysis.

foreign-exchange earnings if the demand for exports were inelastic with respect to price. Prebisch holds the view that price elasticity of demand for
primary products is indeed low (Prebisch II, p. 256), but this is not an important part of his argument. (The significance of price-inelastic demand for
primary products has been given much more attention in the "commentaries"
than in Prebisch's own work.)

The objection to devaluation, in Prebisch's view, is that it will stimulate
exports from the periphery beyond the point which is socially optimal from
the point of view of any one peripheral country. Higher internal prices for
exports (initially) would encourage an increase in the output of exports.
Higher internal prices of imports would also encourage domestic production
of import-substitutes. But exports would increase too much, because the perfectly competitive firms producing exports would equate marginal cost with
price, whereas socially the appropriate calculation would be an equation of
marginal cost with marginal revenue. Since the domestic prices of exports
would fall (from the initial post-devaluation peak—whether they would fall
to levels lower than before devaluation is not clear), social marginal revenue
would be less than price. Since for some, at least, of the world's primary
products, the demand function facing any individual exporting *country* is
probably close to infinitely elastic, the assumption here must be that all the
peripheral countries are pursuing the same policy[24] and that either: (1.) exports are produced under conditions of perfect competition in each country;
or (2.) the decision-making unit in each country is ignoring the policy being
carried out in the other countries exporting the same commodity. One of
these is essential to the mechanism, since supply of exports (which is the same
thing, in Prebisch's model, as the output of exportables) is a function of price,
not of marginal revenue.

For a "demonstration" that devaluation would lead to an increase in exports
beyond the socially optimum point, the reader is referred to the Appendix
(Prebisch II, pp. 269–273). The analysis here, however, is extremely difficult
to follow. First, he is referring here, not to the response to devaluation, but
rather to

> . . . how the process of spontaneous industrialization might operate ac-
> cording to the classical mechanism, assuming that there is free mobility
> of labor and unrestricted competition. We are concerned here only with
> the alternative employment of the surplus manpower in export pro-
> duction and industrial activities: for the sake of simplicity, other aspects
> will be overlooked (Prebisch II, p. 269).

[24]Prebisch makes this explicit on pp. 260–261, and states that he is ". . . considering
the general need of the peripheral countries for industrialization." On this score he is
commendably unselfish and would (justifiably) reject Kindleberger's criticism that he
is ignoring "the competitive effect." Part of this "competition" could be directed, according to Kindleberger, at the developed countries, which are presumably fair game.
But Kindleberger argues also that "an underdeveloped country can expand its sales
it it can out-produce its fellow underdeveloped countries," and this solution Prebisch
refuses to consider. See Charles P. Kindleberger, *Economic Development* (New York:
McGraw-Hill, 1958), p. 247.

Some of these "other aspects," however, would seem to be fairly important. Thus, for the sake of "simplicity" it must be assumed that there is no domestic demand for the export good, nor for any (agricultural or primary) product which may be a very close substitute on the supply side for the export commodity. (Nor, *a fortiori*, can there be any new export good which is a close substitute in supply for existing exports.) All production not devoted to export must be industrial production. But even within this somewhat restrictive simplification it is not clear what the process is. "Spontaneous industrialization" is not defined. All we know is that we start from a position in which there is some industrial production (which is able to compete with imports in the home market) and there is a given quality of "surplus man-power" which needs to be employed. Presumably productivity (in exports? industry? both?) has risen, so that with output constant there is redundant labour. The issue therefore is that of allocating this surplus labour between primary production for export and industrial production for home consumption.

Some additional production for export can take place without any decline in export prices. The extent to which this is possible depends upon the rate of growth at the centre and the centre's income elasticity of demand for imports of the primary product in question. Beyond a certain point, more exports can be sold only at lower prices. (There really should be no distinction made. The only significance of the point — point 0 in Prebisch's diagram — is that before that point is reached export prices are lower than they would otherwise have been; after the point is reached prices are actually falling.) It should be noted again that this does not depend on the demand for primary products being inelastic with respect to price. A larger output can be sold only at declining prices whenever the demand is less than infinitely elastic. Since marginal physical productivity is constant and profits *per unit* are constant (Prebisch II, p. 271), wages are less than prices by a constant amount and the decline in export prices forces wages down in the export-producing sector. Since labour is mobile (and presumably, homogeneous) this forces wages down in the industrial sector as well, making additional, previously extramarginal, industries competitive with imports. Equilibrium is attained when the average product in export production (which is declining because prices of exports are falling) equals the average product in industry (which is declining because as industrial production expands output is expanded and extended to activities where productivity is lower and lower).[25] Wages, of course, are the same throughout, equal in each sector to average product less a constant. But marginal income per person in the export sector is less than wages and less than marginal (equal to average) income in industry. The

[25]Elsewhere, Prebisch seems to feel that undertaking industrial activity will *raise* average productivity. For example, In Prebisch I, p. 15, we read: "As productivity increases with industrialization, wages will rise, thus causing a comparative increase in the prices of primary products. In this way, as its income rises, primary production will gradually obtain that share of the benefits of technical progress which it would have enjoyed had prices declined."

reason for this is the declining price of exports, which means that marginal revenue is less than price. In industry, on the other hand,

> . . . marginal income per person is the same as *per capita* income, from the point of view of the economy as a whole. . . . The fall of wages has brought also a decline of prices in existing industries; but this involves a purely internal transfer, whereas in export activities there is an external loss of income which reduces the increment of income due to the employment of the surplus manpower (Prebisch II, p. 272).

The socially optimum allocation would be to stop increasing export production where marginal product in exports is equal to average product in industry. This can be achieved only by some interference with the free market. The problem, then, is not that the centre's demand is price- or income-inelastic — greater elasticity would postpone the day of reckoning, perhaps, but would not avert it. The problem stems from the fact that exports are produced under perfectly competitive conditions (which may be a valid assumption for parts of Latin America, but surely not for many other countries in the periphery); and that they are produced under conditions of constant marginal physical productivity of labour, which, for primary products, seems inconceivable.

When we apply this analysis to the effects of a devaluation the problem of explaining the origin of the "spontaneous industrialization" is removed. The immediate effect of the devaluation is to raise the domestic prices of both exports and imports. Export production is therefore stimulated, as is the production of at least some of the import-competing goods. Since, as we have noted, there seems always in Prebisch's world to be a redundancy of labour, both of these sectors are able to increase simultaneously. The argument, then, is that the response of the free market to the devaluation would involve an increase in the output of exports that was larger than the optimum and, correspondingly, an increase in the output of industrial, import-competing goods, that was smaller than optimum. It is worth recalling what assumptions underlie this analysis.

(1.) The labour force is perfectly homogeneous and perfectly mobile.

(2.) The periphery as a whole is a monopolist in the market for its exports, or at any rate a sufficiently important seller so that it is faced with a downward-sloping demand curve.

(3.) The export commodity is produced under perfectly competitive conditions *or* the producers of the export commodity (whether private enterprise, government-owned or directed by governmental or para-governmental agencies, such as a marketing board) in each country ignore the fact that other peripheral countries producing the same commodity are also executing the same policies of devaluation and expansion of exports.

(4.) All increased output of the export commodity must be exported. Thus, not only is there no stock-piling of the commodity by marketing boards, but there is no domestic consumption of the export commodity, or else the domestic demand for the export commodity is totally inelastic with respect to both price and income.

(5.) Exports are produced under conditions of constant returns to scale.

(6.) Exports are produced under conditions of constant marginal physical productivity of labour, which in turn implies either: (a.) that labour is the only factor of production; or (b.) that the supply of the other factors of production is infinitely elastic at the prevailing price, which is the "constant unit profit" mentioned above.

It is hardly necessary to point out that this is a rather formidable set of assumptions. Objections to assumptions (5.) and (6.), particularly in the case of agricultural and primary production, are obvious. Assumption (4.) may be a reasonable approximation for some countries and some products in the form in which we have stated it here. But if it is interpreted more broadly it raises a host of new questions. For the assumption that exports are not consumed at home is the same as the statement that there are two sectors in the economy, an industrial, import-competing sector, and a primary-producing, export sector. This is not a "dual economy" problem, since Prebisch raises neither the questions concerned with technological dualism, differences in factor substitutability and the like,[26] nor those involving non-competing groups in the labour market. But the importance of assuming that there are two — and no more than two — sectors is that it limits the number of alternatives available. There is always redundancy in the labour market (though this does not affect the wage level) which can be employed only in the industrial sector, where it runs up against competition from imports which can be overcome by protection or subsidization, or else in the export sector, where it runs into decreasing real returns due to the transfer of income abroad which results from the decline in price of exports. As we have noted previously, there is no room in his discussion for an increase in the output of "domestic goods," such as construction, with high transport costs; or of agricultural products for home consumption, which may be very close substitutes in production for the export commodity; or of "social overhead capital"; or, for that matter, of new exports which may be close substitutes in production for existing goods. On the other hand, there are a number of instances in which Prebisch does seem to be thinking of a third sector (Prebisch I, p. 18, *e.g.*) which consists of domestic services and the like, and in which productivity is very low, so that output in that sector should not be encouraged. In fact, in a number of cases it is this third sector which seems to be the source of the apparently indefinitely large supply of man-power.

An even more troublesome, though related problem is the question of the wage-determination mechanism. In the discussion of the disadvantages resulting from not having "technological density" and in the model presented in the Appendix which we have just examined, it seems clear that the real wage is equal to marginal (which equals the average) product in the export industry.

[26]*Vide, e.g.*, R. S. Eckaus, "The Factor-Proportions Problem in Under-Developed Areas," *The American Economic Review*, Vol. XLV (September, 1955), pp. 539–565; Dale W. Jorgenson, "The Development of a Dual Economy," *Economic Journal*, Vol. LXXI (June, 1961), pp. 309–334.

Since this is constant, real wages in fact depend on the terms of trade. As the price of exports falls, wages fall, and this allows industrial activity, where productivity is lower, to expand. But elsewhere there is the notion that wages are determined by overall, or average, productivity, in the whole economy, as illustrated in footnote 25 on p. 422 and in the following:

> It was pointed out at the beginning of this section that there are two ways of increasing real income. One is through an increase in productivity and the other through a readjustment of income from primary production so as to lessen the disparity between it and income of the great industrial countries.
>
> The second result can be achieved only in so far as the first is accomplished. As productivity and the average real income from industry increase in the Latin-American countries, wages in agriculture and primary production in general will have to rise, as they have in other countries (Prebisch I, p. 47).

These quotations are from Prebisch I, and it is, of course, possible that Prebisch's views changed during the years intervening between publication of the two essays. But whatever the reason, it is clear that there is a difference between the two views of the wage-determination mechanism which needs to be explained. Furthermore, there seems to be a difference in Prebisch's estimation of the productivity in industry in the two cases. If overall productivity rises as a result of industrialization, productivity in industry must be higher than in the production of exports, in which case it is not clear why there is a need for protection of industry. There are two possible explanations for this. One is that Prebisch is implicitly going from a static to a dynamic analysis (which, incidentally, he does frequently throughout both papers) and the rise in productivity which results from industrialization is a long-run result of the working-out of the external economies of industrialization and its overall socio-economic effects, that is, the infant industry, or "infant economy" argument. A different explanation is that the higher productivity resulting from industrialization results from the elimination, or at any rate the diminution, of the third sector, the low productivity domestic services. This is implied elsewhere in Prebisch I (p. 18). But this brings us back to the question of why this third sector cannot consist of "domestic goods" with high transport costs, of agricultural production for home consumption and/or of high-productivity services. What is more serious, there is the problem of how to explain the existence of such a sector in an economy in which labour is mobile and the wage-rate uniform. If productivity in that sector is so low, why does labour not move out of it and into the production of exports until the wage level in exports is brought down (through falling export prices) to that prevailing in domestic service?

Almost all of the preceding discussion has been directed at the formal, analytical structure of Prebisch's arguments. As we stated at the beginning, there is not one, single model, but several. In this sense, we would argue, Prebisch has fallen short of making his case because he has over-stated it. The obvious question then is, can we ferret out from his argument a single, "minimum" model which would be sufficient to justify the policies he proposes? The following is a simplified version which we believe to be logically consistent and sufficient. Its acceptability depends, of course, on its empirical relevance.

Consider two countries, P and C, which are alike with respect to rate of growth of population, rate of increase in *per capita* income (hence rate of increase in productivity per man and in the real wage-rate) and technological density. At the existing exchange rate and wage-rates in the two countries all of P's exports are primary products and all of C's exports are industrial goods. The only difference is that with growth in income the world demand function for C's industrial exports is rising faster than the world demand function for P's primary exports. As a result, an ever increasing proportion of P's incremental population *must* be allocated to industrial production, while in C an ever-increasing proportion of the incremental population *can* — and will — be allocated to industrial production. But P's industrial output can compete (in P's home market) with imports from C only if, through changes in the exchange rate or in the wage-rate, P accepts a deterioration in its terms of trade. Thus, part of the increase in productivity in P accrues to C. So far there has been no need to appeal to differences in market structure, the mechanism of wage-determination or any other asymmetrical imperfections in the working of the market mechanism and perfect competition.

Analytically, the only question remaining is whether there is any tendency for the decline in the terms of trade to stop. Prebisch does not address himself explicitly to this problem, but one gets the impression that he considers the decline in the terms of trade to be a continuing process. There seem, however, to be two equilibrating forces at work. First, as the proportion of the labour force employed in industrial production in P increases, the demand for imports of industrial goods from C should increase at a decreasing rate. Secondly, the fact that the terms of trade for P are declining means that real income *per capita* is not growing as rapidly as in C, so that even with a high income elasticity of demand for imports the absolute increments in imports demanded by P should eventually equal the growth in demand for its exports. Prebisch himself is aware of the latter tendency (Prebisch II, pp. 253–254), but argues that as a result the periphery's growth rate will be less than it would be if the demand for its exports were more income-elastic (or more price-elastic) or the demand for imports less income-elastic. This, indeed, is the heart of the "Prebisch thesis," and, we repeat, it stems from the assumption of different income elasticities of demand, not from alleged differences in market structure and the wage-price mechanism.

The problem thus far is essentially a balance-of-payments problem. Because of the disparities in income elasticities, income in P cannot grow as rapidly as income in C without generating a chronic deficit in the balance of payments. (The protectionism this suggests is of the "exchange-rationing" type discussed on p. 411. Tariffs, multiple exchange rates, or various types of discriminatory controls are frequently proposed — as relatively simple alternatives to more difficult alterations in the internal tax structure — to prevent the high-income groups from "frittering away" precious foreign-exchange reserves by exporting flight capital or importing luxury consumer goods. It would, indeed, be interesting to know the relationship between the apparently high income elasticity of demand for imports and the shape of the income distribution in P.) But the question still remains how fast real income *per capita could* grow in the absence of the balance-of-payments constraint. We are back to the traditional welfare propositions of international trade theory. Ignoring, as Prebisch does, a number of extremely important considerations, such as institutional patterns, the propensity to save and invest, the distribution of income, etc., the absolute growth at any one time is clearly a function of the level of real income. Furthermore, if our goal is to maximize income at some future date it is not obvious that maximizing the rate of growth over the relevant time interval is the most appropriate means to that end. A slower rate of growth of a higher level of income may be better. If "the free play market forces" dictates an increase in exports, and if this maximizes P's income at any — and every — given point in time, this may be preferable to having a lower level of income which is growing at a more rapid rate.[27] Here the empirical questions of world (not domestic) market structure enter. The difficulty is that the periphery (as a group) is a monopolist but not a monopsonist: the world price of its imports is not a function of its demand for imports; and the demand for its exports is likewise independent of its demand for exports. But, though the demand *function* for P's exports is independent of what P does, the *price* of P's exports is directly dependent on the amount it offers for sale on the world market.[28] In a static context this is the only possible interpretation of Prebisch's statement (Prebisch II, p. 255):

> It is not really a question of comparing the industrial costs with import prices but of comparing the increment of income obtained in the expansion of industry with that which could have been obtained in export activities had the same productive resources been employed there.

The two comparisons will yield the same solution (if the international market is in equilibrium) *unless* marginal value product is less than the average in exports and equal to the average (or less, but with a smaller differential) in domestic industrial production, and import prices are not affected. (In a dynamic framework the quoted sentence can be interpreted as a statement of the infant industry argument.)

We can therefore characterize the basic Prebisch thesis as consisting of two components. (1.) A "balance-of-payments" problem, with the demand for

[27]This increase in exports may, of course stop short of complete specialization, since production of exports may begin to run into decreasing returns. Cf. Prebisch II, p. 263, discussing ". . . forces . . . of a Ricardian character." This, incidentally, is one of the many examples of Prebisch's "asides" belying the naivete of his assumptions and "simplifications" in the formal analysis.

[28]The terminology is not Prebisch's, but this is clearly implied in the analysis in the Appendix to Prebisch II, for example.

imports in P tending to grow faster than import demand in C, so equilibrium can be achieved only if P grows more slowly than C. This problem arises from C's inelastic demand (for imports from P) with respect to *income*. (2.) A "real income" problem. This is frequently stated as C's price-inelastic demand for imports from P, but more correctly should be attributed to P's monopolistic position in the world market, which causes the demand for her exports to be less than infinitely elastic with respect to price. The result of this is that "free market," responding to existing relative prices, misallocates resources in P between export industries and import-competing industries, so that aggregate real income in P is not maximized. (It should be remembered, however, that this misallocation is the result of two assumptions about market structure, both of which are necessary: (1.) the monopolistic position of P in the world market *and* either (2.) perfect competition among producers of the export good in each P-country, or (3.) perfectly competitive behaviour on the part of decision-makers in each P-country, each assuming that output of its export good remains constant in the other countries of the periphery).

What remains is a number of empirical questions which must be investigated in order to determine whether the model we have just stated is relevant to the real world. A reasonably careful study of these questions would constitute at least one additional paper, and we shall not attempt it here. We shall, however, indicate the direction that should be followed in such an investigation and the realms that need to be explored.

The "balance-of-payments" component of our "modified Prebisch model" rests on the assumption of a high income elasticity of demand for imports into the periphery and a low income elasticity of demand for imports into the centre. As to the former, even if it proves, on the basis of historical data, to be valid, it is necessary, from a policy-making point of view, to determine the reasons for it. One obvious cause, in the past, for the "scarcity" of foreign exchange in peripheral countries was the capital flight and the high propensity to import of the high-income groups in those countries.[29] A related question is to what extent the high propensity to import has been "programmed" by government development plans requiring large imports of capital goods.[30] This is not to say that such imports are "unjustified," but the question remains whether they should be "built in" to the model as a parameter in describing the economic behaviour of the periphery.

A second question, frequently raised in discussions of the alleged differences in income elasticity of demand facing exporters in the centre as compared with the periphery, pertains to the working of Engel's law. Clearly this applies, if at all, only to the food exports of the periphery (and of the centre, be it remembered), not to industrial raw materials. Empirical studies indicate that Engel's law probably holds, and that income elasticity of demand for food

---

[29]Prebisch makes several references to this, among them Prebisch I, pp. 29, 40.

[30]Cf. Fritz Machlup, "Three Concepts of the Balance of Payments and the So-Called Dollar Shortage," *Economic Journal*, Vol. LX (March, 1950), pp. 46–68.

is less than one. But a corollary of this, also indicated empirically, is that the income elasticity of demand for food is higher among lower-income groups than for high-income groups.[31] As peripheral countries grow, then, as increasing demand for food may compete with growing imports for increasing expenditures. Additionally, a growing demand for the export goods for domestic consumption might be expected, in some countries of the periphery at any rate, to mitigate the misallocation effect with which Prebisch is concerned, since for that part of the domestic output which is consumed domestically, marginal revenue must be equal to average revenue, just as it is in the industrial sector; there is no "transfer abroad" involved. Furthermore, since Engel's law applies to expenditures for housing as well as for food, the possibility of diverting demand from imports to domestic goods as income rises increases in scope, since this is an industry in which, as yet, transport costs are high enough to preclude all but a very small amount of international trade.

Probably more important, for present purposes, than the validity of Engel's law is the question of the low income elasticity of demand, in the centre, for imports of industrial materials. It is not difficult to believe that this elasticity is, in fact, not high. (It has been suggested that it has a value approximately equal to one.) But Prebisch's purported demonstration that is low (Prebisch I, pp. 24 ff.) is open to question on a number of counts. First, he speaks only of the United States, which for obvious reasons (such as sheer size, diversity of economic regions and resource endowments) has in general a low foreign-trade component in national income. Secondly, he speaks of the long-range decline in the import coefficient of the United States. We would argue: (a.) that marginal, rather than average, propensity to import is important here; (b.) that it is the marginal propensity to import *raw materials* that matters, rather than total imports; and (c.) that the period Prebisch is considering, 1919–48, would be expected to contain more years of declining than of rising imports as a share of national income. Since almost two-thirds of the period are accounted for by the Great Depression and by the Second World War and the immediate post-war period, the overall decline in the import coefficient shown in Prebisch's Table V (Prebisch I, p. 24) is not at all surprising.[32]

One of the causes to which the supposed low income-elasticity of demand for raw materials in the centre is frequently attributed is the development of

[31]This is one of the results of a cross-sectional study by Hendrik S. Houthakker, "An International Comparison of Household Expenditure Patterns, Commemorating the Centenary of Engel's Law," *Econometrica*, Vol. 25 (October, 1957), pp. 532–551.

[32]A study has been made for several countries by Calvin Patton Blair, *Fluctuations in United States Imports from Brazil, Colombia, Chile, and Mexico, 1919–1954* (Austin: Bureau of Business Research, the University of Texas, 1959). He concludes that ". . . results do indicate a common general tendency: the United States propensity to import [as a function of gross national product] from each of the four countries shifted downward during the depression and its aftermath, to be lifted again by the stimulus of war demand; and in no case did the import function return to its prewar position" (pp. 33–34). That the function should have risen during the war, while Prebisch's table shows the import coefficient rising only after the end of the war, is, of course, not unexpected, since Prebisch's data are for total imports, from all sources.

synthetic substitutes. We do not dispute this argument, but it should be noted that one of the effects of the appearance of substitutes is to make the *price* elasticity of demand higher. In the case of rubber and certain textiles, for example, one would expect the present price elasticity of demand to be very high indeed.

Related to the question of domestic production of food is that of the possibilities of diversification of exports, especially by the development of joint products or vertical expansion.[33] Both this and the possibilities of increased food production (with respect to Ghana), are illustrated by the following:

> The draft [of a seven-year development plan] states that "Ghana's agriculture has been unable to keep up with the domestic demand for food." emphasis will, therefore, be placed first on agricultural development: expenditure of £G10.8 million on state farms is expected to increase food production to such an extent that food imports costing £G23 million can be eliminated. In industry there will be more emphasis on the processing of raw materials. At least half of Ghana's cocoa exports are to be in the form of processed cocoa rather than of cocoa beans. Timber is to be converted into wood products, plywood, and chipboard. By 1970, it is expected that production of alumina from local bauxite will approach the requirements of the aluminum smelter at Tema.[34]

Clearly, both this type of extension of the export list as well as the readiness with which resources can be shifted from export production to supplying food for domestic consumption will vary greatly from one peripheral country to another. This problem of the extent to which generalization is possible, however, is equally applicable to Prebisch's analysis. As we have previously noted, there are a number of points in his argument at which what Prebisch has observed in Latin America is not obviously relevant for other parts of the periphery. In this connection, as in many others in economic analysis, aggregation is a tool which has greater power than fineness.

Questions for discussion and analysis pertaining to this article may be found at the end of Article 27.

---

[33]Michael Michaely, in his study of concentration in trade, has concluded that ". . . there is no association between the intensity of price fluctuations of exports and the extent of specialization in exports of primary goods. What may have led to the belief that such an association does exist is the disregard of the degree of commodity concentration. . . . It is only because exporters of primary goods are usually countries with highly concentrated exports that they appear to be more vulnerable to violent price fluctuations," *Concentration in International Trade* (Amsterdam: North-Holland Publishing Company, 1962), p. 78. Michaely's discussion of "The Implications of Economic Development" (Chap. 6) is, in general, extremely thoughtful and apt. He seems to feel that on the whole the obstacles to development presented by fluctuations in the terms of trade have been exaggerated, though he recognizes the problem. He is concerned primarily with the problems raised by *fluctuations* in terms of trade rather than with the question of long-run deterioration, and for this reason we have not dealt with his argument at greater length. His work, however, is highly suggestive and could well serve as a guide to further empirical study of *trends* in prices and terms of trade.

[34]Quoted in International Monetary Fund, *International Financial News Survey*, Vol. XV, No. 14 (April 12, 1963), p. 121.

Harry Johnson †

26. ECONOMIC DEVELOPMENT AND INTERNATIONAL TRADE*

Economic growth gives rise to many problems of international economic adjustment.[1] This lecture is concerned with the formal analysis of one group of such problems, the effects of economic growth of various kinds on the growing country's demand for imports and dependence on international trade. The analysis may be treated in either of two ways: as an analysis of the nature of the equilibrium adjustment which growth requires of the international economy; and as a preliminary to analysis of the monetary problems which arise if the mechanism of international adjustment prevents or inhibits the attainment of the required new international equilibrium. The argument employs the standard two-country two-factor model, assuming constant returns to scale in production and perfectly competitive conditions. When we come to analyze the effects of specific types of economic growth, the model will be "concretized" by making assumptions about the nature of the countries and the demand and supply conditions of the goods they produce.

To begin with, let us recapitulate the general nature of the equilibrium established in international trade. Two cases may be distinguished, corresponding to complete and incomplete specialization of the country in production: these are represented in Figures 26-1 and 26-2 (pp. 432-33). In both, quantities of commodities X and Y are measured along the axes, and I_1, I_2, I_3 represent community indifference curves. The domestic production possibilities are represented by fixed quantity OP in the complete specialization case, and by the transformation curve TT in the incomplete specialization case: the terms of trade open to the country on the world market are represented by the slope of the line PC. In equilibrium, the terms-of-trade line is tangent to a community indifference curve at C; and also, in the incomplete specialization case, to the transformation curve at P; the country produces the quantities represented by P (OP of X in Figure 26-1, OR of X and PR of Y in Figure 26-2) and consumes the quantities represented by C (OQ of X and CQ of Y in Figure 26-1, OV of

†Harry G. Johnson, Professor of Economics, University of Chicago.

*From *Money, Trade and Economic Growth* (London: George Allen and Unwin, Ltd., 1961), pp. 75-103. Reprinted by permission of the publisher and the author.

[1]Nationaløkonomisk Tidsskrift, 97 Bund 5-6 Hefte 1959, pp. 253-272.

X and CV of Y in Figure 26-2), exporting PQ of X to pay for imports of QC of Y. The value of the country's national product (national income), measured in terms of import goods, is represented by OM in each case; and the level of satisfaction enjoyed is I_2, as compared with the level I_1 that would be enjoyed if there were no international trade.

The foregoing account assumes that the country faces given terms of trade. In general, the terms of trade will not be given but will be variable and determined by the interaction in the market of the country's own willingness to trade, as determined by its preference system and production capacity (Figure 26-1) or transformation curve (Figure 26-2), and the willingness of the foreign country to trade, as determined by the same factors abroad. The foreign country's willingness to trade can be represented by an offer curve (PF in Figures 26-1 and 26-2) showing the quantities of Y the foreign country would export in return for imports of various quantities of X, the price at which each exchange would occur being shown by the ratio of the quantities of X and Y exchanged. In Figure 26-1, the foreign offer curve has a fixed origin at the point corresponding to the domestic country's productive capacity, and international trade equilibrium is determined by the condition that the point at which an indifference curve is tangent to the (variable) terms of trade line must lie on the foreign offer curve: in Figure 26-2, the origin of the foreign offer curve shifts along the transformation curve, as

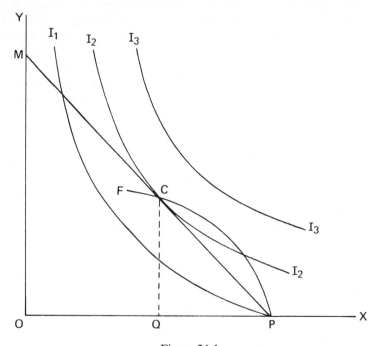

Figure 26-1

domestic production alters; and international trade equilibrium requires, in addition to the condition just stated, that the terms-of-trade line be tangent to the transformation curve at the point from which the offer curve originates. With the insertion of the foreign offer curve *PF*, the "trade triangle" *CPQ* in Figures 26-1 and 26-2 represents the equilibrium of international trade when the terms of trade are variable.

The effect of economic growth is to shift the production point *P* outwards along *OX* in Figure 26-1, and the transformation curve *TT* outwards in Figure 26-2. The analysis of the effects of growth can be pursued in two alternative ways: by assuming a given foreign offer curve and analyzing the new international trade equilibrium that will result from growth, or by considering the effect of growth on the domestic country's demand for imports at the initial terms of trade. The latter is the approach adopted here, both because it enables the isolation of the effects of the growth of the economy and the development of concepts for the analysis of these effects, concepts which are directly applicable to economies whose terms of trade are fixed by the world market, and because, if the foreign offer curve is unchanged, the direction of change of the terms and volume of trade can be predicted from the effect of growth on the country's demand for imports at constant prices.

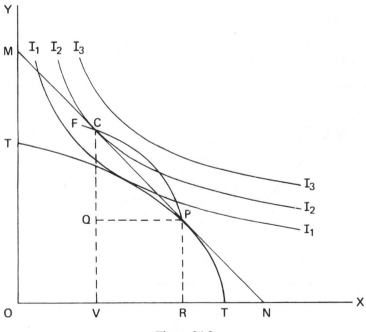

Figure 26-2

The general nature of the effect that economic growth would have on the growing country's demand for imports if growth occurred with unchanged terms of trade is illustrated in Figures 26-3 and 26-4. In each case, the production point shifts from P to P', national income (product) measured in terms of imports from OM to OM', the consumption point from C to C', and the level of satisfaction enjoyed from I_2 to I_3. Imports demanded increase from CQ to $C'Q'$, and exports supplied from QP to $Q'P'$.

The question of economic interest is whether growth will increase the demand for imports more than proportionally to the increase in the value of the national product, in the same proportion as, or less than proportionally to the increase in the value of the national product. From the growing country's point of view, the question is whether growth makes the country relatively less self-sufficient, no more or less dependent on trade, or relatively more self-sufficient. From the point of view of the foreign country, the question is whether the market for its exports expands more than proportionally to, at the same rate as, or less than proportionally to the growth of this country. The three possibilities can be conceptualized in terms of three types of growth: pro-trade-biased growth, which increases the country's demand for imports and supply of exports more than proportionally to output; "neutral" or unbiased growth, which increases the country's demand for imports and supply

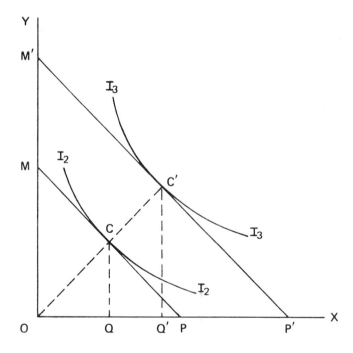

Figure 26-3

of exports in proportion to output; and anti-trade-biased growth, which increases the country's demand for imports and supply of exports less than proportionally to output. Figures 26-3 and 26-4 represent a particular type of
unbiased growth, in which production and consumption of each of the two
goods, and therefore exports and imports, expand proportionally with income
—as shown by the fact that $M'M$, $C'C$, and $P'P$ all meet in the origin. In
addition to the three general types of growth, two extreme cases can be distinguished: ultra-pro-trade-biased growth, in which more than the whole
increase in national income is devoted to the purchase of imports so that the
demand for home-produced goods actually falls and the country becomes
absolutely less self-sufficient; and ultra-anti-trade-biased growth, in which
more than the whole increase in national income is devoted to the purchase
of home-produced goods, so that the demand for imports actually falls and
the country becomes absolutely more self-sufficient.

In the case of complete specialization, the type of growth is determined by
the behaviour of the consumption of importables as the national product
rises. Formally, it can be related to the "output-elasticity of demand for
importables"—the proportional change in quantity of importables demanded, divided by the proportional change in national output which causes
the change in the import demand: growth is pro-trade-biased, neutral, or

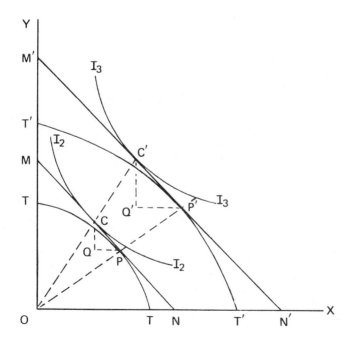

Figure 26-4

anti-trade-biased according as elasticity exceeds, equals, or falls short of one, ultra-anti-trade-biased if the elasticity is negative and ultra-pro-trade-biased if the elasticity exceeds the original ratio of national income to imports (an alternative way of expressing a negative output-elasticity of demand for exportables). The ranges of shift of the consumption point corresponding to the five possible types of growth are illustrated in Figure 26-5.

If growth is due to some other cause than population change, income per head will rise, and the type of growth will depend on the average income-elasticity of demand for imports: if imports are luxury goods, growth will be pro-trade-biased, if they are necessary goods growth will be anti-trade-biased; if imports are inferior goods growth will be ultra-anti-trade-biased and if exports are inferior goods growth will be ultra-pro-trade-biased. If, on the other hand, growth is due to population increase alone, it may be presumed that income per head will fall, so that in aggregate demand luxury goods will behave like necessities and conversely; the net effect of growth on demand will depend on the relations between population size and income per head, and between income per head and consumption per head of the good consumed, and a luxury good may appear inferior in aggregate consumption. To simplify the following argument, and also because it seems reasonable

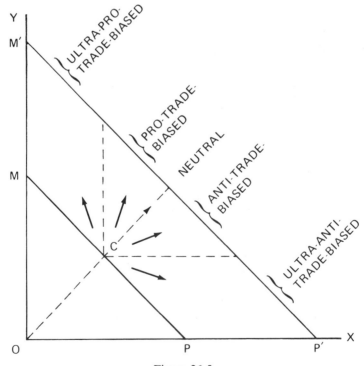

Figure 26-5

to do so, the cases of ultra-bias in the consumption shift will henceforth be ignored.

In the case of incomplete specialization, the effect of growth on the demand for imports depends on the combined behaviour of consumption and production. For analytical purposes it is convenient to consider separately the effects on the country's self-sufficiency of the consumption and production shifts associated with growth, before considering their combined effect. The consumption shift has already been analyzed (the term "demand for import-ables" rather than "demand for imports" has been used deliberately to permit the argument to be extended to the case in which some importable goods are produced at home). The production shift can similarly be classified into five types, which can be formally described in terms of an "output-elasticity of supply of importables." If this elasticity exceeds one, so that domestic produc-tion of importables increases more than proportionally to national income and the country's production pattern becomes more self-sufficient, growth is anti-trade-biased; if the elasticity is negative, so that domestic production of importables falls, growth is ultra-pro-trade-biased; and so on. The ranges of shift of the production point corresponding to these types are shown in Figure 26-6. The determinants of the production shift will be discussed later;

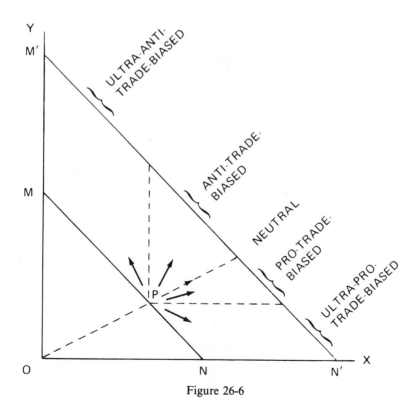

Figure 26-6

it would be possible, but is not worth while, to develop an analysis of output-elasticity of supply in terms of luxury, necessary and inferior production paralleling the analysis of output-elasticity of demand in terms of luxury, necessary and inferior consumption already presented.

The effect of growth on the demand for imports is the combined result of its effects on consumption demand and domestic supply; and the addition of the effects on the consumption and production shifts is complicated. If both shifts are biased in the same direction, or one is neutral, the combined effect is clearly pro-trade-biased or anti-trade-biased. If, however, the two shifts are biased in opposite directions, the net effect cannot be simply assessed. Because consumption of imports initially exceeds domestic production of them, biases of the same degree (as measured by the deviation from unit output-elasticity) but in opposite directions will not cancel out; instead, the bias on the consumption side will dominate unless the production shift is sufficiently more biased than the consumption shift. In other words, the degrees of bias must be compared. But where there is ultra-bias in the production shift and the possibility of contrary ultra-bias in the consumption shift is ruled out, some simplification is possible: ultra-anti-trade-bias in the production shift is sufficient to make the effect of growth ultra-anti-trade-biased, and ultra-pro-trade-bias in the production shift is sufficient to prevent growth being ultra-anti-trade-biased on balance.

The relation between the output-elasticities of consumption and production of importables, the production and consumption biases, and the overall bias of growth can be shown geometrically in terms of Figure 26-7, which reproduces Figure 26-4 but for clarity omits the transformation and indifference curves. The proportional changes in aggregate output, consumption of importables and production of importables are respectively:

$$\frac{MM'}{OM} = \frac{NN'}{ON}, \frac{CC'}{FC} = \frac{NN'}{FN}, \text{ and } \frac{PP'}{GP} = \frac{NN'}{GN}.$$

The output-elasticity of consumption of importables is $\dfrac{CC'}{FC} \div \dfrac{MM'}{OM} = \dfrac{ON}{FN}$,

and the output-elasticity of production of importables is $\dfrac{PP'}{GP} \div \dfrac{MM'}{OM} = \dfrac{ON}{GN}$.

The proportional change in demand for imports is $\dfrac{CC'}{HC} = \dfrac{PP'}{HP} = \dfrac{QQ'}{HQ}$,

and the output-elasticity of demand for imports is $\dfrac{CC'}{HC} \div \dfrac{NN'}{ON}$. The magnitude of the latter, and hence the overall bias of growth, can be determined simply by comparing the slopes of OH and MN. If OH and MN are parallel, as in Figure 26-7, $\dfrac{C'C}{HC} = \dfrac{NN'}{ON}$, the output-elasticity of demand for imports is unity and growth is neutral; if OH lies to the right of a line through O parallel to MN, $\dfrac{C'C}{HC} > \dfrac{NN'}{ON}$, the elasticity exceeds unity, and growth is pro-trade-biased; conversely, if OH lies to the left of the line through O parallel to MN, the elasticity is less than unity and growth is anti-trade-biased. By extension, if $C'C$ and $P'P$ meet in H at an obtuse angle growth is ultra-pro-trade-biased, while if H lies to the right of MN growth is ultra-anti-trade-biased. The bias of the consumption shift can be measured by the excess of the output-elasticity of consumption of importables over unity, and of the production shift by the excess of unity over the output-elasticity of production of importables (so that pro-trade-bias is positive and anti-trade-bias negative in each case). On these definitions the consumption bias is represented in Figure 26-7 by $\dfrac{FO}{FN}$ and the production bias by $\dfrac{GO}{GN}$; $\dfrac{GO}{GN}$ is larger than $\dfrac{FO}{FN}$, thus demonstrating the point previously stated that where the biases are opposed the production bias must be larger than the consumption bias if the latter is not to predominate.

Ultra-pro-trade-biased growth and ultra-anti-trade-biased growth have been described as extreme cases, in terms of their effects on the growing country's self-sufficiency or dependence on trade. Before proceeding to discuss the likely effects on trade of growth due to particular causes, it seems appropriate to notice an alternative conception of extreme types of growth, a conception in terms of economic welfare which really belongs at a later stage of the argument but which it is convenient to introduce at this stage.

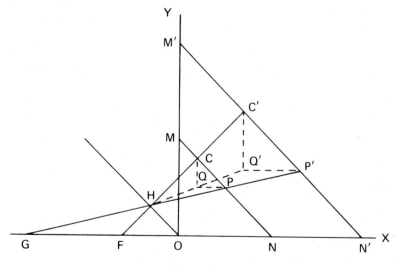

Figure 26-7

Let us assume that only the one country is growing, and consider the nature of the new international trade equilibrium that will result from its increased production, and the economic welfare that will be derived from it. Normally, at least so far as the argument up to this stage has taken us, we might expect that growth would increase the country's demand for imports, thereby worsening its equilibrium terms of trade and so imposing a loss of economic welfare as a partial offset to the gain in welfare associated with a higher level of production. This suggests two possible extreme cases. The first is the case in which the growing country's demand for imports falls instead of rises, so that its terms of trade improve and the benefit from increased production is augmented by a gain on the terms of trade; this case will occur when growth is ultra-anti-trade-biased, possible causes of which will appear in subsequent analysis. The other extreme is the case in which the terms of trade turn unfavourable to such an extent that the welfare loss from this cause more than offsets the gain from increased production, so that the country's growth leaves it worse off on balance. This is the case which Jagdish Bhagwati has described as "immiserizing growth";[2] it is probably a *curiosum,* but worth analyzing.

The simplest way of doing so is to illustrate the possibility of growth which leads to no welfare gain; this possibility is depicted in Figures 26-8 and 26-9, for the two cases of complete and incomplete specialization. In both figures, C_e on the pre-growth indifference curve I_2 is the consumption point when growth has occurred and the terms of trade moved against the country sufficiently to preserve international trade equilibrium; in Figure 26-9, P_e is the new equilibrium production point on the new transformation curve.

In the complete specialization case, zero-gain growth obviously requires that foreign demand for the country's exports be inelastic. With a higher price of imports and the same level of indifference, consumption of importables and therefore imports demanded must fall. For this to correspond to full international equilibrium, the foreigner must accordingly reduce the quantity of imports supplied when their price rises, or, what is the same thing, spend less of his goods on this country's exports when the price of the latter falls. This necessary condition for zero-gain growth in the complete specialization case is illustrated in Figure 26-8, where PF and $P'F'$ represent the (given) foreign offer curve drawn through the pre-growth and post-growth production points. In the incomplete specialization case, consumption of importables must also fall; but the demand for imports does not necessarily fall, since domestic production of importables may fall by more than consumption of them. Thus, zero-gain growth in this case requires *either* that the foreign demand for the country's exports be inelastic *or* that the country's growth be ultra-pro-trade-biased.

[2]Jagdish Bhagwati, "Immiserizing Growth: A Geometrical Note," *Review of Economic Studies,* XXV(3), No. 68 (June, 1958), pp. 201–205.

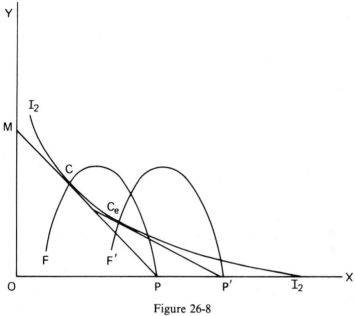

Figure 26-8

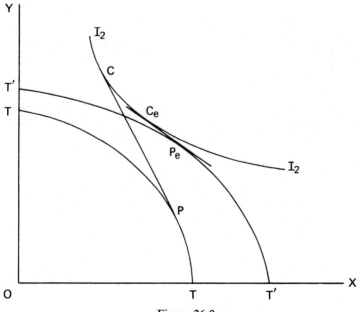

Figure 26-9

To return to the main line of the argument, the concepts of neutral, pro-trade-biased, anti-trade-biased, and ultra-pro- and ultra-anti-trade-biased growth, together with the distinction between the consumption, the production, and the overall effect of growth, must now be applied to analyzing the effects of different types of growth. Following convention, we shall be concerned with three types of economic growth — technical progress, population increase, and capital accumulation — which are assumed to be analytically separable. And we shall consider their effects in two types of economies, one which exports manufactured goods in exchange for foodstuffs — a "manufacturing country" — and one which exports foodstuffs in exchange for manufactured goods — an "agricultural country." Both countries are assumed to be only partially specialized — this is the more interesting case, and can readily be adapted to the case of complete specialization.

To make the analysis more concrete, it is assumed that food is labour-intensive in production and a necessary good in consumption, while manufactures are capital-intensive in production and a luxury good in consumption. Further, it is assumed that capital is better off than labour, so that the average and marginal propensities to consume manufactures are higher for capital than for labour, and the average and marginal propensities to consume food are higher for labour than for capital.

In considering the effects of growth, it is convenient to distinguish between technical progress, which alters the production functions of the economy, and population increase and capital accumulation, which increase the quantity of a productive factor without altering the production function. The effects of factor accumulation are the simplest to deal with, and will therefore be discussed first. For reasons which will become clear in the course of the argument, it is necessary to consider the production effects before the consumption effects.

The production effect of factor accumulation, for the simple model we are using, is given by a rather simple proposition sometimes described as "the Rybczynski theorem;[3] if the terms of trade are constant, and one factor accumulates, there will be an absolute reduction in the production of the good which uses that factor less intensively, and the production of the good using that factor more intensively will increase by more than the value of the total increase in output. The proof of this proposition starts from the fact that, to keep the relative prices of the goods constant, it is necessary to keep factor prices constant, because an increase in the relative price of a factor will increase the relative cost of the good which uses that factor more intensively. To keep factor prices constant, it is necessary to keep the ratio of one factor to the other in each industry constant, since it is this ratio which determines the relative marginal productivities and therefore the relative prices of the factors.

---

[3]T. M. Rybczynski, "Factor Endowment and Relative Commodity Prices," *Economica*, N. S., XXII, No. 88 (November, 1955), pp. 336–341. I first encountered the argument in a paper read by W. M. Corden in November, 1954.

How is this to be done when the amount of one factor increases? Suppose there is an increase in the quantity of capital: then if labour and capital together are shifted out of the labour-intensive into the capital-intensive industry, labour will be released from the labour-intensive industry in greater quantities than are required to operate the released capital in the capital-intensive industry; and the surplus will be available to operate the additional capital.

This point can be illustrated by means of the production box-diagram, as in Figure 26-10. In the diagram AF represents the initial endowment of labour, and AM the initial endowment of capital; production indifference curves for food are drawn in the box with F as origin, and for manufactures with M as origin; the points of tangency of indifference curves from the two origins, which constitute efficient allocations of resources between the two industries, form the contract curve FPM. Suppose that P is the pre-growth production point, the economy producing P_f food by using FL of labour and FC of capital in agriculture, and P_m of manufactures by using LA of labour and BC of capital in manufacturing; the labour/capital ratios in food and manufactures respectively are shown by the slopes of FP and MP, and the exchange ratio between labour and capital is given by the slope of the common tangent to P_f and P_m at P.

Now suppose that capital increases to AM', shifting the origin of the manufactures production indifference curves to M' and altering the contract curve to

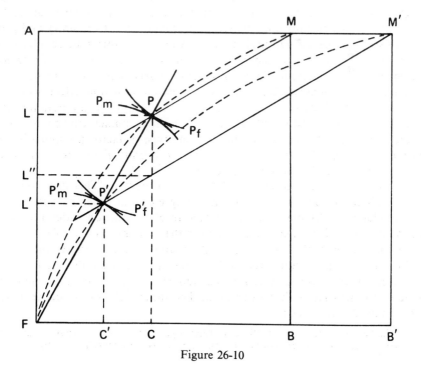

Figure 26-10

FP'M'. At *P'*, the point on the new contract curve with the same labour:
capital ratio in each industry and therefore the same exchange ratio between
factors as at *P*, production of food P'_f is lower than at *P*. The reduction of
food production from P_f to P'_f releases *LL'* of labour and *CC'* of capital
from agriculture; only *L'L''* of the labour released is required to co-operate
with *CC'* capital in manufactures, leaving *LL''* free to operate the additional
capital *MM'*.

It follows from the foregoing argument that capital accumulation will reduce agricultural production and increase manufacturing production at constant terms of trade. Capital accumulation in the manufacturing country will
therefore have an ultra-pro-trade-biased production effect; whereas capital
accumulation in the agricultural country will have an ultra-anti-trade-biased
production effect. Conversely, population growth will reduce manufacturing
output and increase agricultural output; thus the production effect of population growth will be ultra-anti-trade-biased in the manufacturing country
and ultra-pro-trade-biased in the agricultural country.

It also follows from the previous argument that, at constant terms of trade
(and so long as the country remains incompletely specialized), all of the increase in output goes as income to the factor which is accumulating. On our
assumption of differing marginal and average propensities to consume the
goods, capital accumulation will increase the average proportion of income
spent on manufactures, and population growth will increase the average
proportion of income spent on food. Hence, the consumption effect of capital
accumulation will be anti-trade-biased in the manufacturing country and pro-
trade-biased in the agricultural country, while the consumption effect of
population growth will be the reverse in the two countries. As explained
earlier, an ultra-anti-trade-biased production effect will dominate the consumption effect while an ultra-pro-trade-biased production effect will rule
out an ultra-anti-trade-biased total effect. Hence, capital accumulation in the
agricultural country and population growth in the manufacturing country will
be ultra-anti-trade-biased, while the opposite type of factor accumulation in
each country may be anything from ultra-pro-trade-biased to anti-trade-
biased, but will not be ultra-anti-trade-biased.

Let us now turn to the effects of technical progress. This is a complex
problem, because such progress may not only go on at different rates as between industries, but may also affect factors of production differentially in
the industry in which it occurs, as well as in the economy as a whole. A technique for dealing with biased technical progress, which permits the whole
problem to be dealt with in a relatively simple fashion, has only recently been
published by two young American economists.[4] The following argument
employs a somewhat modified version of their technique. As before, we begin
with the production effect.

---

[4]R. Findlay and H. Grubert, "Factor Intensity, Technological Progress, and the
Terms of Trade," *Oxford Economic Papers*, N. S., II, No. 1 (February, 1959), pp. 111–
121.

Let us begin with the simplest case of technical progress, "neutral" technical progress, defined as progress which reduces the quantities of the two factors required to produce a given quantity of output in the same proportion. Neutral technical progress has the initial effect of increasing the output of the industry in which it occurs, and lowering its cost of production at the initial factor prices. We are interested in the effect on production at constant relative prices and costs of the goods. In order to restore the initial relative prices, factors must shift from the other industry into this one: as they do so, the price of the factor used relatively intensively in this industry rises, and the price of the factor used relatively intensively in the other industry falls, so altering the relative costs of the goods and restoring the initial price ratio. Thus, neutral technical progress in an industry leads to expansion of the output of that industry at the expense of the other, at given terms of trade; in other words, neutral progress is ultra-biased. It follows that neutral progress in manufacturing has an ultra-pro-trade-biased production effect in the manufacturing country, and an ultra-anti-trade-biased production effect in the agricultural country; while the effects of neutral progress in agriculture are exactly the reverse.

Now consider technical progress which is biased, in the sense that it alters the optimum ratio of one factor to the other employed at the initial factor prices in the industry in which progress occurs. Such progress may be described as saving the factor whose optimum ratio to the other is reduced.[5] Biased progress has a dual initial effect: it lowers the cost of production in the industry, and it releases a quantity of the factor it saves. Its effects are therefore the same as those of a neutral technical change,[6] combined with an increase in the supply of the factor which is saved by the biased progress.

Again we are interested in the effect on production at constant commodity prices. As in the case of neutral technical progress, the reduction in cost requires a shift of factors into the industry where the progress has occurred. As in the case of factor accumulation, the factor released by progress must be absorbed by an expansion of production of the good which uses the factor relatively intensively, at the expense of production of the other good.

It follows that if technical progress saves the factor which is used relatively intensively in the industry where the progress occurs, both factors operate in the same direction, and the production effect will be even more ultra-biased than if progress were neutral. But if progress saves the factor used relatively intensively in the other industry, the two effects — cost-reducing and factor-saving — work in opposite directions, and the production effect may vary

---

[5]The bias is defined in terms of the effect of progress on the optimum factor ratio, rather than in terms of the relative reductions in quantities of factors required per unit of output, because progress may increase the quantity of one factor required per unit of output.

[6]Neutral technical progress (increased output in the industry) if the cost-saving effect outweighs the bias effect so that less of both factors is required per unit of output than before, neutral technical regress (reduced output in the industry) if more of the other factor is required per unit of output than before.

from one to the other extreme of ultra-bias, depending on the balance of cost-reducing and factor-saving effects.

The argument can be illustrated by reference to Figure 26-11, which is reproduced (with emendations) from Findlay and Grubert. Capital is measured on the vertical axis, labour on the horizontal. The country's factor-endowment ratio is OR. The line through P_m and P_f represents the pre-progress factor price ratio, tangent to a manufacturing production indifference curve at P_m and an agricultural production indifference curve at P_f, these curves representing quantities of equal cost and value at the initial price ratio. OP_m and OP_f are the optimum factor-ratios in the two industries; and the allocation of production between the industries must be such that the two ratios, each weighted by the proportion of the labour force in the industry where the ratio is used, average out to the endowment ratio OR.

This diagram, incidentally, can be used to establish the Rybczynski theorem. Suppose that capital is accumulated, increasing the endowment ratio to OR'; for OP_m and OP_f to average out to the higher level OR', the weight of OP_m must increase and that of OP_f decrease. That is, a larger proportion of the unchanged labour force must be employed in the capital-intensive manufacturing

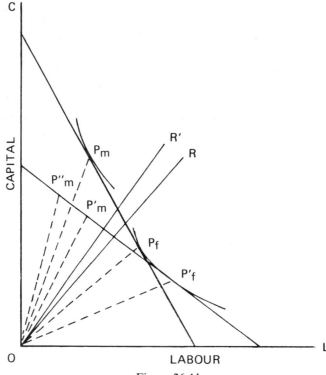

Figure 26-11

industry, and a smaller amount of labour in the labour-intensive food industry. Since capital/labour ratios are constant, production must vary with the amount of labour employed, falling in the labour-intensive industry.

To return to the effects of technical progress, suppose that there is technical progress in manufacturing, which shifts the production indifference curve for manufactures towards the origin O. At the initial factor prices, the cost of the quantity of manufactures represented by this indifference curve would now be less than the cost of the quantity of foodstuffs represented by the (unchanged) production indifference curve for agriculture. To keep the costs of the quantities of the goods equal, and so maintain the initial price ratio, factor prices must alter in favour of capital and against labour, to the factor-price ratio given by the new common tangent to the two production indifference curves, $P'_m P'_f$. As factor prices alter, labour will be substituted for capital in both industries.

The new capital/labour ratio in foodstuffs OP'_f is necessarily lower than the original one, owing to the substitution of cheaper labour for more expensive capital. If progress in manufacturing is capital-saving, neutral, or only slightly labour-saving, the capital/labour ratio in manufactures will also be lower than originally, as illustrated by P'_m. With a lower equilibrium capital/labour ratio in both industries, resources must have shifted out of the labour-intensive industry (foodstuffs) into the capital-intensive industry (manufactures) to maintain the overall average endowment ratio OR. Thus, progress of these types in manufacturing will be ultra-biased towards production of manufactures.

But if progress is sufficiently strongly labour-saving to offset the substitution effect of cheaper labour, the new capital/labour ratio in manufactures will be higher than the original. And with a higher capital/labour ratio in the one industry and a lower ratio in the other, the overall endowment ratio might have been maintained by a shift of resources in either direction (and to any extent) between the industries. Thus, in this case the effect of technical progress in manufacturing may lie anywhere between the extremes of ultra-bias towards production of manufactures, and ultra-bias towards production of foodstuffs.

What about the consumption effect of technical progress? The restoration of the initial relative cost ratio involves lowering the relative price of the factor used less intensively in the industry where progress has occurred, and raising the price of the other. Thus, more than the whole of the increase in national income due to progress goes to that factor which is used intensively in the industry in which the progress has occurred. In consequence, the proportion of expenditure out of national income on the good for which this factor's average and marginal propensity to consume is relatively high rises. It is even possible that total expenditure on the good preferred by the factor from which income is redistributed will fall; it will do so if the reduction in consumption due to straight income redistribution exceeds the increase in consumption due to the net increase in national income which accrues to the favoured factor. But it seems permissible to exclude this possibility of ultra-biased consumption effects through income-redistribution as an exceptional one. On this basis, it follows that progress in manufacturing, which reduces the income of labour and the proportional demand for food, will have an anti-trade-biased consumption effect in the manufacturing country and a pro-trade-biased consumption effect in the agricultural country; while the consumption effects of progress in agriculture will be the reverse.

Remembering that cases of ultra-anti-trade-biased and ultra-pro-trade-biased consumption effects have been excluded by assumption, the conclusions about the total effects of technical progress to which the foregoing analysis leads can be summarized as follows.

(A.) The following types of progress will be ultra-anti-trade-biased:
    (1.) Neutral technical progress in agriculture in the manufacturing country;
    (2.) neutral technical progress in manufacturing in the agricultural country;
    (3.) capital-saving technical progress in manufacturing in the agricultural country;
    (4.) labour-saving technical progress in agriculture in the manufacturing country.

(B.) The following types of progress will be ultra-pro-trade-biased to anti-trade-biased, but not ultra-anti-trade-biased:
    (1.) Neutral technical progress in manufacturing in the manufacturing country;
    (2.) neutral technical progress in agriculture in the agricultural country;
    (3.) capital-saving technical progress in manufacturing in the manufacturing country;
    (4.) labour-saving technical progress in agriculture in the agricultural country.

(C.) The following types of progress can be biased in any way whatever from ultra-pro-trade-biased to ultra-anti-trade-biased:
    (1.) capital-saving technical progress in agriculture in either country;
    (2.) labour-saving technical progress in manufacturing in either country.

In brief, progress which is neutral or saves the factor used relatively intensively in the industry in which it occurs will be ultra-anti-trade-biased if it occurs in a country's import-competing industry, and ultra-pro-trade-biased to anti-trade-biased but *not* ultra-anti-trade-biased if it occurs in a country's export industry; progress which saves the factor used relatively intensively in the other industry than that in which the progress occurs may have any effect whatsoever.

The production, consumption, and total effects of growth of the various types analyzed in the argument so far on the growing country's demand for imports and supply of exports are summarized in the accompanying Table 26-1. The results in many cases are rather indefinite. It should perhaps be

Table 26-1

The Effects of Economic Growth

Type of Growth	Manufacturing Country			Agricultural Country		
	Production Effect	Consumption Effect	Total Effect	Production Effect	Consumption Effect	Total Effect
Capital accumulation	UP	A	UP to A	UA	P	UA
Population Growth	UA	P	UA	UP	A	UP to A
Neutral technical progress						
(a.) manufacturing	UP	A	UP to A	UA	P	UA
(b.) agriculture	UA	P	UA	UP	A	UP to A
Capital-saving technical progress						
(a.) manufacturing	UP	A	UP to A	UA	P	UA
(b.) agriculture	UA to UP	P	UA to UP	UP to UA	A	UP to UA
Labour-saving technical progress						
(a.) manufacturing	UP to UA	A	UP to UA	UA to UP	P	UA to UP
(b.) agriculture	UA	P	UA	UP	A	UP to A

A: anti-trade-biased
P: pro-trade-biased
UA: ultra-anti-trade-biased
UP: ultra-pro-trade-biased

remarked that the chief reason why this is so lies in our original assumption that each factor prefers to consume the product in which it is employed intensively so that progress in that product, by redistributing income towards that factor, increases the relative demand for the product. If each factor preferred the product in which it was used less intensively, the consumption and production effects of progress would work in the same direction in many cases, giving unambiguous results. This may be confirmed by scrutiny of the summary Table 26-1: if factors' preferences for goods were the opposite of those assumed, the effects of growth of the types discussed would be *either* ultra-anti-trade-biased, *or* pro-trade-biased to ultra-pro-trade-biased, except in cases of capital-saving progress in agriculture and labour-saving progress in manufactures.

There are two further possible results of technical progress, suggested by Figure 26-11, which should be mentioned, though it does not seem worth while to develop them in full. The first is that technical progress in one industry may reduce costs there so much that the country specializes completely on that product. In Figure 26-11, the production indifference curve shifts so far towards the origin that either no common tangent exists, or the common tangent implies factor ratios inconsistent with the endowment ratio and nonnegative production. This case is simply the extreme example of an ultra-biased production effect.

The second possibility arises when progress is so saving of the factor used intensively in the industry in which it occurs as to make the optimum ratio of that factor to the other at the initial factor prices lower than the endowment ratio in both industries. In this case, the saved factor cannot be absorbed (at the initial factor price ratio) by a shift of factors between industries; its relative price must fall, so that the consumption effect of progress is biased against the industry in which it occurs. The production effect of this kind of progress will entail complete specialization on the good in which progress occurs, at the initial commodity prices, provided that it can be assumed that with the original technology, the relative factor-intensities of the two industries would be the same at any factor price ratio. This assumption ensures that, as the price of the saved factor falls, the relative cost of producing the product in which progress has occurred, using the pre-progress technique, will fall, Thus, it will never pay to produce the other product.[7] But since the

---

[7]If factor-intensities with the old technique can reverse as the price of the saved factor falls, it is possible for there to exist a common tangent to the new production indifference curve for the industry where progress has occurred and the production indifference curve for the other industry such that (a.) the optimum factor ratios lie on opposite sides of the endowment ratio, (b.) the cost of production with the new technique is lower than with the old, in the industry where progress has occurred. In this case the country remains incompletely specialized at the initial commodity prices, this being made possible by a reversal of relative factor intensities in the two industries; the production effect here may be anywhere between the extremes of bias. The writer is indebted to Messr. Findlay and Grubert for pointing out in correspondence the importance of condition (b.), and so permitting the correction of an error in the original formulation of the argument.

reduction in the price of the saved factor will reduce the cost of producing this product with the old technique more than it will reduce the cost of producing it with the new technique, it is possible that, before the optimum factor-intensity with the new technique is raised to the endowment ratio, the old and new techniques become cost-indifferent. In this case, specialization will be accompanied by the use of that mixture of old and new techniques which demands factors in the average proportion of the country's endowment ratio.

The next step is to analyze the effect of growth in the two countries together, that is, of the growth of the world economy. If growth of the same type is going on in the two countries, conclusions about the movement of the terms of trade between them (i.e. between manufactures and food) can be drawn directly from the Table in many cases. For example, capital accumulation and neutral or capital-saving technical progress in manufactures turn the terms of trade in favour of the agricultural country, population growth and neutral or labour-saving technical progress in food turns the terms of trade in favour of the manufacturing country. But capital-saving progress in agriculture and labour-saving progress in manufactures may turn the terms of trade either way.

In the general case, with population increasing, capital accumulating, and technical progress being applied in both countries, the movement of the terms of trade will depend on the bias and the rate of growth in each country. This dependence can be expressed in the following formula:

$$R_{pm} = \frac{\varepsilon_a R_a - \varepsilon_m R_m}{\eta_a + \eta_m - 1},$$

where R_{pm} is the rate of increase (decrease if negative) of the relative price of manufactures, R_a is the rate of growth of output in the agricultural country and ε_a its output-elasticity of demand for imports, R_m and ε_m are the rate of growth and output-elasticity of demand for imports of the manufacturing country, η_a and η_m are the two countries' price-elasticities of demand for imports, and $\eta_a + \eta_m - 1$ is the "elasticity factor" which determines the proportion of the initial value of trade by which a country's trade balance would improve if the price of its export good fell. The sense of the formula is that $\varepsilon_a R_a$ and $\varepsilon_m R_m$ are the rates of increase in the countries' demands for each other's goods; if these are unequal, equilibrium must be maintained by a relative price change whose magnitude will vary inversely with the elasticity factor.

Consideration of the effects of growth on the terms of trade suggests a concept of "balanced growth" — growth of the two countries at rates which keep the terms of trade between them constant. Balance in this sense requires $\varepsilon_a R_a = \varepsilon_m R_m$; obviously, it is impossible if the output-elasticities of demand have opposite signs, the growth of one country being ultra-anti-trade-biased. In any case, the concept is of very limited usefulness, since "balance" does not imply equal rates of growth of total output, let alone output per head. All that is implied by growth not being "balanced" in this sense is that one of the countries is gaining not only by the growth of its own output but by an improvement in its own terms of trade, while the benefit the other derives from the growth of its output is reduced by a worsening of its terms of trade; it is even possible, as has been shown earlier, for a country to be worse off as the result of growth. If complete specialization is assumed, so that bias depends on consumption only, "balanced growth" implies slower growth in the agricultural country unless growth is due to population increase.

In conclusion, some remarks on the extension of the analysis beyond the confines of the two-country two-good two-factor model seem called for. In the first place, recognition of a third factor, land, used predominantly in agriculture, introduces the classical problem of diminishing returns. If returns diminish strongly enough, the conclusions concerning the effects of population growth may be reversed — if there is no outlet on the land, the growing population may be forced into manufacturing. Second, allowance for a multiplicity of products introduces a variety of complications: rising income may lead to demands for foreign products formerly considered not worth their cost as compared with domestic substitutes; technical progress may be random, leading to sudden reversals of comparative advantage — for example, giving a capital-rich country a comparative advantage in producing a formerly labour-intensive product; and capital accumulation or population increase may alter a country's comparative advantage in particular goods — so that, for example, it may shift from labour-intensive to capital-intensive products in both manufacturing and agriculture. Thirdly, recognition of intermediate products which may be traded, and of the network of intersectoral transactions, greatly complicates the simple connection assumed in the foregoing between domestic demand for and supply of final goods, and the volume of international trade. Fourthly, allowing for the presence of many countries means that the movement of the terms of trade between manufactures and agricultural products depends on the nature and rate of growth in all countries together. One consequence of this is as follows: in the two-country model, "general" growth of one country will tend to increase its demand for imports, so that if the other country does not grow or grows only slowly it will benefit from a favourable movement of its terms of trade; but if there are two groups of countries, the effect of world growth on a particular country depends not only on the relative rates of growth of the two groups, but also on its individual rate of growth as compared with the growth rates of others in its group. A country may lose by a low rate of growth because the rapid growth of others in its group turns the terms of trade against it.

Questions for discussion and analysis pertaining to this article may be found at the end of Article 27.

Bibliography

[1] Akerman, Johan. "The Problem of International Balance in Progressive Economies." *Economia Internazionale*, IV, No. 2 (March, 1951).

[2] Asimakopulos, A. "A Note on Productivity Changes and the Terms of Trade." *Oxford Economic Papers*, N.S., IX, No. 2 (June, 1957).

[3] Aubrey, H. G. "The Long-Term Future of United States Imports and Its Implications for Primary Producing Countries." *American Economic Review*, XLV, No. 2 (May, 1955).

[4] Baldwin, R. E. "Patterns of Development in Newly Settled Regions." *Manchester School of Economic and Social Studies*, XXIV, No. 2 (May, 1956).

[5] Balogh, T. "Static Models and Current Problems in International Economics." *Oxford Economic Papers*, N.S., I, No. 2 (June, 1949).

[6] ———. *The Dollar Crisis: Causes and Cure.* Oxford: Blackwell, 1949.

[7] ———. "The Dollar Crisis Revisited." *Oxford Economic Papers*, VI, No. 3 (September, 1954).

[8] ———. "Progrès Technique et Bien-Être Internationale." *Économie Appliquée*, VII, No. 4 (October-December, 1954).

[9] ———. "Factor Intensities of American Foreign Trade and Technical Progress." *Review of Economics and Statistics*, XXXVII, No. 4 (November, 1955).

[10] Bensusan-Butt, D. M. "A Model of Trade and Accumulation." *American Economic Review*, XLIV, No. 4 (September, 1954).

[11] Bernstein, E. M. "American Productivity and the Dollar Payments Problem." *Review of Economics and Statistics*, XXXVII, No. 2 (May, 1955).

[12] Bhagwati, J. "Immiserizing Growth: A Geometric Note." *Review of Economic Studies*, XXV(3), No. 68 (June, 1958).

[13] ———. "International Trade and Economic Expansion." *American Economic Review*, XLVIII, No. 5 (December, 1958).

[14] ———. "Growth, Terms of Trade and Comparative Advantage." *Economia Internazionale*, XII, No. 3 (August, 1959).

[15] Black, J. "Economic Expansion and International Trade: A Marshallian Approach." *Review of Economic Studies*, XXIII(3), No. 62 (June, 1956).

[16] Black, J. and P. Streeten. "The Balance and Terms of Trade and Economic Growth." *Économie Appliquée*, X, No. 2 (April, 1957).

[17] ———."Appendix: A Mathematical Note on the Growth of a Two-Sector Economy." *Oxford Economic Papers*, N.S., IX, No. 3 (October, 1957).

[18] Brems, H. "The Foreign Trade Accelerator and the International Transmission of Growth." *Econometrica*, 24, No. 3 (July, 1956).

[19] Bruton, H. J. "Productivity, the Trade Balance and the Terms of Trade." *Economia Internazionale*, VIII, No. 3 (August, 1955).

[20] Caves, Richard. *Trade and Economic Structure.* Cambridge, Massachusetts: Harvard University Press, 1960. Especially Chapters V, VI, IX.

[21] Chenery, Hollis. "Patterns of Industrial Growth." *American Economic Review,* L, No. 4 (September, 1960).

[22] _____. "Comparative Advantage and Development Policy." *American Economic Review,* LI, No. 1 (March, 1961).

[23] Clark, Colin. "The Fruits of Economic Progress." *Economia Internazionale,* I, No. 1 (January, 1948).

[24] Corden, W. M. "Economic Expansion and International Trade: A Geometric Approach." *Oxford Economic Papers,* N.S., VIII, No. 2 (September, 1956).

[25] Croome, Honour. "The Dollar Siege." *Lloyds Bank Review,* N.S., No. 17 (July, 1950).

[26] Devons, E. "Statistics on United Kingdom Terms of Trade." *Manchester School of Economic and Social Studies,* XXII, No. 3 (September, 1954).

[27] Findlay, R. and H. Grubert. "Factor Intensities, Technological Progress, and the Terms of Trade." *Oxford Economic Papers,* N.S., XI, No. 1 (February, 1959).

[28] Gottlieb, M. "Optimum Population, Foreign Trade, and the World Economy." *Population Studies,* III, No. 2 (September, 1949).

[29] Haberler, G. "Dollar Shortage." In *Foreign Economic Policy for the United States,* edited by S. E. Harris.

[30] _____. *International Trade and Economic Development.* Cairo: National Bank of Egypt, 1959.

[31] Henderson, P. D. "Retrospect and Prospect: The Economic Survey 1954." *Bulletin of the Oxford University Institute of Statistics,* XVI, No. 3 (June, 1954).

[32] _____. "Some Comments." *Bulletin of the Oxford University Institute of Statistics,* XVII, No. 1 (February, 1955).

[33] Heuss, E. "Foreign Trade Between Countries with Different Rates of Growth of Productivity." *Aussenwirtschaft,* XI, No. 4 (December, 1956).

[34] Hicks, J. R. "An Inaugural Lecture: The Long-Run Dollar Problem." *Oxford Economic Papers.* N.S., V, No. 2 (June, 1953), reprinted in J. R. Hicks. *Essays in World Economics.* Fairlawn: Oxford University Press, 1959.

[35] _____. "A Further Note on Import Bias." In *Essays in World Economics.* Fairlawn: Oxford University Press, 1959.

[36] Johnson, H. G. "Equilibrium Growth in an International Economy." *Canadian Journal of Economics and Political Science,* XIX, No. 4 (November, 1953).

[37] _____. "Increasing Productivity, Income-Price Trends and the Trade Balance." *Economic Journal,* LXIV, No. 255 (September, 1954).

[38] _____. "Economic Expansion and the Balance of Payments." *Bulletin of the Oxford University Institute of Statistics,* XVII, No. 1 (February, 1955).

[39] _____. "Economic Expansion and International Trade." *The Manchester School of Economic and Social Studies,* XXIII, No. 2 (May, 1955).

[40] _____. *International Trade and Economic Growth.* London: Allen and Unwin, 1958. Part II; this reproduces the 1953, 1954, and May 1955 articles, the last with revisions.

[41] _____. "Economic Development and International Trade." *Pakistan Economic Journal,* IX, No. 4 (December, 1959).

[42] Kemp, M. C. "Technological Change, the Terms of Trade and Welfare." *Economic Journal,* LXV, No. 259 (September, 1955).

[43] Kindleberger, C. P. "Anciens et Noveaux Produits dans le Commerce International." *Économie Appliquee,* VII, (July-September, 1954).

[44] _____. *The Dollar Shortage.* Cambridge, Massachusetts, and New York: Technology Press of Massachusetts Institute of Technology, 1951 and New York: Wiley, 1951.

[45] _____. "The Terms of Trade and Economic Development." *Review of Economics and Statistics,* XL, No. 1, Part 2, Supplement (February, 1958). With comments by H. W. Singer and G. M. Meier.

[46] Kurihara, K. K. "The International Compatibility of Growth and Trade." *Economia Internazionale,* XIII, No. 3 (August, 1960).

[47] Laursen, S. "Productivity, Wages and the Balance of Payments." *Review of Economics and Statistics,* XXXVII, No. 2 (May, 1955).

[48] Letiche, J. M. "Differential Rates of Productivity Growth and International Imbalance." *Quarterly Journal of Economics.* LXIX, No. 3 (August, 1955).

[49] _____. *Balance of Payments and Economic Growth.* New York: Harper and Brothers, 1959, Part II.

[50] Lewis, W. A. "World Production, Prices and Trade, 1870-1960." *Manchester School of Economic and Social Studies,* XX, No. 2 (May, 1952).

[51] _____. "Economic Development with Unlimited Supplies of Labour." *Manchester School of Economic and Social Studies,* XXII, No. 2 (May, 1959).

[52] _____. "Unlimited Labour: Further Notes." *Manchester School of Economic and Social Studies,* XXVI, No. 1 (January, 1958).

[53] MacDougall, G. D. A. "A Lecture on the Dollar Problem." *Economica,* XXI, No. 83 (August, 1954).

[54] _____. *The World Dollar Problem.* London: Macmillan, 1957. Especially Chapters III-VI, Appendices VI — A, B and C.

[55] Machlup, F. "Dollar Shortage and Disparities in the Growth of Productivity." *Scottish Journal of Political Economy,* 1, No. 3 (October, 1954).

[56] Marris, R. L. "The Methodology of Long-Term Economic Policy Analysis." *Bulletin of the Oxford University Institute of Statistics,* XVII, No. 1 (February, 1955).

[57] Martin, K. "The Terms of Trade of Selected Countries, 1870-1938." *Bulletin of the Oxford University Institute of Statistics,* X, No. 11 (November, 1948).

[58] _____. "Capital Movements, The Terms of Trade and the Balance of

Payments." *Bulletin of the Oxford University of Statistics,* XI, No. 11 (November, 1949).

[59] Meade, J. E. *The Theory of International Economic Policy, Volume I: The Balance of Payments.* London: Oxford University Press, 1951. Especially pp. 45–7, 82–4, 114–15.

[60] _____ *The Theory of International Economic Policy, Volume I: The Balance of Payments. Mathematical Supplement.* London: Oxford University Press, 1951. Especially Chapter VIII.

[61] _____ *The Theory of International Economic Policy, Volume II: Trade and Welfare.* London: Oxford University Press, 1955. Especially Part III, Appendix 8.

[62] _____ *The Theory of International Economic Policy, Volume II: Trade and Welfare. Mathematical Supplement.* London: Oxford University Press, 1955. Especially Chapter XIX.

[63] Mehta, F. A. "Changes in the Terms of Trade as an Income Factor in World Trade, 1929–1938." *Indian Economic Review,* III, No. 3 (February, 1957).

[64] _____ "The Effects of Adverse Income Terms of Trade on the Secular Growth of Underdeveloped Countries." *Indian Economic Journal,* IV, No. 3 (July, 1956).

[65] Meier, G. M. "A Note on the Theory of Comparative Costs and Long Period Developments." *Economia Internazionale,* V, No. 3 (August, 1952).

[66] Mishan, E. J. "The Long-Run Dollar Problem: A Comment." *Oxford Economic Papers,* N.S., VII, No. 2 (June, 1955).

[67] Myint, Hla. "The Gains from Trade and the Backward Countries." *Review of Economic Studies,* XXII(3), No. 59 (June, 1955).

[68] _____ "The 'Classical Theory' of International Trade and Underdeveloped Countries." *Economic Journal,* LXVIII, No. 270 (June, 1958).

[69] North, D. C. "Location Theory and Regional Economic Growth." *Journal of Political Economy,* LXIII, No. 3 (June, 1955).

[70] Nurkse, R. "A New Look at the Dollar Problem and the United States Balance of Payments." *Economia Internazionale,* VII, No. 1 (February, 1954).

[71] _____ "Internal Growth and External Solvency." *Bulletin of the Oxford University Institute of Statistics,* XVII, No. 1 (February, 1955).

[72] _____ "Relation Between Home Investment and External Balance in the Light of British Experience 1945–55." *Review of Economics and Statistics,* XXXVIII, No. 2 (May, 1956).

[73] _____ *Patterns of Trade and Development.* Stockholm: University of Stockholm Press, 1959.

[74] Pigou, A. C. "Long-Run Adjustments in the Balance of Trade." *Economica,* XX, No. 79 (August, 1953).

[75] Prebisch, R. "Commercial Policy in the Underdeveloped Countries." *American Economic Review,* XLIX, No. 2 (May, 1959).

[76] Ramaswami, V. K. "The Effects of Accumulation on the Terms of Trade." *Economic Journal,* LXX, No. 279 (September, 1960).

[77] Rostow, W. W. "The Terms of Trade in Theory and Practice. *Economic History Review,* Second Series, III, No. 1 (1950).

[78] Rybczynski, T. M. "Factor Endowment and Relative Commodity Prices." *Economica,* XXII, N. S. No. 88 (November, 1955).

[79] Sargent, J. R. "Productivity and the Balance of Payments: A Three-Country View." *Bulletin of the Oxford University Institute of Statistics,* XVII, No. 1 (February, 1955).

[80] Savosnick, K. M. "The Box Diagram and the Production Possibility Curve." *Ekonomisk Tidsskrift,* LX, No. 3 (September, 1958).

[81] Seton, F. "Productivity, Trade Balance and International Structure." *Economic Journal,* LXVI, No. 264 (December, 1956).

[82] Singer, Hans W. "The Distribution of Gains Between Investing and Borrowing Countries." *American Economic Review, Papers and Proceedings,* XL, No. 2 (May, 1950).

[83] Streeten, P. "Productivity Growth and the Balance of Trade." *Bulletin of the Oxford University Institute of Statistics,* XVII, No. 1 (February, 1955).

[84] Tatemoto, M. "Productivity Growth and Trade Balance." *Osaka Economic Papers,* VI, No. 1 (September, 1957).

[85] Tinbergen, J. "The Influence of Productivity on Economic Welfare." *Economic Journal,* LXII, No. 245 (March, 1952).

[86] Triantis, S. G. "Economic Progress, Occupational Redistribution and International Terms of Trade." *Economic Journal,* LXIII, No. 251 (September, 1953).

[87] United Nations (Raul Prebisch). *The Economic Development of Latin America and its Principal Problems.* Lake Success: United Nations, 1950.

[88] Verdoorn, P. J. "Complementarity and Long-Range Projections." *Econometrica,* XXIV, No. 4 (October, 1956).

[89] Viner, J. *International Trade and Economic Development.* Oxford: Clarendon Press, 1953.

[90] ———— "Stability and Progress: The Poorer Countries' Problem." In *Stability and Progress in the World Economy,* edited by D. Hague. London: Macmillan, 1958.

[91] Williams, J. H. *Economic Stability in the Modern World.* The Stamp Memorial Lecture, University of London: 1952.

Melville Watkins†

27. A STAPLE THEORY OF ECONOMIC GROWTH*

The staple approach to the study of economic history is primarily a Canadian innovation; indeed, it is Canada's most distinctive contribution to political economy. It is undeveloped in any explicit form in most countries where the export sector of the economy is or was dominant.[1] The specific terminology — staple or staples approach, or theory, or thesis — is Canadian, and the persistence with which the theory has been applied by Canadian social scientists and historians is unique.

The leading innovator was the late Harold Innis in his brilliant pioneering historical studies, notably the cod fisheries and the fur trade,[2] others tilled the same vineyard[3] but it is his work that has stamped the "school." His concern was with the general impact on the economy and society of staple production. His method was to cast the net widely. The staple approach became a unifying theme of diffuse application rather than an analytic tool

†Melville H. Watkins, Professor of Political Economy, University of Toronto. Financial assistance for the summer of 1961 is gratefully acknowledged from the Ford Foundation. For helpful comments on earlier drafts of this paper, the author is indebted to J. H. Dales, W. T. Easterbrook, J. I. McDonald, A. Rotstein, and S. G. Triantis of the University of Toronto, and C. P. Kindleberger of the Massachusetts Institute of Technology.

*From *The Canadian Journal of Economics and Political Science*, Vol. XXIX (May, 1963), pp. 141–158. Reprinted by permission of the author and the publisher.

[1]The American economic historian, Guy S. Callender, however, devoted considerable attention to the importance of international and interregional trade in staples in the United States, an aspect of American growth which has been much neglected but has recently been revived by Douglass C. North. See Callender, *Selections from the Economic History of the United States, 1765-1860* (Boston: 1909), and North, *The Economic Growth of the United States, 1790-1860* (Englewood Cliffs, N.J.: 1961).

[2]See his *The Fur Trade in Canada: An Introduction to Canadian Economic History* (2d ed., Toronto: 1956); *The Cod Fisheries: The History of an International Economy* (2d ed., Toronto; 1954). For a collection of his writings in the Canadian field, see *Essays in Canadian Economic History* (Toronto: 1957). For a complete bibliography of his writings, see Jane Ward, *Canadian Journal of Economics and Political Science*, (May, 1953), pp. 236–244.

[3]W. A. Mackintosh is sometimes given credit as a co-founder of the staple theory; see his "Economic Factors in Canadian History," *Canadian Historical Review*, IV (March, 1923), pp. 12–25, and "Some Aspects of a Pioneer Economy," *Canadian Journal of Economics and Political Science*, II (November, 1936), p. 457–463.

fashioned for specific users. There was little attempt to limit its application by the use of an explicit framework.[4] Methodologically, Innis' staple approach was more technological history writ large than a theory of economic growth in the conventional sense.[5]

Once solidly entrenched in Canadian studies, the staple approach has now fallen on more uncertain days as its relevance has come to be questioned by Canadian economic historians.[6] The strongest attack has come from Kenneth Buckley who maintains that it is "practical and efficacious" as a theory of economic growth to 1820, but that thereafter "other sources of national economic growth and change" are impossible to ignore; he concludes that Canadian economic historians should "replace the notion of an opportunity structure determined by geography and natural resources with a general concept of economic opportunity without specifying determinants."[7] Vernon C. Fowke's emphasis on agriculture serving the domestic market as an impetus to investment and hence to economic growth in central Canada prior to Confederation involves a devaluation of the role of staple exports.[8] W. T. Easterbrook has argued, after extensive review of the literature, that the staple theory no longer constitutes — and apparently ought not to — an adequate unifying theme for the study of Canadian development.[9] On the other hand, Hugh G. J. Aitken has remained satisfied with the approach. His own recent writings have been focused on the new resource industries of the twentieth century;[10] in commenting on Buckley's paper he suggested that the staple approach was relevant at least to 1914,[11] and he has subsequently maintained that "it is still true that the pace of development in Canada is determined fundamentally by the exports that enable Canada to pay its way in the world."[12]

---

[4]This point has often been noted; see, for example, Richard E. Caves and Richard H. Holton, *The Canadian Economy: Prospect and Retrospect* (Cambridge, Mass.: 1959), p. 30; and W. T. Easterbrook, "Problems in the Relationship of Communication and Economic History," *Journal of Economic History*, XX (December, 1960), p. 563.

[5]Kenneth Buckley makes this point strongly; see his "The Role of Staple Industries in Canada's Economic Development," *Journal of Economic History*, XVIII (December, 1958), p. 442.

[6]For its use in communications study — where, following the later Innis, the media became the resource or staple — see Marshall McLuhan, "Effects of the Improvements of Communication Media," *Journal of Economic History*, XX (December, 1960), pp. 566–575; and the *Gutenberg Galaxy* (Toronto: 1962), particularly pp. 164–166.

[7]"The Role of Staple Industries," pp. 444, 445.

[8]Vernon C. Fowke, *The National Policy and the Wheat Economy* (Toronto: 1957), Chap. 2.

[9]W. T. Easterbrook, "Trends in Canadian Economic Thought," *South Atlantic Quarterly*, LVIII (Winter, 1959), pp. 91–107; and "Recent Contributions to Economic History: Canada," *Journal of Economic History*, XIX (March, 1959), pp. 76–102.

[10]Hugh G. J. Aitken, "The Changing Structure of the Canadian Economy" in Aitken *et. al., The American Economic Impact on Canada* (Durham, N.C., 1959), and *American Capital and Canadian Resources* (Cambridge, Mass.: 1961).

[11]"Discussion," *Journal of Economic History*, XVIII (December, 1958), p. 451.

[12]*American Capital and Canadian Resources*, p. 74.

The sample is small, but so too is the number of practicing Canadian economic historians. There would appear to be declining confidence in the relevance of the staple approach, especially if consideration is given to what has been said as well as what has been written. But, curiously, the decline has been paralleled by rising interest among non-Canadians who may or may not refer to Innis and Canada. The leading advocate of the staple approach today is Douglass C. North, whose work may well have set the stage for a reconsideration of the causes of American economic growth from the American Revolution to the Civil War.[13] Two American economists, Richard E. Caves and Richard H. Holton, have critically re-examined the staple approach from the viewpoint of modern economic theory as a prelude to forecasting the state of the Canadian economy in 1970, and have given it a surprisingly clean bill of health.[14] R. E. Baldwin has provided a brilliant theoretical article on the impact of staple production on an economy, and both North and Caves and Holton have acknowledged their indebtedness to him.[15] Mention must also be made of the analytical approach used by Jonathan V. Levin in his study of the role of primary product exports in Peru and Burma,[16] of the implications for the staple approach of the application of modern income and growth theory to the classic problem of the transfer mechanism for capital imports in the Canadian balance of payments, particularly in the great boom before the First World War,[17] and of the distinction made by Harvey S. Perloff and Lowdon Wingo, Jr., between "good" and "bad" resource exports in the context of American regional growth.[18]

The simultaneous waning of the reputation of the staple approach among Canadians and its rise elsewhere has created a gap in the literature which this paper will attempt to bridge. It will argue that the staple theory can fruitfully

[13]Douglas C. North, "Location Theory and Regional Economic Growth," *Journal of Political Economy*, LXII (June, 1955), pp. 243–258: "International Capital Flows and the Development of the American West," *Journal of Economic History*, XVI (December, 1956), pp. 493–505; "A Note on Professor Rostow's 'Take-off' into Self-sustained Growth," *Manchester School of Economic and Social Studies*, XXVI (January, 1958), pp. 68–75; "Agriculture and Regional Economic Growth," *Journal of Farm Economics*, XLI (December, 1959), pp. 943–951; *The Economic Growth of the United States, 1970–1860.*

[14]Richard C. Caves and Richard H. Holton, *The Canadian Economy*, Part I.

[15]R. E. Baldwin, "Patterns of Development in Newly Settled Regions," *Manchester School of Economic and Social Studies*, XXIV (May, 1956), pp. 161–179.

[16]Jonathan V. Levin, *The Export Economies: Their Pattern of Development in Historical Perspective* (Cambridge, Mass.: 1960).

[17]G. M. Meier, "Economic Development and the Transfer Mechanism: Canada, 1895–1913," *Canadian Journal of Economics and Political Science,* XIX, (February, 1953), pp. 1–19; J. C. Ingram, "Growth and Canada's Balance of Payments," *American Economic Review,* XLVII (March, 1957), pp. 93–104; John A. Stovel, *Canada in the World Economy* (Cambridge, Mass.: 1959).

[18]Harvey S. Perloff and Lowdon Wingo Jr., "Natural Resource Endowment and Regional Economic Growth" in Joseph J. Spengler, editor, *Natural Resources and Economic Growth* (Washington: 1961), pp. 191–212; this article draws on Harvey S. Perloff, Edgar S. Dunn Jr., Eric E. Lampard, and Richard F. Muth, *Regions, Resources and Economic Growth* (Baltimore: 1960).

be limited to a distinct type of economic growth; restate a staple theory so constrainted in more rigorous form, primarily by drawing on the literature cited in the paragraph above; contrast this staple theory with other models of economic development; and finally, consider again the relevance of a staple approach to the Canadian case.

I

The linking of economic history and the theory of economic growth is a prerequisite to further advance in both fields. One obvious link lies in the development of theories appropriate to particular types of economic growth. The staple theory is presented here not as a general theory of economic growth, nor even a general theory about the growth of export-oriented economies, but rather as applicable to the atypical case of the new country.

The phenomenon of the new country, of the "empty" land or region overrun by the white man in the past four centuries, is, of course, well known. The leading examples are the United States and the British dominions. These countries had two distinctive characteristics as they began their economic growth: a favourable man/land ratio and an absence of inhibiting traditions.[19] From these initial features flow some highly probable consequences for the growth process, at least in the early phase: staple exports are the leading sector, setting the pace for economic growth and leaving their peculiar imprint on economy and society; the importation of scarce factors of production is essential; and growth, if it is to be sustained, requires an ability to shift resources that may be hindered by excessive reliance on exports in general, and, in particular, on a small number of staple exports. These conditions and consequences are not customarily identified with underdeveloped countries, and hence are not the typical building blocks of a theory of economic growth. Rather, the theory derived from them is limited, but consciously so in order to cast light on a special type of economic growth. Because of the key role of staple exports it can be called a staple theory of economic growth.

II

The fundamental assumption of the staple theory is that staple exports are the leading sector of the economy and set the pace for economic growth. The limited — at first possibly non-existent — domestic market, and the factor proportions — an abundance of land relative to labour and capital — create a comparative advantage in resource-intensive exports, or staples. Economic development will be a process of diversification around an export base. The central concept of a staple theory, therefore, is the spread effects of the export

---

[19]Both features are recognized by W. W. Rostow in *The United States in the World Arena* (New York: 1960), p. 6; the first is also cited by Bert F. Hoselitz, "Patterns of Economic Growth," *Canadian Journal of Economics and Political Science*, XXI (November, 1955), pp. 416–431.

sector, that is, the impact of export activity on domestic economy and society. To construct a staple theory, then, it is necessary to classify these spread effects and indicate their determinants.

Let us begin with the determinants. Assume to be given the resource base of the new country and the rest-of-the-world environment — the international demand for and supply of goods and factors, the international transportation and communication networks, the international power structure. The sole remaining determinant can then be isolated, namely, the character of the particular staple or staples being exported.

A focus on the character of the staple distinguished Innis' work. C. R. Fay expressed the point most succinctly: ". . . the emphasis is on the commodity itself: its significance for policy; the tying in of one activity with another; the way in which a basic commodity sets the general pace, creates new activities and is itself strengthened or perhaps dethroned, by its own creation."[20] The essence of the technique has been thrown into sharp relief by Baldwin. Using the method of ideal types, he contrasts the implications of reliance on a plantation crop and a family farm crop respectively for the economic development of an area exporting primary products. The important determinant is the technology of the industry, that is, the production function, which defines the degree of factor substitutability and the nature of returns to scale. With the production function specified and the necessary *ceteris paribus* assumptions — including the demand for goods and the supply of factors — a number of things follow: demand for factors; demand for intermediate inputs; possibility of further processing; and the distribution of income.

These determine the range of investment opportunities in domestic markets, or the extent of diversification around the export base. If the demand for the export staple increases, the quantity supplied by the new country will increase. This export expansion means a rise in income in the export sector. The spending of this income generates investment opportunities in other sectors, both at home and abroad. By classifying these income flows, we can state the staple theory in the form of a disaggregated multiplier-accelerator mechanism. In Hirschman's terms, the inducement to domestic investment resulting from the increased activity of the export sector can be broken down into three linkage effects: backward linkage, forward linkage, and what we shall call final demand linkage.[21] The staple theory then becomes a theory of capital formation; the suggestion has been made but not yet elaborated that it is such.

Backward linkage is a measure of the inducement· to invest in the home-production of inputs, including capital goods, for the expanding export sector. The export good's production function and the relative prices of inputs will determine the types and quantities of inputs required. Diversification will be

---

[20]C. R. Fay, "The Toronto School of Economic History," *Economic History*, III (January, 1934), pp. 168–171. See also W. T. Easterbrook, "Problems in the Relationship of Communication and Economic History," p. 563.

[21]Albert O. Hirschman, *The Strategy of Economic Development* (New Haven: 1958), Chap. 6.

the greatest where the input requirements involve resources and technologies which permit of home-production. The emphasis usually placed in studies of economic development on barriers to entry into machinery production suggests a high import content for capital-intensive staples, and hence a small backward linkage effect. Caves and Holton, however, emphasize the importance of capital-intensive agriculture in supplying linkage to domestic agricultural machinery production. Theory and history suggest that the most important example of backward linkage is the building of transport systems for collection of the staple, for that can have further and powerful spread effects.

Forward linkage is a measure of the inducement to invest in industries using the output of the export industry as an input. The most obvious, and typically most important, example is the increasing value added in the export sector; the economic possibilities of further processing and the nature of foreign tariffs will be the prime determinants.

Final demand linkage is a measure of the inducement to invest in domestic industries producing consumer goods for factors in the export sector. Its prime determinant is the size of the domestic market, which is in turn dependent on the level of income — aggregate and average — and its distribution.

The size of the aggregate income will vary directly with the absolute size of the export sector. But a portion of the income may be received by what Levin has called "foreign factors" — factors which remit their income abroad — rather than "domestic factors." To the extent that income received by foreign factors is not taxed away domestically, final demand linkage will be lessened. The servicing of capital imports is a case in point. Primary producers are notoriously susceptible to indebtedness, and the burden will be greater the more capital-intensive the staple. Leakage can also result from wages paid to migratory labour and from immigrants' remittances.

The average level of income, that is, the *per capita* income of the domestic factors, depends on the productivity of "land" or the resource content of the staple export, for other factors are importable. The distribution of income, on present assumptions, is determined by the nature of the production function of the staple, in Baldwin's models being relatively unequal for the plantation crop and relatively equal for the family farm crop.

The impact of these two market dimensions on final demand linkage can be seen by classifying consumer spending in two ways. First, consumer spending may be either on home-produced goods or on imports, and the higher the marginal propensity to import the lower the final demand linkage. Secondly, it may be either on subsistence goods and luxuries, or on a broad range of goods and services; the latter are more likely to lend themselves to those economies of mass production which lie at the heart of on-going industrialization, while luxury spending — other than for labour-intensive services — is likely, given the tendency to ape the tastes of more advanced countries, to be directed towards imported goods, that is, to create in Levin's terminology "luxury importers."

Final demand linkage will tend to be higher, the higher the average level of income and the more equal its distribution. At a higher level of income, consumers are likely to be able to buy a range of goods and services which lend themselves to domestic production by advanced industrial techniques. Where the distribution is relatively unequal, the demand will be for subsistence goods at the lower end of the income scales and for luxuries at the upper end. The more equal the distribution the less likelihood of opulent luxury importers and greater the likelihood of a broadly based market for mass-produced goods.

The discussion of the linkages so far has assumed that investment is induced solely by demand factors. But on the supply side the expansion of the export sector creates opportunities for domestic investment which may or may not be exploited. Consideration must be given to the relationship between staple production and the supply of entrepreneurship and complementary inputs, including technology.

The key factor is entrepreneurship, the ability to perceive and exploit market opportunities. Entrepreneurial functions can be fulfilled by foreigners, and to the extent that this makes available technical and marketing skills the result can be advantageous to the new country. But the literature on economic development, and particularly on the dual economy, raises many doubts as to the adequacy of foreign entrepreneurship. It may flow freely into the export and import trades, but fail to exploit domestic opportunities. Exports may be regarded as safer, in part because they earn directly the foreign exchange necessary to reimburse foreign factors, but largely because export markets are better organized and better known than domestic markets. Foreign domination of entrepreneurship may militate against its general diffusion.

An adequate supply of domestic entrepreneurship, both private and governmental, is crucial. Its existence depends on the institutions and values of society, about which the economist generalizes at his peril. But the character of the staple is clearly relevant. Consider, for example, Baldwin's polar cases. In the plantation case, the dominant group with its rentier mentality on the one hand, and the mass of slaves who are prevented from bettering themselves on the other, can produce a set of institutions as inimical to entrepreneurial activity as is to be found in any tradition-ridden society. Business pursuits may be castigated as "money grubbing"; education — which, as North has emphasized, is very important — is likely to be confined to the élite and to slight the development of technical and business skills; political activity tends to be devoted to the defense of the *status quo*. On the other hand, in the family-farm case, as in wheat areas, the more equal distribution of income can result in attitudes towards social mobility, business activities, education, and the role of government which are more favourable to diversified domestic growth. These are gross differences; the more subtle ones could be worked out for specific staples.

Even where domestic entrepreneurship is forthcoming, its effectiveness rests on the availability of labour and capital, both foreign and domestic. The "push" from the old countries has in the past created a highly elastic supply of labour, although not, as the slave trade attests, without some resort to the use of force. But the individual receiving country has to create conditions sufficiently favourable to the inflow of labour to compete with other receiving countries. The original staple may create a social structure which is unattractive to the immigrant with skills suitable for the development of domestic economic activity. Where the staple is land-intensive, as is fur, the staple producers may find it in their own self-interest to discourage immigration and settlement. The transport technologies associated with particular staples provide varying passenger fares and hence differential stimuli to immigration. The availability of labour domestically will depend on the competing attractions of staple production and the quality of the labour force that has resulted from the exploitation of the particular staple. The staple activity may attract excess labour through non-pecuniary advantages: the romantic life of the fur trader and the aristocratic life of the planter are frequently alleged to have had detrimental consequences for other sectors of the economy. The quality of the labour force is significantly related to education.

Foreign capital, both in substance and in preference for foreign trade over domestic industry, is difficult to distinguish from foreign entrepreneurship, which we have already discussed. The availability of capital domestically will depend on the extent of domestic saving and the biases of the savers in placing their funds. The amount of saving will be determined by the production function for the staple. For example, Baldwin argues that savings will be higher with the skewed income distribution of the plantation crop than with the equal distribution of the family-farm crop. This would be the conventional view, although the opposite would be true if it were assumed that saving was encouraged by greater investment opportunities at home or discouraged by a greater concern with consumption for status in a more hierarchical society. But the amount of saving may not matter greatly. For domestic savers, like foreign capitalists, may be biased against domestic activities; they may prefer to expand the export industry further or to invest in the import trade. They may also prefer to invest abroad, for in an open economy capital can flow out as well as in. It is only when there are abundant opportunities in domestic markets waiting to be exploited that the amount of domestic saving will significantly determine the rate of investment.

The technology applied in domestic sectors is likely, to the extent that it is up to date, to be substantially borrowed from abroad. The newness of the country will minimize the difficulties of adapting borrowed technology and create a potential minimum growth rate not significantly lower than that achieved by advanced economies. The inflow of foreign technology will be facilitated by the inflow of foreign entrepreneurship and capital. To the extent that innovation is necessary and possible in the export sector, confidence may be gained by domestic entrepreneurs which will facilitate creative responses in domestic sectors. As domestic entrepreneurship emerges, innovations should become more appropriate to domestic factor proportions and the requirements of the domestic market.

A historically relevant theory must allow not only for the differing character of particular staples but also for the impact of the resource base of the new country and the international environment. For any particular new country the initial conditions can vary, and these conditions can change over time, both autonomously and as a result of the actions of the new country consequent on its success in exploiting its particular staple or staples.

Although these points are important, it is difficult to say much in general about them. For any given inducement to invest offered by the market, an appropriate resource base is necessary; the best of all possible staples will do little to encourage development if the resource base is sufficiently bad, and the impact of a particular staples can vary widely depending on the resource base of the particular country.[22] The resource base itself can change through discovery, and success in staple production, at least for some staples, may expedite the process.[23]

So too the international environment can vary in its suitability for the development of new countries. Staple producers begin as colonial outposts of old countries and differences among the latter, in their markets for staples, their supplies of factors for export, their institutions and values, and their colonial policies, will affect growth prospects. Change can take place in any of these dimensions: in foreign demand and foreign supply, which can destroy old staples and create new ones; in transport facilities, which can cheapen internationally traded goods; in the "push" of factors from the old countries and the "pull" from other new countries; in colonial policy and in the frequency of wars which can either encourage or discourage growth. And the new country, to the extent that it is successful, may gain power to mould the environment to suit its needs. It can develop a transport system adequate for both domestic and export requirements; it can pursue a commercial policy by which it can cause further processing of its exports and promote import-competing industry without unduly interfering with the optimal allocation of its resources.

What is the likely growth path of a staple economy? Growth is initiated by an increase in demand for a staple export. If the spread effects are potent, as the export sector grows so too will the domestic sectors. The result will be increasing demand for factors. Domestic slack, if it exists at all, will be quickly absorbed, and the continuation of growth will depend on the ability to import scarce factors. If the supply of the foreign factors is elastic, the customary

---

[22]North's book is weakened by his failure adequately to appreciate the importance of the resource base. He applies Baldwin's polar cases to the American South and West in the period prior to the Civil War, but has very probably exaggerated their efficacy in explaining rates and types of development by understating differences in the general resource base which favoured the West.

[23]Note the Canadian mineral discoveries consequent on railway building and hence linked ultimately to the development of the western wheat economy.

tendency for expansion of one sector — in this case exports — to affect domestic sectors adversely by driving up factor prices is mitigated. This explains the very strong booms that are a feature of growth in staple economies.[24]

But what of the nature of growth in the long run? In a staple economy, as in any other, sustained growth requires an ability to shift resources at the dictates of the market — what C. P. Kindleberger calls "a capacity to transform." Particular export lines can create prosperity, but typically only for a short time. Over the longer pull they cease to be profitable either because of diminishing returns on the supply side, or adverse shifts in demand consequent on competition from cheaper sources of supply or from synthetics, or because of the income-inelasticity of foreign demand, or simply because of changes of taste. This tendency can be slowed up by attempts to improve marketing and by seeking out cost-reducing innovations. The possibility of the latter depends on the character of the staple; for example, because of the physical properties of the plants, cotton production was historically much more resistant to mechanization than wheat-growing. But the law of diminishing returns cannot be checked indefinitely. Sustained growth, then, requires resource flexibility and innovation sufficient to permit shifts into new export lines or into production for the domestic market.

The probability of long-run success for the staple economy is significantly increased by its two distinctive initial features: a favourable man/land ratio and an absence of inhibiting traditions. The first implies a relatively high standard of living which facilitates expanding domestic markets and substantial factor mobility. The fact that new countries do not start their development with population pressing against scarce resources gives them an enormous advantage over the typical underdeveloped country. Especially, they have neither a large subsistence agricultural sector severely limiting markets for domestic industry, nor a pool of cheap labour permitting industrialization to proceed with only limited impact on the incomes of much of the population. Subsequent population growth, in part by immigration, means that the size of population is closely related to economic opportunity at a relatively high standard of living. The second feature, the lack of traditions, means that institutions and values must be formed anew, and although there will be a substantial carry-over from the old world, the process will be selective and those transferred are likely to take a form more favourable to economic growth.

These are substantial advantages, and go far to explain the extraordinary success of some new countries. But even for the staple economy, historians have insisted that the process of growth is not without pitfalls. It is frequently alleged, at least implicitly, that the achievement of a higher level of national

---

[24]On external diseconomies generated by an expanding sector when factor supplies are inelastic, see Marcus Fleming, "External Economies and the Doctrine of Balanced Growth," *Economic Journal*, LXV (June, 1955), pp. 241-256. On the character of export-led booms in Canada, see the literature cited in footnote 17.

income masks deficiencies in the structural balance of an economy. W. W. Rostow charges that the high levels of welfare achieved in new countries by exploiting land and natural resources will delay their reaching the "take-off" stage.[25] If the concept of take-off is interpreted as meaning simply the growth and diversification of the manufacturing sector, this argument runs counter to the staple theory. Rostow's claim, however, is no more than an untested hypothesis. He has not outlined the specific mechanism by which primary exports delay industrialization. It is not clear that he is saying anything more than that if a country has a comparative advantage in primary exports it will perforce have a comparative disadvantage in manufactures. This static view communicates nothing about the process of growth in a world where factor supply can be highly elastic and the composition of imports can shift radically over time. The first peril, then, is illusory.[26]

A more real difficulty is that the staple exporters — specifically, those exercising political control — will develop an inhibiting "export mentality," resulting in an overconcentration of resources in the export sector and a reluctance to promote domestic development. Our previous comments on the social and political structure associated with particular staples are relevant here, but the literature on economic development in general is replete with other hypotheses and examples. Easterbrook, developing a theme of Innis', has commented that bureaucratic institutions concerned with "playing it safe" tend to emerge in the face of the initial uncertainties of a marginal status, and then to persist.[27] In the Cuban case, H. C. Wallich emphasizes the importance of the "sugar mentality" which "gives sugar an economic and political dominance even greater than its true weight in the economy."[28] H. W. Singer has pointed out that, when export earnings are high, the country is able to finance development but lacks the incentive to do so; when the earnings are low, the incentive exists but the means are lacking.[29] In Canada, there is evidence of a boom-and-bust psychology; excessive optimism causes booms to proceed beyond their proper limits,[30] while depressions are met by resort to tariffs which are "second best" in the short run and probably inappropriate in the long run and which persist once introduced.[31] One is led

---

[25]W. W. Rostow, *The Stages of Economic Growth* (Cambridge: 1960), p. 36.

[26]North, after appeal to the American case, reaches a similar conclusion.

[27]See his "The Climate of Enterprise," *American Economic Review*, XXXIX (May, 1949), pp. 322–335; "Uncertainty and Economic Change," *Journal of Economic History*, XIV (Autumn, 1954), pp. 346–360; "Long Period Comparative Study: Some Historical Cases," *Journal of Economic History*, XVII (December, 1957), pp. 571–595.

[28]Henry C. Wallich, *Monetary Problems of an Export Economy* (Cambridge, Mass.: 1960), p. 12.

[29]H. W. Singer, "The Distribution of Gains between Investing and Borrowing Countries," *American Economic Review*, XL (May, 1950), p. 482.

[30]The classic example is the building of two additional transcontinental railways during the wheat boom, 1896–1913. The general phenomenon is noted by A.F.W. Plumptre, "The Nature of Economic Development in the British Dominions," *Canadian Journal of Economics and Political Science*, III, (November, 1937), pp. 489–507.

[31]The high correlation between depressions and tariff increases is noted by (contd.)

to conclude that staple economies are often believed to be much more at the mercy of destiny than they actually are. As Levin has demonstrated in his study of Burma, planning can alter income flows, thereby strengthening linkages and increasing domestic investment.

The serious pitfall is that the economy may get caught in a "staple trap." Sustained growth requires the capacity to shift attention to new foreign or domestic markets. The former requires a favourable combination of external demand and available resources. The latter requires a population base and level of *per capita* income that permit taking advantage of the economies of scale in modern industrialism. Both require institutions and values consistent with transformation, and *that* requires the good fortune of having avoided specialization in the wrong kind of staple, such as Baldwin's plantation crop. If the staple is unfavourable or if stagnation persists for any extended period because of a weak resource base, the staple economy can take on the character of the traditional underdeveloped country in both respects stressed by Rostow. First, institutions and values can emerge which are inimical to sustained growth, and the process of remoulding will be difficult. Second, a population problem can be encountered as the population initially established through immigration continues to expand through natural increase. Persistent unemployment and underemployment will become characteristic of the economy. Immigration may be replaced by emigration, as resort is had to the Irish solution. In the absence of alternative opportunities, factors will tend to accumulate excessively in the export sector or in subsistence agriculture. In the former case, growth may become "immiserized" as the terms of trade turn against the country.[32] In the latter, the economy will face a problem common to most underdeveloped countries: development will depend on the interdependent growth of agriculture and industry. In any event, the initial opportunities for easy growth will no longer exist.

If the pitfalls are avoided — if the staple or staples generate strong linkage effects which are adequately exploited — then eventually the economy will grow and diversify to the point where the appelation "staple economy" will no longer suffice. Population growth will come to result more from natural increase than from immigration. *Per capita* income will rise beyond the level consistent with any customary definition of underdevelopment. With the gaining of entrepreneurial confidence and the expanding opportunities of domestic markets, domestic entrepreneurs will persistently usurp markets from foreign suppliers.[33] A well-developed secondary manufacturing sector serving domestic markets and possibly even foreign markets will emerge.

J. H. Young, *Canadian Commercial Policy*. Study done for the Royal Commission on Canada's Economic Prospects (Ottawa: 1957).

[32]For a formal presentation of the theory of immiserizing growth, see J. Bhagwati, "Immiserizing Growth: A Geometric Note," *Review of Economic Studies*, XXV (June, 1958), pp. 201–205, and "International Trade and Economic Expansion," *American Economic Review*, XLVIII (December, 1958), pp. 941–953.

[33]This mechanism has recently been emphasized by Hirschman, *The Strategy of Economic Development*, 120 ff.

Staple exports and imports of manufactured goods may fall as a percent of national income. If "land" remains relatively abundant, this may not happen; that should not be taken as proof of backwardness, however, for it may be no more than the momentary outcome of the operation of the law of comparative advantage.

III

We have taken pains throughout to emphasize the special character of the staple theory. Consideration of the range of relationships possible between foreign trade and economic development will underline the point. In a recent synthesis of the literature, Kindleberger has put forth three models relating foreign trade and economic development; these cover cases where foreign trade is respectively, a leading, a lagging, and a balancing sector of the economy.[34] In the model in which it leads, autonomous foreign demand, typically accompanied by technological change in the developing country, sets the pace, and economic development is a process of diversification around an export base. The staple economy is clearly a special case of this model.

In the model in which foreign trade lags, domestic investment leads, tending to create pressure on the balance of payments which is met by import-substitution. A large number of underdeveloped countries believe that this is the relevant model. The restrictive nature of the commercial policy of developed countries, combined with the tendency for import demand to expand more rapidly than income in the early stages of development — chiefly because of the need to import capital goods and possibly also industrial raw materials and food — lend credence to this belief. The contrast between the leading and lagging models is that between development based on trade-expansion and development based on trade-contraction.

The model in which foreign trade is the balancing sector covers the case of trade-expansion which is not demand-led, but rather based on autonomous supply pushes in the export sector. It applies to the case where domestic investment leads, creating balance of payments difficulties which are met by pushing exports rather than by limiting imports. A trade pattern based on exporting manufactures, in order to import food and take the strain off domestic agriculture, has been espoused by both W. Arthur Lewis and the late Ragnar Nurkse, and is a particular version of the balancing case.[35]

Kindleberger's classification applies to countries already in the process of development. The limitations of the staple theory emerge most clearly when we consider the case where export production is superimposed on a pre-existing subsistence economy. For the staple economy, the export sector can

---

[34]C. P. Kindleberger, *Economic Development* (New York, Toronto, London: 1958), Chap. 14.

[35]W. Arthur Lewis, *The Theory of Economic Growth* (Homewood, Ill.: 1955); Ragnar Nurkse, *Patterns of Trade and Development*, Wicksell Lectures, 1959 (Stockholm: 1959).

be an engine of growth; for the subsistence economy, the consensus appears to be that the export sector will have either limited or adverse effects on the economy. The linkage effects are likely to be slight, regardless of the character of the export good, because of the internal structure of the underdeveloped country, including the existence of non-competing groups in the domestic and foreign sectors.[36] Even where groups are competing, if there is disguised unemployment in the subsistence sector, increases in productivity in the export industry will not bring increases in real wages; these depend on raising productivity in the subsistence sector and to this exports make little or no contribution.[37] The country might have been better off it if had never exported in the first place. Growth may have become immiserized, as was previously noted. Domestic factors may have been drawn into export production when they could have been more productively applied to domestic manufacture.[38] Investments made complementary to the export sector may generate pecuniary external economies which excessively encourage primary export production.[39] Imports which flood in as a result of exporting may destroy existing handicraft production, and if the export sector does not absorb the labour which is displaced, the gains from trade may be negative.[40] If exports and domestic investment compete for available saving, then a rise in the export volume can directly reduce the rate of growth of income.[41]

IV

The closeness of the link between the staple approach and Canadian historical research makes it unlikely that the application of a more explicit theory will add much to our understanding of Canadian economic development. Nevertheless, a few comments are in order, both to clear up some specific ambiguities and to resolve the issue of the relevance of the staple theory to Canada's economic development, past and present.

(1.) The cod fisheries and the fur trade were clearly the leading sectors of the early period. Neither staple required much permanent settlement, although as the fur trade came to rely less on the Indian and penetrated further west and as the cod fisheries shifted from the green cure to the dry cure — an example of forward linkage — the impetus to settlement increased. In New

---

[36]H. Myint, "The Gains from International Trade and the Backward Countries," *Review of Economic Studies,* XXII (1954–55), pp. 129–142.

[37]W. Arthur Lewis, "Economic Development with Unlimited Supplies of Labour," *Manchester School,* XXII (May, 1954), pp. 139–141.

[38]Singer, "The Distribution of Gains."

[39]Lewis, *The Theory of Economic Growth,* p. 348.

[40]G. Haberler provides a geometric demonstration of a case where free trade is harmful, given rigid factor prices. "Some Problems in the Pure Theory of International Trade," *Economic Journal,* LX (June, 1950), pp. 223–240. The argument is extended in Steffan Burenstam Linder, *An Essay on Trade and Transformation* (New York, Stockholm: 1961), Chap. 2.

[41]R. J. Ball, "Capital Imports and Economic Development: Paradoxy or Orthodoxy," *Kyklos,* XV (1962), fasc. 3, pp. 610–623.

France the distribution of income consequent on the fur trade may have been such as to lower final demand linkage — although it would hardly bear comparison with that resulting from a plantation crop — and the aristocracy may have been as much feudal as *bourgeois* in its attitudes, although the drive of men such as Jean Talon should not be forgotten. But neither the character of the staple nor the Frenchness of the colony explain the slow growth relative to the American colonies. Rather, what is fundamental was poor location compared with New England for supplying the West Indies market. This limited the diversity of exports and thus retarded the development of commercial agriculture, lumbering, and above all the carrying trade and shipbuilding which were then the keys to development. A small population base, established more for reasons of imperial design than of economics *per se*, grew rapidly by natural increase. In the face of limited economic opportunities, labour accumulated in subsistence agriculture and New France came to approximate a dual economy, with a compact agricultural community of *habitants* and the moving frontier of the fur traders, which had only limited contacts one with another.[42] By the time of the Conquest the colony had clearly taken on some of the coloration of an "old" society and was partly ensnared in the staple trap.

In the Atlantic colonies, New England's success in developing an aggressive commercial economy around the fisheries shows that the character of cod as a staple can hardly explain the slow growth of Nova Scotia and Newfoundland. Rather, proximity to the markets of the West Indies and southern mainland colonies and, to a lesser extent, good agricultural land and the possibility of a winter fishery, were the prerequisites that were lacking. The effects of a poor location and a weak resource base — the latter being particularly applicable to Newfoundland — were intensified by the frequency of imperial conflict and the commercial and military aggressiveness of New England. The result militated against either England or France taking the effort that was necessary to create an environment favourable to further development. The area was not so much trapped as buffeted about and ignored.

Absence of economic opportunity because of geographic factors was the crucial constraint on both continental and maritime developments. Innis' method has obscured this point and has led to exaggerated emphasis on the character of the staples, particularly of fur. But if the nature of the staples is insufficient to explain the absence of rapid growth, lack of diversified development imprints more clearly the character of those staples around which some success is found and increases the probability that their peculiar biases will persist in institutions and values. Thus, with fur came the life of the *habitant* and the vision of a centralized transcontinental economy; with cod, parochialism and a commitment to the sea.

---

[42]Dietrich Gerhard, "The Frontier in Comparative View," *Comparative Studies in History and Society,* I (March, 1959), pp. 205–229.

(2.) Fowke has argued that commercial agriculture in Upper Canada rose above the subsistence level prior to the 1840's in the absence of substantial external demand. Although allowance must be made for "shanty demand" linked to timber exports, the point is conceded, and with it the implication that some growth is possible without exports as the leading sector. But the quality of the growth that took place was unimpressive. The census of 1851 shows industrial development to be confined to flourmills and sawmills, both of which were on an export basis, and to the small-scale production of the simpler types of manufacture for the local market.[43] The population and income levels that had been attained were not sufficient to sustain a large or technologically sophisticated manufacturing sector. Buckley rightly insists that the economy became more complex after 1820 and that the range of economic opportunity widened, but this does not mean that staple exports ceased to be of critical importance.

(3.) One of Buckley's criticisms of the staple approach is its tendency "to ignore any section once the staple which created or supported it is no longer expanding," and he cites as an example the slighting of Quebec's economic development since the decline of the fur trade.[44] His point has some validity, at least so far as Quebec is concerned, but the neglect is not inherent in a properly stated staple theory of economic growth. As the new country (or region) ages, whether it be successful or unsuccessful, it takes on the character of an old country and becomes amenable to analysis as such. In Quebec in the nineteenth century, it is clear that the expansion of timber and ships as staple exports, the entrepreneurial drive and accumulated capital of the English commerical class carried over from the fur trade, and emigration which relieved the pressure of population on scarce resources combined to lessen the probability that the region would become too deeply enmeshed in the staple trap. Nevertheless, it is the interrelationship between agriculture and industry in the context of a rapidly growing population that should be made the focus of study, as one would expect to be done for any presently underdeveloped country. Statistics on the relative rates of growth of Ontario and Quebec indicate, incidentally, that if one gives credence to the alleged anti-commercial attitudes of the French Canadian, then, given the less favourable man/land ratio Quebec inherited from New France, what needs to be explained is the remarkable success of Quebec.

(4.) The period of Canadian economic history on which most controversy has focused recently has been the "Great Depression" of 1873-96. So long as it could be properly regarded as a great depression, it was amenable to the staple approach. Its bad reputation was based on the slow growth of population and persistent emigration, and this could be linked to the failure of the western wheat economy to expand in a sustained fashion in the face of a trend

[43]O. J. Firestone, "Development of Canada's Economy, 1850–1890" in *Trends in the American Economy in the Nineteenth Century* (Princeton: 1960), pp. 217–252.

[44]Buckley, "The Role of Staple Industries," p. 447.

decline in the world price of wheat. The absence of rapid extensive growth made it possible for the period to be passed over quickly in the history books, and to be remembered more for the attempts that were made to promote development than for the actual growth achieved. Recent research, however, particularly the statistical work of Firestone, McDougall, Hartland, and Bertram,[45] makes it impossible to continue to regard these years as a great depression; they witnessed, in fact, an impressive increase in real *per capita* income, comparable to that in the United States, considerable industrial expansion, and substantial capital inflow.

The growth in real income can be attributed partly to the export sector. Exports did fall as a percentage of national income. Nevertheless, the real value of exports grew absolutely; there were important shifts in the composition of exports which generated new investment, from wood products to agriculture, and within the latter, from grain to animal products, with cattle and cheese emerging as the new staples; probably exports became more highly manufactured — the growth of cheese factories is striking — and more capital-intensive; railway building provided an important stimulus to growth and its *primum causum* was the expectation of large exports of western grain.

Exports, then, continued to play their conventional role as a leader sector. They can hardly be given full credit, however, for the increase in real income of this period. Factor increments shifted from export markets to domestic markets with a success inconsistent with a markedly backward economy. Yet the extent to which the adaption was made to a declining stimulus from the export sector should not be exaggerated. The decade rates of growth of manufacturing after 1870 are not comparable to those of the first decade of the twentieth century when exports were expanding rapidly, and at the end of the century Canadian industry was still backward relative to that of such countries as Britain, the United States, and Germany. There was substantial net emigration in every decade from 1861 to 1901. The Canadian economy was not growing fast enough to generate employment opportunities for increments to the labour force by natural increase; while this may be no cause for concern from an international perspective, contemporary political debate and newspaper comment leaves no doubt that Canadians regarded this steady outflow of population as evidence of an unsatisfactory performance by the economy.

(5.) A restatement of the staple theory might be expected to cast new light on the hoary issue of the long-run impact of the Canadian tariff. A conventional argument has been that the tariff permanently increases the population

---

[45]O. J. Firestone, *Canada's Economic Development, 1867–1953* (London: 1958), and "Development of Canada's Economy, 1850–1900"; Duncan M. McDougall, "Immigration into Canada, 1851–1920," *Canadian Journal of Economics and Political Science,* XXVII (May, 1961), pp. 162–175; Penelope Hartland, "Canadian Balance of Payments since 1868" in *Trends in the American Economy in the Nineteenth Century,* pp. 717–755; Gordon W. Bertram, "Historical Statistics on Growth and Structure of Manufacturing in Canada, 1870–1957," Canadian Political Science Association Conference on Statistics (June 10–11, 1952).

because export industries are less labour-intensive than import-competing industries.[46] Young would appear to have effectively disposed of this line of reasoning,[47] but there may be some validity to the population-sustaining argument for a tariff if one looks at its effect in a boom period, such as 1896 to 1913. It is clear that, by reducing the marginal propensity to import, the tariff increases employment in import-competing industries. At the same time, the fact that factors are in highly elastic supply limits the extent to which costs rise for the export industries, while the sheer strength of the boom, which is being further increased by investment in import-competing industries, keeps imports high in spite of the tariff, thus tending to eliminate foreign repercussion. The tariff would appear to increase employment opportunities, and thereby the population-sustaining capacity of the economy. If, as is probable, the infant industry argument is not valid, however, then the real income has been lowered. We return to the customary view that the Canadian tariff has increased population while lowering real income. But there is an important qualification, as a result of which population may not be increased in the long-run. The tariff will tend to strengthen a boom which is already excessive and thus to increase the problems of readjustment that have to be faced eventually. To the extent that these problems are not otherwise solved, emigration to the United States with its higher wages is likely to be greater than it would have been in the absence of the tariff.

(6.) The period 1896 to 1913 was undeniably an example of a classic staple boom. But the industrial development which was achieved in its wake so increased the complexity of the Canadian economy as to make it impossible to continue to use staple industries as the unifying theme of economic growth, or so the implicit reasoning seems to run in the best of the textbooks.[48] The notion of a discontinuity in Canadian economic development in the early twentieth century, though superficially attractive, is difficult to maintain, as Caves and Holton have demonstrated. The manufacturing sector appears to have been filling in slowly over a long period of time, without passing through any critical stage of economic maturity. Patterns of short-run change consistent with the staple theory are to be found in all three periods of rapid growth in this century, 1900–1913, 1920–1929, and 1946–1956: the rate of investment closely reflects the demand for exports, current and prospective; production for domestic markets expands around the export-base, replacing imports; excessive optimism leads to over-expansion in the export sector and complicates the subsequent problems of readjustment; and the quantity of saving adjusts itself to investment demand, in part by inducing capital imports.

[46]W. A. Macintosh, *The Economic Background of Dominion-Provincial Relations, A Study Prepared for the Royal Commission on Dominion-Provincial Relations* (Ottawa: 1939), p. 84ff.; and Clarence L. Barber, "Canadian Tariff Policy." *Canadian Journal of Economics and Political Science*, XXI (November, 1955), pp. 513–530.

[47]Young, *Canadian Commercial Policy*, p. 89.

[48]W. T. Easterbrook and H. G. J. Aitken, *Canadian Economic History* (Toronto: 1956).

Is the staple theory, then, relevant to Canada today, or has it been long irrelevant? Does the evidence adduced by Caves and Holton on the common character of growth patterns in the twentieth century, which could be extended to include the boom of the 1850's, reflect historical necessity or historical accident? Is Canada unable to grow at a satisfactory rate unless exports lead, or able to do so but relieved of the necessity until now by good luck? There is no doubt that luck is a neglected factor in Canadian economic history. Nevertheless, the fundamental fact is the pervasive interdependence with the North Atlantic community, and particularly with the United States. Canada is a small and open economy, a marginal area responding to the exogenous impact of the international economy. The basic determinants of Canadian growth are the volume and character of her staple exports and the ability to borrow, adapt, and marginally supplement foreign technology. These guarantee for Canada a minimum rate of growth that cannot diverge too widely from that achieved elsewhere, particularly in the United States. They create no assurance, however, of a rate of growth sufficient to maintain full employment, even if the expansion of the labour force be limited to natural increase. The probability that borrowed technology and staple exports will provide a sufficient impetus to the economy has diminished as staples have become more capital-intensive.

That expanding exports and satisfactory economic growth have been correlated in the past is clear. How this is interpreted depends on a judgment as to the freedom of action that Canada possesses. The emphasis increasingly placed by economists on the link between the inefficiency of Canadian secondary manufacturing industry and the Canadian tariff[49] suggests that the major difficulty is an inhibiting export mentality, the elimination of which lies within Canadian control. From this point of view, economic institutions and political values, an inefficient structure of industry combined with an unwillingness to do anything about it, have in the past prevented Canada from growing at a satisfactory rate in the absence of a strong lead from primary exports, but this need not be true for the indefinite future.

---

[49]See H. E. English, "The Role of International Trade in Canadian Economic Development since the 1920's," unpublished doctoral thesis, University of California, 1957; S. Stykolt and H. C. Eastman, "A Model for the Study of Protected Oligopolies," *Economic Journal,* LXX (June, 1960), pp. 336–347; Roger Dehem, "The Economics of Stunted Growth," *Canadian Journal of Economics and Political Science,* XXVIII (November, 1962), pp. 502–510.

Questions for Discussion and Analysis

Article 23

1. *The systems of taxation are apparently quite different in the developed and underdeveloped countries. Comment.*
2. *Would it be better in an underdeveloped country to levy a property tax on the value of the crop produced or on the value of the land? (Both of these methods are in current use.)*
3. *Marketing boards for commodities produced in a country are a source of revenue to the country. Do they serve any other purpose?*
4. *How does one compare the relative desirability of the systems of taxation currently in existence in two underdeveloped countries? How would you test to see which is the better system for possible implementation in a third country?*

Article 24

5. *The first step in defining an economic plan is defining the goals of the society and the economy. Comment.*
6. *Political machinations have been blamed for making poor utilization of the resources made available in planning. What better tools could be used than political ones in determining what projects should be undertaken?*
7. *Precisely how much power should the planning office have? At one extreme no one pays any attention to the office, and at the other it has life or death control over every activity in the economy!*
8. *Why is there "over-optimism" concerning the benefits of planning?*
9. *Could planning be harmful to an economy?*

Article 25

10. *State clearly and succinctly the Raul Prebisch argument for protection in developing countries. What, if any, parts of the "Prebisch thesis" do you disagree with? How does it differ from standard development and trade theory?*
11. *What is Prebisch's objection to devaluation? How can this objection be handled with orthodox theory?*
12. *According to Prebisch, what are the benefits of protectionism? How does Flanders counter these arguments? What is "counter-vailence"? How do price elasticity, income elasticity, and the terms of trade fit into the Prebisch thesis?*

Article 26

13. Describe in very general terms the effects of economic growth on a country's imports and exports.
14. How do pro-trade-biased growth, anti-trade-biased growth, and neutral (or unbiased) growth differ?
15. Discuss the "Rybczynski theorem."

Article 27

16. Watkins states that "the fundamental assumption of the staple theory is that staple exports are the leading sector for the economy and set the pace for economic growth." Are staple exports, then, a _necessary_ pre-condition for economic growth or merely a _sufficient_ pre-condition for growth?
17. If foreign entrepreneurship can be used to provide the necessary linkages to promote economic growth, why have so many countries expropriated foreign owned companies and replaced the foreign management with nationals?
18. What types of staple commodities would be ideal from the point of view of the supplying country, and what types of staples prove to be of minimal use in providing the requisites of development?
19. What is a "staple trap"? What countries are currently in such a trap, and how might they have avoided being caught?
20. What is the relationship between the staple theory and Rostow's first stage of development? Is there a relationship between the staple theory and the Take-Off?
21. Can the staple theory be viewed as a special case of the unbalanced approach to economic development, since the unbalanced approach to development requires focus on forward and backward linkages and this is the key to the staple theory of development.

Section VI

CONCLUSIONS

In the conclusion of a volume of selections on economic development, there are a number of possible courses of action. It is possible to select a few survey articles, showing the state of the art as of the moment in an effort to provide a comprehensive review for the reader. It is possible to provide a last dose of sage advice from some leading economists on the development process. Or it is possible to try to add a few more missing links to the understanding of the problems of development. The last course is the one chosen. Only two articles appear: the first, by Evsey Domar, among other things, looks at the role of the developed countries, particularly the United States, relative to the developing societies; the second, by Walter Johnson, concerns itself with something that is often ignored, the costs of economic development.

The direction to be given in developing an economy is the subject of Evsey Domar's short paper. He recommends that minimal disturbance be made to the private sector in the allocation of productive resources, and that any direction in the form of planning be "macro" rather than "micro" in its scope. He admits that profit maximization has its defects in planning for an economy, but points out that it is a very fine place from which to start, and that alternative allocations of resources can be judged by their impact on enterprise profits. He then points out that voices have been raised condemning the use of a capitalistic system in pursuing development. There is the complaint that capitalism thrives on personal greed (indeed, the invisible hand of the individual working to better his own position is the vehicle through which capitalism is supposed to work) and greed is not at all a noble thing. He asserts that greed is one personal attribute that the world has in abundance, whereas patriotism, love of motherhood, code heroism, and the like are always subject to shortage.

Domar's statement at the beginning of section IV that "economic change without political change is impossible . . ." may cause conservative economists to ask for definitions of terms in order that the revolutionary flavor may be removed from it, but Domar's point is that receptivity to political change may take place regardless, with rather disastrous results to policies which have been made in the expectation of the existing order's permanence.

Domar is talking about the role of the large, powerful, developed nations with regard to the less developed. His proposals for foreign aid, and military aid in particular, are based, of course, on the recent history of the United States.

And now, having spent many pages discussing the beauties of economic development and the benefits of development, some small time must be spent in looking at the costs of development. And Johnson does this in the final selection of this section.

"Increasing per capita income and providing economic security are desirable goals." This appears to be a reasonable statement, and almost all students of economics would agree that it was a true statement if it were reworded slightly: "Increasing per capita income and providing economic security, all else being equal, are desirable goals." The *costs* of economic development with a high rate of growth must be considered as well as the *benefits* that come from the development process. In asking the question "Is economic growth desirable?", we point out that there are real costs to increasing the rate of growth of income in a society.

The alternatives to economic growth considered in the United States are thought to be a higher level of employment, greater stability of the purchasing power of the currency, a more equitable distribution of income, and a better balance of the streams of international payments. Tradeoffs among these five goals of national economic policy can be and are specified, and a mixture of them is chosen. Economic growth *may* involve the sacrifice of some quantum of achievement in the four remaining areas. Bringing about the increase in real per capita income in the less developed countries also involves real cost.

W. L. Johnson also discusses a more subtle, less quantifiable set of costs, more closely identifiable with many non-Western societies and popularized in economics by W. A. Lewis. Johnson considers a catalogue of possible costs, including the decline of social bonds, the decline of religion and traditional values, and the decline of workmanship and crafts. Now, not all of the costs considered in this catalogue are real costs, and some of the evils which have been attributed to economic growth are not evils at all, according to Lewis, *et al.* But Johnson cautions that certainly the maximization of the rate of growth without cognizance of these factors can be costly. But all of this is simply a restatement of the old adage that too much virtue can easily result in the generation of a vice.

If this is the case and there are tradeoffs in which increased rates of economic growth can be generated through incursion of additional costs, then the matter is simply one of specifying the proper trade.

In concluding the short perusal of the literature that is available in a volume of this nature, the student could do very well to return and read the two selections in Section I again. Leibenstein's reminders as to the limitations of economic theory in the analysis of economic development and Bauer's plea for the interdisciplinary approach should now be more meaningful than upon the first reading. In addition, the "intellectually curious" reader is urged to sample some of the extensive suggested readings, by topic, in the Bibliography that follows the Appendix in this volume. Finally, to get some feel for the general orders of magnitude of the relevant social-economic data in developing countries, the reader is invited to scrutinize the Appendix.

Evsey Domar †

28. REFLECTIONS ON ECONOMIC DEVELOPMENT *

I have tried to analyze the friendship of my Friday Niters. I trace it back thirty years to the time when I came to Wisconsin and had given up my first ideas of teaching. I began simply to tell my classes personal stories of my mistakes, doubts and explorations, just as they happened to occur to me, injecting my generalizations, comparisons and all kinds of social philosophies . . .

John R. Commons, *Myself*

If the establishment of the John R. Commons Lecture is a new experiment for Omicron Delta Epsilon, so is its preparation for me. For these "Reflections" are not a research paper but a discourse. They contain no formulas, mathematical appendices, statistical tables, and footnotes, the indispensable props of my other efforts. I believe that it behooves an economist between ages of maturity and senility to engage in such a discourse occasionally, and Commons' words give me the courage to try. But they do not remove my fear that this discourse, like many such, will be trivial.

I

In a game of free associations among economists, the expression "economic development" is likely to be followed by "model" and "plan." A plan usually aims at maximizing the rate of growth of consumption or income either by solving an explicit system of equations (and inequalities), or by selecting a preliminary target rate and adjusting it by iteration. In either case, a so-called bill of final goods (or its equivalent) is customarily drawn up and is combined with a matrix of input coefficients to find the required inputs (labor, capital, materials, foreign exchange), and the resulting outputs. Soviet planners prefer to begin with a target list of several important outputs (like steel, fuel, power, etc.), rather than with that of final products, and even though their use of input-output techniques, at least until recent years, has been less

†Evsey D. Domar, Professor of Economics, Massachusetts Institute of Technology.
*From *The American Economist,* Vol. X (Spring, 1966), pp. 5–13. Reprinted by permission of the author and the publisher.

explicit and elegant than ours, the difference in approach, from the point of view of this lecture, has been slight.

Obviously, a reliable matrix of input coefficients is the heart of this planning process, and clearly the change in the coefficients, that is the saving on the various inputs over time, must constitute an important ingredient of growth. Since I have promised to avoid formulas, let me merely state that the average relative change in the coefficients named by Leontief the "Index of Structural Change," and similar to Solow's "Indes of Technical Change," and to Kendrick's "Index of Total Productivity," accounts for a large fraction of the rate of growth of income in advanced countries: some 40 or 50 percent of the total rate of growth, and perhaps some 70–80 percent of the rate of growth of income per capita. We know less about the behavior of such indexes in underdeveloped countries, but it stands to reason that a similar, though possibly less pronounced, phenomenon must exist there as well.

Now the remarkable fact is that the planner usually takes the changes in most input coefficients as given, that is as determined outside of the plan itself. This attitude is a tribute to his common sense: he knows that the planning organization can do little to achieve the proper reductions. The Russians have indeed tried, both by appeal to socialist patriotism and by direct command, to regulate thousands upon thousands of coefficients, which they call "norms," (of which an enterprise may have as many as five hundred). The truth is that Soviet planners (by their own admissions) simply do not know which norms should be reduced in what enterprise and by how much, and are loath to allow any increases, however necessary they may be. Their attempts to regulate norms from above have produced little more than straight jackets for their managers, who try to escape from them by misreporting and cheating. The French have done more explicit planning than other Western countries; but even they, to my knowledge, have not tried to prescribe specific norms to firms.

In contrast, most governments of advanced Western and of socialist countries have been quite successful (depending of course on your standards) in achieving a reasonable degree of macro-equilibrium. The Russians, for instance, have had no serious inflation since their monetary reforms of the late nineteen-forties, and mass unemployment has been unknown in the West for a quarter of a century.

This success in macro-planning, combined with the obvious inability of a government, even as strong and as dedicated to all kinds of planning as the Soviet, to enforce, and even to know, the correct micro-decisions, strongly suggests that at the present state of economic knowledge governments should concentrate their activities in the macro-sphere. And they should promulgate some general rules and incentives to insure that the correct micro-decisions are made, as they should be made, in a decentralized manner, on the spot, by those who have the necessary detailed information. There is no clear dividing line designating macro and micro-decisions; the existence of externalities, increasing returns, monopolies, large risks, and ignorance reduces the effectiveness of decentralized decisions and calls for government interference, particularly in underdeveloped countries where markets are small (see below) and many investment decisions have important external effects. I cannot suggest any simple general rules for the division of functions; much depends on the historical setting in particular countries and on the *relative* ability, efficiency and honesty of government functionaries. But I do suggest that a government begin its planning activities in the macro-area and move into the micro-area only if and when clearly necessary, with the burden of the proof for each such move being placed on the government.

It is this optimum and ever-shifting division between centralized and decentralized decision-making that is, in my opinion, the central economic problem of today, rather than the questions of private versus public ownership of the means of production. It was Oscar Lange who clearly perceived the problem in his classical essay on socialism, and not Karl Marx.

Following Lange, the managers of enterprises, private or public, should be instructed to select the least expensive method of production and to equate marginal cost with price (as a general rule subject to proper qualifications and exceptions). But I do not know of any practical way of enforcing this instruction except by ordering the managers to maximize profits, with prices set by the market under competitive conditions, and by the government or some other body under monopolistic ones. The maximization of profits, though under certain important restrictions, has now become the declared policy of the Soviet government.

I fully realize how abstract my simple suggestions are, and I do not imply that the quest for profits in the real world will indeed result in a Pareto optimum. There is no shortage of studies showing the limitations of this method of resource allocation, particularly in underdeveloped countries. It is only that I do not know of any better method for enforcing economic discipline and preventing wholesale waste. The future may present us with a wider choice.

Economic efficiency is served by the pursuit of profits no better than the acquisition of knowledge is by the pursuit of good grades. Neither method is esteemed by intellectuals. A student can get good grades by choosing easy courses, flattering teachers, and even by cheating on examinations. With a small highly motivated group of students better stimuli are available, as they are in the economic world. But what are we to do in the age of mass education and of mass production? Should we prescribe the Soviet-type norms to our students, that is the exact number of hours to be spent (by each student individually or by all?) on each subject, with their study hours policed by a horde of proctors, supervised in their turn by super-proctors? And what is to prevent a student from spending the prescribed number of hours looking into the assigned book and thinking of something else?

In the privacy of our faculty lounges we discount the significance of students' grades and stress instead their intelligence, imagination, creativeness, research ability, and other attributes not necessarily reflected in grades. But, if a student with a poor record is to claim these attributes, the burden of proof must be on him.

Similarly, planning agencies, investment banks, international lenders, and foreign donors will have plenty of opportunity, in the privacy of their well-appointed offices, to re-examine the submitted projects (particularly when externalities are involved or the price system is defective) and rank them not necessarily in order of the expected rate of profit; nor should a manager's performance be judged on that basis alone. But the burden of the justification for an unsatisfactory profit rate, actual or expected, should rest with enterprise managers and project sponsors.

So far I have tried to by-pass the question of private as against public ownership of the means of production, or of capitalism versus socialism, and concentrate instead on the making of economic decisions under either system. I have no general solution to this complex question independently of time or place. I wish (though I do not hope) that this question could be discussed with less passion, and that our government would not try to force capitalism on unwilling people, even though my own advice to the underdeveloped countries is to try capitalism first. Their governments are simply not yet ready to undertake the very complex and difficult task of managing their economies. Few governments are. Can you imagine the mismanagement, waste and corruption which would accompany an attempt by the government of my own Commonwealth of Massachusetts to take over its economy? A sharp movement toward socialism in an underdeveloped country invariably antagonizes and frequently destroys the class of capitalist owners and managers who are so scarce there to begin with; their replacement by socialist administrators is a slow and painful process involving much waste. And when all is said and done, it remains true, particularly in underdeveloped countries, that a capitalist owner has a stronger attachment to *his own* resources than a state-appointed official has for the *public* wealth. As President Johnson once remarked, "The best fertilizer for land is the footprint of its owner."

II

I have little hope that my advice to the underdeveloped countries — to experiment with an essentially market-oriented capitalist economy — will be welcome to most of their intellectuals and to many government officials. Since my advice is strikingly unoriginal and is likely to be joined by the majority of American economists, it is worth while inquiring into the reasons for its rejection. Let me list several.

(1.) The market mechanism strives to satisfy effective demand for goods and services which depends on the existing distribution of income and wealth.

Granted a lopsided distribution, which is true of many underdeveloped countries, how can one justify the resulting production and importation of luxuries (including sojourns in Miami and on the Riviera) for the few rather than food and shelter for the many? Of course, the distribution of wealth can and should be corrected by taxation, wider access to education, and other measures, but what underdeveloped government is strong enough to attack the holders of wealth? And what is the use of running an efficient economy for a wrong purpose?

(2.) As a disciplinary device (this being its main function) the profit criterion can be harsh and unfair. It can punish the most well-intentioned and hard-working person and throw riches to the unscrupulous speculator. It is easy to forget this and to join Schumpeter in extolling the selection process supposedly rewarding the able and bankrupting the weakling, but how would we enjoy being on the receiving end? No wonder that the current Soviet reforms oriented toward the market and profits are opposed by many Soviet managers, who would gain freedom but lose security. And who are we to complain, being, as most of the members of this assembly undoubtedly are, either holders of tenure positions or aspirants for them?

(3.) The next objection is directed not so much against the market economy as such, as against its capitalist incarnation. To put it bluntly, capitalism is an unappetizing system. It runs not on the higher human motivations, but on the lowest — selfishness and greed, which are regularly denounced by the keepers of our conscience on Sundays (and Saturdays), and put to good use the rest of the week. It is hard to love an economic system in which public welfare is merely a by-product of the pursuit of gain.

Perhaps I am making a virtue out of necessity, but there is a great advantage in propelling an economic system by greed because greed is so abundant. No civilization, to my knowledge, has ever suffered from a shortage. The Russians have tried to run their economic system on much higher fuels — patriotism and social consciousness — but when they run out of these precious propellants, as they invariably do, they resort to brute force. Lately they have talked more and more about, "material self-interest" of the managers and workers in a language reminiscent of the testimony of our business men at congressional tax hearings. But I have to admit that by running our economy on greed we fail to develop moving forces of higher quality, and we suffer from their shortage in our political and social life.

We know that the pursuit by each person of his selfish ends, under proper restrictions and conditions, can result in a reasonably efficient allocation of resources and a good deal of personal freedom, because selfishness need not be forced. On the whole, the practice of *modern* capitalism may be better than its theory (while the opposite may be true of socialism), but it is the theory that attracts intellectuals, and the theory of capitalism is difficult to explain to a person not versed in economics, and particularly to one from an underdeveloped country whose impression of *its* capitalism (symbolized, I imagine, by a picture of peasants devoured by a horde of money-lenders and tradesmen) is altogether different. In a growing economy like ours where national wealth, roughly speaking, doubles every generation, and where abject poverty is relatively rare, one may be tolerant of other people's making fortunes. Not so, however, in a country with a long history of stagnation (even if no longer present) where the gain for one implies the loss for another. If, to borrow an historical term, our present economic system may be named "Enlightened Capitalism," one would not so honor its predecessors, nor the capitalist or semi-capitalist systems found in most underdeveloped countries today.

(4.) The less enlightened phases of capitalism, through which most Western countries passed in their own time were long remembered for their exploitation of women and children, miserable wages, high profits, repressive taxes, and other ills, which, however horrible in themselves, were nevertheless conducive to capital accumulation and economic development *and were permitted to exist by the ideology of the time.* Many underdeveloped countries are more backward today than Europe was on the eve of the Industrial Revolution, but the ideology of their intellectuals, largely imported from the advanced countries, has little tolerance for such a process. Impressed as we are with the skills and knowledge which underdeveloped countries can obtain from the advanced ones, we may forget that one such import — medical knowledge — has inflicted upon them a growth of population which Europe has not experienced in all her history. Similarly, many ideological imports, appropriate for our state of economic development, are not at all suited for theirs. Besides, they lack the immunity to ideas which we, from long association with them (and with TV commercials) have developed. Hence, the tendency to carry ideas to the extreme. If we are bored with the profit motive, they are apt to reject it altogether. If the pensions paid under our social security system are modest, in Uruguay (according to the *New York Times)* one can retire with a full income at the age of fifty-five. Marxism, I would venture to suggest, as a protest against the social and economic conditions of the working classes of the nineteenth century, has done the Western countries much more good than harm. (How mild does the *Communist Manifesto* of 1848 sound to-day!) But when exported to Russia and China it started a conflagration. One cannot embargo ideas, and it is the import of Western ideas into the underdeveloped countries that contributes to the rejection of capitalism.

(5.) The last reason for this rejection which I would like to offer (there must be many others) is *impatience.* As seen by the intellectuals from the underdeveloped countries, what does this system have to offer? First, the development and export of agricultural and mining products, with all the uncertainties of the world demand for them. Then, a gradual expansion of light industries, beginning with food, textiles, and the like, and the refining of minerals. All through this period they will be threatened with inflation to which a market economy easily succumbs when it tries to move fast, and their dependence on advanced countries for technical help, machinery, spare parts, materials, and foreign exchange in general, will continue and even increase. And finally, after a long period of apprenticeship during which their rich are likely to get richer, and the poor — poorer (at least for a while), they will eventually reach our present standard of living from which we, at the time, will be miles away.

Realistically speaking, perhaps there is no faster method. But how unexciting this prospect is! Soviet economic literature of the nineteen-twenties, reflecting this feeling, was obsessed with speed. Capitalist countries must be overtaken not in generations, but in ten-fifteen years. No other promise could have satisfied the Soviet leadership of the time, nor the Chinese leaders of today.

Suppose, while driving to a very important appointment (or final examination) you suddenly have a flat tire. Twenty minutes later you are ready to go on, but you know how long the trip takes, and you know that you will be terribly late if you follow your usual route. What are you to do? Presently, stopping for a traffic signal, you notice a left turn which you have never taken before. It is in the generally correct direction, but it may lead nowhere and delay you even more. In desperation, you make the turn. You will probably fail. But — who knows — perhaps you will discover a new and faster route and make your appointment after all. You *know* that otherwise you are bound to be late.

According to what I call the "Gerschenkron Law" (which is a bit tautological, but interesting nevertheless), the more backward a country is, the greater are the tensions arising in it and the more radical are its industrialization methods. England got along without any special innovations; France and particularly Germany, developed the investment banks. The big push in Russia and Japan in the last century came from the government. Russian innovations since 1928 and Chinese since 1949 have been most radical, and yet one wonders what Africa will do in her time. We may disapprove of these costly, even if heroic, methods of development, but we must understand the preference for them by many intellectuals in underdeveloped countries.

III

I suspect that you are becoming impatient with my superficial sketch and want to hear the answer to the basic question — what can we do about all this? My first suggestion is not to get excited. Economic development is a difficult and complex process, hard to deal with, because contrary to some of our favorite models, it is essentially not a capital but a human problem. I cannot prove this, but I can illustrate. Take Colombia (my favorite underdeveloped country) and Japan. In 1958 the per capita income of Japan ($285) was, according to the U.N. sources, a bit below that of Colombia ($301). By now it is probably twice as high. But Japan must be making better use of its capital, so its capital per person is perhaps only some 50–70 percent higher than that of Colombia. Imagine now that the Colombian capital is suddenly increased to the Japanese per capita level. The standard of living of (at least some) Colombians will rise, and even their balance of payments may improve, but no economic miracles will happen. Now reduce the Colombian capital to its original level, but replace the seventeen million Colombians with seventeen million Japanese. Need I continue?

The human problems in economic development and in our War on Poverty at home are similar: in both cases the victim must acquire the middle-class mentality, so much abused by intellectuals: ambition, willingness to accept discipline, ability to work hard and efficiently, to learn, to save and invest, to exercise foresight, and so on. It is curious that most of these virtues would please both a good New England puritan (if any are still left there) and a good Russian communist. Indeed, the human ideal of the two creeds is strikingly similar, and for good economic reasons, though the puritan would naturally stress one's responsibility to God, and the communist — to socialism.

So far this looks not like an economic, but a psychological problem which might best be left to our colleagues on the floor or in the other building. But our colleagues have proved singularly ineffective (or much wiser than we are); hence, the operationally-minded economist must do what he can do. We cannot increase human happiness directly but we increase a person's income and his choice of occupations, improve his health and widen his horizon, in the hope that these changes will make him happier. Similarly, we cannot change the human beings and the society in the underdeveloped countries directly, but we can suggest some reasonably practical measures with helpful direct and indirect effects. Here are a few:

(1.) Education (including technical assistance). This is the most direct way of transforming both individuals and societies — witness the Soviet and Chinese efforts and recall the striking achievements of the Jesuits in the past. Statistics of the number of souls saved by Christian missionaries in Africa are unfortunately unavailable, but how often one sees the phrase "educated in missionary schools" in the biographies of African leaders. To be sure, education contains some risks — dissatisfied intellectuals, Ph.D.'s refusing to return home, barely literate youngsters rejecting manual work, and others — but these risks must be taken. We cannot hope to educate the millions in underdeveloped countries, but we can train teachers, help finance selected areas, set standards of excellence, and hope for the "demonstration effect." At present, aid to formal education comprises only some two or nine percent (depending on the denominator used) of our foreign aid. Why should it not be magnified ten or twenty times? Surely it will do much more good and much less harm than military aid.

(2.) Birth control. Hardly any comments are needed here. Perhaps future historians will ridicule our concern with a population of *only* three billions in the presence of empty spaces in much of the Americas, Africa, Australia and Northern Asia, just as we, until recently, ridiculed Malthus. But what matters now is not the opinions of future historians but the growth in the number of mouths to feed, children to educate, and men to be provided with jobs.

(3.) Economic integration. By area and population many underdeveloped countries look large. My favorite Colombia is larger than France, West Germany and Italy combined; and it contains 17 million people. But her GNP in 1963 was hardly $5 billion, about a third of that of the state of Massachusetts, and less than the GNP generated by the Boston Metropolitan Area. International income comparisons are notoriously inexact, and perhaps Colombia's income is understated. But a part of her population is still engaged in subsistence farming and is therefore almost outside of the market. Even with a generous correction, Colombia is small by market size, and there are of course many smaller countries. For that matter, the GNP of *the whole of South America* was estimated (by the parity method) at some $45 billion in 1963, much less than the $67 billion of New York State alone. All of Africa was rated at some $40 billion with some $11 billion generated by the Union of South Africa. Without the latter, the African GNP was below that of the state of Ohio. But New York and Ohio are parts of a larger economic entity, while neither South America nor Africa comprises one.

We should persuade, push and even bribe the underdeveloped countries into forming free trade areas and common markets. Only then will they really benefit from economies of scale and of specialization and will be able to reduce the risks inherent in foreign trade. The argument that their economies are similar to one another and that they therefore trade more with the advanced countries than among themselves makes just as little sense as a similar argument that might have been presented to our Founding Fathers in regards to the thirteen American states.

(4.) Emergency assistance in case of natural calamities, famines, epidemics and the like. The humanitarian reasons for such aid require no comments.

Beyond these four obvious suggestions, foreign aid policy becomes rather complex. It is certainly most proper for us to help the less developed countries to accelerate their development (particularly if we recognize that we are partly responsible for their predicament), and it is in our own interest to do so. The problem is how to help these societies to change themselves rather than to hinder the change, since it is difficult to aid a country without adding strength to its ruling classes and to its government, however unenlightened both may be. It may also not be easy to avoid the creation of the patron-client relationship between the recipient and the donor, which is most unhealthy for both sides. It is very tempting to force reforms on the recipient by the promise of aid. But such reforms can remain on paper, and our insistence that they be carried out according to the agreement made is apt to cause mutual animosity. Besides, seldom is our knowledge about the country sufficient to assure us of the correctness of our stand.

If I have run out of simple positive suggestions, let me make a negative one: that military aid be given only under exceptional circumstances. The sight of Indians and Pakistanis fighting each other with American and British tanks is a good example of the harm that our good intentions can cause. And let us not forget that Trujillo rose to power in the Dominican Republic on the shoulders of American-trained constabulary. In our obsession with fighting communism we tend to over-emphasize the effectiveness of military means; we seem to have forgotten Lenin's dictum that it is not the rifle that fires but the man who pulls the trigger.

IV

Above all, let me repeat, we should not get excited every time a riot, a coup, a revolution or a counter-revolution sweeps some underdeveloped country. Economic change without political change is impossible, and the latter does have a nasty habit of not always proceeding in a nice, evolutionary and democratic manner. What the present-day advanced countries have accomplished over generations, the underdeveloped ones must do in a few decades, and usually with weak and inefficient governments. If France has gone through five republics, four major revolutions and several near-revolutions in less than two hundred years, surely each underdeveloped country is entitled to its quota of political upheavals concentrated into a short span of time.

During this process many underdeveloped countries will enjoy spells of democratic rule interspersed with military, rightist, leftist, tyrannical, benevolent, and all sorts of dictatorships. It is altogether possible that *in the middle* of their developmental process some will go communist. I would venture to suggest that communism is an experience (some would say — a disease) of adolescence. No advanced country has yet succumbed to it (except by foreign force, like East Germany and Czechoslovakia), while Russia and other East European countries are beginning to recover from it as their economies develop. The Chinese are not entirely wrong in questioning the purity cf the present-day Russian communism, and perhaps the Africans will question the Chinese variety some day. It was comfortable to think that communists could seize power only after a long and exhausting war (Russia, China, Yugoslavia), or under foreign pressure (the rest of Eastern Europe). Cuba has destroyed this pleasant belief, and the state of Kerala in India has shown that communists can win even a reasonably fair election. Some day they may repeat this feat in a whole country, and it will be particularly galling to us if that country has grown to adolescence with our aid, and if the communist leaders were trained in American-organized or aided schools.

I do not wish communism on any country, advanced or underdeveloped, but we must realize that the chances for our *effective* interference are small. If we only knew how to save a country during those critical years some action might be recommended. But our performance in Russia and China in the past, and in Viet Nam and in the Dominican Republic at present has revealed a striking degree of ignorance and ineptitude. Indeed, it is likely that in our anxiety to permit only an orderly change we may inhibit any change, and thus create the most favorable conditions for a communist victory. The recent House resolution authorizing our intervention in Latin American countries to save them from communism which was, by the way, opposed by the would-be victims of our benevolence — the irony of it! — is a rare example of political stupidity, to put it mildly. At best it will be ineffective; at worst, it will give the respective regimes a false sense of security and lead them into traps from which we will be unable to rescue them when the time comes.

For her role in defeating Napoleon, Russia enjoyed a brief spell of good will from other European countries. But Russian opposition to every popular movement which threatened the existing order in Europe eventually made her the most hated country on that continent. We also enjoyed a period not only of international good-will but of real affection at the close of World War II. Need I belabor my parallel?

Questions for discussion and analysis pertaining to this article may be found at the end of Article 29.

Walter Johnson †

29. THE COSTS OF ECONOMIC DEVELOPMENT*

The drive toward economic development that exists throughout the world exists since the benefits of a developed society are obvious to all. A rising level of national income and increasing productivity of the labor force allow higher standards of living, may provide for a distribution of income in which larger numbers of the populace rise above a subsistence standard of income, may allow the choice between leisure and labor while providing a basic modicum of the goods and services necessary for life, and is virtually necessary for full membership in the community of nations.

The achievement of the benefits of economic development is the subject of virtually all of the literature dealing with the problems of the underdeveloped societies. The various descriptions of the underdeveloped country focus sharply on statistics which show the extent to which progress must be made in order to emerge as the equal of the world's leaders. Statistics on birth and death rates, literacy, rate of growth of income or per capita income, percent urbanization, and the like from the underdeveloped country are compared with those from nations such as Canada, Sweden, the United States and West Germany to show the extent to which countries are in need of development aid and of development itself.

A large part of the literature of development deals with the strategies of development, and concerns itself with whether a broad push is needed to insure rising per capita income, whether a basic level of investment is the key to emergence, how the generation of capital (whether physical, intangible, or human) allows the progress of growth, and so forth. Again, the assumption is that the benefits of economic growth can be achieved if the "proper" prescription is recognized and then taken.

Much the same can be said about the whole subject of the control of the size of population and the structure of population. It is only recently that the emergence of the "affluent society" has caused new concern with the growth of population in developed societies. The recent literature applies the two

†Walter L. Johnson, Associate Professor of Economics, University of Missouri — Columbia. For helpful comments on earlier drafts of this paper, the author is indebted to David R. Kamerschen, University of Missouri — Columbia.
*An unpublished manuscript. Reprinted by permission of the author.

hundred year old warnings of Malthus relative to overpopulation to the underdeveloped countries, cites the economic costs of rapid population growth and of a population structure which does not provide for a large percentage of productive laborers in the population, bewails the atrophy in the non-economic "quality of life," and so forth.

There has been, unfortunately, all too little said about the costs of growing pains associated with a heady growth rate and economic development. And these costs can be great — very great! Any society has, at all times, a number of possible growth rates that it may pursue under different growthmanship strategies. For each of these rates there is a different cost involved, with higher and higher rates involving greater sacrifice on the part of the people and on the resources of the society. The proper rate of growth for a society is the one where the benefits of increasing the rate of growth slightly are weighted against and balanced with the costs of achieving that rate of increase. The goal of a society, then, is one of *optimization* of the rate of growth, not of *maximization* of that rate. "Damn the torpedoes" and "Full speed ahead" may be a policy which achieves the desired end of winning naval battles, but is not the one which inexorably produces the desired flow and composition of national product. In other words, economists do not preach that man can live by GNP alone. Rather they emphasize that what nations should seek is the *optimal* (read "best") and not the *maximal* (read "largest") volume of goods and services. Thus, an opulent nation such as the United States may be growing too fast relative to the concomitant costs and constraints involved.

But what is the real benefit of economic growth and development? It is tempting to point out that wealth and income are related to personal satisfaction and the maximization of utility in a society (which is something that all economists favor). But this may not be the case at all. Increasing standards of living may simply induce even higher aspirations on the part of people, making them unhappier than they were before "development" began. The use of the "*micro* quantity theory of money" — i.e., more money is better than less money for the individual — is one of the more common errors and one of the most easy to make in justifying high growth rates. J. J. Spengler of Duke University has said "You only have revolutionaries emerge when their bellies are full." Aspirations which may have been limited in the absence of any dynamism shown in the economy may rise rapidly with the emergence of the first signs of development when the people realize that things are not what they should be. Personal satisfaction may decline, not increase. The benefit of growth is that it increases the number of options open to the society and to the members of the society in pursuing economic activity. Higher levels of income allow choices to be made between labor and leisure, industrialization or assistance to agriculture, more or less religious and national holidays, and so forth. These choices are possible since the society has the resources to allocate after providing for the basic subsistence of its people.

There are two ways in which the costs of economic development might be categorized: a list of the costs to the traditional society in moving toward a more modern society, and a consideration of the tradeoffs involved in accepting a higher rate of growth.

W. Arthur Lewis (*Theory of Economic Growth*, George Allen & Unwin, Ltd.: 1955) for instance has presented a list — cataloguing some of these costs:

(1.) The economizing spirit necessary for development may lead directly to materialism.

(2.) Growth and development promote individualism, but in doing so tend to break down the social structure. An individual becomes more cognizant of his responsibilities for his self and less aware of his responsibilities to family and to tribe.

(3.) Focusing national interest on economic matters forces an orientation toward reason which may prejudice the religious beliefs of the people and force a shift toward atheism.

(4.) In the development of the new skills necessary for a technologically oriented society, the old handicrafts and skills will die.

(5.) The economies of scale inherent in development require the mobilization of capital, and the separation of ownership from the use of the capital. He becomes an employee rather than an independent man, and is thus subjugated to the corporation.

(6.) Man becomes a slave of the clock and loses independence of action. He reports to work at some given hour and leaves according to schedule.

(7.) Large scale production leads to the growth of cities. Cities become the home of the slums of a country, and grow at the expense of the villages.

(8.) Growth is dependent on the inequitable distribution of income, and providing of incentives for hard work guarantees that inequalities will persist.

In cataloguing the alleged costs of economic development, Lewis is very careful to point out that some of the things listed as costs are not *necessarily* costs at all. A change in social structure is not perforce evil. The use of reason may or may not prejudice the religious beliefs of the people. Development of the new skills, along with the division of labor does not require that specifications for products be relaxed in mass production nor that the older skills are redundant to the society. The fact that large scale production involves large organizations in which some men are employed who do not own the capital of the productive process does not necessarily mean that large industries are inherently bad. Further, being a clock slave in a factory is little different than being a clock slave in a one man shop. The growth of slums and the ugliness and blight of cities *may* be a result of the development; if so, it is a result of poor planning of the implementation of development rather than the development itself. Inequities in the distribution of income and wealth may be remedied in large part through taxation and subsidies.

In conclusion, then, Lewis points out that certain of the alleged costs of economic development are not necessary requisites to development and that certain of the "costs" such as a reorganization of the social structure with the emergence of greater individualism, are not costs at all.

An alternative view of the calculation of the costs involved in economic development can be taken, emphasizing the tradeoffs involved in growth. Three of these tradeoffs are considered to be of prime importance:

(1.) In attempting to increase the rate of growth we sacrifice current leisure for current work.

(2.) In increasing the growth rate, current consumption is traded for future consumption.

(3.) The greater the rate of growth and change, the greater is the difficulty in changeover with resultant temporary unemployment of resources.

It is, of course, possible to have the burden of increasing the growth rate fall on either leisure or on current consumption or both.

The important thing to remember is that the incremental cost of each equal addition to the growth rate will be higher as the growth rate increases. Sacrifice of the first units of consumption for increased growth will not be particularly painful, but further sacrifices begin to strike into "necessities" and become very painful indeed. Also, giving up some idle time for increased labor is not particularly onerous for some amounts of labor per week. After a point, however, it becomes increasingly burdensome to the labor force to increase the length of the work week further.

The optimal growth rate is that which gives benefits in form of a larger flow of income which are just equal to the cost of achieving the last increment of growth. As long as the benefits of growth are greater than the costs of achieving those benefits, a transfer to growth is in order; but, when the marginal benefits of the increased flow of future goods are just equal to the (rising) marginal costs of achieving them, further shifts can only reduce society's achievements, since the cost of further increases in the growth rate will be greater than the benefits arising from it.

The two listings of costs are probably not complete. The social costs of pollution and the emergence of large slums are hinted at in Lewis' listing, and are not a part of the cost side of the tradeoffs mentioned earlier. The cost of the loss of national resources consumed in haste that could well have been saved are not mentioned in either listing. There are a number of costs borne by society that do not appear in the felicitous calculus of the individual in making the "hard" decisions relative to development.

Some of the examples of social costs incurred in development and growth are painfully obvious to Americans: air that kills plant life and forces eyes to water, streams that will not support life, and the sprawl of the slum. All of these are avoidable, and all represent a decay in the order of things that has occurred as a product of development. To the extent that they have occurred the society is less than it would have been in the absence of development and a cost has been undergone for which the development project has not been forced to pay. In the economist's jargon, there are "social costs" as well as private costs involved in economic growth. However, in a free enterprise society, profit maxizing firms do not include social costs in their decision-making algorithm. In a large measure this is the reason that government's role in the development drama being acted out in most of the world today is not unlike that of the Danish prince in Hamlet.

Certain of the costs of development are rather subtle, and slow in coming. The decline of the game fields of East Africa to the point where it is virtually certain that certain species will not persist is a cost that is very hard to calculate in terms of dollars (or East Africa shillings) but a cost to East Africans and to all human beings nevertheless.

While Lewis is very careful to point out that many of the alleged costs in his listing of reasons for opposition to economic development are not costs at all, to the extent that there is validity in any of them, costs to society are positive and in general nontrivial in magnitude.

Equilibration of marginal costs and marginal benefits is, of course, the correct course of action in selecting the proper growth rate for a society. Positive rates of interest (sometimes quite high in societies which have relatively little capital) require that the returns from investment projects be discounted quite heavily in the computation of the present value of the worth of a project. Many costs, however, are born in the very short run, and do not bear discounting so heavily since they are close on the time horizon. Thus, a project that promises large returns in the distant future may not be worthwhile from the point of maximization of the value of societies wealth. By the same token, recognition of the costs of immiserization of the masses in order to provide growth for the future and a larger stream of production at some future date might result, in certain countries in a lessening of the desire for immediate development at any cost.

In conclusion, then, there are different things that economists have identified in considering the "costs" of development. On the one hand, the older order in a developing country probably will give way to some new order if development proceeds. This may or may not involve cost. Or, it is possible to view the costs of development as the foregone alternatives to development. It is this latter method of calculation that can provide the decision maker with information on which to make his choice between additional development and fulfilling some other need of the economy. Incanting over a computer full of numbers and burning incense on the console of the machine is not sufficient, however, if only the costs seen in the private market place (and benefits, for that matter) are brought to play in selecting the proper rate of growth. The social costs of development are great, and their neglect virtually guarantees that the growth rate selected will be above that which is in the present best interest of society.

Questions for Discussion and Analysis

Article 28

1. *Is there any real distinction between "macro-planning" and and "micro-planning"?*
2. *What valid reasons are there for the rejection of the capitalist model by developing countries?*
3. *Domar ranks economic integration along with education and birth control in promoting economic development. Why should he give it such prominence?*
4. *Is economic change without political change impossible?*

Article 29

5. *How would one go about measuring the costs to society of undertaking a particular development project?*
6. *Is a change in the social order and social values necessarily a cost? Might these changes be a cost? How?*
7. *Under what conditions should the United States seek to arrest or even reduce its rate of growth?*

APPENDIX

Basic Economic Data for the Less Developed Non-Communist Areas

Country	Population (1966) Total	Population (1966) Rate of growth	Area Total	Area Agricultural land Percent of total area	Area Agricultural land Acres per capita	GNP per capita (1965 est.)[a]	Electric power per capita	Education Literacy[b]	Education Pupils as percent of population[c]	Health—people per doctor	Export trade—main export Item
	Millions	Percent	1000 sq. miles	Percent	Acres	Dollars	KWH per year	Percent	Percent	Number	Item
Developed areas[d]	635	1.2	12,400	39	5	2,110	3,740	96	19	780	....
United States	197	1.4	3,600	47	6	3,500	5,950	98	23	690	....
Less developed areas	1,600	2.5	26,400	26	3	180	155	37	12	4,000	....
Africa[e]											
Including South Africa	270.7	2.4	11,300	31	8	155	200	18	9	11,400	....
Excluding South Africa	252.5	2.4	10,800	27	8	125	80	17	8	17,700	....
Algeria	12.1	2.9	920	19	9	225	95	15	19	12,800	Petroleum.
Botswana	0.6	3.0	222	72	177	60	(*)	20	12	22,000	Cattle carcasses.
Burundi	2.9	2.5	11	71	2	50	5	(*)	5	65,000	Coffee.
Cameroon	5.3	2.1	183	35	8	130	212	10	12	26,900	Coffee, cocoa.
Central African Republic	1.4	2.0	238	10	11	90	16	15	9	40,000	Diamonds, cotton.
Chad	3.5	2.0	496	40	37	70	5	5	5	81,900	Cotton.
Congo (Brazzaville)	1.0	2.5	132	2	2	140	45	20-25	19	12,500	Wood, diamonds.
Congo (Kinshasa)	16.3	2.3	906	22	8	80	160	30-40	14	30,100	Copper.
Dahomey	2.4	2.9	43	18	2	70	8	5	6	20,100	Palm products.
Ethiopia	20.5	1.4	457	66	10	58	12	5	2	61,400	Coffee.
Gabon	0.5	0.7	103	2	3	300	84	10-15	17	5,700	Wood, manganese.
Gambia	0.3	2.2	4	19	1	85	22	10	4	18,200	Peanuts.
Ghana	8.0	2.7	92	22	2	285	68	20-25	17	12,000	Cocoa.
Guinea	3.6	3.0	95	(*)	(*)	73	49	10	6	28,400	Alumina.
Ivory Coast	3.9	2.3	125	(*)	(*)	251	57	20	10	18,600	Coffee, wood.

Kenya	9.6	3.0	225	10	1	90	55	20–25	11	9,700	Coffee, tea.
Lesotho	0.9	1.7	12	94	8	58	(*)	35	20	23,000	Wool, mohair.
Liberia	1.1	1.6	43	37	9	199	248	10	8	11,700	Iron ore, rubber.
Libya	1.7	3.7	679	6	17	542	83	30	12	4,000	Petroleum.
Malagasy Republic	6.6	3.5	230	62	14	90	21	35	11	10,300	Coffee, vanilla.
Malawi	4.1	3.0	46	19	1	41	13	5–10	9	43,100	Tobacco, tea.
Mali	4.7	2.1	465	(*)	(*)	65	6	5	4	40,000	Livestock, peanuts.
Mauritania	0.9	2.2	419	36	104	138	6	1–5	3	30,300	Iron ore.
Mauritius	0.8	2.8	1	66	0.4	231	139	60	23	3,700	Sugar.
Morocco	13.7	3.1	172	35	3	196	96	10–15	10	10,800	Phosphates.
Niger	3.4	3.0	489	14	13	75	6	1–5	2	64,700	Peanuts.
Nigeria	ƒ43.6	ƒ2.1	357	24	1	114	28	30–35	8	26,500	Petroleum, cocoa.
Rhodesia, Southern	4.4	3.2	150	17	4	240	966	20	17	7,700	Tobacco.
Rwanda	3.2	3.1	10	71	1	50	4	5–10	12	143,700	Coffee, tin ore.
Senegal	3.6	2.3	76	28	4	195	58	5–10	7	15,200	Peanuts & products.
Sierra Leone	2.3	2.2	28	82	6	150	38	10	7	14,200	Diamonds, iron ore.
Somali Republic	2.6	2.9	28	34	21	60	4	5	6	31,900	Bananas, livestock.
Sudan	13.9	2.9	246	12	6	104	13	10–15	1	29,500	Cotton.
Tanzania	10.7	1.9	967	50	11	71	22	15–20	4	19,700	Sisal, cotton.
Togo	1.7	2.7	363	42	3	95	6	5–10	7	23,100	Phosphates, cocoa.
Tunisia	4.8	2.5	22	60	5	200	77	25–35	11	10,200	Olive oil, phosphates.
Uganda	7.7	2.5	63	16	1	87	76	25	18	12,600	Coffee, cotton.
Upper Volta	5.0	2.0	91	18	2	53	4	5–10	7	63,500	Livestock.
Zambia	3.8	2.9	288	41	20	227	798	40	12	8,900	Copper.
East Asia:[g]											
Including Japan	380	2.2	1,700	17	0.5	320	550	70	17	2,300	....
Excluding Japan	281	2.7	1,560	17	0.6	130	90	60	15	5,200	....
Burma	25.3	2.1	262	13	0.9	71	24	60	9	9,300	Rice.
Cambodia	6.2	2.1	70	16	1.2	132	14	31	13	25,000	Rice and rubber.
China (Taiwan)	13.2	2.8	14	25	0.2	215	490	78	22	1,500	Sugar.
Hong Kong	3.8	4.7	0.4	13	0.1	421	650	71	21	2,800	Clothing and textiles.
Indonesia	106.9	2.3	576	12	0.4	100	19	43	11	41,000	Rubber and oil.
Korea, South	29.1	2.8	38	22	0.2	102	110	71	22	2,600	Fish and plywood.
Laos	2.7	2.4	91	8	2.0	66	7	15	6	49,000	Tin.
Malaysia	9.7	3.0	128	17	1.5	305	250	43	18	6,500	Rubber and tin.
Philippines	33.5	3.4	116	37	0.9	161	150	72	19	1,700	Sugar and coconuts.
Singapore	1.9	2.7	0.2	22	.02	500	500	60	24	2,300	Rubber and oil.
Thailand	32.4	3.1	198	21	0.8	123	34	68	16	7,300	Rice and rubber.
Vietnam, South	16.6	2.8	66	35	0.9	115	39	40–50	13	16,600	Rubber.

(continued on next page)

Basic Economic Data (Continued)

Country	Population (1966) Total	Population (1966) Rate of growth	Area Total	Area Agricultural land Percent of total area	Area Agricultural land Acres per capita	GNP per capita (1965 est.)[a]	Electric power per capita	Education Literacy[b]	Education Pupils as percent of population[c]	Health—people per doctor	Export trade—main export Item
	Millions	Percent	1000 sq. miles	Percent	Acres	Dollars	KWH per year	Percent	Percent	Number	
Latin American Republics	236.9	2.9	7,710	25	5	385	400	66	16	1,800	....
Argentina	22.7	1.6	1,084	50	16	718	690	91	17	670	Grain and meat.
Bolivia	4.2	2.4	424	13	8	145	130	32	14	3,830	Tin.
Brazil	84.0	3.0	3,280	15	4	270	410	61	13	2,500	Coffee.
Chile	9.0	2.4	286	17	3	485	670	84	20	1,770	Copper.
Colombia	18.5	3.0	440	17	3	284	320	62	14	2,280	Coffee.
Costa Rica	1.6	3.8	20	30	2	395	430	84	21	2,200	Coffee.
Dominican Republic	3.7	3.6	19	26	1	265	140	64	17	1,620	Sugar.
Ecuador	5.3	3.4	112	19	3	222	110	68	17	2,990	Bananas.
El Salvador	3.0	3.2	8	51	1	273	140	48	15	4,520	Coffee.
Guatemala	4.8	3.3	42	19	1	305	90	38	10	4,190	Coffee.
Haiti	4.8	2.3	11	31	0.4	70	20	10	6	14,980	Coffee.
Honduras	2.3	3.1	43	38	4	223	80	45	13	6,640	Bananas.
Mexico	44.2	3.5	760	52	6	455	400	71	18	2,020	Cotton.
Nicaragua	1.7	3.5	57	13	3	355	190	50	13	2,370	Cotton.
Panama	1.3	3.2	29	18	3	495	400	78	20	1,920	Bananas, petroleum.
Paraguay	2.1	2.6	157	27	14	221	60	68	19	1,660	Meat.
Peru	12.0	3.1	514	16	4	367	330	61	20	2,150	Fishmeal, copper.
Uruguay	2.8	1.4	72	86	14	573	640	91	15	880	Wool and meat.
Venezuela	9.0	3.4	352	21	5	882	920	80	19	1,280	Petroleum.
British Honduras	0.1	3.1	9	2	1	370	(*)	89	29	3,700	Timber and citrus.

Guyana	0.7	2.8	83	13	10	298	310	80	25	2,110	Sugar.
Jamaica	1.8	2.6	4	45	1	489	450	85	20	2,040	Bauxite and sugar.
Surinam	0.4	2.9	55	0.3	0.3	392	690	80	23	2,240	Bauxite.
Trinidad and Tobago	1.0	3.0	2	35	0.4	646	930	80	23	2,550	Petroleum.
Near East Total[g]	128.6	2.5	2,526	32	3.0	290	210	36	13	2,400	....
Cyprus	0.6	1.5	4	57	2.1	702	563	76	17	1,400	Minerals.
Greece	8.6	0.5	51	68	2.6	650	483	82	15	750	Tobacco.
Iran	24.0	2.5	636	11	1.9	253	98	15–20	11	3,200	Oil.
Iraq	8.4	3.2	173	35	4.6	233	147	20	16	4,800	Oil.
Israel	2.7	2.6	8	53	1.0	1,325	1,615	90	22	430	Diamonds, citrus.
Jordan	2.0	3.0	38	12	1.4	244	82	35–40	19	4,700	Vegetables & fruits.
Kuwait	0.5	h12.0	6	(*)	(*)	3,196	1,369	47	17	800	Oil.
Lebanon	2.6	2.5	4	27	0.3	450	299	86	15	1,400	Fruits.
Saudi Arabia	6.9	1.7	772	i43	31.0	225	(*)	5–15	i3	12,700	Oil.
Syrian Arab Republic	5.9	3.0	71	69	5.6	197	63	35	14	5,500	Cotton.
Turkey	31.9	2.5	301	70	4.2	261	159	46	14	3,200	Tobacco.
United Arab Republic	30.4	2.7	386	3	0.2	160	177	30	14	2,500	Cotton.
Yemen Arab Republic	4.1	(*)	75	(*)	(*)	120	(*)	10	2	54,000	Coffee.
South Asia Total	653.3	2.4	1,961	43	0.8	100	70	25	11	6,300	....
Afghanistan	15.4	2.0	254	19	1.9	83	12	5–10	j2	29,300	Fruits, nuts, karakul.
Ceylon	11.6	2.9	25	29	0.4	145	37	70–80	24	4,600	Tea.
India	499.0	2.4	1,263	54	0.9	101	77	24	12	5,800	Tea, textiles.
Nepal	10.3	2.0	54	13	0.4	73	2	5–10	4	42,200	Rice.
Pakistan	117.0	2.6	365	27	0.5	97	36	20	8	7,700	Jute and mfrs.

Source: *Proposed Foreign Aid Program FY 1968*, Summary presentation to the Congress, Agency for International Development (Washington, D.C., U.S. Government Printing Office, 1967), Table 3, pp. 291–297.

*Not available.
a GNP data unadjusted for inequalities in purchasing power among countries.
b Includes very rough estimates for many countries.
c Primary and secondary school pupils.
d Generally Australia, Canada, Western Europe, Japan, New Zealand, South Africa, and the United States.
e Egypt is included under Near East. Totals include countries not listed.
f Estimate pending study of recent census figure of 55.6 million. General economic data are based on pre-census series.
g Total for countries listed.
h Reflects heavy immigration in recent years.
i Mostly grazing land.
j Public education only.

BIBLIOGRAPHY

[The reader should also consult the references given in the various articles in this text; especially those provided at the end of Articles 16, 17, 19 and 26.]

Section I

Bauer, Peter T. "International Economic Development." *Economic Journal,* Vol. 69 (March, 1959), pp. 105–123.

Boulding, Kenneth E. "In Defense of Statics." *Quarterly Journal of Economics,* Vol. 69 (November, 1955), pp. 485–502.

Boulding, Kenneth E. "The Relations of Economic, Political, and Social Systems." *Social and Economic Studies,* Vol. 11 (December, 1962), pp. 351–362.

Gerschenkron, A. *Economic Development in Historical Perspective.* Cambridge: Harvard University Press, 1962.

Hunter, John M. "Underdeveloped Nations." *Business Topics,* Vol. 10, No. 2 (Spring, 1962), pp. 17–30.

Myint, Hla. "An Interpretation of Economic Backwardness." *Oxford Economic Papers,* N.S. Vol. 6 (June, 1954), pp. 132–163.

Myint, Hla. "Economic Theory and the Underdeveloped Countries." *Journal of Political Economy,* Vol. 73 (October, 1956), pp. 477–491.

Nell, Edward J. "Theories of Growth and Theories of Value." *Economic Development And Cultural Change,* Vol. 16 (October, 1967), pp. 15–26.

Ranis, Gustav. *The United States and the Developing Economies.* New York: W. W. Norton, 1964.

Reynolds, Lloyd. "The Content of Economic Development." *American Economic Review,* Vol. 59 (May, 1969), pp. 401–408.

Seers, Dudley. "Why Visiting Economists Fail." *Journal Of Political Economy,* Vol. 70 (August, 1962), pp. 325–328.

Section II

Alonzo, William. "Urban and Regional Imbalances in Economic Development." *Economic Development and Cultural Change,* Vol. 17 (October, 1968), pp. 1–14.

Bauer, P. T. and Basil Yamey. "Economic Progress and Occupational Distribution." *Economic Journal,* Vol. 61 (December, 1951), pp. 741–755.

Beckerman, W. and R. Bacon. "International Comparison of Income Levels: A Suggested New Measure." *Economic Journal,* Vol. 76 (September, 1960), pp. 518–536.

Bennett, Merrill K. "International Disparities in Consumption." *American Economic Review,* Vol. 41 (September, 1951), pp. 632–649.

Benveniste, Guy and William E. Moran, Jr. *Handbook of African Economic Development.* Prager, 1962.

Cameron, Rondo. "Economic Development: Some Lessons of History for Developing Nations." *American Economic Review,* Vol. 57 (May, 1967), pp. 312–324.

Chenery, Hollis B. and Lance Taylor. "Development Patterns: Among Countries and Over Time." *Review of Economic and Statistics,* Vol. 50 (November, 1968), pp. 391–416.

Eckaus, Richard S. "The Factor Proportions Problem in Underdeveloped Areas." *American Economic Review,* Vol. 45 (September, 1955), pp. 539–565.

Ellis, Howard S. "How Culture Shapes Economic Growth." *Arizona Review,* Vol. 20, No. 1 (January, 1971), pp. 1–9.

Galenson, Walter. "Economic Development and the Sectoral Expansion of Employment." *International Labour Review,* Vol. 87, No. 6 (June, 1963), pp. 505–519.

Hauser, Philip M. "Demographic Indicators of Economic Development." *Economic Development and Cultural Change,* Vol. 7 (January, 1959), pp. 98–116.

Hoselitz, Bert F. "Non-economic Factors in Economic Growth." *American Economic Review,* Vol. 47 (May, 1957), pp. 28–41.

Kuznets, Simon. "Developed and Underdeveloped Countries: Some Problems of Comparative Analysis." *Zeitschrift fur die Gesamte Staatswissenschaft,* Vol. 124 (February, 1968), pp. 96–107.

Letwin, William. "Four Fallacies About Economic Development." *Daedalus,* Vol. 92 (Summer, 1963), pp. 396–414.

Nutter, G. Warren. "On Measuring Economic Growth." *Journal of Political Economy,* Vol. 65 (February, 1957), pp. 51–63.

Rottenberg, Simon. "Income and Leisure in an Underdeveloped Country." *Journal of Political Economy,* Vol. 60 (April, 1952), pp. 95–101.

Spengler, Joseph J. "Economic Factors in Economic Development." *American Economic Review,* Vol. 47 (May, 1957), pp. 42–56.

Wolf, Charles F. "Institutions and Economic Development." *American Economic Review*, Vol. 45 (December, 1955), pp. 867–883.

Section III

Adelman, Irma. *Theories of Economic Growth and Development*. Stanford: Stanford University Press, 1961.

Baran, Paul A. *The Political Economy of Growth*. Monthly Review, Inc., 1957.

Bruton, Henry J. "Contemporary Theorizing on Economic Growth." In *Theories of Economic Growth*. Edited by Bert F. Hoselitz. New York: Free Press, 1960.

Chamber of Commerce of the United States. *World Population: Prospects and Problems*, 1966.

Chayanov, A. V. *The Theory of the Peasant Economy*. Homewood: Richard D. Irwin for the American Economic Association, 1966.

Denison, E. F. *Why Growth Rates Differ: Postwar Experience in Nine Western Countries*. Brookings Institution, 1967.

Fei, John C. H. and Gustav Ranis. "A Theory of Economic Development." *American Economic Review,* Vol. 51 (September, 1961), pp. 533–565.

Fei, John C. H. and Gustav Ranis. *Development of the Labor Surplus Economy*. Homewood: Richard D. Irwin, 1964.

Galbraith, John K. *Economic Development*. Geneva: Houghton Mifflin, 1964.

Georgescu-Roegen, N. "Economic Theory and Agrarian Economics." *Oxford Economic Papers*, Vol. 12 (February, 1960), pp. 1–40.

Hagen, Everett E. "The Process of Economic Development." *Economic Development and Cultural Change*, Vol. 5 (April, 1957), pp. 193–215.

Hagen, Everett E. "How Economic Growth Begins: A Theory of Social Change." *Journal of Social Issues*, Vol. 19, No. 1, pp. 20–34.

Hagen, Everett E. *On the Theory of Social Change*. Homewood: Dorsey Press, 1962.

Hahn, Frank H. and R. C. O. Mathews. "The Theory of Economic Growth: A Survey." *Economic Journal,* Vol. 74 (December, 1964), pp. 779–902.

Hirschman, Albert O. *The Strategy of Economic Development*. New Haven: Yale University Press, 1958.

Johnston, B. F. and J. W. Mellor, "The Role of Agriculture in Economic Development." *American Economic Review*, Vol. 51 (September, 1961), pp. 571–581.

Jorgensen, Dale M. "Surplus Agricultural Labor and the Development of a Dual Economy." *Oxford Economic Papers*, Vol. 19 (November, 1967), pp. 281–312.

Kuznets, Simon. "The Economic Requirements of Modern Industrialization." In *Economic Growth and Structure*. New York: Norton, 1965.

Lewis, W. A. "Economic Development with Unlimited Supplies of Labour."
Manchester School, Vol. 22 (May, 1954), pp. 139–191; "Unlimited Supplies
of Labour: Further Notes," *Idem,* Vol. 26 (January, 1958), pp. 1–32.

McClelland, David C. *The Achieving Society.* New York: Free Press, 1967.

Meade, James E. *A Neo-Classical Theory of Economic Growth, Revised
Edition.* Unwin University Books, 1962.

Myrdal, Gunnar. *Rich Lands and Poor.* New York: Harper & Row, 1957.

Nelson, Richard R. "A Theory of Low-Level Equilibrium Trap." *American
Economic Review,* Vol. 46 (December, 1956), pp. 894–908.

Oshima, Harry T. "Economic Growth and the 'Critical Minimum Effort.' "
Economic Development and Cultural Change, Vol. 7 (July, 1959), pp. 467–
476.

Oshima, Harry T. "Income Originating in the Models of Harrod and Domar."
Economic Journal, Vol. 69 (September, 1959), pp. 443–451.

Rosenstein-Rodan, Paul N. "Problems of Industrialization of Eastern and
South-Eastern Europe." *Economic Journal,* Vol. 53 (June-September,
1943), pp. 202–211.

Rostow, W. W. *The Stages of Economic Growth.* New York: Cambridge
University Press, 1960.

Schumpeter, Joseph A. *The Theory of Economic Development.* Cambridge:
Harvard University Press, 1934.

Scitovsky, Tibor. "Two Concepts of External Economies." *Journal of Polit-
cal Economy,* Vol. 62 (April, 1954), pp. 143–151.

Scitovsky, Tibor. "Growth — Balanced or Unbalanced." In *Allocation of
Economic Resources,* M. Abramovitz, *et. al.,* Stanford: Stanford University Press, 1959, pp. 207–217.

Swamy, Dalip S. "Statistical Evidence on Balanced and Unbalanced Growth."
Review of Economics and Statistics, Vol. 49 (August, 1967), pp. 288–303.

Tinbergen, Jan and H. C. Bos. *Mathematical Models of Economic Growth.*
McGraw-Hill, 1962.

Section IV

Adelman, Irma. "An Econometric Analysis of Population Growth." *American Economic Review,* Vol. 53 (June, 1963), pp. 314–339.

Aubrey, Henry G. "Investment Decisions in Underdeveloped Countries."
In *Capital Formation and Economic Growth.* National Bureau of Economic Research, 1955.

Baranson, J. *Technology for Underdeveloped Areas: An Annotated Bibliography.* New York: Pergamon Press, 1967.

Barnett, Harold J. and Chandler Morse. *Scarcity and Growth.* Baltimore:
John Hopkins Press, 1963.

Becker, Gary S. "An Economic Analysis of Fertility." In *Demographic and
Economic Change in Developing Countries.* National Bureau of Economic
Research, 1960.

Chamberlain, Neil W. *Beyond Malthus: Population and Power.* Basic Books, Inc., 1970.

Clark, Colin. "The Fundamental Problems of Economic Growth." *Weltwirtschlaftliches Archiv*, Vol. 94, No. 1 (March, 1965) pp. 1–9.

Coale, A. J. and E. M. Hoover. *Population Growth and Economic Development in Low Income Countries.* Princeton: Princeton University Press, 1958.

Coale, Ansley J. "Population and Economic Development." *The Population Dilemma*, 2nd ed. Englewood Cliffs: Prentice Hall, 1969.

Cochrane, Willard W. *The World Food Problem: A Guardedly Optimistic View.* New York: Crowell, 1969.

Daly, Herman E. "The Population Question in Northeast Brazil: Its Economic and Idealogical Dimensions." *Economic Development and Cultural Change*, Vol. 18, No. 4, Part I (July, 1970), pp. 536–574.

Davis, Kingsley, and Judith Blake. "Social Structure and Fertility: An Analytical Framework." *Economic Development and Cultural Change*, Vol. 4 (April, 1956), pp. 211–235.

Davis, Kingsley. "The Amazing Decline of Mortality in the Underdeveloped Areas." *American Economic Review*, Vol. 46 (May, 1956), pp. 305–318.

Davis, Kingsley. "Population." *Scientific American,* Vol. 209 (September, 1963), pp. 62–71.

Eckaus, Richard S. "Technological Change in Less Developed Areas." In *Development of the Emerging Countries*, Robert E. Asher (ed.). Brookings Institution, 1962.

Eckaus, Richard S. "Notes on Invention and Innovation in Less Developed Countries." *American Economic Review*, Vol. 56 (May, 1966), pp. 98–109.

Eckstein, Otto. "Investment Criteria for Economic Development and the Theory of Intertemporal Welfare Economic." *Quarterly Journal of Economics*, Vol. 71 (February, 1957), pp. 56–85.

Enke, Stephen. "Population and Growth: A General Theory." *Quarterly Journal of Economics* (February, 1963), pp. 55–70.

Enke, Stephen. "The Economic Case for Birth Control in Underdeveloped Countries." *Challenge*, Vol. 15, No. 5 (May-June, 1967), pp. 30–31, 41–43.

Galenson, Walter and Harvey Leibenstein. "Investment Criteria, Productivity, and Economic Development." *Quarterly Journal of Economics* (August, 1955), pp. 343–370.

Hagen, Everett E. "Population and Economic Growth." *American Economic Review*, Vol. 49 (June, 1959), pp. 310–327.

Harbison, Fredrick. "Entrepreneurial Organization as a Factor in Economic Development." *Quarterly Journal of Economics*, Vol. 70 (August, 1956), pp. 364–379.

Hicks, W. Whitney. "A Note on the Burden of Dependency in Low Income Areas." *Economic Development and Cultural Change* Vol. 13 (January, 1965), pp. 233–235.

Kamerschen, David R. "The Statistics of Birth Rate Determinants." *Journal of Development Studies*, Vol. 7 (April, 1971), pp. 293–303.

Kim, Young Chim. "Sectoral Output-Capital Ratios and the Level of Economic Development: A Cross-Sectional Comparison of Manufacturing Industry." *Review of Economics and Statistics*, Vol. 51, No. 4 (November, 1969), pp. 453–458.

Kirk, Dudley and Dorothy Nortman. "Population Policies in Developing Countries." *Economic Development and Cultural Change*, Vol. 15 (January, 1967), pp. 129–142.

Leff, Nathaniel. "Dependency Rates and Savings Rates." *American Economic Review*, Vol. 59, No. 5 (December, 1969), pp. 886–896.

Leibenstein, Harvey. "Incremental Capital-Output Ratios and Growth Rates in the Short-Run." *Review of Economics and Statistics*, Vol. 48 (February, 1966), pp. 20–27.

Miller, Morris. "The Scope and Content of Resources Policy in Relation to Economic Development." *Land Economics*, Vol. 37, No. 4 (November, 1961), pp. 291–310.

Nurkse, Ragnar. *Problems of Capital Formation in Underdeveloped Countries and Patterns of Trade and Development.* Fairlawn: Oxford University Press, 1967.

Ohlin, Goran. *Population Control and Economic Development.* Development Center of the Organization for Economic Cooperation and Development, 1967.

Paglin, Morton. "Surplus Agricultural Labor and Development: Facts and Theories." *American Economic Review*, Vol. 55 (September, 1965), pp. 815–833.

Papanek, Gustav F. "The Development of Entrepreneurship." *American Economic Review*, Vol. 52, No. 2 (May, 1962), pp. 46–58. Also E. E. Hagen's "Discussion" pp. 59–61.

Papanek, Gustav F. *Pakistan's Development: Social Goals and Private Incentives.* Cambridge: Harvard University Press, 1967.

Pesek, Boris P. "Kuznets' Incremental Capital-Output Ratios." *Economic Development and Cultural Change*, Vol. 12 (October, 1963), pp. 22–33.

Sen, Amartya K. "On Optimizing the Rate of Saving." *Economic Journal*, Vol. 71 (September, 1961), pp. 479–496.

Spengler, Joseph J. "The Population Problem: Yesterday, Today, Tomorrow." *Southern Economic Journal*, Vol. 27 (January, 1961), pp. 249–266.

Spengler, Joseph J. "Demographic Factors and Early Modern Economic Development." *Daedalus*, Vol. 97, No. 2 (Spring, 1968), pp. 433–446.

Villard, Henry H. "Some Notes on Population and Living Levels." *Review of Economics and Statistics*, Vol. 37 (May, 1955), pp. 189–195.

Section V

Balassa, Bela. "Toward a Theory of Economic Integration." *Kyklos*, Vol. 14 (1961), pp. 1–14.

Balassa, Bela. "Growth Strategies in Semi-Industrial Countries." *Quarterly Journal of Economics*, Vol. 84, No. 1 (February, 1970), pp. 24–47.

Balogh, Thomas. "Economic Policy and the Price System." *Economic Bulletin for Latin America*, (March, 1961).

Bronfenbrenner, Martin. "The Appeal of Confiscation in Economic Development." *Economic Development and Cultural Change*, Vol. 3 (April, 1955), pp. 201–218; "Second Thoughts on Confiscation." *Idem* (July, 1963), pp. 367–371.

Chenery, Hollis B. "Comparative Advantages and Development Policy." *American Economic Review*, Vol. 51 (May, 1961), pp. 18–51.

Curries, Lauchlin. *Accelerating Development: The Necessity and the Means.* New York: McGraw-Hill, 1966.

deVries, Berend A. "The Export Performance of Developing Countries." *Finance and Development,* Vol. 5, No. 2 (March, 1968), pp. 2–7.

Dorrance, Grace S. "The Effect of Inflation on Economic Development." *International Monetary Staff Papers*, Vol. 10 (March, 1963), pp. 1–47.

Friedman, Milton. "Foreign Economic Aid: Means and Objectives." *Yale Review* (June, 1958), pp. 500–516.

Griffin, K. B. and J. L. Enos. "Foreign Assistance: Objectives and Consequences." *Economic Development and Cultural Change*, Vol. 18, No. 3 (April, 1970), pp. 313–317.

Gurley, John G. and Edward S. Shaw. "Financial Structures and Economic Development." *Economic Development and Cultural Change*, Vol. 15 (April, 1967), pp. 257–268.

Harberler, Gottfried. "International Trade and Economic Development." *National Bank of Egypt Fiftieth Anniversary Commemoration Lectures,* 1959.

Hagen, Everett E. *Planning Economic Development.* Homewood: Richard D. Irwin, 1963.

Hirschman, Albert O. "Economic Policy in Underdeveloped Countries." *Economic Development and Cultural Change*, Vol. 5 (July, 1957), pp. 362–370.

Hirschman, Albert O. "The Political Economy of Import-Substituting Industrialization in Latin America." *Quarterly Journal of Economics*, Vol. 82 (February, 1968), pp. 1–32.

Host-Madsen, Poul. "Balance of Payments Problems of Developing Countries." *Finance and Development*, Vol. 4, No. 2 (June, 1967), pp. 118–124.

Johnson, Harry G. *Economic Policies Toward Less Developed Countries.* New York: Praeger, 1967.

Lerner, Daniel and Wilbur Schram (eds.). *Communication and Change in the Developing Countries.* Honolulu: East-West Center Press, 1967.

Lewis, W. Arthur. *Development Planning: The Essentials of Economic Policy.* New York: Harper and Row, 1966.

Little, I. M. D. and J. M. Clifford. *International Aid.* Chicago: Aldine Publishing Co., 1966.

Lotz, Joergen R. and Elliot R. Morss. "A Theory of Tax Level Determinants for Developing Countries." *Economic Development and Cultural Change*, Vol. 18, No. 3 (April, 1970), pp. 328–341.

Prebisch, Raul. "The Role of Commercial Policies in Underdeveloped Countries." *American Economic Review*, Vol. 49 (May, 1959), pp. 251–273.

Prebisch, Raul. "The Economic Development of Latin America and Its Principal Problems." *Economic Bulletin for Latin America*, Vol. 7 (February, 1962), pp. 1–22.

Pincus, John. *Trade, Aid, and Development*. New York: McGraw-Hill, 1967.

Rosenstein-Rodan, Paul N. "International Aid for Underdeveloped Countries." *Review of Economics and Statistics*, Vol. 43 (May, 1961), pp. 107–138.

Singer, Hans W. "Distribution of Gains Between Investing and Borrowing Countries." *American Economic Review*, Vol. 40, (May, 1950), pp. 472–492.

Slater, Courtenay. "External Debt and Economic Development: Some Empirical Tests of Macroeconomic Approaches." *Southern Economic Journal*, Vol. 36, No. 3 (January, 1970), pp. 252–262.

Solow, Robert M. "Some Problems of the Theory and Practice of Economic Planning." *Economic Development and Cultural Change.* Vol. 10 (January, 1962).

Spengler, Joseph J. "Bureaucracy and Economic Development." In *Bureaucracy and Political Development*, Joseph La Palombara. Princeton: Princeton University Press, 1964, pp. 199–232.

Stolper, Wolfgang F. *Planning Without Facts: Lessons in Resource Allocation from Nigeria's Development*. Cambridge: Harvard University Press, 1966.

Streeten, Paul. "The Frontier of Development Studies: Some Issues of Development Policy." *Journal of Development Studies*, Vol. 4, No. 1 (October, 1967), pp. 2–24.

Tinbergen, Jan. *The Design of Development*. Baltimore: John Hopkins Press, 1958.

Tinbergen, Jan. "Social Factors in Economic Development." *Zeitscheift fur die Gesamte Staatswissenschaft*, Vol. 124 (September, 1968).

Tobin, James. "Economic Growth as an Objective of Government Policy." *American Economic Review*, Vol. 54 (May, 1964), pp. 1–20.

Viner, Jacob. *International Trade and Economic Development*. New York: Free Press, 1962.

Ward, Richard S. "Absorbing More Labor in LDC Agriculture." *Economic Development and Cultural Change*, Vol. 17 (January, 1969), pp. 178–188.

Section VI

Chamber of Commerce of United States. "What Is Economic Growth?" In *The Promise of Economic Growth*. Washington, D.C., 1961.

Enke, Stephen. "Economists and Development: Rediscovering Old Truths."
    Journal of Economic Literature, Vol. 7 (December, 1969), pp. 1125–1139.
Higgins, Benjamin. "The Primrose Path to Economic Development." *Chal-
    lenge*, Vol. 15, No. 3 (January-February, 1967), pp. 30–31, 42.
Lewis, W. Arthur. "Is Economic Growth Desirable?" In Appendix, *The
    Theory of Economic Growth*. London: Allen and Unwin, 1955.
Mishan, E. J. *Technology and Growth: The Price We Pay*. New York:
    Praeger, 1970.

Appendix

For a demonstration of what can be done with limited data, see:

Kindleberger, Charles P. *Economic Growth in France and Britain, 1851–1950*.
    Simon and Schuster, 1969.
Lundberg, Erik. *Instability and Economic Growth*. New Haven: Yale Uni-
    versity Press, 1968.

For data see:

Adelman, Irma and Cynthia Taft Morris. *Society, Politics and Economics
    Development: A Quantitative Approach*. Baltimore: John Hopkins Press,
    1967.
Agency for International Development. *Proposed Foreign Aid Program, FY
    1968*, 1968.
Ginsburg, Norton. *Atlas of Economic Development*. Chicago: University of
    Chicago Press, 1961.
Hagen, Everett E. and Oli Hawrylyshyn. "Analysis of World Income and
    Growth, 1955–1965." *Economic Development and Cultural Change*, Vol.
    18, No. 1, Part II (October, 1969), pp. 1–69.
Kuznets, Simon. "Quantitative Aspects of the Economic Growth of Nations."
    Economic Development and Cultural Change, various issues, e.g., July,
    1960.
Russett, Bruce M., *et al. World Handbook of Political and Social Indicators*.
    New Haven: Yale University Press, 1964.

General

A. *Textbooks*

Baldwin, Robert E. *Economic Development and Growth*. New York: John
    Wiley and Sons, 1966.
Bauer, Peter T. and Basil S. Yamey. *The Economics of Underdeveloped
    Countries*. Chicago: University of Chicago Press, 1957.
Bruton, Henry J. *Principles of Development Economics*. Englewood Cliffs:
    Prentice-Hall, 1965.
Buchanan, Norman S. and Howard S. Ellis. *Approaches to Economic De-
    velopment*. New York: Twentieth Century Fund, 1955.

Burmeister, Edwin and Rodney Dobell. *Mathematical Theories of Economic Growth*. New York: Macmillan, 1971.

Caincross, A. K. *Factors in Economic Development*. London: George Allen & Unwin Ltd., 1962.

Clark, Colin. *Conditions of Economic Progress*, 3rd ed. New York: Macmillan, 1957.

Enke, Stephen. *Economics for Development*. Englewood Cliffs: Prentice-Hall, 1963.

Gill, T. Richard. *Economic Development: Past and Present*. Englewood Cliffs: Prentice-Hall, 1963.

Hagen, Everett E. *The Economics of Development*. Homewood: Richard D. Irwin, 1968.

Heilbroner, Robert L. *The Great Ascent*. New York: Harper and Row, 1963.

Higgins, Benjamin. *Economic Development*. Rev. ed. New York: W. W. Norton & Co., Inc., 1968.

Kindleberger, Charles P. *Economic Development*, 2nd ed. New York: McGraw-Hill, 1965.

Krause, Walter. *Economic Development*. Belmont: Wadsworth Publishing Co., 1961.

Kunkel, John H. *Society and Economic Growth*. Fairlawn: Oxford University Press, 1970.

Leibenstein, Harvey. *Economic Backwardness and Economic Growth*. New York: John Wiley & Sons, Inc., 1957.

Lewis, W. Arthur. *The Theory of Economic Growth*. London: George Allen & Unwin, 1955.

Mountjoy, Alan B. *Industrialization and Underdeveloped Countries*. Rev. ed. Chicago: Aldine Publishing Co., 1967.

Myint, Hla. *The Economics of Developing Countries*. New York: Praeger, 1964.

Myrdal, Gunnar. *Asian Drama: An Inquiry into the Poverty of Nations*. New York: Pantheon Books, 1968.

Pepelasis, Adamantios, Leon Mears, and Irma Adelman. *Economic Development*. New York: Harper & Row, 1961.

Singer, Hans W. *International Development: Growth and Change*. New York: McGraw-Hill, 1964.

Villard, Henry H. *Economic Development*. Rev. ed. New York: Holt, Rinehart & Winston, Inc., 1963.

Wilcox, Clair, Willis D. Weatherford, Jr., Holland Hunter, and Morton S. Baratz. *Economics of the World Today*. 2nd ed. New York: Harcourt, Brace, & World, Inc., 1966.

Zimmerman, L. J. *Poor Lands, Rich Lands*. New York: Random House, 1965.

B. *Books of Readings (And/Or Essays)*

Agarwals, A. N., and S. P. Singh (eds.). *The Economics of Development.* Fairlawn: Oxford University Press, 1958.

Black, Eugene R. *The Diplomacy of Economic Development and Other Papers.* New York: Atheneum, 1963.

Chandrasekhar, S. *Asia's Population Problems.* New York: Praeger, 1967.

Domar, Evsey D. *Essays in the Theory of Economic Growth.* Fairlawn: Oxford University Press, 1957.

Falkus, Malcolm E. (ed.). *Readings in the History of Economic Growth.* Fairlawn: Oxford University Press, 1968.

Feinstein, Otto. (ed.). *Two Worlds of Change: Readings in Economic Development.* Anchor Books, 1964.

Hahn, Frank H., (ed.). *Readings in the Theory of Growth.* New York: St. Martins Press, 1971.

Hauser, Philip M. (ed.). *The Population Dilemma.* 2nd edition. Englewood Cliffs: Prentice Hall, 1969.

Hoselitz, Bert F. (ed.). *Theories of Economic Growth.* New York: Free Press, 1960.

Kuznets, Simon. *Economic Change.* New York: W. W. Norton, 1953.

Kuznets, Simon. *Six Lectures on Economic Growth.* New York: Free Press, 1959.

Kuznets, Simon. *Postwar Economic Growth: Four Lectures.* Cambridge: Harvard University Press, 1964.

Kuznets, Simon. *Economic Growth and Structure.* New York: W. W. Norton, 1965.

Meir, Gerald M. (ed.). *Leading Issues in Development Economics.* 2nd ed. Fairlawn: Oxford University Press, 1970.

Morgan, T., G. W. Betz, and N. K. Choudry. (eds.). *Readings in Economic Development.* Belmont: Wadsworth, 1963.

Myint, Hla. *Economic Theory and Underdeveloped Countries.* Fairlawn: Oxford University Press, 1971.

Novack, David E. and Robert Lekachman. (eds.). *Development and Society.* New York: St. Martins Press, 1964.

Okun, Bernard and Richard W. Richardson. (eds.). *Studies in Economic Development.* New York: Holt, Rinehart & Winston, 1961.

Phelps, Edmund S., (ed.). *The Goal of Economic Growth.* New York: W. W. Norton, 1962.

Ranis, Gustav (ed.). *The United States and the Developing Countries.* New York: W. W. Norton, 1964.

Ranis, Gustav. *Government and Economic Development.* New Haven: Yale University Press, 1971.

Schiavo-Campo, Salvatore and Hans W. Singer (eds.). *Perspectives of Economic Development.* Geneva: Houghton Mifflin, 1970.

Shannon, Lyle W. (ed.). *Underdeveloped Areas.* New York: Harper & Row, 1957.

Spregelglas, Stephen and Charles J. Welsh. (eds.). *Economic Development: Challenge and Promise.* Englewood Cliffs: Prentice-Hall, Inc., 1970.

Tangri, Shanti and H. Peter Gray (eds.). *Capital Accumulation and Economic Development.* Lexington: D. C. Heath and Co., 1967.

Theberge, James D. (ed.). *Economics of Trade and Development.* New York: John Wiley & Sons, Inc., 1968.

Ward, Richard J. (ed.). *The Challenge of Development.* Chicago: Aldine Publishing Company, 1967.